T0368276

PARADOX BEYOND NATURE

An Eastern Orthodox and Roman Catholic Dialogue on the Marian Homilies of Germanos I, Patriarch of Constantinople (715—730)

Gregory E. Roth

authorHOUSE®

AuthorHouse™
1663 Liberty Drive
Bloomington, IN 47403
www.authorhouse.com
Phone: 1-800-839-8640

Published by AuthorHouse   04/16/2012

ISBN: 978-1-4685-7202-5 (sc)
ISBN: 978-1-4685-7203-2 (e)

Library of Congress Control Number: 2012905932

Nihil obstat: François Rossier, S.M., STD

Vidimus et approbamus: Bertrand A. Buby, S.M., STD—Director
Johann G. Roten, S.M., PhD, STD—Examinator
Thomas A. Thompson, S.M., PhD–Examinator
Luigi Gambero, S.M., STD—Examinator

Contents

Abbreviations

Sources

PG

Migne, J. P. *Patrologiae cursus completus, seu bibliotheca universalis, integra, uniformis, commoda, oeconomica, omnium ss. patrum, doctorum scriptorumque ecclesiasticorum : series graeca.* Patrologia Graeca. Vol. 98. [Parisiis]: Migne, 1857.

Gharib
Germanos

Gharib, Georges, et al. *Germano de constantinopoli. testi mariani del primo millennio.* Ed. Georges Gharib. Vol. II. Padri e altri autori bizantini (VI-XI sec.). Rome: Città Nuova Editrice, 1988.

Piana

La Piana, George. *Le rappresentazioni sacre nella letteratura bizantina dalle origini al sec. ix, con rapporti al teatro sacro d'occidente.* Grottaferrata,: Tip. italo-orientale "S. Nilo", 1912.

Works on Germanos

Horvath or
H*
* in data
analysis

"Germanos of Constantinople and the Cult of the Virgin Mary, Mother of God, Mediatrix of All Men." *De cultu mariano saeculis VI-XI; acta congressus mariologici mariani internationalis in Croatia anno 1971 celebrati. 1972.* Pontificia academia mariana internationalis.

Perniola or
P*
* in data
analysis

Perniola, Erasmo. *La mariologia di san Germano, patriarca di Constantinopoli.* Roma: Edizioni Padre Monti, 1954.

Other Works

Cunningham *Wider* Cunningham, Mary B. *Wider Than Heaven: Eighth-Century Homilies of the Mother of God*. Popular Patristic Series. Vol. 35. Crestwood, NY: St. Vladimir's Seminary Press, 2008.

Cunningham *Preach* Cunningham, Mary B. "Preaching and the Community." *Church and People in Byzantium*. Eds. Rosemary Morris, et al. Birmingham, England: Centre for Byzantine, Ottoman and Modern Greek studies, University of Birmingham, 1990. 39-40.

Cunningham *Typology* Cunningham, Mary B. *The Meeting of the Old and the New: The Typology of Mary the Theotokos in Byzantine Homilies and Hymns*. Studies in Church History, the Church and Mary. Ed. R. N. Swanson. Rochester, NY: Ecclesiastical History Society/Boydell Press, 2004.

Daley *Dormition* *On the Dormition of Mary: Early Patristic Homilies*. Trans. Brian E. Daley, S.J. Crestwood, NY: St. Vladimir's Seminary Press, 1998.

Meyendorff *Divine* Germanus. *On the Divine Liturgy*. Trans. Paul Meyendorff. Crestwood, N.Y.: St. Vladimir's Seminary Press, 1984.

Lexicons

Lampe

Lampe, G. W. H. *A Patristic Greek Lexicon.* xlix, 1568 p. in 5 vols. Oxford: Clarendon Press, 1961.

LSJ

Liddell, Henry George, et al. *A Greek-English Lexicon.* New ed. Oxford: Clarendon Press, 1966. Liddell, Henry George, et al. *Greek-English Lexicon : A Supplement.* Oxford: Clarendon Press, 1968.

Forward

This work has been a long time in the writing. I started translating the homilies of Germanos I, Patriarch of Constantinople (715-730) in the 1980's. My fascination with Byzantine Homilies grew as I started a course of studies at the International Marian Research Institute (IMRI) in Dayton, Ohio. My first contact with IMRI was to present Mary in Ecumenism from the Orthodox Christian tradition. Once in the STL/STD program I wrote all my papers on Byzantine subjects; most included a translation of one of Germanos' homilies. One of the promises I made to myself at the beginning of my studies was that I would not limit myself only to Byzantine subjects—I, as an Orthodox Priest, wanted to understand both approaches to Mariology. This dissertation is one of the results of that commitment.

I am grateful for the education and patience that the faculty of IMRI have given me. There have been several people who have helped me with this work. Mary B. Cunningham helped by her earlier publications and also by generously sending me a more complete text of the Annunciation Homily. Fr. Brian Daley, S.J., answered numerous enquiries connected with his translations of the Dormition Homilies. Fr. Luigi Gambero also was always available by e-mail to answer questions. Fr. Bertand A. Buby, my advisor, helped to direct my dissertation and Fr. Johann G. Roten sent e-mails when I needed encouragement to do this work. Others such as Dr. Paul Meyendorff, my friend from seminary days, and Dr. John Duffy, chair of the Harvard University Classics Department and Stephen J. Shoemaker of the University of Oregon answered my early enquiries about text. Dr. Engelhardt assisted me by e-mail correspondence, face to face conversations and encouragement. Many others from the past, my teachers Fr. Schmemann and Fr. Meydendorff and Fr. George MacRae S.J. gave me courage to do academic work. But it is to my Presbytera Catharine P. Roth, Ph.D, and Metropolitan Kallistos (Timothy Ware) that I own the most. Catharine put up with many visits to talk to the Patriarch (our code for I'm headed to the basement to work on Germanos) as well as much editing. His Eminence invited me to lecture on many occasions while we were in the United Kingdom and so put faith in me and what I had to say.

In 2008 the University of Cincinnati provided Catharine with a Tytus Fellowship and warmly welcomed my research for this dissertation. To all these individuals I give my warmest thanks.

But finally, like Germanos, I want to acknowledge my debt to Mary, the Theotokos, without whose obedience to God none of this would ever have happened.

Very Reverend Archpriest Gregory E. Roth
Feast of the Annunciation 2010

Rhetorical Terms
and Definitions

Elements of persuasion:
(1) how to choose a subject, known as invention (εὕρησις or *inventio*) with guidelines for the best techniques for choosing a subject; (2) how to arrange the material, known as argumentation (τάξις or *dispositio*); (3) how to compose, the proper use of figures of speech, the right denotation or connotation—style (λέξις or *elocutio*) was also considered to be a clue as to the trustworthiness of the speaker; (4) how to memorize the speech so as to deliver it in a natural fashion (μνήμη or *memoria*)—among the ways of doing this could be the creation of an imaginative scene which would help both the rhetor and the hearers to remember it because of the striking figures of speech, or the images of the persons or the events); (5) how to use one's voice, pauses, gestures, etc. known as delivery (ὑπόκρισις or *pronunciatio*).

Symbouleutic devices: (1) μῦθος, myth; (2) χρεία, ethical thought; and (3) γνώμη, a maxim or saying.

Dicanic devices: (1) ἀνασκευή the refutation of a given statement; (2) κατασκευή, confirmation of a given statement; (3) εἰσφορὰ νόμος, discussion of whether a given law was good or bad; and (4) κοινὸς τόπος, amplification of a given topic, *communis locus.*

Panegyric devices: (1) ἐγκώμιον, encomium; (2) ψόγος, the opposite of encomium; (3) σύγκρισις, comparison; and (4) ἠθοποιΐα, characterization.

Note: All three categories used ἔκφρασις, description (of people, places, and things) and διήγημα, narrative. Θέσις, the posing of a question of general interest, was used in symbouleutic and panegyrical progymnasmata. In Byzantine history more attention was paid to these two categories than to the dicanic.

Rhetorical Forms used by Christian homilists:

Ἠθοποιΐα (ethopoeia): contemplation of the thoughts of various characters. Such as Samson's thoughts upon being blinded or what the Virgin thought upon seeing her son change water into wine, etc.

Ἐγκώμιον (encomium): form of praise of individuals. Often used to praise the lives of saints.

Σύνκρισις (comparison): Often used as part of an encomium. In homilies it was used as an exhortation to lead a good life. Byzantine homilists never tired of comparing the works of God with those of the Devil, the grossness of heathenism with the beauty of the life of a saint. The technique was already biblical—witness the comparison of the wise and foolish virgins (Mt. 25.1-13).

Ἔκφρασις is most often used to describe nature and, as a special category, works of art. It was particularly attractive to the medieval mind. Works of art lent themselves particularly well to ἔκφρασις since they were immobile and fixed in form, and thus could be dealt with in detail. Ἔκφρασις is also one of the most thoroughly Christianized forms. The many descriptions of the heavenly majesty in the religious poetry of Byzantium serve as an example of ekphrasis.

Μῦθος (myth): Provided an answer to the ethical demand of the religious mind. It may have been popular because its fictional appeal gave freedom from the confines of dogma and the strictures of doctrinal prescriptions.

Χρεία: the development of a quotation of a specific author, was practiced in Byzantium with an eye to its application to preaching of the Gospel. Within the Christian empire the exegesis of scriptural meaning, the quotations of the early Fathers, and the vast body of catenae literature were the main uses of χρεία.

Forms of argumentation in Byzantine homiletical rhetoric:

Argumentation was an inductive form concerned with social, contingent, debatable matters focused upon specific events; and rhetoric could only argue for what is probable. These traditional values were called 'final topics' or 'major aims' (τέλεα κεφάλαια) of the rhetorical speech. A list of these included that which is right (δίκαιος), lawful (νόμιμος), advantageous (συμφέρων), honorable (καλός), pleasant (ἡδύς), easy (ῥάδιος), feasible (δυνατός), and necessary (ἀναγκαῖος).

Criteria for argumentation: However, a syllogism might arise deductively from a cultural phenomenon by finding its major premise. This inferred proposition (ἐνθύμημα) can be seen in a New Testament form in the Beatitudes in Matthew. Supporting arguments could be non-inventive or invented. Non-invented proofs were those that the rhetor did not create. These proofs were highly prized by early Christians because they established the truth of what was being said. 'Witnesses,' 'oracles,' 'oaths,' 'miracles,' and 'prophetic predictions' were just a few of the forms of non-invented proofs. Examples would include arguments from 'the opposite,' 'the same,' 'the greater,' 'the lesser,' etc. Another form of proof available to the rhetor was the material that he could use as examples. Among these were historical examples (παράδειγμα), analogy (παραβολή), and fable (μῦθος). Paradigm was taken from history, and analogy and fable were taken from the worlds of nature and normal social practice.

The standard form of argumentation: was called *thesis* (θέσις), consisted of: (1) an introduction (προοίμιον) that acknowledged the situation, addressed the audience, and established the ethos of the speaker; (2) a statement of the case that rehearsed the circumstances, clarified the issue (stasis) and established the proposition with a reason (ratio, αἰτία) or by appeal to the final topics; (3) the supporting arguments that gave examples using the customary strategies from the topics; and (4) the conclusion that summarized the argument and pressed for its acceptance. These were the forms used with judical and deliberative rhetoric. Epideictic oratory followed a somewhat different outline that demonstrated the person's virtues and established the basis for his honors or memorial.

Introduction

In recent years several Roman Catholic scholars have commented on how different the Byzantine theological tradition is from theirs—not in the sense of saying that the conclusion of the Byzantine and Roman Catholic traditions are at odds with each other, but in that the way theology is done is different. Byzantine theological reflection is the subject of this dissertation: specifically, reflection on the person of Mary, the Theotokos, the Mother of God.

Brother John Samaha, S.M., in a short article of only eight or so pages asks and answers the question: Is there a Byzantine Mariology?[1] Relying heavily on Fr. Alexander Schmemann's articles[2], Bro John crafts an insightful article that asks and answers the question at hand. Father Brian E. Daley, S.J., provides insights into one of the aspects of Byzantine homilies that puzzle many Catholic Mariologists. Fr. Daley comments on the "show" oratory that is so clearly evident in Byzantine homilies.[3] These two Roman Catholic theologians go a long way in explaining why there are often difficulties in understanding between Orthodox and Roman Catholic Mariologists. René Laurentin comments:

> Oriental thought loves mystery, Western, analytical clarity. Marian thought in the East is contemplative and poetic. Its inventiveness consists in translating the same basic facts into continually renewed symbols which give new brightness to the truth and, now and then, bring out-or suggest some hidden

---

[1]   Brother John M. Samaha, S.M. "Is There a Byzantine Mariology?" (2008): http://www.ignatiusinsight.com/. May 21, 2008. <http://www.ignatiusinsight.com/features2007/samaha_marybyzantine_sept07.asp >.

[2]   Alexander Schmemann, "Mary in Eastern Liturgy." *Marian Studies* 19 (1968) and "On Mariology in Orthodoxy." *Marian Library Studies* 2 (1970). Both are reprinted in *The Virgin Mary*. St. Vladimir's Seminary Press, 1995.

[3]   *On the Dormition of Mary: Early Patristic Homilies.* Introduced and Trans. Brian E. Daley, S.J. Crestwood, NY: St. Vladimir's Seminary Press, 1998.

aspect. Latin Marian thought (above all, the most committed) proceeds, on the contrary, by analysis, comparison, reasoning, syllogism. It distinguishes, constructs, forms notions and words answering to the divisions of its rational analysis; it is by choice specialized, systematic, and organized into theses. Finally, it has a way of multiplying juridical notions with which the Orthodox mentality often finds it impossible to cope.[4]

The burden of this dissertation is to illustrate some of the aspects of this difficulty: to illustrate an approach to doing Mariology in a Byzantine way that takes into account the uniqueness of the Byzantine experience of doing theology.

Upon entering an Orthodox Church one is immediately aware of being in a specific space that is designed for a spiritual purpose. It is quite clearly arranged for a purpose; however, this purpose is not straightforward, but perhaps mysterious. Physically it seems like many other churches. There are clear distinctions in the arrangements of the various spaces. There is a nave, an altar, etc. But what sets this building apart from many others is the way these spaces are decorated. There are pictures and lots of pictures designated as icons. One is faced with coming to terms with them, both their very existence and also their arrangement. They are a puzzle because their arrangement, at first, seems repetitive with the same figure appearing over and over again. Many of these figures are familiar to both Western and Eastern Christians through a long history of sacred art. The two most familiar figures are those of Jesus Christ and His Mother, Mary. While the iconographic program of an Orthodox Church cannot be immediately attributed to the Middle Byzantine period, the very existence and theology that allows icons as a part of worship was its primary theological question.

Canon Laurentin sets out an agenda for a mutual project:

> Psychologically, methodologically, conceptually. the division between us is deep.

> Here once again, the work of the ecumenical dialogue will be a return to the sources, to the Scriptures and the Greek Fathers

---

4   René Laurentin, *The Question of Mary*. 1st. ed. New York: Holt, 1965. 132.

and Byzantine homilists, who are also our Fathers. This is a rather wide foundation; but it would be important for both sides to take part in this work, and to a certain degree jointly, for in the last few centuries Orthodox theology has also neglected its own tradition. Such a work would, therefore, lead to the recovery of important things by both sides. On the Catholic side, it would enrich our sense of what the Mystery is, and of the manifestation of God in humanity of which Mary is the sign. It would lead us to look again at not a few recent and particular notions which we tend to handle without reserve, as if they were absolute and adequate. (Thus. the distinction between objective and subjective redemption on which is based the whole question of "co redemption" in modern mariology is itself an importation from Protestant theology.) In general, the Orthodox would reject any work on the subject which gave the impression of setting up structures and quasi-autonomous functions having in themselves their own efficacy quite independently of the God who works all things in all men. In a dialogue established along these lines, it would have to be shown in what sense our Latin formulae are modes of expression basically equivalent to what the East expresses according to another pattern of thought.[5]

Germanos I, seventy-fourth Bishop of Constantinople, and thirtieth Patriarch, is one of the most important players at the beginning of the iconoclastic controversy, and continues to be a source of theological and Mariological reflection. Indeed, one could rightly claim that he stands at the end of one theological era and the beginning of another. It is the burden of this dissertation to illustrate Germanos' own formulation of Middle Byzantine Marian Homilies—a formulation that has influenced later generations of theologians. Germanos' Marian devotion has often been the cause of some puzzlement on the part of Roman Catholic Mariologists and theologians.[6] In his remarkable article cataloguing the titles given to

---

[5]   Laurentin 133

[6]   "… nine discourses in the extravagant rhetorical style of the later Byzantines." From: Written by J.P. Kirsch. Transcribed by Robert B. Olson. *The Catholic Encyclopedia*, Volume VI. Published 1909. New York: Robert Appleton Company. September 1, 1909. http://www.newadvent.org/cathen/06484a.htm

Mary by Germanos, Father Tibor Horvath, S.J. comments that Germanos' " . . . praises and eulogies of Mary have almost no limit . . ."[7]

First, it is an argument of this dissertation that Germanos' Mariology illustrates the unique theological process of Byzantine Orthodoxy. Whatever, later theological interpretations one might draw from Germanos' Marian corpus, an important criteria in interpreting it is to allow Germanos' *Weltanschauung* to be an important contributor to understanding Germanos' Mariology.

Second, that unique theological process is the direct result of the Byzantine educational process. Centuries of traditional education were codified in the highest level of education, rhetoric. Men such as Germanos were trained in rhetoric. The exercises learned in the *Progymnesmata* were applied to all forms of Byzantine expression including poetical and homiletical works. It is this that accounts for much of the uniqueness of expression found in Middle Byzantine works.

Third, we shall look at homiletical productions by Germanos: The Homily on the Belt of the Theotokos and the double acrostic homily on the Annunciation. We shall also look at Germanos' two homilies on the Presentation of the Theotokos in the Temple,[8] and the two/three homilies on the Dormition.[9]

---

[7]   "Germanos of Constantinople and the Cult of the Virgin Mary, Mother of God, Mediatrix of All Men". *De cultu mariano saeculis VI-XI*; Acta Congressus Mariologici Mariani Internationalis in Croatia anno 1971 celebrati. 1972. Pontificia Academia Mariana Internationalis, 285.

[8]   These four homilies have recently been published by Mary B. Cunningham *in Wider Than Heaven: Eighth-Century Homilies of the Mother of God.* Popular Patristic Series. Vol. 35. Crestwood, NY: St. Vladimir's Seminary Press, 2008. I have supplied my own translations, some of which were done in the late 1980s and 90s. They are intended to be used as 'working' translations and not finished literary pieces. Also parts of them were translated by Catharine P. Roth, Ph.D., especially the Second Homily on the Dormition and the additional parts of the Annunciation Homily.

[9]   *On the Dormition of Mary: Early Patristic Homilies.* Trans. Brian E. Daley, S.J. Crestwood, NY: St. Vladimir's Seminary Press, 1998. 153-81. Fr. Daley's translation and commentary are first rate. Daley also agrees with contemporary scholarship that the first Dormition homily and the second should be considered as one homily.

Fourth, we shall analyze Germanos' approach to Mary as found in these homilies, and compare it to the approaches of Perniola and Horvath, whose earlier works represent forms of Western Roman Catholic Mariology.[10] These comparisons will be substantiated by providing two examples of the type of questions and answers derived from this analysis.

Finally, we shall provide several lists drawn from Germanos' homilies in the hope of supplying useful data for both Orthodox and Roman Catholic Mariologists, and a continuing dialogue with regard to an historical-critical approach to Germanos as a representative of Middle Byzantine homilist.

---

[10]   These two scholars have provided and article in the case of Horvath and a dissertation on the part of Perniola. In both cases they were concerned with Germanos' Mariology and provide a Roman Catholic view of Germanos. "Germanos of Constantinople and the Cult of the Virgin Mary, Mother of God, Mediatrix of All Men." *De cultu mariano saeculis* VI-XI; acta congressus mariologici mariani internationalis in Croatia anno 1971 celebrati. 1972. Pontificia Academia Mariana Internationalis. And, Erasmo Perniola, *La mariologia di San Germano, Patriarca di Constantinopoli*. Roma: Edizioni Padre Monti, 1954.

Chapter One

1.1 Life of Germanos

There are few dates that we can set definitely for the life of Germanos I, Patriarch of Constantinople.[11] We know that he died in 733 on his family's estate in Plantonion near Constantinople.[12] He was born into a noble family sometime around 630 to 650. A letter attributed to Pope Gregory II states

---

[11] The difficulty can be illustrated by Lucian Lamza, Patriarch Germanos I. Von Konstantinopel (715-730) : Versuch einer endgültigen chronologischen Fixierung des Lebens und Wirkens des Patriarchen: mit dem griechisch-deutschen Text der Vita Germani am Schluss der Arbeit. Würzburg: Augustinus-Verlag, 1975.

[12] The most complete list of sources for Germanos' life is found in Germanus, On Predestined Terms of Life. Trans. Charles Garton and Leendert Gerrit Westerink. Arethusa Monographs. Vol. VII. Buffalo: Dept. of Classics, State University of N.Y. at Buffalo, 1979.

Principal sources for his life are (1) Theophanes, Chronographia, of which the best edition is by C. de Boor, 2 vols. (Leipzig 1883, repro Hildesheim 1963)-see index for references to Germanos; (2) the brief ancient Vitae, notably (a) the Menologion Basilii, Migne PC 117, 451-452, and (b) the synaxaria, notably the Synaxarion constantinopolitanum, aeta sanctorum 63 (Brussels 1902) 677-679, and one from MS. D (Paris. 1587) given at the foot of cols. 677-678 of the same work; (3) an anonymous ninth-century Vita ed. by A. Papadopulos-Kerameus, Μαυρογορδάτειος Βιβλιοθήκη 1 (Constantinople 1884), Appendix 1-17; (4) allusions in St John Damascene, Nikephoros, Georgios Hamartolos, Kedrenos, and Zonaras. Among the secondary sources we wish to record indebtedness, not spelled out in detail in what follows, to Migne, PC 98, 9 ff., including the Vita by G. Henschen (1681); O. Bardenhewer, Geschichte der altkirchlichen Literatur (Freiburg 1932, repro Darmstadt 1962) 48 ff.; H. G. Beck, Kirche und theologische Literatur im byzantinischen Reich (Munich 1959) 473 *ff*; the article by W. M. Sinclair in Smith and Wace's Dict. of Chr. Biogr. Boston 1880, repro New York 1967); the article by F. Cayre in the Dict. De Theol. Cath. 6 (Paris 1924) 1300-1309; that by J. Darrouzes in the Dict. de Spiritualité 6 (Paris

that he was ninety-five while still patriarch in the late 720s.[13] Although the authenticity of the letter is doubted, if it is accepted, Germanos would have been born about the early 630s. The synaxaria also report divergent dates and ages for Germanos.[14]

Germanos' life was one full of strife. His father, Justinian, became embroiled in the dynastic strife around the imperial throne and was directly implicated in the assassination of Constans II at Syracuse in 668. Germanos' father was executed and Germanos was castrated, according to Theophanes. It is reasoned that this was the time when Germanos chose to enter the clergy at St. Sophia's by direction of the emperor, Constantine IV. According to an anonymous ninth-century Vita, he was said to be no more than twenty when he entered the clergy in 668, an account that would put his birth at 648/50.[15] Germanos' career seems to have been successful from the beginning. He is reported to have risen to be head of the clergy at St. Sophia's, and was devoted to the study of Scripture and to contemplation. As a noble he must have been afforded the best education that the capital of the empire had to offer. That strong rhetorical education and his devotion to Scripture and contemplation served him well in his writings and homiletical work. He is also reported to have been hard working in church affairs. He is said to have been instrumental, along with Patriarch George I, in persuading the Emperor to write to Rome for help in convoking the sixth Ecumenical Council (680-81). It is also claimed that Germanos exercised an important role in the Council of Trullo—the Quinisext Council (685-695)—that met to deal with a number of disciplinary canonical issues that were not taken up during the two earlier Ecumenical Councils. It was after these councils that Germanos was appointed Metropolitan of Cyzicus.[16] In Germanos' time Cyzicus was still an important see.[17]

1967); that in the Oxf. Dict. of the Christian Church 2 (Oxford 1974); and the Cambridge Medieval History 4.1 (Cambridge 1966).

[13] See PL 89, 517 B; also quoted in Henschen's Vita, PG 98 30 C
[14] See Garton vi.
[15] See Garton vi for this date.
[16] There is no evidence for this except in the ninth-century Vita, although it seems to be widely held. We also do not know when Germanos became the Metropolitan of Cyzicus.
See Lamza 71.
[17] As ecclesiastical metropolis of Hellespontus, Cyzicus had a catalogue of bishops beginning with the first century; Lequien (I, 747) mentions fifty-nine. A more complete list is found in Nicodemos, in the Greek "Office of St.

1.2 Monothelite Controversy

In 711 an army officer named Philippicus assumed the throne after assassinating Justinian II. During Philippicus' reign the issue of Monothelitism was raised again by the Emperor. In 712 he called a local synod with the purpose of rehabilitating the Monothelites. Germanos found himself in a difficult position in that he had been one of the main players at the Sixth Ecumenical Council, and now as Metropolitan of Cyzicus he was expected to bow to the Emperor's demands and sign a document that rehabilitated Monothelitism. Germanos signed.[18] Whatever his reason for signing was, he seems to have learned from this event. Philippicus destroyed the depiction of the Sixth Ecumenical Council in the imperial palace and removed an inscription from the Milton gate in front of the palace that commemorated the council. He replaced them with portraits of himself and the Patriarch Sergius.[19] This action must have stuck in Germanos' mind when Leo III took a similar course with iconoclasm.

Germanos was a man of controversy, both political and theological. In his life he paid the price of that controversy; so it should come as no surprise that there is controversy about his life and his work. When he was born, when he died, how he handled the issues surrounding Monothelitism and, for that matter, the beginnings of the iconoclastic controversy have all been called into question by his contemporaries and modern scholars. What is clear is that he was a man of his age who made major contributions to the life of the Byzantine world and its Church. All these issues seem to have come together in bringing Germanos to the

---

Emilian" (Constantinople, 1876), 34-36, which has eighty-five names. We may mention the famous Arian Eunomius; St. Dalmatius; St. Proclus and St. Germanus, who became Patriarchs of Constantinople; and St. Emilian, a martyr in the eighth century. Gelasius, an historian of Arianism, who wrote about 475, was born at Cyzicus. From: Written by S. Vailhé. Transcribed by Gerald M. Knight. From: Written by S. Vailhé. Transcribed by Gerald M. Knight. *The Catholic Encyclopedia,* Volume IV. Published 1908. New York: Robert Appleton Company.

[18] There is conjecture that Germanos signed because he remembered the consequences of disloyalty to the Emperor during his youth. See Lamza 75-85.

[19] See Doom, 82.

throne as well as in his resignation fifteen years later.[20] Germanos was to serve as Patriarch during the short reigns of Anastasios II (713-715)[21] and Theodosios III (715-717)[22] and the longer reign of Leo III (717-741). Germanos was enthroned on August 11, 715 after the death of John VI (712-715). In his capacity as Ecumenical Patriarch, Germanos convened a synod that officially reestablished the Catholic faith and anathematized the Monothelites.[23] Germanos also seems to have been instrumental in securing the bloodless resignation of Theodosius III that made way for Leo to ascend the Byzantine throne.[24]

1.3 Iconoclastic Controversy

Germanos' relationship with the new Emperor was harmonious at first. According to the *Vita* and much hagiographical literature, Germanos required of Leo, before his coronation, an oath not to make any innovations in church doctrine.[25] On the Feast of the Annunciation in 717 Germanos crowned Leo.

With the coronation of Leo III "the Roman oikumene had finally been transformed into Byzantium."[26] Later on December 25, 718, Germanos baptized Leo's only son, the future Constantine V (741-775), and crowned Leo's wife Maria.[27]

---

[20] See Lamza, 86 to 103 concerning the politics both ecclesiastical and secular surrounding his enthronement.

[21] Artemios; secretary of Philippikos; deposed & entered monastery, later revolted & was executed.

[22] tax-collector; abdicated and entered monastery

[23] Lamza, 107 and Grumel *Regestes*, vol. II, 1 disagree on the date of this council. Lamza sets its date in 716 and Grumel in 715.

[24] Lamza, 107.

[25] Garton, ix.

[26] Alexander Schmemann, The Historical Road of Eastern Orthodoxy. Crestwood, N.Y.: St. Vladimir's Seminary Press, 1977. 200

[27] Theophanes, ed. de Boor, p. 400, 2-3). It should be noted that Δεκεμβρίου is de Boor's own emendation, on the basis of Anastasius' octavo kalendas Ianuarias (Chronographia, II, 258, 31); all the Greek codices available to him have Οκτωβρίου. Gero comments: "One wonders why the empress was not crowned simultaneously with Leo some years before. A slight possibility exists, it seems, therefore, that Maria was Leo's second wife, and that Anna, Artavasdus' wife, was only Constantine's half-sister." Stephen Gero.

Leo, the general, as Emperor was confronted with a turbulent political climate. The Byzantine Empire was besieged by Arab armies. In 717 Leo was aware that an Arab army was en route to attack Constantinople. Leo prepared the military and led a procession to the sea walls holding a cross. Reaching the sea, he struck the waters to drive away the invading Arabs in imitation of Moses during the Exodus. Meanwhile, the Patriarch Germanos and the clergy processed around the city walls carrying icons. On the Feast of the Dormition in 718 the Arabs started to withdraw from the City. Both the Emperor and the Patriarch claimed that it was their actions that saved the city. The Emperor is in some accounts from the east proclaimed a great Moses.[28] In other accounts the Patriarch is proclaimed the one who turned away the Arabs by the power of the Theotokos.[29] From this date Germanos led an all night vigil on the eve of the Dormition to give thanks to the Theotokos for saving her city. Both the Emperor and the Patriarch were present at this vigil as would be appropriate. Germanos' homilies on these occasions that emphasized the role of the clergy and disregarded the role of the Leo III and the army caused enmity to grow between the two.[30]

Germanos is chiefly remembered for his stand on Iconoclasm. Elements of Iconoclasm had been of concern for the Church for most of its history. [31] As Patriarch, Germanos was faced with some iconoclastic clergy in Asia Minor. It is from Germanos' correspondence in three letters and his *De Haeresibus et Synodis* that we get a contemporary picture of the issues of iconoclasm in the early eighth century.[32] Germanos' *De Haeresibus et Synodis* was written after his deposition, perhaps as early as 730. The first of the three letters was to John of Synada, which was to be

---

Byzantine Iconoclasm During the Reign of Constantine V, with Particular Attention to the Oriental Sources. Louvain: Corpus SCO, 1977. 9 n.4.

[28] See Gero, Leo 37-38.

[29] See Gero, Leo 36

[30] Judith Herrin. *The Formation of Christendom.* 1st Princeton paperback print., with revisions and ill. ed. Princeton, N.J.: Princeton University Press, 1989. 320.

[31] See Adrian Fortescue "Iconoclasm." *The Catholic Encyclopedia.* 1910 ed, 1910. Vol. VII. Also Lamza, 134-5. For a longer explanation see, G. Ostrogorsky, "Les Débuts De La Querelle Des Images." *Mélanges Charles Diehl.* Vol. I. vols. Paris, 1930. 236-38 or H.-G. Beck, "Die griechische Kirche im Zeitalter des Ikonoklasmus." *Handbuch der Kirchengeschichte.* Ed. H.-G. Beck. Vol. III. vols. Freiburg: I. Halbband, 1966., 33-34.

[32] *PG* 98, 77-80.

delivered to Constantine of Nacolia.[33] The second letter is to Constantine, upbraiding him for not having delivered the first letter to John.[34] The third letter is to Thomas of Claudiopolis, who is accused of a deliberate act of iconoclasm.[35] In these letters and his *De Haeresibus et Synodis* we can get some idea of the level of iconoclastic activity in the early part of the century, and of Germanos' theological perspective on the issue of icons.[36] At this early stage Germanos does not seem to be aware of Leo's iconoclastic leanings.[37]

According to Theophanes the first act of willful destruction of icons by Leo took place in the autumn of 726.[38] He also places it after the volcanic eruption near Thera and Therasia. Both Theophanes[39] and Nicephorus[40] report that Leo viewed this as a sign from God, and he immediately began his iconoclastic policies.[41] The first act was the destruction of the famous Chalce image.[42] According to Nicephoros the Emperor's action caused an uprising in the Helladic and Cycladic themes.[43] It is, perhaps, because of the popular support for icons that Germanos was not forced to abdicate the Ecumenical Throne until 730.[44] Also the support for the Iconophiles on the part of the Roman Pontiff, Gregory II, meant that Leo had a difficult political situation

---

[33]   Mansi, XIII 100BC

[34]   Mansi, XIII 105B-108A

[35]   Mansi, XIII 108A-127A

[36]   Gero, *Leo* 87-9.

[37]   See Gero, *Leo* 85-93 for a fuller exposition of the importance of these letters and their content.

[38]   *Chronographia,* ed. DeBoor and Theophanes, and Turtledove, Harry. *The Chronicle of Theophanes : An English Translation of Anni Mundi 6095-6305 (A.D. 602-813).* Philadelphia: University of Pennsylvania Press, 1982. 96-8.

[39]   *Chronographia,* ed. DeBoor and Turtledove, 96-98.

[40]   *Breviarium,* ed. De Boor, 57, 21-27.

[41]   For an exposition of Leo's earlier policies see Gero, *Leo* 94-5 and Ostrogorsky, *Les débuts* 238-42.

[42]   For a history of the this icon see André Grabar and Foundation Schlumberger pour les études byzantines, *L'iconoclasme Byzantin; Dossier Archeologique.* Paris: College de France, 1957. 130-42 or Cyril A. Mango, *The Brazen House; a Study of the Imperial Palace of Constantinople.* København: I kommission hos Munksgaard, 1959. 108-148

[43]   *Breviarium* ed. De Boor, 57, 27-58.

[44]   See Gero *Leo* 94 n.4.

on his hands.[45] Although Gregory II was ordered by Leo III to destroy the images in Rome and call a general council to forbid their use,

> Gregory answered, in 727, by a long defense of the pictures. He explains the difference between them and idols, with some surprise that Leo does not already understand it. He describes the lawful use of, and reverence paid to, pictures by Christians. He blames the emperor's interference in ecclesiastical matters and his persecution of image-worshippers. A council is not wanted; all Leo has to do is to stop disturbing the peace of the Church. As for Leo's threat that he will come to Rome, break the statue of St. Peter (apparently the famous bronze statue in St. Peter's), and take the pope prisoner, Gregory answers it by pointing out that he can easily escape into the Campagna, and reminding the emperor how futile and now abhorrent to all Christians was Constans's persecution of Martin I. He also says that all people in the West detest the emperor's action and will never consent to destroy their images at his command (Gregory II, *Ep. I ad Leonem*). The emperor answered, continuing his argument by saying that no general council had yet said a word in favour of images; that he himself is emperor and priest (*basileus kai hiereus*) in one and therefore has the right to make decrees about such matters. Gregory writes back regretting that Leo does not yet see the error of his ways. As for the former general Councils, they did not pretend to discuss every point of the faith; it was unnecessary in those days to defend what no one attacked. The title "Emperor and Priest" had been conceded as a compliment to some sovereigns because of their zeal in defending the very faith that Leo now attacked. The pope declares himself determined to withstand the emperor's tyranny at any cost, though he has no defense but to pray that Christ will send a demon to torture the emperor's body that his soul be saved, according to 1 Corinthians 5:5.[46]

---

[45] Germanos' letter to Pope Gregory is lost to us, as is the letter from Pope Gregory to Germanos. Both Gregory and Germanos came to their thrones in 715 and Gregory survived until 731.

[46] Adrian Fortescue, "Iconoclasm." *The Catholic Encyclopedia*. 1910 ed, 1910. Vol. VII.

1.4 Abdication and Final Years

Finally in 730 on January 7, Leo convened a *silentium*. Theophanis gives this account in the *Chronographia:*

> In this year Maslama attacked the land of the Turks. When they met one another in battle men fell on both sides. Maslama became fearful and withdrew in flight through the mountains of Khazaria.

> In the same year the lawbreaking Emperor Leo raged against the true faith. He brought in the blessed Germanos and began to entice him with coaxing words. The blessed chief prelate told him, "We have heard there will be a condemnation of the holy and revered icons, but not during your reign." When the Emperor forced him to say during whose reign, he said, "During the reign of Konon." The Emperor said, "In fact, my baptismal name is Konon." The patriarch said, "Heaven forbid, my lord, that this evil should come to pass through your rule. For he who does it is the forerunner of the Antichrist and the over thrower of the incarnate and divine dispensation." Because of this the tyrant became angry; he put heavy pressure on the blessed man, just as Herod once had on John the Baptist. But the patriarch reminded him of his agreements before he became Emperor: he had given Germanos a pledge secured by God that he would in no way disturb God's church from its apostolic laws, which God had handed down. But the wretch was not ashamed at this. He watched Germanos and contended with him, and put forth statements to the effect that if he found Germanos opposing his rule, he would condemn the holder of the throne like a conspirator and not like a confessor.

> In this Leo had Germanos' pupil and synkellos Anastasios as an ally. He was on good terms with Anastasios because Anastasios agreed with his impiety: the successor to the throne was an adulterer. The blessed patriarch was not unaware that Anastasios was crooked; imitating his Master, he wisely and gently reminded him of what betrayal entailed, as if to another

Iscariot. But when he saw Anastasios had inalterably gone astray, he turned to him so that Anastasios stepped on the back of his robe. When Anastasios went in to the Emperor, Germanos said, "Don't hurry, for you will enter the gate through which the chariots come." Anastasios was troubled by this statement, as by other things he had heard, but was unaware of its prophetic nature. It came true at last after fifteen years, in the third year of Constantine the persecutor (the twelfth indiction). This persuaded everyone that it had been foretold to the senseless man by divine grace. For once Constantine had reconquered the Empire after the revolt of his brother-in-law Artavasdos, he beat Anastasios and paraded him backwards in the hippodrome with other enemies of the Emperor. Naked and seated on an ass, he was brought in through the gate the chariots used, because with the Emperor's enemies he had renounced Constantine and crowned Artavasdos, as will be revealed in its own place.

In Byzantium the champion of pious doctrines—the holy and marvelous priest Germanos—was in his prime, fighting against the wild beast who bore the name Leo ["lion"] and against his henchmen. In the elder Rome Gregory, a holy and apostolic man who held the same throne as had the prince Peter, caused Rome, Italy, and all the west to secede from both political and ecclesiastical obedience to Leo and his Empire. In Syrian Damascus the priest and monk John Chrysorrhoas (the son of Mansur), an excellent teacher, shone in his life and his words. But since Germanos was under his control, Leo expelled him from his throne. Through letters Gregory openly accused Leo of what was known to many, and John subjected the impious man to anathemas.

On January 7 of the thirteenth indiction—a Saturday—the impious Leo convened a *silentium* against the holy and revered icons at the tribunal of the nineteen Akkubita. He even summoned the holy patriarch Germanos, thinking he could persuade him to subscribe to opposing the holy icons. But in no way would the noble servant of Christ obey Leo's abominable, wicked doctrine. He rightly taught the true doctrine, but bade farewell to his position as chief prelate. He gave up his surplice and, after many instructive words, said, "If I am Jonah, cast me into the sea. For, Emperor, I cannot make innovations in the faith without an ecumenical conference." He went off to the Platanaion and went into seclusion at his ancestral home, having been patriarch for fourteen years, five months, and seven days. On the twenty-second of this same January they chose Anastasios, who was misnamed the pupil and synkellos of the blessed Germanos, since he agreed with Leo's impiety. He was appointed false bishop of Constantinople because of his all-embracing hunger for power. As I said before, Gregory the pope of Rome refused to accept Anastasios and his libelli and, through letters, condemned Leo for his impiety; he also split off Rome and all Italy from his rule. The tyrant was furious, and stepped up his persecution of the holy icons. Many clerics, monks, and pious laymen were endangered because of their true concept of the faith and were crowned with the crown of martyrdom.[47]

Germanos returned to his family home. His last years were spent in continued writing. His *De Haeresibus et Synodis* was written there. Like so much in his life his date of death (perhaps on May 12, 733) is conjecture. He was buried at the monastery of Chora. Even in death he was controversial. He was anathematized by the council of Hiereia in 754 and rehabilitated by the Second Council of Nicaea in 787.

---

[47]   Turtledove, 98-100

Chapter Two

Rhetorical Education in Middle Byzantium

Byzantine theology and the Mariology that it produced were both the immediate heirs of that political, cultural, and historical entity called Byzantium. The inheritor of the Greek/Roman tradition in government, thought, and life-orientation, Byzantium arose out of the crisis of the collapse of the Western Roman Empire. The Orthodox East, along with the others, responded to this religious lacuna, and produced great religions and cultures that were to dominate the Mediterranean, Asia Minor, and each other for a millennium.

One cannot understand the literature of the Byzantine Empire in either its secular or religious forms unless one is aware of the history of rhetoric.[48]

---

[48] Much of the information in this section is the result of a careful reading and further research on the basis of three authors. George Alexander Kennedy. *The Art of Persuasion in Greece.* A History of Rhetoric. Vol. I. Princeton, N.J.: Princeton University Press, 1963. *Greek Rhetoric under Christian Emperors.* Princeton, N.J.: Princeton University Press, 1983. *A New History of Classical Rhetoric.* Princeton, N.J.: Princeton University Press, 1994. *Progymnasmata: Greek Textbooks of Prose Composition and Rhetoric.* Leiden; Boston: Brill, 2003.

George L. Kustas, "The Evolution and Function of Byzantine Rhetoric." *Viator* (1970). Mary B. Cunningham, "Preaching and the Community." *Church and People in Byzantium.* Eds. Rosemary Morris, et al. Birmingham, England: Centre for Byzantine, Ottoman and Modern Greek studies, University of Birmingham, 1990. 39-40. "Innovation or Mimesis in Byzantine Sermons?" *Originality in Byzantine Literature, Art and Music : A Collection of Essays.* Ed. Anthony Robert Littlewood. Oxford [England]: Oxbow Books, 1995. 67-80.

2.1 Classical Rhetorical Education

Rhetoric arose during the sixth and fifth centuries B.C.E. Its power is attested by the legend that it was the force that banished the tyrants and gave the Greeks democracy.[49] The rules of rhetoric were learned by the trial-and-error experiences in the councils of the oligarchies and the assemblies of the people.[50] Rhetoric developed as a way for the Greeks to successfully present their cases before the courts, and their thought on matters of public policy and for making public speeches. As successful elements of these presentations began to be analyzed, soon theories of rhetoric were developed.[51] Rhetoric became the tool, the techniques by which educated men communicated in the courts, in philosophical discussion, in deliberations on public matters and on ceremonial occasions. This tool, rhetoric, "By the first-century B.C.E . . . had been thoroughly enculturated, the system of techniques fully explored, the logic rationalized, and the pedagogy refined. Rhetoric permeated both the system of education and the manner of public discourse that marked the culture of Hellenism on the eve of the Roman age."[52] This process of adapting rhetoric to contemporary political realities was also the Byzantine pattern.

Early in the history of Byzantium an anonymous author stated that the function of rhetoric varied with the type of polity. "Among the ancient Lacedaimonians rhetoric served the aims of oligarchy; among the Athenians, democracy; we practice it in faith and orthodoxy under an empire."[53] Rhetoric, which had been developed since the time of Aristotle, was pressed into service by the Byzantine Empire. It was to be used by the Orthodox Church to communicate its thought in all the literary forms.

---

[49] See Vincent Farenga, "Periphrasis on the Origin of Rhetoric." *Modern Language Notes* 94/5,1033-55.
[50] See Donald L. Clark, *Rhetoric in Greco-Roman Education.* (New York: Columbia University Press, 1957); and George A. Kennedy, *The Art of Persuasion in Greece,* vol. 1 *A History of Rhetoric,* Princeton: Princeton University Press, 1963
[51] See Burton L. Mack, *Rhetoric and the New Testament,* in New Testament Series, ed. Dan O. Via, Jr. (Minneapolis: Fortress Press, 1990) 26-7. Mack presents a clear, short history of the development of rhetoric to which I am indebted for clearing up some of the ambiguities in earlier histories of rhetoric.
[52] Mack, 28
[53] *Prolegomenon Sylloge,* ed. H. Rabe (Leipzig 1925) 41. 7-9. Translation from George L. Kustas, "The Function and Evolution of Byzantine Rhetoric," *Viator 1* (1970): 55.

For the Greeks of later antiquity and the Byzantines the study of rhetoric in its most demanding and scientific elements was only for the few who could meet the demands of such study. Most education ended with the grammatical school, that taught the rudiments of rhetoric and prepared citizens for "systematic thinking in judicial and deliberative issues, in which all citizens may be assumed to have some interest, and in matters which can be discussed at the level of probability."[54] Throughout the course of antiquity the immediate purposes for rhetoric changed, as did the manner of teaching it. What is clear is that in later antiquity three specific characteristics arose that taken together form the milieu out of which arose the Orthodox Church's rhetorical response to meeting the challenges of proclaiming and defining its beliefs.

The first of these characteristics is the influence of the Neo-Platonic philosophers, and especially the Second Sophistic.[55] The Neo-Platonists, beginning with Porphyry, reorganized philosophy on a dialectical basis. The process of division and definition was taught to the students on the basis of the stasis theory. Rhetoric became the teaching of clear, systematic thinking applied to judicial and deliberative issues. Byzantine rhetoric is the heir of the Second Sophistic,[56] for which there seems to be no clear terminus, just the creation of the Byzantine use of it in the Byzantines' literary and artistic life. There is, however, a clear development of the tools of literary works. Beginning in the second century A.D. the literary practices and ideals of the Second Sophistic began to be codified into a system. These treatises make up the Byzantine rhetorical tradition which in turn constituted the educational curriculum. During the course of the next fifteen hundred

---

[54] George Kennedy, *Greek Rhetoric Under Christian Emperors,* vol. 3, A History of Rhetoric (Princeton: Princeton University Press, 1983). 53

[55] The expression Second Sophistic was first used by Philostratus in his *Lives of the Sophists.* There does seem to be some disagreement over the dating of the Second Sophistic but what is clear is that it took on a different color after the second century (AD) with the introduction of Neo-Platonism. The Second Sophistic was at base a contest between philosophy and rhetoric for the preeminence in education. For a fuller account of the history of the literature of the Second Sophistic see in Albin Lesky, *A History of Greek Literature,* trans. James Willis and Cornelis de Heer, (London: Methuen & Co Ltd, 1966) the sub-headings "The Second Sophistic" and "The Second Sophistic in the Later Era" in the chapter "The Empire" 829-844 and 870-874.

[56] George L. Kustas, "The Evolution and Function of Byzantine Rhetoric," *Viator,* 1 (1970) 55-

years they are copied, commented upon, edited and on occasion altered to meet the demands of the Christian Empire.[57] Thus the education of *homo byzantinus* is an education in rhetorical technique and its style.

A second characteristic is the use of the progymnasmata as an educational tool. The progymnasmata, a set of exercises in types of rhetorical composition, were introduced at the level of basic grammatical education and continued on in higher studies. It is in the study of progymnasmata, even more than the theory of style, that we can see the basis of rhetorical composition in late antique and Byzantine rhetoric.

The third characteristic is the adoption of the commentary method. For the pagan philosophical schools, commentary was made on the works of Plato and Aristotle. They were in the form of written versions of the lectures of the philosophers of both Antiquity and Late Antiquity. For Christians, they took the form of exegesis of the Greek Bible.

Although rhetoric was applied to a new religion, it was not a break with the past. Byzantine civilization understood itself to be in continuity with all of its history, Greek and Roman, and its cultural and educational heritage and ideals remained from late antiquity on. Contemporary needs were not seen as a break with the past. Kustas states:

> Precisely because the tradition (educational, etc.) remained alive there never developed in Byzantium a uniquely Christian rhetoric existing as an entity apart and distinct from its Sophistic forebears. The changes within this received framework are slow and sometimes subtle, but, for all that, . . . a clear pattern of development.[58]

---

[57] As a measure of this process one can look at the tenth century alphabetical encyclopedia *Suda* that is a gold mine of information on classical and Christian writers, historical personages, unusual words and Attic vocabulary. It is a collection of abridged earlier works. Within the *Suda,* only a few rhetorical words are mentioned and Kennedy's *Rhetoric Under Christian Emperors* suggests that this is because rhetorical terminology was too well known to be given special treatment (page 313). For the text of the *Suda* see *Suidae Lexicon*, ed. Ada Adler, 5 vols (Leipzig: Teubner, 1928-38). Also see the Suda on line: http://www.stoa.org/sol.

[58] George L. Kustas, "The Function and Evolution of Byzantine Rhetoric," *Viator* 1 (1970 55-56.

During the period of the Second Sophistic handbooks were developed which helped to organize knowledge about the art of persuasion. These handbooks dealt with such subjects as: (1) how to choose a subject, known as invention (εὕρησις or *inventio*) with guidelines for the best techniques for choosing a subject; (2) how to arrange the material known as argumentation (τάξις or *dispositio*); (3) how to compose, the proper use of figures of speech, the right denotation or connotation—style (λέξις or *elocutio*) was also considered to be a clue as to the trustworthiness of the speaker; (4) how to memorize the speech so as to deliver it in a natural fashion (μνήμη or *memoria*)—among the ways of doing this could be the creation of an imaginative scene which would help both the rhetor and the hearers to remember it because of the striking figures of speech, or the images of the persons or the events);[59] (5) how to use one's voice, pauses, gestures, etc. known as delivery (ὑπόκρισις or *pronunciatio).* But it is to the progymnasmata we must turn to gain a more in-depth picture of rhetoric and the educated Byzantine's mind.

Two codifications seem to have been wide spread in Byzantium: Hermogenes, a second and third century CE rhetorician from Tarsus, and Aphthonius of Antioch from the fourth and fifth century.

> Kustas points out that there were many other texts known to the Byzantines. He states: "One can trace the influences of Theon, Hermagoras, and Menander, and record the use of rhetorical masters such as Dionysius of Halicarnassus, Demetrius, Synesius, and Aristides, particularly after the tenth century; but they come much less to the fore than the ever present and ever used outlines of Hermogenes and his commentator, Aphthonius.[60]

---

[59] See *Rhetorica ad Herennium,* trans. Harry Caplan, Loeb Classical Library (Cambridge MA: Harvard University Press, 1954) III. xvi. 28-xxiv.40.

[60] George L. Kustas, "Byzantine Rhetoric" 56. See also footnote number two in Kustas for further documentation. An English translation of Aphthonius can be found in Ray Nadeau's "The Progymnasmata of Aphthonius" in *Speech Monographs,* 19 n. 4 (1952) 264-285.

Hermogenes's writings were not original, but they were clear and well arranged. He presented the only attempt to cover the whole of rhetoric.[61] Rhetoric which had earlier severed the law and the court became the servant of higher education, and its proper use the mark of an educated Byzantine.[62] The Neo-Platonists adopted Hermogenes not long after his death and there were many commentaries made on his work in the third century. Iamblichus enhanced Hermogenes' reputation by declaring in his favor over the claims of the rival system.[63] Syrianus, the fifth-century Athenian scholar, was the author of the earliest commentary.[64]

Aphthonius, however, was the commentator through whom Hermogenes was best known in Byzantium. In his Progymnasmata (the school exercises) Aphthonius presented a number of exercises that helped to develop the style and techniques laid down by Hermogenes.[65] Aphthonius created a simple exposition with examples for each of the types of rhetoric outlined. Nothing, including his examples, can be considered to be his own creation.

In his Progymnasmata there are fourteen progymnasmata divided by the scholiasts into three categories, symbouleutic, dicanic, and panegyrical.[66] Within the first category, symbouleutic, there are: (1) μῦθος, myth; (2) χρεία, ethical thought; and (3) γνώμη, a maxim or saying.[67] In the dicanic there were four: (1) ἀνασκευή the refutation of a given statement;

---

[61] Προγυμνάσματα, Περὶ στάσεων, Περὶ εὑρέσεως, Περὶ ἰδεῶν, Περὶ μεθόδου δεινότητος. Rabe in *Opera Hermogenis* comments that Περὶ εὑρέσεως and Προγυμνάσματα incerta erant." Whether or not Rabe's contention that they are spurious, a contention that most recent scholars accept, it remains a fact that both were used in the form we find in the *Opera Hermogenis* throughout the history of Byzantium.

[62] See Albin Lesky, *A History of Greek Literature,* trans. James Willis and Cornelis de Heer (London: Methuen & Co Ltd, 1966), 829-844. Lesky presents a short history of the contest between philosophy and rhetoric for dominance in the educational world of Late Antiquity.

[63] See, Christ-Schmid-Stählin, *Geschichte der griechischen Litteratur* 7.2.2, ed. 6 (Munich 1924) 934—936.

[64] *Syriani in Hermogenem commentaria*, ed. H. Rabe (Leipzig 1892—1893) 2 vols.

[65] Τὰ δὲ τοῦ Αφθονίου προγυμνάσματα εἰσαγωγή τίς ὄντα πρὸς ἐκεῖνα.

[66] This division is at least as old as Aristotle. See *Rhetores graeci* 2.567.7; Carmariotes, Epitome, *Rhetores graeci* 1.120.10, and for more see Kustas, footnote 10.

[67] For the Greek definitions of these categories see Kustas, footnote 11.

(2) κατασκευή, confirmation of a given statement; (3) εἰσφορὰ νόμος, discussion of whether a given law was good or bad; and (4) κοινὸς τόπος, amplification of a given topic, *communis locus*. The first two, ἀνασκευή and κατασκευή, continued to be used by Christians apologists to counter the pagans' myths. The κοινὸς τόπος, according to Cicero, played on two emotions in particular: *indignatio* and *misericordia*. In many homilies and epistles these two emotions were evoked.

The third category, panegyric, contained four types as well: (1) ἐγκώμιον, encomium; (2) ψόγος, the opposite of encomium; (3) σύγκρισις, comparison; and (4) ἠθοποιΐα, characterization. All three categories used ἔκφρασις, description (of people, places, and things) and διήγημα, narrative. Θέσις, the posing of a question of general interest, was used in symbouleutic and panegyrical progymnasmata. In Byzantine history more attention was paid to these two categories than to the dicanic.[68]

2.2 Byzantine Rhetorical Usage

Although all of the categories were always present in Byzantine history, some were more thoroughly developed than others. This affords us our first opportunity to see the relationship between rhetoric and art in the Byzantine Empire. During the Middle Ages the art of letter writing, epistolography, was developed. The heyday of epistolography was during the Roman age, and it went hand in hand with an emphasis on individual portraiture and character expression that is so marked a feature of Roman portrait art. As a form it falls under ἠθοποιΐα.[69] During the fifth century the pseudo-Libanius traditon recognized 41 distinct types of letters.[70] By the time of the late tradition there were 113 different possibilites.[71]

Epistolography owes its development as a genre not to the pagans but to Christianity. St. Paul's Epistles, letters, had a great impact upon Byzantium. Much of early Christianity was transmitted by letters such as those of Ignatius of Antioch, Clement of Rome, and numerous others. The need to clarify Christian theology which arose with the demands of the Emperor Constantine, and its increased visibility as a licit religon,

---

[68] See Kustas
[69] See Nicholaus, Progymnasmata, ed. J. Felten (Leipzig 1913) 67.2
[70] See Ἐπιστολιμαῖοι χαρακτῆρες, ed. V. Weichert (Leipzig 1910) 14
[71] See V. Weichert (Leipzig 1910) 34

contributed to the need to write letters. The Cappadocians and their letters were incorporated in the Christian canon of epistolography and frequentily cited by the rhetoricians of the later centuries together with their pagan predecessors. It was the Cappadocians who gave to epistolography its eminently practical Christian character.[72]

Because of Christianity's emphasis on the importance of the individual and his/her unique relationship to the Creator,[73] other literary forms, such as general histories, theological treatises, and even scientific tracts, come to be dedicated to particular individuals. An anonymous scholium on Apthonius states that ἠθοποιΐα is the perfect kind of progymnasma and in this capacity contributes to the ἐπιστολιμαῖος χαρακτήρ.[74] But it was in homilies that the Christian homilist through his address to his congregation was able to display his virtuosity, just like the orator of the pagan era.

Ἠθοποιΐα was practiced by both Christian and pagan orator. In literature pious Christians did not contemplate the thoughts of Ajax before his suicide or Danaë's reaction to Zeus's golden shower.[75] However, they did contemplate Samson's thoughts upon being blinded or what the Virgin thought upon seeing her son change water into wine or—in a mixture of pagan and Christian—Hades's remarks on learning of Lazarus's resurrection.[76]

Ἐγκώμιον one can also trace on three different levels: (1) pagan prescriptions from the pagan tradition; (2) Christians using the outer pagan structure, but with Christian models; and (3) encomium is used to guide and adorn other forms of literature.[77]

---

[72] J. Kykutris, Pauly-Wissowa, Real-Encyclopädie supp. 5 s.v. "Epistolographie" col.219.24 and 219.34.

[73] See Constable and Kazhdan concerning the reasons for success of the Christians in the world of the first few centuries C.E.: "Homo byzantinus and God" in *People and Power in Byzantium:* An Introduction to Modern Byzantine Studies, (Washington D.C.: Dumbarton Oaks Center for Byzantine Studies, 1982). Also for a more in-depth history of the whole period see Peter Brown, *The Making of Late Antiquity,* (Cambridge, MA: Harvard University Press, 1978).

[74] See *Rhetores graeci* 2.52.1

[75] See, for Ajax: Libanii opera, ed. R. Foerster (Leipzig 1925), 8.384*ff.*; for Danaë: Nicephorus Basilaces, *Rhetores graeci* 1. 476.

[76] See Nicephorus Basilaces, *Rhetores graeci* 1. 476*ff,* where pagan and Christian themes are presented side by side.

[77] See the panegyrics of the Cappadocians and later Fathers in honor of the Christian martyrs, the catalogue of praises in saints' lives, the extolling of

Σύνκρισις, the third of the forms of the panegyrical, also cuts across the other rhetorical types and affects them all. Simile is the simplest form of σύγκρισις and is indispensible to the encomium. Indeed, this was a major form of comparison: how much better was this man compared to a lesser man,[78] or how much better this mosaic is than that of Zeuxis, or this icon puts Pheidias to shame.[79] It was, however, in the homilies with their exhortations to lead a good life that we find comparisons used most effectively. Byzantine homilists never tired of comparing the works of God with those of the Devil, the grossness of heathenism with the beauty of the life of a saint. The technique was already biblical—witness the comparison of the wise and foolish virgins (Mt. 25.1-13). It must also have impressed itself upon the early fathers as they tried to define the dogmatic issues which needed to be dealt with as they defined Christian doctrine. Indeed, Gregory of Nazianzus encourages the use of mythology as a form of σύγκρισις, when he instructs a friend in the principles of effective writing.[80]

Ἔκφρασις is most often used to describe nature and, as a special category, works of art. It was particularly attractive to the medieval mind. As Guignet points out, works of art lent themselves particularly well to ἔκφρασις since they were immobile and fixed in form, and thus could be dealt with in detail.[81]

Ἔκφρασις is also one of the most thouroughly Christianized forms. The many descriptions of the heavenly majesty in the religious poetry of Byzantium—indeed, all of the liturgical poetry—serve as attestation of it Christian development. In the time of the Macedonian Renaissance and

---

the virtues of the Fathers in reverence of the exegete for the Gospel text, and the praise of the Lord of Heaven and other persons of the Christian pantheon through homily and hymn. Also see Kustas, footnote 23, for a comment on ψόγος and its fortunes at the hands of the Byzantines.

[78] Encomium was written with a great deal of what we would call 'falsehood.' But we must remember that it was a literary form. If the emperor, in fact, did not lead his troops in person it made no difference to the literary form—he led them in the ecomiastic spirit. The form demanded that he 'lead' his armies.

[79] See M. Guignet, *St. Grégoire de Nazianze et la rhétorique* (Paris 1911) 189.

[80] See Letter 46, PG 37.96A

[81] *St. Grégoire* 207

the revival of the interest in classical art, it is used to describe this very Christian art as well.[82]

Aphthonius defined μῦθος as "a false saying which mirrors the truth."[83] The use of fables in prose and verse during the period of the second Sophistic continued in Byzantium. Μῦθος answered the ethical demand of the religious mind. It may have been popular because its fictional appeal gave freedom from the confines of dogma and the strictures of doctrinal prescriptions.[84]

Χρεία, the development of a quotation of a specific author, was practiced in Byzantium with an eye to its application to preaching of the Gospel. Nicephorus Basilaces, a twelfth-century writer and professor of exegesis and author of a rhetorical manual, urged the use of Sophocles as a model of χρεία. Within the Christian empire the exegesis of scriptural meaning, the quotations of the early Fathers, and the vast body of catenae literature were the main uses of χρεία.

Χρεία reached its highest achievement in Byzantium homilies. The power and the beauty of Byzantine homilies is often achieved due to χρεία. An example of the application of χρεία in Byzantine homilies is found in C. Mango's translation of Photius' (810-895) homilies giving an example of the rich use of the rhetorical tradition.[85]

Before we look at homilies we must understand something of the theories of argumentation. Within rhetoric there were the three 'species': (1) judicial, (2) deliberative, and (3) epideictic. Within each of these were two subtypes. In judicial there were accusation and defense; in deliberative there were persuasion and dissuasion; and in epideictic there were praise and blame. Rhetorical performance was able to address a wide range of

---

[82] See Psellus: *Tzetzae allegoriae Iliadis; accedunt Pselli allegoriae,* ed. J. Boissonade (Paris 1851(363-365; *M. Pselli scripta minora 2: Epistulae,* ed E. Kurtz (Milan 1941) letter 188, 207-209. Also, C. Mango, "Antique statuary and the Byzantine beholder." *Dumbarton Oaks Papers* 17 (Washington 1963) 65: a description of an antique relief of Odysseus and Polyphemus by Contantine Manasses.

[83] 1.6 ἔστι δὲ μῦθος λόγος ψευδὴς εἰκονίζων τὴν ἀλήθειαν.

[84] See Kustas, "Function and Evolution of Byzantine Rhetoric," *Viator* 1 (1970 62.

[85] See C. Mango, *The Homilies of Photius, Patriarch of Constantinople: English Translation, Introduction and Commentary* (Cambridge, MA: 1958).

subjects and circumstances. Almost any human occasion could be viewed as debatable and approached rhetorically.[86]

Rhetoric in all three of its 'species' was not concerned with creating conceptual systems within which natural and rational orders could be defined as was philosophy. Rhetoric whose origin was in the judical and political assemblies of Greece, could not be expected to function under the same theories of argumentation as philosophy. Two results became clear: (1) rhetoric was concerned with social, contingent, debatable matters focused upon specific events; and (2) rhetoric could only argue for what is probable. Therefore, the most important evidence introduced in rhetorical debate came from the legal and cultural traditions of society, and not from the natural order—whose data could only be at best, illustrative. Rhetoric's proofs came to be called *pisteis,* which were commonly shared perspectives of those in debate. Therefore, in arguing a particular case persuasion would be determined by the degree to which traditional views and values could be marshaled in support of a given argument.[87] These traditional values were called 'final topics'or 'major aims' (τέλεα κεφάλαια) of the rhetorical speech. A list of these included that which is right (δίκαιος), lawful (νόμιμος), advantageous (συμφέρων), honorable (καλός), pleasant (ἡδύς), easy (ῥάδιος), feasible (δυνατός), and necessary (ἀναγκαῖος). These were not rigidly defined and so changed over time.

Argumentation required that three logical criteria be met: (1) a clear position had to be taken; (2) reasons for that position had to be given immediately; and (3) proofs had to be given supporting that position. Hence, rhetorical argumentation was inductive, using maxims or social and cultural traditions. However, a syllogism might arise deductively from a cultural phenomena by finding its major premise. This inferred proposition (ἐνθύμημα) can be seen in a New Testa-ment form in the Beatitudes in Matthew. Supporting arguments could be non-inventive or invented. Non-invented proofs were those that the rhetor did not create. These proofs were highly prized by early Christians because they established

86   See Burton L. Mack, *Rhetoric and the New Testament,* New Testament Series ed. Dan O. Via Jr. (Minneapolis: Fortress Press, 1990) 35.
87   It is, of course, Aristotle who in his *The Art of Rhetoric (Ars Rhetorica)* who is credited with working out the distinctions between philosophical and rhetorical argumentation. See Aristotle, *The "Art" of Rhetoric (Ars Rhetorica).* Trans. J.H. Freese, Loeb Classical Library, (Cambridge, MA: Harvard University Press, 1926).

the truth of what was being said. 'Witnesses,' 'oracles,' 'oaths,' 'miracles,' and 'prophetic predictions' were just a few of the forms of non-invented proofs. Examples would include arguments from 'the opposite,' 'the same,' 'the greater,' 'the lesser,' etc. Another form of proof available to the rhetor was the material that he could use as examples. Among these were historical examples (παράδειγμα), analogy (παραβολή), and fable (μῦθος). Paradigm was taken from history, and analogy and fable were taken from the worlds of nature and normal social practice.

The standard form of argumentation, which was called *thesis* (θέσις), consisted of: (1) an introduction (προοίμιον) that acknowledged the situation, addressed the audience, and established the ethos of the speaker; (2) a statement of the case that rehearsed the circumstances, clarfied the issue (stasis) and established the proposition with a reason (ratio, αἰτία) or by appeal to the final topics; (3) the supporting arguments that gave examples using the customary strategies from the topics; and (4) the conclusion that summarized the argument and pressed for its acceptance. These were the forms used with judical and deliberative rhetoric. Epideictic oratory followed a somewhat different outline that demonstrated the person's virtues and established the basis for his honors or memorial.[88]

Rhetorical education was not merely the mark of an educated man in the Byzantine Empire; it was also the requirement for admission to higher offices. Rhetorical education did not end with employment. Education meant both education and culture that went on for a lifetime. Kustas says that progymnasmata can be regarded in some way as a codification of the speculative spirit of the Greek language.[89] For the Byzantine all possibilities had to be considered. Every new variations on the theme of praise were enjoined by encomium. Ἠθοποιΐα was concerned with what so-and-so would say if . . . The possible meanings of a phrase were explored and its implications were developed. Questions such as, should I marry, take a trip, etc., were investigated on one level, while questions on

---

[88] Menander, a third century theorist, said that epideictic oratory is concerned with either praise (encomium) or blame (ψόγος). Menander gives rules for composing praises of countries, cities, harbors, and bays, in honor of birthdays, marriages, embassies, and coronations, as well as funerals. He uses the terms encomium and panegyric interchangeably. For a list of the possible forms of encomium see T. Viljamaa, *Studies in Greek Encomiastic Poetry of the Early Byzantine Period,* vol 2, no. 4 (Helsinki: 1968) 64.

[89] See Kustas, "Function and Evolution of Byzantine Rhetoric" *Viator* 1 (1970) 64.

the development of theological and homiletical topics were handled in a similar manner. Rhetoric, in short, permeated all of Byzantine life, in the streets, the schools and the highest levels of theological reflection.

While probably not so true on the streets of Byzantium, much of this form of reflection was done with a formality that meant the Greek language was Atticised. Certainly the style of rhetorical writing was to use Attic. One of the constant aspects of Byzantine culture was its love-affair with its past.[90] While there was a basic distinction between ἀττικῶς (ῥητορικῶς) and κοινῶς the basic style of rhetorical writing was to use classical Greek.[91] In this development the Byzantine Church participated fully. It is in poetry that the Church makes its greatest contribution to an atticised Greek; while in its homilies atticised Greek was used, the need to communicate with a less educated audience meant that the atticisation was limited. This was a difficulty for the Byzantines. John Chrysostom in *On the Priesthood* cautions "Let a man's diction be beggarly and his verbal composition simple and artless, but do not let him be inexpert in the knowledge and careful statement of doctrine."[92]

For the Christians of Late Antiquity the Holy Scriptures provided the main source for commentary. In the Byzantine Empire Old Testament commentary was on the basis of the LXX, and the New Testament on the Greek text. Certainly not all three styles of rhetoric (judicial, dicanic and panegyric) lent themselves well for the purposes of commentary. In the Byzantine world it is just this that separated Christian rhetorical practice from pagan. Although Christian rhetoric drew its foundation from classical rhetoric, it also reflected the radical theological orientation taught by Jesus and his disciples. Kennedy makes it clear that the source of inspiration for Christians . . . originated in Jewish attitudes toward God and speech found in the Old Testament:

---

[90]   Although the final codification of what was to be Byzantine Attic did not appear until the tenth century, it was developed all along.

[91]   See G. Böhlig, *Untersuchungen zum rhetorischen Sprachgebrauch der Byzantiner* (Berlin 1956) 3ff.

[92]   See St. John Chrysostom, *Six Books on the Priesthood,* trans. G. Neville (London, 1964) IV, 6,121-22. Quoted from: Cunningham, Mary B. "Innovation or Mimesis in Byzantine Sermons?" *Originality in Byzantine Literature, Art and Music: A Collection of Essays.* Ed. Anthony Robert Littlewood. Oxford [England]: Oxbow Books, 1995. 68.

> . . . Christian rhetoric presupposes the intervention of God in
> history and through the Holy Spirit, in the minds of men. For
> the classical ethos of the speaker it substitutes divine authority
> given canonization in the Scriptures and the revelation accorded
> to the Church; for probable argument as a basis of proof it
> substitutes proclamation of the *kergyma*, or divine message, but
> preserves the forms of inductive and deductive argument; for
> supporting evidence it turns to miracles and the acts of martyrs;
> and for pathos the Christian orator threatens damnation or
> promises eternal life. Christian rhetoric has distinctive topics
> and a distinctive style based largely on the language of the
> psalmist and the prophets.[93]

The tension between the classical rhetorical world and the needs of
Christians to communicate their beliefs to that world inevitably meant
that some accommodation was necessary. Indeed, that accommodation
appeared even in the work of St. Paul, who was not able to avoid dialectic in
dealing with matters of Church discipline. Questions of what a Christian's
relationship was to Jewish law illustrate this. In his letter to the Galatians,
and in his dispute with St. Peter, one can clearly see the working of this
dialectic. St. Paul had to interpret the teaching of Jesus by extending the
rational arguments and applying them to new questions.

The apologists of the second century use dialectic to explain the
correctness of the Christian position. In general, the need of the Church
to explain its thought and its zeal to convert pagan society to Christianity
drew it ever more into the realm of classical rhetorical practices. The
Church, although its Scriptures were written in *koiné,* had to utilize Attic
in order to makes its argument acceptable to the pagan world. Christian
exegetes interpreted the Scriptures that required them to use the art of
definition, division, and syllogistic reasoning.

Within the Christian apologists there arose two schools of exegetical
thought: Alexandria and Antioch. The Alexandrian school can best be
represented by Origen. For Origen the Scriptures were the inspired text
that God had arranged in a series of levels of meaning.[94] The lowest was

---

[93] George A. Kennedy, *Greek Rhetoric under Christian Emperors,* vol. 3 *A
      History of Rhetoric,* (Princeton NJ: Princeton University Press, 1983) 180.
[94] *On First Principles* 4.1.11.

the 'corporeal' level of the literary meaning; the moral level is higher, and the theological level is the highest. The last of these levels is the only one that is present throughout all parts of the Scripture, and its elucidation is the chief objective of the exegete and the preacher. In the Alexandrian school the use of allegorical interpretation became the prime characteristic of exegesis and from there it was tranmitted to the West, where it remained a major influence. In the East, however, the School of Antioch predominated, and allegory is consistently used in homilies and poetry but not as often for exegesis. Eastern exegesis in the fourth and fifth centuries was dominated by an acceptance of the literal meaning of the text and the seeking of historical explanation for the content.[95]

Gregory Thaumaturgus in his farewell to Origen in 238 provided the earliest known example of the use of the structure and the topics of classical epideictic oratory to create Christian panegyric. In about 270 C.E. Paul of Samosata, who was excommunicated by a synod of bishops for his view that Jesus was a man who became divine and not God who became a man, was also accused of excessively flamboyant oratorical delivery by Eusebius.[96] Interestingly Eusebius tells us that one of Paul's accusers was Malchion, a presbyter of great faith, who was also head of a sophistic school in Antioch!

With the fourth century and the legitimization of Christianity great changes took place in the relationship of Christianity to rhetoric. Eusebius is credited with the creation of Christian historiography. Through his oratory at I Nicaea (325 A.D.), as well as his written debate, his panegyrics of Constantine, and especially in his *Ecclesiastical History* in ten books, the use of classical rhetorical elements in the service of the Christian Church becomes legitimate too. However, it is classical rhetoric in a Christian key. Although Eusebius was familiar with the conventions of secular historians, he chose to quote extensively from original writings and documents rather than to create speeches for historical characters. In so doing, he sought to establish the authority of his work rather than give it dramatic brilliance. His Greek, both in style and in diction, reflects an elevated *koiné* rather

---

[95] See Christian Schaeubin, *Untersuchungen zu Methode und Herkunft der antiochenischen Exegese* (Theophaneia XXIII0, Cologne: Haustein, 1974.

[96] Eusebius, *Ecclesiastical History,* 7, 29-30 vol. II, trans. J.E.L. Oulton, Loeb Classical Library (Cambridge MA: Harvard University Press, 1964).

than Attic. He follows the model of the Christian preacher and weaves quotations from Scripture into his narrative.

Scholasticus, a fourth-century lawyer, in his history praises Socrates and Plato (3.23) and makes the distinction between philosophy, which is good, and dialectic or *philoneikia*, the love of disputation, which is destructive and, he believes, a major cause of the theological controversies of the fourth century (2.34; 3.22-23). But he also believed in the study of classical philosophy because "the Scriptures do not instruct using the art of reasoning, by means of which we may be enabled successfully to resist those who oppose the truth. Besides, adversaries are most easily foiled when we can use their own weapons against them." (3.16)[97]

Eusebius also demonstrates the feelings of the Church toward panegyric. Here again, Christians of the fourth century chose to adopt and adapt classical rhetorical style to their own ends. Panegyric, which as a public form of speech had been such an important element in classical rhetoric, adopted a particularly Christian character. The earliest example we have is repeated as a whole in Eusebius. It was delivered on the occasion of the reconstruction of the church in Tyre. But unlike a classical rhetorical panegyrist, who would have lauded Bishop Paulinus who headed the reconstruction of the church, Eusebius celebrates primarily the victory of the Church over her enemies—the visible and material church in Tyre is made a symbol for the greater and invisible Church (sections 21, 22, & 26). Quotations and allusions to Scripture are woven into the language and imagery. The forms of verbal amplification (sections 15-16), the use of an extended series of rhetorical questions (sections 17-20), and the use of paraleipsis (sections 43-44) represent classical panegyric. Additonally, in the description of the church at Tyre Eusebius adopts the progymnasmatic form of the exphrasis. And if one were to extend the search for parallels one might find *synkrisis* in his opposition of the Devil and Christ (sections 58-61).[98]

The homily, which in Greek means "conversation," implies an informality in structure, and, in the Christian context, a reliance on authority and inspiration. Its origin seems to have been in the elucidations and applications of the scriptural readings in the Jewish Sabbath services.

---

[97] Text ed. R. Hussey, revised by W. Bright, Oxford Univ. Press, 1893; English translation by A.C. Zeno, *SLN & PNF,* Second Series, II.

[98] See Eusebius, *Ecclesiastical History,* vol. 1. Trans. Kirsopp Lake, Loeb Classical Library (Cambridge, MA: Harvard University Press, 1965).

One can see examples of this in the homilies of Jesus and Paul. Because of their exhortations to live a religious life, homilists were influenced by diatribe and so fell to some extent under the genre of rhetoric with its style; yet they remained primarily tied to the scriptural Greek text.

2.3 Rhetoric and Byzantine Homilies

Homilies and the exegesis of Scripture were very closely related. Exegesis, being the discovery of the truth, corresponded to dialectic in the classical rhetorical tradition. But its source of authority was the *Kerygma*.[99] Due to the homily's close tie to Scripture it took on some of the imagery and rhythmical devices that were common to Hebrew poetry. Some, such as antithesis, assonance, anaphora, and isocolon, were identical with figures of speech in classical rhetoric.

Melito of Sardis, a second century bishop, illustrates the process of mixing biblical and rhetorical figures.[100] The poetry of the Psalms and the rhetoric of the Prophets could be regarded as presenting the mystical perception of the ineffable widom-not-of-this-world, that the Church found to be proper subject matter for the preaching of the *Kerygma*.

Many more examples of the mixing of biblical and rhetorical figures can be given by citing the homilies of Gregory of Nyssa, Gregory Nazianzus, John Chrysostom, Theodore of Mopsuestia, Cyril of Alexandria, Athanasius, Proklus and many, many others. While these examples are interesting, a full development of the history of homiletics during this period is beyond the scope of this inquiry. The documentation for the role of rhetoric and the homilies of the Capadocians alone would easily comprise another paper.[101]

---

[99] The relationship of the homily and rhetoric is best seen in the *De Doctrina Christiana* of St. Augustine. For a closer look see George A. Kennedy, *Greek Rhetoric Under Christian Emperors,* A History of Rhetoric, (Princeton NJ: Princeton University Press, 1983) 183.

[100] Greek use of Biblical figures is largely typological. At a conference in Amiens France, Olivier Clément, an Orthodox lay theologian, emphasized that historically the Orthodox Church has chosen to interpret Scripture and its role in the life of the Church in typological terms.

[101] See George A. Kennedy, *Greek Rhetoric Under the Christian Emperors,* A History of Rhetoric vol. 3, (Princeton NJ: Princeton University Press, 1983) 180-325.

Rhetoric as a system had a long development in Greek history. It was already well established as a tool of discourse in the first century C.E. and continued to be re-applied in the Greek-speaking world during the Byzantine Empire. When Christians began to spread their message to the Greek world, they naturally used the forms that had been created by that society, of which they were a part and, in which they had been educated. Rhetoric played a role in their proclamations of the Christian faith from the apologists to the Ecumenical Councils. In the homilies and the liturgical life of the Church and on those formal occasions during the time of the Byzantine Empire, the Church used rhetoric to proclaim its faith to all who were fellow celebrants of Byzantium.

Finally, the importance of rhetoric's role in the production of Byzantine homilies is well stated by George L. Kustas when he writes: "Rhetoric did not simply provide the machinery of literary endeavor; it was a key element of the Byzantine *Weltanschauung*."[102]

---

[102] George L. Kustas, *Studies in Byzantine Rhetoric* 1.

Chapter Three

The Way of Byzantine Theological Reflection—Poetry, Homily, Iconography, and Liturgy

One of the burdens of this dissertation is to illustrate how theology is done in the Middle Byzantine era. We have much information on the Early and Middle Byzantine era and the way theology was done with regard to the Virgin Mary.[103] We also have much current speculation about the role of the Virgin Mary in the Middle Byzantine era.[104] Some of these volumes contain extensive bibliographies that reflect the current state of the question and underscore the reason for this dissertation.[105] I hope that this dissertation will add to the knowledge of how the Theotokos is viewed from the perspective of the Orthodox Church.

---

[103] See, for example, Hilda Graef, *Mary: A History of Doctrine and Devotion* (New York, 1963) and M. Carroll, *The Cult of the Virgin Mary, Psychological Origins.* (New Jersey, 1986). Also see the classical articles by A. M. Cameron, 'The Theotokos in Sixth-Century Constantinople: A City Finds its Symbol' *JThSt 29* (1978), 79-108 and her 'The Virgin's Robe: an Episode in the History of Early Seventh-Century Constantinople,' *Byz 49 (1979) 42-56.*

[104] See Bissera V. Pentcheva, *Icons and Power: The Mother of God in Byzantium.* University Park, PA: The Pennsylvania State University Press, 2006. and Maria Vassilaki,. *Images of the Mother of God : Perceptions of the Theotokos in Byzantium.* Aldershot, Hants, England ; Burlington, VT: Ashgate, 2005. *Mother of God. Representations of the Virgin in Byzantine Art.* Ed. Maria Vassilaki. Milan and Athens: Benaki Museum, 2000. These volumes have extensive bibliographies.

[105] Averil Cameron in *Mother of God* 3-15, n. 1; the bibliography on the Theotokos is vast, but most authors approach the subject from the Roman Catholic position.

29

In this period, a period of transition with regard to the way in which the Virgin is viewed, we have some clear indications of how Byzantine theological development took place. Niki Tsironis points out that

> There is nothing haphazard about this process: a new theme first emerges in the free images of poetry; it then moves over into the language of religious homilies, which is also poetical but is closer to the liturgical style; it appears next in iconography; and only when the new theme has been fully integrated within all those media can it be adopted and assimilated into liturgical texts—a process which signifies the full incorporation and consolidation of this new theme into the body of Orthodox religious practice.[106]

This process of poetry-homily-iconography-liturgical texts is a natural process in the Byzantine world. During the iconoclastic period we can illustrate this process as homilies shift in their treatment of the Theotokos. Germanos is a good representative of the new theme and the new style in homilies. In his homily on the *Passion of Christ*, Germanos stresses the human qualities of the Theotokos. He sees in her tenderness a confirmation of the human nature which she gave to her Son. "She endures his passion and death in human fashion."[107] Later in the same homily he shows her grief and in a poetic fashion links her grieving and His birth. 'The mother reaches a peak in her lamentations. She conceives still greater sighs. She gives birth to a more extensive weeping. For now she no longer has sight of her son. The sun knew its setting, going below the earth, and it became night for the mother of the Sun. A night of heavy sorrow and disaster."[108] It is here that we meet yet another characteristic of Byzantine poetry and homilies, that of using epithets based on Old Testament typologies.[109]

---

[106] Tsironis, Niki. "From Poetry to Liturgy: The Cult of the Virgin in the Middle Byzantine Era." *The Mother of God : Representations of the Virgin in Byzantine Art.* Ed. Maria Vassilaki. New York: Abbeville, 2004. 91-9.

[107] *PG* 98 269A

[108] *PG* 98 269B, quoted from Tsironis, "From Poetry" 91.

[109] There is a growing literature on the subject of typology and allegory in the Byzantine homilies. See, M. Warner, *Alone of All Her Sex, the Myth and the Cult of the Virgin Mary* (London, 1976). Metropolitan Kallistos (Timothy Ware) *Mary in the Orthodox Tradition* (Wallington, Surrey, 1997). Young,

3.1 Typologies in Byzantine Homilies

For a people that considered itself to be the "New Israel" it was only natural that they should see in Old Testament types the foreshadowing of the stages of salvation history.[110] Typology is basic to both the hymnographical and the homiletical literature of the Orthodox Church. Together they form part of the liturgical worship. While hymns, especially those to the Theotokos, are numerous, they are difficult to classify, since they are scattered throughout the year. As a general rule, homilies to the Theotokos are related specifically to feasts in honor of the Theotokos.[111] Additionally, homilies not only have a specific occasion for their production, but are also frequently identifiable with a specific author and, maybe, place.[112] Homilies lend themselves to easy interpretation, often with agendas unknown to the original authors.[113]

Biblical Exegesis, 192-5. Archimandrite Ephraim Lash, 'Mary in the Eastern Christian Literature', *Epiphany* 1989) 310-21. Cunningham, M.B. "The Meeting of the Old and the New: The Typology of Mary the Theotokos in Byzantine Homilies and Hymns". *Studies in Church History, the Church and Mary.* Ed. R. N. Swanson. Rochester, NY: Ecclesiastical History Society/ Boydell Press, 2004.

[110] See Ch. Hannick, 'Exégèse, typologie et rhétorique dans l'hymnographie byzantine' *DOP* 53 (1999) 207-18.

[111] See Christian Hannick, "The Theotokos in Byzantine Hymnography: Typology and Allegory." *Images of the Mother of God : Perceptions of the Theotokos in Byzantium.* Ed. Maria Vassilaki. Aldershot, Hants, England; Burlington, VT: Ashgate, 2005. xxxii, 383 p.,[22] p. of plates. 70.

[112] While this is generally true, there still are many homilies that are misattributed as well. See, Laurentin, René. 'Table rectificative des pièces mariales inauthentiques ou discutées contenues dans les deux patrologies de migne.' *Court traité de théologie mariale.* Paris, 1954.

[113] It is the contention of this dissertation that if we wish Byzantine homilies to provide evidence for contemporary theological needs it is also important to allow them to speak from their own context. Often allowing them to speak from their own context will yield new insights into contemporary theological issues. Several examples of searching for contemporary theological answers in Middle Byzantine homilies are the great contributions of: Jugie, Martin. Homélies Mariales Byzantines: textes grecs édités et traduits en latin I—II. *PO.* 16.3 (1921); 19.3 (1925) (repr. Turnhout. 1990). Th. Toscani and I. Cozza, *De immaculata deiparae conceptione, hymnologia graecorum ex editis et manuscriptis codicibus cryptoferratensibus* (Rome, 1862). R. Caro.

Germanos frequently used typological references in his homilies. For example, in his first homily on the Presentation in the Temple he calls Mary: (κάλυμμα τῆς νέας διαθήκης)[114] 'the ark of the New Covenant' neatly combining the images of the ark and the New Testament. In the same homily one can see typology dissolving into theology when Germanos proclaims Mary to be:

> 'the all-golden jar, which holds the sweetest delight of our souls, Christ, the manna . . . you surpassed all created beings, O gift of God, untilled earth, un-ploughed field, vine with fair branches, delightful cup, bubbling fountain, Virgin who gave birth and Mother who knew no man, treasure of innocence and pride of holiness.'[115]

And then a little later he exclaims: 'with your well-received and maternally persuasive prayers to your Son, born of you without a father, and to God, the creator of all things.'[116] Clearly Germanos has used some Old Testament terms to designate the New Testament role of the Virgin Mary, and in so doing has proclaimed her as the intercessor for 'all things.'[117]

Typology as an exegetical method provided many ways of connecting the Theotokos to New Testament/Christian theological development. Typologies provided an opportunity to do theology in a rhetorical format. In the process of doing theology, typology moved to allegory where the comparison and transition becomes more developed. Allegory is a rhetorical tool that provides for deeper exegetical investigation.[118] It also occasioned

---

La homilética mariana griega en el siglo V I—II (Marian Library Studies, 3—4) Dayton, OH 1971-72.

[114] PG 98, 384A

[115] PG 98, 309C

[116] PG 98, 309C

[117] A recent study edited by Maria Vassilaki illustrates that there is a growing interest concerning Mary for other than theological purposes. This volume (Mother of God. Representations of the Virgin in Byzantine Art. Milan and Athens: Benaki Museum, 2000) shows that there is a significant number of Byzantinists who are principally interested in the role of Mary as an historical and sociological force in Byzantium.

[118] See Christian Hannick, "The Theotokos in Byzantine Hymnography: Typology and Allegory" 75.

the use of both New Testament and apocryphal literature.[119] This freedom
that the Byzantine exegete felt with regard to creating poetry, homilies,
hymnography and liturgical texts is often misunderstood from a western
European perspective. Hannick points out that this criticism does not
take into account the hymnographic and poetic production of Byzantine
Orthodoxy.[120]

Byzantine theology is liturgical. In reference to Father Alexander
Schmemann's contention that the highest theological statements in
Orthodoxy are found in the midst of the liturgical life (*lex orandi est lex
credendi*),[121] Tsironis points out that:

> We should note that the fully-fledged doctrinal formulations
> characteristic of other Christian denominations are not a feature
> of Orthodoxy: the decrees of the various Ecumenical Councils
> mainly dealt with the condemnation of heresies expounded and
> creating problems within the Church.[122]

In Germanos' homilies we can see the working of the Byzantine
theological mind. Germanos was doing exegesis in a Byzantine fashion. He
was preaching to the public and his exegesis and rhetorical skill were being
evaluated by the public at the same time.[123] Fr. Schmemann states concerning
the process of creating a Byzantine Christian world, 'The meeting of the
new and now more peaceable approach of the new religion and the world
can be described as a meeting which took place on the basis of worship. The
conversion of this world was primarily a liturgiological conversion.'[124]

> Each parameter of what we call Orthodox doctrine was tested
> by the faithful; that is by the Church—in other words by the
> people, in the literal meaning of the Greek word *ekklesia*. Only

---

[119] One of the most common apocryphal sources was the *Protevangelium of
James*. E. de Strycker, *La forme la plus ancienne du protévangile de Jacques*
(*Subsidia Hagiographica,* 33) (Brussels, 1961).
[120] Hannick, 75-6.
[121] Alexander Schmemann, *Liturgy and Tradition: Theological Reflections of
Alexander Schmemann* ed. Th. Fish (Crestwood, NY, 1990), 11-20.
[122] Tsironis 98.
[123] Tsironis, 98.
[124] Schmemann 11-20

after receiving their affirmation and approval was a doctrine entrusted to the liturgy and incorporated within the tradition. This 'filtration process' for the acceptance or rejection of dogma involved the whole Church, clergy and laity as a single body, . . . the adoption of the experimental imagery of poetry and homiletics by religious art, and its subsequent transference through the agency of the *melourgos* into the liturgical life of the Church, where, once established, it would remain alive and unchallenged throughout the centuries. The theoretical background to this process is in complete harmony with Orthodox theory and practice since it confirms the 'power' of the people in the life of the Church.[125]

Germanos' importance (for this dissertation at least) is that he was at the juncture of two important ages in the development of Byzantine Mariology. His dates (630-730 CE) place him at the beginning of the Middle Byzantine period and at the cusp of the iconoclastic controversy. His letters, writings, and homilies make it clear that he was a major player in his era. It is especially in his homilies on the Virgin Mary that we can see the theological process taking place. The Virgin Mary herself perhaps best exemplifies this transition from poetry to homily to liturgy 'as it is the contrast between the striking absence of the ecclesiastical doctrine and the devotion—equally striking—on the part of the faithful which finally elevates the Mother of God to become the very symbol of the Orthodox Church.'[126] Germanos, who was anathematized by the iconoclastic council at Hiereia in 754 and canonized by the Seventh Ecumenical Council in 787, was an important developer of the Orthodox Christian position that she is the guarantor of the Incarnation. Her humanity guaranteed the humanity of Christ, and the willingness of the Virgin Mary to 'lend' her humanity to God was the basis of the theology of the iconodules.[127] Germanos is credited with a large part in the resolution of that controversy.

---

[125] Tsironis, 98-9.

[126] Tsironis, 99.

[127] The literature on the Iconoclastic controversy is very large. See Leslie Brubaker, et al. *Byzantium in the Iconoclast Era (Ca 680-850) : The Sources : An Annotated Survey. Birmingham Byzantine and Ottoman Monographs.* Vol. 7. Aldershot UK: Ashgate, 2001. And others in the bibliography.

3.2 Apophatic and Cataphatic Language

It is well established that Orthodox theology is apophatic in nature.[128] But it is also the case that Orthodox theology uses language apophatically.[129] The theological language of the Orthodox Church is construed to represent the un-representable. This is why it takes its form in the poetical, liturgical, and rhetorical. None of these require the precise definition of cataphatic language. There can be no adequate conceptual grasp of such theological elements as God's essence, or the paradox of Mary. Theological language must maintain a sense of mystery and ineffability about the divine.[130] Words are like icons pointing toward that which is ineffable. Since language could never approach an adequate level to describe God, language could be used in all its apophatic force without the danger that it would be construed as other than a human attempt to describe that which is unable to be described by mere human language.

Much of the misunderstanding that arises in the minds of Catholic Mariologists when reading Byzantine texts is due to their searching for the cataphatic definitions of Western theology.

3.3 Byzantine Mariological Reflection

Byzantine Mariology begins and ends in mystery. Father Schmemann points out:

A student of Mariology in the Orthodox Church may be struck by two apparently contradictory facts: on the one hand, a tremendous richness of Mariological material in the liturgy, yet, on the other hand, a virtual absence of specifically Mariological studies in theology. It is indeed a real paradox of the Orthodox East that the whole of its Mariological experience and piety seems to have permeated its worship but did not provoke any significant theological reflection. We have nothing that would correspond to specialized Mariological treatises in the

---

[128] "Apophatic Theology". Orthodox Wiki. <http://orthodoxwiki.org/Apophatic_theology>.

[129] Peterson, Michael L. *Philosophy of Religion : Selected Readings*. 3rd ed. New York: Oxford University Press, 2007. 426.

[130] Peterson, 426

> West, and in our manuals of dogmatics there are no separate chapters dealing with the place of Mary in the economy of salvation. Thus, the veneration of Mary—so obvious, so central in worship—has not been expressed, analyzed, or evaluated systematically.[131]

This has caused mutual difficulties in understanding each other for the two rich Mariological traditions of the West and the East. This theological conundrum is not easily unraveled. It requires charity on the part of both "lungs of the Church" and an acceptance of differing theological methodologies. A starting point is to recognize that for both Roman Catholics and Orthodox, Mariology is always Christological. Mariology arose in the midst of the great Christological debate of the fourth and fifth centuries. "This means that from the very beginning Mariology was understood as precisely an integral part of *Christology* and thus—ultimately—of the Christian experience of God and man."[132] The council was, as Dr. Paul Meyendorff points out, "laconic" in its definition formulated at the Third Ecumenical Council (Ephesus, 431).[133] But the Byzantines did not develop the same rigorous philosophical/ theological discipline that the Latin West did

3.4 The Role of Philosophy and Orthodox Theology

Dr. H. Tristram Engelhardt, Jr, a physician and ethical philosopher, points to the different roles philosophy has played in the two theological worlds of Western and Eastern Christianity.[134] Dr. Engelhardt contends that philosophy's role in the Byzantine world remains as the handmaid of

---

[131]   Alexander Schmemann, "Celebration of Faith." Trans. John A Jillions. *The Virgin Mary*. Vol. 3. 3 vols. Crestwood, NY: St. Vladimir's Seminary Press, 2001. 85.

[132]   Schmemann, "Mary: The Archetype of Mankind" 49.

[133]   Alexander Schmemann, *"Celebration of Faith."* 7.

[134]   H. Tristram Engelhardt, "Critical Reflections on Theology's Handmaid: Why the Role of Philosophy in Orthodox Christianity Is So Different." *Philosophy & Theology* 18.1 (2006): 53-75. I am grateful to Dr. Engelhard for his permission and encouragement to use his work in this dissertation. A fuller treatment can be found in: Engelhardt, H. Tristram. *The Foundations of Christian Bioethics*. Lisse [The Netherlands]; Exton, PA: Swets & Zeitlinger Publishers, 2000. See especially chapter 4.

theology and contributes only in certain restricted areas to the theological enterprise. Theology appears to be an enterprise separate from the educational system in the Byzantine Empire. For example, in the fifth century the School of Advanced Christian Studies appointed one professor of philosophy among its thirty-one teachers, but no theologians. There were five teachers of rhetoric in this so-called University of Constantinople.[135] He claims that the Byzantine theological enterprise is noetic rather than discursive and that theology is done "as a practice of pursuing a relationship with God through prayer, almsgiving, asceticism and vigils that can lead through grace to an unmediated knowledge of God."[136]

Dr. Engelhardt distinguishes nine senses of philosophy and four senses of theology. He points to the almost completely academic construal of these fields in Western theology and makes distinctions among the senses of philosophy and theology by his claim that only a few of them obtain in the Byzantine Christian theological enterprise.[137]

The nine senses of philosophy are:

1. Philosophy as a way of life involving an immanent pursuit of virtue and human excellence, most especially wisdom (e.g., the Epicureans);

2. Philosophy as a pursuit of immediate knowledge (e.g., noetic knowledge) of a transcendent reality, guided not by special revelation held to have occurred in the past, but by intellectual (i.e., noetic) intuition and or discursive reasoning (e.g., neo-Platonists);

---

[135] Basile Tatakis, *Byzantine Philosophy*." Trans. Nicholas J. Moutafakis. Indianapolis: Hackett, 2003. 11. Other sources are: B. N. Tatakis. *Christian Philosophy in the Patristic and Byzantine Tradition.* Trans. George Dion Dragas. Orthodox Theological Library. Ed. George Dion Dragas. Vol. 4. Rollinsford, NH: Orthodox Research Institute, 2007. Katerina Ierodiakonou, *Byzantine Philosophy and Its Ancient Sources.* Oxford: Clarendon Press, 2002. David Bradshaw. *Aristotle East and West : Metaphysics and the Division of Christendom.* Cambridge ; New York: Cambridge University Press, 2007.

[136] Engelhardt, *Critical Reflections* 56.

[137] For a recent defense of the contribution of philosophy to theological reflection, see John Paul II. 1998. *Fides et Ratio.* Vatican *City:* Libreria Editrice Vaticana.

3. Philosophy as the philosophy of nature in the sense of rational reflection on the structure of reality and on empirical experience (e.g., as undertaken by the Greek Atomists);

4. Philosophy as the discursive, speculative exploration of the nature of being, including metaphysics both general and special (e.g., rational psychology);

5. Philosophy as the pursuit of clarity in claims through engaging and framing conceptual distinctions and through drawing out the implications of particular moral, metaphysical, and epistemological commitments without any view towards making substantive progress in the understanding of morality, epistemology, and metaphysics;

6. Philosophy as the disciplined description and analysis of what is presented to consciousness (e.g., phenomenology);

7. Philosophy as the conceptual analysis of the character and soundness of claims, arguments, and ways of regarding reality and morality (e.g., contemporary analytic and hermeneutic philosophy) towards the goal of making substantive progress in the understanding of morality, epistemology, and metaphysics;

8. Philosophy as the use of reasoning to support and advance the plausibility of one's religious/metaphysical/moral position, although the arguments and analyses offered are not considered sufficient by themselves to establish one's position by sound rational argument (as with the Sophists, many rhetoricians, and early Christian apologists);

9. Philosophy as the pursuit and/or expression of the truth of Christianity guided by the Holy Spirit.[138]

The four theological senses are:

1. discursive reflection on the nature of beings so as to demonstrate the nature and existence of God, as well as the nature of the relation and duties of created beings to their Creator; this sense of theology engages philosophy in the fourth sense, namely, metaphysical reasoning, especially that special metaphysics usually termed natural theology;

2. the discursive analysis and assessment of religious concepts, claims, arguments, and ways of regarding religious truth so

---

[138] *Critical Reflections* 54-5 (footnotes removed)

as to advance religious knowledge. Theology in this sense is a species of the seventh sense of philosophy and is tantamount to the philosophy of religion, with the cardinal difference that the truth of a particular revealed religion is granted as the foundation for philosophical-religious reflection and speculation; not only are the implications of a particular revelation drawn out, but they are combined with philosophical understandings, so that, within this genre of theology, the breadth and depth of theological claims can grow and dogma can develop;

3. theology as a practice of pursuing a relationship with God through prayer, almsgiving, asceticism, and vigils that can lead through grace to an unmediated knowledge of God; theology in this sense occurs through turning from oneself to God—it begins in the will, in repentance and in turning to God, and not in discursive, rational reflection or intellectual contemplation. This sense of theology defines the mind of the Church, which does not change or develop, because the Church is the Body of Christ (Colossians 1:24) and Christ is the same yesterday, today, and forever (Hebrews 8:4).

4. theology as the analysis or exegesis of the theological knowledge acquired through theology in the third sense; such analysis is not strictly dependent on any philosophical account of morality, knowledge, or reality; this form of theology leads to no new knowledge and does not support the development of doctrine, since what it offers must always remain within the confines of theology in the third sense; however, there can be development in the clarity of the expression or formulation of dogmas, which developments can then be of use in responding to heresies.[139]

Among the nine senses of philosophy he contends that the ninth one is equivalent to Orthodox theology.[140] The second and fourth are academic disciplines found within seminaries, and the third one in practice is liturgical-ascetic-noetic rather than academic.[141] Only the third and fourth senses of theology are accepted as Orthodox.

---

[139] *Critical Reflections* 56-7 (footnotes removed)

[140] "This last use of philosophy is materially equivalent to the Orthodox Christian understanding of theology." *Critical Reflections* 55.

[141] *Critical Reflections* 55-6.

It is argued that Orthodox Christianity has affirmed theology in the third and fourth sense, while rejecting a place for the first and second senses of theology. Indeed, it is only theology in the third sense that for Orthodox Christianity *is* theology *sensu stricto.* As a result, it is only the fifth sense of philosophy that properly plays a direct role in Orthodox Christian theology, and then only for theology in the fourth sense, although philosophy in the eighth sense is employed in apologetics, and the ninth sense is materially equivalent to theology in the third sense. These claims amount to holding that Orthodox theology is at its core mystical. [142]

Engelhard's analysis provides a theoretical foundation for understanding the different, although complementary, methods of theological reflection. At base Byzantine theological reflection is liturgical and mystical.

3.5 Liturgy and Mary

Both the liturgical and the mystical are tied together in Byzantine Mariology. Father Schmemann points out that:

The liturgy is the main, if not exclusive *locus* of Mariology in the Orthodox Church. As I said before, Mary has never become the object of any special and separate theological speculation; one would seek in vain for a Mariological treatise in our manuals of dogma. This liturgical veneration has, to be sure, been adorned with much piety, symbolism and allegory, and this has led to questions about the biblical character and justification of these forms.[143]

There is very little said about Mary in the canonical scriptures. Jesus Christ's birth is mentioned by Matthew and Luke. Mark does not mention her at all. And in John's gospel she appears only twice; once at the beginning at the wedding in Cana and at the very end, standing by the Cross. In the Acts of the Apostles she appears only once, where she appears with the

---

[142] *Critical Reflections* 57 also see fn 7.
[143] Schmemann, "On Mariology in Orthodoxy" 61

gathered disciples at prayer. She is not mentioned in any of the other books of the New Testament; not in Paul's epistles nor the other books.[144] On the surface this relative paucity should rule out Mary as a major person in the history of salvation. In what has to be one of the most beautifully crafted statements about the reasons the Orthodox Church has for including her, Father Schmemann states:

Let me put it this way: if our faith in Christ knew nothing of His Mother except that she existed and that her name was Mary, then even this most elementary knowledge would be enough to genuinely know her, to behold in her image, to find within Christian faith and to find likewise within our own hearts all that the Church has seen, heard and come to know in two thousand years.[145]

Within the Byzantine liturgical world we can find feasts of the Virgin Mary, hymns to the Virgin Mary, para-liturgical Marian piety, Marian iconography and homilies that elaborate the Orthodox Church's Marian themes.

The Marian feasts form a highly developed cycle of Marian commemorations. Four of them are counted among the twelve great feasts: the Nativity of the Virgin (September 8), the Presentation of the Theotokos in the Temple (November 21), the Annunciation (March 25), and the Dormition of the Theotokos (August 15).[146] In addition there are a number of lesser Marian feasts such as: the Protection of the Virgin (October 1), the Synaxis of the Theotokos (December 26), and the Conception of the Theotokos (December 9)—to name the best known ones. In addition we should mention the Feast of the Sash of the Theotokos (August 31) on which Germanos preached.

As a general rule each cycle of prayers has at its conclusion a special prayer to the Virgin Mary. These prayers are the so-called *theotokia,* that follow the doxology "Glory to the Father, the Son and the Holy Spirit, now and ever and unto ages of ages."

The icons of the Theotokos form an integral part of each Orthodox Church. Their specific locations, the two most common being the apse and on the iconostasis, have particular theological meaning.[147]

---

[144] I am leaving aside, for the moment, the allegorical and typological references to Mary found in the Old Testament and the Book of the Revelation of John.

[145] Schmemann, "The Mother of God" 15.

[146] One might also include the Presentation of Christ in the Temple (February 22) that is deeply Marian, and is one of the Great Feasts.

[147] For the connection between the placement of icons and the rhetorical tradition in late middle Byzantium see Henry Maguire, "Byzantine Rhetoric, Latin

The best known of the para-liturgical texts must be the *Akathistos* hymn sung during the first four Fridays of Great Lent. There are too many others to mention. But among them are many *Akathistoi*, hymns written after the *Akathistos*.

It should be evident by now that Mariology, in the Byzantine sense, does not make of Mary a particular cult, added to that of Christ; rather it is "an essential dimension of the cult addressed to God and Christ, a quality or tonality of that cult."[148]

3.6 Byzantine Epistemology and Ontology

If one dimension of Byzantine Mariology can be found in the liturgical life of the Church, it must also be said that that dimension is an outgrowth of the process of doing theology in the Byzantine mode. Clearly the knowledge which forms the basis of Mariology must come from some other source that is not discursive. It comes from knowledge gained from spiritual practices such as fasting and prayer within the community of the Orthodox Church. These practices have largely been within the monastic communities. Staretz Sophrony (1896-1993), a late twentieth-century Orthodox theologian, states:

> The rationalist-theologian is concerned with a multitude of problems whose solution he seeks through philosophical speculation. His actual religious experience is not very wide. It proceeds mainly from the rational sphere of his being, not from a lively communion with God. He counts his scientific erudition and intellectual experience as spiritual riches, rating them so highly that all other knowledge takes second place.[149]

Drama and the Portrayal of the New Testament." *Rhetoric in Byzantium : Papers from the Thirty-Fifth Spring Symposium of Byzantine Studies, Exeter College, University of Oxford, March 2001.* Ed. Elizabeth Jeffreys. Aldershot, Hants, England; Burlington, VT: Ashgate, 2003. xii, 215-33.

[148] Schmemann, *Mary in Eastern Liturgy* 90. One friend put it that: "In Western Mariology she is the frosting on the cake; in Byzantine Mariology she is part of the cake mix."

[149] Sophrony. *Saint Siouan the Antonite*. Trans. Rosemary Edmonds. Essex, UK: Stavropegic Monastery of St. John the Baptist, 1991. 190.

This "lively communion with God" does not reject the clarifying role of discursive philosophy, but does not accept philosophy as in any way capable of informing theology, rather, it is the other way around. Engelhard underscores this:

> If one brings these distinctions somewhat recast to the examination of the relationship between philosophy and theology, one can identify not only (1) different understandings of metaphysics or ontology, that is, of the basic nature of reality (the Orthodox recognize that God in His nature is fully transcendent and therefore in His nature incomprehensible, while in the West an *analogia entis* is claimed) and (2) different understandings of the nature of knowledge claims (noetic knowledge for the Orthodox is the primary mode of theological knowledge, while in Western Christianity theology is primarily discursive, so that theology is grounded in experience of God in traditional Christianity and in knowledge about God in Western Christianity), but also (3) different exemplars of good knowledge, (4) different exemplars of reliable knowers (holy men versus learned scholars), and (5) different sociologies of knowledge (much of Orthodox Christian theology is undertaken outside of the academy; while Western Christian theology generally occurs in the academy), all of which is set within different communities of knowers.[150]

Thus Byzantine metaphysics recognizes God as fully transcendent and deems knowledge of God to be primarily apophatic. "To claim (as does Aquinas, for instance) that it [theology] is a science in the Aristotelian sense—one that has God as its subject matter—would have struck the Byzantines as strangely pretentious".[151]

Epistemically theological knowledge *sensu stricto* is only found by participation in the life of the Church. Correct participation in the life of the Church is the *sine qua non* for proper theological reflection. As

---

[150]   Engelhard, *Critical Reflections* 60-1.

[151]   David Bradshaw. *Aristotle East and West : Metaphysics and the Division of Christendom.* Cambridge, U.K. ; New York, NY: Cambridge University Press, 2007.

David Bradshaw puts it, "Orthodox Christianity's apophaticism [is] at the root of the entire [Orthodox] tradition. What is the point of spinning out words about God when He can be known only through practice? On such a view theology, however complex it may become, is ultimately simply the enterprise

of preserving 'the faith once delivered to the saints.'"[152] Orthodox theological epistemology is noetic and empirical.[153] God is viewed not as an essence to be grasped intellectually, but as an *energeia* to be known through participation in the life of the Orthodox Church.[154]

Byzantine theological reflection is multi-faceted. While it is true that one can find instances of similar approaches in the Orthodox world to the West, it is clear that they are not given the same authority as in the West. Empirical and noetic knowledge has been the norm for Orthodox theology. That effort is located in the monastic communities. Orthodox theological schools in the West approach theological education as liturgically based. It is through the liturgy that one learns theology. [155] While this may seem intellectual questionable from a Western perspective[156], it had been the vehicle of Orthodox theology under very trying circumstances and has proven to be effective in teaching the Orthodox faith.[157] Orthodox theology is more implicit than explicit. That is the nature of theology that begins with poetry and ends in liturgical, auricular, noetic knowledge.

---

[152] Bradshaw 221.

[153] Dr. Engelhard suggests that there is a parallel with medicine with regard to the role of philosophy. 63-4.

[154] See Bradshaw 153*ff* for a fuller explanation of the relationship of *energia* and knowledge.

[155] One of the standards for the education of convert clergy to the Orthodox Church is to spend an liturgical year at a seminary before ordination in the Orthodox Church.

[156] M. Gordillo, *Mariologia orientalis*. "Orientalia christiana analecta", 141 (1954) attempts to reconcile the Eastern and Western traditions by taking Western presuppositions for granted. From, Meyendorff *Byzantine Theology*, 235.

[157] One only needs to look at the survival of the Orthodox Church in the USSR to see the power of this form of doing theology.

Chapter Four

Middle Byzantine Homilies Types and Purposes of Homilies

We have established that one of the main influences on Middle Byzantine homilies was the primacy of rhetorical education. There does not appear to be any gap in the influence of rhetoric from pre-Socratic times through the Middle Byzantine era.[158] Part of this was because "Byzantium was constitutionally disposed not to exclude any items of her patrimony, pagan or Christian."[159] It also seems to be the case that "no one ever consciously undertook to construct a full-fledged theory of Christian rhetoric that could substitute for its pagan counterparts or even be added to them. On the other hand, this is not to deny that such a theory exists. It has, however, to be extracted from more general contexts serving other more immediate interests."[160] That "more immediate interest" was the need of the Byzantine Church to communicate its message.

---

[158] Much of the information in this chapter can be found in two sources: George L. Kustas, "Rhetoric and the Holy Spirit." *Originality in Byzantine Literature, Art and Music: A Collection of Essays.* Ed. Anthony Robert Littlewood. vols. Oxford [England]: Oxbow Books, 1995. 29-37.

   Mary B. Cunningham, "Innovation or Mimesis in Byzantine Sermons?" *Originality in Byzantine Literature, Art and Music: A Collection of Essays.* Ed. Anthony Robert Littlewood. vols. Oxford [England]: Oxbow Books, 1995. 67-80. And "Preaching and the Community," *Church and People in Byzantium.* Eds. Rosemary Morris, et al. Birmingham, England: Centre for Byzantine, Ottoman and Modern Greek studies, University of Birmingham, 1990. 39-40.

[159] Kustas, "Rhetoric and the Holy Spirit" 29

[160] Kustas, "Rhetoric and the Holy Spirit" 30

4.1 Middle Byzantine Homilies

To judge for the manuscript evidence, homilies represent one of the most popular literary genres in the Byzantine world.[161] Kennedy stated that "Various types of homilies developed in the early Church including the exegetical, the prophetic and the missionary."[162] Mary Cunningham notes that Kennedy is able only to point to the Second Epistle of Clement to the Corinthians as the sole example of a prophetic sermon.[163] By the Middle Byzantine era the prophetic and the missionary sermon had fallen out of use and the exegetical homilies and those written for the growing number of feasts were more common.[164] It is to these two forms that we must now turn.

The exegetical homily may have grown out of the *haggadah* originally.[165] What is clear is that by the fourth century, Christian homilists were using classical rhetorical techniques, as Ševčenko shows.[166] In addition to the exegetical form, homilies had thoroughly adopted the encomiastic[167] form to celebrate the Christian martyrs and the panegyrical to celebrate the increasing number of feasts.[168] Festal homilies, as might be expected, tend

---

[161] Cunningham comments in her "Preaching and Community" that "For a nearly comprehensive survey and analysis of the manuscripts containing homilies and saints' lives" see Albert Ehrhard,. "Überlieferung und Bestand der Hagiographischen und homiletischen Literatur der griechischen Kirche von den Anfängen bis zum Ende des 16. Jahrhunderts." *Texte und Untersuchungen zur Geschichte der altchristlichen Literatur*. Leipzig: J. C. Hinrichs, 1937. From Cunningham, *Preaching* nt 1 p. 29

[162] George Alexander Kennedy. *Greek Rhetoric under Christian Emperors*. Princeton, N.J.: Princeton University Press, 1983. 182

[163] Cunningham, footnote 3, 77.

[164] See, I Ševčenko, "A Shadow Outline of Virtue: The Classical Heritage of Greek Christian Literature (Second to Seventh Century)," *Age of Spirituality: A Symposium,* ed. K. Weitzmann (New York, 1980), 57.

[165] See, G. Vermes, *Scripture and Tradition in Judaism. Haggadic Studies* (Leiden, 1961); R. Block, "Midrash" *Supplément au dictionnaire de la Bible V,* coll. 1263-80; A.G. Wright, *The Literary Genre Midrash* (New York, 1967). Quoted from Cunningham 77.

[166] Ševčenko, 57*ff*.

[167] See, T.C. Burgess, "Epideictic Literature," *University of Chicago Studies in Classical Philology* 9 (1902), 89-261; D.A. Russell and N.G. Wilson, *Menander Rhetor* (Oxford, 1981)

[168] Many authors illustrates this point by referring to Melito of Sardis' Περί Πάσχα. For a translation find: S.G. Hall (ed. and trans), *Melito of Sardis. On*

to be both exegetical and encomiastic, such as the homilies composed to celebrate the great feasts of the Mother of God.[169] Each homily took its structure primarily (although not exclusively) from the specific form it followed: the exegetical from the *haggadah*, while the encomiastic and the panegyrical took theirs from the classical rhetorical models of the Second Sophistic.[170]

For the purposes of this dissertation I shall refer to these two forms of Middle Byzantine homilies as (1) Exegetical, and (2) Festal. One thing will be immediately clear: they are not distinct forms one from the other as are *kontakia* or *troparia*. Homilies had to meet one practical requirement—they had to be simple enough for them to be understood by their auditors. One of the great orators of the Orthodox Church, John Chrysostom, makes this practical need clear in his treatise *On the Priesthood*:

> Now if I were demanding the polish of Isocrates and the grandeur of Demosthenes and the dignity of Thucydides and the sublimity of Plato, it would be right to confront me with the testimony of Paul. But in fact I pass over all those qualities and the superfluous embellishments of pagan writers. I take no account of diction or style. Let a man's diction be beggarly and his verbal composition simple and artless, but do not let him be inexpert in the knowledge and careful statement of doctrine.[171]

Despite this caution from John Chrysostom it seems probable that, as the influence of the rhetorical style grew, fewer and fewer Byzantines were

---

Pascha and Fragments (Oxford, 1979). Also G. Bonner, "The Homily on the Passion by Melito Bishop of Sardis and some Fragments of the Apocryphal Ezekiel," *Studies and Documents* 12 (London and Philadelphia, 1940).

[169] Cunningham, 'Innovation' 68.

[170] The full development of the panegyrical homily owes its development to the Cappadocians: Basil the Great, Gregory of Nyssa, Gregory Nazianzus. For a discussion of the role of the Cappadocians see I. Ševčenko, "A Shadow Outline of Virtue: The Classical Heritage of Greek Christian Literature (Second to Seventh Century)," *Age of Spirituality: A Symposium,* ed. K. Weitzmann (New York, 1980), 53-57.

[171] John Chrysostom, *Six Books on the Priesthood,* trans. G. Neville (London, 1964) IV, 6, 121-22.

able to understand these "show" pieces.[172] Germanos addresses his hearers in one of his homilies on the Presentation in this manner: " . . . while we, the peculiar people of God, priests and rulers, lay and monastic, slaves and free, craftsmen and farmers, vintners and fishermen, young and old, men and women, . . ."[173] Germanos' hearers encompassed a wide range of educational and theological learning. Each of these, no doubt, expected the Patriarch to speak to them in his homilies—quite a daunting task!

The exegetical homily was by far the most common type of sermon, to judge from the numbers extant. By the fourth or fifth century, one could expect to hear such homilies at the primary liturgical services. At least in this period it seems likely that these homilies were actually preached at the Divine Liturgy.[174] In its purest form it resembles the exegesis of the Jewish Synagogue and does not seem to admit to a classical prototype. Both the Christian and Jewish form are characterized by a literal or moral interpretations of biblical events; they stress miraculous aspects and reject naturalistic interpretations, while suppressing details that might at first glance appear shocking.[175] What separates the Christian and Hebrew exegesis is that for the Christians the exegetical method stressed in every appropriate context the Chalcedonian doctrine of the two natures of Christ. As a general rule, there is no sophisticated argumentation in order to convey this teaching of the two natures. "The central Christian paradox of an incarnate God could be illustrated on a very human level, by means of a dramatic reenactment of the gospel narratives."[176] Important to our study of Germanos are the homilies of Leontios of Byzantium (probably mid-sixth century). Leontios develops the dramatic exegetical

---

[172] There is considerable debate about how much individual Byzantines understood, or even whether they heard the homilies or not. See Cunningham, 'Innovation' 72.

[173] *PG* 98 312 B-C

[174] As Cunningham points out there is still a great deal of work to do on the liturgical context of these homilies. For some clues see B. Goodall, *The Homilies of St John Chrysostom on the letters of St Paul and Titus and Philemon, Prolegomena to an Edition,* University of California Publication in Classical Studies 20 (1979), 65-73, and for Gregory of Nazianzos, H. Hunger, "On the Imitation (Mimesis) of Antiquity," *DOP* 23 (1969), 18.

[175] See J. Daniélou, *Grégoire de Nysse, La vie de Moïse,* SC 1 (Paris, 1968) 16-20.

[176] Cunningham, 'Innovation' 69.

homily.[177] Leontios' homilies are full of dialogues, between principals in the Scriptural passages; there is a orator and an imaginary interlocutor between the Devil and Christ. Leontios also makes use of the rhetorical figures of antithesis, anaphora, and assonance.[178] Exegetical homilies that make use of drama also seem "to encourage a literal, even down-to-earth interpretation of the Scriptures."[179] Later in Germanos' homily on the Annunciation we will see these qualities demonstrated. Theological issues that appear only in an undeveloped form become dramatic realities in these homilies. Questions such as the Trinity, and many Marian doctrines, are dramatized and the latter (not in the Scripture) dogmas are taught to the faithful by means of dramatic homilies. Yet the exegetical homily remains largely conversational in its style.[180]

These homilies are quite straightforward and easy to understand as their heuristic intent would require. The rhetorical device of anaphora, repetition of the first words at the beginning of a phrase, and homoioteleuton, or assonance at their end, created an easy way to remember what was being said. While these pleonasms were part of the Asiatic rhetorical style they were also present in the "folk" genres that relied on formulae and rhyming sequences.[181]

In short, the exegetical homily was generally intended to be heard by a congregation whose theological sophistication was not very high. Leontios of Constantinople can serve as an example of the exegetical homily and its intended congregation. They were certainly fond of the dramatization of biblical episodes:

"... The biblical exegesis which Leontius presents to his congregation cannot be called either intellectual or demanding."[182] Leontius was a popular homilist, ... whose

---

[177] C. Datema and P. Allen, *Leontii presbyteri constantinopolitani, homiliae,* CCSG 17 (Louvain, 1987).
[178] Pauline Allen with C. Datema (trans.) *Leontius, Presbyter of Constantinople: Fourteen Homilies* (Brisbane, 1991), 14-16.
[179] Cunningham, 'Innovation' 72
[180] See Kustas, *Studies* 44
[181] See R. Crosby, "Oral Delivery in the Middle Ages," *Speculum* 11 (1936) 88-110; M.J. Jeffreys, "Formulas in the Chronicle of the Morea," *DOP* 27 (1973), 163-95.
[182] See Allen 5. In fact the entire section that describes Leontius and his congregation paints a familiar picture to today's preacher: 3-8.

greatest quality is his ability to bring the biblical readings of the liturgy to life by dramatising their contents. The biblical figures for their part become the *dramatis personae* of the homilies, who present their ideas and feelings in monologue or dialogues. Thus in the homilies, with the exception of the panegyrical passages, Leontius stays close to the text of the scripture, and systematic expositions are found only rarely.[183]

After the seventh century the style of homily changed. They were "longer, more ornate and literary style prevails; . . ."[184] Sermons were now being written to honor established feasts and were concerned with the interpretation of the scriptural passages that were set for any particular feast. The bulk of surviving homilies from this time appear to be written for the all-night vigils which were held on important feasts. "Some, especially those dedicated to the Theotokos, would have been read out in cycles of three."[185] Yet one is able to make some distinction between festal homilies and Marian homilies. "Whereas the Marian homilies praise the Mother of God, some festal homilies concentrate more on explaining the scriptural readings in a literal fashion."[186] It is also worth noting that about 75% of the homilies we have from the eight and ninth centuries were devoted to the Theotokos.[187]

4.2 Issues in Understanding Middle Byzantine Homilies

There are some issues that present themselves when reading Byzantine Homilies. This is particularly true if one assumes they are the same as Western Christian homilies. The difficulty is raised by Jakov Ljubarskij in

---

[183] Allen, 9.

[184] Cunningham, 'Innovation' 75

[185] Cunningham, 74. Also see M. Cunningham, "Preaching and the Community," in Rosemary Morris (ed.) *Church and People in Byzantium* (Birmingham, 1990), 39-40; C. Chevalier, "Les trilogies homilétiques dans l'élabaration des fêtes mariales, 650-850," *Gregorianum* 18 (1937), 361-78.

[186] Cunningham, *Preaching,* 39.

[187] Tsironis, *Iconoclastic* 35.

his article "How should a Byzantine text be read?[188] Ljudbarskij asks the question: " . . . is there anything peculiar in the works of Byzantine authors that differentiates them from other texts and should make readers deal with them differently?" While confirming that the traditional methods of classical philology are the *conditio sine qua non* to be used by Byzantinists: " . . . (by which I mean the correct interpretation and emendation of the text and the extraction of historical information from it)" he also questions whether this method is enough to base scholarly interpretations on. [189] He points out that many scholars think that there is something particular in the works of Byzantine authors that makes them different from other medieval texts and consequently requires a different approach to them.[190]

Ljubarskij suggests that one can differentiate two contemporary approaches. The first views the Byzantine writer as demonstrating his or her rhetorical skill.[191] These writers were concerned with the rhetorical and disregarded, to an extent, any reality outside of the 'school norms' of rhetoric. In the opinion of Cyril Mango, Byzantine literature had little contact with reality and is a kind of 'distorting mirror.'[192] The second comes from the Byzantines themselves. These interpreters attempt to 'translate' the allegories and metaphors in Byzantine literature into some purely spiritual meaning. Modern interpreters attempt to explain what the Byzantines really meant by the use of allegorical and symbolic references. "So the main task of the modern scholar is to penetrate beneath the surface and try to understand and explain what was in reality meant by the author."[193] This approach is often taken by those who feel an affinity with the visual and theological world of Orthodox Christianity.[194]

---

[188] Jakov Ljubarskij, "How Should a Byzantine Text Be Read?" *Rhetoric in Byzantium: Papers from the Thirty-Fifth Spring Symposium of Byzantine Studies, Exeter College, University of Oxford, March 2001.* Ed. Elizabeth Jeffreys. Aldershot, Hants, England; Burlington, VT: Ashgate, 2003. 117-25.

[189] Ljubarskij 117

[190] Ljubarskij 117

[191] This approach was formulated by Cyril Mango and S. Averintzev. See Ljubarskij 117-8.

[192] This reference to Mango's lecture can be found in *Byzantium and its Image* (Aldershot, 1984), II. Quoted from Ljubarskij 118.

[193] Ljubarskij 118

[194] For example, Sofia Poljakova interpreted Byzantine erotic romances claiming them to be not actions of earthly characters; but, rather representations of Divine Love and similar lofty subjects. See S. Poljakova, *Iz istorii vizantijskogo*

Both of these approaches appear to be one-sided. To contend that 'only' school norms were of concern to the Byzantine writer or preacher is to disregard the theological foundation of the Ecumenical councils and to forget the mission of the Church. They forget the seriousness with which the Byzantines communicated in written or oral forms. Rhetoric had a serious purpose which was to communicate, in the form of homilies, the theological and moral content of the Byzantine mind. That same seriousness in using rhetoric can be seen today in the political rhetoric of contemporary orators or the sermons of 'preachers.' To contend that the sole reality that the Byzantines really meant by the use of allegory and symbols was purely otherworldly is to forget the everyday life of the Byzantine people and the need to communicate felt by the homilist. While one forgets the human character of the Chalcedonian formula, the other forgets the spiritual. Each of these approaches gives a shortsighted interpretation of the Byzantine theological world. Neither of them by itself is adequate to do justice to Byzantine literature and especially to the preaching of the Gospel.

A third approach has been championed by Alexander Kazhdan.[195] Byzantine literature is approached as literature. The same criteria that are applied to literature in general are applied to Medieval Byzantine texts. According to Kazhdan, Byzantine texts have two or even more levels. This polysemy is inherent in every fiction and provides a key to interpreting Byzantine texts. In order to understand the Byzantine text one must be aware of the context within which it was created. That context allows for 'overtones' that nuance the text and give meaning. Ljubarskij illustrates this point by referring to the language and manner of speech found in Germanos' homily on the Annunciation.

> Those who read and listened to Germanos' Homily must have been well aware of the content of the Annunciation story, and Germanos' aim was surely not to retell it but to impress the audience. The way which the patriarch chose is absolutely

---

romana (Moscow, 1979) also see J. Ljubarskij, 'Der byzantinischer Roman in der Sicht der russischen Byzantinistik' found in P. Agapitos and D. Reinsch, eds., *Der Roman im Byzanz der Komnenenzeit* (Frankfurt am Main, 2000), 1924. Refences from Ljubarskij 118.

[195]   A. Kazhdan, *A History of Byzantine Literature* (650-850) (Athens, 1999).

artistic: in a sense the 'overtones' of his Homily are more important than its main content.[196]

This approach to Middle Byzantine homilies and their interpretation seems to meet the criteria for theological interpretation as well as account for the *Weltanschauung*.

If one accepts Kazhdan's contention then this polysemy can be well demonstrated in the use of dialogue in Byzantine preaching. Enlarging upon and referencing Kazhdan's work Mary Cunningham illustrates the usage of dialogue in Byzantine homilies.[197] For our author, Germanos, this provides an insight into his homiletical style. Dialogue can take many forms. It can be used to expound stories. Generally the preacher quotes a particular biblical passage which is in the form of a speech or a dialogue and then builds on it. The homilist then may expound on it by inventing speeches. The Annunciation appears to have been one of the favorite stories which homilists, including Germanos, built upon.

A second from of dialogue would be with the congregation. This form of dialogue appears to be less important in the eighth century than it might have been earlier to Byzantine preachers.[198] Germanos does refer to his auditors on a number of occasions.[199]

Dialogue served several purposes in the eighth century Byzantine world. Cunningham explores the technique by accessing three roles for dialogue: first, how the authority of the preacher was reinforced; second, dialogues used by the homilist to teach the congregation the basic theology of the Christian faith; third, dialogue as a gauge of the individual preacher's

---

[196] Ljubarskij 119; also see M. Cunningham "Dramatic Device or Didactic Tool? The Function of Dialogue in Byzantine Preaching." *Rhetoric in Byzantium: Papers from the Thirty-Fifth Spring Symposium of Byzantine Studies,* Exeter College, University of Oxford, March 2001. Ed. Elizabeth Jeffreys. Aldershot, Hants, England; Burlington, VT: Ashgate, 2003. 111-12.

[197] Mary B. Cunningham, and Pauline Allen. "Dramatic device or didactic tool? The function of dialogue in Byzantine preaching." *Preacher and Audience: Studies in Early Christian and Byzantine Homiletics.* Leiden ; Boston: Brill, 1998. 101-13. Much of this section is taken from this chapter.

[198] Cunningham, Preacher and Audience, 103.

[199] See, for example 292C, 320E and others.

relationship to his congregation.[200] All three of these are present to some degree in Germanos' homilies.

First, the homilist uses scriptural texts freely by glossing them. Only a preacher of authority would do this with the abandon that Germanos illustrates. Both Old Testament and New Testament texts are used freely by Germanos. Germanos gives us an example of this in the dialogue between Christ and Mary to be found in the Dormition homilies:

> "'It is time,' says the Lord, 'to bring you, my mother, [to me]. So as you filled the earth and those on the earth with joy, O blessed one, now make the heavenly places also joyous. Cheer the mansions of my Father. Lead the souls and spirits of the saints. As I see your honorable transfer towards me, accompanied by angels, they are fulfilled faithfully, as through you their part also will settle in my light. Therefore come with rejoicing. Hail even now, as also earlier. (360C)

In this homily Christ continues for many more lines in which Germanos glosses I Cor. 13.12, Ps. 94.4, Zech. 12.11 (LXX). Homilists appeared to be quite aware of their auditors and varied the rhetorical devices. Tsironis[201] points to a new lyricism to be found in the eighth-and ninth-century homilies which Germanos illustrates when he follows a dialogue or a call

---

[200] Behold, again another festival, and a glorious feast of the Mother of the Lord. Behold, the arrival of the blameless bride (*cf.* 2 Peter 3.14). Behold, the first procession of the queen. Behold, an accurate sign of the glory which will surround her. (309B)

Behold, the prelude of the divine grace which will overshadow her. Behold, the brilliant evidence of her exceptional purity. For where entering not many times, but once in the year (*cf.* Leviticus 16.1*ff*), the priest performs the mystical worship, there she is brought by her parents for unceasing residence, to be in the sacred sanctuary of grace. (309C)

[201] On the new lyricism of eighth-and ninth-century homiletics, specifically with reference to those written in honour of the Mother of Cod, see N. Tsironis, *The Lament of the Virgin Mary from Romanos the Melode* to *George of Nicomedia* (unpublished PhD thesis, King's College, London, 1998), 180. See also M. Vassilaki and Tsironis, "Representations of the Virgin and their association with the Passion of Christ," in M. Vassilaki, ed. *Mother of God. Representations of* the *Virgin in Byzantine Art* (Athens, 2000. 453-63. From Cunningham, *Preacher and Audience,* 106.

to participation in a feast by an anaphora such as found in the First Homily on the Presentation:

> So let us eagerly approach together this mutually beneficial, salvific feast of the Mother of God. And bowing before the unapproachable place [the holy of Holies] let us watch the child going toward the second veil, Mary the all-holy Mother of God who put an end to unfruitful sterility, and exchanged the mere shadow of the letter of the law (cf. Hebrews 10.1ff) through the grace of her birth-giving.[202]

> Today, at three years of age, she goes towards her dedication in the temple of the law, she who alone is called the stainless and greatest temple of the high priest and the Lord of all, and in whose bright light is the radiance of divine light which illuminates the darkness of the Law. (293A)

> Today a babe is handed over to a priest, the one who will dedicate the only high-priestly God made flesh as a child at forty days for us, having received in his welcoming arms (cf. Luke 1.22ff.) the uncontainable One who is beyond all human knowing.[203]

> Today a new, pure, unspoiled book which will not be written by hands, but written in gold by the spirit, hallowed with blessings according to the Law, she is brought forward as an acceptable gift.

> Today Joachim, who has wiped away the reproach of childlessness, goes openly down the main road boastfully

---

[202] This is the first reference in this homily to the place of the Virgin as the instrument of the Incarnation.

[203] This is a reference to the Presentation in the Temple of Christ. Germanos makes reference to that event to set the events of the Presentation of the Theotokos in the context of her role in the Incarnation. Mary and Joseph present Jesus to Simeon as Mary was presented to Zacharias by Joachim and Anna. Both presentations were necessary parts of salvation history.

showing off his offspring, and again is shown as a functionary of hallowing according to the Law.

Today also Anna has exchanged the persistence of barrenness for fruitfulness, and becoming inspired by joy, proclaims to the ends of the earth that she has borne a child, embracing to her bosom the one who is wider than the heavens. (293B)

Today the gate of God's temple is opened to receive the entry of the eastward looking, sealed gate of Emmanuel (*cf.* Ezekiel 44.1-3).

Today the sacred Table of the temple joyfully meets and participates in the true divine table of the heavenly soul-feeding bread and by changing to the worship of the bloodless sacrifice begins to shine.

Today she who alone is called the new, god-like, purifying and mercy seat, not made by hands, (*cf.* Hebrews 9.11) for mortals who have drowned in floods of sin, is presented to the mercy seat of the temple. (293C)

Today she who will receive the Holy One of the Holy through the hallowing of the Spirit is placed in the holy of Holies at a pure and innocent age; and she who is marvelously exalted above the Cherubim, makes more holy the holy of Holies by her presence.

Today Mary advances, about whom no matter how much we say, we cannot come close to our goal of adequately praising her. Her beauty far surpasses the power of every tongue and mind. For her greatness is a vast sea, as the Heavenly drop born from her has shown. And therefore her richness is unlimited in its infinitude, and her wealth is inexhaustible. (293D)

'Today' is an important word in Byzantine hymns and homilies, especially when it is connected with the present time of the homily. Byzantine homilists connected the historical event commemorated by the feast with the day on which the homily was preached. In doing so the 'today' had two meanings and as a consequence time was transformed. In this way the feast is not just a commemoration of a past event but provides an avenue for participation in the feast for those attending. Germanos makes this clear at the beginning of the Annunciation Homily:

> With joyful soul let us spiritually celebrate this luminous and ever-glorious memorial of this honorable and royal assembly (*cf.* 1 Peter 2.9), O peoples, nations, and languages (*cf.* Daniel 4.1), and all social classes, and this multitudinous congregation who have come together because of your love for this feast, and the people around [us]. Let us weave with all zeal hymns which are worthy of the Queen who was from the lineage of David. Let us compose a springtime feast of feasts, and a festival of festivals of our hope, our unmistakable proclamation of this feast day (Psalm 81.3). (320E)

> For today, truly, the intellectual powers of heaven have come down from Heaven, and *invisibly celebrate* her with us earthborn [human beings]. (321A)

Germanos doesn't always use the word 'today' to establish the timelessness of the feast and the time in which it is celebrated. In the Second Homily on the Presentation he uses the same rhetorical devise but with 'behold.'

> Behold, again another festival, and a glorious feast of the Mother of the Lord. Behold, the arrival of the blameless bride (*cf.* 2 Peter 3.14). Behold, the first procession of the queen. Behold, an accurate sign of the glory which will surround her. (309B)

> Behold, the prelude of the divine grace which will overshadow her. Behold, the brilliant evidence of her exceptional purity. For where entering not many times, but once in the year (*cf.* Leviticus 16.1*ff*), the priest performs the mystical worship, there she is brought by her parents for unceasing residence, to be in the sacred sanctuary of grace. (309C)

Second, eighth-century homilists used dialogue to teach theology and doctrine. The Homily on the Annunciation provides a good example of teaching dogma by the use of dialogue. This homily is carefully structured. There are two dialogues: the first, on an alphabetical acrostic is between the Angel and Mary, and the second, also on an alphabetical acrostic is between Mary and Joseph. This homily is currently of much interest to several scholars due to its structure.[204] A careful reading of the Greek text illustrates Kazhdan's comment "that the level of style employed in the speeches of the main characters reflects their position in life. Whereas Mary speaks in a simple manner denoting ignorance . . . the archangel adopts a solemn and elevated style which befits his divine habitation and the importance of his message. Even more remarkably, it is noticeable that the Virgin's stylistic level changes and becomes more dignified once she has understood and accepted the archangel's announcement. In her dialogue with Joseph, Mary adopts a highly rhetorical style, employing elaborate compound words which express complex theological ideas."[205]

Finally, the homilies also provide some information about the congregation that is hearing the homilies. This information comes as informal remarks and rhetorical questions. There is some information found in Germanos and we can make some guesses from the context. See the Second Homily on the Presentation for a relative of Germanos. (320A)

---

[204] The text of the homily is problematical. I received the Greek text in this dissertation from Mary Cunningham who had done some work on the various mss.

[205] Kazhdan, Byzantine Literature 62-3. Quote from Cunningham, Preacher and Audience, 111.

Chapter Five

Introduction to Germanos' Homilies

Germanos' homilies on the Virgin Mary trace her life from the time she entered the Temple, through her life as a young woman, her old age and death and to her role as Protector of the Church and the City of Constantinople. While Germanos does not treat of her conception or birth his homilies could be viewed as a type of hagiography. In one sense Germanos presents Mary as a child, a young woman, and an older woman about to die. In this he presents Mary in the three stages of being a woman: a child, a young woman and an old woman—a classical trilogy. Germanos treats each stage with a sensitivity that is borne of pastoral observation and experience. The three-year-old skipping in the Temple, the young woman attempting to make sense of the message of the Angel and her pregnancy and wondering about her child, and the older woman whose life will soon end and her preparation of her home for that event are only some of the examples of his close observation.

The homilies are also more. Over that layer of observation is laid the theological considerations of one who knows that child, young woman, older woman to be the Theotokos—a unique and specific role in salvation history. These two poles along with a deep humility towards her accounts for the tone of the homilies. The style of the homilies is the result of the rhetorical presentation, that rich Byzantine manner of declaiming anything from political to theological discourse.

They constitute a rich biographical treatment of Mary. In particular Mary's personality is developed in the homily on the Annunciation. This homily is good theater. Richly populated with asides from Mary and with dialogues that push the plot on, the homily on the Annunciation constitutes the central act of Mary's life. The homilies on the Dormition portray an older woman who is clearly a leader in the Christian Community. Treated as an elder, and the most intimate companion of Christ, Mary's role as the Theotokos is richly developed as the companion of the members of the Church—the Body of Christ. At the same time the Dormition homilies also develop her role as Mediatrix. Mary's power of Intercession, predicated on her role in the Incarnation and her participation in the resurrection of her Son are guarantees of a continued relationship between the Earth and Heaven.

Mary's biography does not end with her death, but is continued with the homily on the Sash. This homily preached some seven centuries later explores the role of Mary vis à vis her role as Empress and protector of the city of Constantinople. In a profound manner, the Sash homily is a fitting coda to all of Germanos' homilies on Mary.

While Germanos gives us a biographical treatment of Mary he does not give us anything about Mary's conception or birth in any detail. He treats the Presentation in the Temple as a prequel to the rest of her life[206]. In that way, the Presentation is a foretaste of the Annunciation and the Incarnation. In the Presentation homilies Mary is more spoken to or of than speaking. She is the source of the New Dispensation, the New Covenant, but remains primarily observed, unlike her role in the homilies on the Annunciation and the Dormition.

These are richly textured homilies by a master of observation and a rhetorician of some skill. But they are not definitive theological statements. Homilies coming after poetry in the Byzantine theological process are conversations, spoken words at the time of their delivery. That conversation takes place both within and without the homilies. In the former the characters represented in the homilies dialog with each other concerning the theological substance that is presented by the homilist. In the latter, the auditors are invited to share the 'today' of the homily and the theological implications from whatever time they come to the homily. While later generations might include them in collections of homilies which tended to be local collections first and then after some time they became more universally accepted.

Germanos clearly represents the manner of doing theology at one stage of that process, he was not alone; but is a good representative of the way of

---

[206] Liturgically it is common in the Orthodox Church to anticipate major feasts by having a fore-feast. Typically the coming feast will be announced in a short hymn so that the congregation members will be aware of the coming feast.

doing theology in Byzantium. The most one can claim for these homilies is that they represent the thought of one Patriarch of Constantinople at the time they were preached. Indeed, I believe it can be questioned if they were all preached while he was yet Patriarch.

Chapter Six

General Introduction to the Two Presentation Homilies

Germanos' homilies on the Presentation of the Theotokos are perhaps his most important ones. In fact, Germanos' link with this Feast is so strong that "The character of this composition (speaking of a fifth century ivory book cover) is not surprising, especially since the feast of Mary's *eisodos* seems to have been introduced to the Byzantine church in the eighth century by Patriarch Germanos I (715-730)".[207] This also appears to be the time at which the calendar of the Church was becoming more standardized within the Byzantine Empire[208]. The Homily on the Entrance of the Theotokos, however, was not yet universally celebrated outside of Constantinople as we learn from the listing of the Dominical Feast in John of Euboea (*ca.* 442-44).[209] It is clear from the mss evidence in Ehrhard that Germanos' homily Ἰδοὺ καὶ πάλιν (Germanos' second homily on the

---

[207]   Bissera V Pentcheva,. *Icons and Power: The Mother of God in Byzantium.* University Park, PA: The Pennsylvania State University Press, 2006. 138 who is quoting Jacqueline Lafontaine-Dosogne. "Iconographie de l'enfance de la vierge dans l'empire byzantin et en occident." *Mémoires de la Classe des beaux-arts. Collection* in-4o, 2. sér., t. 11, fasc. 3. (1992). 137.

[208]   Lafontaine-Dosogne. Iconographie vol I 24. See n. 4

[209]   Mary Cunningham points out in her introduction to John of Euboea, a mid-eighth century preacher, that he does not include the Feast of the Entrance of the Theotokos in his list of Feasts found in his Homily on the Conception of the Theotokos. M. Cunningham, *Wider than Heaven: Eighth-century Homilies on the Mother of God.* Popular Patristic Series. Vol. 35. Crestwood, NY: St. Vladimir's Seminary Press, 2008, 47. Homily from the same volume 173-195.

Presentation) was the most popular of all of Germanos' homilies, and the most-often chosen of his two homilies on the Presentation.[210]

Like the Dormition homilies the Presentation is from the apocryphal literature. The *Protoevangelium of James* is generally recognized as the source of the story of Mary's entrance into the Temple[211]. The *Protoevangelium of James* was widely read and the Greek text was highly influential in the Byzantine Empire[212]. The *Protoevangelium of James* is divided into three parts each with eight chapters. The first part contains the source material for the birth, dedication and entrance of the Virgin Mary.

Germanos homilies on the Presentation appear to be the first ones.[213]

Presentation #	Incipit:	*PG* 98	*BHG*
1	Θυμηδίας	292C—309B	1103
2	Ἰδοὺ καὶ πάλιν	309B—320B	1104

---

[210] Albert Ehrhard. "Überlieferung und Bestand der hagiographischen und homiletischen Literatur der griechischen Kirche von den Anfängen bis zum Ende des 16. Jahrhunderts". *Texte und Untersuchungen zur Geschichte der altchristlichen Literatur;* Leipzig, J. C. Hinrichs, 1937. I have counted nearly 60 references to Ἰδοὺ καὶ πάλιν in Ehrhard's three volumes.

[211] The *Protoevangelium of James* is quite accessible. On the InterNet one source is "Protoevangelium of James". 2008 May 21 2008. Also TLG has a Greek text. <http://www.newadvent.org/fathers/0847.htm>.

[212] Some indication of the popularity of the *Infancy Gospel of James* may be drawn from the fact that about one hundred and thirty Greek manuscripts containing it have survived. The *Gospel of James* was translated into Syriac, Ethiopic, Coptic, Georgian, Old Slavonic, Armenian, Arabic, Irish and Latin. Though no early Latin versions are known, it was relegated to the apocrypha in the Gelasian decretal, so must have been known in the West. As with the canonical gospels, the vast majority of the manuscripts come from the tenth century or later. The earliest known manuscript of the text, a papyrus dating to the third or early fourth century, was found in 1958; it is kept in the Bodmer Library, Geneva (Papyrus Bodmer 5). Of the surviving Greek manuscripts, the fullest surviving text is a tenth century codex in the Bibliotheque Nationale, Paris (Paris 1454). Quoted from: http://en.wikipedia. org/wiki/Gospel_of_James, May 21, 2008.

[213] "Germain serait ainsi le plus ancien auteur d'une homelie sur la fête. also n. 6. See, Mary Jerome Kishpaugh. *The Feast of the Presentation of the Virgin Mary in the Temple: An Historical and Literary Study*. Washington, D.C.: The Catholic University of America, 1941. 30-1.

The two homilies differ in complexity of style. The first homily is very complex and at time seems to be a rhetorical exercise. While it is written as if Germanos is preaching it to a congregation it would have been difficult to follow and, I believe, lends itself more readily to reading than preaching. The second homily is much simpler, with fewer neologisms[214] and less rhetorical practices. It is probably for these reasons that it was more popular to judge from the mss evidence among the books of homilies.

6.1 Analysis of the Presentation Homilies

Unlike the Dormition homilies the Presentation homilies had little, if any, precedence in Constantinople. In Bissera V. Pentcheva's dissertation she quotes an earlier scholar as the source for her contention that Germanos introduced the feast of the Presentation into the Byzantine Church calendar[215]. If we accept this as a warrantable assumption, then we are hearing in the Presentation homilies a first attempt at presenting this feast to the Church.

Before all else the Presentation is, for Germanos, a sign, a pre-figuration of the role of Mary in salvation history[216]. At the very beginning of his Second Homily on the Presentation he proclaims:

---

[214] Detorakis list 55 words in the first homily and 11 in the second. In addition there is at least one word in the first homily that no one lists. Theodorakis Detorakis, "Αθησαυριστες λεξεισ απο τα εργα του πατριαρχη γερμανου α'." *Lexicographica byzantina : Beiträge zum Symposion zur byzantinischen Lexikographie (Wien, 1.-4. 3._1989).* Eds. Wolfram Hörandner and Erich Trapp. Wien: Verlag der Österreichischen Akademie der Wissenschaften, 1991. vi, 314 p.

[215] Bissera V Pentcheva,. *Icons and Power: The Mother of God in Byzantium.* University Park, PA: The Pennsylvania State University Press, 2006. 138 who is quoting Jacqueline Lafontaine-Dosogne. "Iconographie de l'enfance de la vierge dans l'empire byzantin et en occident." *Mémoires de la classe des beaux-arts. Collection* in-4o, 2. sér., t. 11, fasc. 3. (1992). 137.

[216] The contemporary hymn (troparion) for the Feast of the Entrance of the Theotokos into the temple is: Today is the preview of the good will of God, of the preaching of the salvation of mankind. The Virgin appears in the temple of God, in anticipation proclaiming Christ to all. And let us rejoice and sing to her: Rejoice, O Divine Fulfillment of the Creator's dispensation!

Behold, the first procession of the queen. Behold, an accurate sign of the glory which will surround her.

Behold, the prelude of the divine grace which will overshadow her. Behold, the brilliant evidence of her exceptional purity. For where entering not many times, but once in the year (*cf.* Leviticus 16.1*ff*), the priest performs the mystical worship, there she is brought by her parents for unceasing residence, to be in the sacred sanctuary of grace.

Who ever knew such a thing? Who saw, or who heard, of men now or men of old, that a female was led into the inner holy places of the holy places, which are barely accessible even to men, to live in them and to pass her time in them? Is this not a clear demonstration of the strange miracle to be done for her later? Is it not an evident sign? Is it not an obvious testimony? (309B/C)

In both homilies Germanos addresses an element that appear to oppose this Feast, if not the totality of the veneration of the Theotokos. Immediately he presses his case against those who doubt the role of Mary:

Let them show us, those who wag their tongues against her, and who see as if not seeing, where they ever beheld such things? A maiden from the promise, at the age of three years, is brought as a blameless gift within the third curtain, to live there continuously, and receives petitions from the wealthy men of the people (*cf.* Psalm 45.13). She is sent forth by virgins, brought forward with lamps, welcomed by priests and prophets with uplifted hands! How, when they see the beginning, did they disbelieve in the ending? How, when they had seen the strange and unusual [events] in her case, did they deny those which happened afterwards? For not at random, and as it chanced, did the first things happen concerning her; but all were preludes of the last things. (312A)

Let those who are vainly wise in their own sight tell us: How, when other barren women have given birth, is none of their daughters dedicated in the holy of holies and received by prophets? Could not those who then saw such great things [done] for her say, as also those of the same mind later [said] for her son: "What will this child be?"[217] Yes indeed. But let those of alien mind travel the road of perdition, and let them fall into the pit which they have dug. (312B)

Germanos treats of the themes of Mary as container, ark, throne and many other ways of illustrating that her role as the Mother of God is the reason that she is worthy of honors. He also makes it clear that those who celebrate the Feast need to adopt an appropriate attitude: "For the annual observation of this feast is coming, in which one must be pure to participate. Please follow me gladly, with pure thoughts and in bright garments." (292C)

She is the harbinger of the good news which she ushers in. The result of her coming to the Temple is that the Law and its sterility is replaced. Germanos uses the plight of the parents of Mary as an analogy:

Today Joachim, who has wiped away the reproach of childlessness, goes openly down the main road boastfully showing off his offspring, and again is shown as a functionary of hallowing according to the Law.

Today also Anna has exchanged the persistence of barrenness for fruitfulness, and becoming inspired by joy, proclaims to the ends of the earth that she has borne a child, embracing to her bosom the one who is wider than the heavens. (293B)[218]

The Entrance of the Theotokos has historical and cosmic implications:

---

[217] At Luke 1.66, these words are used about John the Baptist, not about Jesus.

[218] The current hymn (kontakion) for the Nativity of the Theotokos expresses this: By your Nativity, O most pure Virgin, Joachim and Anna are freed from barrenness; Adam and Eve, from the corruption of death. And we, your people, freed from the guilt of sin, celebrate and sing to you: The barren woman gives birth to the Theotokos, the Nourisher of our Life.

Our ancestors (Adam and Eve) who are about to be released from the curse and again inheriting the residence in paradise from which you were cast out: should you not hymn the cause of your salvation, with a fitting encomium and great praises? Indeed you especially ought to shout out, and I with you and with us both all creation [ought] to sing out in joy. (300A)

The priest Zacharias summarizes all the reason Germanos gives for the celebration of the Feast of the Entrance of the Theotokos:

Once again, the forefathers call to the priest: "Receive her who will receive the immaterial and uncontainable fire. Receive her who will be called the container of the Son and Word of the only God and Father. Accept her who has destroyed the reproach of our bareness and sterility. Lead into the sanctuary her who will restore us to the ancient pasture of paradise. Possess her, who endures fear like ours in her own childbearing and will be victorious over the power of death and the tyranny of hell. Enfold her who covers our nature which was stripped bare in Eden. Take the hand of her who binds in swaddling clothes him who puts an end to our uncontrolled and impulsive audaciously spread-out hands. Return to God her who returned us, you who are the priestly celebrant of the expectation of our hopes." (300C)

"Behold, Lord, accept her whom you gave. Receive her whom you provided. Accept her whom you assigned to destroy our bareness, overcoming through her the barrenness of the Law, you have ransomed us through her from the terrible persistence [daily repetition of temple sacrifices?]. House her who so well has housed us, her whom you have chosen, and have foreseen, and have blessed. Draw to yourself her who leans on you and is attracted by your fragrance. You chose her as a lily out of the brambles of our unworthiness. Embrace her who is brought to you with a most radiant complexion. Behold, to you we offer her [as our intercessor] and dedicate ourselves." (300D)

Not only does Mary's Entrance have cosmic implications but Germanos extends the roles of Joachim and Anna to parallel their daughter's:

You have been made known as shining stars as if fixed in the firmament, each of you being a torch-bearer enlightening the murky shadow of the letter and the law which was given in a stormy darkness and each of you surely and unstumblingly guiding the believer in Christ to the new grace of the new light. You have been made known as the shining horns of the new righteous, spiritual temple, holding in your breasts the holy, God-acknowledged, rational altar of the sacred victim. You, if it is not too early to say, have been made known as Cherubim flying around the mercy-seat (*cf.* Exodus 25.18*ff.*) with the nourishment of the Priest who supports the universe. You appeared to cover the mystical and holy Ark of the new covenant of Him who on the Cross wrote the forgiveness of our sin, [forming] a covering which far surpasses the one which long ago was wrought of gold to cover the Ark (*cf.* Exodus 25.10). (301B)[219]

Your rejoicing has become that of the cosmos. Your renown is the universal joy of all men. Fortunate are you who bear the title of parents of such a blessed child. Fortunate are you, who have brought such a blessed gift to the Lord! Fortunate are the breasts by which she was nursed and the womb that carried her (*cf.* Luke 11.27). (301C)

---

[219] See, 308B: "Hail, you who through your birth released the fetters of sterility, who scattered the reproach of childlessness, and sank the curse of the Law (*cf.* Galatians 3.13); and blossomed forth the grace of blessing—by entering the Holy of Holies you perfected the prayers of your parents and the foundation for forgiveness of our sins, fulfilling the perfection of harmony as the leader of the beginning of grace."

Chapter Seven

First Homily on the Presentation of the Theotokos in the Temple Introduction and Commentary

The First Homily on the Presentation of the Theotokos in the Temple

This homily is both the more complex and the longer of the two homilies on the Presen¬tation of the Theotokos. A general outline may be found in an introduction, a body and a concluding prayer.

The first homily begins with Germanos declaring that every festival fills all who celebrate it from a treasury. However, this feast "attracts the soul and body with spiritual joy in proportion to the preeminence of the excellent child of God (Mary)." He invites those who are present to participate in the Feast of the Presentation and counsels them that they must do so "with pure thoughts and in bright garments" as they "hasten to pick the precious flowers from the private meadow of the Mother of God." Following two quotations from the Song of Songs, he then sets the scene of the presentation and introduces for the first time the themes of the Temple/ the Law and the sterility of the Law before Christ, proclaiming that through the grace of Mary's birth-giving the shadow of the letter of the Law is made bright. Germanos ties the concept of the role of Mary in the Incarnation and the change that it made to the relationship of humankind to God. He is perhaps making reference to Hebrews 10.1*ff* when he speaks of the shadow of the law.[220]

Germanos then launches on a long anaphora on the word 'today' and weaves the themes of the three-year-old child, the Temple (its architecture), the Law, sterility (of the Law and Mary's parents Joachim and Anna), Mary's

---

[220] It is, perhaps, to Hebrews with its theme of the OT law and the NT church that this homily is most related.

purity, the role of Zacharias in both the Presentation of Mary and Christ's Presentation (*cf.* Luke 1.22*ff*), Mary as the Wider-than-the-Heavens, the cosmos and Mary's beauty. In this series of anaphoras Germanos plays on the comparisons and contrast between what were the perceptions of humans before Christ and the wonders that are evident in the light of the Incarnation. In the final anaphora he returns to the theme of the impossibility of adequately lauding this event of the Presentation of Mary in the Temple.

> And therefore her richness is unlimited in its infinitude, and her wealth is inexhaustible. For while it is possible for everyone in everything else to be sated, it is not possible in this feasting to give too much sweetness in her hymns and festivals. And hence, the material is without limit of praises starting with her. And since the well is unfailing and not diminished by the drawing out but as much as is drawn out is refilled 100 or 10,000 fold, those who draw out cannot cease. For the mystery overflows and the plant grows taller even than the incorporeal minds, not to mention the incarnate minds, in the compassion of the all-rich and pure maiden! (293D/269A)

Germanos then returns to the number 'three' and recites a Biblical history of 'three' ending with the Niceno-Constantinopolitan formulation of the Incarnation:

> When, at last, the One, All-Holy, unoriginate Trinity, deigned to be contained in the belly of the Virgin Mother, through the good will of the Father and of the Son and by the overshadowing of the Holy Spirit, then it was necessary for her who had been glorified by the same number to be most brilliantly consecrated, and because of this she is brought into the temple at three years ofage. Her Fashioner and Son puts all things finally and surely in order. (296 D)

The number three is of importance for both the persons of the Holy Trinity and also the age of Mary when she is brought to the Temple. Having established that it was necessary for Mary to be brought to the Temple at the age of three he then goes on to elaborate the possible thoughts of Mary's parents in an ethopoeia of Anna. In another series of anaphoras Germanos illustrates again the history that is Mary's. Anna directs both historical and contemporary people in the procession that is to take Mary to her Entrance in the Temple. Mary's parents allow Mary to go into the temple. With Mary's entrance into the Temple, the Temple is made brighter and more beautiful because of her presence. Joachim, Anna, Zacharias, the prophets and the forefathers are overjoyed by her entrance.

In what sounds a great deal like a chorus in a Greek play, the forefathers call on Zacharias to take Mary into the Temple:

> Once again, the forefathers call to the priest: "Receive her who will receive the immaterial and uncontainable fire. Receive her who will be called the container of the Son and Word of the only God and Father. Accept her who has destroyed the reproach of our barenness and sterility. Lead into the sanctuary her who will restore us to the ancient pasture of paradise. Possess her, who endures fear like ours in her own childbearing and will be victorious over the power of death and the tyranny of hell. Enfold her who covers our nature which was stripped bare in Eden. Take the hand of her who binds in swaddling clothes him who puts an end to our uncontrolled and impulsive audaciously spread-out hands. Return to God her who returned us, you who are the priestly celebrant of the expectation of our hopes. (300C)

> "Behold, Lord, accept her whom you gave. Receive her whom you provided. Accept her whom you assigned to destroy our barenness, overcoming through her the barenness of the Law, you have ransomed us through her from the terrible persistence [daily repetition of temple sacrifices?]. House her who so well has housed us, her whom you have chosen, and have foreseen, and have blessed. Draw to yourself her who leans on you and is attracted by your fragrance. You chose her as a lily out of the brambles of our unworthiness. Embrace her who is brought to you with a most radiant complexion. Behold, to you we offer her [as our intercessor] and dedicate ourselves." (300D)

Germanos paints Mary's parents in most gracious tones. Zacharias speaks to them in what could only be called an ode of the life of Mary and her parents.

> So then Zacharias having received the child, probably first addresses the parents saying: "O causes of our salvation, what shall I say to you? What shall I call [you]? I am astonished seeing what kind of fruit you have brought forth, such a one as by her purity attracts God to dwell within her. For never yet has anyone existed or will anyone exist who shines forth in such beauty. You (Joachim and Anna) are seen as the two double rivers flowing out of paradise, (*cf.* Genesis 2.10¬15) carrying a lamp more precious than gold and precious stones, who in the beauty of her blameless virginity and her dewy sparkling illuminates the whole earth. (301A) You have been made known as shining stars as if fixed in the firmament, each of you being a torch-bearer enlightening the murky shadow of the letter and the law which was given in a stormy darkness and each of you surely and unstumblingly guiding the believer in Christ to the new grace of the new light. You have been made known as the shining horns of the new righteous, spiritual temple, holding in your breasts the holy, God-acknowledged, rational altar of the sacred victim. You, if it is not too early to say, have been made known as Cherubim flying around the mercy-seat (*cf.* Exodus 25.18ff.) with the nourishment of the Priest who supports the universe. You appeared to cover the mystical and holy Ark of the new covenant of Him who on the Cross wrote the forgiveness of our sin, [forming] a covering which far surpasses the one which long ago was wrought of gold to cover the Ark (*cf.* Exodus 25.10). (301B) Your rejoicing has become that of the cosmos. Your renown is the universal joy of all men. Fortunate are you who bear the title of parents of such a blessed child. Fortunate are you, who have brought such a blessed gift to the Lord! Fortunate are the breasts by which she was nursed and the womb that carried her (cf. Luke 11.27). (301C)

Germanos then paints a picture of the purpose of Mary and in part prayer, part litany, Joachim, Anna, Zacharias, the prophets' and the forefathers' rejoicing is expanded to the rejoicing of the cosmos, and continues to illustrate some of the implications of Mary's Entrance into the Temple. Throughout this section Germanos compares the old with the new. While not disparaging the old he sees its completion in the new, seeing a cosmic meaning in all of this. Finally he concludes: "Thus the fulfillment of the divine mystery was accomplished through an initiative from God. Thus the infant grew and was strengthened, and all the opposition which was given to us by the curse of Eden was weakened." And the purpose of Mary's Entrance into the Temple was:

> Hail, you who through your birth released the fetters of sterility,
> who scattered the reproach of childlessness, and sank the curse
> of the Law (cf. Galatians 3.13); and blossomed forth the grace
> of blessing – by entering the Holy of Holies you perfected the
> prayers of your parents and the foundation for forgiveness of
> our sins, fulfilling the perfection of harmony as the leader of the
> beginning of grace. (308B)

There follows a set of acclamations (χαῖρε) illustrating the salvific work accomplished by God through Mary. He then concludes the homily with a prayer that is redolent of the Great Litany in the Divine Liturgy:

> But O most blameless and all-laudable, most holy one, offering
> to God greater than all created things, untilled earth, unplowed
> field well-pruned vineyard, most joyous wine bowl, gushing
> spring virgin birth-giver and husbandless mother, treasure
> of purity and ornament of holiness, by your acceptable and
> motherly-persuasive petitions to your son, born from you
> without a father, and the God Creator of all, following the
> furrows of good ecclesiastical order, steer us from the floods
> of heresies and scandals to the calm and harbor where ships do
> not sink.* Clothe the priests brilliantly with righteousness and
> the joy of glorious blameless pure faith. [As for] those orthodox
> lords who have obtained you as a diadem and robe sea-purple
> and supremely golden dye, or pearl, or precious stone and the
> undefiled ornament of their own royalty, wielding their scepters
> in peace and stability; subject to them and spread under their

feet the unfilial barbarian nations who blaspheme against you and the God [born] from you.

Guard [them] in the hour of battle along with the army which always relies on your aid. Confirm [them] to go obediently by God's command with the well-directed servitude of good order. Crowning with victorious trophies your city which holds you as tower and a foundation, protect [her], girding [her] with strength. Keep the dwelling-place of God always as the beauty of the temple. Preserve those who praise you from all misfortune and distress of soul. Providing rescue for the captives, appear as a succor to those who are strangers, homeless, and friendless. Stretch out your protective hand for all the world, so that in joy and gladness we may celebrate your festival with the rites which we are now most gloriously performing. In Christ Jesus the King of all and our true God, to whom [be] glory and power, along with the holy Father, the source of life, and the coeternal Spirit, one in essence and sharing the throne, now and ever and to the ages of the ages. Amen. (308C/D & 309A).

Chapter Eight

First Homily on the Presentation of the Theotokos in the Temple
Translation

Θυμηδίας μὲν

[292C]

A sermon on the presentation of the all-holy Theotokos (in the Temple) by our holy father Germanos, Archbishop of Constantinople.

1—Every divine festival, whenever it is celebrated, spiritually fills those who are present from a treasury and divinely flowing spring. But even more and beyond other feasts does this recently hymned festival, brilliantly celebrated, attract the soul with holy joy and gives more joy in proportion to the preeminence of the excellent child of God. For the annual observation of this feast is coming,[221] in which one must be pure to participate. Please follow me gladly, with pure thoughts and in bright garments. Let us hasten to pick the precious flowers from the private meadow of the Mother of God.

---

[221] At first look the contrast between "the recently hymned festival" and "For the annual observation is coming," may confuse the reader. However, I believe Germanos is referring to the practice of signaling the coming (a foretaste) of a feast by singing some of the hymns before the feast actually takes place. This custom of the Orthodox Church is still practiced today.

[292D]

And let us be anointed with the perfume of her roses, as Solomon says in the beautiful verse of his Song: "Who is that who comes up from the wilderness, perfumed with myrrh and frankincense, with all the fragrant powders of the merchants?" (Song of Songs 3.6)—"Come hither from Lebanon, my bride; come hither from Lebanon" (Song of Songs 4.8)

[293A]

So let us eagerly approach together this mutually beneficial, salvific feast of the Mother of God. And bowing before the unapproachable place [the holy of Holies] let us watch the child going toward the second veil, Mary the all-holy Mother of God who put an end to unfruitful sterility, and exchanged the mere shadow of the letter of the law (*cf.* Hebrews 10.1*ff*) through the grace of her birth-giving.[222]

2—Today, at three years of age, she goes towards her dedication in the temple of the law, she who alone is called the stainless and greatest temple of the high priest and the Lord of all, and in whose bright light is the radiance of divine light which illuminates the darkness of the Law.

[293B]

Today a babe is handed over to a priest, the one who will dedicate the only high-priestly God made flesh as a child at forty days for us, having received in his welcoming arms (*cf.* Luke 1.22*ff.*) the uncontainable One who is beyond all human knowing.[223]

Today a new, pure, unspoiled book which will not be written by hands, but written in gold by the spirit, hallowed with blessings according to the Law, she is brought forward as an acceptable gift.

---

[222] This is the first reference in this homily to the place of the Virgin as the instrument of the Incarnation.

[223] This is a reference to the Presentation in the Temple of Christ. Germanos makes reference to that event to set the events of the Presentation of the Theotokos in the context of her role in the Incarnation. Mary and Joseph present Jesus to Zacharias as Mary was presented to Zacharias by Joachim and Anna. Both presentations were necessary parts of salvation history.

Today Joachim, who has wiped away the reproach of childlessness, goes openly down the main road boastfully showing off his offspring, and again is shown as a functionary of hallowing according to the Law.

Today also Anna has exchanged the persistence of barrenness for fruitfulness, and becoming inspired by joy, proclaims to the ends of the earth that she has borne a child, embracing to her bosom the one who is wider than the heavens.

[293C]

Today the gate of God's temple is opened to receive the entry of the eastward looking, sealed gate of Emmanuel (*cf.* Ezekiel 44.1-3).

Today the sacred Table of the temple joyfully meets and participates in the true divine table of the heavenly soul-feeding bread and by changing to the worship of the bloodless sacrifice begins to shine.

Today she who alone is called the new, god-like, purifying and mercy seat, not made by hands, (*cf.* Hebrews 9.11) for mortals who have drowned in floods of sin is presented to the mercy seat of the temple.

[293D]

Today she who will receive the Holy One of the Holy through the hallowing of the Spirit is placed in the holy of Holies at a pure and innocent age; and she who is marvelously exalted above the Cherubim, makes more holy the holy of Holies by her presence.

3—Today Mary advances, about whom no matter how much we say, we cannot come close to our goal of adequately praising her. Her beauty far surpasses the power of every tongue and mind. For her greatness is a vast sea, as the Heavenly drop born from her has shown. And therefore her richness is unlimited in its infinitude, and her wealth is inexhaustible.

[296A]

For while it is possible for everyone in everything else to be sated, it is not possible in this feasting to give too much sweetness in her hymns and festivals. And hence, the material is without limit of praises starting with her. And since the well is unfailing and not diminished by the drawing out (cf. John 4.14) but as much as is drawn out is refilled 100 or 10,000 fold, those who draw out cannot cease. For the mystery overflows and the plant grows taller even than the incorporeal minds, not to mention the incarnate minds, in the compassion of the all-rich and pure maiden!

[296B]

4—And her own parents presented to God the one who had reached three years of age. But how great is the three-fold number and exceedingly honored and for everyone a cause of all security! With three stones David slew the infamous Goliath (cf. 1 Samuel 17.40ff.), and Elijah the Tishbite, as by three circuits he brought thus the flame of fire onto water (cf. 1 Kings 18.34ff.), prepares [men] to believe. And for an equal number of days Jonah was carried about in the breast of the beast covered with water (cf. Jonah 2.1ff.). He is declared an image of God who managed the whale. And in like time the children boldly walked about in the furnace nourished by the heavenly dew (cf. Daniel 3.49ff.)[224]. And my Lord Jesus' ministry was for a period of three encircling years,

[296C]

cleansing me from the stain of my transgression and at another time healing every disease and weakness. And to a similar number of disciples he revealed the mystical appearance of His own glory upon the mountaintop (cf. Matthew 17.1). And by spending three days he raised the souls of those imprisoned in the shadows of hell from the ages [past]. And what more? See with me the number three even in the greatest things. For the cause of all and the divine source of perfection has chosen to be praised in three blessings, in three characters, that is in three natures, and if indeed we need to say the same thing with "in three persons" in one essence, as a perfect number without confusion, a collective unity; neither is the deficient poverty dishonored, nor either is a vain fantasy indulged by a greater number with many origins. Thus that Gregory [says] who is great in divine matters and accurate in theology [Gregory of Nazianzus].

---

[224] All of these references are also part of the canons sung during matins in the Orthodox Church.

[296D]

When, at last, the One, All-Holy, unoriginate Trinity, deigned to be contained in the belly of the Virgin Mother, through good will of the Father and of the Son and by the overshadowing of the Holy Spirit, then it was necessary for her who had been glorified by the same number to be most brilliantly consecrated, and because of this she is brought into the temple at three years of age. Her Fashioner and Son puts all things finally and surely in order.

5—When she who is the nourisher of our lives had been weaned, her parents fulfill the commitment which they had promised.

[297A]

They call together, as it is reported, all the virgins in the region to go after her as torch-bearers. Delighted by the procession of the lamp-bearers, she walks without turning back.

And the barren and unfruitful Anna with foresight lifts her hands to God and says in a loud distinct voice, "Come with me, let us rejoice together, all women and men who rejoiced at her birth, even more now, as I dedicate to the Lord this divinely beautiful and holy gift recently received from my own womb. Come with me, chorus leaders, with singers and instrumentalists, and joyfully begin new songs in a new way, not as did Moses' sister Miriam (cf. Exodus 20-21) but with my daughter as the leader.

[297B]

Come with me also, you neighbors and strangers and keep up with me in giving thanks with great joy for a good childbirth and even more in dedicating the fruit of my pains of childbirth to the holy places: sing with joy a divinely inspired song. Come with me also, company of the prophets, the assembly of the elect, ordering aright the resonating glorious hymns through the Holy Spirit of our God: let us sing a hymn. For there the word vibrates with prophetic sound, and thereby is severed all opposing evil speech.

6—But come with me, David the forefather and ancestor of God[225] and make ever more harmonious music striking your harp in the giving of hymns on the strings of the spirit (cf. I Samuel 16.23) with your God-inspired voice,

[297C]

guiding more clearly her escort of virgin companions, as "The virgins after her are led along to the king, those who are with her are led along" (Ps 44:15, LXX). For behold the crowd leads the young women in song on the way. The daughter of the King is led to the holy house and with praises and songs into the holy temple, she who will accomplish Your word, the one you yourself called daughter, my regal child, for you said: "All glory is given to the daughter of the King who resides within [the temple] dressed in gold-fringed robes," of a pure and spotless virginity, and in the similar way you will have said, "embroidered with incomparable beauty" (Ps 44:14 LXX).

Come here David bringer of dawn's light[226]: "Who is this who shines out like the dawn, is as fair as the moon, and bright as the sun?" "How gracefully you walk in your sandals!" (Cant 7:2)

[297D]

"How beautiful and pleasant you are" (Cant 7:7) the one who shall be clothed in the Sun (Rev 12:1) and will bring forth a new wonder under the Sun! (cf. Ec. 1:9-10)

Come, loud-voiced Ezekiel, holding the divine scroll of the life-creating Spirit and crying your holy words to the eastward oriented and sealed gate (Ezekiel 44:1) which only God goes through; and anyone else in holy orders, or all the rest of the choir of spectators, raise your voices, having seen accomplishment of thing that have been prophesized. But what?

---

[225] David was the ancestor of both Mary and Joseph, see Luke 3.23-38 and Mathew 1.1-17.

[226] ἡωσφῶν, attested only here

[300A]

Our ancestors who are about to be released from the curse and again inheriting the residence in paradise from which you were cast out: should you not hymn the cause of your salvation, with a fitting encomium and great praises? Indeed you especially ought to shout out, and I with you and with us both all creation [ought] to sing out in joy.

7—Probably with these thoughts the chaste Anna, having accepted this course with her loving husband, sends forth her for whom she had felt the pangs of childbirth. With the lamp-bearing virgins they reach the temple, whose gates open to receive the mystical gate of God Emmanuel, and the threshold of the temple is blessed by Mary's footsteps.

[300B]

For, on the one hand, the house is brightened by the lamps, but even more, the house is brilliantly illuminated by the luminance of the true lamp. By her entry the temple's beauty is adorned. The vestments of the horn of the altar of sacrifice are made more royal by the purple-hued garment of her virginity. Zacharias rejoices that he is found worthy to receive the Mother of God. Joachim is glad, confirming the outcome of the oracles. Anna is joyful at the sanctification of her child. The forefathers jump for joy, escaping the captivity of condemnation. The prophets are delighted, and with them all who are yet to come in this age of grace also leap for joy.

8—And thus the child of God is led in [and] takes her place by the horns, as her parents offer their vows, and the priest gives his blessing.

[300C]

Once again, the forefathers call to the priest: "Receive her who will receive the immaterial and uncontainable fire. Receive her who will be called the container of the Son and Word of the only God and Father. Accept her who has destroyed the reproach of our bareness and sterility. Lead into the sanctuary her who will restore us to the ancient pasture of paradise. Possess her, who endures fear like ours in her own childbearing and will be victorious over the power of death and the tyranny of hell.

Enfold her who covers our nature which was stripped bare in Eden. Take the hand of her who binds in swaddling clothes him who puts an end to our uncontrolled and impulsive audaciously spread-out hands. Return to God her who returned us, you who are the priestly celebrant of the expectation of our hopes."

[300D]

"Behold, Lord, accept her whom you gave. Receive her whom you provided. Accept her whom you assigned to destroy our bareness, overcoming through her the barrenness of the Law, you have ransomed us through her from the terrible persistence [daily repetition of temple sacrifices?]. House her who so well has housed us, her whom you have chosen, and have foreseen, and have blessed. Draw to yourself her who leans on you and is attracted by your fragrance. You chose her as a lily out of the brambles of our unworthiness. Embrace her who is brought to you with a most radiant complexion. Behold, to you we offer her [as our intercessor] and dedicate ourselves."

[301A]

9—These are the harmonious [words] of the righteous [people], this is the dance of the God-loving couple, these is the beautifully arranged inscription of the ancestors of God. So then Zacharias having received the child, probably first addresses the parents saying: "O causes of our salvation, what shall I say to you? What shall I call [you]? I am astonished seeing what kind of fruit you have brought forth, such a one as by her purity attracts God to dwell within her. For never yet has anyone existed or will anyone exist who shines forth in such beauty. You are seen as the two double rivers flowing out of paradise, (*cf.* Genesis 2.10-15) carrying a lamp more precious than gold and precious stones, who in the beauty of her blameless virginity and her dewy sparkling illuminates the whole earth.

[301B]

You have been made known as shining stars as if fixed in the firmament, each of you being a torch-bearer enlightening the murky shadow of the letter and the law which was given in a stormy darkness and each of you surely and unstumblingly guiding the believer in Christ to the new grace of the new light. You have been made known as the shining horns of the new righteous, spiritual temple, holding in your breasts the holy, God-acknowledged, rational altar of the sacred victim. You, if it is not too early to say, have been made known as Cherubim flying around the mercy-seat (*cf.* Exodus 25.18*ff.*) with the nourishment of the Priest who supports the universe. You appeared to cover the mystical and holy Ark of the new covenant of Him who on the Cross wrote the forgiveness of our sin, [forming] a covering which far surpasses the one which long ago was wrought of gold to cover the Ark (*cf.* Exodus 25.10).

[301C]

Your rejoicing has become that of the cosmos. Your renown is the universal joy of all men. Fortunate are you who bear the title of parents of such a blessed child. Fortunate are you, who have brought such a blessed gift to the Lord! Fortunate are the breasts by which she was nursed and the womb that carried her (*cf.* Luke 11.27).

10—Come to me, child, child higher than the heavens. Come, you who are seen as a child but are known as God's workshop. Come hallow rather the gateway of the holy place, for you, so to speak, are not purified and hallowed by this [gate]: but instead you hallow it more.

[301D]

Come gaze upon the Holy of Holies and the awesome treasury, You who will become the inexhaustible, unsearchable treasure. Come into the entry doors of the Bema, you who destroy the doors of death. Gaze upon the veil (*cf.* Exodus 26.31*ff.*), you who enlighten through your lightning flash those who are blinded by their dull-sighted tastes. Give to me your hands as I lead you like a babe and hold my hand exhausted by old age and weakened by earthly-minded zeal in transgressing the commandment, and lead me to life.[227] For behold I keep you as a staff in old age and a prop for

---

[227] Perhaps a prayer of Germanos even though the words are put into Zacharias' mouth.

the weariness that comes naturally with old age. Behold, I see you as one who will become a support for those who have descended to death.

[304A]

Approach in order to venerate the table, you who are called the living, undefiled table, which has been spoken of in many symbols. Make your way through the courts of the whole sanctuary breathing out as an odor of incense (*cf.* Exodus 30.1*ff.*). You have become more fragrant than myrrh, you who have been proclaimed by the God-chosen tongue of the spirit-filled prophet to be a censer. Go up, go up to the steps of the holy house. Daughters of Jerusalem taking pleasure in the beauty of your comeliness joyously compose a hymn. The kings of the Earth call you blessed. Your ascent of the steps is recognized as divine and delightfully shown as a God-supported ladder to the great patriarch Jacob (*cf.* Genesis 28.12*ff.*). Sit down O Lady, for it is proper to you as the Queen glorified above all earthly kingdoms to be seated upon such steps.

[304B]

This holy place is a fitting dwelling for you who are the throne of the Cherubim. Behold, as Queen of all I have attributed, as it is fitting to you, the most honorable throne. Do you yourself raise up those who have been cast down. And now with David I cry unto you: 'Hear O daughter consider and incline your ear; forget not your people and your father's house; and the king will desire your beauty.' (Psalm 45.11 *ff.*)"

11—And with this the old man restrained himself, although he had thoughts enough for many more encomia.[228] And the parents went away, and the child having been consecrated to God remained behind. And angels did their duty of feeding with fear, and the maiden was fed by immaterial beings, whether with immaterial or material food.[229]

---

[228] Perhaps Germanos is speaking of himself here although the words are those of Zacharias.

[229] A similar theme appears in Germanos' homily on the Annunciation: You saw me, didn't you, O blessed one, when you were in the Holy of Holies, and when you received nourishment from my fiery hands? I am Gabriel, who always stand before the glory of God. (325C)

[304C]

Thus the fulfillment of the divine mystery was accomplished through an initiative from God. Thus the infant grew and was strengthened, and all the opposition which was given to us by the curse of Eden was weakened (*cf*. Genesis 3.16*ff*.).

12—But come now, assembly dear to God, whatever power is in our childish thoughts, with one voice let us proclaim the χαῖρε to the Virgin (*cf*. Luke 1.28), not being able adequately to hymn her perfect feast; but excusing our weakness as far as possible, since God is pleased with what is within our power. For the only [woman] known as virgin and mother has surpassed all thought, and the cause is clear. For what virgin has given birth, or after giving birth has preserved her virginity undefiled, except you alone, who truly bore God in the flesh for us, all-blessed maiden?

[304D]

13—Therefore hail, forgiveness of transgressions given by God for us filthy ones, who are denuded by the death-dealing and soul-destroying food of Eden, as you put on the sea-purple robe which represents God-given forgiveness today for your entrance to the holy of holies in your glorious garment not made by hands (*cf*. Genesis 3.17), O bride of God.

[305A]

Hail, you who today call together all the prophetic assembly for the beginning of your most brilliant and venerable Entrance, with well-tuned cymbals as with musical instruments striking up the divine-sounding strain and dancing in spiritual joy.

14—Hail to you who by the rhythm of your footsteps trample down my terrible leader—that serpent with his crooked-minded, good-hating diabolical nature—who has counseled me toward transgression (*cf*. Genesis 3.1-13). But you controlling your changeable, visible, and corrupt nature continue to journey along toward the heavenly, holy and even eternal tent.

Hail to you who have radiantly shown this day of joy and gladness (*cf.* Psalm 45.15 LXX) of your torch-lit Entrance upon those who have been caught by the shadow of death and the abyss of infirmity—you who bear witness that the divinely-ordained destruction of darkness shall come about through you, O most wonderful Mary.

[305B]

Hail, bright cloud (*cf.* Exodus 19.16) who continues to drop divine spiritual dew upon us (*cf.* Exodus 16.13), you who today by your holy entrance into the Holy of Holies have made to shine the all-brilliant Sun upon those who remain in the shadow of death. A fountain pouring out God, from which the rivers of divine knowledge pour out the bright clear water of orthodoxy and drown out the company of the heretics.

15—Hail, delightful and rational paradise of God, which today is planted in the east by the omnipotent right hand of his will (*cf.* Genesis 2.8), who have blossomed forth the beautiful lily and the unfading rose for those who in the west have drunk the bitter soul-destroying plague of death, on whom the life-giving tree has sprouted forth to the intimate knowledge of the truth. Those who have tasted from it are made immortal.

[305C]

Hail, sacred, undefiled, most pure palace of the omnipotent God. You are wrapped in his grandeur and guide us all with your mystical joy. Right now you are being established in the court of the Lord, in his holy Temple, in which is located the decorated bridal chamber not made by hands of the bridegroom (*cf.* Psalm 19.5-6). Through you, the Word which was married to the flesh willingly wished to reconcile those wanderers (*cf.* Romans 5.10) who through their own private will had been separated.

[305D]

16—Hail, new Zion and holy Jerusalem, holy city of the great king—within his citadels God has shown himself a sure defense (*cf.* Psalm 47.3*ff.* LXX)—and [God] making kings subject to the veneration of your glory, and preparing all the world to celebrate in great joy the feast of your

Entrance. Truly golden and brilliant . . . You the seven-lighted lamp stand (*cf.* Exodus 25.31) enkindled by the unapproachable Light and filled by the oil of purity, and giving the rising of its gleam to the blind in the darkness of sin.

[308A]

Hail, O fertile (Ps. 67.15-17 LXX) shady mountain (Hab. 3.3) in whom the rational lamb has been nourished, he who has set aside our sins, from whom the stone not made by hands was quarried (Dan. 2.34), he who has crushed the sacrificial idols and "the head of the cornerstone has become marvelous in our eyes" (Ps. 117.22, 23).

17—Hail, holy throne of God, the divine gift, house of glory, the most beautiful splendor and elect treasure and universal propitiation, and "heaven declaring the glory of God," (Psalm 18.2 LXX) the Orient who has raised the unapproachable radiant one, who sends forth from the highest heaven his warmth (Psalm 18.7LXX)—that is to say his managing forethought—from which no one ever can hide.

[308B]

Hail, you who through your birth[230] released the fetters of sterility, who scattered the reproach of childlessness, and sank the curse of the Law (*cf.* Galatians 3.13); and blossomed forth the grace of blessing—by entering the Holy of Holies you perfected the prayers of your parents and the foundation for forgiveness of our sins, fulfilling the perfection of harmony as the leader of the beginning of grace.

18—Hail, most blessed Mary (*cf.* Luke 1.28), the holiest of the holy ones, higher than the heavens, more glorious than the Cherubim and more honorable than the Seraphim, more blessed than all of creation. You are the dove who bears the olive branch to us in your glorious and splendid entry into the Temple announcing a saving refuge from the spiritual deluge

---

[230] This is one of the few references to Mary's own birth to be found in Germanos.

(*cf.* Genesis 8.11). "The wings of a dove covered with silver, its pinions with green gold" (Ps. 67.14 LXX)

[308C]

struck by the lightning of the all holy and illuminating Spirit, the all-gold container (*cf.* Exodus 16.33) who bore Christ, the manna, the sweet sweetness of our souls.

19—But O most blameless and all-laudable, most holy one, offering to God greater than all created things, untilled earth, unplowed field (*cf.* Ezekiel 19.10), well-pruned vineyard, most joyous wine bowl, gushing spring (*cf.* Ezekiel 17.6), virgin birth-giver and husbandless mother, treasure of purity and ornament of holiness, by your acceptable and motherly-persuasive petitions to your son, born from you without a father, and the God Creator of all, following the furrows of good ecclesiastical order, steer us from the floods of heresies and scandals to the calm and harbor where ships do not sink.[231]

[308D]

Clothe the priests brilliantly with righteousness (*cf.* Psalm 131.16 LXX) and the joy of glorious blameless pure faith. [As for] those orthodox lords who have obtained you as a diadem and robe sea-purple and supremely golden dye, or pearl, or precious stone and the undefiled ornament of their own royalty, wielding their scepters in peace and stability; subject to them and spread under their feet the un-filial barbarian nations who blaspheme against you and the God [born] from you.

[309A]

Guard [them] in the hour of battle along with the army which always relies on your aid. Confirm [them] to go obediently by God's command with the well-directed servitude of good order. Crowning with victorious trophies your city which holds you as tower and a foundation, protect [her],

---

[231] ἀπόντιστος here only—ἀκαταπόντιστος in Theodore the Studite and Nicholas Mysticus

girding [her] with strength. Keep the dwelling-place of God always as the beauty of the temple. Preserve those who praise you from all misfortune and distress of soul. Providing rescue for the captives, appear as a succor to those who are strangers, homeless, and friendless. Stretch out your protective hand for all the world, so that in joy and gladness we may celebrate your festival with the rites which we are now most gloriously performing. In Christ Jesus the King of all and our true God, to whom [be] glory and power, along with the holy Father, the source of life, and the coeternal Spirit, one in essence and sharing the throne, now and ever and to the ages of the ages. Amen

Chapter Nine

References to Mary in the First Homily on the Presentation of the Theotokos in the Temple by Germanos, Patriarch of Constantinople (715-730)

PG 98 Location	Greek	English	OT/NT Reference
Germanos introduces his homily by declaring that there are great befits to those who celebrate any divine festival. But this one gives more joy because it is a festival of Mary, that preeminent child.			
292C	ὅτῳ καὶ ὑπεραναβαινούσης τῆς ἐξαρχούσης Θεόπαιδος	to the preeminence of the excellent child of God	
292C	τῆς θεομήτορος	the Mother of God	
Germanos extends his metaphor of the "private meadow of the Mother of God". Perhaps he is referring to the fact that none of this homily's origin is found in the canonical scriptures. So, he invites his auditors to "Please follow me gladly, with pure thoughts and in bright garments. Let us hasten to pick the precious flowers from the private meadow of the Mother of God."			
292D	«Τίς αὕτη ἡ ἀναβαίνουσα ἀπὸ τῆς ἐρήμου, ὡς στελέχη καπνοῦ τεθυμιαμένη, σμύρναν καὶ λίβανον ἀπὸ πάντων κονιορτῶν μυρεψοῦ;»	"Who is that who comes up from the wilderness, perfumed with myrrh and frankincense, with all the fragrant powders of the merchants?"	Song of Songs 3.6
292D	«Δεῦρο ἀπὸ Λιβάνου, νύμφη μου, δεῦρο ἀπὸ Λιβάνου.»	"Come hither from Lebanon, my bride; come hither from Lebanon."	Song of Songs 4.8

Germanos sets the scene of the Presentation. This event is seen as the end of the old Law with its sterility and proclaims that through the Incarnation "the shadow of the letter of the Law is made bright."			
293A	τῆς Θεομήτορος	the Mother of God	
Germanos then launches on a long anaphora on the word 'today' and weaves the themes of the three-year-old child, the Temple (its architecture), the Law, sterility (of the Law and Mary's parents Joachim and Anna), Mary's purity, the role of Zacharias in both the Presentation of Mary and Christ's Presentation (*cf.* Luke 1.22*ff*), Mary as the Wider-than-the-Heavens, the cosmos and Mary's beauty.			
293A	παῖδα . . . χωροῦσαν	the child going	
Here in 293A Germanos says that Mary is going toward the "second veil" while in the Second homily on the Presentation he says that Mary "is brought as a blameless gift within the third curtain" 312A.			
293A	Μαρίαν τὴν πάναγνον καὶ Θεομήτορα	Mary the all-holy Mother of God	
293A	τὴν ἀκαρπίας στείρωσιν διαλύσασαν	who put an end to unfruitful sterility	
293A	καὶ νομικοῦ γράμματος σκιὰν τῇ τοῦ τόκου χάριτι διελάσασαν.	and exchanged the mere shadow of the letter of the law through the grace of her birth-giving	(*cf.* Hebrews 10.1*ff*)
293A	Σήμερον γὰρ τριετίζουσα πρόεισι τῷ νομικῷ ναῷ ἀνατεθησομένη	Today, at three years of age, she goes towards her dedication in the temple of the law,	
293A	ἡ **ναὸς** ἀκηλίδωτος καὶ ὑπέρτατος μόνη χρηματίσασα τοῦ ἀρχιερέως καὶ τῶν ἁπάντων τελετάρχου Κυρίου	she who alone is called the stainless and greatest temple of the high priest and the Lord of all	
293A	καὶ ἐν τῇ ἰδίᾳ μαρμαρυγῇ τῆς θεολαμποῦς αἴγλης, τὴν ἐν τῷ γράμματι ἀχλὺν διελοῦσα	and in whose bright light is the radiance of divine light which illuminates the darkness of the Law.	
Germanos underlines a parallel between the life of Mary and Jesus by referring to Zacharias as the priest that receives both Mary and Jesus at their presentations. Both of Mary's parents are introduced as well and Germanos makes a reference to their renewed status because of the birth of Mary. "Today Joachim, who has wiped away the reproach of childlessness, goes openly down the main road boastfully showing off his offspring, and again is shown as a functionary of hallowing according to the Law. Today also Anna has exchanged the persistence of barrenness for fruitfulness, and becoming inspired by joy, proclaims to the ends of the earth that she has borne a child, embracing to her bosom the one who is wider than the heavens."			

293B	Σήμερον βρέφος	Today a babe	
293B	ὁ καινότατος καὶ καθαρώτατος ἀμόλυντος τόμος, οὐ χειρὶ γραφησόμενος	a new, pure, unspoiled book which will not be written by hands	
293B	ἀλλὰ πνεύματι χρυσωθησόμενος, ταῖς κατὰ νόμον εὐλογίαις ἁγιαζομένη	but written in gold by the spirit, hallowed with blessings according to the Law	
293B	χαριστήριον δῶρον	an acceptable gift	

Mary is seen as "the eastward looking, sealed gate of Emmanuel, a confirmation of her Virginity.

293C	τὴν ἀνατολόβλεπτον καὶ ἐσφραγισμένην τοῦ Ἐμμανουὴλ	the eastward looking, sealed gate of Emmanuel	(*cf.* Ezechiel 44.1-3)
293C	Σήμερον ἡ ἱερὰ τοῦ ναοῦ τράπεζα λαμπρύνεσθαι ἄρχεται, πρὸς ἀναιμάκτους θυσίας τὴν μεταβίβασιν μετηλλαχυῖα τῇ τῆς οὐρανίου καὶ ψυχοτρόφου ἄρτου τραπέζης θείας προσκυνήσεως μεθέξει καὶ γλυκυτάτῳ ἀσπασμῷ	Today the sacred Table of the temple joyfully meets and participates in the true divine table of the heavenly soul-feeding bread and by changing to the worship of the bloodless sacrifice begins to shine.	
293C	ἱλαστήριον καινόν τε καὶ θεοειδέστατον καθαρτικόν τε καὶ ἀχειρότευκτον χρηματίσασα	Today she who alone is called the new, god-like, purifying and mercy seat, not made by hands	(*cf.* Hebrews 9.11)
293C	Σήμερον ἡ τὸν τῶν ἁγίων Ἅγιον εἰσδεξομένη Πνεύματος ἁγιασμῷ	Today she who will receive the Holy One of the Holy through the hallowing of the Spirit	
293D	ἀπειροκάκῳ καὶ ἀδαήμονι ἡλικίᾳ	at a pure and innocent age	
293D	τοῖς τῶν ἁγίων Ἁγίοις ἁγιωτάτως καὶ εὐκλεῶς ἁγιασμῷ μείζονι, . . . Χερουβὶμ δόξης ὑπεραρθεῖσα θαυμασιωτάτως ἐναποτίθεται	she who is marvelously exalted above the Cherubim, makes more holy the holy of Holies by her presence	
293D	ἡ Μαρία	Mary	

293D	τοῦ αἴνους τῷ πάσης ὑπερ-αρθῆναι καλλονῇ γλώσσης τε καὶ νοὸς ἐξεστη-κότως, προάγει	Her beauty far surpasses the power of every tongue and mind	
293D	Πέλαγος γὰρ ἀχανὲς τὰ ταύτης μεγαλεῖα	For her greatness is a vast sea	
293D	Διὸ δὴ τοῦ χάριν καὶ ἄληπτος τῇ ἀπειρίᾳ ὁ ταύτης πλοῦτος πέφυκε, καὶ ἡ αὐτῆς τρυφὴ ἀδάπανος	And therefore her richness is unlimited in its infinitude, and her wealth is inexhaustible	

Germanos returns to one of his constant themes that of how impossible it is for humans to adequately praise Mary: "For while it is possible for everyone in everything else to be sated, it is not possible in this feasting to give too much sweetness in her hymns and festivals. And hence, the material is without limit of praises starting with her. And since the well is unfailing and not diminished by the drawing out (cf. John 4.14) but as much as is drawn out is refilled 100 or 10,000 fold, those who draw out cannot cease. For the mystery overflows and the plant grows taller even than the incorporeal minds, not to mention the incarnate minds, in the compassion of the all-rich and pure maiden!"

296A	Ἐν τῷ κατοίκτρῳ γὰρ τὸ μυστήριον ὑπερβλύζει καὶ βλαστάνον ὑπερανίσταται καὶ ἀΰλους νόας, μὴ ὅτι γε ἐνύλους, τῆς πανολβίου καὶ πανάγνου κόρης!	For the mystery overflows and the plant grows taller even than the incorporeal minds, not to mention the incarnate minds, in the compassion of the all-rich and pure maiden!	

Germanos then returns to the number 'three' and recites a Biblical history of 'three' ending with the Nicaea-Constantinopolitan formulation of the Incarnation. 296B/C

296B	τριετῆ χρόνον τετελεκυῖαν	the one who had reached three years of age	
296D	παρθενομήτορος κόρης γαστρὶ	the belly of the Virgin Mother	

Germanos sees Mary's entrance and residence in the Temple to be a necessary preparation to her consecration: ἱερουργεῖσθαι λαμπρότατα. In this he appears to be in agreement with many of the Greek fathers who see the Annunciation to be the point of her consecration. In doing this Germanos says: "Her Fashioner and Son puts all things finally and surely in order" 296D

296D	ἔδει δὲ καὶ ταύτην τῷ αὐτῷ τοῦ ἀριθμοῦ δεδοξασμένην κλέει ἱερουργεῖσθαι λαμπρότατα	then it was necessary for her who had been glorified by the same number to be most brilliantly consecrated	
296D	Ἤδη μὲν οὖν ἀπογαλακτισθείσης αὐτῆς τῆς ἡμετέρας ζωῆς τροφοῦ	she who is the nourisher of our lives had been weaned	

Having established that it was necessary for Mary to be brought to the Temple at the age of three he then goes on to elaborate the possible thoughts of Mary's parents in an ethopoeia of Anna. This section tells of the arrangements for the procession of Mary to the Temple. 297A-300C.

297A	ἀμεταστρεπτεὶ βαδίσῃ	she walks without turning back	
297A	δῶρον θεοκαλλώπιστον	this divinely beautiful and holy gift	
297A	ἀλλὰ τῆς ἐξ ἐμέθεν γεγεννημένης ἀφηγουμένης	my daughter as the leader	
297B	τὴν τῶν ἐμῶν ὠδίνων καρποφορίαν	the fruit of my pains of childbirth	
297C	«ἀπενεχθήσονται τῷ Βασιλεῖ παρθένοι ὀπίσω αὐτῆς, αἱ πλησίον αὐτῆς ἀπενεχθήσονται.»	"The virgins after her are led along to the king, those who are with her are led along"	(Ps 44:15, LXX)
297C	ἡ τοῦ Βασιλέως. . θυγατέρα.	The daughter of the King	
297C	ἐμὴ παῖς βασιλικώτατα	my regal child	
297C	«Πᾶσα ἡ δόξα γὰρ, ἔφης, τῆς θυγατρὸς τοῦ βασιλέως ἔσωθεν ἐν κροσσωτοῖς χρυσοῖς,» περιβεβλημένη τῇ ἀμιάντῳ καὶ ἀσπίλῳ παρθενίᾳ, καὶ πεποικιλμένη τῇ ἀσυγκρίτῳ καλλονῇ, ὁμοιοτρόπως λελέξων·	"All glory is given to the daughter of the King who resides within [the temple] dressed in gold-fringed robes," of a pure and spotless virginity, and in the similar way you will have said, "embroidered with incomparable beauty".	(Ps 44:14 LXX)
297C	δεῦρ' ἴθι, Δαυῒδ ἠωσφῶν· «Τίς αὕτη ἡ ἐκκύπτουσα ὡσεὶ ὄρθρος, καλὴ ὡς σελήνη, ἐκλεκτὴ ὡς ἥλιος; τί ὡραιώθησαν διαβήματά σου ἐν ὑποδήμασι;»	Come here David bringer of dawn's light1: "Who is this who shines out like the dawn, is as fair as the moon, and bright as the sun?" "How gracefully you walk in your sandals!"	(Cant 7:2)
297D	«Τί ὡραιώθης καὶ τί ἡδύνθης,»	"How beautiful and pleasant you are"	(Cant 7:7)
297D	ἡ τὸν ἥλιον περιδυσομένη	the one who shall be clothed in the Sun	(Rev 12:1)

297D	καὶ καινὸν ὑπὸ τὸν ἥλιον προσάξουσα θέαμα!	will bring forth a new wonder under the Sun!	(*cf.* Ecc 1:9-10)
297D	καὶ κεκράζων τὴν εὐφημίαν τῇ ἀνατολοβλέπτῳ καὶ θεοπαρόδῳ ἐσφραγισμένῃ πύλῃ	the eastward oriented and sealed gate which only God goes through	(Ez 44:1)
300A	καὶ βαλβὶς ἁγιάζεται τῇ τῆς Μαριὰμ ἰχνηλατήσει	the threshold of the temple is blessed by Mary's footsteps	
300B	πλέον δὲ τῇ τῆς μιᾶς λαμπάδος δᾳδουχίᾳ στιλπνοφαῶς κατ-αστράπτεται	the house is brilliantly illuminated by the luminance of the true lamp	
300B	Πορφυρίζονται στολαὶ τῶν κεράτων τοῦ θυσιαστηρίου τῇ ἁλουργοειδεῖ αὐτῆς καὶ παρθενικῇ ἀμφιάσει	The vestments of the horn of the altar of sacrifice are made more royal by the purple-hued garment of her virginity	
300B	ἡ Θεόπαις,	the child of God	

Germanos places an anaphora in the mouths of Mary's parents addressed to Zacharias. 300C/D.

300C	Δέδεξο τὴν δεδεξομένην τὸ ἄϋλον καὶ ἀκατάληπτον πῦρ	"Receive her who will receive the immaterial and uncontainable fire	
300C	δέδεξο τὴν δοχεῖον χρηματίσουσαν τοῦ Υἱοῦ καὶ Λόγου τοῦ Πατρὸς καὶ μόνου Θεοῦ	Receive her who will be called the container of the Son and Word of the only God and Father	
300C	λάβε τὴν τὸ ὄνειδος ἡμῶν τῆς ἀτοκίας καὶ τὴν στείρωσιν ἐκμειώσασαν	Accept her who has destroyed the reproach of our bareness and sterility	
300C	εἰσάγαγε τῷ θυσιαστηρίῳ τὴν εἰς τὴν ἀρχαίαν νομὴν ἡμᾶς τοῦ παραδείσου εἰσοικίσουσαν·	Lead into the sanctuary her who will restore us to the ancient pasture of paradise	
300C	κράτησον τὴν ἐν τῷ ἰδίῳ τόκῳ τὴν καθ' ἡμῶν δειλίαν φερομένην θανάτου ἰσχὺν καὶ ᾅδου τυραννίδα κρατήσουσαν	Possess her who endures fear like ours in her own childbearing and will be victorious over the power of death and the tyranny of hell	

300C	περίπτυξαι τὴν περισκέπουσαν ἡμῶν τὴν ἐν Ἐδὲμ γυμνωθεῖσαν φύσιν	Enfold her who covers our nature which was stripped bare in Eden	
300C	ἐπιλαβοῦ τῆς χειρὸς τῆς σπαργανούσης τὸν τὴν ἡμῶν ἀκρατῆ καὶ ὁρμητικὴν αὐθαδεστάτως ὑφαπλωθεῖσαν χεῖρα συντελοῦντα	Take the hand of her who binds in swaddling clothes him who puts an end to our uncontrolled and impulsive audaciously spread-out hands	
300C	ἀνάθου Θεῷ τὴν ἀναθεῖσαν ἡμᾶς, θεοτελὲς τῶν ἐλπίδων προσδοκίας.	Return to God her who returned us, you who are the priestly celebrant of the expectation of our hopes.	
300D	Ἴδε, Κύριε, ἴδε· ἣν δέδωκας, λάβε· ἣν παρέσχες, εἴσδεξαι· ἣν ἡμῖν διαλύουσαν στείρωσιν ἔνειμας, δέχου· δι' αὐτῆς καὶ νόμου ἀπαιδίαν κατακρίνων, ἐλυτρώσω ἡμᾶς ἐνδελεχισμοῦ δεινοτάτου δι' αὐτῆς· ταύτην καλῶς ἡμᾶς διοικήσασαν ἀπολάμβανε, ἣν ᾑρετίσω, καὶ προώρισας, καὶ ἡγίασας, ἐπίσπασαί σοι προσερειδομένην καὶ τῇ ὀσμῇ σου τεθελγμένην, ἣν ὡς κρίνον ἐξ ἀκανθῶν τῆς ἡμετέρας ἀναξιότητος ἐξελέξω· εὐχρωτάτά σοι προσφερομένην ἐναγκάλισαι. Ἰδού σοι ταύτην παρατιθέμεθα καὶ ἑαυτοὺς ἀνατιθέμεθα.	"Behold, Lord, accept her whom you gave. Receive her whom you provided. Accept her whom you assigned to destroy our bareness, overcoming through her the barrenness of the Law, you have ransomed us through her from the terrible persistence [daily repetition of temple sacrifices?]. House her who so well has housed us, her whom you have chosen, and have foreseen, and have blessed. Draw to yourself her who leans on you and is attracted by your fragrance. You chose her as a lily out of the brambles of our unworthiness. Embrace her who is brought to you with a most radiant complexion. Behold, to you we offer her [as our intercessor] and dedicate ourselves."	

Zacharias now addresses Joachim and Anna. Zacharias ode to Mary's parents paints a picture of them in biblical and cosmic terms.			
301A	τὴν παῖδα	the child	
301A	καρπὸν	fruit	
301A	Τοιοῦτος γὰρ ὅστις τῇ καθαρότητι θέλγει Θεὸν ἐν αὐτῇ οἰκῆσαι	such a one as by her purity attracts God to dwell within her	
301A	Οὐδὲ γὰρ πώποτέ τις γέγονεν ἢ γενήσεται τοιαύτη καλλονῇ διαλάμπουσα	For never yet has anyone existed or will anyone exist who shines forth in such beauty	
301A	Ὑμεῖς ὤφθητε οἱ ἐκ παραδείσου ἀφιγμένοι δύο διπλούμενοι ποταμοί	You are seen as the two double rivers flowing out of paradise	(*cf.* Genesis 2.10-15)
301A	τὴν τῷ κάλλει τῆς ἑαυτῆς ἀμώμου παρθενίας καὶ ταῖς δροσιστικαῖς μαρμαρυγαῖς τὴν ἅπασαν γῆν καταυγάζουσαν	who in the beauty of her blameless virginity and her dewy sparkling illuminates the whole earth	
301B	τὸ τοῦ ἱεροῦ σφαγίου ἡγιασμένον καὶ θεεγκαίνιστον λογικώτατον θυσιαστήριον	the holy, God-acknowledged, rational altar of the sacred victim	
301B	τὸ τῆς κιβωτοῦ κάλυμμα τὴν τῆς νέας διαθήκης	cover the mystical and holy Ark of the new covenant	(*cf.* Exodos 25.10).
With 301C an anaphora on 'come' (Δεῦρο), in the midst of which Zacharias makes some prophesies concerning the child Mary and her work in the redemption of Israel, quoting both Exodus and Genesis. This ends with 304B.			
301C	τοιαύτης παιδὸς γεννήτορες χρηματίσαντες!	who bear the title of parents of such a blessed child	
301C	τοιοῦτον εὐλογημένον δῶρον Κυρίῳ προσάξαντες!	brought such a blessed gift to the Lord!	
301C	παιδίον τῶν οὐρανῶν ἀνώτερον	child higher than the heavens	
301C	βρέφος ὁρώμενον καὶ θεϊκὸν ἐργαστήριον νοούμενον	you who are seen as a child but are known as God's workshop	

301C	Δεῦρο, προπύλαια τοῦ ἁγιαστηρίου ἁγίασον μᾶλλον· οὐ γὰρ σύ, ὡς ἔπος ἔτι φάναι, ταὐτῷ καθαιρομένη ἁγιάζῃ, ἀλλ' ἢ καὶ λίαν ἁγιάζεις	Come hallow rather the gateway of the holy place, for you, so to speak, are not purified and hallowed by this [gate]: but instead you hallow it more	
301D	ἡ κειμήλιον ἄπλετον καὶ ἀνεξερεύνητον γενησομένη	will become the inexhaustible, unsearchable treasure	
301D	ἡ τὰ τοῦ θανάτου πρόθυρα συνθλῶσα	you who destroy the doors of death	
301D	ἡ τοὺς τῇ ἀμβλυοποιῷ γεύσει τετυφλωμένους τῇ σῇ ἀστραπῇ φωτίζουσα	you who enlighten through your lightning flash those who are blinded by their dull-sighted tastes	
301D	Δίδου μοι χεῖράς σε ποδηγοῦντι ὡς βρέφος, καὶ κράτει μου χεῖρα τῷ γήρᾳ κεκμηκότι καὶ τῇ τῆς ἐντολῆς παρεκδύσει γεήφρονι ζήλῳ νενευκότι, καὶ ἄγοις με πρὸς ζωήν	Give to me your hands as I lead you like a babe and hold my hand exhausted by old age and weakened by earthly-minded zeal in transgressing the commandment, and lead me to life.	
301D	Ἰδοὺ γάρ σε κατέχω βακτηρίαν τοῦ γήρους καὶ τῆς ἀσθενησάσης τῷ ὀλισθήματι φύσεως ἀνόρθωσιν	For behold I keep you as a staff in old age and a prop for the weariness that comes naturally with old age	
301D	Ἰδού σε στήριγμα βλέπω γενησομένην τῶν καταβεβηκότων πρὸς θάνατον.	Behold, I see you as one who will become a support for those who have descended to death	
304A	τράπεζαν κεχρηματικέναι σε λογικωτάτην καὶ ἀμόλυντον	who are called the living, undefiled table	
304A	ἐκπνέουσα, καὶ ὑπὲρ μύρον τοῖς ὀσφραινομένοις	more fragrant than myrrh	*cf.* Exodus 30.1*ff*
304A	πύριον	a censer	
304A	τῇ καλλονῇ τῆς ὡραιότητος	the beauty of your comeliness	
304A	μακαρίζουσιν	blessed	

304A	ἡ βάσις θεία γεγνωρισμένη καὶ θεοστήρικτος κλίμαξ δεδειγμένη τῷ πατριαρχικωτάτῳ Ἰακὼβ θυμηρέστατα	Your ascent of the steps is recognized as divine and delightfully shown as a God-supported ladder to the great patriarch Jacob	cf. Genesis 28.12ff
304A	ὦ Δέσποινα	O Lady	
304A	σοὶ τῇ βασιλίσσῃ καὶ ὑπὲρ πάσας τὰς βασιλείας τοῦ κόσμου δεδοξασμένῃ	to you as the Queen glorified above all earthly kingdoms	
304B	τῷ Χερουβικωτάτῳ θρόνῳ	the throne of the Cherubim	
304B	ὡς παντανάσσῃ	Queen of all	
304B	τὴν προκαθεδρίαν	the most honorable throne	
304B	«Ἄκουσον, θύγατερ, καὶ ἴδε, καὶ κλῖνον τὸ οὖς σου, καὶ ἐπιλάθου τοῦ λαοῦ σου καὶ τοῦ οἴκου τοῦ πατρός σου, καὶ ἐπιθυμήσει ὁ βασιλεὺς τοῦ κάλλους σου.»	'Hear O daughter consider and incline your ear; forget not your people and your father's house; and the king will desire your beauty.'	Psalm 45.11 ff.)"
304B	ἡ παῖς	the child	
304B	ἡ κόρη	the maiden	

Germanos now invites his auditors to join in the 'praises' of Mary. "But come now, assembly dear to God, whatever power is in our childish thoughts, with one voice let us proclaim the χαῖρε to the Virgin (cf. Luke 1.28), not being able adequately to hymn her perfect feast; but excusing our weakness as far as possible, since God is pleased with what is within our power."

304C	τὸ βρέφος	the infant	
304C	τῇ Παρθένῳ	the Virgin	
304C	Ὑπερβέβηκε μὲν γὰρ οὖν ἅπασαν ἔννοιαν ἡ μόνη παρθένος καὶ μήτηρ γνωρισθεῖσα	For the only [woman] known as virgin and mother has surpassed all thought	
304C	πανολβία κόρη	all-blessed maiden	
304D	Θεόνυμφε	O bride of God	
305A	τῆς φαεινοτάτης καὶ σεβασμιο-φόρου Προόδου	most brilliant and venerable Entrance	
305A	ἡ τῇ τῶν βημάτων σου ῥυθμίσει καταπατήσασα τὸν δεινόν μοι ποδηγόν	by the rhythm of your footsteps trample down my terrible leader	

305A	καὶ συνοδεύουσαν ἐπιλαβομένη τὴν ὀλισθηρὰν φανεῖσαν φθαρτὴν οὐσίαν πρὸς τὴν ἄϋλον καὶ ἁγίαν ἀγήρω πάλιν σκηνήν.	But you controlling your changeable, visible, and corrupt nature continue to journey along toward the heavenly, holy and even eternal tent.	
305A	καὶ ζόφου διάλυσιν ἐπιμαρτυρουμένη θεοβράβευτον διὰ σοῦ γενήσεσθαι, πανυπερθαύμαστε Μαρία.	you who bear witness that the divinely-ordained destruction of darkness shall come about through you, O most wonderful Mary.	
305B	ἡ νοητικὴν θείαν δρόσον ἡμῖν ἐπιστάζουσα φωτεινὴ νεφέλη	bright cloud who continues to drop divine spiritual dew upon us (*cf.* Exodus 16.13)	(*cf.* Exodus 19.16) & (*cf.* Exodus 16.13)
305B	ἡ τῇ τῶν Ἁγίων ἁγία σήμερον ὑπεισδύσει τοῖς ἐν σκιᾷ θανάτου κατεχομένοις παμφαίνοντα ἥλιον ἐξανατείλασα	you who today by your holy entrance into the Holy of Holies have made to shine the all-brilliant Sun upon those who remain in the shadow of death	
305B	πηγὴ ἡ θεόβρυτος	A fountain pouring out God	
305B	ὁ τερπνότατος καὶ λογικὸς Θεοῦ παράδεισος, σήμερον πρὸς ἀνατολὰς τῆς αὐτοῦ θελήσεως φυτευόμενος δεξιᾷ παντοκράτορι	delightful and rational paradise of God, which today is planted in the east by the omnipotent right hand of his will	(*cf.* Genesis 2.8)
305B	καὶ αὐτῷ τὸ εὐανθὲς κρίνον καὶ ἀμάραντον ῥόδον κυπρίζουσα	who have blossomed forth the beautiful lily and the unfading rose	
305C	τὸ τοῦ παμβασιλέως Θεοῦ ἱερότευκτον ἄχραντόν τε	sacred, undefiled, most pure palace of the omnipotent God	
305C	τὴν αὐτοῦ μεγαλειότητα περιβεβλημένη καὶ ξεναγοῦσά σου τῇ μυσταρχικῇ ἀπολαύσει ἅπαντας	You are wrapped in his grandeur and guide us all with your mystical joy	

305D	ἡ νέα Σιών, καὶ θεία Ἱερουσαλήμ, ἁγία «πόλις τοῦ μεγάλου ἄνακτος Θεοῦ, ἧς αὐτὸς Θεὸς ἐν ταῖς βάρεσι γινώσκεται,»	new Zion and holy Jerusalem, holy city of the great king – within his citadels God has shown himself a sure defense	(cf. Psalm 48.3ff.)
305D	ἡ ὄντως χρυσοειδὴς καὶ φωτεινή . . . ἑπτάφωτος λυχνία τῷ ἀδύτῳ φωτὶ ὑφαπτομένη καὶ τῷ τῆς ἁγνείας ἐλαίῳ πιαινομένη, καὶ τοῖς ἐν ζόφῳ πταισμάτων ἀχλύϊ τυφλώττουσι αἴγλης ἀνατολὴν πιστουμένη	Truly golden and brilliant . . . You the seven-lighted lamp-stand enkindled by the unapproachable Light and filled by the oil of purity, and giving the rising of its gleam to the blind in the darkness of sin	(cf. Exodus 25.31)
308A	πιότατον καὶ κατάσκιον ὄρος	O fertile shady mountain	(Ps. 67.15-17) and (Hab 3.3)
308A	ὁ τοῦ Θεοῦ ἅγιος θρόνος, ἡ θεῖον ἀνάθημα, ἡ δόξης οἶκος, ἡ περικαλλὲς ἀγλάϊσμα, καὶ ἐκλεκτὸν κειμήλιον, καὶ παγκόσμιον ἱλαστήριον, «καὶ Θεοῦ δόξαν διηγούμενος οὐρανός.»	holy throne of God, the divine gift, house of glory, the most beautiful splendor and elect treasure and universal propitiation, and "heaven declaring the glory of God,"	(Psalm 19.2)
308B	ἡ τῇ σῇ γεννήσει στειρώσεως δεσμὰ λύσασα, καὶ ὀνειδισμὸν ἀτεκνίας λικμήσασα, καὶ νομικὴν κατάραν βυθίσασα, καὶ χάριτος εὐλογίαν ἀνθήσασα, καὶ τῇ πρὸς τὰ τῶν ἁγίων Ἅγια εἰσόδῳ εὐχῆς τελείωσιν γονικῆς καὶ θεμέλιον τῆς ἡμῶν ἀφέσεως καὶ χαρμονῆς συμπλήρωσιν τελειώσασα, ὡς χάριτος ἀρχὴν προαγαγοῦσα.	you who through your birth released the fetters of sterility, who scattered the reproach of childlessness, and sank the curse of the Law; and blossomed forth the grace of blessing – by entering the Holy of Holies you perfected the prayers of your parents and the foundation for forgiveness of our sins, fulfilling the perfection of harmony as the leader of the beginning of grace.	(cf. Galatians 3.13)

308B	κεχαριτωμένη Μαρία, ἡ τῶν ἁγίων ἁγιωτέρα, καὶ οὐρανῶν ὑψηλοτέρα, καὶ Χερουβὶμ ἐνδοξοτέρα, καὶ Σεραφὶμ τιμιωτέρα, καὶ ὑπὲρ πᾶσαν κτίσιν σεβασμιωτέρα·	most blessed, the holiest of the holy ones, higher than the heavens, more glorious than the Cherubim and more honorable than the Seraphim, more blessed than all of creation.	Mary (cf. Luke 1.28)
308B	ἡ τῇ ἐνδόξῳ καὶ αἰγληφανεῖ σου Προόδῳ ἔλαιον ἡμῖν κομίζουσα, τὸν τοῦ νοητοῦ κατακλυσμοῦ λυτῆρα, τὸν σωτηριώδη ἡμῖν ὅρμον εὐαγγελιζομένη περιστερά	You are the dove who bears the olive branch to us in your glorious and splendid entry into the Temple announcing a saving refuge from the spiritual deluge.	(cf. Genesis 8.11)
308B/C	ἧς «αἱ πτέρυγες περιηργυρωμέναι καὶ τὰ μετάφρενα ἐν χλωρότητι χρυσίου,» τοῦ παναγίου καὶ φωτιστικοῦ καταστραπτόμενα Πνεύματος· ἡ πάγχρυσος στάμνος, τὸν ἡδύτατον τῶν ψυχῶν ἡμῶν γλυκασμὸν ἤτοι Χριστὸν τὸ μάννα φέρουσα.	"The wings of a dove covered with silver, its pinions with green gold" struck by the lightning of the all holy and illuminating Spirit, the all-gold container who bore Christ, the manna, the sweet sweetness of our souls.	(Ps. 67.14 LXX) (cf. Exodus 16.33)
Germanos brings his 'praises' to an end and then gives a final prayer. 305C to 309A.			
308C	ὦ πανάμωμε, καὶ πανύμνητε, καὶ πανσέβαστε	O most blameless and all-laudable, most holy one	
308C	καὶ πάντων δημιουργημάτων ὑπερφερὲς Θεοῦ ἀνάθημα	offering to God greater than all created things,	
308C	ἀγεώργητε γῆ, ἀνήροτε ἄρουρα, εὐκληματοῦσα ἄμπελος, κρατὴρ εὐφραντικώτατε, κρήνη πηγάζουσα	untilled earth, unplowed field, well-pruned vineyard, most joyous wine bowl, gushing spring,	(cf. Ezechiel 19.10) (cf. Ezechiel 17.6)
308C	Παρθένε γεννῶσα καὶ Μήτηρ ἀπείρανδρε, ἁγνείας κειμήλιον καὶ σεμνότητος ἐγκαλλώπισμα,	virgin birth-giver and husbandless mother, treasure of purity and ornament of holiness	

308C	τὸν ἐκ σοῦ ἀπάτορα, Υἱόν τε καὶ Θεὸν πάντων δημιουργὸν εὐπροσδέκτοις καὶ μητροπειθέσι λιταῖς	by your acceptable and motherly-persuasive petitions to your son	
309A	συνθρόνῳ	the throne	

Chapter Ten

The Second Homily on the Presentation of the Theotokos in the Temple Introduction and Commentary

The second homily is much shorter, only about half the size of the first. It is much less complex; although it uses rhetoric, it appears less burdened with the need to prove its rhetorical worth. It is also clear that Germanos is aware of some contention with regard to the theological importance of Mary.[232]

Germanos begins this homily with an anaphora using 'Behold'. He sets the scene of the Presentation and alludes to the future events of the Annunciation and the Incarnation to which the Presentation testifies. The very fact of a female entering the Holy of Holies and living there is an 'evident sign, and obvious testimony' which should put all those who doubt, those who 'wage their tongues against her,' aright.

> How, when they see the beginning, did they disbelieve in the ending? How, when they had seen the strange and unusual [events] in her case, did they deny those which happened afterwards? For not at random, and as it chanced, did the first things happen concerning her; but all were preludes of the last things. (312A) See also 317B.

---

[232] In two places (312A & 317B) Germanos mentions those who are 'grumbling' or 'grumblers' about the Feast and the importance of the Theotokos in the scheme of the Incarnation.

It is clear that Germanos is deeply involved in a struggle which has profound theological implications. The Patriarch is quite willing to anathematize those who fall short of his theological position on the Theotokos:

> Let those who are vainly wise in their own sight tell us: How, when other barren women have given birth, is none of their daughters dedicated in the holy of holies and received by prophets? Could not those who then saw such great things [done] for her say, as also those of the same mind later [said] for her son: "What will this child be?" Yes indeed. But let those of alien mind travel the road of perdition, and let them fall into the pit which they have dug[233]. (312B)

He then announces to those to whom he is speaking the reason for celebrating this Feast.

> But we, the remnant of God's people, priests and rulers, secular and monastics, slaves and free, craftsmen and farmers, gatherers and fishermen, young and old, men and women: hither, let us eagerly approach the Theotokos, and let us watch the divine mysteries which were accomplished earlier in her. (312B)

Germanos then continues with an ethopoeia of Zacharias in which Zacharias questions Anna as to her reasons for doing such an unheard of thing as to bring a young female to the Temple to be raised there. There follows Anna's response to Zacharias' question in which she tells of her prayers beseeching God to take away her shame at being barren. She also relates briefly her husband's efforts with regard to their barrenness. She also tells of her promise to God of dedicating her child making an 'acceptable gift'. Zacharias accepts Anna's explanation and responds: "Blessed is your root, O all-honored one. Glorified is your womb, you who love your husband. And exceedingly glorious is your offspring, you who love God [or, beloved of God]." Zacharias then 'holding the child

---

[233] There are a number of reasons that this homily was so popular. One of these must have been the strong language Germanos used against those whom he anathematized.

with great joy brings her eagerly into the Holy of Holies,' and in a joyous anaphorical ethopoeia introduces her to the Temple.[234]

Germanos continues his narration of what must have taken place with the introduction of the child, Mary, into the Temple. In a wonderful aside Germanos comments on Mary as both a child and the fulfiller of her future role: " . . . the child skipping and rejoicing, as in a bridal chamber, walked in the Temple of God; being three years old in her chronological age, but more than perfect in divine grace, as foreknown and predestined and chosen for the God and governor of all." Germanos' narration continues with a description of how Mary was treated in the Temple as she grew and when she reached puberty he relates how Joseph is chosen for her. Briefly he relates the event and the importance of the Annunciation and the role of Mary as benefactor of humankind:

> and give to those who celebrate your feast your help, your protection, and your assistance, guarding always by your intercessions these people from every necessity and dangers, and dread diseases, and all kinds of misfortunes, and from the coming just threat of your Son. Set them, as you are the mother of the Master, in a place of comfort, where [there are] light and peace, and the ultimate giving of things desired.[235] (317B)

Immediately Germanos mentions the fate of those who oppose Mary referencing Ps 31.19 and Ps 83.18 and also Luke 1.49:

> "And may the deceitful lips be mute, those which speak lawlessness in arrogance and contempt against you the righteous woman" (*cf.* Psalm 31.19). And let the image of these [people] be brought to naught in your city. Let them be put to shame, and let them die out, and let them perish, and let them know that your name is Mistress (cf. Psalm 83.18). For you alone are

---

[234] At this point Germanos lists a number of names that seem fitting to him for the circumstance of Zacharias' celebrating the Entrance of the Theotokos into the Temple. This is a typical Byzantine flight of fancy and should not be taken as other than a rhetorical embellishment of the ethopoeia.

[235] The description of the place in which Mary will set those who celebrate her feast is echoed in the prayers for the dying and dead in the Orthodox tradition, and, so for the auditors would have special meaning.

Theotokos, most sublime over all the earth; and we bless you in faith, bride of God, and with desire we honor you, and with fear we bow before you, always magnifying you, and solemnly calling you blessed (*cf.* Luke 1.49). (317B) See also 312B.

Germanos then proclaims an anaphora redolent of the macharisms from the Sermon on the Mount in which he mentions all the main participants, places, and future events, in the Presentation:

For blessed truly is your father among men, and blessed is your mother among women, blessed is your household, blessed are your acquaintances, blessed are those who saw you, blessed are those who accompanied you, blessed are those who served you, blessed are the places where you walked, blessed is the Temple into which you were brought, blessed is Zachariah, who took you in his arms, blessed is Joseph, who was betrothed to you, blessed is your couch, blessed is your tomb! For you [are] honor of honors, and reward of rewards, and exaltation of exaltations.[236] (317C)

He then concludes with a prayer in which he mentions "and join me to my relative and fellow servant[237] in the land of the meek, in the tents of the just (*cf.* Psalm 118.15), in the choir of the saints (*cf.* Psalm 116.9); and make me worthy, O protection and joy of all, and brilliant gladness of heart, to rejoice along with her, I beg you, in your truly ineffable joy, of the God and King who was born from you, and in his imperishable bridal-chamber, and in the unceasing and insatiable delight, and in the kingdom which has no evening and no limits.

Both homilies present the Entrance of the Theotokos in the Temple as the completion of the old order and the inauguration of the new order. Germanos uses many metaphors to explain Mary's importance in salvation

---

[236] Such constructions as "honor of honors, and reward of rewards, and exaltation of exaltations" are a rhetorical devise that places them on the highest possible level and allows his auditors to reflect and remember the status of Mary.

[237] We do not know who this relative of Germanos was, but it must have been a woman who followed a life of service to God. Georges Gharib and Luigi Gambero. Testi mariani del primo millennio. Roma: Città Nuova Editrice, 1989. 336 nt. 8.

history. In these homilies on the Entrance of the Theotokos his primary ones are related to the Temple and its worship. It is clear that Mary is the new Temple and as such the Entrance of Mary into the old Temple is an event of such importance that only a great festival can adequately celebrate it, even if mere humans, Germanos included, are not able to do so adequately on their own.

Chapter Eleven

Second Homily on the Presentation of the Theotokos in the Temple

Translation

Ἰδοὺ καὶ πάλιν

[309B]

Of our father among the saints Germanus, archbishop of Constantinople, encomium on the holy Theotokos, when she was brought into the Temple by her parents at the age of three years.

Behold, again another festival, and a glorious feast of the Mother of the Lord. Behold, the arrival of the blameless bride (*cf.* 2 Peter 3.14). Behold, the first procession of the queen. Behold, an accurate sign of the glory which will surround her.

[309C]

Behold, the prelude of the divine grace which will overshadow her. Behold, the brilliant evidence of her exceptional purity. For where entering not many times, but once in the year (*cf.* Leviticus 16.1*ff*), the priest performs the mystical worship, there she is brought by her parents for unceasing residence, to be in the sacred sanctuary of grace.

Who ever knew such a thing? Who saw, or who heard, of men now or men of old, that a female was led into the inner holy places of the holy places, which are barely accessible even to men, to live in them and to pass her time in them? Is this not a clear demonstration of the strange miracle to be done for her later? Is it not an evident sign? Is it not an obvious testimony?

[312A]

Let them show us, those who wag their tongues against her, and who see as if not seeing, where they ever beheld such things? A maiden from the promise, at the age of three years, is brought as a blameless gift within the third curtain, to live there continuously, and receives petitions from the wealthy men of the people (*cf.* Psalm 45.13). She is sent forth by virgins, brought forward with lamps, welcomed by priests and prophets with uplifted hands! How, when they see the beginning, did they disbelieve in the ending? How, when they had seen the strange and unusual [events] in her case, did they deny those which happened afterwards? For not at random, and as it chanced, did the first things happen concerning her; but all were preludes of the last things.

[312B]

Let those who are vainly wise in their own sight tell us: How, when other barren women have given birth, is none of their daughters dedicated in the holy of holies and received by prophets? Could not those who then saw such great things [done] for her say, as also those of the same mind later [said] for her son: "What will this child be?"[238] Yes indeed. But let those of alien mind travel the road of perdition, and let them fall into the pit which they have dug. But we, the remnant of God's people (*cf.* 1 Peter 2.10), priests and rulers, secular and monastics, slaves and free, craftsmen and farmers, gatherers and fishermen, young and old, men and women: hither,

[312C]

let us eagerly approach the Theotokos, and let us watch the divine mysteries which were accomplished earlier in her. How is the all-holy one today led by her parents to the Temple of God through its priests? How does the prophet receive her with his own hands, and bring her into the sanctuary, making no objection, and not saying to her parents, "I do not perform this new practice, and bring a maiden into the holy of holies, to be sheltered there, and to dwell there continuously, where I am assigned to enter once in the year."

---

[238] See, Luke 1.66, where these words are used of John the Baptist, not Jesus.

[312D]

The prophet uttered nothing of this sort, but as if foreseeing what would be, since he was a prophet, assuredly accepting her, and waiting, as after him Simeon [awaited] her son, he receives her willingly (*cf.* Luke 2.25*ff*)

Then perhaps he embraced the mother and addressed her, saying something like this, and holding the child by her hands: "Where are you from, O woman? What is your character, and the purpose of such an undertaking? And how, since you have no model of this kind, have you alone discovered this new and unprecedented action?

[313A]

To bring a maiden to make her tent in the sanctuary? What is your plan? Tell me. And what is your name?"

[313B]

Why have you made me an example in my family, and a shaking of the head in my tribe? Why have you declared me a participant in the curse of your prophets, giving me a childless womb and dry breasts (*cf.* Hosea 9.14)? Why have you made my gifts unacceptable as of a childless [woman]? Why have you left me to become a cause of muttering for my acquaintances, and a mockery for those at hand, and a reproach for my neighbors? Look at [me], Lord; hear [me], Master; have compassion [on me], Holy One. Make me like the birds of heaven, the beasts of the earth, the fish of the sea: because they also are productive before you, Lord. May I not appear worse than the irrational animals, O Most High, I who have been made by you in your likeness and image (*cf.* Genesis 1.26).'

[313C]

Saying these things, and things like them, I added, 'To you, Master, I will assuredly dedicate an acceptable gift, whatever child you may give me, to be that [gift] and to remain in your holy place, as a sacred offering and all-honorable gift, which I have received from you the most generous giver of perfect gifts.' Such things I was crying out to the God in the heavens, being outdoors in my garden, raising my eye to the heavens, beating my breast with my hands. But my husband being all alone on the mountain, and fasting for forty days, was supplicating God with [words] equivalent to these;

[313D]

thus you see the Lord who is ready for mercy and loves souls has bent down and sent an angel to the prayers of both of us, announcing to us the conception of my child. So therefore when [my] nature was bidden by God, it received the seed; for it did not dare to accept it before the divine grace. But when that [grace] preceded, then the closed womb opened its own gates, and receiving the deposit from God, held it in itself, until by the good will of God it brought forth to light that which had been sown in it.

[316A]

And then when [the child] had been weaned, 'I return my vows to God, which my lips sent forth, and my mouth spoke in my tribulation (Psalm 65.13*ff* LXX).' For this reason I assembled the band of virgins with torches, I called the priests together, I gathered my relatives, saying these [words] to all: 'Rejoice with me, all of you, that I am proved today both a mother and a guide; not bringing my child to an earthly king, because it is not fitting, but dedicating this [child] to the heavenly king, as his [own] gift. For the rest, O prophet, receive my god-given daughter. Receive [her] and leading her in, plant her in the place of sanctification, in the prepared dwelling-place of God, making no nosy inquiries, until God who summoned her here is pleased to bring to conclusion the matters concerning her."

[316B]

When Zacharias heard these [words], at once he replied to Anna: "Blessed is your root, O all-honored one. Glorified is your womb, you who love your husband. And exceedingly glorious is your offspring, you who love God [or, beloved of God]." Then holding the child with great joy, he brings her eagerly into the Holy of Holies, perhaps saying things like this to her: "Come here, fulfillment of my prophecy. Come here, completion of the commandments of the Lord. Come here, seal of his covenant. Come here, goal of his counsels. Come here, revelation of his mysteries. Come here, mirror of all the prophets. Come here, refutation of those who utter evil. Come here, joining of [things] long ago separated. Come here, support of things bent down. Come here, renewal of things grown old. Come here, light of those lying in darkness.

[316C]

Come here, new divine gift. Come here, mistress of all born on earth. Enter into the glory of your Lord: for now, into [the glory] here below where men walk, but after a short time, into the [glory] above which is inaccessible to human beings."

So probably the mystic teacher spoke to the child, and set her where it was fitting, and arranged in advance and predestined (cf. Romans 16.25). But the child skipping and rejoicing, as in a bridal chamber, walked in the Temple of God; being three years old in her chronological age, but more than perfect in divine grace, as foreknown and predestined and chosen for the God and governor of all.

She remained in the inner holy of holies, nourished with ambrosial food by an angel, and receiving drink of divine nectar, until her second advance in age-group.[239]

[316D]

And then by the assent of God and the counsel of the priests a lot is drawn concerning her, and Joseph the just is allotted, and receives this holy Virgin according to the dispensation from the Temple of God and his priests, to ensnare the serpent who originated evil, so that he should not attack the undefiled maiden as a virgin, but as a betrothed woman he should pass her by.

[317A]

So the all-pure one was in the house of Joseph the carpenter being protected, until the divine mystery hidden before all the ages (cf. Romans

---

[239]   Sc. Into puberty.

16.25) was fulfilled in her, and from her God was made like mortals. But this needs another treatment and a suitable time; let our discourse be led back again to its subject, and the day of her sending forth today be celebrated with auspicious words. Therefore go, Lady and Mother of God, go to your inheritance, and walk in the halls of the Lord, skipping and rejoicing, nourished and flourishing, awaiting from day to day the coming of the Holy Spirit in you, and the overshadowing of the power of the Most High (*cf.* Luke 1.26), and the conception of your Son, as Gabriel will address you;

[317B]

and give to those who celebrate your feast your help, your protection, and your assistance, guarding always by your intercessions these people from every necessity and dangers, and dread diseases, and all kinds of misfortunes, and from the coming just threat of your Son. Set them, as you are the mother of the Master, in a place of comfort, where [there are] light and peace, and the ultimate giving of things desired. "And may the deceitful lips be mute, those which speak lawlessness in arrogance and contempt against you the righteous woman" (*cf.* Psalm 31.19). And let the image of these [people] be brought to naught in your city. Let them be put to shame, and let them die out, and let them perish, and let them know that your name is Mistress (*cf.* Psalm 83.17-18). For you alone are Theotokos, most sublime over all the earth; and we bless you in faith, bride of God, and with desire we honor you, and with fear we bow before you, always magnifying you, and solemnly calling you blessed (*cf.* Luke 1.49).

[317C]

For blessed truly is your father among men, and blessed is your mother among women, blessed is your household, blessed are your acquaintances, blessed are those who saw you, blessed are those who accompanied you, blessed are those who served you, blessed are the places where you walked, blessed is the Temple into which you were brought, blessed is Zachariah, who took you in his arms, blessed is Joseph, who was betrothed to you, blessed is your couch, blessed is your tomb! For you [are] honor of honors, and reward of rewards, and exaltation of exaltations.

But Oh me, Mistress, my only soul-leader from God, the divine dew of the burning in me, the moisture flowing from God for my parched heart, the bright-shining lamp of my darkened soul, the guide for my journey,

[317D]

the power for my weakness, the clothing of my nakedness, the wealth of my poverty, the healing of my incurable wounds, the removal of tears, the cessation of groaning, the reversal of misfortunes, the lightening of pains, the release of fetters, the hope of my salvation, hear my prayers: have pity on my groaning, and accept my lamentations. Have mercy on me, bending down to my tears.

[320A]

Have compassion on me, as mother of the God who loves mankind. Look down and assent to my supplication, fill up my thirsty desire, and join me to my relative and fellow servant[240] in the land of the meek, in the tents of the just (*cf.* Psalm 118.15), in the choir of the saints (*cf.* Psalm 116.9); and make me worthy, I beg you, O protection and joy of all and brilliant gladness of heart, to rejoice along with her, in your truly ineffable joy, [because] of the God and King who was born from you, and in his imperishable bridal-chamber, and in the unceasing and insatiable delight, and in the kingdom which has no evening and no limit. Yes, Mistress; yes, my refuge, my life and my support, my armor and my boast, my hope and my strength. Grant me with her to enjoy the inexpressible and unceasing gifts in the heavenly mansion.

---

[240] We do not know who this relative of Germanos was, but it must have been a woman who followed a life of service to God. Georges Gharib and Luigi Gambero. *Testi mariani del primo millennio.* Roma: Città Nuova Editrice, 1989. 336 nt. 8. While we do not know the name of Germanos' relative this passage is redolent of the final prayers in the Orthodox funeral and memorial service and should be read as one who is familiar with them as Germanos' auditors would have been.

[320B]

For as the mother of the Most High you have, I know, the power which runs along with the will; and because of this I am bold. Therefore may I not be deprived, all-undefiled Lady, of my expectation (*cf.* Galatians 6.4); but may I obtain this, Bride of God, you who gave birth beyond words to the expectation of all, our Lord Jesus Christ, the true God and Master: to whom is due all glory, honor, and veneration, with the Father who has no beginning, and the life-giving Spirit, now and ever, and to the ages of ages. Amen.

Chapter Twelve

References to Mary in the Second Homily on the Presentation of the Theotokos in the Temple by Germanos, Patriarch of Constantinople (715-730)

PG 98 Location	Greek	English	OT/NT Reference
Germanos begins this homily with an anaphora using 'Behold'. He sets the scene of the Presentation and alludes to the future events of the Annunciation and the Incarnation to which the Presentation testifies. (309B/C)			
309B	Τῆς Μητρὸς τοῦ Κυρίου	the Mother of the Lord	
309B	Τῆς ἀμωμήτου νύμφης	the blameless bride	2 Peter 3.14
309B	τῆς βασιλίδος	the queen	
309B	ἰδοὺ σήμαντρον ἀκριβὲς τῆς ἐσομένης περὶ αὐτὴν δόξης	Behold, an accurate sign of the glory which will surround her	
It is clear that Germanos is aware of some contention with regard to the theological importance of Mary. In two places Germanos mentions those who are 'grumbling' or 'grumblers' about the Feast and the importance of the Theotokos in the scheme of the Incarnation. See, 312B, 317B and in Pres I 305B.			
309C	ἰδοὺ προοίμιον τῆς μελλούσης ἐπισκιάζειν αὐτῇ θείας χάριτος	the prelude of the divine grace which will overshadow her	
309C	ἰδοὺ γνώρισμα τηλαυγὲς τῆς ὑπερβαλλούσης αὐτῆς καθαρότητος	Behold, the brilliant evidence of her exceptional purity	

309C	ἐκεῖ αὐτὴ πρὸς διαμονὴν ἀδιάπαυστον ὑπὸ τῶν αὐτῆς γονέων προσάγεται	there she is brought by her parents for unceasing residence, to be in the sacred sanctuary of grace	
309C	θῆλυ προσαγόμενον εἰς τὰ τῶν ἁγίων ἐνδότερα Ἅγια	a female was led into the inner holy places of the holy places	
309C	ἐν αὐτοῖς κατοικεῖν καὶ ἐνδιατρέφεσθαι;	to live in them and to pass her time in them?	
309C	Ἆρ' οὐκ ἀπόδειξις ἐναργὴς τοῦτο τῆς ἐπ' αὐτῇ γενησο-μένης ξένης εἰς ὕστερον μεγα-λουργίας; Ἆρ' οὐ σημεῖον ἐμφανές; Ἆρ' οὐ τεκμήριον εὔδηλον;	Is this not a clear demonstration of the strange miracle to be done for her later? Is it not an evident sign? Is it not an obvious testimony?	
312A	Κόρην ἐξ ἐπαγγελίας	A maiden from the promise	
312A	αὐτὴν τριετίζουσαν	at the age of three years	

Here in 312A Germanos says that Mary is brought as a blameless gift within the third curtain" while in the first homily on the Presentation he says that Mary going toward the "second veil" 293A.

312A	ὡς δῶρον ἄμωμον	is brought as a blameless gift	
312A	τὸ ἐκεῖσε οἰκεῖν	to live there continuously	
312A	ὑπὸ τῶν πλουσίων τοῦ λαοῦ λιταν-ευομένην	receives petitions from the wealthy men of the people	*cf.* Psalm 45.13
312A	ὑπὸ παρθένων προπεμπομένην· μετὰ λαμπάδων προσαγομένην· ὑπὸ ἱερέων καὶ προφητῶν χερσὶν ὑπτίαις προσλαμβανομένην;	She is sent forth by virgins, brought forward with lamps, welcomed by priests and prophets with uplifted hands!	

Germanos clearly sees that the Presentation of Mary in the Temple is an event that had to take place. In Presentation I he calls it Mary's consecration 296D.

312A	Οὐ γὰρ εἰκῆ, καὶ ὡς ἔτυχε, τὰ περὶ αὐτὴν πρῶτα γεγόνασιν· ἀλλὰ πάνταπροοίμια τῶν ὑστάτων	For not at random, and as it chanced, did the first things happen concerning her; but all were preludes of the last things.	

The Patriarch is quite willing to anathematize those who fall short of his theological position on the Theotokos. In two places (312B & 317B) Germanos mentions those who are 'grumbling' or 'grumblers' about the Feast and the importance of the Theotokos in the scheme of the Incarnation.

312B	εἰς τὰ τῶν ἁγίων ἀνατίθεται Ἅγια, καὶ ὑπὸ προφητῶν προσείληπται;	dedicated in the holy of holies and received by prophets?	
312B	τοιαῦτα καὶ τηλικαῦτα εἰς αὐτήν	such great things [done] for her	
312B	«Τί ἄρα ἔσται τὸ παιδίον τοῦτο;»	"What will this child be?"	Lk 1.66
312C	τῇ Θεοτόκῳ	the Theotokos	
	τὰ εἰς αὐτὴν προτελεσθέντα θεῖα μυστήρια [οἰκονομικῶς]	the divine mysteries which were accomplished earlier in her	
312C	ἡ πανίερος	the all-holy one	
312C	πῶς ὁ προφήτης αὐτοχειρὶ ταύτην εἰσδέχεται, καὶ τοῖς ἀδύτοις εἰσφέρει, οὐδὲν δυσχεράνας	How does the prophet receive her with his own hands, and bring her into the sanctuary	
312C	καὶ κόρην εἰσάγω εἰς τὰ τῶν ἁγίων Ἅγια, πρὸς τὸ ἐν αὐτοῖς αὐλίζεσθαι, καὶ κατοικεῖν ἀδιάσπαστα	bring a maiden into the holy of holies, to be sheltered there, and to dwell there continuously	

Germanos then continues with an ethopoeia of Zacharias in which Zacharias questions Anna as to her reasons for doing such an unheard of thing as to bring a young female to the Temple to be raised there. There follows Anna's response to Zacharias' question in which she tells of her prayers beseeching God to take away her shame at being barren. She also relates briefly her husband's efforts with regard to their barrenness. (312D—316A)

312D	τὴν παῖδα	the child	
312D	κόρην	a maiden	
313C	τέκνον	child	
313D	ἐμῆς παιδός	my child	
316A	τὸ ἐμὸν τέκνον	my child	
316A	τοῦτο	this [child]	
316A	ὡς τούτου δῶρα	as his [own] gift	
316A	τὴν ἐμὴν θεόσδοτον θυγατέρα	my god-given daughter	

Gregory E. Roth

| 316A | ἕως ἂν τὰ κατ' αὐτὴν εὐδοκήσειεν εἰς πέρας ἐλθεῖν, ὁ ταύτην ἐνταῦθα καλέσας Θεός. | until God who summoned her here is pleased to bring to conclusion the matters concerning her | |

At this point Germanos lists a number of names that seem fitting to him for the circumstance of Zacharias' celebrating the Entrance of the Theotokos into the Temple. This is a typical Byzantine flight of fancy and should not be taken as other than a rhetorical embellishment of the ethopoeia. (316B—316C)

316B	ἡ προσαγωγή σου	your offspring	
316B	τὴν παῖδα	the child	
316B	πλήρωσις τῆς ἐμῆς προφητείας	fulfillment of my prophecy	
316B	τέλεσμα τῶν συνταγῶν Κυρίου	completion of the commandments of the Lord	
316B	σφράγισμα τῆς αὐτοῦ διαθήκης	goal of his counsels	
316B	δήλωσις τῶν αὐτοῦ μυστηρίων	revelation of his mysteries	
316B	διόπτρα τῶν προφητῶν ἁπάντων	mirror of all the prophets	
316B	σύλλογε κακῶς διαφωνούντων	refutation of those who utter evil	
316B	σύναψις τῶν πάλαι διεστηκότων	joining of [things] long ago separated	
316B	στήριγμα τῶν κάτω νενευκότων	support of things bent down	
316B	καινισμὸς τῶν πεπαλαιωμένων	renewal of things grown old	
316B	τὸ σέλας τῶν ἐν σκότει κειμένων	light of those lying in darkness	
316C	δώρημα καινότατον καὶ θεῖον	new divine gift	
316C	Δέσποινα τῶν γηγενῶν ἁπάντων	mistress of all born on earth	
316C	τὸ παιδίον	the child	

Germanos reminds his auditors of the contrast between Mary at three and her cosmic role in a lovely reference: "But the child skipping and rejoicing, as in a bridal chamber, walked in the Temple of God; being three years old in her chronological age, but more than perfect in divine grace, as foreknown and predestined and chosen for the God and governor of all."

| 316C | Ἡ παῖς | the child | |

316C	τριετίζουσα μὲν τῷ χρόνῳ τῆς ἡλικίας, ὑπερτελὴς δὲ τῇ χάριτι τῇ θείᾳ, ὡς ἅτε προεγνωσμένη καὶ προωρισμένη	being three years old in her chronological age, but more than perfect in divine grace, as foreknown and predestined	
316D	καὶ τότε νεύματι Θεοῦ, καὶ βουλῇ ἱερέων δίδοται περὶ αὐτῆς κλῆρος	And then by the assent of God and the counsel of the priests a lot is drawn concerning her	
316D	τὴν ἁγίαν ταύτην Παρθένον	this holy Virgin	
316D	ὡς παρθένῳ προσβάλῃ τῇ ἀκηράτῳ κόρῃ	the undefiled maiden as a virgin	
316D	μεμνηστευμένην ταύτην παραδράμῃ	a betrothed woman	
316D	ἡ πανάχραντος	the all-pure one	
317A	Δέσποινα Θεομῆτορ	Lady and Mother of God	

In two places (312A & 317B) Germanos mentions those who are 'grumbling' or 'grumblers' about the Feast and the importance of the Theotokos in the scheme of the Incarnation.

317C	Σὺ γὰρ, τιμὴ τῶν τιμῶν, καὶ γέρας τῶν γερῶν, καὶ ὑψωμάτων ὕψωμα.	you [are] honor of honors, and reward of rewards, and exaltation of exaltations	
317C	Δέσποινα	Mistress	
317C	μόνη τὸ ἐμὸν ἐκ Θεοῦ ψυχαγώγημα	my only soul-leader from God	
317C	τοῦ ἐν ἐμοὶ καύσωνος ἡ θεία δρόσος	the divine dew of the burning in me	
317C	τῆς ξηρανθείσης μου καρδίας ἡ θεόρρυτος ῥανὶς	the moisture flowing from God for my parched heart	
317C	τῆς ζοφερᾶς μου ψυχῆς ἡ τηλαυγεστάτη λαμπὰς	the bright-shining lamp of my darkened soul	
317C	τῆς ἐμῆς πορείας ἡ ποδηγία	the guide for my journey	
317D	τῆς ἀσθενείας μου ἡ δύναμις	the power for my weakness	
317D	τῆς γυμνώσεως ἡ ἀμφίασις	the clothing of my nakedness	
317D	τῆς πτωχείας ὁ πλοῦτος	the wealth of my poverty	

125

Gregory E. Roth

317D	τὸ τῶν ἀνιάτων τραυμάτων τὸ ἴαμα	the healing of my incurable wounds	
317D	ἡ τῶν δακρύων ἀναίρεσις	the removal of tears	
317D	τῶν στεναγμῶν ἡ κατάπαυσις	the cessation of groaning	
317D	τῶν συμφορῶν ἡ μεταποίησις	the reversal of misfortunes	
317D	τῶν ὀδυνῶν ὁ κουφισμὸς	the lightening of pains	
317D	τῶν δεσμῶν ἡ λύσις	the release of fetters	
317D	τῆς σωτηρίας μου ἡ ἐλπίς	the hope of my salvation	
320A	ὡς μήτηρ τοῦ φιλανθρώπου Θεοῦ	as mother of the God who loves mankind	
320A	ἡ πάντων προστασία καὶ χαρά	O protection and joy of all	
320A	καὶ φαιδρὰ θυμηδία	brilliant gladness of heart	
320A	ἐν τῇ χαρᾷ ἐκείνῃ τῇ ὄντως ἀνεκφράστῳ	in your truly ineffable joy	
320A	Δέσποινα	Mistress	
320A	τὸ ἐμὸν καταφύγιον	my refuge	
320A	ἡ ζωὴ καὶ ἡ ἀντίληψις,	my life and my support	
320A	τὸ ὅπλον καὶ τὸ καύχημα	my armor and my boast,	
320A	ἡ ἐλπίς μου καὶ τὸ σθένος μου	my hope and my strength	
320B	ὡς τοῦ Ὑψίστου μήτηρ	as the mother of the Most High	
320B	πανάχραντε Κυρία	all-undefiled Lady	
320B	Θεόνυμφε	Bride of God	
320B	ἡ τὴν τῶν ὅλων προσδοκίαν ὑπὲρ λόγον τεκοῦσα	you who gave birth beyond words to the expectation of all	

Chapter Thirteen

Annunciation Homily
Introduction and Commentary

The homily on the Annunciation is the only one of Germanos' homilies that has a New Testament basis.[241] There is a lot of conjecture as to when this feast originated.

> In the Orient, where the part which Mary took in the Redemption is celebrated by a special feast, 26 December, the Annunciation is a feast of Christ; in the Latin Church, it is a feast of Mary. It probably originated shortly before or after the council of Ephesus (c. 431). At the time of the Synod of Laodicea (372) it was not known; St. Proclus, Bishop of Constantinople (d. 446), however, seems to mention it in one of his homilies. He says, that the feast of the coming of Our Lord and Saviour, when He vested Himself with the nature of man (*quo hominum genus indutus*), was celebrated during the entire fifth century. This homily, however, may not be genuine, or the words may be understood of the feast of Christmas.[242]

The Feast of the Annunciation came to be celebrated nine months before the Nativity. In the Byzantine tradition the feast frequently comes

---

[241]   Lk 1:26-38

[242]   Frederick Holweck. "The Feast of the Annunciation." *The Catholic Encyclopedia.* Vol. 1. New York: Robert Appleton Company, 1907. 23 May 2008 <http://www.newadvent.org/cathen/01542a.htm>

during Great Lent. Nevertheless, it is a feast of great joy and is celebrated with a vesperal liturgy.

> Because the feast of the Annunciation normally comes during the season of Great Lent, the manner of celebration varies from year to year depending upon the particular day on which it falls. If the feast comes on a weekday of Lent, which is the most common case, the Divine Liturgy of the feast is served in the evening with Vespers and thus is celebrated after a full day of total abstinence. When this happens, the fasting rules for the Liturgy of the Presanctified Gifts are followed. The Divine Liturgy of the Annunciation is the only celebration of the eucharistic liturgy of Saint John Chrysostom allowed on a weekday of Great Lent. [243]

Yet another special feature of the Feast of the Annunciation is that of a dialogue between Mary and the Archangel Gabriel.

> A special feature of this feast is the Matinal Canon which has the character of a dialogue between the Archangel Gabriel and the Virgin Mary. Also among the more popular elements of the feast is the Magnification which has the form of our own salutation to the virgin mother with the words of the archangel:[244]

The Greek term for the Feast of the Annunciation is Εὐαγγελισμός, *Evangelismos*, which is the same word for evangelist, and by extension to Good News, Gospel. The Feast is clearly one of the Incarnation.

Germanos' homily on Annunciation is a long dialogical homily. It is a double alphabet. The first words of each of the parts of the dialogue begin with the corresponding Greek letter. The dialogue is in two parts. The first is between the Theotokos and the Archangel Gabriel, in which the Archangel has the daunting task of informing Mary of her role in the Incarnation and convincing her that the news is real and genuinely from

---

[243]   Thomas, V. Rev. Hopko, "Annunciation". 2008. Orthodox Church in America. May 23, 2008. <http://oca.org/OCchapter.asp?SID=2&ID=84>.

[244]   Thomas, V. Rev. Hopko, "Annunciation". 2008. Orthodox Church in America. May 23, 2008. <http://oca.org/OCchapter.asp?SID=2&ID=84>.

God. The second is between Mary and Joseph in which Mary has the daunting task of convincing Joseph that her pregnancy is not due to some dalliance but by the Holy Spirit. The text in *PG* is lacking the last four and one half stanzas beginning with the second one for "X" and going through "Ω". Also two stanzas from the dialogue between Mary and the Archangel are missing. These stanzas have been supplied by La Piana.[245] There seem to be twenty-two words that appear to be unique to Germanos.

The homily appears only three times in Ehrhard and two of those are only partial.

Annunciation#	Incipit:	*PG* 98	*BHG*
1	Τῆς παρούσης τιμίας	320E—340A	1145n
La Piana	Χρυσός, ὡς ἐμοὶ	NA	1049m

The homily seems to have been combined with various texts called chairetismi.[246] This would be a common practice. In some mss the section found in *PG* 98 312A—312C is expanded in both the Σήμερον and the Χαῖρε.[247] Also there is an ending in some mss. For the purposes of this translation I have chosen to use the *PG* text with the additions found by La Piana.[248]

---

[245] George La Piana,. *Le rappresentazioni sacre nella letteratura bizantina dalle origini al sec. ix, con rapporti al teatro sacro d'occidente.* Grottaferrata,: Tip. italo-orientale "S. Nilo", 1912. This volume is very useful for a picture of the role of drama in Byzantine homilies. See especially 313—23 for Germanos' Annunciation homily.

[246] From Χαῖρε, a common greeting.

[247] For example in Georges Gharib and Luigi Gambero. "Testi mariani del primo millennio." Roma: Città Nuova Editrice, 1989. 318—90. Vol. II. IV vols.

[248] La Piana 313-323.

The homily begins with Germanos setting the scene:

> With joyful soul let us spiritually celebrate this luminous and
> ever-glorious memorial of this honorable and royal assembly
> (*cf.* 1 Peter 2.9), O peoples, nations, and languages (*cf.* Daniel
> 4.1), and all social classes, and this multitudinous congregation
> who have come together because of your love for this feast, and
> the people around [us].

In typical fashion Germanos equates the assembly in Constantinople with both Old and New Testament references. Germanos' congregation is a royal one, it is cosmopolitan and multilingual. Germanos claims that they have come out of love for this Feast, and invites his auditors to: " . . . weave with all zeal hymns which are worthy of the Queen who was from the lineage of David. Let us compose a springtime feast of feasts, and a festival of festivals of our hope, our unmistakable proclamation of this feast day (Psalm 81.3)."

Rhetorically this homily makes use of many devices. In the first part of the homily Germanos is at pains to illustrate the paradox of the Incarnation on many levels. Additionally, Germanos appears to have been more concerned with keeping the alphabet going. As a consequence chronology suffers. At several places Germanos quotes from the liturgical literature of the Church. And he challenges those who would not believe in the Incarnation and have difficulty with accepting paradoxical thought with the proclamation:

> For today, truly, the intellectual powers of heaven have come
> down from Heaven, and exalt her with us earthborn [human
> beings] . . . For this living, honorable and God-ruled city ever
> praises her who protects our walls.

Germanos in humility invites the congregation to hear what might have been said when the Archangel comes to Mary.

> But with unworthy lips we, who are among the least, have held
> discourse about these matters. We have learned from the Holy
> Scriptures about this heavenly bride and queen, the Theotokos.
> And so, beloved, let us turn to the God-inspired news which the

archangel Gabriel brought, and let us hear what he said to the blameless lady when he arrived.

In a series of twenty-four double dialogues between the Archangel Gabriel and Mary Germanos investigates the predicament of Mary's questioning the call of God to be the Mother of the Lord and Gabriel's cosmic understanding of the Incarnation. Paradox after paradox is explored. At first Mary sees only a man who has come unannounced to her in private. But paradoxically this man appears to be both an angel and a young man who has a comely form worthy to be painted. Mary is, at first, convinced that he has come to seduce her as was Eve. Gabriel is persistent in his proclamation of "this joyful message." Germanos weaves together the threads of the paradox of what Mary and Gabriel see. Mary views herself as a maiden who is placed in a difficult situation with a man who is telling her things which she does not want to believe, and yet she hears the ring of truth in his words. She is also concerned about how she will be judged if she does become pregnant while still not married to Joseph. Gabriel is concerned that she does not understand the truth of the words which he is proclaiming and that she does not rightly understand the status which she has because of her role in the Incarnation. Finally Gabriel reveals to Mary that Elizabeth, her kinswoman, is pregnant in her old age, and tells Mary that "Zacharias the prophet and beloved of your cousin Elizabeth, will convince your unbelief." Gabriel predicts that "When my words shall come to pass in their own time, then you will understand the power of this incomprehensible mystery. Then you will know the result of my words and the ineffable condescension of the Most High." The dialogue continues with Mary half believing and half doubting. She questions the modality of her conceiving without a man. Mary attempts to get Gabriel to leave and Gabriel makes it clear that he is not a stranger to her for she saw him " . . . when you were in the Holy of Holies, and when you received nourishment from my fiery hands? I am Gabriel, who always stands before the glory of God."

Mary becomes concerned with how Joseph will react to her being pregnant. It is clear by now that Mary accepts the message but is concerned with the consequences to herself and her guardian, Joseph. Germanos' weaving of the event does not follow a straight chronological order, but goes back and forth. It is perhaps driven by the rhetorical device of that alphabetical dialogue. Nowhere is this chronological issue more apparent than when Gabriel says: "Cast away your unbelief, Virgin. For behold, as it seems to me, my words have been accomplished, a lump is rising in your belly. Even if you do not wish it, "with God nothing is impossible". Even before Mary becomes curious about the Child she will bear. Gabriel simply states: "You shall bear the Lord, the Savior, who is one of the life-beginning Trinity. You shall bring unexpected joy to the world, which neither angels nor men have brought; and your name shall be called blessed." The same questions arise once again about Joseph and the repercussions of Mary's bearing a child. The remainder of the first dialogue is a proclamation of the importance of Mary and her role as the Theotokos. Questions about her role are phrased as a paradox that she states:

"How shall the race of men flee to me who am matter and drawn from the earth? And how shall I embrace Christ the Light of the World? And how shall that unsetting Sun be borne by the spiritual moon?" Gabriel does not directly answer this question, but states: "O Virgin, bringer of heavenly joy, joyful and marvelous dwelling place, and propitiation of the whole cosmos, the only truly blessed one among women (Luke 1.42), prepare yourself for the mystical coming of Christ." And finally at the end of the dialogue Mary says: "O young man, messenger of ineffable joy, you have come from the bodiless ones, and speak to one made of clay. How long shall I tolerate you? How long will you continue to speak? "Behold, the servant of the Lord, let it be to me according to your word".

Germanos then transitions to the dialogue between Mary and Joseph. Immediately it is apparent that Mary has gained a new voice. She is sure of herself and confident in the decision she has made. Joseph is not convinced that Mary is blameless and pure, and he immediately begins to question her. Much of the dialogue between Mary and Joseph might be understood as a debate between the law and the Prophets. Joseph is concerned about the judgment—to which Mary responds that he needs to look on her and her pregnancy in another way:

The Theotokos

Fear, rather, the unchangeable judgment of the age to come, O Joseph, which even the angels fear who have never sinned. I do not care for earthly kings and judgments.

132

Joseph

It is written in the Law of Moses. "If one finds a virgin, and lies with her by force, the man shall give to the father of the young woman fifty silver shekels." (Deuteronomy 22.24-25) What will you do with that?

The Theotokos

It is written in the prophets, that "they shall give the sealed book to a man who knows letters and he shall say: 'I am not able to read it' (Isaiah 29.11)." Perhaps then as it seems to me, the prophecy was said about you.

Mary tells Joseph that he shall have all revealed to him in his sleep. The dialogue continues with Joseph telling Mary to leave his house since she has dishonored his house and his grey hair. The dialogue continues for some time raising similar concerns on the part of Joseph. Mary, for her part, is concerned with what will happen to her if Joseph does throw her out of his house.

Wait a little, Joseph. Do not make me secretly a stranger to your house. Just as I have not been accustomed to traveling, I do not know right from left, and I do not understand where to go or where to seek refuge.

Mary continues trying to convince Joseph of her innocence and mentions the event with her cousin Elizabeth's child, John, leaping in her womb to worship Mary's child when they meet. Mary summarizes her plight in an aside:

The day of affliction fell upon me, and blame and suspicion came upon me; and the scrutiny of my betrothed was placed firmly on me; and my pregnancy accused me, and the Angel who cried "Hail" is quickly hidden, and what else I may say I do not know.

Speaking to Joseph Mary pleads:

Behold, you banish me from your house, O Joseph, I do not
know where I shall go. Shall I return to the sanctuary of the
temple? Or shall I go back to my parents? And how shall I look
upon them?

And she says:

I shall hide myself in one of my caves in my town of Bethlehem.
I shall await the appropriate time of my birth-giving. May I
learn who this is to whom I am about to give birth, for I reckon
that the Lord will regard my lowliness.

Joseph continues questioning Mary about the 'stranger' and Mary's
encounter with him. Joseph questions how Mary conceived when she
relates an encounter at her well and says that she could not conceive by
the voice she heard at the well. He accuses her of being like Eve, deceived.
Mary counters by quoting Isaiah 7.14 contending that Joseph does not
believe the prophets. Germanos turns to the Nativity story from Luke's
Gospel. Joseph is puzzled over 'an angel' who appeared to him in a dream
and Mary suggests that it was perhaps the same angel that appeared to her.
The couple make preparations for the birth of the Child and Mary muses
over who that Child is. Joseph is finally convinced claiming:

Yesterday I was thrown down by suspicion, shame I have brought
to your beauty and your loveliness, but now receiving the fullness
from on high, at once I shall give an account and prostrate myself
in reverence to your greatness and bless your name.

The remainder of the homily is missing in Migne's text. In the
translation I use the ending supplied by LaPiana. The coming of the
Magi is predicted, a 'beast of burden' is sought and Joseph expresses his
confidence in the guidance of the angel. Mary recites part of Luke's Gospel
and what appears to be an ending very like many liturgical endings.

O great and marvelous is this day to me. For the powerful one
has done great things for me, and holy is his name. To those

who fear him his mercy is from generation to generation (Luke 1.49*ff*.). To him be glory and power unto the end of the ages. Amen.

Because of the unique nature of this homily it is more difficult to classify how Mary is viewed.[249] In addition to the typologies, allegories, and titles, I have chosen to include actions and events as well as Mary's own reflections on herself.

Time is also a problem. Germanos relies heavily on the New Testament account of the Annunciation. That, of course, is in the past; but additionally there is a cosmological element that is outside of time as it is part of eternity. It is clear that Germanos sees this cosmological preparation as the cause of the Annunciation and the Incarnation, they are events that have been decreed from all eternity. Gabriel states to Mary: "Prepare then for Christ's coming. For I have come to announce to you what has been decreed before the foundation of the cosmos."[250] Horvath, among others, commented on the " . . . curious view of several Greek Fathers according to which Mary conceived Jesus before she gave her consent (*In Annunt.*; PG 98, 328B-C).[251]

The homily should also be viewed as an extended ethopoiia (ἠθοποιΐα). In the case of the Annunciation Homily the narrative is based on the account in Luke with each of the characters—Mary, the Angel and Joseph—being developed in the course of the story.

Mary, for her part, is the one character that grows the most in the dialogue. At the beginning of the homily she is convinced that the Angel is some young man that has come to seduce her.

---

249 For a short explanation from an Orthodox Priest see: www.orthodoxed.org/files/Time_and_Eternity.pdf
     Augustine of Hippo was also concerned with time from the point of view of the Christian perspective. See: http://www.fordham.edu/gsas/phil/klima/augustine/Time%20and%20Eternity%20in%20Augustine.htm

250 Ὁπλίζου λοιπὸν εἰς Χριστοῦ παρουσίαν· ἦλθον γὰρ εὐαγγελίσασθαί σοι τὰ προρρηθέντα, πρὸ καταβολῆς κόσμου. 321C

251 Tibor Horvath. "Germanos of Constantinople and the Cult of the Virgin Mary, Mother of God, Mediatrix of All Men". De cultu mariano saeculis VI-XI; Acta congressus mariologici mariani internationalis in Croatia anno 1971 celebrati. 1972. Pontificia Academia Mariana Internationalis. 298 ftn. 106

> Young man, I see the beauty of your comely form which is
> worthy to be painted, and the radiant vision of your appearance,
> and I hear your words, which I have never heard before, and I
> am suspicious that you have come to lead me astray. (324A)

Mary's first thought is that she has a fiancé whom she does not want to disappoint. She has family who would be disappointed in her if she should give in to this 'young man.' (334C) But the Angel persists in pressing his claim that the message she is hearing is from God and that it is an 'incomprehensible mystery.' (324D) When the Angel tells her that she will be called 'the throne which bears God, the royal seat of the heavenly King,' and that she will obtain 'a royal character' as she is the daughter of the early king David and the Mother of 'the holy Jesus who sits upon the Cherubim,' she protests:

> How shall I become the throne of the Most High? Answer me,
> you who are speaking to me! How can flesh made of clay touch
> the unapproachable light which is brighter than the Sun? You are
> proclaiming impossible news, young man. (324D and 325A)

Mary's puzzlement continues in an aside where she expresses her thoughts: "How shall I know this, that what he says[252] will be accomplished? I am an unwedded virgin, and have not experienced shameful, sweet pleasure. For I am the handmaiden of the Lord who created me." (325B) Mary has made reference to her up-bringing in the Temple and now the Angel reveals to her that he is Gabriel whom she has seen when she 'received nourishment from my fiery hands.' (324D) At this point Mary accepts the 'wondrous vision which Gabriel has laid out for her, but frets about the consequences and that 'Joseph will hand me over to those who judge these things.' (325D) The Virgin has not totally banished doubt from her mind and the conversation between the Angel and her continues, in the course of which he relates to Mary how she will become pregnant and who she will bear. (328B-C) Mary begins to wonder about the child she will bear (328D). Finally Mary accepts the news and summarizes the events:

---

[252] From Piana's manuscript

O young man, messenger of ineffable joy, you have come from the bodiless ones, and speak to one made of clay. How long shall I tolerate you? How long will you continue to speak? "Behold, the servant of the Lord, let it be to me according to your word" (Luke 1.38). (329D)

Mary has grown from a wary young woman confronted with a young man who is not her fiancé into an assured young woman who will have to confront that fiancé and convince him that she has not misbehaved.

Mary's confrontation with Joseph paints the picture of an assured and competent young woman engaging an older recalcitrant man. Joseph's stubborn opposition to Mary's news leads to a debate between them concerning the Scriptural justification for such an event in the Law and the Prophets[253] and concern on Joseph's part for the social ramifications or the judgment of the Sanhedrin.

---

[253] See 332C for example.

Chapter Fourteen

Homily on the Annunciation
Translation

Τῆς παρούσης τιμίας

Homily of Germanos I, Patriarch of Constantinople on the Feast of the Annunciation to the Most Blessed Theotokos

[320 E]

With joyful soul let us spiritually celebrate this luminous and ever-glorious memorial of this honorable and royal assembly (*cf.* 1 Peter 2.9), O peoples, nations, and languages (*cf.* Daniel 4.1), and all social classes, and this multitudinous congregation who have come together because of your love for this feast, and the people around [us]. Let us weave with all zeal hymns which are worthy of the Queen who was from the lineage of David. Let us compose a springtime feast of feasts, and a festival of festivals of our hope, our unmistakable proclamation of this feast day (Psalm 81.3).

[321 A]

For today, truly, the intellectual powers of heaven have come down from Heaven, and *invisibly celebrate* her with us earthborn [human beings].

Today is fulfilled the prophecy of David which says, "Let the heavens rejoice, and let the earth be glad" (Psalm 95.11), for behold now both have been filled with joy.

Today the numerous assembly of festival-loving people puts on white robes.

Today the warm spring has shone on us as after a cold winter, and the golden-rayed sun has risen for us more pleasant and more delightful.

Today the God-planted Eden is opened, and the God-formed Adam settles in her with the goodness of his love for mankind.

Today the ancestral denial is loosed from distress, and the hateful contempt of the foremother and her toilsome punishment has ceased.

Today the hosts above dance together with those on earth; because of this present assembly from the four corners of the earth the whole universe is illuminated with brilliant light.

Today the undefiled Church of Christ is magnified in fitting conformity, and as with golden fringes is glorified with the beauty of the present much-desired day.

Today the Jerusalem below, visible from afar and having a holy name, rejoices greatly with the [Jerusalem] above; and the new Zion, to speak prophetically, is delighted. (Zephaniah 3.14)

Today Bethlehem, the city of David and of the beautiful young maiden, is revealed as a heaven on earth, and is adorned like a very handsome bridegroom.

Today the conspicuous city and territory and every race of men sing this universal festival full of light.

Today the kings of the earth and all peoples (Psalm 148.11) royally celebrate the blessed memory of our blameless queen the Mother of God.

Today the daughters of kings and queens bring garlands for the honor of the royal bridal chamber from [the lands of the] rising of the sun to the setting (Psalm 49.1, 112.3).

Today young women and brides, mothers and virgins, well-born and of every class, bless the mother and virgin and nourisher of our life.

Today the Holy of Holies is praised by all, heaven and earth together, and together they celebrate all the events.

Today the worthily-written book of the prophets is brought into our midst and each of them foretells the grace of the present feast.

Today the patriarch Jacob, making a narrative concerning that mystical and blessed ladder stretching from earth to heaven, rejoices fittingly (Genesis 28.12).

Today Moses that ancient prophet and leader of the people of Israel, tells us clearly about that bush on the mountain Horeb (Exodus 3.2).

Today the notable elder Zachariah in his own prophecy cries out and says, "I saw, and behold a lamp stand all gold, and the lamp on top of it" (Zachariah 4.2).

Today Isaiah the great herald, marvelous among prophets, prophesies shouting: "A rod will arise from the root of Jesse, and a blossom will come up from it" (Isaiah 9.1).

Today the marvelous Ezekiel cries out: "For behold the gate [is] shut and no one will go in, except the Lord God only. And the gate will be shut" (Ezekiel 44.2-3).

Today Daniel the marvelous, tells future events like things already present for a long time: "A stone was cut from the mountain without a hand" (Daniel 2.45)—that is, without a husband.

Today David the groomsman making melody about the virgin, as about another beautiful city, cries out thus: "Glorious things have been spoken about you, city of the great king" (Psalm 86.2).

Today Gabriel the leader of the hosts, running down below the vaults of heaven, greets the Virgin and Theotokos with these words: "Hail, full of grace, the Lord is with you" (Luke 1.28).

Today let all angels and us assume the angelic voice and with him let us bring his praises to the ambassador of joy, saying:

Rejoice greatly, daughter of David the king and true mother of the heavenly king and especially wielding the scepters of the faithful.

Rejoice greatly, daughter of Joachim and Anna, who gave you birth blamelessly by prayer, in the suitable time of their life together.

Rejoice greatly, daughter of David and Virgin Theotokos, truly divine is the encomium, "Blessed is the fruit of your womb" (Luke 1.42).

Hail, full of grace, you who sprouted beyond expectation from the royal tribe of David and from Anna the child of God.

Hail, full of grace, nourished from infancy, growing, having your descent traced, and receiving her nourishment from the hand of an angel and bringing ineffable and truly indescribable joy to all the universe.

Hail, full of grace, the royal purple robe which wrapped the incarnate king of heaven and earth.

Hail, full of grace, the fragrant earth and life-bearing casket and new myrrh-jar of the Spirit, who fill all the universe with the sweet smell of myrrh.

Hail, full of grace, the truly golden censer and the pure and all-holy and undefiled treasure of holiness.

Hail, full of grace, the all-golden and all-blameless beauty and the exceptional and truly marvelous dwelling-place of the Word.

Hail, full of grace, who have raised in flesh the sun which shines eternally on the universe and surrounds the whole creation with goodness.

Hail, full of grace, the all-bright cloud of the life-giving Spirit, who bore the rain of compassion and gave dew to all the creation.

Hail, full of grace, salvation of the earth-born ones, who changed grief into joy, and joined earthly things with the heavenly, and dissolved the dividing wall of enmity.

Hail, full of grace, the God-sealed and God-traversed gate of our life, through which passed the coeternal Word of the God and Father.

Hail, full of grace, untouched plant of holiness and shady tree of compassion and gold-purple lily of true virginity.

Hail, full of grace, heifer who have not borne the yoke, who suckled the fatted calf and carried that heavenly greatness in your womb.

Hail, full of grace, the unspotted lamb, who embraced in your undefiled hands that purple-fleeced sheep which was willingly sacrificed for all.

Hail, full of grace, the blameless and unwedded maiden, who received a strange conception and a childbearing without seed unheard-of by your relatives.

Hail, full of grace, the ark of sanctification (cf. Psalm 131.8), and the God-planted rod of uprightness which blossomed forth the pure flower.

Hail, full of grace, the golden-colored light-bearing lamp stand, and the radiant tent, and the table which holds the life-giving bread in itself.

Hail, full of grace, the cherubic and extremely strange seat of the king of glory, and truly the royal palace of the incarnation of the Word.

Hail, full of grace, in whose protection the living, honorable and God-ruled city ever prides itself.

Hail full of grace, [you are] the golden jar which contained the manna (*cf.* Hebrews 9.4), and [you are] the true royal tabernacle, which the new Bez'alel fittingly adorned in gold (*cf.* Exodus 31.2*ff.*).

Hail full of grace, [you are] the glowing purple God-bearing cloud, and [you are] the spring flowing unfailingly for all.

Hail full of grace, [you are] the lofty high throne of the Maker of all, the redeemer, the administrator of all things in heaven and on earth.

[321 B]

Hail full of grace, [you are] the living temple of the majestic glory, (Psalm 29.9) of him who was incarnate for us, assuming flesh for our salvation.

Hail full of grace, [you are] the carrier of life, nourisher of the nourisher, the one who gives milk to him who caused honey to spring from rocks long ago (*cf.* Deuteronomy 32.13).

Hail full of grace, mountain of God, fertile mountain (*cf.* Psalm 68.15), imposing mountain, uncut mountain, mountain of God's appearing.

Hail full of grace, exceeding great joy of the soul, and object of worship for the whole cosmos, and truly good mediator for all sinners.

Hail full of grace, gate for the afflicted, formidable guardian of those who with pure hearts confess you to be the Theotokos.

Hail full of grace, who for the sake of the salvation of all human kind bore the Master who loves mankind.

[321 C]

Hail full of grace, marvelous and sympathetic refuge of all Christians, and vision higher than any beauty of great achievements.

But with unworthy lips we, who are among the least, have held discourse about these matters. We have learned from the Holy Scriptures about this heavenly bride and queen, the Theotokos. And so, beloved, let us turn to the God-inspired news which the archangel Gabriel brought, and let us hear what he said to the blameless lady when he arrived.

The Angel
Hear, most blessed one, hear the hidden words of the Most High.

"Behold, you shall conceive in your womb, and you shall produce a son, and shall call him Jesus" (Luke 1.31). Prepare then for Christ's coming. For I have come to announce to you what has been decreed before the foundation of the cosmos.

[321 D]

The Theotokos

Depart o man, from my city and my fatherland. Depart quickly from this house. Go a long way from my vestibule, you who speak to me. Do not bring this announcement to me, unworthy as I am (*cf.* Luke 1.41).

The Angel

The Lover of mankind, wishing to fulfill His ancient plan, and having mercy on mankind's wandering, was pleased in his goodness and love for man to become man. Why do you not accept my greeting, O blessed one?

[324 A]

The Theotokos

Young man, I see the beauty of your comely form which is worthy to be painted, and the radiant vision of your appearance, and I hear your words, which I have never heard before, and I am suspicious that you have come to lead me astray.

The Angel

Know truly and believe that I am more amazed at seeing your God-created beauty.

Seeing you I know that I am examining closely the glory of my Lord.

The Theotokos

I have heard a tongue which I do not comprehend. I have beheld an appearance which I have never seen. How should I not be perplexed? I begin to tremble all over. I have obtained a proper suitor, and am not accustomed to speak with strangers.

[324 B]

The Angel

Accept this joyful message which is worthy of being heard, along with the song of praise which is due to you. For "the one who is borne of you, shall be called the son of the Most High" (Luke 1.35), and your son shall be born in the height of hallowed goodness.

The Theotokos

I am afraid and I tremble at your words. I suspect that you have come to deceive me like another Eve. I am nothing like her. What a greeting you bring to a maiden whom you have never seen before!

The Angel

I proclaim to you good news of joy. I proclaim to you unimaginable birth. I proclaim to you the inexplicable coming of the Most High. Perhaps even that purple thread you are holding foretells your royal status.

[324 C]

The Theotokos

Since you are telling this to me, and since you won't stop saying it, for the rest I will say to you that I don't trust this announcement of yours. You come to debase my virginity, and to grieve my betrothed.

The Angel

Zacharias the prophet and the beloved of your cousin Elizabeth, will convince your unbelief. Go to her so that you may learn from him[254] the things that will happen to him.

The Theotokos

Joachim and Anna are my holy and blameless parents, and I their child, how can I be an embarrassment to them? Who will inform them that Mary did not misbehave?

[324 D]

The Angel

When my words shall come to pass in their own time, then you will understand the power of this incomprehensible mystery. Then you will know the result of my words and the ineffable condescension of the Most High.

---

[254]   her

The Theotokos
<*You have heard that*> I am of the House and the ancestry of David. How shall I assist in these awesome, heavenly mysteries? And how shall I be able to conceive the holy Jesus who sits upon the Cherubim?

[325 A]

The Angel
You shall be called the throne which bears God, the royal seat of the heavenly King. As you are Queen and Virgin, and a daughter of [David] the earthly king, so you have a royal character.

The Theotokos
How shall I become the throne of the Most High? Answer me, you who are speaking to me! How can flesh made of clay touch the unapproachable light which is brighter than the Sun? You are proclaiming impossible news, young man.

The Angel
Why? For what purpose, for what reason, have you distrusted my good news, Glorified one? How long will you disobey the angel that was sent to you from heaven? I am not Eve's deceiver—far from it.

[325 B]

The Theotokos
I have seen your many changeable faces, and have heard your most marvelous message, which no one has ever heard. And therefore I cannot accept this good news.

The Angel
Even though my voice and my form terrify you, I know that the words of my mouth shall become a harbinger <of ineffable joy> to you. And all heaven and earth shall bless you <according to your own words> (*cf.* Luke 1.48).[255]

---

[255] Supplements from Piana's manuscript

The Theotokos

How shall I know this, that what he says[256] will be accomplished? I am an unwedded virgin, and have not experienced shameful, sweet pleasure. For I am the handmaiden of the Lord who created me.

[325 C]

The Angel

I shall tell you clearly, that Elizabeth your cousin at this very moment is about to give birth in her old age to a son, and at his birth many shall rejoice and be amazed, for his name will be called John (cf. Luke 1.19).

The Theotokos

You who speak to me, receive [these] gifts from me and leave. Whether you are an angel or a man I do not truly know. I see the vestments of an angel, and in the glance I perceive a man.

The Angel

You saw me, didn't you, O blessed one, when you were in the Holy of Holies, and when you received nourishment from my fiery hands? I am Gabriel, who always stand before
the glory of God.

[325 D]

The Theotokos

I have a pious, holy and righteous fiancé, who is a master carpenter. I am cautious about him lest he may come upon me conversing with you, a stranger, and especially since we are alone.

The Angel

Now I have begun to speak. I am full of eternal words; and for the rest I shall tell you that the Lord who is about to be born of you, is the King of kings, and "will rule over the House of Jacob forever and of his kingdom there shall be no end" (Luke 1.35).

---

[256] From Piana's manuscript

The Theotokos

Now my heart is troubled and I do not know what to make of this wondrous vision. For I believe that your words are true. And Joseph will hand me over to those who judge these things.

[328 A]

The Angel

I cannot comprehend, O holy one, that you are doubtful about me who come to you from on high. Rather, I should be cautious concerning you as you are about to become the mother of my Lord, and I should tremble in your royal presence.

The Theotokos

Your message is strange to me. Your authoritative manner of coming contradicts your words and demeanor. You come into my house and approach me without being announced, as if to a servant girl, not as if you considered me a lady.

The Angel

You have been entirely pure and blameless. I am amazed that you have so much distrusted my words, O full of grace. Behold even as I speak, I think that the King of Glory has made his residence in you, O Queen.

[328 B]

The Theotokos

You are greeting an untried virgin, and an unmarried girl you extol. You know the truth: when and where and "How will this happen to me, since I know no man?" (Luke 1.34)

The Angel

"The Holy Spirit will come upon you, and the power of the Most High will overshadow you, and therefore the holy one who is born of you shall be called the Son of God. Fear not Mary, you have found favor with God" (Luke 1.35 and 1.30).

The Theotokos

You came from heaven and deliver to me a much-anticipated message. You proclaim to me the presence of the Holy Spirit; but how should I not reject and even more disbelieve this paradoxical good news? Tell me, you who speak to me.

[328C]

The Angel

Cast away your unbelief, Virgin. For behold, as it seems to me, my words have been accomplished, a lump is rising in your belly. Even if you do not wish it, "with God nothing is impossible" (Luke 1:37).

The Theotokos

I am a sprout of the root of David. I fear that on me as on him [David] will come unexpected scorn of adultery, and the golden plate of the holy head dress of the priest will show me to be a sinner.[257]

The Angel

You shall bear the Lord, the Savior, who is one of the life-beginning Trinity. You shall bring unexpected joy to the world, which neither angels nor men have ever brought; and your name shall be called blessed.[258]

[328 D]

The Theotokos

Tell me, young man, what kind of savior, am I to bear? For truly your good news is strange even to the spiritual powers of angels, fiery might of archangels, and the commanders of the many-eyed [cherubim].

The Angel

At all times your words are sweet and joyous, O blessed one. It is because of this that I will say to you, your pregnancy is due not to the will of the flesh but to the will of God and the descent of the Holy Spirit (*cf.* John 1.13).

---

[257] See *Protoevangelion Jacobi* 386 re: Conception of John by Elizabeth.

[258] Note the use of unexpected. The play on the Greek.

[329 A]

The Theotokos
Who will persuade Joseph that I shall conceive not by the will of man, but by the descent of the Holy Spirit? For it has never at any time been heard that a virgin has given birth to a child without a man.

The Angel
All the races of men shall take refuge under your compassion. And all tongues of clay shall bless you. And your name shall be spoken from generation to generation (*cf.* Luke 1.50), for through you, the Lord, the light of the world, is about to be born.

The Theotokos
How shall the race of men flee to me who am matter and drawn from the earth? And how shall I embrace Christ the Light of the World? And how shall that unsetting Sun be born by the spiritual moon? *<Or how will the race of men take refuge with me?>*

[329 B]

The Angel
Put on a joyful countenance, O blessed one. You are about to become heaven, a God-containing tabernacle, a living temple of God, wider and higher and more wondrous than the seven firmaments.

The Theotokos
I shiver at the beginning of the paradox of my unusual childbearing. I am concerned about Joseph and I do not know what will happen. But it is good for me to go to the house of Zacharias, to see my kinswoman.

The Angel
You shall become the common propitiation of all Christians. And therefore again I salute you as is fitting, "*<Hail>* O full of grace, the Lord is with you, blessed are you among women, blessed is the fruit of your womb" (Luke 1.38).

[329C]

The Theotokos

I am of royal blood, and spent my earliest childhood in the royal house of Bethlehem, and my childhood I spent blamelessly in the temple; and being a virgin up to now, how can I be called the mother of my child?

The Angel

The Most High searched all the universe, and did not find a mother like you. Certainly, <*as he knew,*> as he wished, as he was pleased, from you, the holy one, he shall become man because of his love for mankind.

[329D]

The Theotokos

I shall praise the Lord in song, "for he has looked upon the lowliness of his handmaiden; for behold from henceforth all generations shall call me blessed" (Luke 1.48) and the people of the Gentiles shall unceasingly praise me.

The Angel

O Virgin, bringer of heavenly joy, joyful and marvelous dwelling place, and propitiation of the whole cosmos, the only truly blessed one among women (Luke 1.42), prepare yourself for the mystical coming of Christ.

The Theotokos

O young man, messenger of ineffable joy, you have come from the bodiless ones, and speak to one made of clay. How long shall I tolerate you? How long will you continue to speak? "Behold, the servant of the Lord, let it be to me according to your word" (Luke 1.38).

[332 A]

The blessed Virgin, worthy of all praise, said all these things, and perhaps even more mystical and fitting things. But let us listen next, beloved ones, if you are willing, to what the righteous Joseph said to her.

Joseph
Undefiled, I received you from the house of the Lord, and an undefiled virgin I kept you in my house. And what is this which I now see, a mother contrary to expectation and not a virgin? Speak to me, Mary. Quickly, tell me the truth.

The Theotokos
You kept me undefiled, as you say, in your house, and I reckon again you have found me pure. From my childhood I have hated the spotted garment of the flesh, and no trace of enjoyment is in me.

[332 B]

Joseph
Fear the judgment seat, the harsh council chamber, the court of the Jewish synagogue which can not be deceived; and tell me the pure truth. Do not hide from me what will happen.[259]

The Theotokos
Fear, rather, the <*terrible*> court and the unchangeable judgment of the age to come, O Joseph, which even the angels fear who have never sinned. Do not be concerned at all for the earthly king and judgment.

[332C]

Joseph
It is written in the Law of Moses. "If one finds a virgin, and lies with her by force, the man shall give to the father of the young woman fifty silver shekels" (Deuteronomy 22.24-25) What will you do with that?

The Theotokos
It is written in the prophets, that "they shall give the sealed book to a man who knows letters and he shall say: 'I am not able to read it' (Isaiah 29.11)." Perhaps then as it seems to me, the prophecy was said about you.

---

[259] what has happened to you

Joseph

Make public, Mary the one who plots against my house. Bring this undisciplined one in here, so that I may cut off his head with a carpenter's sword, in as much as he has dishonored my grey head and besides, the twelve tribes of Israel will mock me.

[332 D]

The Theotokos

You are just and blameless, and my God in all likelihood shall reveal to you that which will happen to me. In sleep He will show you him whom you call a plotter. For I was not accustomed to go to that height where He dwells.

Joseph

Leave my house now quickly, and go to your lover. I shall not feed you again, you will not eat bread at my table, inasmuch as with anguish and scorn, instead of joy, you have dishonored my grey hair.

The Theotokos

Wait a little, Joseph. Do not make me secretly a stranger to your house. Just as I have not been accustomed to traveling, I do not know right from left, and I do not understand where to go or where to seek refuge.

[333 A]

Joseph

Since you are between life and death, tell me the truth, Mary. Who is he that has hunted me? Reveal to me the one who has conversed with you. Tell me what his social class is. Tell me of what city he was, so that having gone there I may bring dishonor on him.

The Theotokos

As the Lord lives, I am pure, and have known no man. He who appeared to me, seemed to me to be an angel, being in human form. He stood at a respectful distance. And while standing, he spoke gently to my unworthy self.

Joseph

There will come to you, and also to me, an old man, the accusation of wife-stealing, and unexpected dishonor from those who judge such matters. The water of testing will examine both of you, even if we are unwilling.

[333B]

The Theotokos

You have heard that my kinswoman, Elizabeth the wife of Zacharias, has even now conceived beyond hope a Prophet and Forerunner. For if he were not a prophet he would not have leapt to worship the Lord hidden inside of me (cf. Luke 1.40).

Joseph

I wonder at you, and am greatly amazed, and I know that you have been spoken of among the Sons of Israel, and the Lord Adonai shall hold me in dishonor, for I by the Holy Spirit received you from the Holy Temple to guard, but I have not guarded your virginity.

[333 C]

The Theotokos

The day of affliction fell upon me, and blame and suspicion came upon me; and the scrutiny of my betrothed was placed firmly on me; and my pregnancy accused me, and the Angel who cried "Hail" is quickly hidden, and what else I may say I do not know.

Joseph

I have seen the roundness of your previously immaculate belly, and I have begun to tremble all over. For tell me, how shall I <*hide you or how shall I*> reveal you? Or how shall I be able to escape the notice of the Jewish Sanhedrin? Leave my house, leave it at once.

The Theotokos

Behold, you banish me from your house, O Joseph, I do not know where I shall go. Shall I return to the sanctuary of the temple? Or shall I go back to my parents? And how shall I look upon them?

[333 D]

Joseph

Even if I keep quiet about your sin, the stones will cry out.[260] And the Holy of Holies will shout aloud, because I received you for safe keeping from the priest who is enrolled there, and I have not guarded your virginity.

The Theotokos

I shall hide myself in one of my caves in my town of Bethlehem. I shall await the appropriate time of my birth-giving. May I learn who this is to whom I am about to give birth, for I reckon that the Lord will regard my lowliness (*cf.* Luke 1.48).

Joseph

Tell me plainly who this stranger is, that betrayer, who at some time like a spy, especially when I was away and not within the walls of the city of Nazareth, came unannounced to my house.

[336 A]

The Theotokos

When I had taken the pitcher to go to my well to draw water that I may drink, a voice came softly to my ear, saying, "Hail Most Blessed the Lord is with you."

Joseph

You did not conceive by a voice, did you? Never has it been heard, that a virgin conceived by the sound of words without a man, nor did our fathers tell us that such an event occurred in the ancient days.

The Theotokos

Is it not written in the Scriptures, "That a virgin shall conceive, and shall bear a child to us" (*cf.* Isaiah 7.14)? You cannot say that the prophets lie, can you? You are mistaken, O Joseph, you are out of your mind about many things.

---

[260] your belly will cry out

[336 B]

Joseph

Now I will say,[261] Mary, that you have followed the path of your mother Eve. She was cast out of paradise because she listened to the whisperer, and you shall be cast out of my house as a guilty woman.

The Theotokos

Now you attack me like a foreigner and a stranger and an accuser. You do not converse with me like a queen, but secretly pursue me from city to city. How I shall defend myself now?

Joseph

Your motherhood is strange, as it seem to me, and not only to me but also to angels and men, and they would not believe this. Who has ever heard that a virgin has borne an infant, and especially without a man?

[336 C]

The Theotokos

It is strange to you, I know. The paradoxical nature of my childbearing astounds your mind. I am not responsible for this condition which has been brought upon me. From infancy I have been accustomed to worship the Lord who made me.

Joseph

Did I not say to you, show me the attacker of my house and I will free you from this accusation? Did I not say to you, go quickly to your lover? What more could you hope for?

The Theotokos

I do not clearly understand in what place he dwells. I truly wished to go to him, to gaze upon his beauty which is worthy to be painted, and to have righteous dialogue with him. For, he said to me "Rejoice," and I am grieved just now.

---

[261] I see

[336 D]

Joseph
How can I not be frightened, and confounded in my sight? For I received you from the temple of my God as a virgin, and I did not guard you. And how shall I bring gifts to my Lord God and fulfill the customs of the law as I have been accustomed to do?

The Theotokos
Believe the prophets of God, and concerning this matter do not allow yourself to sink into greater pain. For you shall find it written in them, "Behold, a virgin shall conceive and bring forth a son, and they shall call his name Emmanuel. (Matthew 1.23)"

[337 A]

Joseph
The high priestly staff prevailed upon me to take you from the house of prayer for safekeeping, and I took possession of you with all the good arrangements in my house. Why Mary, did you not receive the fullness of my hospitality and my deeds?

The Theotokos
As the Lord lives, I have not known the stain of another's bed nor the blame of fleshly desire, but <*I am pure*>; once again as I held the purple thread <*in my hands*>, I heard the voice of an angel saying to me: "Fear not, Mariam, for you have found favor with God (Luke 1.30)."

Joseph
Be content with my house a little longer, for the time of enrollment has come near of Caesar Augustus who is king (*cf.* Luke 2.1ff.). But I fear to enroll you as my wife, much less in the lineage of David.'

[337 B]

The Theotokos
I shall guard your words in my heart, and I shall be content in your house a little longer, and I shall await the time of enrollment and the day

of my giving birth, until we shall bring the tribute to Caesar Augustus, the Emperor who now rules the Romans.

Joseph
Perhaps it was an angel who appeared to me in a dream, and said to me: "Joseph, son of David, fear not to take Mary to you as a wife, for that which shall come of her, is of the Holy Spirit, and she shall produce a son and you shall call his name Jesus (Matthew 1.20*ff*.)."

The Theotokos
Perhaps, my lord, that one whom you saw in a dream was the same one who greeted me with "Hail". But for now, make ready *<a place and>* a cave and seek out a Hebrew woman of our race, who will guard the mystery and will take care of me in the accustomed manner.

[337 C]

Joseph
Surely he will appear and show me the place and the cave. But you, Mary, prepare the swaddling clothes. Whether a prophet or a king is the one about to be born, we do not know, "for he shall be called a Nazarene (Matthew 2.23)."

The Theotokos
I suspect that the one who is about to be born shall be called a king. For it is written in the prophets: "Rejoice greatly, O daughter of Zion. Shout aloud, O daughter of Jerusalem. Lo your King comes to you, righteous and saving (Zachariah 9.9)."[262]

Joseph
He who appeared to me in the dream shall reveal those things which are about to happen to us. I shall be cautious of Herod, for if some one should give away the secret, he will seek to know about the birth of the child.

---

[262] Text from Zachariah 9.9. This is only the first half of the LXX.

[337 D]

The Theotokos
There will appear today in the heavens a sign, for so it is written in the prophets: "A star shall rise out of Jacob, and a man arise out of Israel, and shall crush the leaders of Moab (Numbers 24.17)."

[340 A]

Joseph
Yesterday I was thrown down by suspicion, shame I have brought to your beauty and your loveliness, but now receiving the fullness from on high, at once I shall give an account and prostrate myself in reverence to your greatness and bless your name <*unto the ages, for the Lord has had mercy on his people*>.

[At this point the Migne text ends. The following is LaPiana's text on the basis of a mss.]

The Theotokos
Gold as it seems to me, <and myrrh and incense>, shall be brought to the one about to be born (*cf.* Matthew 2.11) as the prophet and king David said, for "He shall live and the gold of Arabia shall be given to him (Psalm 72.19)."[263]

Joseph
Henceforth, let us feel our way. If you wish an untouched place, as the time comes for the birth, for we shall have need of a beast of burden to go there. For behold I see you extremely gloomy, and I know that you are about to give birth.

The Theotokos
This once examine the prophet Micah. He shall show you the place. For thus he says: "And you Bethlehem of the House of Ephratha, are

---

[263] so that the saying of David will be fulfilled, "All the earth with his glory, may it be so, may it be so." (Psalm 71.2)

not the least among the thousands of Judah, for out of you shall come a governor who shall rule your people Israel (Micha 5.2)."

Joseph

As I think, that angel who appeared to me in a dream will not abandon you until all that has been written shall be fulfilled in that time and he shall go with us upon the road.

The Theotokos

O great and marvelous is this day to me. For the powerful one has done great things for me, and holy is his name. To those who fear him his mercy is from generation to generation (Luke 1.49*ff.*). To him be glory and power unto the end of the ages. Amen.

(In some mss. there is more text added as an ending.)

> But these things the angel said graciously, conversing reverently with the Theotokos, and Joseph likewise replied to the lady full of grace, being at a loss concerning the power of the mystery.
>
> So we people of clay, with what colors of encomium may we describe the virginal image?[264] With what words of praise may we illuminate the undefiled form of the pure one? She [is] the inaccessible sanctuary of incorruption. She [is] the sanctified temple of God. She [is] the golden altar of holocausts (cf. Exodus 30.28). She [is] the divine incense-offering of the covenant. She [is] the holy oil of anointing. She [is] the all-honorable jar of the mystical perfume of nard. She [is] the priestly ephod. She [is] the golden lamp stand always carrying the seven-branched lamp stand. She [is] the ark gilded inside and out, sanctified in body and spirit, in which lay the golden censer, and the golden

---

[264] This passage is borrowed from Proclus, *Laudatio de genitricis Mariae*, chapter 17: F.J. Leroy, *L'homilétique de Proclus de Constantinople* [*Studi e Testi* 247. Vatican City: Biblioteca Apostolica Vaticana, 1967]: 299-324-: (TLG text {2755.005}). Proclus in turn borrowed from the Homily on the Annunciation attributed to Gregory of Nyssa: D. Montagna, "La lode alla theotokos nei testi greci dei secoli iv-vii-" *Marianum* 24 (1962): 536-539- (TLG text {2017.051}).

jar which holds the manna and the other things, about which it is written. She [is] the firstborn heifer which has not known the yoke, of which the ash, the body of the Lord taken from her purifies those who have shared it by (from?) the pollution of sin. She [is] the gate which looks toward the east, which is closed forever by the master's entrance and exit. She [is] the new volume of the new covenant, by which the power of the demons has been sharply stolen, and the captivity of mankind has been swiftly alleviated.[265] *She [is] the three measures of humanity, Greeks, barbarians, and Jews, in which the ineffable wisdom of God has hidden the leaven of his own goodness. She [is] the treasury of spiritual blessing. She [is the ship] which brings the incorruptible royal wealth from Tarshish, from the earthly land of the gentiles carrying the conversion (?) of the Jerusalem above. She [is] the beautiful bride of the songs, who took off the old garment and washed the earthly feet (cf. Song of Songs 5.3), and with modesty received the incorruptible bridegroom in the storeroom of her soul. She [is] the new wagon of the faithful, which carried the living ark of the dispensation and through the two heifers giving birth for the first time directed it on the right road of salvation. She [is] the tent of witness, from which as a young [baby] the true Joshua/Jesus has come forth after the nine-month time of gestation. She [is] the chest made secure outside and inside, adorned with understanding and piety, in which the spiritual Moses is saved from the Pharaoh of the law, whose daughter, that is the church of the gentiles, caring for [him?] in her virginal arms promises to give her the reward of eternal life. She [is] the fifth well of the oath, in which the water of immortality gushes forth, through the incarnate dispensation and presence in the fulfillment of the fifth covenant: for the first was written in reference to Adam; the second in reference to Noah; the third in reference to Abraham; the fourth in reference to Moses; the fifth in reference to the Lord, since he also went forth five times into the vineyard of righteousness to reward the pious workers, at the first hour, and the third, and the sixth and the ninth and the eleventh. She [is] what was the*

---

[265] Cunningham 243

unspotted fleece laid on the universal threshing-floor, on which the rain descending from heaven filled the whole earth with the unstinting gift of good things; dried up by the immeasurable load of evil things, and again dried it up; from the moisture of the passions which sinks into the flesh. She [is] the fruitful olive tree planted in the house of the Lord, from which the Holy Spirit taking bodily matter, brought to the storm-battered nature of mankind the peace which was foretold. She, the ever-flourishing and imperishable paradise, in which the wood of life having been planted brings without hindrance the fruit of immortality to all. She [is] the offering of the new creation, in which the water of life bubbles up. She [is] the joy of virgins, the support of the faithful, the diadem of the Church, the seal of orthodoxy, the coinage of truth, the garment of continence, the decorated robe of virtue, the stronghold of righteousness, the boast of the Holy Trinity, according to the evangelical story: "The Holy Spirit will come upon you, and the power of the Most High will overshadow you, for which reason the holy one which is begotten will be called the Son of God." (Luke 1.35)

But we, O Mother of God, in faith confess, in desire venerate, and in fear bow down, always magnifying you and reverently blessing [you].[266] *For blessed is your father among men, and blessed is your mother among women, blessed is your household, blessed are your relatives, and blessed are your acquaintances, blessed are those who saw you, blessed are those who accompanied you, blessed are those who served you, blessed is Joseph, who was betrothed to you, blessed is your tomb! For you [are] the honor of those who give honor, and reward of old men,*[267] *and exaltation of exaltations.*

But O my only Mistress, my soul-leader from God, the divine dew for my burning, the drop flowing from God for my parched heart, the bright-shining lamp for my darkened soul, the guide

---

[266] From here to the end, cf. Germanos, Homily on the Presentation II, PG 98.317C ff.

[267] text corrupt?

for my inexperience, the power for my weakness, the clothing of my nakedness, the wealth of my poverty, the healing of my incurable wounds, the removal of tears, the cessation of groaning, the reversal of misfortunes, the lightening of pains, the release of fetters, the hope of my salvation, hear my prayers: have pity on my groaning, and accept my lamentations. Have mercy on me, bending down to my tears. Have compassion on me, as mother of the God who loves mankind and is our God. Look down and assent to my supplication, fill up my thirsty desire, and join me to my relative and fellow servant in the land of the meek, in the tents of the just (cf. Psalm 118.15), in the choir of the saints (cf. Psalm 116.9); and make me worthy, O protection and joy of all and brilliant gladness, also in joy to rejoice along with you.[268] *I beg you, to be with you in that truly ineffable joy of the God and King who was born from you and in his imperishable bridal-chamber, and in the unceasing and insatiable delight, and in the kingdom which has no evening and no limit.*

Yes, Lady, my refuge, my life and my support, my armor and my boast, my hope and my strength, grant me to enjoy the inexpressible and unceasing gifts of your Son and your God and our God in the heavenly mansion. For as the mother of the Most High you have, I know, the power which runs along with the will. Because of this I beg, may I not be deprived, all-undefiled Lady, of my expectation (cf. Galatians 6.4), but may I obtain this, Bride of God, you who gave birth to the expectation of all, our Lord Jesus Christ the true God and your Son and Master of all things visible and invisible, to whom is due all glory, honor, and veneration, with the Father who has no beginning, and the all-holy Spirit, now and ever, and to the ages of ages. Amen.

---

[268] The Presentation homily reads ταύτῃ "with her."

Chapter Fifteen

References to Mary in the Homily on the Annunciation of the Theotokos by Germanos, Patriarch of Constantinople (715-730)

PG 98 Location	Greek	English	OT/NT Reference
320E	τῇ ἐκ Δαβὶδ Βασιλίδι	the Queen who was from the lineage of David	
321A	ἐν ᾗ ἡ ἔμψυχος καὶ ἔντιμος καὶ θεοβασίλευτος πόλις, ἀεὶ τειχιζομένη σεμνύνεται	For this living, honorable and God-ruled city ever praises her who protects our walls.	
321A	Χαῖρε, κεχαριτωμένη	Hail full of grace	
321A	ἡ τοῦ μάννα στάμνος ὁλόχρυσος	the golden jar which contained the manna	*cf.* Hebrews 9.4
321A	σκηνὴ ὡς ἀληθῶς πορφυροποίητος	the true royal tabernacle	*cf.* Exodus 31.2*ff*.).
321A	Χαῖρε, κεχαριτωμένη	Hail full of grace	
321A	ἡ διὰ πάντων πορφυρίζουσα θεοβάστακτος νεφέλη	the glowing purple God-bearing cloud	
321A	καὶ πηγὴ πηγάζουσα πᾶσιν ἀέ018ναον	the spring flowing unfailingly for all	
321A	Χαῖρε, κεχαριτωμένη	Hail full of grace	
321A	ὁ θρόνος ὁ ὑψηλὸς καὶ ἐπηρμένος τοῦ τῶν ὅλων ποιητοῦ	the lofty high throne of the Maker of all	

321B	Χαῖρε, κεχαριτωμένη	Hail full of grace	
321B	ὁ ναὸς ὁ ἔμψυχος τῆς μεγαλοπρεποῦς δόξης	the living temple of the majestic glory	Psalm 29.9
321B	Χαῖρε, κεχαριτωμένη	Hail full of grace	
321B	ἡ ζωὴν φέρουσα	the carrier of life	
321B	τρέφουσα τὸν τρέφοντα	nourisher of the nourisher	
321B	γάλα ποτίζουσα, τὸν ἐκ πέτρας μέλι πάλαι πηγάσαντα	the one who gives milk to him who caused honey to spring from rocks long ago	Deuteronomy 32.13
321B	Χαῖρε, κεχαριτωμένη	Hail full of grace	
321B	ὄρος Θεοῦ	mountain of God	
321B	ὄρος πῖον	fertile mountain	cf. Psalm 68.15
321B	ὄρος κατάσκιον	imposing mountain	
321B	ὄρος ἀλατόμητον	uncut mountain	
321B	ὄρος Θεοῦ τὸ ἐμφανές.	mountain of God's appearing	
321B	Χαῖρε, κεχαριτωμένη	Hail full of grace	
321B	ψυχῆς ἀγαλλίαμα	exceeding great joy of the soul	
321B	ὅλου τοῦ κόσμου παγκόσμιον σέβασμα	object of worship for the whole cosmos	
321B	ἁμαρτωλῶν ἀπάντων ἡ ὄντως ἀγαθὴ μεσιτεία	truly good mediator for all sinners	
321B	Χαῖρε, κεχαριτωμένη	Hail full of grace	
321B	θύρα θλιβομένων	gate for the afflicted	
321B	προστασία φοβερά, τῶν εἰλικρινεῖ καρδίᾳ Θεοτόκον ὁμολογούντων σε	formidable guardian of those who with pure hearts confess you to be the Theotokos	
321B	Χαῖρε, κεχαριτωμένη	Hail full of grace	
321B	ἡ φιλάνθρωπον Δεσπότην ὑπὲρ κοινῆς τοῦ γένους τῶν ἀνθρώπων κυοφορήσασα σωτηρίας	who for the sake of the salvation of all human kind bore the Master who loves mankind	
321C	Χαῖρε, κεχαριτωμένη	Hail full of grace	
321C	Χριστιανῶν ἀπάντων θαυμαστὸν καὶ εὐσυμπάθητον καταφύγιον	marvelous and sympathetic refuge of all Christians	

321C	πάσης μεγαλουργοῦ καλλονῆς ὑψηλότερον θέαμα	higher vision of the beauty of great achievements	
321C	τὴν οὐράνιον νύμφην καὶ βασιλίδα καὶ Θεοτόκον	heavenly bride and queen, the Theotokos	
321C	τὴν ἄμεμπτον	to the blameless lady	
321C	δεδοξασμένη	most blessed one	
321C	Ἄκουε, δεδοξασμένη· λόγους ἀποκρύφους Ὑψίστου ἄκουε· «Ἰδοὺ συλλήψῃ ἐν γαστρί, καὶ τέξῃ υἱὸν καὶ καλέσεις τὸ ὄνομα αὐτοῦ Ἰησοῦν.»	"Behold, you shall conceive in your womb, and you shall produce a son, and shall call him Jesus"	Luke 1.31
321C	Ὁπλίζου λοιπὸν εἰς Χριστοῦ παρουσίαν· ἦλθον γὰρ εὐαγγελίσασθαί σοι τὰ προρρηθέντα, πρὸ καταβολῆς κόσμου	Prepare then for Christ's coming. For I have come to announce to you what has been decreed before the foundation of the cosmos	
321D	ταπεινώσει	unworthy as I am	*cf.* Luke 1.41
321D	ἡ κεχαριτωμένη	O blessed one	
324A	σου θεογράφιστον κάλλος	your God-created beauty	
324A	δόξαν Κυρίου μου	the glory of my Lord	
324A	πῶς οὐκ ἐκπλήξομαι	How should I not be perplexed?	
324A	ὅλη δι' ὅλου σύντρομος γεγονυῖα	I begin to tremble all over	
324B	ἐγκώμιον τό σοι πρεπωδέστατον	the song of praise which is due to you	
324B	Δέδοικα καὶ τρέμω σου τοὺς τοιούτους λόγους	I am afraid and I tremble at your words	
324B	ὑπολαμβάνω, ὡς ἄλλην Εὔαν πλανῆσαί με παραγέγονας	I suspect that you have come to deceive me like another Eve	
324B	Ἐγὼ δὲ οὐκ εἰμὶ κατ' ἐκείνην	I am nothing like her (Eve)	
324B	κόρην	a maiden	
324B	τόκον ἀνεννόητον	unimaginable birth	
324B	Τάχα δὲ καὶ ἣν κατέχεις πορφύραν, προμηνύει τὸ βασιλικὸν ἀξίωμα	Perhaps even that purple thread you are holding foretells your royal status	

Gregory E. Roth

324C	ἐξουθενῆσαι ἦλθες τὸ παρθενικόν μου ἀξίωμα	You come to debase my virginity	
324C	οἱ ἐμοὶ γονεῖς τυγχάνουσιν	are my holy and blameless parents	
324C	Τίς ἴδῃ καὶ πληροφορήσῃ ὅτι Μαρία οὐκ ἠτάκτησεν;	Who will inform them that Mary did not misbehave?	
324D	Ἡ ἐξ οἴκου καὶ πατριᾶς Δαβὶδ καταγομένη	I am of the House and the ancestry of David	
324D	πῶς τοιούτοις φρικτοῖς καὶ ἐπουρανίοις ἐξυπηρετήσω μυστηρίοις;	How shall I assist in these awesome, heavenly mysteries?	
324D	Καὶ πῶς Ἰησοῦν τὸν ἅγιον, τὸν ἐπὶ τῶν Χερουβὶμ καθεζόμενον, ἐγὼ πῶς ὑποδέξασθαι δυνήσομαι;	And how shall I be able to conceive the holy Jesus who sits upon the Cherubim?	
325A	Θρόνος θεοβάστακτος	the throne which bears God	
325A	βασιλικὴ καθέδρα τοῦ ἐπουρανίου Βασιλέως κληθήσῃ	You shall be called the royal seat of the heavenly King	
325A	Βασίλισσα καὶ Δέσποινα	Queen and Virgin	
325A	βασιλέως ἐπιγείου θυγάτηρ τυγχάνεις	a daughter of [David] the earthly king	
325A	χαρακτῆρα ἔχεις βασιλικόν	so you have a royal character.	
325A	Θρόνος Ὑψίστου	the throne of the Most High	
325A	πῶς τὸ ὑπὲρ ἥλιον φῶς ἐκεῖνο τὸ ἀψηλάφητον ψηλαφήσει σὰρξ πηλίνη	How can flesh made of clay touch the unapproachable light which is brighter than the Sun?	
325A	δεδοξασμένη	Glorified one	
325B	χαρᾶς ἀνεκλαλήτου πρόξενά σοι2	a harbinger <of ineffable joy> to you	cf. Luke 1.48
325B	μακαρίσαι σε κατὰ τὸ ῥημά σου ὁ οὐρανὸς καὶ ἡ γῆ3	all heaven and earth shall bless you <according to your own words>	cf. Luke 1.48
325B	Κατὰ τί γνώσομαι τοῦτο, ὅτι ἔσται τελείωσις τοῖς ὑπ᾽αὐτου λαλουμένοις4	How shall I know this, that what he says5 will be accomplished?	

325B	καθότι παρθένος ἀθαλάμευτος ἔφω τυγχάνω, καὶ μῶμος ἡδυπαθείας οὐκ ἔστιν ἐν ἐμοί;	I am an unwedded virgin, and have not experienced shameful, sweet pleasure	
325B	Δούλη γάρ εἰμι τοῦ ποιήσαντός με	I am the handmaiden of the Lord who created me	
325C	εὐλογημένη	O blessed one	
328A	δεδοξασμένη	O holy one	
328A	σὲ ὡς Μητέρα Κυρίου μου μέλλουσαν ἔσεσθαι	as you are about to become the mother of my Lord	
328A	σου τὸ βασιλικὸν ἀξίωμα	your royal presence	
328A	τάχα ὡς παιδίσκην	as if to a servant girl	
328A	καὶ οὐχ ὡς δέσποιναν λογισάμενος	not as if you considered me a lady	
328A	καθαρὰ καὶ ἄμεμπτος τυγχάνουσα	entirely pure and blameless	
328A	ἡ κεχαριτωμένη	O full of grace	
328A	βασιλίδι	Queen	
328B	παρθένον ἀπείρανδρον	an untried virgin	
328B	κόρην ἀπειρόγαμον	an unmarried girl	
328B	Μαριάμ	Mary	
328B	εὗρες γὰρ χάριν παρὰ τῷ Θεῷ	you have found favor with God	
328C	Παρθένε	Virgin	
328C	εἰ μὴ βούλει	Even if you do not wish it	
328C	Ῥίζης Δαβιδικῆς βλάστημα τυγχάνω	I am a sprout of the root of David	
328C	καὶ ἔσται τὸ ὄνομά σου εὐλογημένον	your name shall be called blessed.6	
328D	Τέρψις καὶ διόλου γλυκασμός ἐστι τὰ ῥήματά σου, δεδοξασμένη	At all times your words are sweet and joyous, O blessed one	
329A	Ὑπὸ τὴν σὴν εὐσπλαγχνίαν καταφεύξεται πᾶν γένος ἀνθρώπων	All the races of men shall take refuge under your compassion.	
329A	πᾶσα γλῶσσα πηλίνη μακαρίσει σε	all tongues of clay shall bless you	
329A	λαληθήσεται τὸ ὄνομά σου ἐν πάσῃ γενεᾷ, καὶ γενεᾷ	your name shall be spoken from generation to generation	*cf.* Luke 1.50

329A	ὅτι διὰ [τοῦ] σοῦ Κύριος, τὸ φῶς τοῦ κόσμου, μέλλει τίκτεσθαι.	for through you, the Lord, the light of the world, is about to be born	
329A	Ἡλίκη τυγχάνουσα, καὶ ἐκ γῆς τὴν γέννησιν ἔχουσα	who am matter and drawn from the earth	
329A	ὑπὸ τῆς νοητῆς σελήνης βασταχθήσεται	be born by the spiritual moon	
329B	δεδοξασμένη	O blessed one	
329B	οὐρανὸς γὰρ μέλλεις γενέσθαι	You are about to become heaven	
329B	καὶ σκηνὴ Θεοῦ ἔμψυχος	a God-containing tabernacle	
329B	ναὸς θεοχώρητος,	a living temple of God	
329B	ἑπτὰ στερεωμάτων εὐρυχωρότερός τε καὶ ὑψηλότερος καὶ θαυμασιώτερος	wider and higher and more wondrous than the seven firmaments	
329B	Χριστιανῶν ἁπάντων γενήσῃ κοινὸν ἱλαστήριον	You shall become the common propitiation of all Christians	
329B	Κεχαριτωμένη· ὁ Κύριος μετὰ σοῦ· εὐλογημένη σὺ ἐν γυναιξί, καὶ εὐλογημένος ὁ καρπὸς τῆς κοιλίας σου.	"O full of grace, the Lord is with you, blessed are you among women, blessed is the fruit of your womb"	Luke 1.38
329C	Χαρακτῆρα φέρουσα βασιλικὸν, καὶ εἰς τὰ βασίλεια τῆς ἐμῆς Βηθλεὲμ τιθηνήσασα, καὶ εἰς ἅγια ἐκ παιδόθεν ἀμέμπτως διαπρέψασα· καὶ παρθένος λοιπὸν τυγχάνουσα,	I am of royal blood, and spent my earliest childhood in the royal house of Bethlehem, and my childhood I spent blamelessly in the temple; and being a virgin up to now,	
329C	πῶς ἐγὼ μήτηρ ἀκούσω τοῦ παιδός μου;	how can I be called the mother of my child?	
329C	ὡς ηὐδόκησεν	the holy one	
329D	«ὅτι ἐπέβλεψεν ἐπὶ τὴν ταπείνωσιν τῆς δούλης αὐτοῦ· ἰδοὺ γὰρ ἀπὸ τοῦ νῦν μακαριοῦσί με πᾶσαι αἱ γενεαί·»	"for he has looked upon the lowliness of his handmaiden; for behold from henceforth all generations shall call me blessed"	Luke 1.42
329D	καὶ πηλῷ διαλεγόμενος	[you] speak to one made of clay	

329D	«Ἰδοὺ ἡ δούλη Κυρίου, γένοιτό μοι κατὰ τὸ ῥῆμά σου.»	"Behold, the servant of the Lord, let it be to me according to your word"	Luke 1.38
332A	ἡ πανύμνητος καὶ μακαρία Παρθένος	The worthy of all praise blessed Virgin	
332A	Ἄσπιλόν	Undefiled	
332A	παρθένον ἀμόλυντον	an undefiled virgin	
332A	μητέρα παρ' ἐλπίδα καὶ οὐ παρθένον τυγχάνουσαν;	a mother contrary to expectation and not a virgin?	
332A	Μαρία	Mary	
332A	Ἄσπιλόν	undefiled	
332A	ἀμώμητον	pure	
332A	ὅτι ἐκ παιδόθεν ἐμίσησα τὸν ἀπὸ σαρκὸς ἐσπιλωμένον χιτῶνα, καὶ ἴχνος ἡδυπαθείας οὐκ ἔστιν ἐμοί.	From my childhood I have hated the spotted garment of the flesh, and no trace of enjoyment is in me.	
332B	Μαρία	Mary	
332C	Μαρία	Mary	
333A	Μαρία	Mary	
333A	ὅτι καθαρά εἰμι, καὶ ἄνδρα οὐ γινώσκω	I am pure, and have known no man	
333C	Θλίψεως ἡμέρα κατέλαβέ με, καὶ μέμψις ἐξ ὑποψίας ἐπῆλθέν μοι· καὶ ἐξέτασις μνήστορός μου κατεπείγει με· καὶ κυοφόρησις παιδός μου κατηγορεῖ με· καὶ	The day of affliction fell upon me, and blame and suspicion came upon me; and the scrutiny of my betrothed was placed firmly on me; and my	
	ὁ τὸ, Χαῖρε, μοὶ λέξας ἄγγελος τάχα ἀπεκρύβη· καὶ τί λοιπὸν λογίσομαι, οὐκ οἶδα.	pregnancy accused me, and the Angel who cried "Hail" is quickly hidden, and what else I may say I do not know.	
333C	σου τὸν τόκον τῆς πρὶν ἡγνισμένης νηδύος,	the roundness of your previously immaculate belly	
	τὴν ταπείνωσίν μου	my lowliness	
336A	«Χαῖρε, κεχαριτωμένη, ὁ Κύριος μετὰ σοῦ.»	"Hail Most Blessed the Lord is with you."	

171

336A	«Ὅτι Παρθένος ἐν γαστρὶ λήψεται, καὶ παιδίον ἡμῖν τεχθήσεται;»	"That a virgin shall conceive, and shall bear a child to us?"	*cf.* Isaiah 7.14
336B	Μαρία	Mary	
336B	Νῦν λέξω, Μαρία, ὅτι τοῖς ἴχνεσιν Εὔας σῆς μητρὸς ἐξηκολούθησας.	Now I will say, Mary, that you have followed the path of your mother Eve	
336B	Νῦν ἐπῆλθές μοι ὥς τίς ποτε ἀλλογενὴς καὶ ἑτερόφυλος, καὶ κατήγορος,	Now you attack me like a foreigner and a stranger and an accuser.	
336B	οὐχ ὡς βασιλίδι τινὶ διαλεγόμενος·	You do not converse with me like a queen	
336C	τὰ λεγόμενα καὶ καταπλήττει σου τὸν νοῦν τῆς μυστικῆς κυοφορίας τὸ παράδοξον μυστήριον.	The paradoxical nature of my childbearing astounds your mind.	
336D	«Ἰδοὺ ἡ παρθένος ἐν γαστρὶ ἕξει, καὶ τέξεται υἱόν, καὶ καλέσουσι τὸ ὄνομα αὐτοῦ Ἐμμανουήλ.»	"Behold, a virgin shall conceive and bring forth a son, and they shall call his name Emmanuel	Matthew 1.23
337A	Μαρία	Mary	
337A	«Μὴ φοβοῦ, Μαριάμ· εὗρες γὰρ χάριν παρὰ τῷ Θεῷ.»	"Fear not, Mariam, for you have found favor with God	Luke 1.30
337A	γυναῖκα ἐμήν	my wife	
337A	διὰ τὴν Δαυϊτικὴν συγγένειαν	in the lineage of David	
337B	«Ἰωσὴφ υἱὸς Δαβίδ, μὴ φοβηθῇς παραλαβεῖν Μαριὰμ τὴν γυναῖκά σου· τὸ γὰρ ἐν αὐτῇ γεννηθὲν, ἐκ Πνεύματός ἐστιν ἁγίου· τέξεται δὲ υἱόν, καὶ καλέσεις τὸ ὄνομα αὐτοῦ Ἰησοῦν.»	"Joseph, son of David, fear not to take Mary to you as a wife, for that which shall come of her, is of the Holy Spirit, and she shall produce a son and you shall call his name Jesus."	Matthew 1.20*ff.*"
337C	Μαρία	Mary	
At this point the Migne text ends. The following is La Piana's text on the basis of a mss.			

340A	Ὦ μεγάλης μοι καὶ μακαρίας ἡμέρας ταύτης, ὅτι ἐποίησέ μοι μεγαλεῖα ὁ δυνατὸς, καὶ ἅγιον τὸ ὄνομα αὐτοῦ· καὶ τὸ ἔλεος αὐτοῦ εἰς γενεὰν καὶ, τοῖς φοβουμένοις αὐτόν	O great and marvelous is this day to me. For the powerful one has done great things for me, and holy is his name. To those who fear him his mercy is from generation to generation	Luke 1.49*ff*

Chapter Sixteen

General Introduction to Germanos' Homilies on the Dormition

Germanos' homilies on the Dormition of the Theotokos are problematical. The Greek term κοίμησις, koimesis, with its long history might provide a more accurate term, but it proves as problematical as any other.[269] A full history of the Feast is provided by Brian J. Daley, S.J.[270] Father Daley also provides a translation of Germanos' homilies on the Dormition.[271] Xanthopoulos reports that the Emperor, Maurice (539-610),[272] fixed the date of the Dormition on August 15.[273]

The story of the Dormition does not come from the canonical scriptures principally but from the apocryphal *Transitus Mariae,* the earliest Greek document that is attributed to John the Evangelist.[274] Antoine Wenger

---

[269] See, *LSJ* 967-8 and *Lampe* 760
[270] *On the Dormition of Mary: Early Patristic Homilies.* Trans. and Introduction by Brian E. Daley, S.J. Crestwood, NY: St. Vladimir's Seminary Press, 1998. For a treatment of the earlier i.e. pre-Middle Byzantine development see: Stephen J. Shoemaker, *The Ancient Traditions of the Virgin Mary's Dormition and Assumption.* Oxford Early Christian Studies. Oxford: Oxford University Press, 2006, 9-77.
[271] Daley, *Dormition* 153-81.
[272] Maurice was emperor from August 14, 582, when he succeeded his father-in-law Tiberius II, until 602 when Pochas deposed him. He was executed in 610.
[273] *Hist. Eccl.* 17.28 also found in *PG* 147 292.
[274] See, Constantine von Tischendorf. *Apocalypses Apocryphae.* Leipzig, 1866, 95-112. or Justin Perkins and Constantine von Tischendorf. *Apocalypses Apocryphae Mosis, Esdrae, Pauli, Iohannis.* Hildesheim: G. Olms, 1966. Another useful volume is Simon Claude Mimouni. *Dormition et assomption de marie: histoire des traditions anciennes. théologie historique* Paris:

found another, slightly divergent, text that was published in 1955.[275] Both of these documents date from the late fifth to early sixth century and so would have been familiar in Germanos' time.[276]

It is important to realize that the period in which the Feast of the Dormition was developing in the Greek world was also the period in which the person of Christ was being debated in the Councils. Between the years of 381 and 553, the dates of the two Councils of Constantinople, devotion to Mary evolved.[277] The issue of the Mystery of Christ's person, divine and human, was worked out in this period. That formulation proclaimed by the Council of Chalcedon would inevitably require reflection on the role and person of Mary, or the Theotokos as she was proclaimed at the Council of Ephesus in 431.[278] By Germanos' time other implications of the proclamations of the Councils had to be worked out. Those issues of the wills of Christ (Monothelitism) and the issue of how much matter participated in the Incarnation (Iconoclasm) were immediate issues in which Germanos played central roles.[279]

> Germanos would have recognized this sequence of events as described in the Transitus Mariae: although not strictly a gospel of the Nativity notice may here be taken of the account of John the Theologian of the Falling Asleep (koimesis) of the Holy Mother of God or as it is more commonly called "the Passing of Mary" (transitus Mariae). It was originally written in Greek, but

---

Beauchesne, 1995. This volume was originally presented as the author's thesis (doctoral)—Ecole pratique des hautes études, Section des sciences religieuses, 1991. Includes bibliographical references.

[275] Antoine Wenger. *L'assomption de la t.s. vierge dans la tradition byzantine du vie au xe siècle; études et documents.* Paris,: Institut français d'études byzantines, 1955. 210-40. R as this is called can also be found in *Archives de l'Orient chrétien*, 5.
"Documents" (pp. [207-415) in Greek, with French translation, or in Latin. Bibliography: p.[5]-8.

[276] See, Daley, *Dormition* 9

[277] Daley, *Dormition* 11

[278] For a contemporary debate on the importance of the Council of Ephesus and the role of Mary and Marian devotion in the Byzantine world see, Bissera V Pentcheva. *Icons and Power: The Mother of God in Byzantium.* University Park, PA: The Pennsylvania State University Press, 2006. 12-16.

[279] See, Germanos' Life earlier in this dissertation.

appears also in Latin and several other languages. Two years, it seems, after the ascension of Jesus, Mary, who paid frequent visits to the, "Holy tomb of our Lord to burn incense and pray" was persecuted by the Jews and prayed her Son that He would take her from the earth. The archangel Gabriel brings an answer to her prayers and announces that after three days she shall go to the heavenly places to her Son, into true and everlasting life. Apostles from their graves or from their dioceses are summoned to her bedside at Bethlehem and relate how they were occupied when the summons reached them. Miracles of healing are wrought round the dying bed; and after the instantaneous transportation of Mary and the attendant apostles to Jerusalem, on the Lord's Day, amidst visions of angels Christ Himself appears and receives her soul to Himself. Her body is buried in Gethsemane and thereafter translated to Paradise. Judged by its contents which reveal an advanced stage of the worship of the Virgin and also of church ritual, the document cannot have been produced earlier than the end of the 4th or the beginning of the 5th century, and it has a place among the apocryphal documents condemned by the Gelasian Decree. By this time indeed it appears as if the writers of such documents assumed the most unrestricted license in imagining and embellishing the facts and situations regarding the gospel narrative.[280]

Another difficulty that arises with regard to the Dormition homilies of Germanos is how many of them are there? The first two homilies in *PG* 98 appear to be one. Several scholars of the last few decades have suggested that the first homily was divided so as to fit into the scheme of three homilies that would be read at the vigil of Marian Feasts.[281]

---

[280] "The Passing of Mary". 1939. *International Standard Bible Encyclopedia.* Ed. James Orr. Wm. B. Eerdmans Publishing Co. May 21, 2008.

[281] Martin Jugie "Les homélies de saint germain de constantinople sur la dormition de la sainte vierge." *Échos d' Orient* 16 (1913). 219-21; *La Mort et L'assomption de la sainte vierge, étude historico-doctrinale.* Città del Vaticano, 1944. 227 n.1; C. Chevalier, "Les trilogies homolétique dans l'élabortion des fetes mariales, 650-850." *Gregorianum* 18 (1937) 372-5; Luigi Carli. *La morte e l'assunzione di maria santissima nelle omelie greche*

The three homilies are designated:

Dormition #	Incipit:	*PG* 98	*BHG*
1	Ὁ χρεωστῶν	340A—348C	1119
2	Παυσάσθωσαν τῶν αἱρετικῶν	348C—359D	1135
3	Φήμη καλὴ καὶ ἀγαθὴ	360A—372D	1155

It also appears from looking at Ehrhard that it was late that the homilies were separated.[282]

In Ehrhard there are only two references to the second homily appearing separately. The first is in a twelfth century full year collection where it appears alone and without its end.[283] In the second attestation it appears along with the other two homilies in a sixteenth century half-year collection of homilies.[284] Ehrhard comments:

> Die zwei Reden des Germanos Ὁ χρεωστῶν and Παυσάσθωσαν werden hier (vie in anderen Hss) al seine Einheit behandelt, was sie ja auch sind. Der Schluß der letzteren steht auf dem Fol. 165ᵛ: ἀοράτῳ ἐνεργείᾳ τοῦ ὑπὸ σοῦ παρθενικῶς γεννηθέντος Χριστοῦ τοῦ θεοῦ ἡμῶν, ᾧ ἡ δόξα κτλ. = M. *(PG)* 98, 357.[285]

The earliest extant homily is from the seventh century and is by John of Thessalonica. It is a narration of the events leading up to Mary's departure from this life. John was bishop of Thessalonica during a part of the seventh century. He was clearly trying to introduce the feast into the local calendar as can be seen from the introduction to the homily.[286]

---

dei secoli vii, viii. Romae,: Officium libri catholici, 1941. 46*f.* and Mimouni, 168*f.* (all references from Daley, *Dormition 43*).

[282] Albert Ehrhard. "Überlieferung und Bestand der hagiographischen und homiletischen Literatur der griechischen Kirche von den Anfängen bis zum Ende des 16. Jahrhunderts". *Texte und Untersuchungen zur Geschichte der altchristlichen Literatur* ;. Leipzig,: J. C. Hinrichs, 1937.

[283] Ehrhard vol. I 167 Cod. Athen. 1027 m.s. Fol. 260ᵛ

[284] Ehrhard vol. II 101 Cod. Bodl. Barocc. 199 m.s. 10, 375 also see n. 2 98 of the same volumn.

[285] Ehrhard vol. II 117 n. 2.

[286] The Emperor Maurice (582-602) decreed that the Empire should celebrate the feast on August 15 of every year. For some reason Thessalonica seems to

A more complete list of the early versions of the Dormition narrative can be found in M. van Esbroeck's *Lex texts littéraires sur l'assomption avant le Xe siècle.* Daley points out that while van Esbroeck's chronological classification is the system followed by most scholars today, it is also "conjectural in some cases, . . .".[287] From this evidence and the lack of Germanos' usual flowery beginning one would be lead to accept the contention that Germanos' intended it to be part of the first homily and not a separate one. From the manuscript evidence in Ehrhard it would appear that the first homily enjoyed slightly more exposure than the second (third) one.

The texts that I have included of the homilies are from *PG* 98 following the divisions of Combefis that is found in *Novum auctarium* I, 1445-1456 and *PG* 98 340A-348C for the Ὁ χρεωστῶν. *PG* 98 348C-359D for the Παυσάσθωσαν τῶν αἱρετικῶν. And *PG* 98 360A-372D for the Φήμη καλὴ καὶ ἀγαθή.

What happened to Mary after her life on Earth has been a problematical question for many centuries. Despite the enormous amount of research and Pius XII's encyclical, *Munificentissimus Deus* questions still remain unanswered.[288]

Germanos' homilies are quite different from each other. The first (*PG* 340A—348C) and second (*PG* 348C—359D homilies do indeed appear to be one. Fr. Daley believes that they were separated so as to conform to the homilies of St. John of Damascus and Andrew of Crete.

> The scholarly sources that recognize only two homilies of Germanos I on the Dormition of Mary, as far as I can retrieve them now, are Johannes List, in his book *Studien zur Homiletik Germanos I. von Konstantinopel und seiner Zeit (*1939), and Hans-Georg Beck, *Kirche und theologische Literatur des Byzantinischen Reiches* (1959), p. 475. There may be others, too; but it's pretty obvious from the homilies themselves that they are originally two works, and have probably been divided

---

have been slow to adopt it. See, Brian E. Daley "At the Hour of Our Death": Mary's Dormition and Christian Dying in Late Patristic and Early Byzantine Literature. *Dumbarton Oaks Papers,* vol. 55. (2001). Fr. Daley also has a translation and commentary on this homily in *Dormition* 47-70

[287] Daley, *Mary's Dormition.* 72. n. 3.

[288] For a treatment of the last centuries efforts and especially those of Cothenet, Jugie, Wegner and Mimouni see: Shoemaker 9-25.

into three to make them "match" Andrew of Crete's and John of Damascus's.[289]

Germanos gives us an extended homily that is a theological reflection on the Dormition in the first two homilies in PG 98. The third homily is a narrative of the events surrounding the falling asleep of the Mother of God.

---

[289] Private email from Fr. Daley on August 29, 2009. I am grateful to Fr. Daley for always answering any questions I have on his book.

Chapter Seventeen

Introduction and Commentary
First Homily on the Dormition

The first homily can be divided into an introduction (340A-340C), a narration of the scene (340D-341A), and a theological reflection on the Dormition (341B-348C), there appears to be a short, hasty conclusion at the end of 348C.

Germanos begins by declaring that the role of a debtor is to attempt to adequately repay his debt. In the case of the work of Mary this is not possible. Germanos proposes to offer words in an attempt to repay his debt to her.

> He who is not able to provide exchange of deeds thinks fit to
> offer the gift of words to his advocate. Therefore, O Theotokos,
> I dare to praise you who have obtained marvels paradoxical
> gifts that cannot be explained. (340B)

Germanos only hope is to apply Mary's words at the Annunciation to himself: "Regard the lowliness of your servant" (340B) and to rely on her help:

> lift up the mouth of the humble one, and fill me who hunger
> eagerly to sing your praise with the good things of your
> prosperity, so that with my mind led by your assistance I may
> not hesitate to magnify you, Mistress. For you justly said that all
> generations of mankind blessed you—you who are not worthily
> magnified by anyone—you who always feel sympathy for the
> meager and rash poverty of mind of your encomiasts. (340B)

Germanos then introduces the two themes of this homily. "Shall I hymn the praises of your incarnate companionship with humanity, or shall I trumpet in the spirit the glory of your translation from sleep to life? Both are terrible, each is awesome." He then sets out his agenda: "So going on the discourse will take its subject concerning your triumphal songs/rites in narrative, but going forward, let it begin the hymn of the present topic, your honorable and glorious translation, O Mother of God." (340C).

Beginning in the next section (340D) Germanos develops the theme of Mary's life after her falling asleep and her roles both on earth and in heaven. It is clear that Germanos sees the two roles as connected intimately with one another. Mary's role on earth and her role in heaven are both tied to the Incarnation. It is due to the her role in the Incarnation that her role on earth and her person are so highly regarded by man and God. In a reference to the creation story Germanos narrates the fall of man and the discord it caused between humankind and angels and the restoration of that relationship at the time of the Nativity. He begins with a near quote of Prolog of John:

> "in the beginning" was the Word of God the Father (*cf.* Jn. 1.1), at once upon your delivery even the armies of the angels bent down from the heavens, hymning the God who was born from you, and shouting that glory was attributed in the highest places and they cried out that peace had arrived on earth (*cf.* Lk. 2.14). So no longer did they name enmity as a dividing wall between angels and men, heaven and earth, but a harmonious commonwealth and one antiphonal doxology from both angels and men, sent up to God one and trinity. (341A/B).

It is at this point that Germanos deals with the theological issue of the perichoresis of the Father and the Son and clearly weaves the Nicene-Constantinopolitan creed into his homily.

> "From the womb before the morning star I have begotten you." (Psalm 109.3 LXX) Oh sayings full of theology! If before being born from you, the Virgin Mother, this one was only-begotten Son of God, how does the Father say to him, "Today I have begotten you"? It is clear that "today" does not represent a new

beginning of the divinity of the Only-begotten, but declares his corporeal presence among men. (341B)

Germanos ties this together with the Incarnation and Mary in the next few words:

> But the "I have begotten you" reveals the divinely-originate and synergetic communion of the Holy Spirit in the Father. For since the Spirit is not alien to the Father, for by good will and sending of the Father he has come to dwell in you the Virgin and Mother, the Father makes his own the activity of the all-holy Spirit, whence the Father along with the Spirit making new the corporeal procession of the Son from you says, "Today I have begotten you." And this "From the womb before the morning star I begot you" relates to the same expression of faith, that also it reveals the preexisting essence of divinity in the Only-begotten shared with the coeternal essence of the Father, and his incarnate natural and non-imaginary entrance into humanity at the last times from you the Ever-virgin. (341C)

Continuing with these themes Germanos ties up the creation story in Genesis, the Creed and the Nativity narrative in Luke playing on the contrast of light/dark and day/night:

> For Scripture called "womb before the morning star" the generative procession of the Light which was before the heavens and appeared on earth: to show that before all visible and invisible creation the Only-begotten was born from the Father without beginning, Light was born from Light. (344A) And again [Scripture] called your belly "womb", to show also the habitation of the Only-begotten from your flesh; but "before the morning star" has declared the night then before the dawning—morning star, you who well represent the day. Since in the night you bore light for those who sat in darkness (cf. Luke 1.79), [Scripture] called "before the morning star" the hour of your childbirth. For it says, "Shepherds were in the same place outdoors and keeping watch at night." (Luke 2.8) Such was glory shown to the heavenly ones through you, O Theotokos.

> If it had not been new—the angels would not be singing "Glory in the highest," in praise of your ineffable childbearing had it already been glorified. What kind of illumination is this also of earthlings? Because through your blameless flesh man has been made a citizen of heaven, and shepherds associated with angels.

> (344B)The angels descending . . . lifted up to the high and glorified worthiness of God; that is, having learned of the generative relation without beginning of the Father towards the Son before the ages, and not a created consubstantiality.

Germanos returns to the theme of the Incarnation and the womb. To this he ties the role of Mary on earth and in heaven, and questions how Mary could suffer death only according to the flesh. Mary could not leave humankind orphaned:

> For when you were proved to be a God-containing heaven of the most high God, since your bosom [was] able to carry(ing) Him, and again you were called a spiritual earth because of the [God-]containing service of your flesh. Consequently it is easy to believe, that also when you dwelt in this world, you were always a dweller with God; translated from human [life], you never deserted those in the world. But we talk idly—those who are accustomed to venerate you faithfully—why have we not been found worthy to encounter you also in the body? Therefore we call thrice-blessed those spectators who have delighted in your sojourning, since they have obtained you the Mother of life as a companion for their life. (344C)

Germanos continues to develop the theme of Mary's role with humankind. She is viewed as protectoress and one who recognizes those who honor her. (344D/345A). Continuing along this line Germanos stacks up references to the Dormition of Mary and how she did not suffer dissolution of the body. (345C)

It develops the parallel between Jesus and Mary and the necessity that Mary's role in the Incarnation be that of Theotokos whose body is like any human beings. He compares the two graves and says:

You, as one who happens [to have] a body like ours, and because of this not being able to escape the encounter with the common death of mankind, in the same way as your Son and the God of all himself, so to speak, because of his humanity, [like] all of our race, "tasted" of a similar "death in the flesh"(Heb. 2.9): obviously glorifying, along with his own unique and life-creating burial, also the memorial of your life-receiving Dormition, so that the both [graves] received bodies not in appearance only, but did not at all cause corruption. (345D)

In both cases their bodies did not suffer corruptions. Jesus' because He was both God and man and Mary's because she provided the means for the Incarnation.

For it was not possible for you being a God-containing vessel to be destroyed by the dissolution of corpse-corrupting earth. For since he who emptied himself in you was God from the beginning and Life before the ages, and it was necessary for the Mother of Life to become a companion with Life, and to experience death simply as sleep, and through this translation arise as Mother of Life. (345A)

It is that relationship between a mother and her child that Germanos gives as a reason for her Dormition:

For just as a child seeks and desires its own mother, and a mother loves to spend time with her child, so also it suited you who have acquired a child-loving compassion for your Son and God to ascend to him; and also it undoubtedly befitted the God who has mother-loving affection for you to establish for you his companionship and fellowship. (348A)

There follows a short, transitional summary of Germanos' theological argument in which all of the preceding elements are mentioned. And then there is a abrupt end.

Chapter Eighteen

First Homily on the Dormition
of the Theotokos
Translation

ὁ χρεωστῶν

Of our father among the saints Germanos archbishop of Constantinople, first homily on the all-venerable dormition of the holy Theotokos.

[340A]

The debtor always praises his own benefactor. He who is being saved does not fail to recognize the protection of his own savior.

[340B]

He who is not able to provide exchange of deeds thinks fit to offer the gift of words to his advocate. Therefore, O Theotokos, I dare to praise you who have obtained marvels paradoxical gifts that cannot be explained. To you I also, speaking freely, employing your own sayings in exultation. Regard the lowliness of your servant, lift up the mouth of the humble one, and fill me who hunger eagerly to sing your praise with the good things of your prosperity, so that with my mind led by your assistance I may not hesitate to magnify you, Mistress. For you justly said that all generations of mankind blessed you (Luke. 1.48)—you who are not worthily magnified by anyone—you who always feel sympathy for the meager and rash poverty of mind of your encomiasts.

[340C]

What shall I say first, and what shall I keep for second? Shall I hymn the praises of your incarnate companionship with humanity, or shall I trumpet in the spirit the glory of your translation from sleep to life? Both are terrible, each is awesome. So going further the discourse will take its subject concerning your triumphs in narrative, but going forward, let it begin the hymn of the present topic, your honorable and glorious translation, O Mother of God.

[340D]

When you left earthly [places], you obviously entered the heavenly [places]; except earlier you were not lacking participation in the heavenly, nor did you depart from the earthly when you were transferred, since you were made more sublime than the ranks in heaven, and you were revealed as higher than the deeds of earth. For in truth, you beautified the heavens, and you illuminated the earth, O Theotokos. For when the heavens along with the generations of men were established, angels were assigned to tend their life; and to guide, and administer, and guard them, with an unchanging heart of faith towards God. "For he established," it is said, "bounds for the nations according to the number of the angels of God." (Deut. 32.8, Odes 2.8)

[341A]

And it is said, "The angel of the Lord will encircle those who fear [the Lord] and will protect them." (Psalm 33.8 LXX) But of the wretched men then living in error and idolatry, polluting the air with the smoke of sacrifices, for the rest even the angels ceased from companionship with men; for God took away his holy Spirit from them in return. But when you gave birth in the last times to him who "in the beginning' was the Word of God the Father (*cf.* John 1.1), at once upon your delivery even the armies of the angels bent down from the heavens, hymning the God who was born from you, and shouting that glory was attributed in the highest places and they cried out that peace had arrived on earth (*cf.* Luke 2.14). So no longer did they name enmity as a dividing wall between angels and men, heaven and earth (*cf.* Ephesians 2.14),

[341B]

but a harmonious commonwealth and one antiphonal doxology from both angels and men, sent up to God one and trinity. And the Father of his only-begotten Son, bearing witness to his physical birth from you without a father, proclaims to him, "Today I have begotten you." (Psalm 2.7 LXX) And again, "From the womb before the morning star I have begotten you." (Psalm 109.3 LXX) Oh sayings full of theology! If before being born from you, the Virgin Mother, this one was only-begotten Son of God, how does the Father say to him, "Today I have begotten you"? It is clear that "today" does not represent a new beginning of the divinity of the Only-begotten, but declares his corporeal presence among men.

[341C]

But the "I have begotten you" reveals the divinely-originate and synergetic communion of the Holy Spirit in the Father. For since the Spirit is not alien to the Father, for by good will and sending of the Father he has come to dwell in you the Virgin and Mother, the Father makes his own the activity of the all-holy Spirit, whence the Father along with the Spirit making new the corporeal procession of the Son from you says, "Today I have begotten you." And this "From the womb before the morning star I begot you" relates to the same expression of faith, that also it reveals the preexisting essence of divinity in the Only-begotten shared with the coeternal essence of the Father, and his incarnate natural and non-imaginary entrance into humanity at the last times from you the Ever-virgin.

[341D]

For Scripture called "womb before the morning star" the generative procession of the Light which was before the heavens and appeared on earth: to show that before all visible and invisible creation the Only-begotten was born from the Father without beginning, Light was born from Light.

[344A]

And again [Scripture] called your belly "womb", to show also the habitation of the Only-begotten from your flesh; but "before the morning star" has declared the night then before the dawning—morning star, you who well represent the day. Since in the night you bore light for those who sat in darkness (*cf.* Luke 1.79), [Scripture] called "before the morning star" the hour of your childbirth. For it says, "Shepherds were in the same place outdoors and keeping watch at night." (Luke 2.8) Such was the glory shown to the heavenly ones through you, O Theotokos. If it had not been new—the angels would not be singing "Glory in the highest," in praise of your ineffable childbearing, had it already been glorified. What kind of illumination is this also of earthlings? Because through your blameless flesh man has been made a citizen of heaven, and shepherds associated with angels.

[344B]

The angels descending . . . lifted up to the high and glorified worthiness of God; that is, having learned of the generative relation without beginning of the Father towards the Son before the ages, and not a created consubstantiality.

So since, O all-holy Mother of God, heaven, and what is more [the] earth, through you was brought into a place of refuge, how is it acceptable for you to leave mankind orphaned of the sight of you at your translation? Far from us be it to think this! For as when you lived in this world, you were not a stranger to heavenly conversations, neither when you have been transferred have you alienated from mankind your spiritual counsel.

[344C]

For when you were proved to be a God-containing heaven of the most high God, since your bosom [was] able to carry Him, and again you were called a spiritual earth because of the [God-]containing service of your flesh. Consequently it is easy to believe, that also when you dwelt in this world, you were always a dweller with God; translated from human [life], you never deserted those in the world. But we talk idly—those who are accustomed to venerate you faithfully—why have we not been found worthy to encounter you also in the body? Therefore we call thrice-blessed those spectators who have delighted in your sojourning, since they have obtained you the Mother of life as a companion for their life.

[344D]

Otherwise when you walk around in the body with us, so also the eyes of our souls are guided to look upon you daily.

For also, as you kept fellowship in the flesh with our ancestors, likewise also with us you dwell in the spirit. And your great oversight for us characterizes your companionship with us. And we all hear your voice, and the voice of all [comes] to your ears of hearing, and being known by you through your support, we recognize

[345A]

always your protective support. For there is no barrier—I mean not even due to the separation of the soul and body—for you recognize your servants. For you did not abandon those whom you saved, you [did not] leave those whom you gathered together; because your spirit lives always, and your flesh did not endure the corruption of the grave. You oversee all, O Mother of God, and your oversight is upon all, so that even if our eyes do not have the power to see you, all-holy one, you love to dwell in the midst of all, revealing yourself especially to those who are worthy of you. For the flesh does not hinder the power and activity of your spirit, just as wherever it wishes your spirit blows, since it is pure and immaterial: incorrupt and unstained, and a spirit which dwells together with the Holy Spirit, and the chosen one of the only-begotten divinity.

[345B]

You, as it is written, [are] "in beauty" (Cant 2.3 LXX) and your virginal body, altogether holy, altogether pure, altogether the residence of God; so because of this [it is] separated and alien from earthly dissolution. While remaining human it is changed to the sublime life of incorruptibility. This is safe and supremely glorious, ending in life and unsleeping; as it was not possible for this to be controlled by death-dealing confinement, being a God-receiving vessel, and a living temple of the all-holy divinity of the Only-begotten One. Because of these things, we trust that you, O Theotokos, will return home with us.

For truly, truly, and again I will say with thanksgiving: you were not separated from [us] the Christian family even when you departed. You were not made distant, O life of shared imperishability,

[345C]

from this perishing world, but you draw near to those who call upon you. You are found by those who seek you in faith. [All] these things are [indications] of the energy of life—of ever-blowing spirit—and sure visions of the body which does not flow away. For how could dissolution of the body to earth and dust occur in you who from the corruption of death ransomed mankind through the incarnation of your Son? You departed from the earthly ones to show the mystery confirmed of his awesome assumption of humanity, so that when you had endured the exile from temporary [things], the God born from you would be believed to have come forth also a perfect man, the Son of the true Mother, subject to the laws of natural necessities, by the command of a divine decree,

[345D]

and by the order of biological time. You, as one who happens [to have] a body like ours, and because of this is not able to escape the encounter with the common death of mankind, in the same way as your Son and the God of all himself, so to speak, because of his humanity, [like] all of our race, "tasted" of a similar "death in the flesh" (Heb. 2.9): obviously glorifying, along with his own unique and life-creating burial, also the memorial of your life-receiving dormition, so that both [graves] received bodies not in appearance only, but did not at all cause corruption.

[348A]

For it was not possible for you being a God-containing vessel to be destroyed by the dissolution of corpse-corrupting earth. For since he who emptied himself in you was God from the beginning and Life before the ages, it also was necessary for the Mother of Life to become a companion with Life, and to experience death simply as sleep, and through this translation arise as Mother of Life. For just as a child seeks and desires its own mother, and a mother loves to spend time with her child, so also it suited you who have acquired a child-loving compassion for your Son and God to ascend to him; and also it undoubtedly befitted the God who has mother-loving affection for you to establish for you his companionship and fellowship.

[348B]

In this manner having endured the departure from this passing life, you have moved to the imperishable haunts of the eternal ones, where God dwells, with whom you also being a companion, O Theotokos, do not separate yourself from the activity of this [world]. For you have become a corporeal house of rest for him, O Theotokos, and you are called the very place of repose by your translation, all-praised one. "For this is my rest," [Scripture] says, "unto the age of the age;" (Psalm 131.14 LXX) that is, the flesh put on by him from you, O Theotokos—with which we believe that Christ has appeared not only for this present age, but also will be revealed in the coming age, with such flesh from you, coming to judge the living and the dead. So since you are his eternal resting-place, he took you to himself free from corruption,

[348C]

wishing to have you nearby, as one might say, [with] your conversation and compassion. Therefore also whatever you seek from him, he gives with a child's affection, and whatever you seek from him, he fulfills with the power of God: who is blessed unto the ages.

Amen.

Chapter Nineteen

References to Mary in the First Homily
on the Dormition of the Theotokos by
Germanos, Patriarch of Constantinople
(715-730)

PG 98 Location	Greek	English	
Germanos begins this homily with proclaiming his debt. He also makes it clear that neither he nor any other encomiast is able to adequately give thanks or praise to the Theotokos. In the course of doing this he alludes to Mary's song at the Annunciation (Lk 1.46—55).			
340B	Θεοτόκε	O Theotokos	
340B	τὰ τῶν παραδόξων κεκτημένη θαυμάσια	you who have obtained marvels paradoxical gifts	
340B	τῆς ἐπιτυχίας	your prosperity	
340B	ἵνα σοῦ τῇ ἀντιλήψει τὸν νοῦν ποδηγούμενος	with my mind led by your assistance	
340B	Δέσποινα	Mistress	
340B	μακαρίζειν σε πάσας τὰς τῶν ἀνθρώπων γενεάς	all generations of mankind blessed you	
340B	τὴν μὴ παρ' οὐδενὸς ἀξίως μεγαλυνομένην	you who are not worthily magnified by anyone	
340B	σέ, τὴν συμπαθοῦσαν ἀεί, τῇ στενῇ τῶν ἐγκωμιαστῶν σου καὶ προπετεῖ πτωχονοίᾳ.	you who always feel sympathy for the meager and rash poverty of mind of your encomiasts	

Gregory E. Roth

Germanos introduces one of the constant themes in this homily that of Mary's
"incarnate companionship with humanity". From this he will develop, in part, the
theme of Mary's continued presence with Christians.
A second theme that is introduced here is the "Falling Asleep" of Mary. A theme that
will be linked with the Incarnation, Mary's role as Mediatrix and the death of humans.

340C	Τῆς ἐνσάρκου σου μετὰ ἀνθρώπων συναναστροφῆς	your incarnate companionship with humanity	
340C	τῆς ζωοκοιμήτου σου κατὰ πνεῦμα μεταστάσεως τὴν δόξαν	the glory of your translation from sleep to life	
340C	τῆς τιμίας καὶ ἐνδόξου σου, Θεομῆτορ, μεταστάσεως,	your honorable and glorious translation, O Mother of God.	
340C	Θεομῆτορ	Mother of God	

Germanos carefully paints the character of Mary as being both heavenly and earthly (in
the best possible sense). Heaven and earth are not in opposition to each other. Mary is
seen as one who: "beautified the heavens, and . . . illuminated the earth, O Theotokos."
Also Mary is "made more sublime than the ranks in heaven, and [is] revealed as higher
than the deeds of earth." Following Deut 32.8 and Odes 2.8 Germanos introduces the
role of the Angels and their relationship to human kind. In doing this he creates the
image of how creation was before the Fall.

340D	Θεοτόκε	O Theotokos	

Germanos begins his theological reflection on the perichoresis of the Holy Trinity
principally in this section and through 344A. Especially in 341D he seems to be
making a reference to the Nicean-Constantinopolitan Creed when he develops the
theme of light and applying Ps. 109.3 "From the womb before the morning star I begot
you." Also of importance in these sections is that the relationship of angels and human
beings is restored at the Nativity: "a harmonious commonwealth and one antiphonal
doxology from both angels and men, sent up to God one and trinity."

341B	τῆς Παρθένου Μητρὸς	the Virgin Mother	
341C	τῇ Παρθένῳ καὶ Μητρὶ	the Virgin and Mother	
341C	τῆς Ἀειπαρθένου	the Ever-virgin	
344A	καὶ γαστέρα πάλιν, τὴν σὴν ἐσήμανε κοιλίαν, τοῦ δεῖξαι καὶ τὴν σαρκικὴν ἐκ σοῦ τοῦ Μονογενοῦς ἐπιδημίαν	And again [Scripture] called your belly "womb", to show also the habitation of the Only-begotten from your flesh	
344A	τὴν ἡμέραν καλῶς ὑποτιθεμένη	you who well represent the day	

196

344A	Τοιαύτη ἡ προστεθεῖσα διὰ σοῦ τοῖς ἐπουρανίοις δόξα, Θεοτόκε	Such was glory shown to the heavenly ones through you, O Theotokos	
344A	διὰ τῆς σῆς ἀμώμου σαρκὸς	through your blameless flesh	

Germanos returns to the earlier theme of angels and man and Mary (341B & C) as well as the Incarnation.

344B	παναγία Θεομῆτορ	O all-holy Mother of God	
344B	διὰ σοῦ κατεκομίσθη	through you was brought into a place of refuge	

Germanos employs comparison and contrast to develop this section in which he returns to his argument that Mary as a consequence of her participation in the Incarnation has a special relationship to creation and to divine and human life. He also calls her "Mother of Life," a term that is used in the Dormition hymns of the Orthodox Church. Perniola mentions θεοχώρητος among the title that justify Mary's power. 119.

344C	ἐπειδὴ καὶ οὐρανὸς θεοχώρητος ἀνεδείχθης τοῦ ὑψίστου Θεοῦ	when you were proved to be a God-containing heaven of the most high God	
344C	διὰ τὸν χωρητικὸν κόλπον σου πρὸς αὐτοῦ βασταγμοῦ	since your bosom [was] able to carry Him	
344C	γῆ πάλιν αὐτῷ πνευματική	a spiritual earth	

Horvath points out that the same word σύνοικος is used for Mary's dwellings with both God and Man. 290, cf. 356A

344C	σύνοικος ἦσθα διὰ παντὸς τοῦ Θεοῦ	you were always a dweller with God	
344C	μετατεθεῖσα τῶν ἀνθρωπίνων, οὐκ ἐγκατέλιπάς ποτε τοὺς ἐν τῷ κόσμῳ	translated from human [life], you never deserted those in the world	
344C	τὴν Μητέρα τῆς ζωῆς	the Mother of life	

Important to Germanos' theme of Mary as Mediatrix is that she has formed through her actions in the Incarnation a fellowship with both heaven and earth. That fellowship with earth extends to members of the Christian community, the Church, and it is because of that fellowship that Christians can take heart in the face of the human condition and especially death.
"And your great oversight for us characterizes your companionship with us. And we all hear your voice, and the voice of all [comes] to your ears of hearing, and being known by you through your support, we recognize always your protective support. For there is no barrier—I mean not even due to the separation of the soul and body—for you recognize your servants" 344D/345A.

344D 345A	Καὶ τῆς φωνῆς σου πάντες ἀκούομεν· καὶ ἡ φωνὴ τῶν ὅλων πρὸς τὰ σὰ τῆς ἀκροάσεως ὦτα· καὶ γινωσκόμενοι παρὰ σοῦ διὰ τῆς ἀντιλήψεως, ἐπιγινώσκομέν σου προστατικὴν ἀεὶ τὴν ἀντίληψιν	we all hear your voice, and the voice of all [comes] to your ears of hearing, and being known by you through your support, we recognize always your protective support.	
345A	Οὐ γὰρ ἀφῆκας, οὓς διέσωσας· κατέλιπας	you did not abandon those whom you saved	

In 345A Germanos states: " . . . and your flesh did not endure the corruption of the grave." Germanos clearly believes that Mary did not suffer corruption in the grave. Additionally Mary's flesh and spirit are not opposed to each other: "For the flesh does not hinder the power and activity of your spirit, just as wherever it wishes your spirit blows, since it is pure and immaterial; incorrupt and unstained, and a spirit which dwells together with the Holy Spirit, and the chosen one of the only-begotten divinity."

345A	κατέλιπας, οὓς συνήγαγες	you [did not] leave those whom you gathered together	
345A	ὅτι ζῇ σου τὸ πνεῦμα διὰ παντός, καὶ ἡ σὰρξ διαφθορὰν οὐχ ὑπέμεινε ταφῆς	your spirit lives always, and your flesh did not endure the corruption of the grave	
345A	Πάντας ἐπισκέπτῃ	You oversee all	
345A	Θεομῆτορ	O Mother of God	
345A	καὶ ἡ ἐπισκοπή σου, . . . ἐπὶ πάντας	your oversight is upon all	
345A	παναγία	all-holy one	
345A	ἐν μέσῳ σὺ τῶν ἁπάντων ἐμφιλοχωρεῖς	you love to dwell in the midst of all	
345A	ἐμφανίζουσα τοῖς ἀξίοις σου διαφόρως ἑαυτήν	revealing yourself especially to those who are worthy of you	
345A	Ἡ γὰρ σὰρξ οὐκ ἐμποδίζει τῇ δυνάμει καὶ ἐνεργείᾳ τοῦ πνεύματός σου· ὅτιπερ ὅπου θέλει πνεῖ σου τὸ πνεῦμα, ἐπειδὴ καθαρὸν τοῦτο καὶ ἄϋλον· ἄφθαρτον καὶ ἀκηλίδωτον, καὶ τοῦ Πνεύματος τοῦ ἁγίου συνδιαιτικὸν πνεῦμα, καὶ τῆς Μονογενοῦς θεότητος ἐκλεκτόν.	For the flesh does not hinder the power and activity of your spirit, just as wherever it wishes your spirit blows, since it is pure and immaterial; incorrupt and unstained, and a spirit which dwells together with the Holy Spirit, and the chosen one of the only-begotten divinity	

Germanos again makes clear that Mary's body did not suffer any corruption. Mary's companionship with humans is also underlined once again. Perniola references this passage in three different places. 149 fnt 14, 150 fnt 20, 155 fnt 31 Also see 345C also references in Perniola four times 148 fnt 7, 151 fnt 30, 154 fnt 31 and with 345D 154 fnt 29.

345B	Σὺ, κατὰ τὸ γεγραμμένον, «ἐν καλλονῇ·»	You, as it is written, [are] "in beauty"	
345B	τὸ σῶμά σου τὸ παρθενικόν, ὅλον ἅγιον, ὅλον ἁγνόν, ὅλον Θεοῦ κατοικητήριον	your virginal body, altogether holy, altogether pure, altogether the residence of God	
345B	ὡς ἐκ τούτου λοιπὸν καὶ ἀλλότριον χοϊκῆς ἀναλύσεως	[it is] separated and alien from earthly dissolution	
345B	Ἐναλλαγὲν μὲν ὡς ἀνθρώπινον πρὸς ἄκραν ἀφθαρσίας ζωήν	While remaining human it is changed to the sublime life of incorruptibility	
345B	καθ' ὅτιπερ οὐδὲ ἦν δυνατὸν παρὰ νεκροποιοῦ συνκλεισμοῦ τοῦτο κρατηθῆναι	as it was not possible for this to be controlled by death-dealing confinement	
345B	ὡς σκεῦος ὑπάρχον θεηδόχον	being a God-receiving vessel	
345B	καὶ ἔμψυχος ναὸς τῆς τοῦ Μονογενοῦς παναγίας θεότητος	a living temple of the all-holy divinity of the Only-begotten One	
345B	Θεοτόκε	O Theotokos	
345B	οὐκ ἐχωρίσθης κἂν μετέστης τοῦ Χριστιανικοῦ γένους	you were not separated even if you departed from the Christian family	
345B	συναφθαρσίας ζωή	O life of shared imperishability	
345C	ἀλλ' ἐγγίζεις τοῖς ἐπικαλουμένοις σε	you draw near to those who call upon you	
345C	Εὑρίσκῃ τοῖς πιστῶς ἐκζητοῦσί σε	You are found by those who seek you in faith	
345C	ἅτινα ζωῆς εἰσιν ἐνεργείας πνεύματος ἀειπνόου, σώματος ἀδιαρεύστου παραστατικὰ θεωρήματα	[All] these things which are [indications] of the energy of life, of ever-blowing spirit, and [are] sure visions of the body which does not flow away.	

In 345C/D Germanos summarizes his theological position with regard to Mary, the Incarnation and the Dormition. Also mentioned in Perniola 154 fnt 29.

| 345C/D | Πῶς γὰρ εἶχε διάλυσις σαρκὸς πρὸς χοῦν καὶ κόνιν ἀνθυποστρέψαι σε, τὴν ἀπὸ θανάτου καταφθορᾶς, τὸν ἄνθρωπον, διὰ τῆς τοῦ Υἱοῦ σου λυτρωσαμένην σαρκώσεως; Μετέστης γοῦν τῶν ἐπιγείων, τοῦ δειχθῆναι τὸ τῆς φρικτῆς ἐνανθρωπήσεως βεβαιούμενον ἀφαντάστως μυστήριον· ἵνα σοῦ τὴν ἐκδημίαν τῶν προσκαίρων ὑπομεμενηκυίας, ὁ ἐκ σοῦ γεννηθεὶς Θεὸς, πιστευθῇ καὶ τέλειος προελθεῖν ἄνθρωπος, ἐξ ἀψευδοῦς Μητρὸς Υἱὸς, ὑποκειμένης νόμοις φυσικῶν ἀναγκασμάτων, ὅρου θείου κελεύσματι, καὶ χρόνου βιωτικοῦ παρακελεύσει· | For how could dissolution of the body to earth and dust occur in you who from the corruption of death ransomed mankind through the incarnation of your Son? You departed from the earthly ones to show the mystery confirmed of his awesome assumption of humanity, so that when you had endured the exile from temporary [things], the God born from you would be believed to have come forth also a perfect man, the Son of the true Mother, subject to the lows of natural necessities, by the command of a divine decree, and by the order of biological time | |

At this point Daley expresses the view that Germanos expresses the main point of this homily. *cf* fn 7, 167

| 345D | τῆς ὡς μιᾶς τῶν καθ᾽ ἡμᾶς τυγχανούσης σωμάτων | one who happens [to have] a body like ours | |

| 345D | καὶ διὰ τοῦτο μὴ τοῦ κοινοῦ τῶν ἀνθρώπων θανάτου δυνηθείσης ἐκφυγεῖν τὸ συνάντημα | and because of this not being able to escape the encounter with the common death of mankind | |

Here Germanos compares the two burials: one of Jesus and one of Mary

| 345D | καὶ τὸ σὸν τῆς κοιμήσεως ζωοπαράδεκτον μνῆμα· ὥστε ἀμφοτέρων σώματα μὲν ἀφαντάστως ὑπο—δεξαμένων, διαφθορὰν δὲ μηδαμῶς ἐνεργησάντων | the memorial of your life-receiving dormition, so that the both [graves] received bodies not in appearance only, but did not at all cause corruption. | |

Germanos develops the theme of the Mother/Child relationship of Jesus and Mary as a means of understanding the power of Mary and Mediatrix. Horvath mentions this title under Motherhood 286. Perniola references 348A three times: 149 ftn 22, 152 ftn 9 (Incorrectly placed in Dorm II) and 152 ftn 22.

348A	θεοχώρητον . . . ἀγγεῖον	God-containing vessel	
348A	Μητέρα τῆς Ζωῆς	Mother of Life	
348A	σύνοικον ἔδει τῆς Ζωῆς	companion with Life	
348A	καθάπερ ὕπνον τὴν κοίμησιν ὑπολαβεῖν	to experience death simply as sleep	
348A	ὡς ἐγρήγορσιν ὑποστῆναι τὴν μετάστασιν ὡς Μητέρα τῆς Ζωῆς	through this translation arise as Mother of Life	
348A	φιλότεκνα σπλάγχνα	child-loving compassion	
348B	συνδιάγωγος	companion	
348B	Θεοτόκε	O Theotokos	
348B	οὐκ ἀποχωρίζῃ τῆς τούτου συναναστροφῆς	do not separate yourself from the activity of this [world].	
348B	Οἶκος γὰρ αὐτῷ καταπαύσεως σὺ γέγονας σωματικὸς	a corporeal house of rest for him	
348B	Θεοτόκε	O Theotokos	
348B	καὶ τόπος ἀναπαύσεως αὐτὸς χρηματίζει μεταστάσει	you are called the very place of repose by your translation	
348B	πανύμνητε	all-praised one	
348B	«Αὕτη γὰρ, φησὶν, ἡ κατάπαυσίς μου εἰς αἰῶνα αἰῶνος·»	For this is my rest," [Scripture] says, "unto the age of the age;"	Psalm 131.14 LXX
348B	Ἡ ἐκ σοῦ περιβληθεῖσα τούτῳ, Θεοτόκε, σάρξ	the flesh put on by him from you, O Theotokos	
348B	ὡς αἰωνίας σου τούτῳ καταπαύσεως οὔσης	his eternal resting-place	
348B	ἀδιάφθορον	free from corruption	

At this point Combéfis' text in Migne breaks off and begins a second homily. Daley and others contend that this is not the end of this homily and that the second homily in Migne should be considered to be the proper ending of this homily: an opinion with which I agree.

Chapter Twenty

Second Homily
on the Dormition of the Theotokos
Introduction and Commentary

Dormition II (according to Combéfis) continues with a reference to those who oppose the veneration of Mary. It is not clear from the text to whom Germanos is referring as "the ignorant and thunderstruck speeches of the heretics . . .! What is clear is that Germanos considers it not only correct but necessary for Christians to praise Mary because of her childbirth. (348D). He then begins a short meditation comparing Mary and Eve. This meditation begins with the phrase: "Therefore your aid is powerful for salvation, O Theotokos, even needing no other advocate with God." In the context this should be considered to be an hyperbole. Germanos' comparison of Mary and Eve is interesting. Mary frees her ancestor from reproach and Germanos believes that Eve too is redeemed. The comparison of Mary and Eve is a device to illuminate Mary and her role in the Incarnation.

> For you are the mother of the true Life. You leaven the new creation of Adam. You free Eve from reproach. She is the mother of earth; you are the mother of light. Her womb [is the source] of destruction; your belly [is the source] of imperishability. She is the dwelling-place of death; you are the removal from death. She brings eyelids down to earth; you are the unsleeping glory of wakeful eyes. Her children are grief; but your Son is universal joy. (349A) She, as being earth, passed into earth; but you bore Life for us, and passed over to life, and obtained the power to mediate life to mankind, even after death. (349B)

Mary's falling asleep is once again tied to her role in the Incarnation. And since she is not dead because of her Son's love and respect for her, she is also a powerful source of help for his Body, the Christian people. Mary's role in aiding human beings in a spiritual life is illustrated in what could be a litany ending with "if not through you." At the end of each of these a different epithet is given for Mary. She is called: all-holy [lady], Theotokos, Virgin Mother, Mother of God, and Theochoretos (God-containing door). Mary's status as the Mother of God is once again given as the reason for her power as an intercessor. (352A) Mary turns "back the just threats and the verdict of deserved punishment, loving greatly the people who are called by the name of your Son." (352B) Mary is a "vision beyond the understanding of angels," she is "the support of the nation of Christians." Germanos, once again, returns to the difficulty of adequately lauding Mary in a confused section that seems to be missing some text. Germanos continues his praises of Mary's role as a Mediatrix through 353A.

Germanos returns to several of his earlier themes which celebrate her role in the Incarnation, the establishment of Christ's Body, the Church and the nations. Then he returns to the Dormition and its relationship to the Christian people. Germanos draws out the analogy of life and breath and intercession glossing Lamentations 4.20 LXX: "For we are not as attracted by breathing of the air as we are drawn by the shelter of my [your] name, so that in Christ and in you is fulfilled what is written: "You are the breath of our nostrils; in your shelter and your breath we will live." For Germanos the parallels between Mary and Jesus ever return. (356B)

In 356C Germanos mentions icons: "The material painting [color] of your images [icons], Mother of God, illuminates the giving of your gifts to us." Germanos links icons with the Incarnation: "Because of this man is blessed even if he is a sinner, since he has been found to have you as a relative in essence, and through you he is a partaker of the divine nature."

Germanos declares:

> Away with death for you, O Theotokos, because you have brought life to mankind! Away with the tomb for you, since you became the divine foundation of an impregnable fortress! Away with earth poured over you; for you are the re-fashioning, because you have been called Mistress of those who have perished in the substance of clay.

Just as there is a parallel between Mary and Jesus, so there is also one between Mary and the Christian people. While this does not extend to the same level as that between Mary and Jesus, it does assure humans that Mary has not abandoned them by her translation:

> so also we believe that we will see you going with us as a leader even after our departure from the body. For it is not such a pain for the soul, when it is drawn out of the flesh, as it is more painful to be deprived of you, all-pure one. For this reason it is written, "Even if my body sleeps, my heart wakes" (Cant. 5.2 LXX).

Germanos makes reference to the narrative of the Dormition with the Apostles in 357B/C. Germanos seems to be at pains to underline the truth of the human nature of Mary and the consequence of her human nature:

> And even though you have received the inevitability of death due to your human nature, your eye which guards us does not nod nor will it sleep (Ps. 120.4 LXX).

> For your translation does not lack witness, nor is your dormition a deception. Heaven tells the glory (Ps. 19.1 LXX) of those who ran together for you then. (357B)

This time Germanos provides us with a conclusion in which he reiterates the difficulty mentioned at the beginning of adequately hymning the Virgin Mary and adds that she has these honors because she has fulfilled the role of Theotokos:

> so neither is anyone sufficient to magnify your sublimity with voices of praise. You have by yourself your own hymn, because you were shown to be Theotokos. For not even because this has been heard by our ears only from Scriptural narrative, nor again because our fathers reported this to us by completely true tradition (Ps. 43.2 LXX), have you fulfilled the title of Theotokos; but because the deed which you have done among us, properly and truly, without tongue-grace and with orthodox [faith], validates

you as Theotokos by the very facts. And for the sake of this, it was truly fitting that your God-receiving body should not be shut in by deathly corruption, but that the tomb received its own mixture as human, and with a living conclusion of your own life transferring to the heavenly places. For the showing of your flesh is empty, but the finding of your spirit is inseparable from the companionship with mankind, by the invisible operation of Christ our God who was virginally born from you—to whom be glory unto the ages. Amen. (357C/D).

Chapter Twenty-One

Second Homily
on the Dormition of the Theotokos
Translation

Παυσάσθωσαν τῶν αἱρετικῶν

Of the same, second discourse on the Dormition of our most holy Lady the Theotokos and ever-virgin Mary.

[348D]

Let the ignorant and thunderstruck speeches of the heretics cease! Let their unrighteous lips be sealed! "Let all who seek you rejoice and be glad," O Theotokos, "and let them say always: 'Magnified be the Lord,' and those who love [you]" (Ps. 39.17 LXX) magnify your name as is needful, because "the mouth" of Christians "will meditate on your righteousness" (Ps. 34.28 LXX) and your virginity; all day long [they will meditate on] the praise of the holiness of your childbirth. "The poor saw" through you "the wealth of the goodness of God" (Ps. 68.33 LXX; Rom. 2.4). They saw and they said, "The earth is full of the mercy of the Lord." The sinners "have sought God out" through you

[349A]

"and they have been saved" (Ps. 33.3 LXX). They themselves said, "If the Lord had not helped us"—he who was incarnate of a virgin—"in a little he would have settled" in the all-devouring Hades of death, the sinking "of our souls" (Ps. 94.17 LXX). Therefore your aid is powerful for salvation, O Theotokos, even needing no other advocate with God. For you are the mother of the true Life. You leaven the new creation of Adam. You free Eve from reproach. She is the mother of earth; you are the mother of light. Her womb [is the source] of destruction; your belly [is the source] of imperishability. She is the dwelling-place of death; you are the removal from death. She brings eyelids down to earth; you are the unsleeping glory of wakeful eyes (*cf.* Ps. 120.4 LXX and later 357B). Her children are grief; but your Son is universal joy.

[349B]

She, as being earth, passed into earth; but you bore Life for us, and passed over to life, and obtained the power to mediate life to mankind, even after death. "There is no end of your succor" nor is there any danger, so to speak, nor should we humans perceive any when your transfer in living sleep comes into human [awareness], because your advocacy is living, and your intercession is life, and your protection is ceaseless. For if you were not guiding, no one would be made fully spiritual; no one would be worshipping God in spirit (John 4.24). For then is a man spiritual, when you, O Theotokos, became the dwelling-place of the Holy Spirit. No one is filled with divine knowledge, if not through you, all-holy [lady]. No one is saved, if not through you, Theotokos. No one is free from dangers, if not through you, Virgin Mother. No one is redeemed, if not through you, Mother of God.

[349C]

No one receives the gift of mercy, if not through you, Theochoretos. For who among sinners can prevail to such an extent? Who among those not made upright can speak so strongly in his defense? For everyone who is sometimes able to assist,

[352A]

being wary of the cutting-down of the fig tree in the parable (Luke 13.6*ff.*), deferred sending up his supplication to God on our behalf; lest if rejection was given because of the fruitlessness of the promise, the answer seem unacceptable. But you, having a mother's power with God, accomplish succor in surpassing degree even for those extremely sinful. For it is not possible for your voice ever to be disregarded, since God is obedient to you in every way and for every reason and in every situation, as you are his true and pure Mother. Therefore he who suffers tribulation takes blessed refuge with you; he who is sick, clings to you; he who wages war, takes you as armor against his enemies. You repel "spirit and anger and tribulation, dispatched by evil angels" (Ps. 77.49 LXX).

[352B]

You turn back just threats and the verdict of deserved punishment, loving greatly the people who are called by the name of your Son. Therefore your Christian people examining their own [affairs], delegate you to bring their petitions to God with confident speech. They unhesitatingly make bold to entreat you, all-holy Lady, because of [their] experience and the multitude of your bounties towards us, and to constrain you often in supplications. In return who will not bless you (*cf.* Luke 1.48)? You are a vision beyond the understanding of the angels. You are the surpassingly strange good fortune of mankind. You are the support of the nation of Christians. You are the refuge importuned by sinners. You are carried from hour to hour in the mouth of Christians. For if one is merely called Christian, if he even strikes his foot against a stone (Ps. 90.12 LXX), he calls upon your name for help.

[352C]

Therefore anyone who glorifies you does not glorify unceasingly. To glorify you, rather even if he begins insatiably. For it is impossible to praise you as you deserve. [He] desires to magnify you always, because he speaks your praise unceasingly, taking consolation from this need. [For anyone who glorifies you must consider that he should do it without ceasing. And even though he begins with much zeal he will find it impossible to rightly glorify you as you deserve.][290] For although he is greatly in your debt he gives you nothing in return, he multiplies thanksgiving, [just] as you

---

[290] The Greek here is confusing and confused. Fr. Dailey suggest that there is a lacuna here. I have provided what I believe to be a responsible reconstruction/translation of the Greek text.

[multiply] your advocacy. Since he brings to the one who always does good thanksgiving as at the beginning, an all-good gift having no end. Who will not be amazed at your unchanging protection, your immovable refuge, your unsleeping intercession, your unceasing salvation, your secure assistance, your unshakable advocacy, your impregnable wall, your storehouse of enjoyment, your blameless paradise,

[352D]

your safe stronghold, your mighty entrenchment,

[353A]

your strong tower of protection, your harbor for the storm-tossed, your calm for those in turmoil, your surety for sinners, access for the hopeless, restoration of the banished, return of the exiles, reconciliation of those alienated, reunion of those condemned, blessing of those convicted, dew for the soul's drought, drop of water for the withering plant ("for our bones," as it is written, "through you rise up like a plant" (Isaiah 66.14 LXX)), the mother of the lamb and the shepherd, and the one recognized as bringer of all good things. Whatever is yours, is paradoxical, "true, and all together made righteous, all desirable and sweeter than honey and honeycomb; for your servants desire them, in desiring them, great reward [is obtained] from you" (Ps. 18.10-12 LXX). "Who will understand your mercies?" (Ps. 106.43 LXX)

[353B]

But this is sufficient for your praise, one who is worthy of all admiration, for we are not able [to adequately sing] your encomia. For you have from God the great sublime triumph; for which reason you have established a Christian people for him from your flesh, and related by birth to you, you have made conformable to his divinity and to his image which makes us like [him]. "Therefore your name is blessed because of this unto the ages" (Ps. 71.17 LXX). Before the sun [is] your light. Above all the creation is your honor. Before the angels is your greatness. "You [are] higher than the heaven" (Job 11.8) but also wider than the heaven of heavens, and than the holy seventh [heaven] which according to someone in Scripture distinguishes from it. You more than eighth heaven, and if it is possible to speak of any other beyond this: blessed are you to generations of generations;

[353C]

but also in you have all the tribes of the earth been blessed (*cf.* Gen. 12.3 etc.). For there is no place where you are not glorified, nor tribe, from which fruit has not sprouted from you for God; so that even the nations which have not known you in this world, at an acceptable time (Isaiah 49.8; cf. 2 Cor. 6.2) will call you blessed, O Virgin. For when he who is born from you will come "to judge the inhabited world in righteousness" (Ps. 97.9 LXX), "they will see and beat their breasts" (Zach. 12.10 LXX) those who did not wish to confess you in faith as Theotokos. And then they will know,

[356A]

of what a treasure they have deprived themselves by their evil counsel.

But to us Christians who venerate you with a Christian faith as Theotokos, stretch out the mercy of your unchangeable advocacy. For we rightly recognize your falling-asleep to be life, and we trust to have you as a spiritual house-mate. And when tribulation . . . you are near, seeking you we are ransomed. And when again it is time for joy, it is you who bring this. And when among all we are troubled, we trust that you are with us. For as the thirsty man hurries to the spring, so also every faithful soul runs to you, burning to be filled with your assistance. And again as the breath of air blows a life-giving aroma to mankind, so also the breath of every orthodox Christian carries you in the mouth.

[356B]

For we are not as attracted by breathing of the air as we are drawn by the shelter of my [your] name, so that in Christ and in you is fulfilled what is written: "You are the breath of our nostrils; in your shelter and your breath we will live" (Lam. 4.20 LXX). For what race of men, not to speak [only] of Christians, has obtained such glory, has abounded in such support? Angels rejoice in the mansions of the heavens; we delight to spend time in your holy temples. For if the temple of Solomon formerly made a shadow of heaven on earth, how much more when you have become a living temple of Christ, is it not right to adorn your churches as earthly heavens? Stars speak brilliantly in the firmament of heaven.

[356C]

The material painting [color] of your images [icons], Mother of God, illuminates the giving of your gifts to us. For sun and moon carry torches for the one turning of the cycle. Every house and every city and countryside delights in your light. Because of this man is blessed even if he is a sinner, since he has been found to have you as a relative in essence, and through you he is a partaker of the divine nature. "Blessed" truly, and well has this happened to him; or rather "and it will be well" (Ps. 127.2 LXX); for you will not abandon to the end those who are found worthy to receive your succor.

[357A]

Away with death for you, O Theotokos, because you have brought life to mankind! Away with the tomb for you, since you became the divine foundation of an impregnable fortress! Away with earth poured over you; for you are the re-fashioning, because you have been called Mistress of those who have perished in the substance of clay. So in faith we confess that we have you as a companion with us. For if we were not comforted by this, our spirit would have failed in our desire for you. By faith we know that the heavens have been fitted together, as it is written (Heb. 11.3; cf. Gen. 1.1); so also we believe that we will see you going with us as a leader even after our departure from the body. For it is not such a pain for the soul, when it is drawn out of the flesh, as it is more painful to be deprived of you, all-pure one. For this reason it is written, "Even if my body sleeps, my heart wakes" (Cant. 5.2 LXX).

[357B]

And even though you have received the inevitability of death due to your human nature, your eye which guards us does not nod nor will it sleep (Ps. 120.4 LXX *cf.* earlier 349B).

For your translation does not lack witness, nor is your dormition a deception. Heaven tells the glory (Ps. 19.1 LXX) of those who ran together for you then. Earth stands by the truth concerning them. The clouds cry out the honor which was furnished to you from them. And angels report the gift-giving which came to you then—I mean how the apostles came to your side in Jerusalem, as also Habakkuk the prophet from the part of the mountains in one hour snatched up by a cloud, and lifted up by an angelic right hand,

[357C]

stood by the pit of Daniel in Persian Babylon (Daniel 12.32-39 LXX). But as a raindrop poured into the sea adds nothing, nor does the poor man's purse empty the treasury of the rich man, so neither is anyone sufficient to magnify your sublimity with voices of praise. You have by yourself your own hymn, because you were shown to be Theotokos. For not even because this has been heard by our ears only from Scriptural narrative, nor again because our fathers reported this to us by completely true tradition (Ps. 43.2 LXX), have you fulfilled the title of Theotokos; but because the deed which you have done among us, properly and truly, without tongue-grace[291] and with orthodox [faith], validates you as Theotokos by the very facts. And for the sake of this, it was truly fitting that your God-receiving body should not be shut in by deathly corruption,

[357D]

but that the tomb received its own mixture as human, and with a living conclusion of your own life transferring to the heavenly places. For the showing of your flesh is empty, but the finding of your spirit is inseparable from the companionship with mankind, by the invisible operation of Christ our God who was virginally born from you—to whom be glory unto the ages. Amen.

---

[291]   This word (ἀγλωσσοχαρίτως) is attested only here. Lampe suggests it means "without flattering, sincerely". Lampe 20

Chapter Twenty-Two

References to Mary in the Second Homily on the Dormition of the Theotokos by Germanos, Patriarch of Constantinople (715-730)

PG 98 Location	Greek	English	OT/NT References
At this point Combéfis text in Migne breaks off and begins a second homily. Daley, and others, contend that this is not the end of this homily and that the second homily in Migne should be considered to be the proper ending of first homily on the Dormition: an opinion with which I agree.			
Germanos clearly has some group of heretics in mind. Depending on when one dates this homily they could be monothelites or the iconoclasts or, perhaps, he has some much earlier group in mind.			
348D	Θεοτόκε,	O Theotokos	
	«μελετήσει τὴν δικαιοσύνην σου»	"will meditate on your righteousness	Ps. 34.28 LXX
348D	παρθενίαν σου	your virginity	
348D	τῆς ἁγιοσύνης τοῦ τόκου σου	the holiness of your childbirth	
348D	«Εἶδον οἱ πτωχοὶ τὸν» διὰ σοῦ «τῆς χρηστότητος τοῦ Θεοῦ πλοῦτον.»	"The poor saw" through you "the wealth of the goodness of God"	Ps. 68.33 LXX; Rom. 2.4
In this section Germanos puts forward a number of comparisons. Of special interest is the extended comparison of Mary and Eve. His introduction to this comparison is particularly interesting: "Therefore your aid is powerful for salvation, O Theotokos, even needing no other advocate with God. For you are the mother of the true Life. You leaven the new creation of Adam."			

348D 349A	«Τοῦ ἐλέου Κυρίου πλήρης ἡ γῆ.» «Ἐξεζήτησαν» οἱ ἁμαρτωλοὶ διὰ σοῦ «τὸν Θεὸν, καὶ ἐσώθησαν.»	"The earth is full of the the mercy of the Lord." The sinners "have sought God out" through you "and they have been saved"	Ps. 33.3 LXX

Mary's position as Mother is given by Germanos as the reason for her power as an intercessor. Christians need no other human advocate.

349A	«Εἰ μὴ ὅτι Κύριος ἐβοήθησεν ἡμῖν,» ἐκ παρθένου σαρκωθείς, «παρὰ βραχὺ παρῴκησεν ἄν,» ἐν τῷ παμφάγῳ τῆς ἀπονεκρώσεως ᾅδῃ, «τῶν ψυχῶν ἡμῶν»	"If the Lord had not helped us"—he who was incarnate of a virgin—"in a little he would have settled" in the all-devouring Hades of death, the sinking "of our souls"	Ps. 94.17 LXX
349A	Δυνατὴ τοιγαροῦν πρὸς σωτηρίαν ἡ βοήθειά σου, Θεοτόκε, καὶ μὴ χρῄζουσά τινος ἑτέρου πρὸς τὸν Θεὸν παραθέτου	Therefore your aid is powerful for salvation, O Theotokos, even needing no other advocate with God	

Here Germanos begins a comparison of Mary and Eve in the form of an anaphora using Ἐκείνης as the first word. It begins with reference to her: "You leaven the new creation of Adam."

349A	Σὺ γὰρ εἶ τῆς ὄντως ἀληθινῆς Ζωῆς ἡ μήτηρ	For you are the mother of the true Life	
349A	Σὺ εἶ τῆς ἀναπλάσεως τοῦ Ἀδὰμ ἡ ζύμη	You leaven the new creation of Adam	
349A	Σὺ εἶ τῶν ὀνειδισμῶν τῆς Εὔας ἡ ἐλευθερία	You free Eve from reproach	
349A	Ἐκείνη μήτηρ χοός, σὺ μήτηρ φωτός	She is the mother of earth; you are the mother of light	
349A	Ἐκείνης ἡ μήτρα, φθορᾶς· ἡ δὲ σὴ γαστήρ, ἀφθαρσίας	Her womb [is the source] of destruction; your belly [is the source] of imperishability	

Horvath mentions that this is the only place that θάνατος is mentioned in relation to Mary 287.

349A	Ἐκείνη θανάτου κατοίκησις, σὺ μετάστασις ἀπὸ θανάτου.	She is the dwelling-place of death; you are the removal from death	
349A	Ἐκείνη βλεφάρων καταχθονισμός, σὺ γρηγορούντων ὀφθαλμῶν ἀκοίμητος δόξα	She brings eyelids down to earth; you are the unsleeping glory of wakeful eyes	
349A	Ἐκείνης τὰ τέκνα, λύπη· ὁ δὲ σὸς Υἱὸς, παγγενὴς χαρά	Her children are grief; but your Son is universal joy.	
349B	Ἐκείνη ὡς γῆ οὖσα εἰς γῆν παρῆλθε· σὺ δὲ Ζωὴν ἡμῖν ἔτεκες, καὶ πρὸς τὴν ζωὴν ἐπανῆλθες, καὶ Ζωὴν τοῖς ἀνθρώποις, καὶ μετὰ θάνατον, προξενεῖν κατίσχυσα	She, as being earth, passed into earth; but you bore Life for us, and passed over to life, and obtained the power to mediate life to mankind, even after death	

Here is the end of this anaphora that contrasts Mary and Eve. This anaphora is of particular importance as it expresses Germanos' contentions in this homily. See comment immediately below.

Horvath comments that Germanos sees "almost no limit" to his praises of Mary 285.

349B	«Οὐκ ἔστι τῆς ἀντιλήψεώς σου κόρος,»	"There is no end of your succor"	
349B	διότι καὶ ἡ προστασία σου ζῶσα, καὶ ἡ πρεσβεία σου ζωή, καὶ ἡ σκέπη σου διηνεκής	because your advocacy is living, and your intercession is life, and your protection is ceaseless	
349B	Εἰ μὴ γὰρ σὺ προηγοῦ	For if you were not guiding,	

Here begins an anaphora on οὐδεὶς in which Germanos enumerates the results of Mary's intercessions. The refrain "if not through you" εἰ μὴ διὰ σοῦ provides an antiphonal response.

349B	οὐδεὶς πνευματικὸς ἀπετελεῖτο	no one would be made spiritual;	
349B	οὐδεὶς ἐν Πνεύματι τὸν Θεὸν προσεκύνει	no one would be worshipping God in spirit	John 4.24
349B	Θεοτόκε	O Theotokos	

349B	Οὐδεὶς θεογνωσίας ἀνάμεστος	No one is filled with divine knowledge	
349B	εἰ μὴ διὰ σοῦ, παναγία	if not through you, all-holy [lady].	
349B	οὐδεὶς ὁ σωζόμενος	No one is saved	
349B	εἰ μὴ διὰ σοῦ, Θεοτόκε	if not through you, Theotokos	
349B	οὐδεὶς κινδύνων ἐλεύθερος	No one is free from dangers	
349B	εἰ μὴ διὰ σοῦ, Παρθενομῆτορ	if not through you, Virgin Mother	
349B	οὐδεὶς ὁ λελυτρωμένος	No one is redeemed	
349B	εἰ μὴ διὰ σοῦ, Θεομῆτορ	if not through you, Mother of God	
349C	οὐδεὶς ὁ ἐλεούμενος δῶρον	No one receives the gift of mercy	
	εἰ μὴ διὰ σοῦ, Θεοχώρητε	if not through you, Theochoretos	

Germanos now compares the intercession of other humans to those of Mary. Mary's intercessions are clearly more powerful due to her role as mother of the Incarnate Lord. This continues the development of a theme that began in 349A. Germanos also begins an anaphora using the word "you" or "your" that continues to 353A where he ends his praises of the Virgin Mary.

Mary's role as Mediatrix is due to her role as Mother of Christ. Horvath mentions 352A : But you, having a mother's power with God 289.

352A	Σὺ δὲ, μητρῴαν ἔχουσα πρὸς τὸν Θεὸν τὴν ἰσχὺν, καὶ τοῖς καθ' ὑπεροχὴν ἁμαρτάνουσι, καθ' ὑπερβολὴν τὴν συγχώρησιν ἐξανύεις	But you, having a mother's power with God, accomplish succor in surpassing degree even for those extremely sinful.	

Horvath mentions this passage: Οὐδὲ γὰρ ἐνδέχεταί σέ ποτε παρακουσθῆναι as illustrating Mary's power as Mediatrix. Horvath incorrectly ascribes this to 353A and Dormition III. 289.

352A	Οὐδὲ γὰρ ἐνδέχεταί σέ ποτε παρακουσθῆναι, ἐπειδὴ πειθαρχεῖ σοι κατὰ πάντα καὶ διὰ πάντα, καὶ ἐν πᾶσιν ὁ Θεὸς, ὡς ἀληθινῇ αὐτοῦ καὶ ἀχράντῳ Μητρί	For it is not possible for your voice ever to be disregarded, since God is obedient to you in every way and for every reason and in every situation, as you are his true and pure Mother	

352A	Ὅθεν ὁ θλιβόμενος, εὐλόγως πρὸς σὲ καταφεύγει· ὁ ἀσθενῶν, σοὶ προσκολλᾶται· ὁ πολεμούμενος, σὲ τοῖς ἐχθροῖς ἀνθοπλίζει.	Therefore he who suffers tribulation takes blessed refuge with you; he who is sick, clings to you; he who wages war, takes you as armor against his enemies	
352A	«Θυμὸν καὶ ὀργὴν καὶ θλίψιν, ἀποστολὴν δι' ἀγγέλων πονηρῶν,» σὺ μεταβάλλεις.	You repel "spirit and anger and tribulation, dispatched by evil angels"	Ps. 77.49 LXX
352B	Ἀπειλὴν δικαίαν καὶ ψῆφον ἀξιοπαθοῦς καταδίκης σὺ μεταστρέφεις, ἀγαπῶσα μεγάλως τὸν ἐπικεκλημένον τῷ ὀνόματι τοῦ Υἱοῦ σου λαόν.	You turn back just threats and the verdict of deserved punishment, loving greatly the people who are called by the name of your Son	
352B	Ὅθεν καὶ ὁ Χριστιανὸς λαός σου, τὰ καθ' ἑαυτὸν ἀνακρίνων, πρὸς μὲν τὸν Θεὸν παρρησιαστικῶς ὑποστέλλεταί σοι τὰς δεήσεις προσφέρειν.	Therefore your Christian people examining their own [affairs], delegates you to bring their petitions to God with confident speech.	
352B	Σὲ δυσωπεῖν ἀνενδοιάστος θαρρεῖ, παναγία, διὰ τὴν πεῖραν, καὶ τὰ πλήθη τῶν εἰς ἡμᾶς ἀγαθῶν σου, καὶ παραβιάσεσθαί σε πολλάκις ἐν ἱκεσίαις.	They unhesitatingly make bold to entreat you, all-holy Lady, because of [their] experience and the multitude of your bounties towards us, and to constrain you often in supplications.	
352B	Ἀνθ' ὧν τίς σε μὴ μακαρίσει;	In return who will not bless you?	(cf. Luke 1.48)

Horvath mentions that Mary's motherhood surpasses even the understanding of angels 286.

352B	Τὴν τῶν ἀγγέλων ὑπὲρ ἔννοιαν θεωρίαν	You are a vision beyond the understanding of the angels.	

Gregory E. Roth

352B	τὴν ὑπόληψιν τοῦ γένους τῶν Χριστιανῶν	You are the support of the nation of Christians.	
352B	τὸ ὀχλούμενον τῶν ἁμαρτωλῶν προσφύγιον	You are the refuge importuned by sinners.	
352B	τὴν καθ' ὥραν ἐν τῷ στόματι τῶν Χριστιανῶν φερομένην	You are carried from hour to hour in the mouth of Christians.	
352B	Μόνον γὰρ εἰ θροηθῇ Χριστιανός, εἰ καὶ πρὸς λίθον τὸν ἑαυτοῦ προσκόψῃ πόδα, τὸ σὸν ἐπικαλεῖται πρὸς βοήθειαν ὄνομα	For if one is merely called Christian, if he even strikes his foot against a stone, he calls upon your name for help.	(*Ps.* 90.12 LXX)

Daley indicates that there is a lacuna in the text here. It is difficult to see how long this is. It is my opinion that there are some words left out, but that it is not a major omission—perhaps a scribe's error. See ftn 11, 167.

Germanos now compares the intercessory power of human beings and contrasts that with Mary's intercessory prowess. This is the development of a theme that began in 349A. He also returns the the debt that mankind owns to Mary and the impossibility of adequately repaying the debt. See, 340A and B at the beginning of Dormition I for the debtor theme.

352C	Ἐπὰν γὰρ πολλὰ χρεωστῶν οὐδὲν ἀνταποδίδωσί σοι, πληθύνει τὴν εὐχαριστίαν, ὡς σὺ τὴν προστασίαν.	For when although he is greatly in your debt he gives you nothing in return, he multiplies thanksgiving, as you [multiply] your advocacy.	

Germanos begins a long recitation on Mary's attributes as an intercessor. Certain of these attributes are echoes of some of the ektenia in the Great Litany of the Liturgy.

352C	τὴν ἀμετάθετον σκέπην	your unchanging protection	
352C	τὴν ἀμετάστατον καταφυγὴν	your immovable refuge	
352C	τὴν ἀκοίμητον πρεσβείαν	your unsleeping intercession	
352C	τὴν ἀδιάλειπτον σωτηρίαν	your unceasing salvation	

220

352C	τὴν σταθερὰν βοήθειαν	your secure assistance	
352C	τὴν ἀσάλευτον προστασίαν	your unshakable advocacy	
352C	τὸ ἀπόρθητον τεῖχος	your impregnable wall	
352C	τὸν θησαυρὸν τῶν ἀπολαύσεων	your storehouse of enjoyment	
352C	τὸν ἀνέγκλητον παράδεισον	your blameless paradise	
352D	τὸ ἀσφαλὲς ὀχύρωμα,	your safe stronghold,	
352D	τὸ κραταιὸν περιχαράκωμα	your mighty entrenchment	
353A	τὸν ἰσχυρὸν τῆς ἀντιλήψεως πύργον	your strong tower of protection	
353A	τὸν λιμένα τῶν χειμαζομένων	your harbor for the storm-tossed	
353A	τὴν γαλήνην τῶν τεταραγμένων	your calm for those in turmoil	
353A	τὴν τῶν ἁμαρτωλῶν ἐγγυητὴν	your surety for sinners	
353A	τὴν τῶν ἀπεγνωσμένων προσαγωγὴν	access for the hopeless	
353A	τὴν τῶν ἐξορισθέντων ἀνάληψιν	restoration of the banished	
353A	τὴν τῶν ἐκδιωχθέντων ὑποστροφὴν	return of the exiles	
353A	τὴν τῶν ἀλλοτριωθέντων οἰκείωσιν	reconciliation of those alienated	
353A	τὴν τῶν κατακεκριμένων παράθεσιν	reunion of those condemned	
353A	τὴν τῶν καθῃρημένων εὐλογίαν	blessing of those convicted	
353A	τὴν δρόσον τῆς ψυχικῆς αὐχμηρίας	dew for the soul's drought	
353A	τὴν σταγόνα τῆς ἐκτακείσης βοτάνης. «Τὰ γὰρ ὀστᾶ ἡμῶν, ὡς γέγραπται, διὰ σοῦ καθάπερ βοτάνην ἀνατελεῖ·»	drop of water for the withering plant ("for our bones," as it is written, "through you rise up like a plant")	(Isaiah 66.14 LXX)
353A	τὴν τοῦ ἀμνοῦ καὶ ποιμένος μητέρα	the mother of the lamb and the shepherd	

Gregory E. Roth

| 353A | καὶ πάντων τῶν ἀγαθῶν γνωριζομένην πρόξενον | and the one recognized as bringer of all good things | |
| 353A | Ὅσα τὰ σὰ, παράδοξα, «ἀληθινά, δεδικαιωμένα ἐπὶ τὸ αὐτό, ἐπιθυμήματά τε πάντα καὶ γλυκύτερα ὑπὲρ μέλι καὶ κηρίον. Καὶ γὰρ οἱ δοῦλοί σου ποθοῦμεν αὐτά, ἐν τῷ ποθεῖν αὐτά, ἀντάμειψις ἐκ σοῦ πολλή.» | Whatever is yours, is paradoxical, "true, and all together made righteous all desirable and sweeter than honey and honeycomb; for your servants desire them, in desiring them, great reward [is obtained] from you" | (Ps. 18.10-12 LXX). |

Here Germanos declares that " . . . this is sufficient for your praise, one who is worthy of all admiration, for we are not able [to adequately sing] your encomia." See 340 B for and earlier declaration about the difficulty of creating and encomia to Mary. It is my opinion that this should be read as a question although the Greek text does not indicate it as such. Germanos returns to a frequent theme of human beings' (and often specifically his) unworthiness to adequate praise the Theotokos.

Horvath mentions Mary's role as Mediatrix of the Christian people: "Therefore your Christian people examining their own [affairs], delegates you to bring their petitions to God with confident speech." 289

353B	ἀξιάγαστε	one who is worthy of all admiration	
353B	Ἔχεις ἐκ Θεοῦ τὸ μέγα πρὸς θρίαμβον ὕψος	you have from God the great sublimity for triumph	
353B	διότι λαὸν αὐτῷ Χριστιανικὸν ἀπὸ σαρκὸς τῆς σῆς συνεστήσω	for which reason you have established a Christian people for him from your flesh	
353B	καὶ τὸ ὁμοιογενές σου, σύμμορφον τῆς θείας αὐτοῦ καὶ ὁμοιωτικῆς εἰκόνος ἀπειργάσω	and related by birth to you, you have made conformable to his divinity and to his image which makes us like [him].	

Germanos has established that because of Mary's participation in the Incarnation a people—the Christian People—is established. Because they are related by birth to the Theotokos human nature is once again made conformable to God's divinity. In this Germanos is stating the principles established by the ecumenical councils concerning the divinity and humanity of Christ. See especially the council of Chalcedon and the issues of monophysitism.
What follows immediately is a rudimentary hymn to the Theotokos much like "More Honorable than the Cherubim . . ."

safe222

353B	«Εὐλογημένον τοίνυν διὰ τοῦτο τὸ ὄνομά σου εἰς τοὺς αἰῶνας.»	"Therefore your name is blessed because of this unto the ages"	(Ps. 71.17 LXX)
353B	Πρὸ τοῦ ἡλίου τὸ φῶς σου	Before the sun [is] your light.	
353B	Ὑπερτέρα πάσης τῆς κτίσεως ἡ τιμή σου	Above all the creation is your honor	
353B	πρὸ τῶν ἀγγέλων ἡ ὑπεροχή σου	Before the angels is your greatness.	
353B	«Ὑψηλοτέρα σὺ τοῦ οὐρανοῦ·» ἀλλὰ καὶ πλατυτέρα τοῦ οὐρανοῦ τῶν οὐρανῶν	"You [are] higher than the heaven" but also wider than the heaven of heavens,	(Job 11.8)

The following section Fr. Daley references to Basil, *In Hexaemeron* Hom. 3.3. He suggests that the idea of eight heavens appears in Jewish apocalyptic literature. Ftn 13 167

353B	Ὀγδοώτερε, καὶ εἰ ἔστι τις ἕτερος, καὶ ὑπερέκεινα τούτου λέγειν, οὐρανέ· εὐλογημένη σὺ ἐν γενεαῖς γενεῶν	You more than eighth heaven, and if it is possible to speak of any other beyond this: blessed are you to generations of generations;	
353C	ἀλλὰ καὶ εὐλογήθησαν ἐν σοὶ πᾶσαι αἱ φυλαὶ τῆς γῆς	but also in you have all the tribes of the earth been blessed	(*cf.* Gen. 12.3 etc.)
353C	Οὐδὲ γάρ ἐστι τόπος ἔνθα σὺ μὴ δοξάζῃ· οὐδὲ φυλή, ἐξ ἧς οὐκ ἐβλάστησαν διὰ σοῦ καρποὶ τῷ Θεῷ· ὥστε καὶ τὰ μὴ ἐπεγνωκότα σε κατὰ τὸν κόσμον τοῦτον ἔθνη, καινῷ δεκτῷ καὶ αὐτὰ μακαριοῦσί σε, Παρθένε	there is no place where you are not glorified, nor tribe, from which fruit has not sprouted from you for God; so that even the nations which have not known you in this world, at an acceptable time will call you blessed, O Virgin	(Isaiah 49.8; cf. 2 Cor. 6.2)

At the end of 353C and the beginning of 356A Germanos once again refers some who can only be heretics.

353C 356A	Ὅταν γὰρ ὁ ἐκ σου γεννηθεὶς ἥξει «κρῖναι τὴν οἰκουμένην ἐν δικαιοσύνῃ, ὄψονται καὶ κόψονται,» οἱ μὴ Θεοτόκον σε πιστῶς ὁμολογῆσαι θελήσαντες· καὶ τότε γνώσονται, ποίου θησαυροῦ ἑαυτοὺς κακοβούλως ἐζημίωσαν.	For when he who is born from you will come "to judge the inhabited world in righteousness", "they will see and beat their breasts" those who did not wish to confess you in faith as Theotokos. And then they will know, of what a treasure they have deprived themselves by their evil counsel	(Ps. 97.9 LXX) (Zach. 12.10 LXX)
356A	Θεοτόκον	Theotokos	
356A	παράτεινον τῆς ἀμεταθέτου σου προστασίας τὸ ἔλεος	stretch out the mercy of your unchangeable advocacy	
356A	Καὶ τὴν γὰρ κοίμησίν σου, Θεοτόκε, ζωὴν ἡγούμεθα δικαίως	For we rightly recognize your falling-asleep to be life, O Theotokos	

Horvath includes the term σύνοικόν as an indication of Mary's role as Mediatrix 289. His reference to 348B does not use the word but it is yet another illustration of Germanos understanding the close relationship that exists between Mary and the Church.

356A	καὶ σύνοικόν σε πνευματικῶς ἔχειν πεπιστεύκαμεν	and we trust to have you as a spiritual house-mate	
356A	ζητοῦντές σε λυτρούμεθα	seeking you we are ransomed	
356A	ὅταν πάλιν χαρᾶς καιρός, σὺ εἶ ταύτης πρόξενος	when again it is time for joy, it is you who bring this	
356A	καὶ ὅταν ἐν ὅλοις ὑπὸ σοῦ μεριμνώμεθα, μεθ' ἡμῶν σε διάγειν πιστοφορούμεθα	And when among all we are troubled, we trust that you are with us	
356A	Καὶ πάλιν ὥσπερ τὸ τοῦ ἀέρος ἄσθμα ζωτικὴν τοῖς ἀνθρώποις ἐμπνέει τὴν ὄσφρησιν· οὕτω καὶ σὲ παντὸς ὀρθοδόξου Χριστιανοῦ ἐπὶ στόματος προφέρει πνοή	as the breath of air blows a life-giving aroma to mankind, so also the breath of every orthodox Christian carries you in the mouth.	

Germanos uses an analogy to illustrate why the faithful flee to the assistance of Mary: "For as the thirsty man hurries to the spring, so also every faithful soul runs to you, burning to be filled with your assistance." He continues the analogy in part of 356B.

365B	Οὐδὲ γὰρ τοσοῦτον τῆς τοῦ ἀέρος ἀνιμώμεθα ψυχαγωγίας	For we are not as attracted by breathing of the air	

The word Germanos uses here ψυχαγωγίας would be recognized as coming from ψυχαγωγέω a word that has the classical meaning of leading the souls of the departed to the neither world. As such it takes on a meaning that is not easily translated into English.

356B	ὅσον τῆς τοῦ ὀνόματός μου ἀρυόμεθα σκέπης	the shelter of my [your] name	

Horvath mentions this phrase: ὡς ἐν Χριστῷ καὶ ἐν σοὶ τὸ γεγραμμένον πληροῦσθαι as an illustration of how Germanos' " . . . Mariology seems to be some sort of extension of Christology" 285. Also see Dormition III 364A-372C for an extended example of this. Ref. Horvath 285

356B	«Ἀναπνοὴ, φησί, μυκτήρων ἡμῶν σὺ εἶ· ἐν τῇ σκέπῃ σου καὶ πνοῇ ζήσομεν.»	"You are the breath of our nostrils; in your shelter and your breath we will live"	(Lam. 4.20 LXX)

The next few lines represent the Theotokos as the temple of God and clearly refer to the iconographic agenda of Orthodox temples (churches). It is also interesting to see the reference to the heavenly mansions and the earthly temples: a reference that Germanos develops more fully in his writing on the Divine Liturgy.

356B	Εἰ γὰρ ὁ Σολομώντειος ναὸς, πάλαι τὸν οὐρανὸν ἐπὶ τῆς γῆς ἐσκιογράφει	For if the temple of Solomon formerly made a shadow of heaven on earth	
356B	πόσῳ μᾶλλον ἐμψύχου σοῦ ναοῦ γεγονυίας τοῦ Χριστοῦ, μὴ καὶ τὰς Ἐκκλησίας τὰς σὰς, ὡς ἐπιγείους οὐρανοὺς δικαίως ἔστιν ἀνακομπάζειν;	how much more when you have become a living temple of Christ, is it not right to adorn your churches as earthly heavens?	
356B	ἀστέρες λαμπηδογλωσσοῦσιν ἐν τῷ στερεώματι τοῦ οὐρανοῦ·	Stars speak brilliantly in the firmament of heaven.	

Germanos is making a reference to the iconography of the Theotokos where she is represented with stars around her in a blue field.

356C	Θεομῆτορ		Mother of God	

Gregory E. Roth

Germanos' development of the theme of Mary and the sun and moon and their light as seen by all human beings.			
356C	Ἥλιος καὶ σελήνη τὸν ἕνα τοῦ κυκλώματος δᾳδουχοῦσι πόλον· πᾶς οἶκος, καὶ πᾶσα πόλις, καὶ χώρα, τὸ σὸν, ἐκ τοῦ σοῦ γεννηθέντος φωτὸς, ἀγλαΐζεται φῶς.	For sun and moon carry torches for the one turning of the cycle. Every house and every city and countryside delights in your light.	
356C	Διὰ τοῦτο μακάριος κἂν ἁμαρτωλὸς ὁ ἄνθρωπος, ὅτιπερ συγγενῆ σε κατ' οὐσίαν κτησάμενος εὑρέθη, καὶ θείας φύσεως διὰ σοῦ κοινωνὸς	Because of this man is blessed even if he is a sinner, since he has been found to have you as a relative in essence, and through you he is a partaker of the divine nature.	
Mary's paramont role in the Incarnation is here given as the reason for her intercessory power.			
356C	οὐ διαλείψῃ γὰρ τοῖς τὴν σὴν ἀντίληψιν ἕως τέλους ἔχειν ἀξιουμένοις	for you will not abandon to the end those who are found worthy to receive your succor	
In this the final part of this homily Germanos begins an anaphora on Ἐρρέτω "Away" addressed to Mary as Theotokos. For each "Away" Germanos provides a reason directly related to the reason for saying "Away". This section also uses metaphors as a way of showing the Dormition. Perniola references 357A twice,—130 ftn 24, 131 ftn 29			
357A	Ἐρρέτω θάνατος ἐπὶ σοὶ, Θεοτόκε, ζωὴν ὅτι τοῖς ἀνθρώποις προσήγαγες.	Away with death for you, O Theotokos, because you have brought life to mankind!	
357A	Ἐρρέτω τάφος ἐπὶ σοὶ, ἐπειδήπερ ὕψους ἀκαταφράστου θεῖος ἐγένου θεμέλιος.	Away with the tomb for you, since you became the divine foundation of an impregnable fortress!	

226

357A	Ἐρρέτω χοῦς ἐπὶ σοί· ἀνάπλασις γὰρ εἶ, ὅτι τοῖς ἐν ὕλῃ πηλοῦ διαφθαρεῖσι κεχρημάτικας, Δέσποινα.	Away with earth poured over you; for you are the re-fashioning, because you have been called Mistress of those who have perished in the substance of clay	
357A	Οὐκοῦν πίστει σε μεθ᾽ ἡμῶν συνανάστροφον ἔχειν ὁμολογοῦμεν. Εἰ μὴ γὰρ ἐν τούτῳ παρηγορούμεθα, ἐξέλιπεν ἂν τῇ ἐπιθυμίᾳ τῇ πρὸς σέ, τὸ ἡμέτερον πνεῦμα	So in faith we confess that we have you as a companion with us. For if we were not comforted by this, our spirit would have failed in our desire for you.	

Germanos returns to the theme of the heavens, this time giving their fittedness as a reason for believing that Mary, even though she must suffer death as all human beings, will always continue as a companion with humans.

357A	καὶ πίστει τοὺς οὐρανούς, ὡς γέγραπται, κατηρτίσθαι νοοῦμεν· οὕτω καὶ σὲ μετελθοῦσαν συνδιάγωγον καὶ μετὰ τὴν ἐκδημίαν τοῦ σώματος πιστεύομεν ἀναθεωρεῖν	By faith we know that the heavens have been fitted together, as it is written; so also we believe that we will see you going with us as a leader even after our departure from the body	(Heb. 11.3; cf. Gen. 1.1)

With a reference to Cant. 5.2 LXX and Ps. 120.4 LXX Germanos confirms his confidence in the Dormitions of the Theotokos.

357A	Οὐ γὰρ ὀδύνη τοσαύτη τῇ ψυχῇ, τῆς σαρκὸς ὅταν ἀποσπασθῇ, ὅσον ὀδυνηρότερόν σου στερηθῆναι, πανάχραντε. Ὅθεν κατὰ τὸ γεγραμμένον, «Κἂν τὸ σῶμά σου καθεύδει, ἡ καρδία σου ἀγρυπνεῖ.»	For it is not such a pain for the soul, when it is drawn out of the flesh, as it is more painful to be deprived of you, all-pure one. For this reason it is written, "Even if my body sleeps, my heart wakes"	

357B	Καὶ κἂν τὸ ἀπαραίτητον τοῦ θανάτου, τῇ ἀνθρωπίνῃ παρεδέξω φύσει, οὐ νυστάζει, οὐδὲ ὑπνώσει ὁ φυλάσσων ἡμᾶς ὀφθαλμός σου.	even though you have received the inevitability of death due to your human nature, your eye which guards us does not nod nor will it sleep	(Ps. 120.4 LXX).
357B	Οὐκ ἀμάρτυρος γὰρ ἡ μετάστασίς σου· οὐδὲ ψευδὴς ἡ κοίμησις	For your translation does not lack witness, nor is your dormition a deception	
Germanos tells how all of creation is a witness to the Dormition calling upon the heavens, the earth, clouds, the angels and the apostoles as witnesses.			
357B	ὁ οὐρανὸς τῶν ἐπὶ σοὶ τότε συνδραμόντων διηγεῖται δόξαν	Heaven tells the glory of those who ran together for you then	(Ps. 19.1 LXX)
357B	ἡ γῆ, τὴν περὶ αὐτῶν παρίστησιν ἀλήθειαν	Earth stands by the truth concerning them	
357B	αἱ νεφέλαι, τὴν ἐξ αὐτῶν σοι διακονηθεῖσαν βοῶσι τιμήν	The clouds cry out the honor which was furnished to you from them.	
357B	καὶ ἄγγελοι τὴν εἰς σὲ τότε γενομένην ἀπαγγέλλουσι δωροφορίαν	And angels report the gift-giving which came to you	
357B	τὸ πῶς . . . κατὰ τὴν Ἰερουσαλὴμ οἱ ἀπόστολοι παρεγένοντο πρός σὲ	how the apostles came to your side in Jerusalem,	
Germanos recites some similar events from the Old Testament			
357B 357C	καθάπερ καὶ Ἀμβακοὺμ ὁ προφήτης ἐκ μερῶν τῆς Ὀρεινῆς, ἐν ὥρᾳ μιᾷ διὰ νεφέλης ἁρπαγείς, καὶ ἀγγελικῆς δεξιᾶς ὑποληφθείς, ἐν τῇ Περσικῇ Βαβυλῶνι εἰς τὸν λάκκον τοῦ Δανιὴλ παρέστη	as also Habakkuk the prophet from the part of the mountains in one hour snatched up by a cloud, and lifted up by an angelic right hand, stood by the pit of Daniel in Persian Babylon	Daniel 12.32-39 LXX

Once again Germanos uses metaphors to illustrate the futility of human beings attempt to properly praise the Theotokos.

357C	Ἀλλ' ὥσπερ ῥανὶς εἰς θάλασσαν ἐπιχεομένη οὐδὲν προστίθησιν, οὐδὲ βαλάντιον πτωχοῦ, πλουσίου θησαυρὸν ἀποκενοῖ· οὕτως οὐδὲ τὰ ὕψη σου τῶν ἐγκωμίων, ἱκανός τις ἐν λόγων κατευμεγεθῆσαι φωναῖς. Ἔχεις σὺ παρ' ἑαυτῆς τὸν ἴδιον ὕμνον, ὅτιπερ Θεοτόκος ἀνεδείχθης	But as a raindrop poured into the sea adds nothing, nor does the poor man's purse empty the treasury of the rich man, so neither is anyone sufficient to magnify your sublimity with voices of praise. You have by yourself your own hymn, because you were shown to be Theotokos.	
357C	Οὐδὲ γὰρ, ὅτι τοῖς ὠσὶν ἡμῶν παρὰ Γραφικῆς ἐξηγήσεως τοῦτο καὶ μόνον ἠκούσθη· οὐδὲ πάλιν ὅτιπερ οἱ πατέρες ἡμῶν ἀνήγγειλαν ἡμῖν τοῦτο παναληθευούσῃ διηγήσει,	For not even because this has been heard by our ears only from Scriptural narrative, nor again because our fathers reported this to us by completely true tradition	Ps. 43.2 LXX
357C	τὴν προσηγορίαν ἐκληρώσω τῆς Θεοτόκου	have you fulfilled the title of Theotokos	
357C	ἀλλ' ὅτι τὸ ἔργον ὃ εἰργάσω ἐν ἡμῖν, κυρίως καὶ ἀψευδῶς ἀγλωσσοχαρίτως καὶ ὀρθοδόξως, Θεοτόκον σε δι' αὐτῶν βεβαιοῖ τῶν πραγμάτων	but because the deed which you have done among us, properly and truly, without tongue-grace and with orthodox [faith], validates you as Theotokos by the very facts	

357C 357D	καὶ τούτου χάριν, τὸ θεηδόχον σου σῶμα, παρὰ νεκροποιοῦ καταφθορᾶς, ἔπρεπεν ὄντως μὴ συγκλεισθῆναι· ἀλλὰ καὶ τὸν τάφον ὡς ἀνθρώπινον ὑποδέξασθαι τὸ ἴδιον φύραμα· καὶ σοῦ ζωοτελῶς πρὸς τὰ οὐράνια, τῆς οἰκείας μεταστάσης ζωῆς	And for the sake of this, it was truly fitting that your God-receiving body should not be shut in by deathly corruption, but that the tomb received its own mixture as human, and with a living conclusion of your own life transferring to the heavenly places.	

Horvath includes this section as part of Germanos' understanding of Mary as Mediatrix 290

357D	κενὸν μὲν τὸ δειχθῆναι τῆς σαρκός σου· ἀχώριστον δὲ τῆς τῶν ἀνθρώπων συναναστροφῆς εὑρεθῆναι τὸ πνεῦμά σου, ἀοράτῳ ἐνεργείᾳ τοῦ ὑπὸ σοῦ παρθενικῶς γεννηθέντος Χριστοῦ τοῦ Θεοῦ ἡμῶν· ᾧ ἡ δόξα εἰς τοὺς αἰῶνας. Ἀμήν.	For the showing of your flesh is empty, but the finding of your spirit is inseparable from the companionship with mankind, by the invisible operation of Christ our God who was virginally born from you—to whom be glory unto the ages. Amen.	

Chapter Twenty-Three

Third Homily on
the Dormition of the Theotokos
Introduction and Commentary

The Dormition homily found in *PG*98 360A-372D is a narrative of Mary's Dormition. An introduction may be seen in 360A & B. In many respects it is redolent of the earlier homily (homilies). Mary's Dormition is seen as a type for mankind as a whole because of the resurrection of her Son.

> For as once through the mercy of God the bones of mankind were alienated among those on earth, the blameless body of the Theotokos enriched these [bones] which were hardened by corruption,[292] because by the resurrection of him who was born from her they [the bones] were softened by incorruption more than with oil (*cf.* Psalm 54.22 LXX).

The narration begins with Germanos stating the purpose of this homily: "But indeed in a few [words] let us call to mind her ever-memorable translation. For truly the hearing of the exegesis concerning such an event is a source of joy." An angel, tells Mary about her impending Dormition. This occasions a tender speculation on the part of Germanos that illustrates his understanding of the Mother-Child relationship that is so prominent:

---

[292]   Daley's footnote 2: "This statement that Mary's body had already corrupted in the tomb before it was taken up into the presence of God is unusual in early literature on the Dormition."

> "'It is time,' says the Lord, 'to bring you my mother [to me]. Just
> as you filled the earth and those on the earth with joy, O blessed
> one, now make the heavenly places also joyous. Cheer the
> mansions of my Father. Lead the souls and spirits of the saints.
> As I see your honorable transfer towards me, accompanied by
> angels, they are fulfilled faithfully, as through you their part
> also will settle in my light. Therefore come with rejoicing. Hail
> even now, as also earlier. (360C)

As always Germanos is concerned that his auditors know that Mary
does not leave them as 'orphans,' and that Mary's protection parallels
Jesus': "you will not leave those in the world orphaned of your protection;
but as I, although I am not in the world, oversee and care for those in the
world, so also your advocacy will not be taken away from those in the
world until the end." (360D) Mary is to ascend to: " . . . a more living
life, to a joyous rest, to indestructible peace, to a life without cares, to
passionless luxury, to an unlimited sojourn, to unending enjoyment, to
unsetting light, to day without evening, to me Myself, the maker of all and
of you. For where I am, there is eternal life, joy incomparable, residence
unequalled, commonwealth imperishable." (361A) The Transfiguration is
given as an example of Jesus' state and she is told to ask Peter about this.
(361A/B). Once again Mary's Dormition is tied to the Incarnation:

> Death will not boast over you, for you gave birth to Life. You
> became my vessel; the fracture of death-corrupting fall will not
> break this. The shadowing of gloom will not dim this. Come
> willingly to the one who was borne by you. I want to make
> you joyful as a child should, to pay back to you the rent of
> the maternal womb, the wages of wet-nursing, the exchange
> for upbringing, the fulfillment for your affection. Since you
> obtained me as your only-begotten Son, O mother, prefer rather
> to live with me; for I know you have no other child. I proved you
> to be a virgin mother; I also will make you a mother rejoicing
> in her Child. (361C)

Germanos returns to the theme of the debtor, Mary's glory, her roles
as Mediatrix and bridge between life and death and uses a number of

Old Testament types to illustrate Mary's roles. (361D/364A) Mary is counseled to:

> Set down your body in the place of Gethsemane with good cheer, as I before I suffered set down my knees there in a human prayer. For prefiguring your dormition, I myself also bent the knees of my body towards such a place. So as I after the kneeling at that time went forth to my life-giving and willing death on the cross, you also after the laying-down of your remains will immediately be transferred to life.

The narration of the events of the Dormition are picked up at this point with the disciples coming toward Mary. They are the ones who shall bury Mary and it is fitting that it be the Apostles who perform the rites of burial for Mary. (364B).

> Mary rejoices greatly with this news and sets about preparing the place of her death:

> When she heard these messages, the Mother of God rejoiced with great joy, disdaining altogether the temporary life of mankind; and making great lights around her whole house, she calls together her beloved female relatives and neighbors. She sweeps the household, (364C) she decks her bed with flowers, as for the chamber of the marriage of a virgin; [the bed] which until then every night (because of her desire for her Christ and Son) is inundated by the tears of her prayers. "For on my bed," says Scripture, "I have sought him whom my soul has loved" (Cant. 3.1 LXX). She eagerly prepares [the necessities] for her departure. She makes public announcement of her translation, she reveals what has been revealed to her by the angel; she shows the prize which was given to her.(364D)

The preparation having been made the women that were gathered around were weeping and lamenting. They begged Mary not to leave them as orphans:

The women who had been summoned were weeping; those gathered to her side were lamenting, so to speak plowing rivers in the house. They were begging her that they should not be left orphans by her. But she says, "Let the will of my Son and God be done in me. 'For he is my God, and I will glorify him; the God of my Father, and I will exalt him" (Exodus 15.2). He is a Son given birth in the flesh by me, but Father and Creator and God of his own mother. So if you being parents from perishable children and the union of pollution, will not refuse to be separated from these for an instant, how shall I who have obtained God as a Son and maintain my affection singly for him, because without a husband I bore him incorruptibly and virginally, how shall I not be overcome more than you by my affection? For your souls are led to each other to the penalty [the loss] in respect of children; (365A) but I who have been found worthy to have this one as God and Christ and only-begotten, how will I not happily return to him, who is always living and gives life to all?" (365B).

At this point the Disciples arrive, being announced by thunder and storm clouds. The Disciples repeat the circumstances of Mary's imminent departure:

And when they saw her, they bowed before her lovingly, and when they learned the form of the arrival from her, they narrated the following to her: "Because having you as a companion in the sojourn of this world, O Mother of God, (365B) and seeing you like Christ himself we are consoled when we behold [you], we meditate on your translation. But since by divine authority and fleshly attachment to a mother, you have been asked to return to God, we rejoice at what is being accomplished fittingly for you, and turning out advantageously. For we also acquire fulfillment of eternal life in addition to you, and we have obtained you as an intercessor who is being translated to God's side. For it was not suitable for the Mother of God to live in the midst of a crooked and perverted generation (Philippians 2.15), but to pass over to the tents of the heavenly and imperishable dwellings. "(365C)

Mary gives instructions to the Disciples concerning her burial. The Apostle Paul arrives at this point and is greeted by John. The Apostles and Mary welcome him and give him a place of honor. Paul gives what is described as a great encomium for the Virgin of which Germanos repeats only a part. Among the things that are reported is that Paul "will also teach that you (Mary) have been transferred to his side so that it may be made known to the very gentiles that their salvation is strengthened by your (Mary's) intercession . . ." (368B)

Mary dies in the midst of the assembled Disciples and women. Peter appoints Paul to make the prayer over the body of Mary. (368C) The Apostles carry the body of Mary to the tomb. 368D begins with a description of the crowds of people who came out to Mary's funeral:

> An immeasurable crowd flowed to the funeral of the Life-bearer. They were thunderstruck by her sudden departure. They were amazed also at the aerial arrival of the apostles from their dispersion. For the rumor was spread about them in all Jerusalem, that a kind of cloud with lightning and storm coming before the decisive moment, as the spirit whistled through them like a rain and a dew, fell upon the house of the Virgin.

The story of the impious man of the Hebrews follows who loses his hands in an effort to disrupt the funeral. There follows a description of the Apostles and the crowd, the respect of the apostles and the zeal of the crowd to obtain something of the virgin's clothing. Germanos is quick to add that no one touched the body of Mary. (369A) Peter and Paul place the body of Mary in the tomb. Germanos describes Mary's entombment with the snatching away of her body; but this is different:

> And he who snatched it was unseen by all, for it was the invisible God; but the shroud in a light cloud, in the corporeally prophesied light cloud (Isaiah 19.1), in the hands of the apostles then appeared lightly blown by the wind. (369C) The disciples recognized the arrival of Christ with angels to his mother. Being convinced that she was translated by him, they gave glory to God in praise of their voices, also speaking to the people as follows: "Men of Israel, this has now been made known to you

all concerning Mary the mother of Christ according to the flesh, that to us and you together having arrived dead at this tomb, she was taken up from our hands." (369D)

Germanos draws yet another parallel with her Son:

Let no one be shown doubtful in this matter. Let no one accuse us falsely of theft as in the case of Christ's body, also in the case of her remains; but if this is heard from the governor and from your high priests, make the truth free from care and not falsehood. Become witnesses of what you have seen. You young people also become like angels in the body as you have gone today to the tomb. Give your tongue wings for the truth. Do you also say, 'Behold the place where the Virgin is buried, but Mary the life-bearer has been translated.' (369D/372A)

But that is where the parallels end. Mary's assumption is immediate.

She without any dispute became invisible before the tomb was shut with a stone, lest having been laid down without seals and apart from guards she might give the unbelievers a favorable opportunity [to allege] theft. But behold as she was being hymned [in procession] she came to the tomb and she left it empty; and she filled paradise with her own glory, and she has the rest of eternal life, and she is a companion of the luxury of God." Such were the words of the apostles concerning you the mother of God. (372B)

Germanos then promptly ends the homily with a short prayer.

Chapter Twenty-Four

Third Homily on
the Dormition of the Theotokos
Translation

Φήμη καλὴ καὶ ἀγαθή

[360A]

Encomium of our father among the saints Germanos archbishop of Constantinople on the holy and venerable Dormition of our most glorious Lady the Theotokos and ever-virgin Mary.

"A good and excellent reputation fattens the bones," as it is written (Proverbs 15.30). And the exposition concerning the corporeal falling-asleep of the life-bearing and ever-virgin Mary, which is like a divine breath and fragrance of the all-holy flesh of Christ, sanctifies those who sanctify her. For as once through the mercy of God the bones of mankind were alienated among those on earth, the blameless body of the Theotokos enriched these [bones] which were hardened by corruption,[293]

[360B]

because by the resurrection of him who was born from her they [the bones] were softened by incorruption more than with oil (*cf.* Psalm 54.22 LXX). But indeed in a few [words] let us call to mind her ever-memorable

---

[293] Daley's footnote 2: "This statement that Mary's body had already corrupted in the tomb before it was taken up into the presence of God is unusual in early literature on the Dormition."

translation. For truly the hearing of the exegesis concerning such an event is a source of joy.

When Christ our God planned to transfer his life-bearing Mother to his side, by an angel he announces to her the indication of her falling-asleep contrary to the usual; so that not as among the rest of mankind death coming invisibly should make distress for her also as she changes her habitation. For the separation of the body from the soul knows how to grieve the soul even of great men.

[360C]

Therefore so that not leaving without warning she herself might not be disturbed by the natural property of the flesh, as not knowing in advance her own departure (she who bore the God who knows all), an angel is sent to her, encouraging her with words like these from Christ himself:

"'It is time,' says the Lord, 'to bring you my mother [to me]. Just as you filled the earth and those on the earth with joy, O blessed one, now make the heavenly places also joyous. Cheer the mansions of my Father. Lead the souls and spirits of the saints. As I see your honorable transfer towards me, accompanied by angels, they are fulfilled faithfully, as through you their part also will settle in my light. Therefore come with rejoicing. Hail even now, as also earlier.

[360D]

You rightly possess the title "full of grace" in every way. As when you, being about to conceive me, were addressed with "hail," hail also as I seek to receive you at my side. Do not be disturbed as you leave the world which perishes along with its desires. Let its corruption go, since you will not leave those in the world orphaned of your protection; but just as I, although I am not in the world, oversee and care for those in the world, so also your advocacy will not be taken away from those in the world until the end.

[361A]

The unsparing treatment of the flesh will not disturb you; you are ascending to a more living life, to a joyous rest, to indestructible peace, to a life without cares, to passionless luxury, to an unlimited sojourn, to unending enjoyment, to unsetting light, to day without evening, to me myself, the maker of all and of you. For where I am, there is eternal life, joy incomparable, residence unequalled, commonwealth imperishable. So where I am, there you also will be, mother inseparable, with your inseparable Son. Where God is, all goodness, all delight, all radiance. No one seeing my glory has been willing to let this go. No one who has come into my rest has sought again the perishable world. Let Peter be asked, if a similar comparison [was present]

[361B]

of the world and the mountain of Tabor, when on it he beheld my glory for a short time.

When you are living in the world of perishable [things], I revealed my power to you in a vision; when you pass over from life, I will show myself to you face to face (*cf.* I Cor. 13.12). Give to earth its own without tribulation. Your body is mine; and since the ends of the earth are in my hand (Ps. 94.4), no one will snatch anything from my hand. Entrust your body to me, because I also deposited my godhead in your belly. Your god-inspired soul will see the glory of my Father. Your undefiled body will see the glory of his only-begotten Son. Your pure spirit will see the glory of the all-holy Spirit.

[361C]

Death will not boast over you, for you gave birth to Life. You became my vessel; the fracture of death-corrupting fall will not break this. The shadowing of gloom will not dim this. Come willingly to the one who was borne by you. I want to make you joyful as a child should, to pay back to you the rent of the maternal womb, the wages of wet-nursing, the exchange for upbringing, the fulfillment for your affection. Since you obtained me as your only-begotten Son, O mother, prefer rather to live with me; for I know you have no other child. I proved you to be a virgin mother; I also will make you a mother rejoicing in her Child.

[361D]

I will show you to the world that is your debtor, and I will glorify your name even more as you are translated. I will build you as a wall for the world, a bridge for those who are swamped, an ark for those who are being saved, a staff for those who are being led by the hand, an intercession for those who are sinning, and a ladder which has the power to raise mankind to heaven.

Come with rejoicing. Do you open paradise, which your relative and tribeswoman Eve closed. Enter into the joy of your Son. Leave the Jerusalem below. Run up to the heavenly city, because the Jerusalem below [troubles] will be magnified in a short time: "The noise, like the noise," as it is written,

[364A]

"of a pomegranate-orchard being cut down on the plain" (Zechariah 12.11 LXX). Be summoned upwards, and only in appearance [be summoned] to Gethsemane the place of the tomb. I will not leave you orphaned in it for long. I come to you at once, when you have been laid with funeral rites in the tomb, not in order to be conceived again by you (as once and for all I have dwelt in you), but in order rather to receive you to live with me. Set down your body in the place of Gethsemane with good cheer, as I before I suffered set down my knees there in a human prayer. For prefiguring your dormition, I myself also bent the knees of my body towards such a place. So as I after the kneeling at that time went forth to my life-giving and willing death on the cross, you also after the laying-down of your remains will immediately be transferred to life.

[364B]

Behold my disciples are also coming towards you, [those] through whom you will be buried honorably and piously, the spiritual sons of my light—[those] to whom, as you bear witness, I gave the grace of adoption as sons. And indeed when you are buried by them, consider that you are being given funeral rites as from my hands. For it is not fitting for you to receive a funeral from others than from my apostles, in whom the Holy

Spirit dwells, [those] who also fulfill my person, for the honor of your departure, all-pure one.'"

When she heard these messages, the Mother of God rejoiced with great joy, disdaining altogether the temporary life of mankind; and making great lights around her whole house, she calls together her beloved female relatives and neighbors. She sweeps the household,

[364C]

she decks her bed with flowers, as for the chamber of the marriage of a virgin; [the bed] which until then every night (because of her desire for her Christ and Son) is inundated by the tears of her prayers. "For on my bed," says Scripture, "I have sought him whom my soul has loved" (Cant. 3.1 LXX). She eagerly prepares [the necessities] for her departure. She makes public announcement of her translation, she reveals what has been revealed to her by the angel; she shows the prize which was given to her. The prize was a branch, a symbol of victory over death, and a pre-figuration of unwithering life, to confirm that she is going over, that she may prevail over corruption, as also the Christ who received birth from her conquered Hades.

[364D]

Such a branch of a palm-tree, with which also the god-loving children of the Hebrews, when Christ was approaching his passion, as to this one about to become a victor over death, shook with songs of praise, crying out, "Hosanna in the highest;" that is, "Save indeed, [you who are] in the highest." For "Hosanna" among the Hebrews is interpreted as "Save indeed." So as there the branches of the palm-trees foretold the victorious death of Christ with a symbolic demonstration, so also the prize from a palm-tree given to the Theotokos was a fulfillment of victory over death-dealing corruption.

[365A]

The women who had been summoned were weeping; those gathered to her side were lamenting, so to speak plowing rivers in the house. They were begging her that they should not be left orphans by her. But she says,

"Let the will of my Son and God be done in me. 'For he is my God, and I will glorify him; the God of my Father, and I will exalt him" (Exodus 15.2). He is a Son given birth in the flesh by me, but Father and Creator and God of his own mother. So if you being parents from perishable children and the union of pollution, will not refuse to be separated from these for an instant, how shall I who have obtained God as a Son and maintain my affection singly for him, because without a husband I bore him incorruptibly and virginally, how shall I not be overcome more than you by my affection? For your souls are led to each other to the penalty [the loss] in respect of children;

[365B]

but I who have been found worthy to have this one as God and Christ and only-begotten, how will I not happily return to him, who is always living and gives life to all?"

As these things were being said, there comes suddenly a forceful sound of thunder, and a storm cloud which hung low over the earth from which as if some dewy drops the disciples of Christ, landing at the Virgin's house stood together in a crowd. And when they saw her, they bowed before her lovingly, and when they learned the form of the arrival from her, they narrated the following to her: "Because having you as a companion in the sojourn of this world, O Mother of God,

[365C]

and seeing you like Christ himself we are consoled when we behold [you], we meditate on your translation. But since by divine authority and fleshly attachment to a mother, you have been asked to return to God, we rejoice at what is being accomplished fittingly for you, and turning out advantageously. For we also acquire fulfillment of eternal life in addition to you, and we have obtained you as an intercessor who is being translated to God's side. For it was not suitable for the Mother of God to live in the midst of a crooked and perverted generation (Philippians 2.15), but to pass over to the tents of the heavenly and imperishable dwellings."

Saying these things, they were inconsolable with tears. But she says to them, "Rejoice, spiritual children of my child.

[365D]

Remember his words, how at the time of his passion he ordered you not to make the joy of the world into lamentation. Today also as I am transferred to his side, do not make my rejoicing into sorrow but give funeral rites to my body, as I will arrange it on the bed. For I think I am being buried by the very hands of my Son, when I receive a funeral faithfully from you his disciples." (*cf.* 364B)

In the midst of these Paul the apostle arrives, as if the proclamation has moved him from afar. He knocks on the door of the house. John the apostle, who presides over the house, joyfully opens to him,

[368A]

he the virgin who received the Virgin as mother into his own house from Christ himself (John 19.27). The apostles saw Paul, and caught their breath (refreshed themselves?), having given him a place honorably on the raised seat. The Virgin welcomes him joyfully. Paul throws himself at her feet which carried God, and learning for what purpose he himself had arrived, with great and tearful groaning opening his ready and didactic mouth, he makes a great encomium for the Virgin, of which these are a few [words]:

"Rejoice, Mother of life, and subject of my proclamation. Rejoice, the accomplishment of my soul's journey. For even if I have not beheld Christ in the flesh, seeing you in the body, I have the consolation of contemplating Christ, since you provided a body to the bodiless One in which he covered himself.

[368B]

So we satisfy our desire for Christ with your face. I was proclaiming you to the gentiles until yesterday, that you had borne God in the flesh. From now on I will also teach that you have been transferred to his side so that it may be made known to the very gentiles that their salvation is strengthened by your intercession and that they have immovable assistance with God."

And afterwards when many others besides Paul, as we have been able to learn, brought offerings of praise to the Theotokos, the Virgin bids farewell to all. She reclines on the cot which she has spread; she arranges her blameless body as she wished; she gives up her spirit as in sleep. Or to speak rather, she departs from the flesh in awakening, making her leave-taking free from corruption.

[368C]

Therefore as she laid aside with a public cry to Christ [who is] God and her corporeal Son her irreproachable spirit, Peter designates Paul, his fellow leader for Christ, to make the prayer at the remains of the Virgin according to custom. Paul declines, saying that it is fitting for Peter to do this as chief shepherd. Peter in humility nods to Paul, as because of the great labor of his preaching. Paul does not obey at all, keeping the promotion of Christ without novelty for Peter. So Peter makes the prayer. The rest of the apostles raise the cot on their shoulders, with hymns and torches honorably and piously carrying out the body of the Virgin to the tomb.

[368D]

An immeasurable crowd flowed to the funeral of the Life-bearer. They were thunderstruck by her sudden departure. They were amazed also at the aerial arrival of the apostles from their dispersion. For the rumor was spread about them in all Jerusalem, that a kind of cloud with lightning and storm coming before the decisive moment, as the spirit whistled through them like a rain and a dew, fell upon the house of the Virgin. A certain foolish man of the unbelieving Hebrews even then (for these are foolishness of foolishness (Ecclesiastes 1.2), like stumbling-blocks and wranglers always for the manufacturing of discussions stretching out his lawless hands)—"for in the hands of these men

[369A]

unceasingly," it says, "is lawlessness" (Psalm 25.2 LXX)—shakes the pallet of the cot, daring to mistreat the body of the pure one, without hesitation to throw down the corporeal throne of the Most High. His hands are at once cut off, becoming a fearful example for the Jews who behave shamelessly towards Christ. The rest approach the coffin. The apostles shrank back in God-pleasing respect and fear from touching the body of the Virgin. And the disciples because of the great honor and because they recognized that the body was the vessel of the pure one demonstrated praiseworthy cowardice about touching her body. But the faithful of the people struggled for the hallowing of themselves and carrying off anything of her funeral [adornments]. But no one laid hands on her, putting before their eyes especially the rashness of the Hebrew who had been made an example.

[369B]

But by the common opinion and selection of the apostles, Peter and Paul, taking up at one side and the other the shroud which hung loosely over the cot, put the remains in the tomb, weighing their touch with the shroud, the all-glorious and very pious apostles not misusing the laying-on of their hands; because of their desire for God, showing then their evident fear, those who were sublime in humility and heavenly clod-hoppers, honorable working-men and accomplishers of the love of Christ—those who venerated with great honor the Son through his mother and the mother because of the Son, who because of God who became incarnate, nobly gave service to the mother who provided his flesh. So from their hands, as all looked away, the pure body of the Virgin was snatched away.

[369C]

And he who snatched it was unseen by all, for it was the invisible God; but the shroud in a light cloud, in the corporeally prophesied light cloud (*cf.* Isaiah 19.1), in the hands of the apostles then appeared lightly blown by the wind.

The disciples recognized the arrival of Christ with angels to his mother. Being convinced that she was translated by him, they gave glory to God in praise of their voices, also speaking to the people as follows: "Men of Israel, this has now been made known to you all concerning Mary the mother of Christ according to the flesh,

[369D]

that to us and you together having arrived dead at this tomb, she was taken up from our hands. Let no one be shown doubtful in this matter. Let no one accuse us falsely of theft as in the case of Christ's body, also in the case of her remains; but if this is heard from the governor and from your high priests, make the truth free from care and not falsehood. Become witnesses of what you have seen. You young people also become like angels in the body as you have gone today to the tomb. Give your tongue wings for the truth. Do you also say, 'Behold the place where the Virgin has been buried, but Mary the life-bearer was translated. Behold also the shroud

[372A]

without her who was wrapped in it, seeking her who was bound tightly in it, whom it wrapped as a lifeless [body] and now desires to be spread under as for a living [person].'

You women also become myrrh-bearers for her translation. Run, report her transference from the life-receiving tomb.

And you, the place of Gethsemane, are blessed, as you have found glory like Joseph's garden. There Peter and John, running and finding the linen clothes and the handkerchief, believed that Christ had risen. But in you, Gethsemane, all saw, both we the disciples of the Savior and [the crowd] which was gathered in this funeral of the ever-virgin Mary, her who was buried, laid in the tomb, and transferred.

[372B]

She without any dispute became invisible before the tomb was shut with a stone, lest having been laid down without seals and apart from guards she might give the unbelievers a favorable opportunity [to allege] theft. But behold as she was being hymned [in procession] she came to the tomb and she left it empty; and she filled paradise with her own glory, and she has the rest of eternal life, and she is a companion of the luxury of God." Such were the words of the apostles concerning you the mother of God.

But sufficiently I also, all-pure Lady, with the rashness of the words I bring you (for the age will fall short for those who dare to praise you)

[372D]

among these will place my hymn. Remember your Christian servants. Present the prayers of all, the hopes of all. Confirm our faith. Unite the churches. Give victory to the empire. Fight alongside the army. Bring peace to the world, and ransoming all from dangers and temptations, vouchsafe to provide for each the day of reckoning without condemnation. For to whom else shall we flee? You have the words of life which are supplications of your intercession on our behalf before God. For you are the one who always does, and never ceases to do great things with us, and holy is your name which is called blessed by angels and men in all generations of generations (Luke 1.48-50), from now and unto the age of ages. Amen.

Chapter Twenty-Five

References to Mary in the Third Homily on the Dormition of the Theotokos by Germanos I, Patriarch of Constantinople (715-730)

PG 98 Location	Greek	English	OT/NT References
360A	ἡ περὶ τῆς σωματικῆς κοιμήσεως τῆς Ζωοτόκου . . . διήγησις	the exposition concerning the corporeal falling-asleep of the life-bearing . . .	
360A	ἀειπαρθένου Μαρίας	ever-virgin Mary	
"This statement that Mary's body had already corrupted in the tomb before it was taken up into the presence of God is unusual in early literature on the Dormition." See Daley's ftn 2 180. Compare Dorm I 345A.			
360A	τῆς Θεοτόκου	Theotokos	
360B	τῆς ἀειμνήστου μεταστάσεως αὐτῆς	her ever-memorable translation.	
360B	τὴν Ζωοτόκον αὐτοῦ . . Μητέρα	his life-bearing Mother	
360B	τὸ τῆς κοιμήσεως προμηνύει παραστατικόν	her falling-asleep contrary to the usual	
Perniola quotes extensively from 360C-364B. 101-3. This section forms a long speech by Christ to His Mother reassuring her as her death approaches.			
360C	μὴ . . . τῷ φυσικῷ τῆς σαρκὸς ἰδιώματι θορυβηθῇ	she herself might not be disturbed by the natural property of the flesh	

Gregory E. Roth

360C	ὡς μὴ προεγνωκυῖα τὴν ἰδίαν ἔξοδον, ἡ τὸν γνώστην τῶν ὅλων τεκοῦσα Θεὸν	as not knowing in advance her own departure (she who bore the God who knows all)	
360C	τὴν ἐμὴν . . . μητέρα	my mother	

Horvath mentions these next lines as confirmation of the Assumption 288.

360C	Καθὼς οὖν τὴν γῆν καὶ τοὺς ἐν τῇ γῇ χαρᾶς ἐπλήρωσας, κεχαριτωμένη, χαροποίησον καὶ τὰ οὐράνια πάλιν. Φαίδρυνον τὰς τοῦ Πατρός μου μονάς· ψυχαγώγησον, καὶ τῶν ἁγίων τὰ Πνεύματα.	So as you filled the earth and those on the earth with joy, O blessed one, now make the heavenly places also joyous. Cheer the mansions of my Father. Lead the souls and spirits of the saints.	

Daley points out the play on the Greek words for "grace" (χαρίς) and "joy" (χαρά). See, ftn 3, 180. Germanos would have been aware of this and also other implications of the words. As in many other instances in Germanos' homilies, it is good to hear the Greek words and allow them to play on one's perceptions of what he is saying. His auditors also would have picked up on the word "Κεχαριτωμένη" (full of grace) which is a common title for Mary and the greeting of the Angel Gabriel at the Annunciation. *Cf.* Lk 1.28.

360C	τὴν σὴν πρὸς ἐμὲ τιμητικὴν . . . μετάθεσιν	your honorable transfer towards me	

Germanos begins a dialog between Mary and Jesus during which much of their life together and the salvific nature of their relationship to human kind is expressed.

360D	Διὰ πάντων γὰρ ἔχεις τὸ κεχαριτωμένον τῆς προσηγορίας ἀξίωμα. Ὡς ὅταν σὺ μέλλουσα συλλαμβάνειν με, χαίρειν ἐμηνύθης	For through all you have the rank full of grace in your address. As when you, being about to conceive me, were addressed with "hail,"	*Cf.* Lk 1.28
360D	χαῖρε καὶ ἄρτι προσλαμβάνεσθαι ζητουμένη παρ' ἐμοῦ	hail also as you are being sought to be received at my side.	
360D	ἐπεὶ τοὺς ἐν τῷ κόσμῳ τῆς ἀντιλήψεως ὀρφανοὺς οὐκ ἀφήσεις· ἀλλ' ὥσπερ ἐγὼ μὴ ὢν ἐκ τοῦ κόσμου, ἐπιβλέπω καὶ διοικῶ τοὺς ἐν τῷ κόσμῳ· οὕτως καὶ	since you will not leave those in the world orphaned of your protection; but as I, although I am not in the world, oversee	

250

	ἡ σὴ προστασία οὐκ ἀφαιρεθήσεται μέχρι συντελείας ἐκ τῶν τοῦ κόσμου.	and care for those in the world, so also your advocacy will not be taken away from those in the world until the end.	

This is one of the clearest statements of the reason that Mary is such a strong intercessor: like her son, after her dormition, she does not abandon the world but remains an advocate of those left behind.

361A	Μὴ θρυλλήσει σε σαρκὸς ἀφειδίασις	The unsparing treatment of the flesh will not disturb you	

There follows a description of Mary's future residence by her son.

361A	πρὸς ζωοτέραν ἐπανέρχῃ ζωήν, πρὸς ἀνάπαυσιν χαρᾶς, πρὸς εἰρήνην ἀκατάκρατον, πρὸς ἀμέριμνον διαγωγὴν, πρὸς ἀπαθῆ τρυφήν, πρὸς ἀπερίσπαστον διαμονὴν, πρὸς ἀτελεύτητον ἀπόλαυσιν, πρὸς ἄδυτον φῶς, πρὸς ἀνέσπερον ἡμέραν, πρὸς ἐμὲ αὐτόν, τὸν τοῦ παντὸς καὶ σοῦ Ποιητήν.	you are ascending to a more living life, to a joyous rest, to indestructible peace, to a life without cares, to passionless luxury, to an unlimited sojourn, to unending enjoyment, to unsetting light, to day without evening, to me myself, the maker of all and of you	

Germanos illustrates the heavenly world and in some cases draws parallels with what has just been said about Mary's new residence. Germanos creates an emphasis on the comparison by using the words Ὅπου "where" and Οὐδείς "no one". Both comparison and anaphora are rhetorical devices. Horvath mentions the phrase ἀχώριστος μήτηρ as confirming the assumption of the Virgin. It is wrongly ascribed to Dormition II.

361A	Ὅπου γὰρ ἐγώ, ἐκεῖ ζωὴ αἰώνιος, χαρὰ μὴ συγκρινομένη, κατοικία μὴ ἐξισουμένη, πολιτεία μὴ φθειρομένη. Ὅπου τοίνυν ἐγώ, καὶ σὺ μέλλεις ὑπάρχειν, ἀχώριστος μήτηρ, ἐν ἀδιαζεύκτῳ Υἱῷ. Ὅπου Θεός, πᾶσα ἀγαθωσύνη, πᾶσα τερπνότης, πᾶσα φαιδρότης. Οὐδεὶς ἰδὼν τὴν δόξαν μου, παρεᾶσαι ταύτην ἐθέλησεν	For where I am, there is eternal life, joy incomparable, residence unequalled, commonwealth imperishable. So where I am, there you also will be, mother inseparable, with your inseparable Son. Where God is, all goodness, all delight, all radiance. No one seeing my glory has been willing to let this go	

361A 361B	Οὐδεὶς ἐλθὼν εἰς τὴν κατά-παυσίν μου, τά τοῦ φθαρτοῦ πάλιν κατεζήτησεν κόσμου. Πέτρος ἐρωτάσθω, εἰ ὁμοία σύγκρισις τοῦ κόσμου καί τοῦ Θαβωρίου ὄρους, ὅταν ἐν αὐτῷ τὴν ἐμὴν ἐθεάσατο πρὸς ὀλίγον καιρὸν δόξαν	No one who has come into my rest has sought again the perishable world. Let Peter be asked, if a similar comparison [was present] of the world and the mountain of Tabor, when on it he beheld my glory for a short time.	

Germanos presents Christ as saying that He revealed himself to Mary in a vision when she was yet "living in the world of perishable [things]," but with her dormition He will show himself face to face.

361B	Ἐν τῷ κόσμῳ τῶν φθαρτῶν διαγούσης σου, ὀπτασίᾳ τὴν ἐμήν σοι ἐνεφάνιζον δύναμιν· μεταβαινούσης σου τοῦ βίου, πρόσωπον πρὸς πρόσωπον ἐμαυτὸν ὑποδείξω σοι.	When you are living in the world of perishable [things], I revealed my power to you in a vision; when you pass over from life, I will show myself to you face to face.	*cf.* I Cor. 13.12
361B	Ἐμοὶ τὸ σῶμά σου πίστευσον, ὅτι κἀγὼ τῇ κοιλίᾳ σου τὴν ἐμὴν παρεκατεθέμην θεότητα.	Entrust your body to me, because I also deposited my godhead in your belly.	
361B	Ὄψεται τοῦ Πατρός μου τὴν δόξαν ἡ ἔνθεός σου ψυχή.	Your god-inspired soul will see the glory of my Father	
361B	Ὄψεται τοῦ μονογενοῦς αὐτοῦ Υἱοῦ τὴν δόξαν τὸ ἀμίαντον σῶμά σου.	Your undefiled body will see the glory of his only-begotten Son.	
361B	Ὄψεται τοῦ παναγίου Πνεύματος τὴν δόξαν τὸ ἄχραντον πνεῦμά σου	Your pure spirit will see the glory of the all-holy Spirit.	

Horvath mentions this section as confirmation of the Assumption due to the physical relationship between Christ, the Son, and the Virgin, the mother. 288.

361C	Οὐ καυχήσεται θάνατος ἐπὶ σοί· Ζωὴν γὰρ ἐκύησας	Death will not boast over you, for you gave birth to Life	
361C	Σκεῦος ἐμὸν ἐγένου· οὐ ῥαγώσει τοῦτο σύντριμμα θανατοφθόρου καταπτώσεως	You became my vessel; the fracture of death-corrupting fall will not break this	

Interestingly Christ says that He has yet to pay His debt to Mary for all that she did in raising Him.

361C	Ἔρχου προθύμως πρὸς τὸν ὑπὸ σοῦ γεγεννημένον. Εὐφρᾶναί σεβούλομαι τεκνοχρέως· ἀποδοῦναί σοι τὰ τῆς μητρικῆς κοιλίας ἐνοίκια· τῆς γαλακτοτροφίας τὸν μισθόν· τῆς ἀνατροφῆς τὴν ἀντάμειψιν· τοῖς σπλάγχνοις σου τὴν πληροφορίαν	Come willingly to the one who was borne by you. I want to make you joyful as a child should, to pay back to you the rent of the maternal womb, the wages of wet-nursing, the exchange for upbringing, the fulfillment for your affection	
361C	οὐκ ἀντιπερισπάσαι γὰρ οἶδα πρὸς ἑτέρου τέκνου διάθεσιν. Ἐγώ σε παρθένον ἀνέδειξα μητέρα· ἐγώ σε καὶ εὐφραινομένην ἐπὶ Τέκνῳ καταστήσω μητέρα	Since you obtained me as your only-begotten Son, O mother, prefer rather to live with me; for I know you have no other child. I proved you to be a virgin mother	

Jesus' plan for Mary continues with a description of her role as mediatrix. Many of these words are familiar descriptions of Mary's role as mediatrix.

361D	Ἐγώ σοι τὸν κόσμον χρεώστην ἀναδείξω	I will show you to the world that is your debtor	
361D	μετερχομένης πλεῖόν σοῦ τὸ ὄνομα καταδοξάσω	I will glorify your name even more as you are translated	
361D	Ἐγώ σε τεῖχος κοσμικὸν οἰκοδομήσω	I will build you as a wall for the world	

Horvath includes this phrase γέφυραν κλυδωνιζομένων among those pointing to Mary's role as Mediatrix

361D	γέφυραν κλυδωνιζομένων	a bridge for those who are swamped	
361D	κιβωτὸν διασωζομένων	an ark for those who are being saved	
361D	βακτηρίαν χειραγωγουμένων	a staff for those who are being led by the hand	

Horvath mentions πρεσβείαν ἁμαρτανόντων as describing Mary's role as Mediatrix 289

361D	πρεσβείαν ἁμαρτανόντων	an intercession for those who are sinning	
361D	κλίμακα πρὸς οὐρανὸν τοὺς ἀνθρώπους ἀναβιβάζειν ἰσχύουσαν	and a ladder which has the power to raise mankind to heaven	
361D	Ἄνοιξον σὺ τὸν παράδεισον, ὃν ἡ συγγενής σου καὶ ὁμοφυὴς ἀπέκλεισεν Εὔα	Do you open paradise, which your relative and tribeswoman Eve closed	

Germanos compares the heavenly Jerusalem with the earthly one. He makes reference to the destruction of the earthly Jerusalem (ca. 66CE) and at the same time a classical reference by way of Zechariah 12.11 LXX to the pomegranate orchard. For his auditors these references would have also been redolent of the resurrection.

| 361D/ 364A | ἄφες τὴν κάτω Ἰερουσαλήμ· ἀνάδραμε πρὸς τὴν οὐράνιον πόλιν, ὅτι τῆς κάτω Ἰερουσαλὴμ μεγαλυνθήσεται μετὰ μικρὸν «ὁ κοπετός, ὡς κοπετός, κατὰ τὸ γεγραμμένον, ῥοῶνος ἐκκοπτομένου ἐν πεδίῳ.» | Run up to the heavenly city, because the Jerusalem below [troubles] will be magnified in a short time: "The noise, like the noise," as it is written, "of a pomegranate -orchard being cut down on the plain" | (Zechariah 12.11 LXX). |

Germanos makes it very clear that Mary is to die like any human being. Yet she is given the assurance by her Son that He will come quickly and take her to Him.

364A	Προσανακλήθηκαὶ μόνον ἐν σχήματι τῷ Γεθσημανῆ τοῦ μνήματος χωρίῳ	Be summoned upwards, and only in appearance [be summoned] to Gethsemane the place of the tomb	
364A	τοῦ κατατεθῆναί σε κηδευθεῖσαν ἐν τῷ μνημείῳ	when you have been laid with funeral rites in the tomb	
364A	οὐ συλληφθησόμενος πάλιν ὑπὸ σοῦ, ὡς ἐφ᾽ ἅπαξ οἰκήσας ἐν σοί,	not in order to be conceived again by you (as once and for all I have dwelt in you)	
364A	Θὲς ἐν τῷ Γεθσημανῆ χωρίῳ τεθαρρηκότως τὸ σῶμά σου	Set down your body in the place of Gethsemane with good cheer	

Germanos here emphasizes the connection between his death and resurrection and Mary's death and resurrection. It is because Christ first suffered being truly divine and truly human that Mary's dormition and assumption are possible. In this he is following the teachings of the Ecumenical Councils and seems at pains to make this connection. No doubt this is in some manner connected with his recantation of the monothelite heresy. See his life and the monothelite council.

| 364A | καθὼς ἐγὼ πρὸ τοῦ παθεῖν με δι' ἀνθρωπίνην προσευχὴν ἐκεῖσε τὰ γόνατα. Σοῦ γὰρ προτυπούμενος τὴν κοίμησιν, ἔκλινα κἀγὼ πρὸς τὸ τοιοῦτον χωρίον τὰ ἐμὰ τοῦ ἐκ σοῦ σώματος γόνατα. Ὡς οὖν ἐγὼ μετὰ τὴν τότε γονυκλισίαν πρὸς τὸν ζωοποιὸν ἐξῆλθον καὶ ἑκούσιον τοῦ σταυροῦ μου θάνατον, καὶ σὺ μετὰ τὴν κατάθεσιν τοῦ σοῦ λειψάνου πρὸς ζωὴν παραχρῆμα μετατεθήσῃ | as I before I suffered set down my knees there in a human prayer. For prefiguring your dormition, I myself also bent the knees of my body towards such a place. So as I after the kneeling at that time went forth to my life-giving and willing death on the cross, you also after the laying-down of your remains will immediately be transferred to life. | |

The phrase "at that time went forth to my life-giving and willing death on the cross" is an almost direct quote from the Divine Liturgy.

364B	Ἰδοὺ καὶ οἱ ἐμοὶ καταλαμβάνουσι πρὸς σὲ μαθηταί, δι' ὧν τιμίως καὶ εὐλαβῶς ἐνταφιασθίσῃ	Behold my disciples are also coming towards you, [those] through whom you will be buried honorably and piously	
364B	παρ' αὐτῶν ἐνταφιαζομένη, ὡς ἐξ ἐμοῦ χειρῶν λογίζου κηδευομένη	when you are buried by them, consider that you are being given funeral rites as from my hands	
364B	ἐπὶ τιμῇ τῆς ἐξόδου σου, πανάχραντε	for the honor of your departure, all-pure one	
364B	ἡ Θεομήτωρ	Mother of God	

Germanos then tells of the preparations made by Mary for her falling asleep. She sweeps the household, she decks her bed with flowers, as for the chamber of the marriage of a virgin. It is said that: "[the bed] which until then every night (because of her desire for her Christ and Son) is inundated by the tears of her prayers." "For on my bed," says Scripture, "I have sought him whom my soul has loved" (Cant. 3.1 LXX) Perniola quotes this section. 103.

364C	Ἐτοιμάζει προθύμως τὰ πρὸς τὴν ἔξοδον	She eagerly prepares [the necessities] for her departure	
364C	Δημοσιεύει τὴν μετάστασιν	She makes public announcement of her translation	

Once again Germanos draws a parallel between Christ's and Mary's deaths:

364C	Ἦν δὲ τὸ βραβεῖον, φοίνικος κλάδος, σύμβολον νίκης κατὰ θανάτου, καὶ ζωῆς ἀμαράντου προεκτύπωμα· τοῦ πιστωθῆναι μετερχομένην, ὅτι κατα-δυναστεύσειεν τῆς φθορᾶς, ὡς καὶ ὁ ὑπ' αὐτῆς γεννηθεὶς ἐνίκησεν τὸν ᾅδην, Χριστός	she shows the prize which was given to her. The prize was a branch, a symbol of victory over death, and a prefiguration of unwithering life, to confirm that she is going over, that she may prevail over corruption, as also the Christ who received birth from her conquered Hades	

Germanos weaves the branch of a palm-tree and the Entrance into Jerusalem together remembering the "Hosannas in the highest", the "victorious death" and the prize given to His Mother. Perniola references this once—131 ftn 31.

364D	οὕτως καὶ τὸ ἐκ φοίνικος δοθὲν τῇ Θεοτόκῳ βραβεῖον, πληροφόρημα νίκης ὑπῆρχεν θανατοποιοῦ καταφθορᾶς	so also the prize from a palm-tree given to the Theotokos was a fulfillment of victory over death-dealing corruption	

Perniola quotes 365A/B which recounts the reaction of the women attending the Virgin and her response to them concerning her imminent death.

365A	Τὸ θέλημα τοῦ Υἱοῦ μου καὶ Θεοῦ γενέσθω ἐν ἐμοί. «Οὗτος γάρ μου Θεός, καὶ δοξάσω αὐτόν· Θεὸς τοῦ Πατρός μου, καὶ ὑψώσω αὐτόν»	Let the will of my Son and God be done in me. 'For he is my God, and I will glorify him; the God of my Father, and I will exalt him.'	Exodus 15.2
365A	Υἱὸς μὲν σαρκὶ γεννηθεὶς ὑπ' ἐμοῦ· Πατὴρ δὲ καὶ Κτίστης καὶ Θεὸς τῆς ἰδίας οὗτος μητρός	He is a Son given birth in the flesh by me, but Father and Creator and God of his own mother	

Germanos has Mary compare the experience of parents who conceive through the partnership of two human parents with the experience of her giving birth virginally. In so doing, Germanos states unequivally the virgin birth of Jesus and also the place of parental feelings towards their offspring.

365A	Εἰ οὖν ὑμεῖς γονεῖς ὄντες ἐκ φθαρτῶν καὶ ἐκ ῥύπου συναφείας παίδων, οὐ καρτερεῖτε τούτων πρὸς ῥοπὴν χωρισθῆναι, πῶς ἐγὼ Θεὸν Υἱὸν κεκτημένη, καὶ σπλάγχνα μονομερῆ πρὸς αὐτὸν ἐπέχουσα, διότι χωρὶς ἀνδρὸς αὐτὸν ἀφθάρτως καὶ παρθενικῶς ἐκύησα, μὴ μεῖζον ὑμῶν νενίκημαι παρὰ τῶν σπλάγχνων;	So if you being parents from perishable children and the union of pollution, will not refuse to be separated from these for an instant, how shall I who have obtained God as a Son and maintain my affection singly for him, because without a husband I bore him incorruptibly and virginally, how shall I not be overcome more than you by my affection?	
365A 365B	Ὑμεῖς γὰρ ὑπ᾽ ἀλλήλων τὴν ἐπὶ τοῖς τέκνοις ψυχαγωγεῖσθε ζημίαν· ἐγὼ δὲ καὶ Θεὸν τὸν Χριστὸν καὶ μονογενῆ τοῦτον νῦν ἔχειν ἠξιωμένη, πῶς μὴ πρὸς αὐτὸν ἡδέως ἐπαναλύσω, τὸν ἀεὶ ζῶντα καὶ ζωὴν πᾶσι διδόντα	For your souls are led to each other to the penalty [the loss] in respect of children; but I who have been found worthy to have this one as God and Christ and only-begotten, how will I not happily return to him, who is always living and gives life to all?"	
365B	σύνοικον	a companion	
365B	μεταστάσει	translation	
365B	Ἐπεὶ δὲ καὶ θεϊκῇ ἐξουσίᾳ, καὶ σαρκικῇ πρὸς μητέρα προσπαθείᾳ, πρὸς τὸν Θεὸν ἐπεζητήθης ἀναλῦσαι	since by divine authority and fleshly attachment to a mother, you have been asked to return to God	
365C	μεσῖτιν	an intercessor	

257

Gregory E. Roth

Germanos takes Philippians 2.15 as the reason why Mary must fall asleep and go to her Son. Horvath points out that "Further Germanus admits as reason of convenience it is fitting (ἤροζεν) on the grounds of her purity to be taken up from our sinful world." 288 Perniola also mentions this point. 104.		

| 365C | Οὐδὲ γὰρ καὶ ἤρμοζεν τὴν Μητέρα τοῦ Θεοῦ ἐν μέσῳ γενεᾶς σκολιᾶς καὶ διεστραμ-μένης διάγειν, ἀλλ' ἐν σκηναῖς οὐρανίων καὶ ἀφθάρτων διατριβῶν μετελθεῖν | For it was not suitable for the Mother of God to live in the midst of a crooked and perverted generation, but to pass over to the tents of the heavenly and imperishable dwellings. | Philippians 2.15 |

The Apostles/Disciples are inconsolable knowing that Mary will soon go to her Son.

| 365C 365D | Χαίρετε, τέκνα πνευματικὰ τοῦ τέκνου μου. Μνήσθητε τῶν αὐτοῦ ῥημάτων, πῶς ἡμῖν ἐν τῷ καιρῷ τοῦ πάθους μὴ θρῆνον ποιεῖν τὴν χαρὰν προσέταττεν τοῦ κόσμου. Κἀμοῦ δὲ σήμερον πρὸς | But she says to them, "Rejoice, spiritual children of my child. Remember his words, how at the time of his passion he ordered you not to make the joy of the world | |
| | αὐτὸν μετατιθεμένης, μὴ πενθοσθὴν ἐμὴν ἐργάσησθε χαρμονήν· ἀλλὰ τὸ ἐμὸν σῶμα, καθὼς ἐγὼ τοῦτο σχηματίσω πρὸς τῇ κλίνῃ, κηδεύσατε πάντες. Δοκῶ γὰρ ἐκ τῶν χειρῶν αὐτῶν ἐνταφιάζεσθαι τοῦ Υἱοῦ μου, παρ' ἡμῶν τῶν ἐκείνου μαθητῶν κηδευομένη πιστῶς. | into lamentation. Today also as I am transferred to his side, do not make my rejoicing into sorrow (πενθοσθὴν ἁ.λ.), but give funeral rites to my body, as I will arrange it on the bed. For I think I am being buried by the very hands of my Son, when I receive a funeral faithfully from you his disciples." | |

The Apostle Paul now arrives. John the Apostle greets him, which gives Germanos the opportunity to enlarge on the themes . . .

| 368A | τὴν Παρθένον | Virgin | Jn. 19.27 |

Paul is accorded a seat at the High Place (βαθμικῇ): a custom that has liturgical references. Paul seems to have arrived without knowledge of Mary's impending dormition; when he learns of it he makes a great encomium for the Virgin. Of note is Paul's proclamation: "Rejoice, Mother of life, and subject of my proclamation. Rejoice, the accomplishment of my soul's journey. For even if I have not beheld Christ in the flesh, seeing you in the body, I have the consolation of contemplating Christ, since you provided a body to the bodiless One in which he covered himself . . ."

| 368A | ἡ Παρθένος | The Virgin | |

258

368A	Χαῖρε, Μῆτερ τῆς ζωῆς, καὶ τοῦ ἐμοῦ κηρύγματος ἡ ὑπόληψις	"Rejoice, Mother of life, and subject of my proclamation.	
368A	Χαῖρε, τῆς ἐμῆς ψυχαγωγίας ἡ ἐπιτυχία. Εἰ γὰρ καὶ τὸν Χριστὸν σαρκὶ μὴ τεθέαμαι, σὲ βλέπων ἐν σώματι, τὸν Χριστὸν θεωρεῖν παρηγορούμην, τὴν σῶμα τῷ ἀσωμάτῳ χορηγήσασαν ἐν περιβολῇ.	Rejoice, the accomplishment of my soul's journey. For even if I have not beheld Christ in the flesh, seeing you in the body, I have the consolation of contemplating Christ, since you provided a body to the bodiless One in which he covered himself.	

The final moments of the Virgin's life are recounted. Many of the speeches are not reported. Germanos simply says, "And afterwards when many others besides Paul, as we have been able to learn, brought offerings of praise to the Theotokos . . ."

368B	Τὸν οὖν εἰς Χριστὸν πόθον τῷ σῷ προανεπληρούμην προσώπῳ.	So we satisfy our desire for Christ with your person/face.	
368B	Ἐγώ σε τοῖς ἔθνεσιν ἕως χθές, Θεὸν σαρκικῶς ἐκήρυττον γεγεννηκέναι·	I was proclaiming you to the gentiles until yesterday, that you had borne God in the flesh	
368B	ἀπάρτι καὶ πρὸς αὐτὸν μετατεθῆναί σε διδάξω τοῦ γνωσθῆναι αὐτοῖς ἔθνεσιν τὸ σωτήριον αὐτῶν ἐν τῇ σῇ κραταιοῦσθαι πρεσβείᾳ· ὅπως ἔχειν καὶ αὐτὰ προστασίαν πρὸς τὸν Θεὸν ἀμετάθετον	From now on I will also teach that you have been transferred to his side so that it may be made known to the very gentiles that their salvation is strengthened by your intercession and that they have immovable assistance with God."	
368B	τῇ Θεοτόκῳ	the Theotokos	
368B	ἡ Παρθένος	the Virgin	

Germanos then provides a description of Mary's falling asleep.

368B	σχηματίζει τὸ ἄμωμον ἑαυτῆς ὡς ἠβουλήθη σῶμα	blameless body	
368B	διίσταται τῆς σαρκὸς ἐν ἐγρηγόρσει,	she departs from the flesh in awakening	

Gregory E. Roth

368B	ἐλευθέραν φθορᾶς τὴν κατάλειψιν αὐτῆς ποιησαμένη	making her leave-taking free from corruption	
368C	τῷ Χριστῷ καὶ Θεῷ καὶ σωματικῷ αὐτῆς Υἱῷ	Christ [who is] God and her corporeal Son	
368C	τὸ ἀνεπίληπτον ἑαυτῆς πνεῦμα	her irreproachable spirit	
368C	ἐπὶ τῷ λειψάνῳ τῆς Παρθένου	the remains of the Virgin	

Germanos now relates the story of the funeral and burial of the Theotokos. Among the tales is that of the "the foolish man of the unbelieving Hebrews" who while attempting to disrupted the funeral procession attempts to touch the bier and loses his hands. This character appears in the iconography of the Dormition. The apostles who had arrived from various locations are the bier-bearers. Some of the faithful, however, carried off some of her garments in an effort to have some relic of her.

368C	τὸ σῶμα τῆς Παρθένου πρὸς τὸ μνῆμα τιμίως καὶ εὐλαβῶς ἐξοδεύοντες.	honorably and piously carrying out the body of the Virgin to the tomb	
368D	τῆς ζωοτόκου	the Life-bearer	
368D	ἀποικίᾳ	departure	
	Παρθένου	the Virgin	
369A	τῆς ἀχράντου	the pure one	
369A	τὸν ἔνσαρκον θρόνον μὴ ἐνδοιάσας τοῦ Ὑψίστου	the corporeal throne of the Most High	
369A	τοῦ σώματος ἅψασθαι τῆς Παρθένου	touching the body of the Virgin	
369A	ὅτι τὸ σῶμα διεγίγνωσκον ὑπάρχειν τῆς ἁγνῇ	they recognized that the body was the vessel of the pure one	
369A	τοῦ σώματος αὐτῆς	her body	

Mary's remains are placed in the tomb by the apostles. In all of this Germanos attributes the honor shown to Mary to be because of her Son and His Incarnation. At this point as they were looking away Mary's body is snatched away to be with her Son, by the invisible God and the shroud "in a light cloud . . . appeared lightly blown by the wind."

| 369B | τὸ λείψανον | the remains | |
| 369B | οἱ τὸν Υἱὸν διὰ τῆς μητρὸς, τὴν μητέρα διὰ τὸν Υἱὸν ὑπερτίμως σεβασθέντες· οἱ διὰ τὸν ἔνσαρκον γεγονότα Θεόν, τῇ χορηγῷ τῆς σαρκὸς αὐτοῦ, γνησίως τότε δεδουλευκότες Μητρί | those how venerated with great honor the Son through his mother and the mother because of the Son, who because of God who became incarnate, nobly gave service to the mother who provided his flesh. | |

260

Hovath mentions this phrase as evidence of the assumption giving the form of ἀφαιρέω as an example. 287.

369B	τὸ ἄχραντον ἀφηρπάγη τῆς Παρθένου σῶμα	the pure body of the Virgin was snatched away	
369C	Ἔγνωσαν οἱ μαθηταὶ τὴν πρὸς τὴν Μητέρα τοῦ Χριστοῦ σὺν ἀγγέλοις παρουσίαν	The disciples recognized the arrival of Christ with angels to his mother	
369C	ὑφ' οὗ καὶ μεταστᾶσαν αὐτὴν πιστωθέντες	Being convinced that she was translated by him	

The Apostles make proclamation to the people there present. The Apostles' message is redolent of the Gospel accounts of Jesus resurrection and the accusation about His body being stolen away.

369C 369D	Ἄνδρες Ἰσραηλῖται, τοῦτο νῦν γνωστὸν ὑμῖν ἐδείχθη πᾶσι περὶ Μαρίας τῆς κατὰ σάρκα μητρὸς τοῦ Χριστοῦ, ὡς ἅμα ἡμῖν καὶ ὑμῖν ἐπὶ τὸ μνῆμα τοῦτο νεκρὰ παραγενομένη, παρὰ τῶν ἡμετέρων ἀνελήφθη χειρῶν	"Men of Israel, this has now been made known to you all concerning Mary the mother of Christ according to the flesh, that to us and you together having arrived dead at this tomb, she was taken up from our hands	

Germanos then addressing those around the tomb and his hearers concludes the homily using anaphora and exhortation concerning the falling asleep of the Theotokos: "You young people also become like angels in the body as you have gone today to the tomb. Give your tongue wings for the truth." And later: "You women also become myrrh-bearers for her translation. Run, report her transference from the life-receiving tomb." He also addresses Gethsemane and draws a parallel to the burial of Christ by Joseph: "And you, the place of Gethsemane, are blessed, as you have found glory like Joseph's garden."

369D	Μηδεὶς οὖν δύσπιστος ἐν τούτῳ δειχθῇ. Μηδεὶς ἡμῖν ὡς ἐπὶ σώματος τοῦ Χριστοῦ κλοπὴν καὶ ἐν τῷ ταύτης λειψάνῳ ψευδῶς ἐπεγκαλείτω· ἀλλ' ἐὰν ἀκουσθῇ τοῦτο παρὰ τοῦ ἡγεμόνοςκαὶ τῶν ἀρχιερέων ὑμῶν, ἀμέριμνον τὴν ἀλήθειαν, καὶ μὴ τὸ ψεῦδος. ποιήσητε.	Let no one be shown doubtful in this matter. Let no one accuse us falsely of theft as in the case of Christ's body, also in the case of her remains; but if this is heard from the governor and from your high priests, make the truth free from care and not falsehood.	

Horvath mentions the title ἡ ζωοτόκος as reason for the Assumption

Gregory E. Roth

369D 372A	Ἴδε ὁ τόπος, ὅπου τέθαπται μὲν ἡ Παρθένος· μετετέθη δὲ ἡ ζωοτόκος Μαρία. Ἴδε καὶ ἡ σινδὼν χωρὶς τῆς ἔνδον σπαργαν-ωθείσης ἐπι-ζητοῦσα τὴν ἐν αὐτῇ κατα-σφιγχθεῖσαν, ἣν ὡς ἄψυχον ἐσπαργάνου, καὶ ὡς ἐμψύχῳ νῦν ὑποστρωθῆναι ποθεῖ.	Behold the place where the Virgin is buried, but Mary the life-bearer has been translated. Behold also the shroud without her who was wrapped in it, seeking her who was bound tightly in it, whom it wrapped as a lifeless [body] and now desires to be spread under as for a living [person].	
372A 372B	ἐν σοὶ δὲ τῇ Γεθσημανῇ πάντες, οἵ τε μαθηταὶ τοῦ Σωτῆρος ἡμεῖς καὶ ὁ σωρευθεὶς ἐν ταύτῃ τῇ κηδείᾳ τῆς ἀειπαρθένου Μαρίας [ὄχλος] τὴν ταφεῖσαν ἐν τῷ μνημείῳ τεθεῖσαν καὶ μετατεθεῖσαν ἴδομεν.	But in you Gethsemane all saw, both we the disciples of the Savior and [the crowd] which was gathered in this funeral of the ever-virgin Mary, her who was buried, laid in the tomb, and transferred	
372B	γέγονεν ἀφανής	at this became invisible	

Once again Germanos returns to the parallel between the burial of Mary and Christ and the claim that they were stolen away.

372B	τὸ μνῆμα κενὸν ἀφῆκεν	she left the tomb empty	
372B	καὶ τὸν παράδεισον τῆς ἰδίας ἐγέμισε δόξης, καὶ τῆς οὐρανίου ζωῆς τὴν κατάπαυσιν ἔχει· καὶ μετὰ τῆς τοῦ Θεοῦ τρυφῆς συγκάτοικος ὑπάρχει.	and she filled paradise with her own glory, and she has the rest of eternal life, and she is a companion of the luxury of God."	

Germanos ends the speech of the Apostles concerning the falling asleep of the Theotokos and goes on to complete the homily.

372B	τῆς Θεομήτορος	the mother of God	

Germanos ends the homily with a prayer in which he sums up the role of the Virgin Mary as Mediatrix.

372B	πανάχραντε Δέσποινα	all-pure Lady	

Μέμνησο Χριστιανῶν τῶν σῶν δούλων. Παράθου καὶ πάντων δεήσεις, τὰς ὅλων ἐλπίδας. Τὴν πίστιν στερέωσον· τὰς Ἐκκλησίας ἕνωσον· τὴν βασιλείαν τροπαιο-φόρησον· τῷ στρατῷ συμπολέμησον· τὸν κόσμον εἰρήνευσον, καὶ πάντας κινδύνων καὶ πειρασμῶν λυτρουμένη, ἀκατάκριτον ἑκάστῳ τὴν ἡμέραν τῆς ἀνταποδόσεως παρασχεθῆναι δυσώπησον. Πρὸς τίνα γὰρ ἄλλον ἀπελευσόμεθα; Ῥήματα ζωῆς ἔχεις τὰ πρὸς τὸν Θεὸν ὑπὲρ ἡμῶν τῆς σῆς παραθέσεως ἱκετεύματα. Σὺ γὰρ εἶ ἡ πάντοτε ποιήσασα, καὶ ποιεῖν μὴ ἐνδιδοῦσα μεγαλεῖα μεθ᾽ ἡμῶν· καὶ ἅγιον τὸ ὄνομά σου τὸ ἐξ ἀγγέλων καὶ ἀνθρώπων μακαριζόμενον ἐν πάσαις γενεαῖς γενεῶν, ἀπὸ τοῦ νῦν, καὶ ἕως τοῦ αἰῶνος τῶν αἰώνων. Ἀμήν.	Remember your Christian servants. Present the prayers of all, the hopes of all. Confirm our faith. Unite the churches. Give victory to the empire. Fight alongside the army. Bring peace to the world, and ransoming all from dangers and temptations, vouchsafe to provide for each the day of reckoning without condemnation. For to whom else shall we flee? You have the words of life which are supplications of your intercession on our behalf before God. For you are the one who always does, and never ceases to do great things with us, and holy is your name which is called blessed by angels and men in all generations of generations, from now and unto the age of ages. Amen.	Luke 1.48-50

Chapter Twenty-Six

The Sash of the Theotokos Homily
Introduction and Commentary

Germanos' homily on the Sash of the Theotokos is important to our study. It is the only one of the homilies specifically related to a unique location in Constantinople. That location in the copper market, or the Chalkoprateia, was one of the three most eminent churches dedicated to the Theotokos in Constantinople.[294] The other two were the shrines of Blachernae, and Hodegêtria. The Hodegêtria contained the Icon from which the church took its name and the Blachernae contained the robe of the Theotokos.[295] The legends surrounding the Sash's coming to Constantinople are confusing as is much of the Sash's subsequent history.[296] What is clear is that the Sash was at the Chalkoprateia in the time of Germanos. We know that there were ceremonies connected with the Chalkoprateia as well as the other Marian Churches. Xanthopoulos in his early fourteenth century text, which likely contains Anagnostes' sixth century text, reports:[297]

---

[294] John Wortley. "The Marian Relics at Constantinople." *GRBS* 45 (2005): 171.

[295] There is much confusion between the Robe and the Sash. See Wortley, *Relics* 176-9. See also: Cyril A. Mango, "Notes on Byzantine Monuments." *Dumbarton Oaks Papers* 23 (1969-70): 369-75. Professor Mango gives a full account of the state of the octagonal substructure next to the ruined church of St. Mary Chalkoprateia. When I visited the site in 1992 there was very little left and I had to search for some time and then get permission to see the area. Only parts of the walls remained.

[296] See Wortley, *Relics* 171-2, 174-77

[297] Angelidi, "Un texte patriographique;" 114; Angelidi and Papamasrorakis, "The Veneration of the Hodegetria" 373-74; A. Berger, *Untersuchungen zu den Patria Konstantinopoleos* (Poikila Byzantina 8) (Bonn: Habelt, 1988), 376. The synaxarium for April 10 illustrates the general understanding as

> She [Pulcheria] built from the very foundations three supremely
> great sanctuaries of those dedicated to the Mother of God, of
> which the one at the Chalkoprateia carries the name the holy
> *soros*, where she deposited the holy girdle of the Theometor . . .
> In it [the Chalkoprateia] a vigil and a *litania* [procession] were
> decreed to be held on Wednesdays and to advance together with
> light-emitting candles.[298]

The homily on the Sash of the Theotokos is also important because
it illustrates the juncture which the Byzantine Empire had reached. That
juncture would change the Marian cult from one that was relic-based
to one that was icon-based. Germanos stood at the juncture that forever
changed the Byzantine World.[299]

The homily is an iconodule declaration. It seems reasonable to assume
that it was preached during Germanos' reign as Patriarch, since the
reconsecration of such a church would have naturally fallen to the Patriarch,
and so it would have been preached some time between 715 and 730. That
would place it at the very beginning of the iconoclastic controversy. It is
clear that he is preaching at the rededication of the Temple—perhaps after
reconstruction due to damage from an earthquake.[300] It is also clear that the
issues of icons and their role in the political and theological issues of the
day are on Germanos' mind. It is clear that Germanos bases his theology
on the 82nd canon of the Quinisext Council. That canon is of immense
significance since it is the first official conciliar statement concerning icons.
The implications of the canon are: First, there are "potential theological
consequences in the choice of an iconography." Second, it "introduces a
need to police the visual," and so admits the possibility of an iconoclasm.
Third, it "makes the body of Christ central to the definition of Christian

---

practiced in the Orthodox Church: Καὶ ἡ ἀνακόμισις τῆς τιμίας ζώνης τῆς
ὑπεραγίας Θεοτόκου ἀπὸ τῆς ἐπισκοπῆς Ζήλας εἰς τὴν βασιλίδα τῶν πόλεων,
ἐν ἔτει ἑξακισχιλιοστῷ τετρακοσιοστῷ πεντηκοστῷ, ἐπὶ τῶν βασιλέων
Κωνσταντίνου καὶ Ῥωμανοῦ τῶν Πορφυρογεννήτων· μετὰ δὲ ταῦτα ὕστερον
ἀπετέθη ἐν τῇ ἁγίᾳ σορῷ τῶν Χαλκοπρατείων, μηνὶ αὐγούστῳ λα'.

[298] Bissera V Pentcheva, *Icons and Power: The Mother of God in Byzantium*.
University Park, PA: The Pennsylvania State University Press, 2006. 120
[299] Pentcheva 48 and n. 74
[300] Constantinople suffered many earthquakes during this period. See *DOP* 54
for a listing of earthquakes up to 1000 C.E.

representation," thus tying it with the Christology of the preceding six Councils. Fourth, it implies a "privileging" of New Testament knowledge over that of the Old Testament. The Incarnation is understood to mark a change in God's relationship with his world of matter, and how God's presence can be represented visually.[301] In this homily Germanos clearly states his position and claims that Mary is also an important guarantor of the role of representation in iconography by virtue of her singular role in the Incarnation.

The text for the homily is taken from *PG* 98. It appears only a few times in the collections of homilies according to Ehrhard. At times the authorship of another homily on the Sash is wrongly attributed to Germanos.[302] In the earliest manuscripts Δεδοξασμένα ἐλαλήθη is properly attributed to Germanos, and Τίς ὁ φαιδρὸς σύλλογος οὗτος is listed as anonymous. Later manuscripts attribute Τίς ὁ φαιδρὸς σύλλογος οὗτος correctly to Niketas the Paphlagonian,[303] and also (incorrectly) to Michael, the monk and synkellos.[304]

Additionally, there are also some incorrect attributions of the proper homily for August 31, the menological date for the celebration of the Sash.[305]

The text I have used for translation is from *PG* 98 372-384. It is the text of Combefis found in *Originum rerumque Constantinopolitarum manipulus* 232-241.[306]

---

[301] See C. Barber, *Figure and Likeness: On the Limits of Representation in Byzantine Iconoclasm.* Princeton, NJ: Princeton University Press, 2002. 45-6 for the preceding four implications. The literature on the issues of the Iconoclastic controversy is extensive. See, for example: Kenneth Parry, *Depicting the Word: Byzantine Iconophile Thought of the Eighth and Ninth Centuries.* The Medieval Mediterranean: Peoples, Economies and Culture, 400-1453. Ed. Michael Magdalin Whitby, Paul Kennedy, Hugh Abulafia, David Arbel, Benjamin Meyerson,Mark. Vol. 12. Leiden; New York: E.J. Brill, 1996. And Niki. Tsironis, "The Mother of God in the Iconoclastic Controversy." *Mother of God: Representations of the Virgin in Byzantine Art.* Ed. Maria Vassilaki. Milan: Skira, 2000. 26-39.

[302] See Ehrhard vol. III 255.

[303] For his work see *PG* 105

[304] Died about the year 845; a synkellos is a church administrator.

[305] See Ehrhard, vol. III 649 n.1. The date for the celebration of the Blachernae is July 2.

[306] *BHG* Appendix III 144.

I could locate no critical text.

Sash #	Incipit:	*PG* 98	*BHG*
1	Δεδοξασμένα ἐλαλήθη	372D—384A	1086

The homily can be divided into an introduction (372D—373C), the body of the homily (373C—381D) and a final prayer (beginning at 381C and ending at 384A). These divisions are artificial and serve only to delineate general sections. In the homily Germanos develops several themes that relate the city of Constantinople to its protectress, the Theotokos, and the role of Mary in the Incarnation, as well as a rationale for the veneration of the relics and, consequently, also icons. Germanos also makes clear with what attitude human beings must approach all of these events that assure the salvation of human beings properly worshiping God, and Mary's special role in that ethopoeia to mankind. Mary's role as intercessor and protector is linked with the God's concern for humankind.

The homily on the sash begins with calling Constantinople in effect the city of God. Germanos paraphrases David's song about Zion found in Psalm 86:

> Truly and undebatably calling you "the city of the great king,"
> the truly elect city and surpassing all other cities, not due to
> the height of the buildings nor the loftiness of the hills, but due
> to the greatness of the divine virtues, and by purity. (*cf.* Gal.
> 4.21) . . . In whom the King of kings and the Lord of lords
> dwells, in whom all the fullness of divinity resided bodily. (*cf.*
> Col. 2.9) (373A)

It also becomes immediately clear that Germanos has in mind some who do not accept the sanctity of the relics which reside in Constantinople. Constantinople is the 'spiritual Zion.' She is:

> A a city not enrolling her subjects under a mortal and earthly
> king, but under a heavenly [king] who escorts them to eternal
> life, and provides his kingdom to those who follow him.
> (373C)

Germanos finds it incomprehensible that anyone can deny the role of Constantinople, especially since the simple folk still remember the pagan past of antiquity. Those who would deny Constantinople its proper role have broken not only with the past but also with the present and are denying what must seem evident to anyone who is aware of the sanctity which the city has because of the presence of the Temple whose feast they are celebrating. All of this is due to the Theotokos' protection for the city.

> then what should one say about the God-glorified, ever-praised,
> all-pure and blameless maiden? If she bears the title of living
> city of the king, Christ, then justly also her most-holy temple,
> of which we celebrate today the festival, is and is called the
> glorified city. (373B)

Having established the theological reason, bolstered by an observation on the persistence of human belief, Germanos begins the body of his homily by addressing his auditors and giving the specific raison d'être for his Patriarchal presence, the newly rebuilt Temple. Germanos continues to weave his reasons for what he insists is the proper manner for celebrating this feast from his observations of the human condition and his insistence that there is a proper manner required of all those who wish to properly celebrate the feast.

> And the Blameless one rejoices in those of us who renewed
> in virtues, and in the godly pious citizenship, in this manner
> shall celebrate in purity the pure feast of the pure one; and as if
> we were about to approach her presence, in like manner, as we
> come to this holy temple, let us bring into order all things, and
> let us transform all things to the better, in act and in word and
> thought. Let nothing of ours be unworthy of today, neither the
> walking of the feet, not laughing, nor word; do not be turned
> aside by unsuitable clothing. What do I say? Let us also set in
> order our desires. (373C/D & 376A)

Germanos then confronts those who he calls 'grumblers,' those who doubt the Truth of the relics. His argument is made by analogy with other containers which take on the odor of that which they have contained even after being emptied.

For if a vessel contains an unguent for only a short time and then is emptied yet the odor of the unguent remains for a long time. This being true, what might one say about the Sash, and that truly unemptied and holy myrrh—I mean the true and blameless body of the Theotokos, and the Sash that was tied about her middle, embracing her for a long time? Would not the fabric preserve the odor for a long time, and would not those who draw near with faith and love be filled? A sweet smell, not like that of women's perfume, but a divine and august fragrance, driving away the passions of the soul and body.

And if the soulless vessel as we said, having associated with the lifeless myrrh, is able to partake of this quality, what also shall we say concerning this Sash which was near to the dwelling place of the living God? Shall we not run up to it? Shall we not fall before it? Shall we not ask to receive from it purity of body and soul in every way? But what [more]? (376B/C)

Having made such a comparison Germanos then launches into a set of anaphoras on the swaddling clothes and the sash which end in an acclamation and a prayer to the Theotokos and her role in the life of humans and the power she has due to her role as the one through whom the Incarnation took place.

Therefore certainly your help is a power for salvation, Oh Theotokos, and no other mediator is needed before God. This we know, and have experienced in many requests and your warm response; ungrudgingly we have received the answers to our petitions, and we flee to you, your people, your inheritance, your flock, (*cf.* Lk. 12.32) the one which is adorned by the name of your Son. There is truly no end to your magnificence; and there are no boundaries to your help. (380B)

Mary's role as intercessor for mankind is developed with reference to those who earlier were mentioned as 'grumblers' and all who opposed her birth-giving. Those who praise Mary are not limited to this earthly city. In a reference taken from the anaphora of the Divine Liturgy, Germanos sets the scene:

For you having a maternal freedom of speech and strength towards your Son, by your petitions and intercessions you have saved us who were condemned by our sins, and did not dare to look to the heights of heaven, and you redeem us from eternal punishment. . . . Praising you in it, we think that we are joining with the choir of the angels. For what race of men without being Christians enjoys such glory and has such a defense and advocacy? Who gazing in faith, when he has gazed at your worthy Sash, Theotokos, is not filled with delight? Who fervently falling down before it, vainly lifts up offerings of praise? Who contemplating your character, does not forget immediately his tribulation? 381A/B

In what serves as a final prayer Germanos uses a short anaphora intertwining the themes of the container and the fire that would consume a human being who comes into such close proximity with God.

But oh urn from which we who were set on fire by terrible things have drunk the manna of refreshment!

Oh table through whom we who have hungered have been filled with the bread of life!

Oh lamp by whom we who have sat in darkness, have been illuminated by a great light!

You have been given by God the dignity and praise that is fitting to you, do not reject also our unworthy [praise] which we bring you out of desire. Do not reject the praise of our filthy lips, all-hymned one, brought to you out of kind feelings!

Do not abominate the prayerful words of our unworthy tongues!

But according to the measure of our desire, oh glorified one of God, grant to us the forgiveness of sin, the enjoyment of eternal life, and the deliverance from all harm. (*cf.* Ps. 33.14)

Behold the most faithful gathering which surrounds you from this your holy dwelling, which is rich in having you as Lady, patroness and

Mistress, which has come together to sing heart-felt hymns, Theotokos, and is looked after by your holy oversight, take these people out of all misfortune and tribulation; from all disease, all harm, all contumely rescue them. With all joy, all health, all grace by your strong hand fill [these people] in the coming of your Son, our man-loving God, when we shall be judged, as you have motherly boldness and strength and have led us out from the eternal fire; make us worthy to attain eternal good things, by the grace and love of your Son Jesus Christ to whom be glory and might unto the ages of ages. Amen. (381C/D/384A

One cannot read this homily without seeing the iconodules' manifesto about the power of matter to contain God. While this homily seems to have been preached on the occasion of the re-consecration of the Church in the copper market, it provided Germanos with an opportunity to confirm on the basis of the importance of relics their immediate connection with the Incarnation, and to declare that the power of matter to illustrate the relationship between God and man is shown in the Virgin Mary and her role in salvation history. It was the fact of the Incarnation that assured that God, humans, and matter were not theologically incompatible, but rather humans could see through matter the presence of God in His world.

Chapter Twenty-Seven

Homily on the Sash of the Theotokos Translation

Δεδοξασμένα ἐλαλήθη περὶ σοῦ

[372D]

A homily of our father among the saints Germanos, Archbishop of Constantinople, upon the occasion of the rebuilding of the imperial temple[307] of our most holy Lady Theotokos and the holy swaddling clothes of Our Lord Jesus Christ.

"Glorious things of you are spoken, city of God."[308] (Psalms 86.4)

[373A]

To us holy David sang this in the Spirit, and in another place, being foresighted, he spoke concerning your great glory. Truly and undebatably calling you "the city of the great king," the truly elect city and surpassing all other cities, not due to the height of the buildings nor the loftiness of the hills, but due to the greatness of the divine virtues, and by purity: Mary the most chaste and surpassingly unblemished Theotokos (*cf.* Gal. 4.21).

---

[307] Mary Cunningham comments that the word ναός means "temple" and points out that here and elsewhere it is used by Orthodox as a title for the church building. See *Wider Than Heaven: Eighth-Century Homilies on the Mother of God.* Trans. Mary Cunningham. Popular Patristic Series. Crestwood, NY: St. Vladimir's Seminary Press, 2008. 247.

[308]

In whom the King of kings and the Lord of lords dwells, in whom all the fullness of divinity resided bodily. (*cf.* Col. 2.9)

[373B]

She is truly the glorious city, the spiritual Zion. She it was, I suppose, whom the God-inspired David foretold. But if one should call her house the glorified city, he would not speak outside the good and the true. For if those whose names are applied to countries save their memory in appellations for a long time, but of others whose names it is not right for us to bear on our lips, to whom are built steles and temples, and idols even up to today, even if only by reputation, the [names] remain, as if they were still around—they have hung on the ears of the simpler folk—then what should one say about the God-glorified, ever-praised, all-pure and blameless maiden? If she bears the title of living city of the king, Christ, then justly also her most-holy temple, of which we celebrate today the festival, is and is called the glorified city:

[373C]

a city not enrolling her subjects under a mortal and earthly king, but under a heavenly [king] who escorts them to eternal life, and provides his kingdom to those who follow him.

But hearing of the feast, worthy and august listeners, in this hall, do not suppose that it receives the name of inaugural from newly constructed buildings nor from newly made buildings, but from that which is renewed by the Spirit, by which our inner man, stripping off the ancient and tattered garment of sin; and putting on the new [garment] of piety, becomes a free citizen of the new life. (*cf.* 2 Cor. 4.17) And the Blameless one rejoices in those of us who renewed in virtues, and in the godly pious citizenship, in this manner shall celebrate in purity the pure feast of the pure one;

[373D]

and as if we were about to approach her presence,

[376A]

in like manner, as we come to this holy temple, let us bring into order all things, and let us transform all things to the better, in act and in word and thought. Let nothing of ours be unworthy of today, neither the walking of the feet, not laughing,[309] nor word; do not be turned aside by unsuitable clothing. What do I say? Let us also set in order our desires. And let mercy go forth before all things (Judges 11,17), by which God is served, so that being new in soul and body, we may today celebrate anew, this feast of God's most pure mother according to the flesh.

[376B]

For in this city is shown forth both the disposition and veneration of the holy, honorable Sash of the Theotokos and the all holy and most worthy[310] swaddling clothes of her Son. That Sash, which wrapped around her body, and surrounded in the womb the hidden God. That Sash, which beautifully adorned the container of God, and most venerably.

That Sash, that was enriched by the all-pure drips of milk of the most-pure one. And let no one of the grumblers, (*cf.* Judges 16) think it unreasonable that we shall speak as to things having life, and we shall offer our praises.[311]

[376C]

For if a vessel contains an unguent for only a short time and then is emptied, yet the odor of the unguent remains for a long time. This being

---

[309] Mary Cunningham mentions that this is a strange Greek expression: μὴ γέλως ὀδόντων whose meaning is presumably to laugh showing the teeth. Cunningham, *Wider*, 248 ftn 3.

[310] Mary Cunningham emends the word πανακράντων to παναχράντων. The former does not appear in either a search of the *TLG* or Lampe (except in this passage of Germanos). Ἄκραντος does appear in *LSJ*, in Pindar, etc. However the meaning is "unfulfilled," "fruitless," "idle," which would be inappropriate here. The adjective πανάχραντος is a regular epithet of the Theotokos.

[311] While it is not clear that Germanos is addressing the iconoclast party, he seems to have some group in mind who are protesting in some manner the veneration of relics. Mary Cunningham in a long footnote gives a bibliography pertaining to the question. Cunningham, *Wider* 249, ftn. 5.

true, what might one say about the Sash, and that truly unemptied and holy myrrh—I mean the true and blameless body of the Theotokos, and the Sash that was tied about her middle, embracing her for a long time? Would not the fabric preserve the odor for a long time, and would not those who draw near with faith and love be filled? A sweet smell, not like that of women's perfume, but a divine and august fragrance, driving away the passions of the soul and body.[312]

And if the soulless vessel as we said, having associated with the lifeless myrrh, is able to partake of this quality, what also shall we say concerning this Sash which was near to the dwelling place of the living God? Shall we not run up to it? Shall we not fall before it? Shall we not ask to receive from it purity of body and soul in every way? But what [more]? Shall we not speak to it as to one living, and shall we not bring pious songs? Yes, let us do this!

[376D]

Oh Sash, you have girded about the well of Life, and offer life to those who honor you, in fact eternal life![313]

Oh Sash, you give to the loins of those who turn to you mortification on the one hand, and on the other hand, manliness and energy in the practice of virtue!

Oh Sash, you bound up and restrained the weakness of our nature and you hobble both our seen and unseen enemies!

For such things happen to me being pierced by the all holy One and being carried away by the force of my words, I have forgotten about the winding sheet. And it is no wonder! A mother-loving Son rejoices in His

---

312 Mary Cunningham mentions the history of the noun ἐλάτειρα (from the verb ἐλαύνω). Of interest is that the word was used in late antiquity to mean exorcisers (Lampe 445). Cunningham suggests that it is possible that "there may be a deliberate juxtaposition with classical and late antique meanings, but Germanos is in fact describing the healing power of the scent that is preserved in the Virgin's and Christ's articles of clothing." See Cunningham, *Wider* 250 ftn. 6

313 The Greek phrase: Ὦ ζώνη, ἡ τὴν τῆς ζωῆς πηγὴν περιζώσασα, καὶ ζωὴν παρέχουσα τοῖς σὲ τιμῶσιν αἰώνιον! does play on the words "ζώνη" and "ζωῆς" as Mary Cunningham points out. See Cunningham, *Wider* 250 ftn. 8. Much is lost in translation here and elsewhere in Germanos' homilies.

Mother being glorified. But yielding to the law of our nature, even if the matter is beyond our nature,

[377A]

as is fitting we honor first the Mother. For the Lord surely will not reject the all holy One. For he deigned to come forth from her as truly human, and he deigned to be called her Son. The all-compassionate One will accept our human boldness. But having mentioned the swaddling clothes, again I return to the Mother. For she prepared them with her hands. And she wrapped the great Lord, who was a child, in these swaddling clothes. And carrying him on her lap she gave milk to him who granted breath and substance to every kind of being.

[377B]

But Oh swaddling clothes, you bound the liberating Lord, and you let loose [the] cords of our transgressions![314] (*cf.* Prov. 5.22)

Oh swaddling clothes, you bound tightly the mighty Lord, and you strengthened the weakness of our race!

Oh swaddling clothes, you guarded and enfolded faith, and you fettered the enemy and overthrew him!

And Oh swaddling clothes and venerable Sash! Grant sanctification, strength, propitiation and health to me and to those who draw near in love and venerate your holy temple.

Oh venerable Sash, that surrounds and cares for your city, and without plotting kept it safe from the attacks of barbarians.[315]

---

[314] Germanos all but forgets the swaddling clothes. See Cunningham, *Wider* 251 ftn. 9.
[315] Constantinople was besieged numerous times in its history. In Germanos time the most see especially the Arab siege in 714. For an interesting study of the walls of Constantinople, see Stephen R.Turnbull and Peter Dennis. *The Walls of Constantinople Ad 324-1453.* Fortress. Oxford: Osprey Publishing, 2004 48

[377C]

Oh radiant Sash, which honorably surrounded the very venerable body of the Mother of the incorruptible God, and thence was surrounded by incorruption, and continued to remain intact and incorruptible, as this true tradition has come down to us.[316]

But we are attempting the impossible, and are urging ourselves on beyond, to leap over the trench, and we are attempting to honor [the swaddling clothes and the sash] worthily in words, which is impossible even to the angels.

What is more, Oh honorable Sash of the all-honorable Mother of God,[317] surround with truth our loins, with righteousness and meekness. Make us inheritors of eternal and blessed life, (cf. Titus 3.7) and unassailed by enemies both visible and invisible.

[377D]

And guard our faith unshaken. Oh all pure Sash of the all pure One, guard unharmed from any kind of insult your inheritance, your people in upright faith, and save [them] through the godly life. May we have you as strength and aid, a wall and a tower a harbor and a safe refuge.[318]

But you are to me, Oh most pure, all good and most compassionate Lady, the consolation of Christians, the warmest encouragement of the afflicted, the ready refuge of sinners, do not forsake us orphans of your aid.[319] For if by you we should be forsaken, then to whom shall we flee? And what shall we become, Oh all holy Theotokos? The breath and the life of Christians,

---

[316] See also Cunningham, *Wider* 251 ftn. 10.

[317] The phrase: ὦ τιμία τῆς ὑπερτίμου τοῦ Θεοῦ Μητρὸς ζώνη demonstrates the difficulty of translation from Greek to English. Mary Cunningham points it out as an instance of metaclisis, a rhetorical device that is seldom used in English. See Cunningham, *Wider* 252 ftn. 12.

[318] This phrase is a familiar petition in the litanies of the Orthodox Church.

[319] See, Dormition I, 344B; Dormition III 360D, 364A for references to being orphaned.

[380A]

for just as our bodies have breath as a sign of its living energy, so also your all holy name continually being carried forth on the lips of your servants in all times and places and points, is not [only] a sure sign of life, wellbeing and aid, but a defender. Shelter us under the wings of your great goodness. (*cf*. Ps. 17.8) Guard us through your intercession.

Supply to us life eternal, Oh reliable hope of Christians. For we beggars, impoverished in the way of life and works of God, having seen the wealth of goodness offered to us through you, (*cf*. Ps. 31.9), let us say: "The mercy of the Lord fills the earth."[320] (Ps 33.5)

We had been driven away from God in the multitude of our sins, but through you we sought after God and found him, and having found him we were saved.

[380B]

Therefore certainly your help is a power for salvation, Oh Theotokos, and no other mediator is needed before God. This we know, and have experienced in many requests and your warm response; ungrudgingly we have received the answers to our petitions, and we flee to you, your people, your inheritance, your flock, (*cf*. Luke. 12.32) the one (flock) which is adorned by the name of your Son. There is truly no end to your magnificence;[321] and there are no boundaries to your help. Your good works are innumerable. For no one is saved except through you, Oh holy one. (*cf*. Acts 4.12)

No one is ransomed from bad things, except through you, all blameless one, no one receives gifts except through you, all holy one.

---

[320] Ps. 32:5

[321] Horvath comments that "The Marian devotion of Germanus I, Patriarch of Constantinople from 715-730 (born c. 634, d. 733), resembles that of St Bernard of Clairvaux. His praises and eulogies of Mary have almost no limit." "Germanos of Constantinople and the Cult of the Virgin Mary, Mother of God, Mediatrix of All Men". *De cultu mariano saeculis VI-XI;* Acta congressus mariologici mariani internationalis in croatia anno 1971 celebrati. 1972. Pontificia Academia Mariana Internationalis. 285.

No one receives grace except through you all venerable one.[322]

[380C]

Wherefore, who would not praise you? (Luke. 1.48 *ff*) Who would not magnify you? If not worthily, at least heartily, Oh glorious one, Oh blessed one, Oh you who received magnification from your Son and your God as great and wondrous, wherefore all generations shall praise you.

Who then but you, after your Son, takes such thought for the race of men?

Who then defends us by taking our part in tribulation?

Who then going so swiftly before us delivers us from overtaking temptations?

[380D]

Who then through prayer fights so strongly on behalf of us sinners?

Who then defends so outspokenly those who have little hope of amendment of life?

[381A]

For you having a maternal freedom of speech and strength towards your Son, by your petitions and intercessions you have saved us who were condemned by our sins, and did not dare to look to the heights of heaven, and you redeem us from eternal punishment. (*cf.* Ps. 32.7) On which account the afflicted one flees to you, the one who is wronged runs to you; the one constrained by terrible troubles, appeals for your help.

---

[322] Mary Cunningham comments on this passage "Germanos seems to go further in this homily than do other preachers in extolling Mary's central role in obtaining God's mercy for humankind." See Cunningham, *Wider* 253 ftn. 14. However, one must read this homily not in parts but as a whole. See, a few line later the reason: "Oh you who received magnification from your Son and your God as great and wondrous." And elsewhere where Mary's role in the Incarnation is clearly tied to her role as Mediatrix. See also 380B where εἰ μὴ διὰ σοῦ is repeated in the anaphora so that it becomes clear that Germanos views Mary as a necessary agent "through" whom salvation comes.

All your own, Theotokos (Luke. 5.26), is paradox, all above nature, all beyond words and power. Therefore also your protection is beyond understanding. For you have reconciled and established the estranged, the persecuted, those who had become enemies, by your birth-giving you have made children and heirs. (*cf.* Rm. 8.17) You have extended your hand of aid to those who have been plunged into the sea of every kind of sin, rescuing them from the waves.

[381B]

You continue to protect your servants from the attacks of the evil one, you continue to preserve those who flee only to your holy name. You haste to ransom those who call upon you in all needs, and all sorts of temptation, Oh all blameless one. For this reason we speedily flee to your temple; and standing in it we know ourselves to be in heaven.[323]

Praising you in it, we think that we are joining with the choir of the angels. For what race of men without being Christians enjoys such glory and has such a defense and advocacy? Who gazing in faith, when he has gazed at your worthy Sash, Theotokos, is not filled with delight? Who fervently falling down before it, vainly lifts up offerings of praise? Who contemplating your character,[324] does not forget immediately all his tribulation?

[381C]

But those approaching your holy temple, in which you have seen fit to be deposited your honorable Sash, the swaddling clothes of your Son and our God, (the deposition of which we celebrate today), it is not possible to describe how great a joy, how great a delight they have in the enjoyment [of this feast].

But oh urn from which we who were set on fire by terrible things have drunk the manna of refreshment! Oh table through whom we who have hungered have been filled with the bread of life! Oh lamp by whom we

---

[323] An Orthodox Temple can be referred to as a type of Heaven on earth.

[324] Mary Cunningham translates this phrase as referring to an image of the Virgin or the Sash. It is a difficult passage. See Cunningham, *Wider* 254 ftn. 16.

who have sat in darkness, have been illuminated by a great light! You have been given by God the dignity and praise that is fitting to you:

[381D]

do not reject also our unworthy [praise] which we bring you out of desire. Do not reject the praise of our filthy lips, all-hymned one, brought to you out of kind feelings! Do not abominate the prayerful words of our unworthy tongues! But according to the measure of our desire, oh glorified one of God, grant to us the forgiveness of sin, the enjoyment of eternal life, and the deliverance from all harm. (*cf.* Ps. 33.14) Behold the most faithful gathering which surrounds you from this your holy dwelling, which is rich in having you as Lady, patroness and Mistress,

[384A]

which has come together to sing heart-felt hymns, Theotokos, and is looked after by your holy oversight, take these people out of all misfortune and tribulation; from all disease, all harm, all contumely rescue them. With all joy, all health, all grace by your strong hand fill [these people] in the coming of your Son, our man-loving God, when we shall be judged, as you have motherly boldness and strength and have led us out from the eternal fire; make us worthy to attain eternal good things, by the grace and love of your Son Jesus Christ to whom be glory and might unto the ages of ages.

Amen.

Chapter Twenty-Eight

References to Mary in the Homily on the Sash of the Theotokos by Germanos, Patriarch of Constantinople (715-730)

PG 98 Location	Greek	English	OT/NT Reference
The introduction of this homily extends from 372D through 373C. Initially Germanos appears to be talking about the City of Constantinople. However, in 373B he appears to be drawing a parallel between the City and the Theotokos. It is also clear that Germanos is concerned with separating the relics of the sash and the swaddling clothes from the still present idols of the pagan past: "For if those whose names are applied to countries save their memory in appellations for a long time, but of others whose names it is not right for us to bear on our lips, to whom are built steles and temples, and idols even up to today, even if only by reputation, the [names] remain, as if they were still around—they have hung on the ears of the simpler folk—then what should one say about the God-glorified, ever-praised, all-pure and blameless maiden?"(373B).			
372D	ὑπεραγίας Δεσποίνης ἡμῶν Θεοτόκου	our most holy Lady Theotokos	
373B	καὶ πανυμνήτου κόρης τῆς παναχράντου καὶ παναμώμου	the God-glorified, ever-praised, all-pure and blameless maiden	
373B	πόλις ἔμψυχος τοῦ βασιλέως ἐχρημάτισε Χριστοῦ	living city of the king, Christ	

Gregory E. Roth

The body of the homily extends from 373C through 381D. Germanos begins by addressing his auditors concerning the purpose of the feast: "But hearing of the feast, worthy and august listeners, in this hall, do not suppose that it receives the name of inaugural from newly constructed buildings nor from newly made buildings, but from that which is renewed by the Spirit . . ." Germanos refers to his auditors again at the beginning of the final prayer in 381C.

373C	ἡ πανάμωμος	the Blameless one	

Germanos begins an argument from analogy concerning the sash. According to Germanos the sash is similar to any vessel that contains an unguent. Like that vessel that retains the smell of the ungent even after being emptied, so too the sash that contained (was worn by) the Theotokos retains her odor. But he is quick to add that it is: "not like that of women's perfume, but a divine and august fragrance, driving away the passions of the soul and body." 376B

376A	τοῦ Θεοῦ κατὰ σάρκα Μητρὸς	God's most pure mother according to the flesh	
376B	τοῦ Θεοῦ κιβωτὸν	the container (ark) of God	
376B	τῆς παναχράντου	the most-pure one	
376C	τὸ καθαρώτατον . . .τῆς Θεοτόκου σῶμα καὶ παναμώμητον	the most pure and blameless body of the Theotokos	
376C	τὸ ἔμψυχον τοῦ Θεοῦ Λόγου προσεγγισάσης κατοικητήριον	the dwelling place of the living God	

Germanos then begins an anaphora on Ὦ concerning the sash and the swaddling clothes. Germanos also mentions what appears to be a personal religious experience like the one described in the anaphora. He also realizes that he has forgotten the swaddling sheet since he was "carried away by the force of my words." He debates very shortly whether he should mention the swaddling clothes or the sash first and opts for the sash, since it "is fitting we honor first the Mother." Because "a mother-loving Son rejoices in His Mother being glorified. But yielding to the law of our nature, even if the matter is beyond our nature," his reason for this raised the special relationship that Mary has with her Son and provides an insight into the theological content that allows the privileges and responsibilities that Mary has: "For the Lord surely will not reject the all holy One. For he deigned to come forth from her as truly human, and he deigned to be called her Son."

376D	τῆς ζωῆς πηγήν	the well of Life	
376D	τῆς πανάγνου	all holy one	
376D	Μητρὸς	Mother	

Although there are only two references to Mary in 377A, it develops the theme of the Mother and the Child and the paradoxical relationship of a human mother and a divine Son.

284

| 377A | τῇ Μητρὶ | Mother | |
| 377A | τὴν τεκοῦσαν | Mother | |

377B contains an anaphora on both the swaddling clothes and the sash. 377C develops the theme of the incorruptible God and the incorruptible sash.

| 377C | ἡ τῆς τοῦ ἀφθάρτου Θεοῦ Μητρὸς Μητρὸς τὸ ὑπέρσεμνον σῶμα σεμνοπρεπῶς προσεγγίσασα | which honorably surrounded the very venerable body of the Mother of the incorruptible God | |
| 377C | τῆς ὑπερτίμου τοῦ Θεοῦ Μητρὸς | all-honorable Mother of God | |

377D applies the result of Mary's status to her people (the Church)

377D	τῆς παναχράντου	the all pure One	
377D	ὦ πάναγνε, καὶ πανάγαθε, καὶ πολυεύσπλαγχνε Δέσποινα	Oh most pure, all good and most compassionate Lady	
377D	τὸ τῶν Χριστιανῶν παραμύθιον	the consolation of Christians	
377D	τὸ τῶν θλιβομένων θερμότατον παρηγόρημα	the warmest encouragement of the afflicted	
377D	τὸ τῶν ἁμαρτανόντων ἑτοιμότατον καταφύγιον	the ready refuge of sinners	
377D	ὦ παναγία Θεοτόκε	Oh all holy Theotokos	
377D	ἡ τῶν Χριστιανῶν πνοὴ καὶ ζωή	the breath and the life of Christians	

380A continues to develop the theme of Mary and her people.

380A	σὸν πανάγιον ὄνομα	your all holy name	
380A	ζωῆς καὶ θυμηδίας καὶ βοηθείας οὐχὶ τεκμήριον ἀλλὰ πρόξενον	[Mary's all holy name is] not [only] a sure sign of life, wellbeing and aid, but a defender	
380A	ἡμᾶς πτέρυξι τῆς σῆς ἀγαθότητος	under the wings of your great goodness	Ps 17.8
380A	Φρουρήσῃς ἡμᾶς ταῖς μεσιτείαις σου	Guard us through your intercession	

Gregory E. Roth

380A	Παράσχοις ἡμῖν τὴν αἰώνιον ζωήν	Supply to us life eternal	
380A	Χριστιανῶν ἐλπὶς ἀκαταίσχυντε	a reliable hope of Christians	
380A	Ἡμεῖς γὰρ οἱ πτωχοὶ θείων ἔργων καὶ τρόπων, τὸν διὰ σοῦ παρασχεθέντα ἡμῖν τῆς χρηστότητος πλοῦτον θεασάμενοι	For we beggars, impoverished in the way of life and works of God, having seen the wealth of goodness offered to us through you	
380A	ἐζητήσαμεν διὰ σοῦ τὸν Θεὸν, καὶ εὕρομεν· καὶ εὑρόντες ἐσώθημεν.	but through you we sought after God and found Him, and having found him we were saved	

380B contains Germanos' understanding of Mary as Mediatrix, a meditation which continues until 380C where Germanos draws the conclusion "Wherefore, who would not praise you?" and links Mary and Jesus together in another anaphora on σ☐ "you."

380B	Δυνατὴ τοιγαροῦν πρὸς σωτηρίαν ἡ βοήθειά σου	Therefore certainly your help is a power for salvation	
380B	Θεοτόκε	Oh Theotokos	
380B	καὶ μὴ χρῄζουσά τινος ἑτέρου πρὸς Θεὸν μεσίτου	and no other mediator is needed before God	

Horvath mentions this passage along with ones in Dormition II (349B) and Presentation I (296A) as representing "almost no limit" to Germanos' praises and eulogies to Mary: 285

380B	Τοῦτο καὶ ἡμεῖς ἐπιστάμενοι, οὐ μὴν ἀλλὰ καὶ πείρᾳ μαθόντες ἐξ ὧν πολλάκις αἰτοῦντές σε τὴν θερμοτάτην ἡμῶν ἀντίληψιν	This we know, and have experienced in many requests and your warm response; ungrudgingly we have received the answers to our petitions	
380B	Οὐκ ἔστιν ὄντως τῆς σῆς μεγαλειότητος πέρας· οὐκ ἔστι τῆς σῆς ἀντιλήψεως κόρος	There is truly no end to your magnificence; and there are no boundaries to your help	
380B	Οὐκ ἔστι τῶν σῶν εὐεργεσιῶν ἀριθμός	Your good works are innumerable	
380B	Οὐδεὶς γὰρ ὁ σωζόμενος εἰ μὴ διὰ σοῦ	For no one is saved except through you	

380B	παναγία	Oh holy one	
380B	πανάμωμε	all blameless one	
380B	πάναγνε	all holy one	

At this point Germanos draws a conclusion expressing his contention that Mary's intercession should seem self-evident to anyone and links Mary and her Son together in their concern for mankind. This might be read as a veiled reference to the Incarnation. The anaphora is carried through 380D.

380C	τὴν δεδοξασμένην	Oh glorious one	
380C	τὴν μεμακαρισμένην	Oh blessed one	
380C	σὲ τὴν μεγαλεῖα σχοῦσαν παρ' αὐτοῦ τοῦ σοῦ Υίοῦ καὶ Θεοῦ ὡς μεγάλα καὶ θαυμαστά ὅθεν σε καὶ γενεαὶ πᾶσαι γεραίρουσιν	Oh you who received magnification from your Son and your God as great and wondrous, wherefore all generations shall praise you.	
380C	Τίς οὕτως ἀντιληπτικῶς τῶν ἡμετέρων προΐσταται θλίψεων;	Who then defends us by taking our part in tribulation?	
380C	Τίς οὕτως ὀξέως προφθάνων ῥύεται τῶν ὑπερχομένων ἡμῖν πειρασμῶν.	Who then going so swiftly before us delivers us from overtaking temptations?	
380C	Τίς οὕτω τοῦ τῶν ἀνθρώπων γένους μετὰ τὸν σὸν Υίὸν ὡς σὺ προνοεῖται;	Who then but you, after your Son, takes such thought for the race of men?	

In 381A/B "Mary's role as intercessor for mankind is developed with reference to those who earlier were mentioned as 'grumblers' and all who opposed her birthgiving. Those who praise Mary are not limited to this earthly city."

380D	Τίς τοσοῦτον, τῶν ἁμαρτωλῶν ἱκεσίαις ὑπερμαχεῖ;	Who then through prayer fights so strongly on behalf of us sinners?	
380D	Τίς τῶν ἀδιορθώτων κατὰ τοσοῦτον ἀντιφωνητικῶς ὑπεραπολογεῖται;	Who then defends so outspokenly those who have little hope of amendment of life?	
381A	Σὺ γὰρ μητρῷαν ἔχουσα πρὸς τὸν σὸν Υίὸν τὴν παρρησίαν καὶ τὴν ἰσχὺν	For you having a maternal freedom of speech and strength towards your Son	

381A	σαῖς ἐντεύξεσι καὶ σαῖς μεσιτείαις καὶ σώζεις, καὶ τῆς αἰωνίου λυτροῦσαι κολάσεως	by your petitions and intercessions you have saved . . . and you redeem us from eternal punishment.	Ps 32.7
381A	Ὅλα τὰ σὰ, Θεοτόκε, παράδοξα, ὅλα ὑπὲρ φύσιν, ὅλα ὑπὲρ λόγον καὶ δύναμιν	All your own, Theotokos, is paradox, all above nature, all beyond words and power	Lk. 5.26
381A	Διὰ τοῦτο καὶ ἡ προστασία σου, ὑπὲρ ἔννοιαν	Therefore also your protection is beyond understanding	
381A	Τοὺς γὰρ ἀπωσμένους, τοὺς ἐκδεδιωγμένους . . . κατήλλαξας καὶ ᾠκείωσας	For you have reconciled and established the estranged, the persecuted	
381B	πανάμωμε	Oh all blameless one	
381B	Θεοτόκε	Theotokos	

Germanos begins his conclusion. He again turns to an anaphora on Ὦ. There is a final petition to Mary whose role as Mediatrix is linked to the Incarnation. Germanos addresses once again his auditors (earlier mentioned in 376C) and enumerates the expectations with which his hearers have come to the "temple."

381C	στάμνε	urn	
381C	τράπεζα	table	
381C	λυχνία	lamp	
381D	Κυρίαν καὶ προστάτιν καὶ Δέσποιναν	Lady, patroness and Mistress	
384A	Θεοτόκε	Theotokos	
384A	καὶ ἐπισκοπῇ σου θεία ἐπισκεψαμένη	is looked after by your holy oversight	
384A	ὡς μητρῴαν ἔχουσα παρρησίαν τε καὶ ἰσχὺν	having motherly boldness and strength	

Chapter Twenty-Nine

Germanos' Mariology General Notes on the Analysis of Germanos' Homilies

Any new analysis of the homilies of Germanos must take into account the efforts of five scholars. Martin Jugié, A.A.[325] (1878-1954), P. Erasmo Perniola,[326] Tibor Horvath S.J.[327] (1927-2008), Mary Cunningham[328] and Brian Daley, S.J.[329]. The latter two have recently contributed translations of the homilies of Germanos with short comments. They also have provided me with much assistance through email and mail. Father Perniola's and Father Horvath's close studies of the homilies and texts are of primary concern for this analysis, as they provide a similar methodological approach. Father Jugié's work is also referenced with regard to Germanos only.

---

[325] Father Jugié's contribution to Marian studies are many. Of interest here is: "Les Homélies de saint germain de constantinople sur la dormition de la sainte vierge." *Échos d'Orient* 16 (1913). *La mort et l'assomption de la sainte vierge, étude historico-doctrinale.* Città del Vaticano, 1944. *L'immaculee conception dans l'ecriture sainte et dans la tradition orientale.* Romae,: Officium Libri Catholici, 1952.

[326] Father Perniola's contribution to Marian studies is: *La mariologia di san germano, patriarca di constantinopoli.* Roma: Edizioni Padre Monti, 1954.

[327] Father Horvath's contribution to Marian studies is: *Germanos of Constantinople and the Cult of the Virgin Mary, Mother of God, Mediatrix of All Men.* De cultu mariano saeculis VI-XI; acta congressus mariologici mariani internationalis in croatia anno 1971 celebrati. 1972. Pontificia Academia Mariana Internationalis.

[328] Mary Cunningham's contributions to Byzantine studies are many. Of interest here is: *Wider Than Heaven: Eighth-Century Homilies of the Mother of God.* Popular Patristic Series. Vol. 35. Crestwood, NY: St. Vladimir's Seminary Press, 2008.

[329] Father Daley's of interest here is: *On the Dormition of Mary : Early Patristic Homilies.* Crestwood, NY: St. Vladimir's Seminary Press, 1998.

This analysis is done on the basis of the text we have of Germanos' Marian homilies, and some references to other writing attributed to him. The analysis does not make reference to other writers of middle Byzantine era. Scholars such as J. List have provided us with references to parts of Germanos writings and his contemporaries.[330] Nor does this analysis attempt to apply later theological understandings to Germanos.

Germanos' style is that of a Byzantine rhetorician.[331] Germanos' homilies evidence both a considerable knowledge of the LXX and the New Testament, as well as a strong pastoral concern. He does not hesitate to use the apocrypha, especially the narratives of the nativity and the dormition of the Virgin.[332] He has been considered by some as " . . . one of the greatest mariologists in the VIII century. His homilies are important for the history of Marian theology and spirituality;"[333] Father Gambero relates that "his (Germanos') name is quoted among the witnesses of the last two Marian dogmas solemnly proclaimed by the Catholic Church, namely the Immaculate Conception and the Assumption." Neither of these dogmas is investigated here[334]. With regard to the Immaculate Conception one can only say what Father Gambero says about Mary's spiritual motherhood: "Germanus did not grasp the doctrine of Mary's spiritual motherhood; nonetheless, through his insistence on her presence among us and on her maternal concern for her children, he helped in opening the way for this doctrine.[335] With this assessment Jugié agrees: "Comme beaucoup d'autres Pères, saint Germain n'a pas aperçu toutes les conséquences du privilège de la conception immaculée.[336]

---

[330] See, J. List, "Studien zur Homiletik Germanos I. von Konstantiople und seiner Zeit." *Texte und Untersuchungen zur byzantinisch-neugriechischen Literatur* 29 (1939). I have found List particularly useful in sorting out some textual issues especially with regard to the Homily on the Annuciation.

[331] Luigi Gambero, "Germanus of Constantinople, Andrew of Crete, John Damascene: Their Marian Doctrine and Their Involvement in the Iconoclastic Controversy." Dayton, OH: International Marian Research Institute, 1990. 4.

[332] Gambero (1990) 3, 9.

[333] Gambero (1990) 3.

[334] For an Orthodox perspective on the question of the Immaculate concept of the Virgin Mary and the search for its presence in Byzantine authors see, John Meyendorff, *Byzantine Theology: Historical Trends and Doctrinal Themes.* New York: Fordham University Press, 1979. 146-50.

[335] Gambero (1990) 10.

[336] Martin Juge. L'assomption de la sainte Vierge 559.

Germanos is unique in the form that his devotion to Mary takes: "Germanus was a great devotee of the bl, [sic] Virgin. He praises her through words peculiar to him, with a simple and tender style. He calls himself Mary's slave and wants to magnify her as best he can, even though the holy Virgin could never be praised suitably."[337] He can be fairly said to be " . . . very much interested in those aspects of Marian dogma, which underline the relationship between Mary and human creatures; and, therefore, he emphasizes in an original and unique way the doctrine of Mary's mediation and intercession."[338]

Germanos also speaks from a deep knowledge of the Patristic tradition. While there appears to be only one attributable to a specific patristic father[339], one can hear the fathers woven into each homily.

For each of the homilies I have provided. The Greek text, an English translation, an introduction and commentary for each set of homilies, a compilation of the Greek/English texts with included commentary, and an analysis. In addition I have provided references to important considerations related to Mary and Germanos. The analysis is intended to be instructive as to the two approaches to the interpretation of Byzantine homilies. Generally, it can be said that the Roman Catholic approach is to find theological statements and draw conclusions on the basis of words. The Orthodox approach is more literary, more poetical, more narrative—a process in which the individual words take on less theological import and more narrative/poetic intent as rhetorical statements. Byzantine interpretations are (in the absence of definite doctrinal statements, such as by the Ecumenical councils) suggestive and often lack the kind of precise statements that Western Mariologists would like.[340]

Note: In doing my analysis of Germanos I have referenced Perniola and Horvath by using the letters 'P' and 'H' in the fourth column where appropriate. I have also given page and footnote numbers as well as in the case of Perniola. For example: (P 118 ftn.31).

---

[337] Gambero (1990) 3.
[338] Gambero (1990) 4.
[339] Pres I 296C and the end of the Annunciation Homily ftn 11.
[340] A very useful essay on this can be found in: John Meyendorff, *Byzantine Theology: Historical Trends and Doctrinal Themes*. See, especially chapter 12. 151-67.

Chapter Thirty

Ancestors of Mary

The ancestors in Germanos' homilies include Adam and Eve and all the Old Testament figures. The ancestors appear in all but the Homily on the Sash. They are most numerous in the First Homily on the Presentation some sixteen times. They appear as Mary's parents, Joachim and Anna, the first ancestors, Adam and Eve, and as singers such as David and Solomon, Prophets and Patriarchs, such as Ezekiel, Zacharias and the sister of Moses, Miriam. Aaron appears in Anna's ancestry along with David and Solomon and Zacharias' wife, Elizabeth in the Second Homily on the Presentation. David, Jacob, Zacharias and Elizabeth are mentioned in the Annunciation Homily. No specific ancestors are mentioned in the Homilies on the Dormition except for Eve and Adam. And no ancestors are mentioned in the Homily on the Sash.

It appears that for Germanos the ancestors are important as representatives of the people from which Mary comes. In this he is different only in degree from his contemporary Andrew of Crete (660—740) whose homily "On the Nativity of Our Supremely Holy Lady, the Theotokos, with proof that she descends from the seed of David" is concerned with Mary's direct ancestors as a matter of theological and soteriological importance.[341]

The ancestors are of both cosmological and anthropological importance. For Germanos there is an intimate relation between the cosmos and the ancestors and Mary. The ancestors are most often mentioned in the First

---

[341] A recent translation with notes can be found in M.B. Cunningham, *Wider Than Heaven: Eighth-Century Homilies of the Mother of God.* Popular Patristic Series. Vol. 35. Crestwood, NY: St. Vladimir's Seminary Press, 2008. 85—105.

Homily on the Entrance into the Temple. But this relationship with the cosmos, ancestors and Mary is found in the Annunciation homily and is put in the mouth of the Virgin: "<*You have heard that*> I am of the House and the ancestry of David. How shall I assist in these awesome, heavenly mysteries? And how shall I be able to conceive the holy Jesus who sits upon the Cherubim?" (324D) It is this relationship of Cosmos, ancestors and the Incarnation that is celebrated when Zacharias addresses Mary's parents in the First Homily on the Entrance: "Your rejoicing has become that of the cosmos. Your renown is the universal joy of all men. Fortunate are you who bear the title of parents of such a blessed child. Fortunate are you, who have brought such a blessed gift to the Lord! Fortunate are the breasts by which she was nursed and the womb that carried her (*cf.* Luke 11.27). (301C)"

The ancestors are seen as dancing for joy at the prospect of their release from their captivity as Zacharias proclaims when Mary is presented to him: "Zacharias rejoices that he is found worthy to receive the Mother of God. Joachim is glad, confirming the outcome of the oracles. Anna is joyful at the sanctification of her child. The forefathers jump for joy, escaping the captivity of condemnation. The prophets are delighted, and with them all who are yet to come in this age of grace also leap for joy." (300B) Mary is the cause of the ancestors' salvation as Zacharias says in the same Homily (301A) Note that the ancestors is more includes not just those of the past, but also those to come, That is that the ancestors is short hand for all of the human race.

This dance is harmonious but harmony extends to the whole cosmos as the world is brought into the right relationship with God. In this Eve and Mary are used as comparisons in the Second Homily on the Dormition. Germanos compares the result of Eves disobedience and Mary's obedience in this rhetorical device :

> . . . you are the mother of the true Life. You leaven the new creation of Adam. You free Eve from reproach. She is the mother of earth; you are the mother of light. Her womb [is the source] of destruction; your belly [is the source] of imperishability. She is the dwelling-place of death; you are the removal from death. She brings eyelids down to earth; you are the unsleeping glory of wakeful eyes (*cf.* Ps. 120.4 LXX and later 357B). Her children are grief; but your Son is universal joy. (349A)She,

as being earth, passed into earth; but you bore Life for us, and passed over to life, and obtained the power to mediate life to mankind, even after death. (349B)

Ancestors can be individuals such as Mary's own parents. Ancestors can be used to represent all of humankind, they can be past and future generations. Time and again Germanos calls upon individuals to proclaim God's presence in His world. (297D) Germanos creates an image in which the ancestors are harmoniously and joyfully dancing because God has acted in His world and because Mary has been obedient to Him in becoming a willing participant in the Incarnation of His Son. At the very beginning of Mary's obedience to God, as her parents present her in the Temple, an ancestor of Mary is called upon: " . . . come with me, David the forefather and ancestor of God and make ever more harmonious music striking your harp in the giving of hymns on the strings of the spirit (cf. I Samuel 16.23) with your God-inspired voice," (297A) to lead the procession of virgins who escort Mary to the Entrance in the Temple.

Chapter Thirty-One

Mary's Conception, Childhood
and Mary as Gift

There is no homily on the conception of Mary among Germanos' homilies. It appears that the earliest homily on the subject was preached by John of Euboea[342]. Mary Cunningham points out that there is little evidence concerning him[343]. She also suggests that we can date him only by a reference in his homily on the Massacre of the Innocents to 742 or 744[344]. The source of John's homily on the conception of Mary is the Protoevangelion of James. While being unsophisticated in rhetorical style, John still is able to employ apostrophes, dialogue and colorful ekphrasis.[345] John's homily is primarily concerned with Mary's parents Joachim and Anna—much as Germanos does in a more sophisticated rhetorical style in the First and Second Homilies on the Presentation. Both Germanos' homilies and John's share a tenderness toward the plight of Anna especially.[346]

Perniola lists twenty-one instances in Germanos homilies which he contends are indications of Mary's Immaculate Conception. Twelve of these in the First Homily on the Presentation, two in the Second Homily on the Presentation, one in the Annunciation, two each in the First Homily and the Second Homily on the Dormition, one in the Third Homily on the

---

[342] M.B. Cunningham, *Wider Than Heaven: Eighth-Century Homilies of the Mother of God.* Popular Patristic Series. Vol. 35. Crestwood, NY: St. Vladimir's Seminary Press, 2008, 45—7.

[343] Cunningham, 46

[344] Cunningham, 46

[345] See, Cunningham, 46 and the homily 173—195.

[346] See, sections on Mothers and Mary as Mother in Germanos and Virginity—Sterility in this dissertation.

Dormition and one in the Sash Homily. Fifteen of Perniola's citations can be found in the rhetorical devise of anaphora where Germanos is praising Mary and frequently employs Old Testament typologies in an effort to link cosmologically Mary to the fulfillment of the promise of God to His people. None of these references provide us with any substantive evidence that Germanos believed or did not believe in the Immaculate Conception of Mary.

In Germanos' homilies Mary's birth and conception are mentioned only twice. First, in the First Presentation Homily Joachim and Anna call together all the virgins to be torch-bears and Anna says:

> They call together, as it is reported, all the virgins in the region to go after her as torch-bearers. Delighted by the procession of the lamp-bearers, she walks without turning back.

> And the barren and unfruitful Anna with foresight lifts her hands to God and says in a loud distinct voice, "Come with me, let us rejoice together, all women and men who rejoiced at her birth, even more now, as I dedicate to the Lord this divinely beautiful and holy gift recently received from my own womb. Come with me, chorus leaders, with singers and instrumentalists, and joyfully begin new songs in a new way, not as did Moses' sister Miriam (*cf.* Exodus 20-21) but with my daughter as the leader. (297A)

Anna's call is to "all women and men who rejoiced at her birth". Clearly Germanos views this as a call to their immediate neighbors, but also turns it into something of a cosmological event and a proclamation of Mary's role as the one who is the sign of the new covenant as Moses' sister Miriam is of the old.

The second instance occurs in the Second Presentation Homily. Once again it is Anna who speaks, this time to Zacharias in explaining why she was so bold as to bring her daughter to the Temple. Anna has just related her prayer to the Lord asking for a child and now says:

> thus you see the Lord who is ready for mercy and loves souls has bent down and sent an angel to the prayers of both of us, announcing to us the conception of my child. So therefore when

[my] nature was bidden by God, it received the seed; for it did not dare to accept it before the divine grace. But when that [grace] preceded, then the closed womb opened its own gates, and receiving the deposit from God, held it in itself, until by the good will of God it brought forth to light that which had been sown in it. (313C/D)

Does "So therefore when [my] nature was bidden by God, it received the seed; for it did not dare to accept it before the divine grace. But when that [grace] preceded, then the closed womb opened its own gates, and receiving the deposit from God, held it in itself, until by the good will of God it brought forth to light that which had been sown in it." mean that Mary was Immaculately conceived? Or does it mean that it was God's will to bid Anna's nature at that point? Perniola states that Germanos was inclined to believe that Mary's conception was a virginal one. And that here he is saying that he believes in the Immaculate Conception. And he gives as evidence not only this section in the Second Presentation Homily but also that because of Mary's Immaculate Conception she was freed from the corruption of the tomb.[347]

While Perniola's interpretation seems plausible it seems that it raises questions that mitigate such a bold statement. Such as, if Anna conceived Mary Immaculately, why did Germanos not use this as one of the Angel's arguments in the Annunciation Homily? And why did the Seventh Ecumenical Council not then also affirm Germanos' position on the Immaculate Conception? And why has the Orthodox Church allowed

---

[347] E questo tanto più in quanto San Germano inclina a credere, come altrove abbiamo detto, che la concezione di Maria sia stata una concezione verginale. «Subito infatti, egli scrive, al comando di Dio, la natura generò la prole, né ciò era stato possibile prima I della grazia divina; ma come essa per prima vi fece il suo ingresso, la matrice fino allora chiusa, aprì le sue porte, e ritenne presso di sé il dono ricevuto da Dio, fino a quando, per volere dello stesso Signore, quello che era stato concepito, venne alla luce»

Non solo quindi la fecondità di Anna è frutto della grazia. di Dio, ma anche la Vergine che essa genera sarebbe un dono che Dio stesso affida alle sue viscere.

Ed è ancora in virtù della sua immacolata concezione che Maria è liberata dalla corruzione del sepolcro, causata dal peccato. Perniola, Erasmo. *La mariologia di san germano, patriarca di constantinopoli.* Roma: Edizioni Padre Monti, 1954. 130

the question of the Immaculate Conception of Mary to be one of the theologumena?

It appears that all we can claim is that Germanos doesn't give a definite answer to this question and we need to leave our answer ambiguous as well.

Both of the Presentation Homilies give us glimpses of the childhood of Mary, but only as connected with her Entrance in to the Temple.

Chapter Thirty-Two

Cosmos, Man and Mary

For Germanos both his cosmology and anthropology arise from the biblical account of creation. In this Germanos follows the Genesis account of creation. It is given as a fact that all of creation is God's work. In the Second Homily on the Dormition Germanos confirms this position: "In/ by faith we know that the heavens have been fitted together, as it is written (Heb. 11.3; cf. Gen. 1.1)"[348]. Man, God's final creation, because of his status is made master over all of creation. He is tasked with giving names to all things. In this man is a co-creator with God and man is acting in a manner that is constitutive of his very being.[349] That synergistic relationship is broken by the Fall. The Fall changes both the cosmos and man. Following Paul in Romans the Fathers saw that "the earth is cursed because of you" and "the creation was made subject to vanity and servitude but not as if it was supposed to be that way" [350] Both the cosmos and man became subject to an un-natural evolution. It is that un-natural evolution which man calls the "natural state."

> The Fall had repercussions in that it perverted not only the initial relationship between God and man but also the relationship between man and the cosmos. Nature is not at all demonic, but the disturbed relationship of man with the world deprives the

---

[348] Germanos gives this reference to Heb 11.3 and a possible reference to Gen 1.1 as a reason for Mary's Falling Asleep and her continued presence with humankind. Dorm II 357A.

[349] See, Paul Evdokimov, *The Art of the Icon : A Theology of Beauty*. Redondo Beach, Calif. ; [United Kingdom]: Oakwood Publications, 1990. 99-120 for a good account of the Orthodox view of cosmology and anthropology.

[350] Evdokimov 99

world of its center, man, and thereby alters its nature. It is left estranged.[351]

In the First Homily on the Dormition Germanos describes the original cosmology:

> For when the heavens along with the generations of men were established, angels were assigned to tend their life; and to guide, and administer, and guard them, with an unchanging heart of faith towards God. "For he established," it is said, "bounds for the nations according to the number of the angels of God." (Deut. 32.8, Odes 2.8)(340D)

And he also describes the result of the Fall and the disorder that it brought: "But of the wretched men then living in error and idolatry, polluting the air with the smoke of sacrifices, for the rest even the angels ceased from companionship with men; for God took away his holy Spirit from them in return." 341A

Anna goes on to describe the result of her prayers and those of her husband. The result of their supplications is that they are granted the child for whom they prayed. Germanos makes it clear that this is a sign that the natural order is restored cosmologically since the word of Anna conceiving the Theotokos is delivered by an angel:

> thus you see the Lord who is ready for mercy and loves souls has bent down and sent an angel to the prayers of both of us, announcing to us the conception of my child. So therefore when [my] nature was bidden by God, it received the seed; for it did not dare to accept it before the divine grace. But when that [grace] preceded, then the closed womb opened its own gates, and receiving the deposit from God, held it in itself, until by the good will of God it brought forth to light that which had been sown in it. (Presentation II, 313D)

A sign of the disorder of the cosmos is found in two forms of sterility. First, the sterility of the Law and that of Anna, the mother of the Theotokos.

---

[351]   Evdokimov 100.

In the Second Homily on the Presentation Anna describes the consequences of the Fall and the un-naturalness:

> Why have you made me an example in my family, and a shaking of the head in my tribe? Why have you declared me a participant in the curse of your prophets, giving me a childless womb and dry breasts (*cf.* Hosea 9.14)? Why have you made my gifts unacceptable as of a childless [woman]? Why have you left me to become a cause of muttering for my acquaintances, and a mockery for those at hand, and a reproach for my neighbors? Look at [me], Lord; hear [me], Master; have compassion [on me], Holy One. Make me like the birds of heaven, the beasts of the earth, the fish of the sea: because they also are productive before you, Lord. May I not appear worse than the irrational animals, O Most High, I who have been made by you in your likeness and image (*cf.* Genesis 1.26).' (313B)[352]

In the natural order of the cosmos Anna should be able to conceive. In both Homilies on the Presentation Germanos shows a deep and intimate knowledge of the disappointments that arise because of the Fall.[353]

The Virgin's Entrance into the Temple is a sign that the work of God is to restore the proper order of the cosmos and human beings' role in it. Mary's residence in the Temple allows her to become 'God's workshop'. Once again Germanos views this event to have cosmological significance: "Come to me, child, child higher than the heavens. Come, you who are seen as a child but are known as God's workshop (θεϊκὸν ἐργαστήριον).

---

[352] Perniola lists this as a definite reference to the Immaculate Conception. E questo tanto più in quanto San Germano inclina a credere, come altrove abbiamo detto, che la concezione di Maria sia stata una concezione verginale. «Subito infatti, egli scrive, al comando di Dio, la natura generò la prole, né ciò era stato possibile prima della grazia divina; ma come essa per prima vi fece il suo ingresso, la matrice fino, allora chiusa, aprì le sue porte, e ritenne presso di sé il dono ricevuto da Dio, fino A quando, per volere dello stesso Signore, quello che era stato concepito, venne alla luce.» Non solo quindi la fecondità di Anna è frutto della grazia di Dio, ma anche la Vergine che essa genera sarebbe un dono che Dio stesso affida alle sue viscere. See, Erasmo Perniola, *La mariologia di san germano, patriarca di constantinopoli.* Roma: Edizioni Padre Monti, 1954. 130 ftn. 26

[353] For more on sterility see the separate section on sterility and virginity.

Come hallow rather the gateway of the holy place, for you, so to speak, are not purified and hallowed by this [gate]: but instead you hallow it more." (Presentation I 301C)

Using the metaphor of light and the morning star Germanos describes how the Nativity of Christ restored the possibility of that right relationship between God, man, the angels and creation.

> And again [Scripture] called your belly "womb", to show also the habitation of the Only-begotten from your flesh; but "before the morning star" has declared the night then before the dawning—morning star, you who well represent the day. Since in the night you bore light for those who sat in darkness (*cf.* Luke 1.79), [Scripture] called "before the morning star" the hour of your childbirth. For it says, "Shepherds were in the same place outdoors and keeping watch at night." (Luke 2.8) Such was glory shown to the heavenly ones through you, O Theotokos. If it had not been new—the angels would not be singing "Glory in the highest," in praise of your ineffable childbearing had it already been glorified. What kind of illumination is this also of earthlings? Because through your blameless flesh man has been made a citizen of heaven, and shepherds associated with angels.(344A)

And in this Mary becomes, through the Incarnation, the instrument of the re-establishment of that synergy. "For when you were proved to be a God-containing heaven of the most high God, since your bosom [was] able to carry(ing) Him, and again you were called a spiritual earth because of the [God-]containing service of your flesh." (344C).

Mary is lauded as:

> Before the sun [is/was] your light. Above all the creation is your honor. Before the angels is your greatness. "You [are] higher than the heaven" (Job 11.8) but also wider than the heaven of heavens, and than the holy seventh [heaven] which according to someone in Scripture distinguishes from it. You more than eighth heaven, and if it is possible to speak of any other beyond this: blessed are you to generations of generations; (353B)

And "Angels rejoice in the mansions of the heavens; we (human beings) delight to spend time in your holy temples" (356B) And

> But when you gave birth in the last times to him who "in the beginning' was the Word of God the Father (*cf.* John 1.1), at once upon your delivery even the armies of the angels bent down from the heavens, hymning the God who was born from you, and shouting that glory was attributed in the highest places and they cried out that peace had arrived on earth (*cf.* Luke 2.14). So no longer did they name enmity as a dividing wall between angels and men, heaven and earth, but a harmonious commonwealth and one antiphonal doxology from both angels and men, sent up to God one and trinity. And the Father of his only-begotten Son, bearing witness to his physical birth from you without a father, proclaims to him, "Today I have begotten you." (Psalm 2.7 LXX) And again, "From the womb before the morning star I have begotten you." (Psalm 109.3 LXX) (341A/B)

It is because of this understanding of cosmology that Mary is frequently praised as "wider than the heavens" which is a type of the Incarnation.[354] The cosmological dimensions of Mary's participation in this the angel says:

> Hear, most blessed one, hear the hidden words of the Most High.

> "Behold, you shall conceive in your womb, and you shall produce a son, and shall call him Jesus" (Luke 1.31). Prepare then for Christ's coming. For I have come to announce to you what has been decreed before the foundation of the cosmos.[355] (Annunciation 321C)

---

[354] The "Wider that the Heavens" icon shows Jesus seated on the lap the Theotokos who has her hands spread out wide. It generally appears in the apse of an Orthodox Church directly over the altar.

[355] ". . . before the foundation of the cosmos." Means before time. See, Evdokimov, *Icon* 102.

It is important to keep in mind that for the Byzantine Christian "the entire content of the Christian faith depends upon the way in which the question "Who is Jesus Christ?" is answered."[356] The Incarnation is a cosmic event. In the hymn for Vespers on December 24 this is expressed:

> "What shall we present unto Thee, O Christ,
>
> For Thy coming to earth for us men?
>
> Each of Thy creatures brings Thee a thank-offering:
>
> The angels—singing; the heavens—a star;
>
> The Wise Men—treasures; the shepherds devotion;
>
> The earth—a cave; the desert—a manger;
>
> But we offer Thee the Virgin-Mother. O Eternal God, have mercy upon us"
>
> Stichera by Patriarch Anatolios on "O Lord, I have cried unto Thee"
>
> And also in the canon at Matins:
>
> "Today the whole creation rejoices and is jubilant,
>
> For Christ is born of the Virgin".
>
> Christmas Canon, 9th song[357]

Within the Orthodox tradition the faithful are taught theological meaning in the form of the canons and the kontakia and troparia. These poetical compositions form the basis of the teaching of the Orthodox Church.[358]

---

[356] John. Meyendorff, *Byzantine Theology: Historical Trends and Doctrinal Themes*. New York: Fordham University Press, 1979. 151

[357] http://www.orthodoxchristian.info/pages/Christmas_hymns.html

[358] Alexander Schmemann, Liturgy and Tradition: Theological Reflections of Alexander Schmemann ed. Th. Fish (Crestwood, NY, 1990), 11-20.

Chapter Thirty-Three

The Cult of the Theotokos

A good deal can be learned about the cult of the Virgin Mary from Germanos' homilies. But why the cult? According to Germanos the cult of Mary is because the world is in debt for her roles as the mother, the mediatrix and due to her protection. In his homilies on the Falling Asleep of the Virgin Germanos has Jesus say to his mother: "I will show you to the world that is your debtor, and I will glorify your name even more as you are translated." (Dorm III, 361D)

That debt can not be repaid: "For although he is greatly in your debt he gives you nothing in return, he multiplies thanksgiving, [just] as you [multiply] your advocacy." (Dorm. III, 362D) But "the debtor always praises his own benefactor. He who is being saved does not fail to recognize the protection of his own savior. (Dorm. I, 340A). Mary's Divine Motherhood is the source of her power. Mary clearly has a guiding hand in the affairs of the state and the Church.

The reason for the world's debt becomes clear as Germanos recounts the deeds of the Virgin with regard to the good estate of those who are followers of her Son. In the First Homily on the Entrance, in the final prayer, Germanos expresses the reasons for the cult of the Virgin:

> But O most blameless and all-laudable, most holy one, offering to God greater than all created things, untilled earth, unplowed field (*cf.* Ezekiel 19.10), well-pruned vineyard, most joyous wine bowl, gushing spring (*cf.* Ezekiel 17.6), virgin birth-giver and husbandless mother, treasure of purity and ornament of holiness, by your acceptable and motherly-persuasive petitions to your son, born from you without a father, and the God Creator of all, following the furrows of good ecclesiastical order, steer

us from the floods of heresies and scandals to the calm and
harbor where ships do not sink.* (308C)

Clothe the priests brilliantly with righteousness (*cf.* Psalm
131.16 LXX) and the joy of glorious blameless pure faith. [As
for] those orthodox lords who have obtained you as a diadem
and robe sea-purple and supremely golden dye, or pearl, or
precious stone and the undefiled ornament of their own royalty,
wielding their scepters in peace and stability; subject to them
and spread under their feet the un-filial barbarian nations who
blaspheme against you and the God [born] from you. (308D)

Guard [them] in the hour of battle along with the army which
always relies on your aid. Confirm [them] to go obediently
by God's command with the well-directed servitude of good
order. Crowning with victorious trophies your city which holds
you as tower and a foundation, protect [her], girding [her] with
strength. Keep the dwelling-place of God always as the beauty
of the temple. Preserve those who praise you from all misfortune
and distress of soul. Providing rescue for the captives, appear as
a succor to those who are strangers, homeless, and friendless.
Stretch out your protective hand for all the world, so that in
joy and gladness we may celebrate your festival with the rites
which we are now most gloriously performing. In Christ Jesus
the King of all and our true God, to whom [be] glory and power,
along with the holy Father, the source of life, and the coeternal
Spirit, one in essence and sharing the throne, now and ever and
to the ages of the ages. Amen (309A)

Mary's power as intercessor is a direct result of her Divine Motherhood,
and this naturally leads on to her special relationship with the Body of
Christ, the Church. At the end of the Dormition Homilies Germanos
expresses the dependence of the Christian people and the state on Mary's
intercessions:

For to whom else shall we flee? You have the words of life
which are supplications of your intercession on our behalf
before God. For you are the one who always does, and never

ceases to do great things with us, and holy is your name which is called blessed by angels and men in all generations of generations (Luke 1.48-50), from now and unto the age of ages. Amen. (372C)

Frequently Germanos recounts Mary's role vis à vis her roles as protectress of the City of Constantinople. Not surprisingly many of these occur in the Homily on the Sash that celebrates the re-consecration of the Church of the Sash of the Theotokos in the copper market.

You continue to protect your servants from the host of evil, you continue to preserve those who flee only to your holy name. You continue to anticipate ransoming those who call upon you in all needs, and all sorts of temptation, Oh all blameless one. For which reason we speedily flee to your temple; and standing in it we know ourselves to be in heaven.

We praise you in it joining with the choir of the angels. For what race of men is well off without being Christians and having such a defense and advocacy? Who gazing in faith, when he has gazed at your worthy Sash, Theotokos, is not filled with delight? Who fervently falling down before it, vainly lifts up offerings of praise. (381B/C)

The Cult and the Festivals that are celebrated are not delineated in Germanos Homilies[359]. However, the calls to celebrate the various feasts give us some idea of how Germanos viewed the proper attitude toward them.

Every divine festival, whenever it is celebrated, spiritually fills those who are present from a treasury and divinely flowing spring. But even more and beyond other feasts does this recently hymned festival (The Entrance into the Temple), brilliantly celebrated, attract the soul with holy joy and gives more joy

---

[359] In Germanos *On the Divine Liturgy* little information is given as to festivals and Mary is only mentioned a few times.

in proportion to the preeminence of the excellent child of God.
(292C)

And he encourages those at the Feast:

Let us hasten to pick the precious flowers from the private
meadow of the Mother of God.(292C)

And let us be anointed with the perfume of her roses, as
Solomon says in the beautiful verse of his Song: "Who is that
who comes up from the wilderness, perfumed with myrrh and
frankincense, with all the fragrant powders of the merchants?"
(Song of Songs 3.6)—"Come hither from Lebanon, my bride;
come hither from Lebanon" (Song of Songs 4.8) (292D)

So let us eagerly approach together this mutually beneficial,
salvific feast of the Mother of God. (293A)

We also can get an idea of the make-up of the congregation
from his homilies.

But we, the remnant of God's people (*cf.* 1 Peter 2.10), priests
and rulers, secular and monastics, slaves and free, craftsmen
and farmers, gatherers and fishermen, young and old, men and
women: hither, (312B)

let us eagerly approach the Theotokos, and let us watch the
divine mysteries which were accomplished earlier in her.
(312C)

We can also learn that there was an element that was in some way
opposed to the cult, or at least, to part of it. In an interesting part of the
First Homily on the Entrance Germanos says: "Let those who are vainly
wise in their own sight tell us: How, when other barren women have given
birth, is none of their daughters dedicated in the holy of holies and received
by prophets? Could not those who then saw such great things [done] for
her say, as also those of the same mind later [said] for her son: "What

will this child be?"[360] Yes indeed. But let those of alien mind travel the road of perdition, and let them fall into the pit which they have dug." We have no specifics about this group, but we can catch the general tone of a controversy in Constantinople. (312B)

Germanos near the end of the Homily on the Sash gives his reasons for the Cult of the Virgin: "Who then, but you after your Son, would take thought of the race of men? Who then defends us by taking our part in tribulation?" (380C).

The Cult and the celebrations and prayers that are part of it in Germanos' time suggest that Germanos, at least, found in the Virgin an approachable, loving and powerful ally in the spiritual life. She was Mother, Mediatrix and Protector and that was enough to justify devotion to her. In the First Homily on the Entrance Germanos in his development on the number three relates how his spiritual and physical life was made better: "And my Lord Jesus' ministry was for a period of three encircling years, cleansing me from the stain of my transgression and at another time healing every disease and weakness." (296B/C) Later in the same homily he places words in the mouth of the priest Zacharias which might be Germanos own prayer: "Hail to you who by the rhythm of your footsteps trample down my terrible leader—that serpent with his crooked-minded, good-hating diabolical nature—who has counseled me toward transgression. (305A) At the end of the same homily Germanos illustrates Mary's power of intercession and the power of her example in her own Falling Asleep, and his hope to be joined once more with a female relative who has preceded Germanos in death:

Have mercy on me, bending down to my tears. (320A)

Have compassion on me, as mother of the God who loves mankind. Look down and assent to my supplication, fill up my thirsty desire, and join me to my relative and fellow servant[361] in

---

[360] At Luke 1.66, these words are used about John the Baptist, not about Jesus.
[361] We do not know who this relative of Germanos was, but it must have been a woman who followed a life of service to God. Georges Gharib and Luigi Gambero. *Testi mariani del primo millennio.* Roma: Città Nuova Editrice, 1989. 336 nt. 8. While we do not know the name of Germanos' relative this passage is redolent of the final prayers in the Orthodox funeral and memorial service and should be read as one who is familiar with them as Germanos' auditors would have been.

the land of the meek, in the tents of the just (*cf.* Psalm 118.15), in the choir of the saints (*cf.* Psalm 116.9); and make me worthy, I beg you, O protection and joy of all and brilliant gladness of heart, to rejoice along with her, in your truly ineffable joy, [because] of the God and King who was born from you, and in his imperishable bridal-chamber, and in the unceasing and insatiable delight, and in the kingdom which has no evening and no limit. Yes, Mistress; yes, my refuge, my life and my support, my armor and my boast, my hope and my strength. Grant me with her to enjoy the inexpressible and unceasing gifts in the heavenly mansion. (320A)

Germanos' hope borne of his trust in the intercession and example of Mary is once again placed in the mouth of Zacharias when Germanos, an old man prays:

Gaze upon the veil (*cf.* Exodus 26.31*ff.*), you who enlighten through your lightning flash those who are blinded by their dull-sighted tastes. Give to me your hands as I lead you like a babe and hold my hand exhausted by old age and weakened by earthly-minded zeal in transgressing the commandment, and lead me to life. For behold I keep you as a staff in old age and a prop for the weariness that comes naturally with old age. (Pres I, 301D)

While we can gather little from Germanos on the order of the celebration of the festivals of the Virgin Mary, we can gather an understanding of the reasons for her cult. For Germanos it was first in gratitude for the work of Mary in the history of salvation—for the Incarnation, the mothering of the Lord, the suffering of Mary, the example of Mary as the leader (the new Miriam) of the new dance of the new covenant, her power of intercession and protection, and her love, concern, and companionship with the members of the Body of Christ—the Church. Germanos homilies read as deeply pastoral and intimately connected with the human experience as he illustrates time an again in brilliant moments of reflection on Mary and the human condition.

Chapter Thirty-Four

Eve and Mary

Germanos views Eve as the counterpart to Mary, the cosmological ancestor and anthropologically as the mother of mankind in its fallen state. But he does not condemn Eve. Eve, to be sure, is the one who is deceived as Mary says in the Homily on the Annunciation: "I am afraid and I tremble at your words. I suspect that you have come to deceive me like another Eve. I am nothing like her. What a greeting you bring to a maiden whom you have never seen before!" (324B) But she is also freed from reproach (Dorm. I, 349A) It is the serpent who is condemned in Germanos cosmology for evil: "And then by the assent of God and the counsel of the priests a lot is drawn concerning her, and Joseph the just is allotted, and receives this holy Virgin according to the dispensation from the Temple of God and his priests, to ensnare the serpent who originated evil, so that he should not attack the undefiled maiden as a virgin, but as a betrothed woman he should pass her by."(Pres. II, 316D) And, "Hail to you who by the rhythm of your footsteps trample down my terrible leader—that serpent with his crooked-minded, good-hating diabolical nature—who has counseled me toward transgression (*cf.* Genesis 3.1-13)." (Pres. I, 305A)

Eve is the first mother. Cosmologically Eve represents, with Adam, the failure of the human race to reach God's intended purpose for mankind. Eve is mentioned by name only in the Annunciation Homily and the Second Dormition Homily. Eden is mentioned in the First Homily on the Presentation (300C) and, the serpent in mentioned in the Second Homily on the Presentation (316D). One also must include Eve among the ancestors that are part of the chorus found in the First Homily on the Presentation (300 A/B/C). Time and again, Eve is seen as the counterpart to Mary. Mary and Eve are compared in the Second Homily on the Dormition:

For you are the mother of the true Life. You leaven the new creation of Adam. You free Eve from reproach. She is the mother of earth; you are the mother of light. Her womb [is the source] of destruction; your belly [is the source] of imperishability. She is the dwelling-place of death; you are the removal from death. She brings eyelids down to earth; you are the unsleeping glory of wakeful eyes (cf. Ps. 120.4 LXX and later 357B). Her children are grief; but your Son is universal joy. She, as being earth, passed into earth; but you bore Life for us, and passed over to life, and obtained the power to mediate life to mankind, even after death. (349A/B)

And Mary's obedience is viewed as releasing Eve who is Mary's tribeswoman:

"Do you open paradise, which your relative and tribeswoman Eve closed" (Dorm III, 361D).

In the Homily on the Annunciation Eve is clearly seen as a type after which women are likely to follow. Mary, herself, acknowledges this in her conversation with the angel: "I am afraid and I tremble at your words. I suspect that you have come to deceive me like another Eve. I am nothing like her. What a greeting you bring to a maiden whom you have never seen before!" (324B). And Mary has to be assured by the angel that he is not a 'beautiful' young man but an angel bring the news of her impending pregnancy for God. "Why? For what purpose, for what reason, have you distrusted my good news, Glorified one? How long will you disobey the angel that was sent to you from heaven? I am not Eve's deceiver—far from it." (325A) And Joseph accuses Mary of following the path of her mother Eve. (336B)

So, Eve cosmologically is the source of death as we saw above in the comparison of Mary and Eve. And Mary cosmologically is the source of Life and joy. Eve is compared with the Earth and Mary with Heaven.[362]

---

[362] Perniola in commenting on 349A/B states: L'antitesi non poteva essere enunziata in termini più forti. Eva, la madre della polvere, della corruzione, della morte, delle umiliazioni e dei dolori del genere umano; Maria invece madre della luce, immunità dalla corruzione, liberazione dalla morte, trionfo ed allegrezza per tutti. Eva, tratta dalla terra, alla terra fece ritorno; Maria al contrario, non solo ci diede la Vita, ma alla Vita fece ritorno; e quello che più

Father John Meyendorff provides a valuable Orthodox perspective on the role of Mary as the 'new Eve' and the difficulties that arise from approaching Byzantine texts from a Western perspective:

> Byzantine homiletic and hymnographical texts often praise the Virgin as "full prepared," "cleansed," and "sanctified." But these texts are to be understood in the context of the doctrine of original sin which prevailed in the East: the inheritance from Adam is mortality, not guilt, and there was never any doubt among Byzantine theologians that Mary was indeed a mortal being.

> The preoccupation of Western theologians to find in Byzantium ancient authorities for the doctrine of the Immaculate Conception of Mary has often used these passages out of context . . .

> Quotations can easily be multiplied, and they give clear indications that the Mariological piety of the Byzantines would probably have led them to accept the definition of the dogma of the Immaculate Conception of Mary as it was defined in 1854, *if only* they had shared the Western doctrine of original sin. But it should be remembered—especially in the context of the poetical, emotional, or rhetorical exaggerations characteristic of Byzantine liturgical Mariology—that such concepts as "purity" and "holiness" could easily be visualized even in the framework of pre-Christian humanity, which was considered as mortal, but not necessarily "guilty". In the case of Mary, her response to the angel and her status as the "new Eve" gave her a special relation to the "new race" born of her.[363]

In Byzantine theodicy guilt and inclination to sin are not a universal result of the Fall. There is always the possibility that an individual human life, and the choices made by the human being, can participate in God as a theothesized human life.[364]

---

conta si è che dall'alto dei cieli conserva il potere di accordare la vita agli uomini.

[363] John Meyendorff, *Byzantine Theology: Historical Trends and Doctrinal Themes.* New York: Fordham University Press, 1979. 147-8.

[364] See, the chapters on "Mary the Cosmos and Man" and "Mary as Exemplar of Theothesized Humanity.

Chapter Thirty-Five

Mary as Intercessor and Protector

Germanos often comments on how difficult it is to adequately praise Mary. How the human race is in her debt, and laments that he and, for that matter, the whole Church are not able to offer thanks to Mary. He describes the world, himself, and other humans as debtors to Mary. All three instances occur in the Dormition Homilies:

> The debtor always praises his own benefactor. He who is being saved does not fail to recognize the protection of his own savior. (340 A, Dorm I)

> I will show you to the world that is your debtor, and I will glorify your name even more as you are translated. (361D, Dorm III)

> For although he is greatly in your debt he gives you nothing in return, he multiplies thanksgiving, [just] as you [multiply] your advocacy (362C, Dorm III)

The debt is owed to Mary because of her role in the salvation of humankind. She is, first and foremost, the human instrument of the Incarnation. She is the primary intercessor/protector of the Church and the city of Constantinople. She is the icon of what the human condition in life may be[365] and the assurance that death has been transformed by the resurrection in her Falling Asleep—she is the companion of all the living. And it is because of this that she is the intercessor who humans entrust with their petitions to God.

---

[365] See, section entitled: "Mary as Exemplar of theothesized humanity."

Mary's role, that of mother, gives to her special a relationship with Jesus. The love of a child for his mother is the reason that Mary will not suffer the same death as other humans. Her body which has been the throne, the container, etc of God could not be consigned to the grave. Jesus as the Son comes to Mary before her Fall Asleep and reassures her:

> Come willingly to the one who was borne by you. I want to
> make you joyful as a child should, to pay back to you the rent
> of the maternal womb, the wages of wet-nursing, the exchange
> for upbringing, the fulfillment for your affection. (Dorm. III,
> 361C)

The reciprocity of this relationship is given as a reason for the treatment Mary receives at her burial: "those how venerated with great honor the Son through his mother and the mother because of the Son, who because of God who became incarnate, nobly gave service to the mother who provided his flesh" (Dorm. III, 369B). It is from this relationship that Mary has "a maternal freedom of speech and strength towards your Son" (Sash, 381A).

Germanos develops this relationship between Jesus and Mary. It is also, for Germanos, the source of Mary's power as an intercessor: "For it is not possible for your voice ever to be disregarded, since God is obedient to you in every way and for every reason and in every situation, as you are his true and pure Mother" (Dorm. II, 352A)[366] And "Therefore also whatever you seek from him, he gives with a child's affection, and whatever you seek from him, he fulfills with the power of God: who is blessed unto the ages."(348C).

Mary's role as an Intercessor is also that of a protector. Not only does she protect individual members of the Church when they ask, but also she is requested to protect the Church and the city of Constantinople: "Crowning with victorious trophies your city which holds you as tower and a foundation, protect [her], girding [her] with strength." (Pres. I, 309A)[367]

Mary is also the protector of and companion of the Church over which she has direction: "And your great oversight for us characterizes

---

[366] Also see, 308C, 348C and other references to her power as a mother for intercession.

[367] Especially look at the Sash homily.

your companionship with us. And we all hear your voice, and the voice of all [comes] to your ears of hearing, and being known by you through your support, we recognize always your protective support." (Dorm I, 344D/345A). In the Third Homily on the Dormition those around Mary, and by extension the Church, pleads not to be left a orphans at her Falling Asleep.[368] Jesus, himself, tells Mary:

> You rightly possess the title "full of grace" in every way. As when you, being about to conceive me, were addressed with "hail," hail also as I seek to receive you at my side. Do not be disturbed as you leave the world which perishes along with its desires. Let its corruption go, since you will not leave those in the world orphaned of your protection; but just as I, although I am not in the world, oversee and care for those in the world, so also your advocacy will not be taken away from those in the world until the end. (360D)

Mary's companionship with the Church after her Falling Asleep heralds a new relationship with humans. One in which Mary and her companions are united in a special manner from which grows the assurance that Mary's power is mediated to human kind as a gift for all sinners who are willing to ask for her aid:

> Because having you as a companion in the sojourn of this world, O Mother of God, and seeing you like Christ himself we are consoled when we behold [you], we meditate on your translation. But since by divine authority and fleshly attachment to a mother, you have been asked to return to God, we rejoice at what is being accomplished fittingly for you, and turning out advantageously. For we also acquire fulfillment of eternal life in addition to you, and we have obtained you as an intercessor who is being translated to God's side. (Dorm III, 365B/C)

> Therefore your Christian people examining their own [affairs], delegate you to bring their petitions to God with confident speech. They unhesitatingly make bold to entreat you, all-holy

---

[368]   See, 360D, 364A.

> Lady, because of [their] experience and the multitude of your
> bounties towards us, and to constrain you often in supplications.
> In return who will not bless you (*cf.* Luke 1.48)? You are a
> vision beyond the understanding of the angels. You are the
> surpassingly strange good fortune of mankind. You are the
> support of the nation of Christians.(Dorm. II, 352A/353A)

As the Angel in the Annunciation Homily predicts: "You shall become the common propitiation of all Christians. And therefore again I salute you as is fitting, "<*Hail*> O full of grace, the Lord is with you, blessed are you among women, blessed is the fruit of your womb" (Luke 1.38). (329B)

Not only is Mary's intercession powerful but it is necessary to human salvation. In the Second Homily on the Dormition after comparing Mary and Eve he says:

> because your advocacy is living, and your intercession is life,
> and your protection is ceaseless. For if you were not guiding,
> no one would be made fully spiritual; no one would be
> worshipping God in spirit (John 4.24). For then is a man fully
> spiritual, when you, O Theotokos, became the dwelling-place
> of the Holy Spirit. No one is filled with divine knowledge, if
> not through you, all-holy [lady]. No one is saved, if not through
> you, Theotokos. No one is free from dangers, if not through
> you, Virgin Mother. No one is redeemed, if not through you,
> Mother of God.

No one receives the gift of mercy, if not through you, Theochoretos. (349B/C)[369]

This anaphora on 'no one' when read in its context becomes a cosmological statement of the work of God in salvation history. Germanos also compares the Intercessions of Mary with the saints and clearly finds hers to be different. Horvath points out that "Unlike the saints who just serve (διακονεῖν) and distribute God's grace and benefits, Mary is

---

[369]   Also see, Sash 380B.

αἰτοθμένη Intercessor who like the mother of an emperor possesses a certain motherly authority . . ."[370].

Germanos appears to have had experience with the power of Mary's Intercessions and her guidance. In the First Homily on the Presentation he addresses Mary:

> But Oh me, Mistress, my only soul-leader from God, the divine dew of the burning in me, the moisture flowing from God for my parched heart, the bright-shining lamp of my darkened soul, the guide for my journey, (317D)

> the power for my weakness, the clothing of my nakedness, the wealth of my poverty, the healing of my incurable wounds, the removal of tears, the cessation of groaning, the reversal of misfortunes, the lightening of pains, the release of fetters, the hope of my salvation, hear my prayers: have pity on my groaning, and accept my lamentations. Have mercy on me, bending down to my tears. (320A)

All of this is especially poignant when Germanos, in the final prayer in the Second Homily on the Presentation pleads with Mary:

> Have compassion on me, as mother of the God who loves mankind. Look down and assent to my supplication, fill up my thirsty desire, and join me to my relative and fellow servant[371] in the land of the meek, in the tents of the just (cf. Psalm 118.15), in the choir of the saints (cf. Psalm 116.9); and make me worthy,

---

[370] Tibor Horvath. "Germanos of Constantinople and the Cult of the Virgin Mary, Mother of God", Mediatrix of All Men. De cultu mariano saeculis VI-XI; acta congressus mariologici mariani internationalis in Croatia anno 1971 celebrati. 1972. Pontificia Academia Mariana Internationalis. 289.

[371] We do not know who this relative of Germanos was, but it must have been a woman who followed a life of service to God. Georges Gharib and Luigi Gambero. *Testi mariani del primo millennio.* Roma: Città Nuova Editrice, 1989. 336 nt. 8. While we do not know the name of Germanos' relative this passage is redolent of the final prayers in the Orthodox funeral and memorial service and should be read as one who is familiar with them as Germanos' auditors would have been.

I beg you, O protection and joy of all and brilliant gladness of heart, to rejoice along with her[372], in your truly ineffable joy, [because] of the God and King who was born from you, and in his imperishable bridal-chamber, and in the unceasing and insatiable delight, and in the kingdom which has no evening and no limit. Yes, Mistress; yes, my refuge, my life and my support, my armor and my boast, my hope and my strength. Grant me with her to enjoy the inexpressible and unceasing gifts in the heavenly mansion.

For as the mother of the Most High you have, I know, the power which runs along with the will; and because of this I am bold. Therefore may I not be deprived, all-undefiled Lady, of my expectation (*cf.* Galatians 6.4); but may I obtain this, Bride of God, you who gave birth beyond words to the expectation of all, our Lord Jesus Christ, the true God and Master: to whom is due all glory, honor, and veneration, with the Father who has no beginning, and the life-giving Spirit, now and ever, and to the ages of ages. Amen. (317D—320A/B)

---

[372] This is a reference to Germanos' relative.

Chapter Thirty-Six

Motherhood and Mary as Mother

Mothers and their role in salvation history form, perhaps, the most universal part of Germanos' Mariology. Across his narrative mothers from Eve to Mary are placed in cosmological and anthropological roles. Germanos also reaches the heights of his rhetorical efforts when speaking of motherhood.

Eve is the first mother. Cosmologically Eve represents, with Adam, the failure of the human race to reach God's intended purpose for mankind. Eve is mentioned by name only in the Annunciation Homily and the Second Dormition Homily. With the exception of the Second Homily on the Dormition Eve is not seen as the mother. When she is, she is viewed as the counterpart to Mary's motherhood both on the cosmological and anthropological levels.[373]

The second prominent women in Germanos' homilies is Anna, the mother of the Theotokos. Anna appears in both of the Presentation Homilies and in the Homily on the Annunciation[374]. In both homilies she is the driving force behind the conception of Mary. In both instances she represents the Old Testament mother (along with Elizabeth, the other mother in Germanos). She is represented as pleading with God to have an end to her sterility and bareness[375]. Germanos leaves to Anna the task of explaining to Zacharias (the husband of Elizabeth) the priest why Mary

---

[373] See the section in this dissertation on Eve and also see 349A/B for the counterpart of Mary and Eve.

[374] See, 324C

[375] See the section of virginity and sterility for a more complete development of this theme.

should be accepted into the Temple.[376] In the course of explaining this she tells of her prayer to the Lord and in doing so echoes the wants and wishes of the Old Covenant for the New Covenant. Zacharias welcomes Mary into the Temple with these words:

> Then holding the child with great joy, he brings her eagerly into the Holy of Holies, perhaps saying things like this to her: "Come here, fulfillment of my prophecy. Come here, completion of the commandments of the Lord. Come here, seal of his covenant. Come here, goal of his counsels. Come here, revelation of his mysteries. Come here, mirror of all the prophets. Come here, refutation of those who utter evil. Come here, joining of [things] long ago separated. Come here, support of things bent down. Come here, renewal of things grown old. Come here, light of those lying in darkness. (Pres II, 316B).

Cosmologically Anna is pleading for all things to be restored to the original order of the creation. She says: "

> Why have you made me an example in my family, and a shaking of the head in my tribe? Why have you declared me a participant in the curse of your prophets, giving me a childless womb and dry breasts (*cf.* Hosea 9.14)? Why have you made my gifts unacceptable as of a childless [woman]? Why have you left me to become a cause of muttering for my acquaintances, and a mockery for those at hand, and a reproach for my neighbors? Look at [me], Lord; hear [me], Master; have compassion [on me], Holy One. Make me like the birds of heaven, the beasts of the earth, the fish of the sea: because they also are productive before you, Lord. May I not appear worse than the irrational animals, O Most High, I who have been made by you in your likeness and image (*cf.* Genesis 1.26).' (Pres II, 313B)

---

[376] See, 312D/313A "Then perhaps he embraced the mother and addressed her, saying something like this, and holding the child by her hands: "Where are you from, O woman? What is your character, and the purpose of such an undertaking? And how, since you have no model of this kind, have you alone discovered this new and unprecedented action? To bring a maiden to make her tent in the sanctuary? What is your plan? Tell me. And what is your name?"

Zacharias, the priest and prophet (Pres. II, 312D) responds to Anna's story of her quest to be a mother by pronouncing her: ""Blessed is your root, O all-honored one. Glorified is your womb, you who love your husband. And exceedingly glorious is your offspring, you who love God [or, beloved of God]."(Pres. II, 316B). And in the First Homily on the Presentation Zacharias says to Mary's parents: "Your rejoicing has become that of the cosmos. Your renown is the universal joy of all men. Fortunate are you who bear the title of parents of such a blessed child. Fortunate are you, who have brought such a blessed gift to the Lord! Fortunate are the breasts by which she was nursed and the womb that carried her" (*cf.* Luke 11.27).

Anna is also the instigator and arranger of the procession that brings her daughter to the temple.

> And then when [the child] had been weaned, 'I return my vows to God, which my lips sent forth, and my mouth spoke in my tribulation (Psalm 65.13*ff* LXX).' For this reason I assembled the band of virgins with torches, I called the priests together, I gathered my relatives, saying these [words] to all: 'Rejoice with me, all of you, that I am proved today both a mother and a guide; not bringing my child to an earthly king, because it is not fitting, but dedicating this [child] to the heavenly king, as his [own] gift. For the rest, O prophet, receive my god-given daughter. Receive [her] and leading her in, plant her in the place of sanctification, in the prepared dwelling-place of God, making no nosy inquiries, until God who summoned her here is pleased to bring to conclusion the matters concerning her."(Pres. II, 316A)

The second Old Covenant mother is Elizabeth. She appears in the Homily on the Annunciation and her pregnancy appears to be the pivotal point for belief in the Incarnation for both Mary and Joseph. The angel closes his case to Mary for her belief in what he is saying and the message he brings by saying: "I shall tell you clearly, that Elizabeth your cousin at this very moment is about to give birth in her old age to a son, and at his birth many shall rejoice and be amazed, for his name will be called John" (cf. Luke 1.19).(325C) And Joseph is almost persuaded of Mary's innocence and the truth of the Incarnation when Mary states: "You have heard that my kinswoman, Elizabeth the wife of Zacharias, has even now conceived beyond hope a Prophet and Forerunner. For if he were not a prophet he would not have leapt to worship the Lord hidden inside of me" (cf. Luke 1.40).(333B).

Mary as mother is present in each of the homilies. In the two Presentation homilies references to Mary as mother are more commonly related to her future role. Frequently they are titles such as 'the Mother of God,' 'Virgin Mother,' 'Mary the all-holy Mother of God,' 'Mother of the Lord,' 'Lady and Mother of God,'. Occasionally Germanos uses the theological term 'Theotokos'. Sometimes he references a function of motherhood: "she who is the nourisher of our lives". Phrases that also use the role of mother, or its functions, in comparisons that are frequently paradoxical: 'the only [woman] known as virgin and mother,' 'virgin birth-giver and husbandless mother.' 'Bride of God, you who gave birth beyond words to the expectation of all'. Typologies also abound in connection with Mary's Divine Maternity: 'mystical and holy Ark,' 'delightful and rational paradise of God,' 'sacred, undefiled, most pure palace of the omnipotent God,' 'holy throne of God, the divine gift,' and 'the all-gold container.'

The two Presentation homilies are concerned with the Entrance of Mary into the Temple in preparation for her Divine Maternity. They are concerned with the unique event of an introduction of a young female into the Temple and what is more to live in the Holy of Holies[377]. Mary is in these homilies a " . . . child skipping and rejoicing, as in a bridal chamber, walked in the Temple of God; being three years old in her chronological age, but more than perfect in divine grace, as foreknown and predestined and chosen for the God and governor of all." (316C)

The Annunciation Homily is concerned with Mary's role in the Incarnation[378]. This unique homily in Germanos corpus is a dialogue among three persons: Mary, Joseph and the Angel. The Angel is the only one of the three who seems to understand the implications of the Divine Maternity from the beginning:

Hear, most blessed one, hear the hidden words of the Most High.

"Behold, you shall conceive in your womb, and you shall produce a son, and shall call him Jesus" (Luke 1.31). Prepare

---

[377]   See, 312C, 312D, 316B and other places.

[378]   See the Introduction to the Annunciation Homily for the development of the characters in this homily.

then for Christ's coming. For I have come to announce to you what has been decreed before the foundation of the cosmos. (321C)

He understands the purpose of his coming and attempts to tell Mary what it is:

> The Lover of mankind, wishing to fulfill His ancient plan, and having mercy on mankind's wandering, was pleased in his goodness and love for man to become man. (321D)

Mary appears to be less sure about the message at the beginning of the homily and only becomes convinced toward the end of the first dialogue. Joseph does not enter the homily as an actor until the second half and is very slow to comprehend the truth of Incarnation. Through most of the dialogue Joseph appears to more concerned with what will be thought of him for not guarding Mary's virginity and the reaction of the Jewish authorities to her pregnancy. In fact one of his solutions is the throw Mary out of his house:

> Leave my house now quickly, and go to your lover. I shall not feed you again, you will not eat bread at my table, inasmuch as with anguish and scorn, instead of joy, you have dishonored my grey hair. (332D)

and

> Even if I keep quiet about your sin, the stones will cry out. And the Holy of Holies will shout aloud, because I received you for safe keeping from the priest who is enrolled there, and I have not guarded your virginity. (333D)

It is only after the Angel appears to him in a dream that Joseph becomes aware that Mary is part of a much greater plan than he is able to imagine.[379]

---

[379] See 337B *ff*

The Dormition homilies view the Virgins Motherhood in three ways. First, he sees in Mary's motherhood a normal relationship between a parent and her child. Jesus gratitude to her is one of the reasons given for Mary's Falling Asleep and the trust between them is given as one of the reasons that Jesus gives to Mary that she not be concerned with her impending death[380].

Second, Mary's motherhood is given as a reason that she should not suffer corruption:

> You, as it is written, [are] "in beauty" (Cant 2.3 LXX) and your virginal body, altogether holy, altogether pure, altogether the residence of God; so because of this [it is] separated and alien from earthly dissolution. While remaining human it is changed to the sublime life of incorruptibility. This is safe and supremely glorious, life-accomplishing [it's life ended] and unsleeping; as it was not possible for this to be controlled by death-dealing confinement, being a God-receiving vessel, and a living temple of the all-holy divinity of the Only-begotten One. Because of these things, we trust that you, O Theotokos, will return home with us. (345B)[381]

Third, Mary's motherhood is extended to those who form the Body of Christ, the Church.

> For also, as you kept fellowship in the flesh with our ancestors, likewise also with us you dwell in the spirit. And your great oversight for us characterizes your companionship with us. And we all hear your voice, and the voice of all [comes] to your ears of hearing, and being known by you through your support, we recognize always your protective support. For there is no barrier—I mean not even due to the separation of the soul and body—for you recognize your servants. For you did not abandon those whom you saved, you [did not] leave those whom you gathered together; because your spirit lives always, and your flesh did not endure the corruption of the grave.

---

[380] See 357C, 361C
[381] Also see 345C, 357B, 357D, 364A.

You oversee all, O Mother of God, and your oversight is upon all, so that even if our eyes do not have the power to see you, all-holy one, you love to dwell in the midst of all, revealing yourself especially to those who are worthy of you. For the flesh does not hinder the power and activity of your spirit, just as wherever it wishes your spirit blows, since it is pure and immaterial; incorrupt and unstained, and a spirit which dwells together with the Holy Spirit, and the chosen one of the only-begotten divinity. (344D/345A)

She is called a 'companion with life', and her intercessions for the Church are always honored: "Therefore also whatever you seek from him, he gives with a child's affection, and whatever you seek from him, he fulfills with the power of God: who is blessed unto the ages." (348C)[382]

In Germanos' homily on the Sash Mary's motherhood is illustrated in two ways. First, with reference to her care for Jesus as a small child. Both the Sash and the swaddling clothes are mentioned as garments that came into intimate contact with Mary and Jesus: "And Oh swaddling clothes and venerable Sash! Grant me sanctification, strength, propitiation and health to me and to those who draw near in love and venerate your holy temple." (377B)

Second, Mary's motherhood is viewed as providing protection both for the city of Constantinople and the Christian people.

> Therefore certainly your help is a power for salvation, Oh Theotokos, and no other help is needed to (find) God. This we know, and have experienced in many requests and your warm response, ungrudgingly we have received the answers to our petitions, and we flee to you, your people, your inheritance, your flock, (*cf.* Luke. 12.32) the one (flock) which is becoming beautiful by the call of your Son. (380B)[383]

The Divine Maternity of Mary gives rise to a rich set of allusions to motherhood. The majority of them are typological. Epithets such as: 'the golden jar,' 'carrier of life,' 'nourisher of the nourisher,' 'throne,' 'royal

---

[382] Also see 349C, 352A, 353A, 353B,
[383] See also 373B, 373C, 381A/B

seat.' 'God-containing tabernacle,' 'temple,' are to be found in Germanos' homilies[384].

The Divine Maternity is clearly of both cosmological and anthropological importance in Germanos' theology[385].

---

[384] See my listings of the references to Mary in Germanos' Homilies found with each homily in this dissertation.

[385] A word needs be said about both Perniola's and Horvath's work on this subject. Horvath lists words that he believes are important to the development of the theme of 'Motherhood'. He gives 13 references which I have listed. Perniola includes the Divine Maternity as part of the 13th and 14th chapters labeled 'Il Prodigio della Vergine Madre' and 'La Concezione Immacolata de Maria' and to a lesser extent in the remaining parts of his dissertation, Perniolas reference are much more thorough.

Chapter Thirty-Seven

Parallels between Jesus and Mary

Horvath at the very beginning of his article on Germanos states: "It looks as though he (Germanos) were trying to apply to our Lady within the limits of Orthodoxy, the various functions, titles and names of Jesus. So his Mariology seems to be some sort of extension of Christology (ὡς ἐν Χριστῷ καὶ ἐν σοὶ τὸ γεγραμμένον πληροῦσθαι·)"[386] (Dorm II, 356B). Father Horvath's statement is, perhaps, too tentative. There are numerous parallels between Jesus and His Mother. All of them are the direct result of the Incarnation and the role of the Theotokos in Jesus' life and that of His Church. While there are references to the parallels in all the homilies it is in the Dormition Homilies that they are most explicit.

Three parallels that stand out are those of the two Entrances: the Εἰσόδος which literally means 'entrance' and the Ὑπαπαντή which literally means 'meeting.' The source for the Entrance of the Theotokos is outside the canonical scriptures and the source for the Meeting is from Luke 2. To my knowledge Germanos does not mention this parallel.

The second parallel is the burials. This parallel Germanos does mention in the Dormition Homilies: "Set down your body in the place of Gethsemane with good cheer, as I before I suffered set down my knees there in a human prayer. For prefiguring your dormition, I myself also bent the knees of my body towards such a place. So as I after the kneeling at that time went forth to my life-giving and willing death on the cross, you

---

[386]   Tibor Horvath, S.J. "Germanos of Constantinople and the Cult of the Virgin Mary, Mother of God, Mediatrix of All Men." *De cultu mariano saeculis VI-XI; acta congressus mariologici mariani internationalis in croatia anno 1971 celebrati. 1972.* Pontificia Academia Mariana Internationalis, 285.

also after the laying-down of your remains will immediately be transferred to life." (Dorm. III, 364A).

A third parallel is that of the Assumption and the Ascension, which is not developed within Germanos' homilies.

Equally common are the parallels that are drawn because of the relationship that Mary has with her Son. Father Perniola lists many such parallels drawing conclusions concerning both the dogmas of the Immaculate Conception[387] and the Assumption[388].

---

[387] See, Erasmo Perniola, *La mariologia di san germano, patriarca di constantinopoli.* Roma: Edizioni Padre Monti, 1954, 191 ftn. 3 and others listed in the References to the Parallel Events found in the appendix.

[388] Perniola, see the References to the Parallel Events found in the appendix.

Chapter Thirty-Eight

Mary as Queen and Empress

Words such as queen, mistress, royal are used by Germanos to designate Mary's status as Empress. The majority of these happen in the Annunciation Homily and are put in the mouth of the Angel. There are occasions where Mary applies the term to herself, both of these occur in the Annunciation Homily. In the first instance Mary is speaking to the Angel and is claiming that she comes from royal blood.: "I am of royal blood, and spent my earliest childhood in the royal house of Bethlehem, and my childhood I spent blamelessly in the temple; and being a virgin up to now, how can I be called the mother of my child?"(329C). In the second instance Mary is speaking to Joseph who is still unconvinced of the instigator of Mary's pregnancy which Mary deems to be quite an unsatisfactory way of dealing with her and says: :Now you attack me like a foreigner and a stranger and an accuser. You do not converse with me like a queen, but secretly pursue me from city to city. How I shall defend myself now?" (336C)

The titles queen and mistress and are applied to Mary in the Presentation Homilies in a predictive manner. All but one are spoken by Zacharias, the priest who receives Mary in the Temple. The one exception is put in the mouth of Anna, Mary's mother.

In the Dormition homilies Mary is only given the title of mistress. In these instances she is the 'Mistress of those who have perished in the substance of clay' ((357A). Clay being a term for human beings.

In the Homily on the Sash the terms patroness and Mistress are applied to her as the protector of the faithful and by extension of the City of Constantinople.

Behold the most faithful gathering which surrounds you from this your holy dwelling, which is rich in having you as Lady, patroness and Mistress. (381D/384A)

Chapter Thirty-Nine

Virginity and Sterility

Both Horvath and Perniola treat Mary's virginity with reference to the Immaculate Conception. Both present strong evidence for the probability that Germanos held some opinion (theologumenon[389]) concerning Mary's conception. Fr. Horvath makes the claim that "It seems that this text most explicitly expresses Germanus' faith in the Immaculate Conception." [390] This statement is found in the First Homily on the Presentation. He especially quotes 293C: Today she who alone is called the new, god-like, purifying and mercy seat, not made by hands, (cf. Hebrews 9.11) for mortals who have drowned in floods of sin is presented to the mercy seat of the temple. He presents as evidence the Greek words that Germanos uses in this passage. This is, however a particularly difficult poetic passage and illustrates the short-comings of depending on one word or group of words to confirm a theological position that is, at best unclear in the Greek[391].

He presents as evidence the Greek words that Germanos uses in this passage. Perniola gives twenty-one possible references to the Immaculate Conception in Germanos' homilies. The majority of these come from that

---

[389] A theologumenon is an opinion that is not contrary to the faith but is not a matter of dogma. See, Lev Gillet, "The Immaculate Conception and the Orthodox Church". 1983. <u>Chrysostom</u>. (August 1 2008).

[390] Tibor Horath S.J. "Germanos of Constantinople and the Cult of the Virgin Mary, Mother of God, Mediatrix of All Men". De cultu mariano saeculis VI-XI; acta congressus mariologici mariani internationalis in Croatia anno 1971 celebrati. 1972. Pontificia Academia Mariana Internationalis. 286

[391] Σήμερον τῷ ἱλαστηρίῳ ἀνατίθεται ἡ μόνη τοῖς τῶν βρότων ἐσφαλλομένοις διεξαχθεῖσιν ἀμπλακημάτων ἐπιρροαῖς, ἱλαστήριον καινόν τε καὶ θεοειδέστατον καθαρτικόν τε καὶ ἀχειρότευκτον χρηματίσασα.

same homily.[392] Both authors quote 293C. Perniola's much more complete references appear to be the result of considerable knowledge of Byzantine thought and in some instances make connections that on first reading would not appear to the Western Christian mind to be evidence, but do in fact contain relevant evidence[393].

The total virginity of the Theotokos has been an accepted necessary condition of the Incarnation from the time of the first ecumenical councils. In Germanos' homilies this has both physical and cosmological significance. Germanos sees Mary's virginity as not only a guarantee of the truth of the Incarnation[394] but also plays with the concept of virginity and barrenness[395]. In the First Homily on the Presentation he clearly states this:

> Today a babe is handed over to a priest, the one who will dedicate the only high-priestly God made flesh as a child at forty days for us, having received in his welcoming arms (*cf.* Luke 1.22*ff.*) the uncontainable One who is beyond all human knowing.[396]

> Today a new, pure, unspoiled book which will not be written by hands, but written in gold by the spirit, hallowed with blessings according to the Law, she is brought forward as an acceptable gift.

---

[392] Erasmo Perniola *La mariologia di san germano, patriarca di constantinopoli.* Roma: Edizioni Padre Monti, 1954. He finds 12 of the 21 in the First Homily on the Presentation.

[393] See for example his reference to 313B. 130 ftn. 26

[394] For the only [woman] known as virgin and mother has surpassed all thought, and the cause is clear. For what virgin has given birth, or after giving birth has preserved her virginity undefiled, except you alone, who truly bore God in the flesh for us, all-blessed maiden? (304C)

[395] Hail, you who through your birth released the fetters of sterility, who scattered the reproach of childlessness, and sank the curse of the Law (*cf.* Galatians 3.13); (308B)

[396] This is a reference to the Presentation in the Temple of Christ. Germanos makes reference to that event to set the events of the Presentation of the Theotokos in the context of her role in the Incarnation. Mary and Joseph present Jesus to Zacharias as Mary was presented to Zacharias by Joachim and Anna. Both presentations were necessary parts of salvation history.

Today Joachim, who has wiped away the reproach of childlessness, goes openly down the main road boastfully showing off his offspring, and again is shown as a functionary of hallowing according to the Law.

Today also Anna has exchanged the persistence of barrenness for fruitfulness, and becoming inspired by joy, proclaims to the ends of the earth that she has borne a child, embracing to her bosom the one who is wider than the heavens. (293B)

Clearly it is God's plan[397] that the barrenness of Joachim and Anna should result in this "maiden from the promise" (312A). To Germanos this promise is not only the promise made by Joachim and Anna to each other in their marriage, nor solely the promise made to dedicate the child, but also the completion of the promise contained in the Old Testament. "Today, at three years of age, she goes towards her dedication in the temple of the law, she who alone is called the stainless and greatest temple of the high priest and the Lord of all, and in whose bright light is the radiance of divine light which illuminates the darkness of the Law." (293A). The result of this conception is to complete the promise of the Temple worship and makes a reference to the Church's liturgical assembly and its role as the New Jerusalem:

Today the gate of God's temple is opened to receive the entry of the eastward looking, sealed gate of Emmanuel (cf. Ezekiel 44.1-3).

Today the sacred Table of the temple joyfully meets and participates in the true divine table of the heavenly soul-feeding bread and by changing to the worship of the bloodless sacrifice begins to shine

Today she who alone is called the new, god-like, purifying and mercy seat, not made by hands, (cf. Hebrews 9.11) for mortals

---

[397] Thus the fulfillment of the divine mystery was accomplished through an initiative from God. (304C)

who have drowned in floods of sin is presented to the mercy
seat of the temple. (293C)

It is fitting that Mary procession to the Temple then should be lead by
"all the virgins in the region to go after her as torch-bearers." (297A) This
is a royal procession which also is referenced to Psalms of David:

"The virgins after her are led along to the king, those who are
with her are led along" (Ps 44:15, LXX). For behold the crowd
leads the young women in song on the way. The daughter of
the King is led to the holy house and with praises and songs
into the holy temple, she who will accomplish Your word, the
one you yourself called daughter, my regal child, for you said:
"All glory is given to the daughter of the King who resides
within [the temple] dressed in gold-fringed robes," of a pure
and spotless virginity, and in the similar way you will have said,
"embroidered with incomparable beauty" (Ps 44:14 LXX).
(297C)

Virginity and childbearing/barrenness are also mixed together in
Germanos. In his Annunciation homily the angel convinces Mary of the
truth of the proclamation he brings from God by telling her that Elizabeth is
about to give birth to a son in her old age, read past the time of childbearing:
"I shall tell you clearly, that Elizabeth your cousin at this very moment is
about to give birth in her old age to a son, and at his birth many shall rejoice
and be amazed, for his name will be called John" (cf. Luke 1.19). (325C)
(also 324C and 333B). Mary is understandable concerned with the presence
of this beautiful young man and her virginity. She expresses her fear and
consternation at the persistence of the angel by saying to him: "Since you
are telling this to me, and since you won't stop saying it, for the rest I
will say to you that I don't trust this announcement of yours. You come to
debase my virginity, and to grieve my betrothed" (324C) Much of the first
half of the Annunciation Homily is concerned with Mary virginity in the
face of the stranger with whom she is having a conversation. In the second
half of the Annunciation Homily Mary defends her virginity to Joseph
who doesn't believe that Mary could conceive without the aid of a man.
At the beginning of the second half Joseph states the situation as he sees
it: "Undefiled, I received you from the house of the Lord, and an undefiled

virgin I kept you in my house. And what is this which I now see, a mother contrary to expectation and not a virgin? Speak to me, Mary. Quickly, tell me the truth." (332A) Mary attempts to relate the circumstances of her meeting with the angel to Joseph who is slow to be convinced: "As the Lord lives, I am pure, and have known no man. He who appeared to me, seemed to me to be an angel, being in human form. He stood at a respectful distance. And while standing, he spoke gently to my unworthy self." (333A). Mary and Joseph are engaged in a debate centering on the Law and the Prophets. Joseph quotes the Law: "It is written in the Law of Moses. "If one finds a virgin, and lies with her by force, the man shall give to the father of the young woman fifty silver shekels" (Deuteronomy 22.24-25) What will you do with that?" (332C) and Mary counters with: "Is it not written in the Scriptures, "That a virgin shall conceive, and shall bear a child to us" (*cf.* Isaiah 7.14)? You cannot say that the prophets lie, can you? You are mistaken, O Joseph, you are out of your mind about many things." (336A) Yet again Elizabeth's pregnancy is employed, this time by Mary to illustrate that she is telling the truth about her pregnancy: "You have heard that my kinswoman, Elizabeth the wife of Zacharias, has even now conceived beyond hope a Prophet and Forerunner. For if he were not a prophet he would not have leapt to worship the Lord hidden inside of me (cf. Luke 1.40)".(333B) Mary further comforts Joseph by saying: "Believe the prophets of God, and concerning this matter do not allow yourself to sink into greater pain. For you shall find it written in them, "Behold, a virgin shall conceive and bring forth a son, and they shall call his name Emmanuel. (Matthew 1.23)" (336D). Finally Joseph is visited by the angel and tells Mary about it:

The Theotokos

I shall guard your words in my heart, and I shall be content in your house a little longer, and I shall await the time of enrollment and the day of my giving birth, until we shall bring the tribute to Caesar Augustus, the Emperor who now rules the Romans.

Joseph

Perhaps it was an angel who appeared to me in a dream, and said to me: "Joseph, son of David, fear not to take Mary to you as a wife, for that which shall come of her, is of the Holy Spirit, and she shall produce a son and you shall call his name Jesus (Matthew 1.20*ff*.)."(337B)

Germanos accepts the theological position of the Council of Ephesus (341) and the dogmatic definition of Mary as the Theotokos. He also contrasts sterility and Mary's virginity on a cosmic scale. At the same time Germanos equates barrenness/sterility and the Law: "Accept her whom you assigned to destroy our barrenness, overcoming through her the barrenness of the Law" (Pres. I, 300D) and "Hail, you who through your birth released the fetters of sterility, who scattered the reproach of childlessness, and sank the curse of the Law" (*cf.* Galatians 3.13)(Pres. I 308B)

The Entrance of Mary into the Temple brings to a close the Old Covenant and at the Incarnation replaces it with the New Covenant: "let us watch the child going toward the second veil, Mary the all-holy Mother of God who put an end to unfruitful sterility, and exchanged the mere shadow of the letter of the law (*cf.* Hebrews 10.1*ff*) through the grace of her birth-giving". (Pres I, 293A).

Mary's virginity is also important in the Dormition Homilies. In these homilies her virginity is not questioned, but is an established fact of cosmic and anthropological significance. Once again Germanos relates the Incarnation, Mary's virginity and its significance to humans: "If before being born from you, the Virgin Mother, this one was only-begotten Son of God, how does the Father say to him, "Today I have begotten you"? It is clear that "today" does not represent a new beginning of the divinity of the Only-begotten, but declares his corporeal presence among men."(Dorm I, 341B), and it is due to Mary's character as having that beauty that attracts God (theosis) that she does not suffer the common fate of bodily dissolution. "You, as it is written, [are] "in beauty" (Cant 2.3 LXX) and your virginal body, altogether holy, altogether pure, altogether the residence of God; so because of this [it is] separated and alien from earthly dissolution." (Dorm. I, 345B). The special Mother/Child relationship which Mary and Jesus have is also important to the Dormition and once again Mary's virginity is mentioned, and this time it is clear that it is her perpetual virginity that is spoken of: "Since you obtained me as your only-begotten Son, O mother, prefer rather to live with me; for I know you have no other child. I showed/proved you to be a virgin mother" (Dorm. III, 361C).

In the homily on the Sash Mary's virginity is mentioned but it does not form separate category as it does in the other homilies.

Chapter Forty

Analysis of Old Testament Usage[398]

Germanos uses the Old Testament in three ways: First, he quotes directly. Of the 119 allusions to the Old Testament 62 are direct quotes from the Septuagint (LXX). Second, he alludes to Septuagintal passages some 57 times. Third, he uses words and symbols found in the LXX in a typological manner.

An example of the first usage is at the beginning of the Sash homily where Germanos is applying the praise of Zion to Constantinople and by extension to the Theotokos. "Glorious things of you are spoken city of God" found in Psalm 86.42 in the LXX. These direct quotes in Germanos are generally assumed to be transformed by the Incarnation and so take on additional meanings[399].

Allusions to the LXX appear to be almost equal in number to direct quotations. Germanos, for examples alludes to Ezekiel 44,1-3 when referring to the virginity of the Theotokos. This occurs in the First Homily on the Presentation where he 'gate' and creates a double meaning for it: "Today the gate of God's temple is opened to receive the entry of the eastward looking, sealed gate of Emmanuel". First there is the actual gate of the Temple and then he uses the term 'eastward looking sealed gate of Emmanuel' to refer to Mary's virginity.

Typologies abound in Germanos' homilies. Typology as an exegetical method provided many ways of using LXX language to connect the Theotokos to New Testament/Christian theological development. Typologies provided an opportunity to do theology in a rhetorical format.

---

[398] Note: All numbers are approximate. In some instances it is difficult to designate the specific passage in the LXX. Allusions provide and even more difficult situation.

[399] See, "Issues in Understanding Middle Byzantine Homilies" and "Rhetorical Education in Byzantium" earlier in this dissertation.

In the process of doing theology, typology moves to allegory where the comparison and transition becomes more developed. And so provides for deeper exegetical investigation.[400] For example the Ark of the Covenant found in Exodus 20.10 can be transformed into a type of the womb and then become a proclamation of the transformation of the relationship that God has with his people from the Old Testament to the New Testament, the old covenant to the new covenant: "You appeared to cover the mystical and holy Ark of the new covenant of Him who on the Cross wrote the forgiveness of our sin, [forming] a covering which far surpasses the one which long ago was wrought of gold to cover the Ark" (Pres I, 301B).

Germanos frequently quotes directly from the LXX, and often uses types from the Old Testament. He would have been quoting and alluding to the Septuagint (LXX)[401]. It is clear that Germanos knew the Old Testament well, and in particular he used the Psalms in his homilies. I have provided a compilation of known quotes and allusions found in the texts of his homilies with no guarantee of completeness.

Homily	Total Allusions	Direct Quotes	Most Used (numbs)
Presentation I	47	15	Psalms (12)
Presentation II	10	1	Psalms (5)
Annunciation	13	9	Psalms (4)
Dormition I	6	6	Psalms (4)
Dormition II	25	21	Psalms (15)
Dormition III	9	7	Psalms (2)
Sash	9	3	Psalms (6)
Total:	119	62	Psalms (48)

---

[400] See, Christian Hannick,. "The Theotokos in Byzantine Hymnography: Typology and Allegory" 75.

[401] The LXX came in many recensions. This fact alone makes it difficult to be precise in designating direct quotes and allusions. See, MLA citation. Vander Heeren, Achille. "Septuagint Version." *The Catholic Encyclopedia.* Vol. 13. New York: Robert Appleton Company, 1912. 6 Mar. 2010 <http://www.newadvent.org/cathen/13722a.htm>.

Chapter Forty-One

Analysis of New Testament Usage[402]

Germanos uses the New Testament in four ways: First, he quotes directly. Of the 70 allusions to the New Testament 25 are direct quotes. Second, he alludes to New Testament passages some 45 times. Third, he uses words and symbols found in the New Testament in a typological manner. Several of these allusions and typologies have their origin in the LXX and have been used by the various New Testament authors Fourth, he gets narrative from the Gospel of Luke.

Direct quotes, with seven exceptions, come from the Gospels, and the vast majority of those from Luke. The largest number of direct quotes, and allusions, are found in the Homily on the Annunciation. These quotations from Luke are concerned with the Annunciation and are worked into the fabric of the Annunciation Homily and its unique rhetorical structure. New Testament narrative is especially apparent in the Annunciation Homily.

Homily	Total Allusions	Direct Quotes	Most Used (numbs)
Presentation I	11	2	Luke
Presentation II	9	1	Luke
Annunciation	25	15	Luke
Dormition I	6	2	Luke
Dormition II	7	2	Luke
Dormition III	5	2	None
Sash	7	1	Luke
Total:	70	25	Luke

---

[402] Note: All numbers are approximate. I have followed the designations found in PG 98 with some additions from Mary Cunningham in a private message concerning the text of the Annunciation Homily.

Homily	Total Allusions	Direct Quotes	Most Used (numbs)
Presentation I	11	2	Luke
Presentation II	9	1	Luke
Annunciation	25	15	Luke
Dormition I	6	2	Luke
Dormition II	7	2	Luke
Dormition III	5	2	None
Sash	7	1	Luke
Total:	70	25	Luke

Book		PG 98	Homily
Mt.			
Direct Quote	1.23	336D	Annunciation
	1.20	337B	Annunciation
	2.23	337C	Annunciation
Allusion	17.1	296C	Presentation I
	2.11	340A	Annunciation
	21.9	364D	Dormition III
Lk.			
Direct Quote	1.66	312B	Presentation II
	1.34	328B	Annunciation
	1.35	328B	Annunciation
	1.30	328B	Annunciation
	1.37	328C	Annunciation
	1.38	329B	Annunciation
	1.48	329D	Annunciation
	1.38	329D	Annunciation
	1.30	337A	Annunciation
	1.49*ff*	340A	Annunciation
	1.48	340B	Dormition I
	2.8	344A	Dormition I
	13.6*ff*	352A	Dormition II
	1.48—50	372D	Dormition III
	1.48*ff*	380C	Sash
	5.26	381A	Sash
Allusion	1.22	293B	Presentation I
	11.27	301C	Presentation I
	1.28	304C	Presentation I
	1.28	308B	Presentation I
	2.25*ff*	312D	Presentation I
	1.26	317A	Presentation I

	1.49	317B/C	Presentation II
	1.41	321D	Annunciation
	1.19	325C	Annunciation
	1.35	325D	Annunciation
	1.50	329A	Annunciation
	1.42	329D	Annunciation
	1.40	333B	Annunciation
	1.48	333D	Annunciation
	1.79	336A	Annunciation
	2.1*ff*	337A	Annunciation
	2.4	341A	Dormition I
	1.48	344A	Dormition I
	1.28	352B	Dormition II
	12.32	380B	Sash
Jn.			
Direct Quote	4.24	349B	Dormition II
	19.27	365D/A	Dormition III
Allusion	4.14	296A	Presentation I
	1.13	328D	Annunciation
	1.1	341A	Dormition I
Acts			
Direct Quote			
Allusion	4.12	380B	Sash
Rom.			
Direct Quote	2.4	348D	Dormition II
Allusion	5.10	305C	Presentation I
	16.25	316C	Presentation II
	16.25	317A	Presentation II
	8.17	381A	Sash
1 Cor.			
Direct Quote			
Allusion	13.12	361B	Dormition III
2 Cor.			
Direct Quote			
Allusion	6.2	353C	Dormition II
	4.17	373C	Sash
Gal.			
Direct Quote			
Allusion	3.13	308B	Presentation I
	6.4	320B	Presentation II
	4.21*ff*		Sash

Phil.			
Direct Quote	2.15	365C	Dormition III
Allusion			
Col.			
Direct Quote			
Allusion	2.9	373A	Sash
Heb.			
Direct Quote	11.3	357A	Dormition II
Allusion	10.1*ff* 9.11 9.4 2.9	293A 293D 321A 345D	Presentation I Presentation I Annunciation Dormition I
I Pet.			
Direct Quote			
Allusion	2.10 2.9	312B 320E	Presentation II Annunciation
2 Pet.			
Direct Quote			
Allusion	3.14	309B	Presentation II
Rev.			
Direct Quote	12.1	297D	Presentation I
Allusion			

Chapter Forty-Two

Mary as Exemplar of Theothesized Humanity

Germanos clearly views Mary as a person who has the experience of *theosis*[403]. Indeed Mary is the exemplar of *theosis* for all humans. In order to understand Germanos' soteriology we must look at the Orthodox development of the theology of the Fall, its anthropological theory, the role of the ancestors, and Mary's role as the restorer citizenship to the Christian people.

Theosis had a long history before Germanos and is still used in Orthodox theology[404]. What is critical is to understand that all of soteriology depends on the Incarnation, first and always, and all else devolves from that event. Patristic anthropology begins with mankinds' state in the Garden and man's rejection of his God-given place in Paradise.

> The cause of man's rejection of God was—and is—pride. [Note that this is the opposite of obedience.] It is an abuse of the self-determination given to man by God when He created him according to His image. Along with the angels, man is created

---

[403] Theosis or theopoiesis does not appear in Germanos' homilies or any of his other writings. Wilhelm Blum published an attempt at understanding Germanos' understanding of theodicy in "Die Theodizee des Patriarchen Germanos I. Von Konstantinopel." *Vigiliae Christianae* 28.4 (1974): 295-303. His attempt on the basis of Germanos' *On the Way of Life* (PG 98, 89-132) is an attempt to analyze Germanos' thought by close analysis of specific words and comparison with Greek philosophers.

[404] A search of the TLG yields over 100 attestation to the word and its cognates beginning with Hippolytus in the third century AD and it appears in Ecumenical Councils, the Cappadocians, and John of Damascus.

'unsinful by nature, yet free in his will. Unsinful does not mean that man is not capable of sin: only the Divine is incapable of sin. Man who did not have sin in his nature, invented sin by misuse of his freedom of choice (προαίρεσις).Thus he had the possibility (ἐξοθσία) of remaining in harmony with the good and progressing in goodness through the cooperation of divine grace. But he also had the power (ἐξοθσία) to turn his back on the good and place himself in evil; this God allows because of the human right of freedom of choice: . . . Evil, as a state of inauthentic existence, as a state of death and rejection of God who is the source of life, is not the 'nonexisting' (μή ὤν) but neither is it a particular 'essence' since it has no separate being. Evil is the corruption of existence. In the words of St Basil, 'evil is not a living and animate essence; it is a disposition in the soul which opposes virtue; this attitude develops in the slothful because of their alienation from the good'.[405]

By the eighth-century theologians had developed the concept of theosis in the east in a non-Augustinian direction[406]. To the Greek Fathers the Creation and the Expulsion of Adam and Eve from Paradise was a cosmic event. The term Fall or Ancestral guilt (προπατορικὴ ἁμαρτία) was the term they used for Augustine's 'original sin/guilt'. An understanding of the terms and the distinct meanings of them is necessary for an understanding of Germanos' language concerning the deification of the Theotokos. Looking at Germanos with twenty-first century western theological eyes yields only seemingly insurmountable difficulties.

---

[405] Maximos Aghiorgoussis,. "Sin in Orthodox Dogmatic." *St. Vladimir's Theological Quarterly* 21.4 (1977) 183-4. Quoted from: Kimball, Virginia M. "The Immaculate Conception in the Ecumenical Dialogue with Orthodoxy: How the Term *Theosis* Can Inform Convergence." *Mary for Time and Eternity : Papers on Mary and Ecumenism given at International Congresses of the Ecumenical Society of the Blessed Virgin Mary at Chester (2002) and Bath (2004), a Conference at Woldingham (2003) and Other Meetings in 2005.* Eds. William McLoughlin and Jill Pinnock. Leominster: Gracewing, 2007. 189. Much of the original research for this section came from the articles in this book.

[406] See, Kimball, 176, ftn. 8.

The critical point of discussion is how the meaning of that early Eastern prayer was embraced in the *locus* of Eastern praxis. The interpretation of Eastern prayers concerning the All-Holy One, *Panagia,* may have been interpreted by Catholics in an evolving process within a nineteenth-century soteriological emphasis quite different from the soteriology intended at the time of composition of the liturgical lyrics. This is the prime reason for returning to theological and liturgical sources to examine the early ages and the contextual actuality of what Eastern liturgical and theological embrace was at the time.[407]

Germanos is every bit as concerned with the proper understanding of the role of the Theotokos in salvation history as anyone. What he does is place it in a cosmological context that would have been familiar to his contemporaries. When he uses words that might be translated into terms such as 'immaculate', 'pure', 'all-pure', etc he does not use them in the manner that later theologians of Augustinian bent do. Germanos is thoroughly a Byzantine.

The patristic fathers, beginning with Irenaeus, made a distinction between image and likeness[408]. For them likeness (ὁμοίωσις) denoted a state that far surpassed what human beings in their own nature were capable of[409]. But Adam and Eve were disobedient and so lost the likeness while Mary was obedient and heard the word of God, and retained the likeness. Germanos expresses the result in his Second Homily on the Dormition in a comparison of the consequences of Mary and Eve's distinctive choices:

> For you are the mother of the true Life. You leaven the new creation of Adam. You free Eve from reproach. She is the mother of earth; you are the mother of light. Her womb [is the source] of destruction; your belly [is the source] of imperishability. She is the dwelling-place of death; you are the removal from death. She brings eyelids down to earth; you are the unsleeping glory of wakeful eyes (*cf.* Ps. 120.4 LXX and later 357B). Her

---

[407]   Kimball, 186.

[408]   For a fuller treatment of the question see, Kimball 200-08.

[409]   See, Jules Gross. *The Divinization of the Christian According to the Greek Fathers.* 1st ed. Anaheim, Calif.: A & C Press, 2002. 61. From Kimball 198.

> children are grief; but your Son is universal joy. She, as being
> earth, passed into earth; but you bore Life for us, and passed
> over to life, and obtained the power to mediate life to mankind,
> even after death. (349A/B)

Germanos explores the effects of the Fall, obedience and disobedience in the person of the Theotokos in his First Homily on the Presentation. In an anaphora Zacharias addresses the child Mary and says: "Enfold her who covers our nature which was stripped bare in Eden." (300C) And "Therefore hail, forgiveness of transgressions given by God for us filthy ones, who are denuded by the death-dealing and soul-destroying food of Eden, . . ."(304D) In a series of "chaires" Zacharias says: "Hail to you who by the rhythm of your footsteps trample down my terrible leader—that serpent with his crooked-minded, good-hating diabolical nature Hail to you who by the rhythm of your footsteps trample down my terrible leader—that serpent with his crooked-minded, good-hating diabolical nature—who has counseled me toward transgression" (305A).

The result of Adam and Eve's disobedience is visited on the mind of the Virgin Mary as she converses with the Archangel in the Annunciation Homily: "I am afraid and I tremble at your words. I suspect that you have come to deceive me like another Eve. I am nothing like her. What a greeting you bring to a maiden whom you have never seen before!" (324B) A concern that the Archangel addresses at little later: "Why? For what purpose, for what reason, have you distrusted my good news, Glorified one? How long will you disobey the angel that was sent to you from heaven? I am not Eve's deceiver—far from it." (325A). And Joseph accuses Mary of wrong doing in their dialogue in the second part of the Annunciation Homily: "Now I will say, Mary, that you have followed the path of your mother Eve." (336B). Mary's obedience results in the reopening of paradise to her relative and tribeswoman Eve (Dormition III 361D) as Mary is told in the Second Homily on the Dormition: "You leaven the new creation of Adam. You free Eve from reproach". (349A) In a curious comment at the end of the Second Homily on the Presentation the serpent is accused of originating evil and Mary is given to Joseph by lots: "And then by the assent of God and the counsel of the priests a lot is drawn concerning her, and Joseph the just is allotted, and receives this holy Virgin according to the dispensation from the Temple of God and his priests, to ensnare the serpent who originated evil, so that he should not attack the undefiled maiden as a virgin, but as a betrothed woman he should pass her by." (316D).

At the Entrance of the Theotokos into the Temple Germanos employees the Ancestors as a chorus that encourage her parents in their resolve to leave Mary at the Temple. "Come with me, chorus leaders, with singers and instrumentalists, and joyfully begin new songs in a new way, not as did Moses' sister Miriam (cf. Exodus 20-21) but with my daughter as the leader. (297A) The ancestors have much to gain as they are released from the effects of their "ancestral sin (προπατορικὴ ἁμαρτία) by Mary's Entrance: "Our ancestors who are about to be released from the curse and again inheriting the residence in paradise from which you were cast out: should you not hymn the cause of your salvation, with a fitting encomium and great praises? Indeed you especially ought to shout out, and I with you and with us both all creation [ought] to sing out in joy." (297D/300A) Both the heirs of the Old Testament and the New Testament rejoice together: "The forefathers jump for joy, escaping the captivity of condemnation. The prophets are delighted, and with them all who are yet to come in this age of grace also leap for joy." (300B).

The consequences of Mary's obedience and the obedience of her parents to God at the Entrance in the Temple is that the possibility of human kind being once again able to achieve theosis is restored. For Mary's Entrance is characterized by the forefathers choral request to Zacharias to: "Enfold her who covers our nature which was stripped bare in Eden."(300C) Our nature is clothed with the possibility of attaining a 'likeness' or deification. In an apt phrase Paul Evdokimov says: "For the anthropology and cosmology of the Christian Orient, nature has kept something of its initial and predetermined status. The Fall did not touch the image of God in man. It was only reduced to ontological silence by destroying the likeness, that is, the actualization of the image."[410]

The relationship that humans and angels had before the Fall is restored: "Because through your blameless flesh man has been made a citizen of heaven, and shepherds associated with angels" (344A) at the Nativity of Christ. Cosmologically God, Humans, Angels and all the world is back in its proper order. Mary's obedience has resulted in "The stripping off of the ancient bonds of sin; and the freshness of the enveloping pity, being a free

---

[410] Paul Evdokimov. *The Art of the Icon : A Theology of Beauty*. Redondo Beach, Calif. ; [United Kingdom]: Oakwood Publications, 1990 112.

citizen of the new life. (*cf.* 2 Cor. 4.17) And the Blameless one rejoices in these, who are pleasing, and in the godly pious, renewed citizenship, . . ." (Sash 373C)

John of Damascus (b. ca. 675), a contemporary of Germanos, "presents the deification of the Christian as a return to original perfection."[411] It seems reasonable to assume that Germanos would have been aware of current theological trends and so we might expect to find a similar emphasis in his work. For John of Damacus

> Using the physical theory of divinization, John of Damascus describes a soteriological event in Christ where human nature is ignited like molten iron. 'We were really sanctified when [ἀφ' οὗ] the Logos-god became flesh, having been likened to us in everything except sin, when He was mingled with our nature without confusion, and when, without changing it [ἀμεταβλήτως`, He deified [ἐθέωσε] the flesh by the mutual penetration [περιχώρησις] without fusion, of His divinity and His flesh.'[412]

For mankind it is Mary, the agent of the Incarnation and mediatrix, who according to Germanos passes on this restored 'likeness' which transforms even the image of a painting:

> The material painting [color] of your images [icons], Mother of God, illuminates the giving of your gifts to us. For sun and moon carry torches for the one turning of the cycle. Every house and every city and countryside delights in your light. Because of this man is blessed even if he is a sinner, since he has been found to have you as a relative in essence, and through you he is a partaker of the divine nature. "Blessed" truly, and well has this happened to him; or rather "and it will be well" (Ps. 127.2 LXX); for you will not abandon to the end those who are found worthy to receive your succor. 356C Dorm II

---

[411]   Kimball 208
[412]   Kimball 208

But if mankind recognizes the Theotokos as truly in the image and likeness of God, it must have been that God first recognized her. Germanos paints an icon of a dual attraction. Mary to God and God to Mary. In his First Homily on the Presentation he uses parts of the Song of Song to illustrate that beauty of Mary that so attracted God.

> "Who is that who comes up from the wilderness, perfumed with myrrh and frankincense, with all the fragrant powders of the merchants?" (Song of Songs 3.6)—"Come hither from Lebanon, my bride; come hither from Lebanon" (Song of Songs 4.8) 292D

Zacharias says:

> Draw to yourself her who leans on you and is attracted by your fragrance. You chose her as a lily out of the brambles of our unworthiness. Embrace her who is brought to you with a most radiant complexion. Behold, to you we offer her [as our intercessor] and dedicate ourselves." 300D

In the Homily on the Annunciation the Angel relates God's search for Mary: "The Most High searched all the universe, and did not find a mother like you. Certainly, <*as he knew,*> as he wished, as he was pleased, from you, the holy one, he shall become man because of his love for mankind"(329C) And the Angel early in the first dialogue confirms that Mary's beauty is that of one who has drawn close to the likeness of God: "Know truly and believe that I am more amazed at seeing your God-created beauty." (324A)

Seeing you I know that I am examining closely the glory of my Lord.

Germanos explains that God is attracted to Mary because of her uniqueness among all of creation:

> "O causes of our salvation (speaking to Mary's parents), what shall I say to you? What shall I call [you]? I am astonished seeing what kind of fruit you have brought forth, such a one as by her purity attracts God to dwell within her. For never yet has anyone existed or will anyone exist who shines forth in such beauty. You are seen as the two double rivers flowing

out of paradise, (*cf.* Genesis 2.10-15) carrying a lamp more precious than gold and precious stones, who in the beauty of her blameless virginity and her dewy sparkling illuminates the whole earth. 301A

Mary becomes the bride of God and her Entrance into the Temple is as a bride entering her bridal chamber. Quoting from Psalm 19 Germanos says:

Right now you are being established in the court of the Lord, in his holy Temple, in which is located the decorated bridal chamber not made by hands of the bridegroom (*cf.* Psalm 19.5-6).

And at the Annunciation Mary is called the " . . . heavenly bride and queen" 321C.

Clearly Mary is attractive to God. Through her mankind once again becomes attractive to God as well. The restoration of the 'likeness' of God to human kind is substantiated in Mary and many saints through out the story of the Church.

Mary is the bride of God in two ways. First, she is the bride because she bears His Son. Second, she is the bride because she is the leader of Christ s' bride, the Church. Germanos views Mary as the one who because of her union, both at the Incarnation, and through theosis, establishes the Church and renews the citizenship of mankind.

For you have from God the great sublime triumph; for which reason you have established a Christian people for him from your flesh, and related by birth to you, you have made conformable to his divinity and to his image which makes us like [him]. 353B Dormition II

That citizenship provides mankind with the possibility of his own theosis. Germanos' ecclesiology is both cosmological and temporal. With Mary at its head the Church is: "A city not enrolling those under her hand in a mortal and earthly kingdom, but in one which is redolent with heavenly and eternal life, and she represents a kingdom in herself to those who are sworn to her." (373C Sash) At the same time it is a place for those who owe both God and Mary thanks for the salvation that is accessible. It provides both forgiveness for the ancestral sin (προπατορικὴ ἁμαρτία) and a place where citizenship in paradise may be gained. In his Homily on the Sash Germanos expresses this relationship: "The stripping off of the ancient bonds of sin; and the freshness of the enveloping pity, being a free citizen of the new life. (*cf.* 2 Cor. 4.17) And the Blameless one rejoices in these, who are pleasing, and in the godly pious, renewed citizenship, . . ." (373C) Sash. In this citizenship humans have the advocacy of Mary:

> But to us Christians who venerate you with a Christian faith as Theotokos, stretch out the mercy of your unchangeable advocacy. For we rightly recognize your falling-asleep to be life, and we trust to have you as a spiritual house-mate. And when tribulation . . . you are near, seeking you we are ransomed. And when again it is time for joy, it is you who bring this. And when among all we are troubled, we trust that you are with us. For as the thirsty man hurries to the spring, so also every faithful soul runs to you, burning to be filled with your assistance. And again as the breath of air blows a life-giving aroma to mankind, so also the breath of every orthodox Christian carries you in the mouth. 356A Dorm II

Mary's theothesized humanity is also a blessing on the Church and an exemplar of what is possible for other humans: "Because of this man is blessed even if he is a sinner, since he has been found to have you as a relative in essence, and through you he is a partaker of the divine nature." (Dorm. II, 356C) An advocacy whose surety is based on Mary's role in the Incarnation and demonstrated in Mary's Falling Asleep[413].

---

[413] See the treatment of the Dormition in this dissertation.

Chapter Forty-Three

The Paradox of Mary

Paradox is dearly beloved by the Byzantine mind. There appear to be some sixteen instances of reference to paradox in Germanos' Marian homilies. Neither Perniola or Horvath mention paradox as an element of Germanos' Homilies. It is an unfair assumption that they did not recognize paradox for they did implicitly but they were asking different questions of the text. Of the sixteen, or so, references to paradox only one instance is singled out by them. It is the same reference—296A in the First Homily on the Entrance. Horvath quotes only a few words which with an earlier reference to 293C he claims as support for Germanos' belief in the Immaculate Conception of Mary.[414]

Perniola[415] quotes 296A as evidence of the power of Mary. Germanos' allusion to the story of the Woman of Samaria[416] is used as a way of expressing the immeasurable bounty of God. But it is the final line: "For the mystery overflows and the plant grows taller even than the incorporeal minds, not to mention the incarnate minds, in the compassion of the all-rich and pure maiden!" that provides the paradox in that the mystery of God's action is embodied in the beauty of the Virgin Mary and her presentation in the Temple which Germanos describes a little later in the Second Homily on the Presentation. These lines which are preceded by an anaphora on

---

[414] See Tibor Horvath, S.J. "Germanos of Constantinople and the Cult of the Virgin Mary, Mother of God, Mediatrix of All Men". *De cultu mariano saeculis VI-XI*; acta congressus mariologici mariani internationalis in croatia anno 1971 celebrati. 1972. Pontificia Academia Mariana Internationalis.

[415] Erasmo Perniola, *La mariologia di san germano, patriarca di constantinopoli.* Roma: Edizioni Padre Monti, 1954. 116 ftn. 21.

[416] The story of the woman of Samaria is one of the pre-Lenten Gospels read in the Orthodox Church at the Divine Liturgy.

the word 'today' provide a conclusion of sorts to the announcement of the feast and underscore its importance. Germanos explains the paradox in this manner and links it with the Annunciation:

> Who ever knew such a thing? Who saw, or who heard, of men now or men of old, that a female was led into the inner holy places of the holy places, which are barely accessible even to men, to live in them and to pass her time in them? Is this not a clear demonstration of the strange miracle to be done for her later? Is it not an evident sign? Is it not an obvious testimony? (309C)

It is in the Homily on the Annunciation that Germanos uses paradox most frequently. The first times are in the conversation of Mary with the Angel, where the paradox of Mary's impending pregnancy is at first incomprehensible to Mary just as it is the Lucan account of the event. What the angel has come to announce Mary does not trust and says so: "Since you are telling this to me, and since you won't stop saying it, for the rest I will say to you that I don't trust this announcement of yours. You come to debase my virginity, and to grieve my betrothed." (324C) This state of affairs continues for some time even though the angel brings forward convincing arguments and demonstrates clearly to Mary that God can work miracles and even calls on Zacharias, the priest who received Mary in the Temple, to convince her. (324C) The angel calls the Incarnation an 'incomprehensible mystery' whose power Mary will only understand: "When my words shall come to pass in their own time, then you will understand the power of this incomprehensible mystery. Then you will know the result of my words and the ineffable condescension of the Most High." Mary, herself, still not convinced calls the Incarnation "paradoxical good news" (328B) The angel tells Mary that she is already pregnant in 328C providing and instance about which Horvath comments concerning the attitude held by several Greek Fathers.[417] The questions appears to be resolved a little later when Mary asks the question about the child she will bear as she, just as every mother has. But she also enunciates the mystery and her role in it: "Tell me, young man, what kind of savior, am I to bear? For truly your good news is strange even to the spiritual powers of

---

[417] Horvath 298 ftn 106. He also gives a short explanation of this.

angels, fiery might of archangels, and the commanders of the many-eyed [cherubim]." (328D) The angel then tells her, in counter distinction to the earlier statement in 328B "Put on a joyful countenance, O blessed one. You are about to become heaven, a God-containing tabernacle, a living temple of God, wider and higher and more wondrous than the seven firmaments." (329B)[418] And Mary states: "I shiver at the beginning of the paradox of my unusual childbearing."(329B)

The second half of the Annunciation Homily has Mary explaining the paradox to Joseph and Mary says to him: "The paradoxical nature of my childbearing astounds your mind." 336C.

In the Dormition Homilies paradox functions as an explanation of Mary's privileged status as the Mother of God. Germanos begins the First Homily by expressing his debt to the Theotokos. He is aware that he cannot offer adequate thanksgiving to Mary but pleads with her that just as she recognized her own lowliness so too he hopes she will accept and recognize his lowliness and accept what he is able to do in the homily. It is in this context that he acknowledges her as having "obtained marvels paradoxical gifts" (340B). In the Second Homily on the Dormition he acknowledges her as "a vision beyond the understanding of the angels." (352B) and she is "the surpassingly strange good fortune of mankind." (352B) Mary's servants, the Church is protected by her. In what could well be a prayer that is redolent of many prayers for her protection in the Orthodox tradition[419] he states that it is a paradox that those who are not able to adequately thank Mary are yet under her protection and so '"Whatever is yours, is paradoxical, "true, and all together made righteous, all desirable and sweeter than honey and honeycomb; for your servants desire them, in desiring them, great reward [is obtained] from you" (Ps. 18.10-12 LXX). "Who will understand your mercies?"' (Ps. 106.43 LXX) (353A) In the very different Third Homily on the Dormition Mary states the paradox of

---

[418] My explanation is the rhetorical structure demanded what amounts to a denial of Mary's will. Sequence of events is not as important as the argument of the homily. This, of course, is a theologically and philosophically problematic argument. This juxtaposition of these two verses 328B and 329B serve to confirm my contention that the rhetoric demands precede the theological ones. To 'explain' a mystery inevitably places language in a position that it will always fall short of satisfying.

[419] This prayer sounds very much like the anaphora of the Liturgy of St. Basil the Great.

the Incarnation and her relationship with her Son: "He is a Son given birth in the flesh by me, but Father and Creator and God of his own mother." (365A) It is safe to say that Mary's dormition is based on this paradoxical good news for mankind. It is also clear that this paradox is not a violation of the natural order but very much part of it. Christ, as any child would, treats His mother in a particularly natural way in that he being both her Son and her Creator chooses to take her to Himself at her dormition.

In the Homily on the Sash all of this is repeated when Germanos says: "All your own, Theotokos (Luke. 5.26), paradox, all above nature, all beyond words and power. Through which also is your protection that is beyond understanding." (381A) This is the only specific reference to paradox in this homily, but it is clear that paradox is, for Germanos, a fitting designation for the Theotokos and all that she means cosmologically and anthropologically in salvation history.

Germanos views Mary as set of paradoxes all beyond Nature. She is paradoxical because she is born of a barren woman, and as an only child is given by Anna and Joachim into the care of the Temple, where she astonished the priest Zacharias by her beauty and her childishness. She is paradoxical because she does not fit into the normal categories that a Jewish woman should inhabit, she enters the Holy of Holies providing the first encounter between the law and God's resolution of the human predicament of sin and grace. She is paradoxical because she has a special relationship with God, the nature of which illustrates a reciprocal attraction between God and Mary and human beings. She is paradoxical because she is both a Mother and a Virgin, an unnatural violation of the normal reproductive order. She is paradoxical because she is the 'Bride unwedded', a position which allows her to plumb the depths of human disappointment and grief and the profundity of human joy at the same time. She is paradoxical because she is allowed to live by Joseph and is not put to the test of the 'waters', even though she is bearing the Child of Another. She is paradoxical because she has a role and power that no one else has, a position vis à vis the twin dominions of the Church and the City of Constantinople. She is paradoxical because she is finite while the Mother of the Infinite, she is the 'Wider than the Heavens' and yet remains a human woman. She is paradoxical because she lent her humanity to God and so guarantees the Incarnation and the possibility of human salvation, yet she remains fully human and provides the first example of a human theosis.

Chapter Forty-Four

Conclusions

Father Perniola in the conclusion of his dissertation on Germanos says that it would be superfluous, if not tedious, to attempt to summarize and repeat, albeit briefly, what has already been widely done—good advice! In the introduction I presented the problem of understanding Byzantine theological statements from a Western theological position. This is particularly true in Mariology. In the *Question of Mary* Father Laurentin summarized the problem:

> Oriental thought loves mystery, Western, analytical clarity. Marian thought in the East is contemplative and poetic. Its inventiveness consists in translating the same basic facts into continually renewed symbols which give new brightness to the truth and, now and then, bring out-or suggest some hidden aspect. Latin Marian thought (above all, the most committed) proceeds, on the contrary, by analysis, comparison, reasoning. syllogism. It distinguishes, constructs, forms notions and words answering to the divisions of its rational analysis; it is by choice specialized, systematic, and organized into theses. Finally, it has a way of multiplying juridical notions with which the Orthodox mentality often finds it impossible to cope.[420]

I have attempted to present some of the elements of the difficulties that arise when viewing Germanos' homilies from a Western Christian perspective. This I've done from an historical analysis of the educational processes of the Byzantine Empire. Following the lead of many eminent

---

[420]   René Laurentin, *The Question of Mary*. 1st. ed. New York: Holt, 1965. 132.

scholars, I presented the Byzantine educational system and its rhetorical education. After some analysis of the elements of rhetoric I applied this to Byzantine theological reflection. In the course of which I looked at the position of philosophy and theology from the point of view of both Western and Eastern tradition. The results was that the Byzantine position did not accept philosophy in all the ways that it was in the West. I then looked at Middle Byzantine homilies and the requirements for these "conversations" as the Greek word for homily means. Again using the collective writings of several scholars I presented the concept of the process of Byzantine theological reflection as beginning in poetry moving to homilies (which were also poetry), iconography and then to liturgy. Having established this background I was able to analyze Germanos' Marian Homilies in the light of Germanos' world.

I presented my own translations of Germanos' Marian homilies and for each provided introductions and commentaries. This allowed me to do a close and careful study of each of the homilies and to list references to Mary in each as well as provide commentary in both the commentary on the homily and in the analysis. This permitted me to comment in the analysis on the various passages and also on both Perniola's and Horvath's interpretations. In many cases the matter of interpretation came down to the perspective of the authors including myself. No attempt was made to determine 'rightness' of interpretation.

I also provided some other analysis on the basis of themes. In many of these I have listed both Perniola's and Horvath's context. Again with no 'rightness' attributed to them. In a few instances I found miss-attributions and have so noted them and provided the correct attributions. I have provided some analysis of thematic treatments in Germanos with commentary on many of them. I also have provided analysis of the Old Testament and New Testament usage of Germanos in his homilies. All of this is done in the effort to open up dialogue on Germanos' homilies and to provide a opportunity for both Western and Eastern Mariologists to converse.

Finally, I have attempted to provide a deeper look into the dynamics of these 'conversations' concern Mary and her role in salvation history. It is my hope that the dialogue about which Canon Laurentin spoke may indeed happen[421]. My only wish is that I have provided a useful way of looking at Middle Byzantine Homilies that will enable that dialogue.

---

[421] René Laurentin, *The Question of Mary*. 133.

Appendix

Horvath and the Mariology
of Germanos Data

PG 98	Homily	Section	Page	Text
Introduction				
349B	Dorm II	Intro	285	οὐκ ἔστι τῆς ἀντιλήμψεώς σου κόρος
356B	Dorm II	Intro		ὡς ἐν Χριστῷ καὶ ἐν σοὶ τὸ γεγραμμένον πληροῦσθαι
380—381, 384	Annunciation	Intro	285	
I Virginity				
49A	Haeresibus	Virginity	285	παρθένος
373B	Annunciation	Virginity	285	πανάχραντος
373B	Annunciation	Virginity	285	ὑπεράγνός
373B	Annunciation	Virginity	285	ἁγιασμῷ μείζονι
293C	Pres I	Virginity	286 IM?	ἀνατίθεται ἡ μόνη τοῖς τῶν βρότων ἐσφαλλομένοις διεξαχθεῖσιν ἀμπλακημάτων ἐπίρροαῖς, ἱλαστήριον καινόν τε καὶ θεοειδέστατον καθαρτικόν τε καὶ ἀχειρότευκτον χρηματίσασα
296A	Pres I	Virginity	286 IM?	πανολβίου καὶ πανάγνου κόρης

II Motherhood				
339B	Dorm I	Motherhood	286	Θεοτόκος
300C	Pres I	Motherhood	286	(δέδεξο τὴν) δοχεῖον (χρηματίσουσαν τοῦ Υἱοῦ καὶ Λόγου τοῦ Πατρὸς καὶ) μόνου Θεοῦ
304A—305BC	Pres I	Motherhood	286	παλάτιον, ναός, πόλις, παστὰς τοῦ νοητοῦ, λογικώτατον θυσιαστήριον, τράπεζα
348A	Dorm I	Motherhood	286	Θεοχώριτον ἀγγεῖον
344C	Dorm I	Motherhood	286	οὐρανὸς θεοχώρητος ἀνεδείχθής τοῦ ὑψίστου Θεοῦ
340B	Dorm I	Motherhood	286	δέσπινα
304A	Pres I	Motherhood	286	βασίλισσα
160A	Ltr J Synnada	Motherhood	286	πάσης ὁρατῆς καὶ ἀοράτου κτίσεως ὑπερτέρα
304A/B 308B	Pres I	Motherhood	286	Ref above
292C	Pres I	Motherhood	286	θεοπαῖς
304D	Pres I	Motherhood	286	Θεονύμφη
305B	Pres I	Motherhood		πανυπερθαύμαστε
352B	Dorm II	Motherhood		τὴν τῶν ἀγγέλων ὑπὲρ ἔννοιαν θεωρίαν
III Assumption				
340C	Dorm II	Assumption	287	ζωοκοίμητος (neologism)
345D	Dorm II	Assumption	287	Parallel deaths
346B 348A/C	Dorm II	Assumption	288	Σκεῦος ὑπάρκου θεηδόχον (nt 35)
348A	Dorm II	Assumption	287	μετάστασις
348B	Dorm II	Assumption	287	Προλαμβάνω (action) ἐγρήγορσις κοίμησις
349A	Dorm II	Assumption	287	θάνατος
357D	Dorm II	Assumption	288	μονογενοῦς παναγίας θεότητος (nt 35)
360C	Dorm III	Assumption	287	Τῷ φυσικῷ τῆς σαρκὸς ἰδιώματι

360C	Dorm III	Assumption	288	Cheer earth and heaven
361A	Dorm III	Assumption	288	ἀχώριστος μήτηρ
361C	Dorm III	Assumption	288	Her body belonged to Christ
364C	Dorm III	Assumption	287	ἔξοδος
365C	Dorm III	Assumption	288	ἤρμοζεν
366A	Dorm III	Assumption	287	Consequences of God's will
369C	Dorm III	Assumption	287	ἀφαιρέω
369D	Dorm III	Assumption	288	ζωοτόκος
470	Dorm III	Assumption	287	Tomb was empty
IV Mediatrix				
301B	Pres I	Mediatrix	289	κάλυμμα τῆς νέας διαθήκης
304A 361D	Pres I Dorm III	Mediatrix	289	θεοστήρικτος κλίμαξ
304C	Pres I	Mediatrix	289	βάσις θεία
304D	Pres I	Mediatrix	289	Remission of sin? Recompensation?
305B	Pres I	Mediatrix	289	πηγή ἡ θεόβρυτος
305C	Pres I	Mediatrix	289	Missascribed is 305B
305D	Pres I	Mediatrix	290	God becomes know in her
306D/ 356B	Pres I Dorm II	Mediatrix	290	Θεογνωσία ?
308A 293C 302C 329D	Pres I Pres I Pres I Annunciation	Mediatrix	289	πανκόσμιον ἱλαστήριον τοῦ κόσμου πάντος ἱλαστήριον
309 (?)	Pres II	Mediatrix	289	σήμανδρον ἀκριβές—Text not found
316C	Pres II	Mediatrix	288	ὡς ἄτε προεγνωσμένη καὶ προωρισμένη καὶ ἐκλελεγμένη τῷ πάντων Θεῷ καὶ ταμία.
321B	Annunciation	Mediatrix	288	ἁμαρτωλῶν ἁπάντων ἡ ὄντως ἀγαθὴ μεσιτεία
329C	Annunciation	Mediatrix	288	Latin reference

344C	Dorm I	Mediatrix	290	σήνοικος
348B/356A	Dorm II	Mediatrix	289	σήνοικος
352A	Dorm II	Mediatrix	289	Μητρῴαν ἔχουσια πρὸς τὸν Θεὸν τὴν ἰσχὺν
353A	Dorm II	Mediatrix	289	οὐδὲ γὰρ ἐνδέχεταί σέ πότε παρακουσθῆναι
353B	Dorm II	Mediatrix	289	διότι λαὸν αὐτῷ Χριστιανικὸν ἀπὸ σαρκὸς τῆς σῆς συνεστήσω
357D	Dorm II	Mediatrix	290	ἀχώριστον δὲ τῆς τῶν ἀνθρώπων συναναστροφῆς
361D	Dorm III	Mediatrix	289	πρεσβεία
361D/365C	Dorm III	Mediatrix	288	γέφθρα
380B	Zone	Mediatrix	288	μεσῖτις
380B	Zone	Mediatrix	289	Salvation?
384A	Zone	Mediatrix	289	ἐπισκοπῆ σουθεία
V. Devotion and Cult				
304C & 318C	Pres I Pres II	Cult	291	Joy in honorning Mary Latin reference
306D	Pres I	Cult	290	Latin reference, Greek probably 305D God is making the kings honor the Theotokos
317A/B	Pres II	Cult	291	Mary will help all
340B	Dorm I	Cult	291	A great desire which his soul thirsts to satisfy
353C—356A	Dorm II	Cult	290	All places, nations, etc are called to honor the Theotokos
361D	Dorm III	Cult	290	χρεώστην
VI. Psychologists				
185B—C	Ep to Thomas of Claudiopolis	Psychologists	294	
376C	Zone	Psychologists	293	πόθῳ
376D	Zone	Psychologists	294	ἀνδριαν

VII. Theologian				
162A—B 305B & 309A 317A—B 319B	Ep to John of Synnada Pres I Pres I Pres II Pres II	Theologian	295	Mary as mediatrix is the cause of Germanos' devotion
305C	Pres I	Theologian	296	Mary takes human nature to heaven
308A	Pres I	Theologian	296	Ps. 19,6
345B	Dorm I	Theologian	296	μεθ' ἡμῶν σε, Θεοτόκε, πιστεύομεν περινοστεῖν
349B—C	Dorm II	Theologian	296	Οὐδεὶς θεογνωσίας ἀνάμεστος, εἰ μὴ διὰ σοῦ, παναγία· οὐδεὶς ὁ σωζόμενος, εἰ μὴ διὰ σοῦ, Θεοτόκε· οὐδεὶς κινδύνων ἐλεύθερος, εἰ μὴ διὰ σοῦ, Παρθενομῆτορ· οὐδεὶς ὁ λελυτρωμένος, εἰ μὴ διὰ σοῦ, Θεομῆτορ·
357A & 361A	Dorm II Dorm III	Theologian	296	Οὐκοῦν πίστει σε μεθ' ἡμῶν συνανάστροφον ἔχειν ὁμολογοῦμεν
365C	Dorm III	Theologian	296	ἐν μεσῖτίν σε πρὸς Θεὸν μεθισταμένην κεκτήμεθα
368A368A/B	Dorm III	Theologian	295	σὲ βλέπων ἐν σώματι, τὸν Χριστὸν θεωρεῖν παρηγορούμεν, τὴν σῶμα τῷ ἀσωμάτῳ χορηγήσασαν ἐν περιβολῇ
376C—D	Zone	Theologian	295	
376D	Zone	Theologian	295	
381B	Zone	Theologian	296	ἐν αὐτῷ ἑστῶτες, ἐν οὐρανῷ ἑστάναι νομίζομεν

VIII. Historian				
61B	De hairesibus, 48	Historian	297	Against Apollinarios
328B—C cf. 324C, 325B	Annunciation	Historian	298	In the interest of the history of Mariology it should be mentioned that Germanus follow (sic) the curious view of several Greek Fathers according to which Mary conceived Jesus before she gave her consent.
324C, 325B cf 328B—C	Annunciation	Historian	298	During the discussion with the Angel Mary is seen as rather incredulous, and gives a hard time to the Angel who seeks to convince here and conquer her disbelief. Her disbelief, however, is presented a defense of her virginity for which she therefore deserves credit rather than blame. The Patrologist should recall that Germanus was talking as if he were admitting a special inspiration given to the Fathers of the Church. He called the θεωφόρος, i.e. God-bearing or inspired men *(De vitae termino, 5:* PG 98, 100C; cf. also PG 98, 192A, 193B, and the Second Council of Nicaea, θεηγορῷ; DS 600).

341D cf 61B	Dorm I	Historian	297	Mary is not merely Virgin, but truly mother.
375A Ep to the Armenians 140C, Ep to John of Synnada 160D, Letter of Gregory II 152A	Zone	Historian	297	Jesus was a real human born of Mary. Also see other instances in the letters

Perniola and Mary in Germanos Data

PG98	Homily	Chapter in Perniola 13	ftn	Page
293A	Pres I	Il Prodigio	27	117
293B	Pres I	Il Prodigio	8	112
293B	Pres I	Il Prodigio	30	118
293B	Pres I	Il Prodigio	36	118
293C (297D)	Pres I	Il Prodigio	35	118
293C—304A	Pres I	Il Prodigio	28	117
293D—296A	Pres I	Il Prodigio	21	116
297D (293C)	Pres I	Il Prodigio	35	118
300D	Pres I	Il Prodigio	18	114
301A (308C)	Pres I	Il Prodigio	31	118
301B (308C)	Pres I	Il Prodigio	31	118
304A(3)	Pres I	Il Prodigio	32	118
304A(3)	Pres I	Il Prodigio	33	118
304A(3)	Pres I	Il Prodigio	40	118
304C/D	Pres I	Il Prodigio	22	116
305B(2)	Pres I	Il Prodigio	41	118
305B(2)	Pres I	Il Prodigio	42	118
305B/C	Pres I	Il Prodigio	39	118
305C	Pres I	Il Prodigio	37	118
305C	Pres I	Il Prodigio	38	118
305D (308A)	Pres I	Il Prodigio	34	118
308A	Pres I	Il Prodigio	43	118
308A (305D)	Pres I	Il Prodigio	34	118
308B	Pres I	Il Prodigio	48	119
308C (301A)	Pres I	Il Prodigio	31	118
316C	Pres II	Il Prodigio	19	114
316D—317A	Pres II	Il Prodigio	20	115
321 A	Annunciation	Il Prodigio	45	119
321B	Annunciation	Il Prodigio	7	112
324A	Annunciation	Il Prodigio	23	116
325D	Annunciation	Il Prodigio	3	112
328C	Annunciation	Il Prodigio	4	112
329A	Annunciation	Il Prodigio	5	112
329C	Annunciation	Il Prodigio	6	112
332A	Annunciation	Il Prodigio	15	113
341A/B	Dorm I	Il Prodigio	12	113

344C	Dorm I	Il Prodigio	44	119
361C	Dorm III	Il Prodigio	14	113
376B	Zone	Il Prodigio	9	112
377A	Zone	Il Prodigio	10	112
377B	Zone	Il Prodigio	11	112
PG98	Homily	Chapter in Perniola 14	ftn	Page
293A	Pres I	Immac	9	127
293B	Pres I	Immac	11	127
293C	Pres I	Immac	16	128
297A	Pres I	Immac	17	128
300B	Pres I	Immac	25	130
300D	Pres I	Immac	32	132
301A	Pres I	Immac	18	128
304D	Pres I	Immac	19	128
305A	Pres I	Immac	20	128
305B	Pres I	Immac	22	128
305C	Pres I	Immac	12	127
308C	Pres I	Immac	13	127
312A	Pres II	Immac	14	127
313B	Pres II	Immac	26	130
321A	Annunciation	Immac	10	127
345B	Dorm I	Immac	27	131
345C	Dorm I	Immac	28	130
357A	Dorm II	Immac	24	130
357A	Dorm II	Immac	29	131
364D	Dorm III	Immac	31	131
373A	Sash	Immac	15	128
PG98	Homily	Chapter in Perniola 15		Page
293C	Pres I	Corredentrice	21	142
300A	Pres I	Corredentrice	11	141
301D	Pres I	Corredentrice	12	141
304D	Pres I	Corredentrice	17	141
305A	Pres I	Corredentrice	18	142
305B	Pres I	Corredentrice	19	142
321A	Annunciation	Corredentrice	15	141
321B	Annunciation	Corredentrice	13	141
324B	Annunciation	Corredentrice	6	139
324B	Annunciation	Corredentrice	9	140
325A	Annunciation	Corredentrice	7	139
328C	Annunciation	Corredentrice	14	141
329C/D	Annunciation	Corredentrice	16	141
336B	Annunciation	Corredentrice	8	140
348B (349C)	Annunciation	Corredentrice	22	142
349A	Dorm II	Corredentrice	10	140

349C (348B)	Dorm II	Corredentrice	22	142
353B	Dorm II	Corredentrice	20	142
PG98	**Homily**	**Chapter in Perniola 16**	**ftn**	**page**
340C (349B)	Dorm I	Assumption	8	149
345B	Dorm I	Assumption	14	149
345B	Dorm I	Assumption	20	150
345B	Dorm I	Assumption	31	155
345C	Dorm I	Assumption	7	148
345C	Dorm I	Assumption	30	151
345C	Dorm I	Assumption	31	154
345C/D	Dorm I	Assumption	29	154
348A	Dorm I	Assumption	22	149
348A	Dorm I	Assumption	9	152
348A/B	Dorm I	Assumption	23	152
348B/C	Dorm I	Assumption	25	152
349B (340C)	Dorm I & II	Assumption	8	149
357A	Dorm II	Assumption	32	155
357B	Dorm II	Assumption	5	148
357C	Dorm II	Assumption	27	153
361B	Dorm III	Assumption	21	151
361C	Dorm III	Assumption	28	154
364D	Dorm III	Assumption	11	149
365D	Dorm III	Assumption	6	148
368B	Dorm III	Assumption	10	149
368B	Dorm III	Assumption	18	150
369C	Dorm III	Assumption	12	149
369C	Dorm III	Assumption	14	150
369D(372A)	Dorm III	Assumption	13	149
372A(369D)	Dorm III	Assumption	13	149
372A	Dorm III	Assumption	15	150
PG98	**Homily**	**Chapter in Perniola 17**	**ftn**	**page**
305A	Pres I	Viventi	5	161
321A	Annunciation	Viventi	3	161
344B (345A)	Dorm I	Viventi	7	162
345A	Dorm I	Viventi	1	160
345A	Dorm I	Viventi	6	162
345A	Dorm I	Viventi	12	164
345A (344B)	Dorm I	Viventi	7	162
345C	Dorm I	Viventi	13	165
348C	Dorm I	Viventi	10	164
349A	Dorm II	Viventi	2	161
353B	Dorm II	Viventi	4	161
360D	Dorm III	Viventi	8	164
361D	Dorm III	Viventi	9	163

PG98	Homily	Chapter in Perniola 18	ftn	page
317 A/B	Pres II	Grazie	3	168
317D	Pres II	Grazie	4	168
320A	Pres II	Grazie	5	169
345A	Dorm I	Grazie	1	168
348C	Dorm I	Grazie	7	170
349A	Dorm II	Grazie	6	170
349B/C	Dorm II	Grazie	8	171
349C (352A)	Dorm II	Grazie	9	171
352A(349C)	Dorm II	Grazie	9	171
352A (353A)	Dorm II	Grazie	10	171/172
356C	Dorm III	Grazie	11	172
365C	Dorm III	Grazie	2	168
377C (381B)	Zone	Grazie	12	174
384A	Zone	Grazie	13	176
PG98	Homily	Chapter in Perniola 19	ftn	page
292C	Pres I	Culto	15	183
292D—293A	Pres I	Culto	16	183
308—309	Pres I	Culto	22	186
312C	Pres II	Culto	8	181
325B	Annunciation	Culto	5	180
329A	Annunciation	Culto	6	180
340A/B	Dorm I	Culto	4	180
352C	Dorm II	Culto	1	179
352C/353B	Dorm II	Culto	2	180
353C—356A	Dorm II	Culto	9	181
356A/B	Dorm II	Culto	12	182
356B	Dorm II	Culto	13	183
357A	Dorm II	Culto	14	183
372C	Dorm III	Culto	23	186
373C	Zone	Culto	7	181
373C—376A	Zone	Culto	17	184
376B	Zone	Culto	18	184
376B/C	Zone	Culto	19	184
376D—377B/C	Zone	Culto	21	185
380A	Zone	Culto	11	182
380C	Zone	Culto	10	182
381B/C	Zone	Culto	20	184
PG98	Homily	Chapter in Perniola 20	ftn	page
293C	Pres I	Somiglianza	16	193
293D	Pres I	Somiglianza	3	191
296D	Pres I	Somiglianza	4	191
300A	Pres I	Somiglianza	5	191
301A	Pres I	Somiglianza	18	193

321A	Annunciation	Somiglianza	17	193
324A	Annunciation	Somiglianza	20	193
345D	Dorm I	Somiglianza	13	192
348A/B	Dorm I	Somiglianza	6	192
360D	Dorm III	Somiglianza	7	192
361A	Dorm III	Somiglianza	8	192
361D	Dorm III	Somiglianza	2	190
364A	Dorm III	Somiglianza	10	192
364C/D	Dorm III	Somiglianza	11	192
365C	Dorm III	Somiglianza	21	193
368A	Dorm III	Somiglianza	22	193
372A/B	Dorm III	Somiglianza	12	192
376D—377D	Zone	Somiglianza	1	189
381D	Zone	Conclusion		200

References to the Ancestors of Mary and Other Old Testament Figures in Germanos I, Patriarch of Constantinople (715-730)

PG 98 Location	Greek	English	Homily
292D	Εὐμυρίσωμεν ὡς ἐκ καλύκων ῥοδόχρουν αὐτῆς. καλλονὴν ἀναβαίνουσαν πλήρη θυμιαμάτων, ὡς Σολομῶντι ἐν τοῖς Ἄσμασιν φάσκοντι καλῶς ἐστίχισται· «Τίς αὕτη ἡ ἀναβαίνουσα ἀπὸ τῆς ἐρήμου, ὡς στελέχη καπνοῦ τεθυμιαμένη, σμύρναν καὶ λίβανον ἀπὸ πάντων κονιορτῶν μυρεψοῦ;»—«Δεῦρο ἀπὸ Λιβάνου, νύμφη μου, δεῦρο ἀπὸ Λιβάνου.»	And let us be anointed with the perfume of her roses, as Solomon says in the beautiful verse of his Song: "Who is that who comes up from the wilderness, perfumed with myrrh and frankincense, with all the fragrant powders of the merchants?" (Song of Songs 3.6)—"Come hither from Lebanon, my bride; come hither from Lebanon" (Song of Songs 4.8)	Presentation I (P183 ftn. 16)
293B	Σήμερον Ἰωακεὶμ τὸ τῆς ἀπαιδίας ὄνειδος ἀποσμηξάμενος, ἀναφανδὸν ταῖς λεωφόροις μεγαλαυχικώτατα δείξων πρόεισιν οἰκείαν γονήν, καὶ πάλιν μυσταγωγὸς τῆς κατὰ νόμον ἁγιαστείας δείκνυται. Σήμερον καὶ	Today Joachim, who has wiped away the reproach of childlessness, goes openly down the main road boastfully showing off his offspring, and again is shown as a functionary of hallowing according to the Law.	Presentation I (P 112 ftn. 8, 118 ftns. 30 & 36, 127 ftn. 11

	Ἄννα τὸν τῆς ἀτεκνίας ἐνδελεχισμὸν, εὐτεκνίᾳ ἀμείψασα, ἀπλέτῳ χαρμονῇ ἔνθους γινομένη τοῖς πέρασι καρπὸν διακηρυκεύεται κεκτῆσθαι, στέρνοις ἐναγκαλισαμένη τὴν τῶν οὐρανῶν πλατυτέραν.	Today also Anna has exchanged the persistence of barrenness for fruitfulness, and becoming inspired by joy, proclaims to the ends of the earth that she has borne a child, embracing to her bosom the one who is wider than the heavens.	
296B	Καὶ ταύτην μὲν οἱ οἰκεῖοι γεννήτορες, τριετῆ χρόνον τετελεκυῖαν, Θεῷ ἀναφέρουσιν.	And her own parents presented to God the one who had reached three years of age.	Presentation I
297A	Καὶ προέφθασεν ἡ στείρα τε καὶ ἄκαρπος Ἄννα χεῖρα αὐτῆς τῷ Θεῷ διδοῦσα καὶ μεγαλοφωνότατα διαρρήδην βοῶσα· Δεῦτέ μοι, φησὶν, συγχαίρετε, αἵτινές τε καὶ ὅσοι τῇ γεννήσει συνειλεγμένοι, μειζόνως, ἄρτι τὴν ἐξ ἐμῶν σπλάγχνων ἀνατιθεμένη Κυρίῳ δῶρον θεοκαλλώπιστον ἡγιασμένον. Δεῦτέ μοι, ἀρχιχοροί, θυμηρέστατα μετὰ χορῶν καὶ τυμπανιστριῶν, νέον ᾆσμα καινὸν ἐπᾴδουσαι προεξάρχοιτε· οὐ τῆς Μωσέως Μαριὰμ προοδοποιούσης, ἀλλὰ τῆς ἐξ ἐμέθεν γεγεννημένης ἀφηγουμένης.	And the barren and unfruitful Anna with foresight lifts her hands to God and says in a loud distinct voice, "Come with me, let us rejoice together, all women and men who rejoiced at her birth, even more now, as I dedicate to the Lord this divinely beautiful and holy gift recently received from my own womb. Come with me, chorus leaders, with singers and instrumentalists, and joyfully begin new songs in a new way, not as did Moses' sister Miriam (cf. Exodus 20-21) but with my daughter as the leader.	Presentation I (P 128 ftn. 17)
297B	Ἀλλ' ἄγε μοι, Δαυῒδ ὁ προπάτωρ καὶ θεοπάτωρ, μελουργικώτατα τὴν κινύραν τινάσσων ταῖς τοῦ πνεύματος νευραῖς ἐμμελέστερον ἤχει, τῷ θεοπνεύστῳ σου στόματι	But come with me, David the forefather and ancestor of God and make ever more harmonious music striking your harp in the giving of hymns on the strings of the spirit (cf. I Samuel 16.23) with your God-inspired voice,	Presentation I

297C	δεῦρ᾽ ἴθι, Δαυῒδ ἡωσφῶν· «Τίς αὕτη ἡ ἐκκύπτουσα ὡσεὶ ὄρθρος, καλὴ ὡς σελήνη, ἐκλεκτὴ ὡς ἥλιος; τί ὡραιώθησαν διαβήματά σου ἐν ὑποδήμασι;»	Come here David bringer of dawn's light[7]: "Who is this who shines out like the dawn, is as fair as the moon, and bright as the sun?" "How gracefully you walk in your sandals!" (Cant 7:2)	Presentation I
297D	Πάρεσο, μεγαλόφωνος Ἰεζεκιὴλ, τὴν κεφαλίδα θεόθεν κατίσχων τοῦ ζωοποιοῦ Πνεύματος καὶ κεκράζων τὴν εὐφημίαν τῇ ἀνατολοβλέπτῳ καὶ θεοπαρόδῳ ἐσφραγισμένῃ πύλῃ,	Come, loud-voiced Ezekiel, holding the divine scroll of the life-creating Spirit and crying your holy words to the eastward oriented and sealed gate	Presentation I (P 118 ftn 35)
297D 300A	Οἱ προπάτορες τῆς ἀρᾶς ἀπολυθησόμενοι καὶ τῆς ἧς ἐξεβλήθητε τρυφῆς, τὴν οἴκησιν πάλιν ἀποκληρούμενοι· ἆρ᾽ οὐχ τὴν αἰτίαν ὑμνήσετε τῆς σωτηρίας, ἀραρότοις ἐγκωμίοις καὶ μεγίσταις αἰνέσεσιν; ἢ καὶ μάλιστα ὑμῖν ἐστι κεκραγέναι καὶ με σὺν ὑμῖν καὶ πᾶσαν μετ᾽ ἀμφοτέροις τὴν κτίσιν ἀγαλλιᾶσθαι.	Our ancestors who are about to be released from the curse and again inheriting the residence in paradise from which you were cast out: should you not hymn the cause of your salvation, with a fitting encomium and great praises? Indeed you especially ought to shout out, and I with you and with us both all creation [ought] to sing out in joy.	Presentation I
300A	Ταύταις, ὡς εἰκὸς, ταῖς διανοίαις ἢ τοῖς διαβήμασιν ῥυθμίζουσα ἑαυτὴν ἡ σώφρων Ἄννα, σὺν τῷ γλυκυτάτῳ ὁμοζύγῳ τὴν ἐξ αὐτῶν ὠδινηθεῖσαν προπέμποντες	Probably with these thoughts the chaste Anna, having accepted this course with her loving husband, sends forth her for whom she had felt the pangs of childbirth.	Presentation I

---

[7]   ἡωσφῶν, attested only here

300B	Χαίρει Ζαχαρίας ἠξιωμένος δέξασθαι τὴν Θεομήτορα· εὐφραίνεται Ἰωακεὶμ τὴν τῶν χρησμῶν ἔκβασιν βεβαιῶν τῇ τελειώσει τῆς ἀποδόσεως. Γέγηθεν ἡ Ἄννα τῆς αὐτῆς γονῆς τῇ ἀφιερώσει· σκιρτῶσι προπάτορες τὴν τῆς κατακρίσεως εἷρξιν ὑπεκφεύγοντες· τέρπονται οἱ προφῆται, καὶ σὺν αὐτοῖς ἅπασα ἡ ἐν χάριτι ἡλικία χαρμονικῶς προσκιρτᾷ.	Zacharias rejoices that he is found worthy to receive the Mother of God. Joachim is glad, confirming the outcome of the oracles. Anna is joyful at the sanctification of her child. The forefathers jump for joy, escaping the captivity of condemnation. The prophets are delighted, and with them all who are yet to come in this age of grace also leap for joy.	Presentation I
300C	Πάλιν οἱ γεννήτορες βοῶσιν τῷ ἱερεῖ·	Once again, the forefathers call to the priest:	Presentation I
301A	Ταῦτα τὰ τῶν δικαίων σύμφωνα· οὗτοι οἱ κρότοι τοῦ θεοφιλοῦς ζεύγους· αὕτη ἡ καλλισύλλεκτος ἐπιγραφὴ τῶν θεοπατόρων.	These are the harmonious [words] of the righteous [people], this is the dance of the God-loving couple, these is the beautifully arranged inscription of the ancestors of God.	Presentation I (P 118 ftn. 31, 128 ftn. 18)
301A	Τοιγαροῦν ὁ Ζαχαρίας τὴν παῖδα δεδεγμένος, πρῶτα τοῖς γονεῦσιν εἰκότως προσφθέγγεται· Ὦ τῆς ἡμετέρας σωτηρίας αἴτιοι, τί ὑμᾶς προσείπω; Τί καλέσω;	So then Zacharias having received the child, probably first addresses the parents saying: "O causes of our salvation, what shall I say to you? What shall I call [you]?	Presentation I
301C	Ὑμετέρων ἡ χαρμονὴ κοσμικὴ γεγένηται· ὑμῶν τὸ κλέος ἅπασιν εὐφροσύνη ἐξήκουσται. Μακάριοι ὑμεῖς, τοιαύτης παιδὸς γεννήτορες χρηματίσαντες! Εὐλογημένοι ὑμεῖς, τοιοῦτον εὐλογημένον δῶρον Κυρίῳ προσάξαντες! Μακάριοι μασθοὶ οἷς ἐτιθηνήθη, καὶ γαστὴρ ᾗ βεβάστακται	Your rejoicing has become that of the cosmos. Your renown is the universal joy of all men. Fortunate are you who bear the title of parents of such a blessed child. Fortunate are you, who have brought such a blessed gift to the Lord! Fortunate are the breasts by which she was nursed and the womb that carried her (cf. Luke 11.27).	Presentation I

304A	ἡ βάσις θεία γεγνωρισμένη καὶ θεοστήρικτος κλίμαξ δεδειγμένη τῷ πατριαρχικωτάτῳ Ἰακὼβ θυμηρέστατα.	Your ascent of the steps is recognized as divine and delightfully shown as a God-supported ladder to the great patriarch Jacob (*cf.* Genesis 28.12*ff.*).	Presentation I (P 118 ftns 32, 33, 40)
304D/305A	Χαίροις, ἡ τῇ ἐξάρξει σήμερον τῆς φαεινοτάτης καὶ σεβασμιοφόρου Πρόδου θίασον ἅπαντα προφητικὸν ἐπαγείρουσα, μουσικοῖς ὥσπερ ὀργάνοις εὐηχεστάτοις κυμβάλοις θεοφωνότατον ἀλαλαγμὸν ὑπανακρούοντας καὶ ἐν εὐφροσύνῃ ψυχαγωγῶς χορεύοντας.	Hail, you who today call together all the prophetic assembly for the beginning of your most brilliant and venerable Entrance, with well-tuned cymbals as with musical instruments striking up the divine-sounding strain and dancing in spiritual joy.	Presentation I (P 116 ftn 22, 128 ftns 19 & 20)
313A	Ἐγώ, φησίν, ἡ χαριτώνυμος Ἄννα τῷ ὑποφήτῃ, γένους μὲν πέφυκα ἱερατικοῦ,	"I am Anna," she says, "with the name favored by the interpreter/ expounder. I was born of a priestly	Presentation II
	φυλῆς Ἀαρωνείτιδος, ῥίζης προφητικῆς καὶ βασιλικῆς.	family, of the tribe of Aaron, of a prophetic and royal stock (*cf.* Exodus 28, 1*ff.*).	
313A	Τοῦ γὰρ Δαβὶδ καὶ Σολομῶντος, καὶ καθεξῆς ὄρπηξ καθέστηκα· συγγενὴς δέ, καὶ τῆς σῆς γαμετῆς Ἐλισάβετ.	For of David and Solomon and their descendants I am an offshoot; and a relative also of your wife Elizabeth.	Presentation II
324D	Ἤ <Ἤκουσας, ὅτι> ἐξ οἴκου καὶ πατριᾶς Δαβὶδ καταγομένη <τυγχάνω>, πῶς <οὖν> τοιούτοις φρικτοῖς καὶ ἐπουρανίοις ἐξυπηρετήσω μυστηρίοις; Καὶ πῶς Ἰησοῦν τὸν ἅγιον, τὸν ἐπὶ τῶν Χερουβὶμ καθεζόμενον, ἐγὼ πῶς <u>ὑποδέξασθαι δυνήσομαι</u> <ὑποδέξομαι>;	*<You have heard that>* I am of the House and the ancestry of David. How shall I assist in these awesome, heavenly mysteries? And how shall I be able to conceive the holy Jesus who sits upon the Cherubim?	Annunciation

325A	Θρόνος θεοβάστακτος, καὶ βασιλικὴ καθέδρα τοῦ ἐπουρανίου Βασιλέως κληθήσῃ, καθότι Βασίλισσα καὶ Δέσποινα, καὶ βασιλέως ἐπιγείου θυγάτηρ τυγχάνεις, καὶ χαρακτῆρα ἔχεις βασιλικόν	You shall be called the throne which bears God, the royal seat of the heavenly King. As you are Queen and Virgin, and a daughter of [David] the earthly king, so you have a royal character.	Annunciation
325D	«καὶ βασιλεύει ἐπὶ τὸν οἶκον Ἰακώβ, καὶ τῆς βασιλείας αὐτοῦ οὐκ ἔσται τέλος.»	"will rule over the House of Jacob forever and of his kingdom there shall be no end" (Luke 1.35).	Annunciation
328C	Ῥίζης Δαβιδικῆς βλάστημα τυγχάνω, καὶ δέδοικα πῶς ἐπέλθοι κάμοὶ <μοὶ> κοίτης ἀλλοτρίας ἀπροσδόκητος ἐξουθενισμός	I am a sprout of the root of David. I fear that on me as on him [David] will come unexpected scorn of adultery,	Annunciation
329B	Συμφέρει μοι οὖν, εἰς οἶκον Ζαχαρίου ἀπελθεῖν, πρὸς τὴν ἐμὴν συγγενίδα.	But it is good for me to go to the house of Zacharias, to see my kinswoman.	Annunciation
333B	Ἠκούσθη σοι ὅτι καὶ Ἐλισάβετ, ἡ τοῦ Ζαχαρίου, καὶ συγγενίς μου, κατὰ τὸν καιρὸν τοῦτον, προφήτην καὶ Πρόδρομον παρ' ἐλπίδα συνέλαβεν. Εἰ μὴ γὰρ <γὰρ μὴ> προφήτης ἐτύγχανεν, οὐκ ἂν διὰ τῶν σκιρτημάτων προσεκύνει τὸν ἐν ἐμοὶ κρυπτόμενον Κύριον.	You have heard that my kinswoman, Elizabeth the wife of Zacharias, has even now conceived beyond hope a Prophet and Forerunner. For if he were not a prophet he would not have leapt to worship the Lord hidden inside of me (cf. Luke 1.40).	Annunciation
337B	«Ἰωσὴφ υἱὸς Δαβίδ, μὴ φοβηθῇς παραλαβεῖν Μαριὰμ τὴν γυναῖκά σου· τὸ γὰρ ἐν αὐτῇ γεννηθέν, ἐκ Πνεύματός ἐστιν ἁγίου· τέξεται δὲ υἱόν, καὶ καλέσεις τὸ ὄνομα αὐτοῦ Ἰησοῦν.»	"Joseph, son of David, fear not to take Mary to you as a wife, for that which shall come of her, is of the Holy Spirit, and she shall produce a son and you shall call his name Jesus (Matthew 1.20ff.)."	Annunciation

337D	«Ἀνατελεῖ ἄστρον ἐξ Ἰακώβ, καὶ ἀναστήσεται ἄνθρωπος ἐξ Ἰσραήλ, καὶ θραύσει τοὺς ἀρχηγοὺς Μωάβ.»	"A star shall rise out of Jacob, and a man arise out of Israel, and shall crush the leaders of Moab (Numbers 24.17)."	Annunciation
337A	διὰ τὴν Δαυϊτικὴν συγγένειαν	in the lineage of David	Annunciation
344D	Καὶ γάρ, ὡς μετὰ τῶν ἀρχαιοτέρων ἡμῶν ἐν σαρκὶ συνεπολιτεύου, ὁμοίως καὶ μεθ' ἡμῶν τῷ πνεύματι συνοικεῖς·	For also, as you kept fellowship in the flesh with our ancestors, likewise also with us you dwell in the spirit.	Dormition I
349A	Σὺ εἶ τῆς ἀναπλάσεως τοῦ Ἀδὰμ ἡ ζύμη. Σὺ εἶ τῶν ὀνειδισμῶν τῆς Εὔας ἡ ἐλευθερία	You leaven the new creation of Adam. You free Eve from reproach	Dormition II
349A	Ἐκείνη μήτηρ χοός, σὺ μήτηρ φωτός	She is the mother of earth; you are the mother of light	Dormition II
349A	Ἐκείνης ἡ μήτρα, φθορᾶς· ἡ δὲ σὴ γαστήρ, ἀφθαρσίας	Her womb [is the source] of destruction; your belly [is the source] of imperishability	Dormition II
349A	Ἐκείνη θανάτου κατοίκησις, σὺ μετάστασις ἀπὸ θανάτου.	She is the dwelling-place of death; you are the removal from death	Dormition II
349A	Ἐκείνη βλεφάρων καταχθονισμός, σὺ γρηγορούντων ὀφθαλμῶν ἀκοίμητος δόξα	She brings eyelids down to earth; you are the unsleeping glory of wakeful eyes	Dormition II
349A	Ἐκείνης τὰ τέκνα, λύπη· ὁ δὲ σὸς Υἱός, παγγενὴς χαρά	Her children are grief; but your Son is universal joy.	Dormition II
349B	Ἐκείνη ὡς γῆ οὖσα εἰς γῆν παρῆλθε· σὺ δὲ Ζωὴν ἡμῖν ἔτεκες, καὶ πρὸς τὴν ζωὴν ἐπανῆλθες, καὶ Ζωὴν τοῖς ἀνθρώποις, καὶ μετὰ θάνατον, προξενεῖν κατίσχυσα	She, as being earth, passed into earth; but you bore Life for us, and passed over to life, and obtained the power to mediate life to mankind, even after death	Dormition II
361D	Ἄνοιξον σὺ τὸν παράδεισον, ὃν ἡ συγγενής σου καὶ ὁμοφυὴς ἀπέκλεισεν Εὔα	Do you open paradise, which your relative and tribeswoman Eve closed	Dormition III
There are no direct references to ancestors of Mary in the Homily on the Sash.			

References to the Assumption of Mary in Germanos I, Patriarch of Constantinople (715-730)

PG 98 Location	Greek	English	Homily
304A	Καθέσθητι, ὦ Δέσποινα· καὶ πρέπει γάρ σοι τῇ βασιλίσσῃ καὶ ὑπὲρ πάσας τὰς βασιλείας τοῦ κόσμου δεδοξασμένῃ, ἐν τοιαύτῃ βαθμίδι ἐφέζεσθαι.	Sit down O Lady, for it is proper to you as the Queen glorified above all earthly kingdoms to be seated upon such steps.	Presentation I
340C (349B)	ζωοκοιμήτου	translation from sleep to life	Dormition I (P Assumption 149 ftn. 8)
The following references from Dormition I are mislabeled in Horvath 287			
344B	τῇ μεταστάσει	at your translation	Dormition I
344B	οὐδὲ μετα[τε]θεῖσα	have been transferred	Dormition I
345B	Σὺ, κατὰ τὸ γεγραμμένον, «ἐν καλλονῇ·» καὶ τὸ σῶμά σου τὸ παρθενικὸν, ὅλον ἅγιον, ὅλον ἁγνὸν, ὅλον Θεοῦ κατοικητήριον· ὡς ἐκ τούτου λοιπὸν καὶ ἀλλότριον χοϊκῆς ἀναλύσεως. Ἐναλλαγὲν μὲν ὡς ἀνθρώπινον πρὸς ἄκραν ἀφθαρσίας ζωήν· σῶον δὲ τοῦτο καὶ ὑπερένδοξον, ζωοτελὲς καὶ ἀκοίμητον· καθ' ὅτιπερ οὐδὲ ἦν δυνατὸν παρὰ νεκροποιοῦ συγκλεισμοῦ τοῦτο κρατηθῆναι, ὡς σκεῦος ὑπάρχον θεηδόχον, καὶ ἔμψυχος ναὸς τῆς τοῦ Μονογενοῦς παναγίας θεότητος.	You, as it is written, [are] "in beauty" (Cant 2.3 LXX) and your virginal body, altogether holy, altogether pure, altogether the residence of God; so because of this [it is] separated and alien from earthly dissolution. While remaining human it is changed to the sublime life of incorruptibility. This is safe and supremely glorious, life-accomplishing [it's life ended] and unsleeping; as it was not possible for this to be controlled by death-dealing confinement, being a God-receiving vessel, and a living temple of the all-holy divinity of the Only-begotten One.	Dormition I (P Assumption 149 ftn. 14 150 ftn. 21 155 ftn. 31)

| 345C/D | Πῶς γὰρ εἶχε διάλυσις σαρκὸς πρὸς χοῦν καὶ κόνιν ἀνθυποστρέψαι σε, τὴν ἀπὸ θανάτου καταφθορᾶς, τὸν ἄνθρωπον, διὰ τῆς τοῦ Υἱοῦ σου λυτρωσαμένην σαρκώσεως; Μετέστης γοῦν τῶν ἐπιγείων, τοῦ δειχθῆναι τὸ τῆς φρικτῆς ἐνανθρωπήσεως βεβαιούμενον ἀφαντάστως μυστήριον· ἵνα σοῦ τὴν ἐκδημίαν τῶν προσκαίρων ὑπομεμενηκυίας, ὁ ἐκ σοῦ γεννηθεὶς Θεός, πιστευθῇ καὶ τέλειος προελθεῖν ἄνθρωπος, ἐξ ἀψευδοῦς Μητρὸς Υἱός, ὑποκειμένης νόμοις φυσικῶν ἀναγκασμάτων, ὅρου θείου κελεύσματι, καὶ χρόνου βιωτικοῦ παρακελεύσει· σοῦ, τῆς ὡς μιᾶς τῶν καθ' ἡμᾶς τυγχανούσης σωμάτων, καὶ διὰ τοῦτο μὴ τοῦ κοινοῦ τῶν ἀνθρώπων θανάτου δυνηθείσης ἐκφυγεῖν τὸ συνάντημα· ὃν τρόπον καὶ ὁ σὸς Υἱὸς καὶ πάντων Θεός, καὶ αὐτός, ὅσον εἰπεῖν, διὰ τὸν παντὸς ἀποθνήσκοντα τοῦ γένους ἡμῶν ἄνθρωπον, τοῦ ὁμοίου σαρκικῶς «ἀπεγεύσατο θανάτου»· παραδοξάσας δηλαδή, κατὰ τὸν ἴδιον αὐτοῦ καὶ ζωοποιὸν τάφον, καὶ τὸ σὸν τῆς κοιμήσεως ζωοπαράδεκτον μνῆμα· ὥστε ἀμφοτέρων σώματα μὲν ἀφαντάστως ὑποδεξαμένων, διαφθορὰν δὲ μηδαμῶς ἐνεργησάντων. | For how could dissolution of the body to earth and dust recur in you who from the corruption of death ransomed mankind through the incarnation of your Son? You departed from the earthly ones to show the mystery confirmed of his awesome assumption of humanity, so that when you had endured the exile from temporary [things], the God born from you would be believed to have come forth also a perfect man, the Son of the true Mother, subject to the laws of natural necessities, by the command of a divine decree, and by the order of biological time. You, as one who happens [to have] a body like ours, and because of this not being able to escape the encounter with the common death of mankind, in the same way as your Son and the God of all himself, so to speak, because of his humanity, [like] all of our race, "tasted" of a similar "death in the flesh"(Heb. 2.9): obviously glorifying, along with his own unique and life-creating burial, also the memorial of your life-receiving dormition, so that the both [graves] received bodies not in appearance only, but did not at all cause corruption. | Dormition I (P Assumption 148 ftn. 7 154 ftn. 29 151 ftn. 30) |

348A	τὴν μετάστασιν	translation	Dormition I
348A	κοίμησιν	falling asleep	Dormition I
348A	ἐγρήγορσιν	waking up	Dormition I
348B	τῶν περαινομένων	the departure	Dormition I
348A/B/C	Οὐδὲ γὰρ ἐνεδέχετό σε θεοχώρητον οὖσαν ἀγγεῖον. τῆς ἀναλύσεως νεκροφθόρῳ διαρρυῆναι χοΐ. Ἐπειδὴ γὰρ ὁ κενωθεὶς ἐν σοί, Θεὸς ἦν ἀπ᾽ ἀρχῆς, καὶ ζωὴ προαιώνιος, καὶ τὴν Μητέρα τῆς Ζωῆς σύνοικον ἔδει τῆς Ζωῆς γεγονέναι, καὶ καθάπερ ὕπνον τὴν κοίμησιν ὑπολαβεῖν, καὶ ὡς ἐγρήγορσιν ὑποστῆναι τὴν μετάστασιν ὡς Μητέρα τῆς Ζωῆς. Ὥσπερ γὰρ τέκνον τὴν ἰδίαν ζητεῖ καὶ ποθεῖ μητέρα, καὶ μήτηρ συνδιάγειν τῷ τέκνῳ φιλεῖ, οὕτως καὶ σὲ φιλότεκνα σπλάγχνα πρὸς τὸν Υἱόν σου καὶ Θεὸν κεκτημένην, ἥρμοσεν πρὸς αὐτὸν ἐπανελθεῖν· καὶ τὸν Θεὸν δέ, μητροφιλῆ διακρατοῦντα πρὸς σὲ στοργήν, συνδίαιτόν σοι τὴν ἑαυτοῦ καὶ πάντως ἔπρεπε καταστῆναι συνομιλίαν. Τούτῳ δὲ τρόπῳ τὴν ἀποβίωσιν τῶν περαινομένων πεπονθυῖα, πρὸς τὰς ἀφθάρτους τῶν αἰωνίων μετώκησας διατριβάς, ὅπου Θεὸς ἐναυλίζεται, μεθ᾽ οὗ καὶ σὺ συνδιάγωγος οὖσα, Θεοτόκε, οὐκ ἀποχωρίζῃ τῆς τούτου συναναστροφῆς. Οἶκος	For it was not possible for you being a God-containing vessel to be destroyed by the dissolution of corpse-corrupting earth. For since he who emptied himself in you was God from the beginning and Life before the ages, and it was necessary for the Mother of Life to become a companion with Life, and to experience death simply as sleep, and through this translation arise as Mother of Life. For just as a child seeks and desires its own mother, and a mother loves to spend time with her child, so also it suited you who have acquired a child-loving compassion for your Son and God to ascend to him; and also it undoubtedly befitted the God who has mother-loving affection for you to establish for you his companionship and fellowship. In this manner having endured the departure from this passing life, you have moved to the imperishable haunts of the eternal ones, where God dwells, with whom you also being a companion, O Theotokos,	Dormition I (P Assumption 149 ftn. 9 152 ftn. 22 152 ftn. 23 152 ftn. 25

γὰρ αὐτῷ καταπαύσεως σὺ γέγονας σωματικὸς, Θεοτόκε, καὶ τόπος ἀναπαύσεως αὐτὸς χρηματίζει μεταστάσει, πανύμνητε. «Αὕτη γὰρ, φησίν, ἡ κατάπαυσίς μου εἰς αἰῶνα αἰῶνος·» τουτέστιν, Ἡ ἐκ σοῦ περιβληθεῖσα τούτῳ, Θεοτόκε, σάρξ· μεθ᾽ ἧς οὐ μόνον εἰς τὸν παρόντα τοῦτον αἰῶνα ἐπιφανεὶς ὁ Χριστὸς ἐπιστεύθη, ἀλλὰ καὶ κατὰ τὸν μέλλοντα αἰῶνα, σὺν τῇ τοιαύτῃ σου σαρκὶ, ἐρχόμενος κρῖναι ζῶντας καὶ νεκροὺς ἐμφανισθήσεται. Ἄρα οὖν, ὡς αἰωνίας σου τούτῳ καταπαύσεως οὔσης, πρὸς αὐτὸν ἀδιάφθορον προσελάβετό σε, πλησιοχώρως, ὡς εἴποι τις, τῶν σῶν λαλιῶν καὶ σπλάγχνων ἔχειν σε θέλων· διὸ καὶ ὅσα ζητεῖς παρ᾽ αὐτοῦ, τεκνοπενθῷ ἐπιδίδωσι, καὶ ὅσαπερ αἰτεῖς ἐξ αὐτοῦ, θεοδυνάμως ἀποπληροῖ· ὁ ὢν εὐλογητὸς εἰς τοὺς αἰῶνας. Ἀμήν.	do not separate yourself from the activity of this [world]. For you have become a corporeal house of rest for him, O Theotokos, and you are called the very place of repose by your translation, all-praised one. "For this is my rest," he/it says, "unto the age of the age;" (Psalm 131.14 LXX) that is, the flesh put on by him from you, O Theotokos – with which we believe that Christ has appeared not only for this present age, but also will be revealed in the coming age, with such flesh from you, coming to judge the living and the dead. So since you are his eternal resting-place, he took you to himself free from corruption, wishing to have you nearby, as one might say, [with] your conversation and compassion. Therefore also whatever you seek from him, he gives with a child's affection, and whatever you seek from him, he fulfills with the power of God: who is blessed unto the ages. Amen.	

Perniola lists the 348 A—C as part of the Second Dormition Homily, they are part of the First Dormition Homily.			
349B (340C)	ζωοκοιμήτου	translation from sleep to life	Dormition I / Dormition II (P Assumption 149 ftn. 8)

388

357 A	Ἐρρέτω θάνατος ἐπὶ σοί, Θεοτόκε, ζωὴν ὅτι τοῖς ἀνθρώποις προσήγαγες. Ἐρρέτω τάφος ἐπὶ σοί, ἐπειδήπερ ὕψους ἀκαταφράστου θεῖος ἐγένου θεμέλιος. Ἐρρέτω χοῦς ἐπὶ σοί· ἀνάπλασις γὰρ εἶ, ὅτι τοῖς ἐν ὕλῃ πηλοῦ διαφθαρεῖσι κεχρημάτικας, Δέσποινα.	Away with death for you, O Theotokos, because you have brought life to mankind! Away with the tomb for you, since you became the divine foundation of an impregnable fortress! Away with earth poured over you; for you are the re-fashioning, because you have been called Mistress of those who have perished in the substance of clay.	Dormition II (P 155 ftn. 32)
357B	Οὐκ ἀμάρτυρος γὰρ ἡ μετάστασίς σου· οὐδὲ ψευδὴς ἡ κοίμησις.	For your translation does not lack witness, nor is your dormition a deception.	Dormition II (P Assumption 148 ftn. 5)
357C/D	ἱκανός τις ἐν λόγων κατευμεγεθῆσαι φωναῖς. Ἔχεις σὺ παρ' ἑαυτῆς τὸν ἴδιον ὕμνον, ὅτιπερ Θεοτόκος ἀνεδείχθης. Οὐδὲ γὰρ, ὅτι τοῖς ὠσὶν ἡμῶν παρὰ Γραφικῆς ἐξηγήσεως τοῦτο καὶ μόνον ἠκούσθη· οὐδὲ πάλιν ὅτιπερ οἱ πατέρες ἡμῶν ἀνήγγειλαν ἡμῖν τοῦτο παναληθευούσῃ διηγήσει, τὴν προσηγορίαν ἐκληρώσω τῆς Θεοτόκου· ἀλλ' ὅτι τὸ ἔργον ὃ εἰργάσω ἐν ἡμῖν, κυρίως καὶ ἀψευδῶς ἀγλωσσοχαρίτως καὶ ὀρθοδόξως, Θεοτόκον σε δι' αὐτῶν βεβαιοῖ τῶν πραγμάτων· καὶ τούτου χάριν, τὸ θεηδόχον σου σῶμα, παρὰ νεκροποιοῦ καταφθορᾶς, ἔπρεπεν ὄντως μὴ συγκλεισθῆναι·	so neither is anyone sufficient to magnify your sublimity with voices of praise. You have by yourself your own hymn, because you were shown to be Theotokos. For not even because this has been heard by our ears only from Scriptural narrative, nor again because our fathers reported this to us by completely true tradition (Ps. 43.2 LXX), have you fulfilled the title of Theotokos; but because the deed which you have done among us, properly and truly, without tongue-grace[8] and with orthodox [faith], validates you as Theotokos by the	Dormition II (P Assumption 153 ftn. 27)

---

[8]   This word (ἀγλωσσοχαρίτως) is attested only here. Lampe suggests it means "without flattering, sincerely". Lampe 20

	ἀλλὰ καὶ τὸν τάφον ὡς ἀνθρώπινον ὑποδέξασθαι τὸ ἴδιον φύραμα· καὶ σοῦ ζωοτελῶς πρὸς τὰ οὐράνια, τῆς οἰκείας μεταστάσης ζωῆς·	very facts. And for the sake of this, it was truly fitting that your God-receiving body should not be shut in by deathly corruption, but that the tomb received its own mixture as human, and with a living conclusion of your own life transferring to the heavenly places	
360C	Καθὼς οὖν τὴν γῆν καὶ τοὺς ἐν τῇ γῇ χαρᾶς ἐπλήρωσας, κεχαριτωμένη, χαροποίησον καὶ τὰ οὐράνια πάλιν. Φαίδρυνον τὰς τοῦ Πατρός μου μονάς· ψυχαγώγησον, καὶ τῶν ἁγίων τὰ Πνεύματα. Ὁρῶντα γὰρ τὴν σὴν πρὸς ἐμὲ τιμητικὴν καὶ ἐξ ἀγγέλων δορυφορουμένην μετάθεσιν, πληροφοροῦνται πιστῶς, ὡς διὰ σοῦ καὶ ἡ τούτων μερὶς ἐν τῷ ἐμῷ κατοικήσει φωτί.	So as you filled the earth and those on the earth with joy, O blessed one, now make the heavenly places also joyous. Cheer the mansions of my Father. Lead the souls and spirits of the saints. As I see your honorable transfer towards me, accompanied by angels, they are fulfilled faithfully, as through you their part also will settle in my light.	Dormition III
361B	Δὸς ἀθλίπτως τῇ γῇ τὰ ἴδια. Ἐμὸν τὸ σὸν σῶμα· καὶ ἐπειδὴ ἐν τῇ χειρί μου τὰ πέρατα τῆς γῆς, οὐχ ἁρπάζει τις οὐδὲν ἐκ τῆς χειρός μου. Ἐμοὶ τὸ σῶμά σου πίστευσον, ὅτι κἀγὼ τῇ κοιλίᾳ σου τὴν ἐμὴν παρεκατεθέμην θεότητα. Ὄψεται τοῦ Πατρός μου τὴν δόξαν ἡ ἔνθεός σου ψυχή. Ὄψεται τοῦ μονογενοῦς αὐτοῦ Υἱοῦ τὴν δόξαν τὸ ἀμίαντον σῶμά σου. Ὄψεται τοῦ παναγίου Πνεύματος τὴν δόξαν τὸ ἄχραντον πνεῦμά σου.	Give to earth its own without tribulation. Your body is mine; and since the ends of the earth are in my hand (Ps. 94.4), no one will snatch anything from my hand. Entrust your body to me, because I also deposited my godhead in your belly. Your god-inspired soul will see the glory of my Father. Your undefiled body will see the glory of his only-begotten Son. Your pure spirit will see the glory of the all-holy Spirit.	Dormition III (P 151 ftn. 21)

361C	Horvath mentions this section as confirmation of the Assumption due to the physical relationship between Christ, the Son, and the Virgin, the mother. 288.		Dormition III
361C	Οὐ καυχήσεται θάνατος ἐπὶ σοί· Ζωὴν γὰρ ἐκύησας. Σκεῦος ἐμὸν ἐγένου· οὐ ῥαγώσει τοῦτο σύντριμμα θανατοφθόρου καταπτώσεως. Οὐκ ἀμαυρώσει τοῦτο ζόφου κατασκιασμός. Ἔρχου προθύμως πρὸς τὸν ὑπὸ σοῦ γεγεννημένον. Εὔφρᾶναί σεβούλομαι τεκνοχρέως· ἀποδοῦναί σοι τὰ τῆς μητρικῆς κοιλίας ἐνοίκια· τῆς γαλακτοτροφίας τὸν μισθόν· τῆς ἀνατροφῆς τὴν ἀντάμειψιν· τοῖς σπλάγχνοις σου τὴν πληροφορίαν. Μονογενῆ με κεκτημένη, μῆτερ, Υἱὸν, συνοικῆσαί μοι μᾶλλον προτίμησον· οὐκ ἀντιπερισπάσαι γὰρ οἶδα πρὸς ἑτέρου τέκνου διάθεσιν. Ἐγώ σε παρθένον ἀνέδειξα μητέρα· ἐγώ σε καὶ εὐφραινομένην ἐπὶ Τέκνῳ καταστήσω μητέρα.	Death will not boast over you, for you gave birth to Life. You became my vessel; the fracture of death-corrupting fall will not break this. The shadowing of gloom will not dim this. Come willingly to the one who was borne by you. I want to make you joyful as a child should, to pay back to you the rent of the maternal womb, the wages of wet-nursing, the exchange for upbringing, the fulfillment for your affection. Since you obtained me as your only-begotten Son, O mother, prefer rather to live with me; for I know you have no other child. I showed/proved you to be a virgin mother; I also will make you a mother rejoicing in her Child.	Dormition III (P 154 ftn. 28)
361D	Ἐγώ σοι τὸν κόσμον χρεώστην ἀναδείξω, καὶ μετερχομένης πλεῖον σοῦ τὸ ὄνομα καταδοξάσω. Ἐγώ σε τεῖχος κοσμικὸν οἰκοδομήσω, γέφυραν κλυδωνιζομένων, κιβωτὸνδιασωζομένων, βακτηρίαν χειραγωγουμένων, πρεσβείαν ἁμαρτανόντων, καὶ κλίμακα πρὸς οὐρανὸν τοὺς ἀνθρώπους ἀναβιβάζειν ἰσχύουσαν.	I will show you to the world that is your debtor, and I will glorify your name even more as you are translated. I will build you as a wall for the world, a bridge for those who are swamped, an ark for those who are being saved, a staff for those who are being led by the hand, an intercession for those who are sinning, and a ladder which has the power to raise mankind to heaven.	Dormition III

361D 364A	Ἔρχου μετ' εὐφροσύνης. Ἄνοιξον σὺ τὸν παράδεισον, ὃν ἡ συγγενής σου καὶ ὁμοφυὴς ἀπέκλεισεν Εὔα. Εἴσελθε εἰς τὴν χαρὰν τοῦ Υἱοῦ σου· ἄφες τὴν κάτω Ἰερουσαλήμ· ἀνάδραμε πρὸς τὴν οὐράνιον πόλιν, ὅτι τῆς κάτω Ἰερουσαλὴμ μεγαλυνθήσεται μετὰ μικρὸν «ὁ κοπετός, ὡς κοπετός, κατὰ τὸ γεγραμμένον, ῥοῶνος ἐκκοπτομένου ἐν πεδίῳ.»	Come with rejoicing. Do you open paradise, which your relative and tribeswoman Eve closed. Enter into the joy of your Son. Leave the Jerusalem below. Run up to the heavenly city, because the Jerusalem below will be magnified in a short time: "The noise, like the noise," as it is written, "of a pomegranate-orchard being cut down on the plain" (Zechariah 12.11 LXX).	Dormition III
364C/ 364D	Δημοσιεύει τὴν μετάστασιν, δηλοποιεῖ τὰ παρ' ἀγγέλου πρὸς αὐτὴν δηλωθέντα· δεικνύει καὶ τὸ δοθὲν αὐτῇ βραβεῖον. Ἦν δὲ τὸ βραβεῖον, φοίνικος κλάδος, σύμβολον νίκης κατὰ θανάτου, καὶ ζωῆς ἀμαράντου προεκτύπωμα· τοῦ πιστωθῆναι μετερχομένην, ὅτι καταδυναστεύσειεν τῆς φθορᾶς, ὡς καὶ ὁ ὑπ' αὐτῆς γεννηθεὶς ἐνίκησεν τὸν ᾅδην, Χριστός. Τοιοῦτον τὸ βραβεῖον τοῦ φοίνικος, ἐν ᾧ καὶ οἱ θεοφιλεῖς τῶν Ἑβραίων παῖδες ἐπὶ τὸ πάθος ἐγ)γίζοντι τῷ Χριστῷ, ὡς νικητῇ τούτῳ μέλλοντι γίνεσθαι τοῦ θανάτου, δοξολογητικῶς ἐπέσεισαν, κράζοντες· «Ὡσαννὰ ἐν τοῖς ὑψίστοις·» τουτέστι,	She makes public announcement of her translation, she reveals what has been revealed to her by the angel; she shows the prize which was given to her. The prize was a branch, a symbol of victory over death, and a pre-figuration of un-withering life, to confirm that she is going over, that she may prevail over corruption, as also the Christ who received birth from her conquered Hades. Such a prize/branch of a palm-tree, in/ with which also the god-loving children of the Hebrews, when Christ was approaching his passion, as to this one about to become a victor over death, shook with songs of praise,	Dormition III (P 149 ftn. 11)

392

	Σῶσον δή, ὁ ἐν ὑψίστοις. Τὸ γὰρ Ὡσαννὰ παρ' Ἑβραίοις σῶσον δὴ μεθερμηνεύεται. Ὥσπερ οὖν ἐκεῖ τὰ βαΐα τῶν φοινίκων νικητικὸν τὸν τοῦ Χριστοῦ προεμήνυον συμβολικῇ τῇ ὑποδείξει θάνατον, οὕτως καὶ τὸ ἐκ φοίνικος δοθὲν τῇ Θεοτόκῳ βραβεῖον, πληροφόρημα νίκης ὑπῆρχεν θανατοποιοῦ καταφθορᾶς.	crying out, "Hosanna in the highest;" that is, "Save indeed, [you who are] in the highest." For "Hosanna" among the Hebrews is interpreted as "Save indeed." So as there the branches of the palm-trees foretold the victorious death of Christ with a symbolic demonstration, so also the prize from a palm-tree given to the Theotokos was a fulfillment of victory over death-dealing corruption.	
365C	Germanos takes Philippians 2.15 as the reason why Mary must fall asleep and go to her Son. Horvath points out that "Further Germanus admits as reason of convenience it is fitting (ἤροζεν) on the grounds of her purity to be taken up from our sinful world." 288		Dormition III
365D	Μνήσθητε τῶν αὐτοῦ ῥημάτων, πῶς ἡμῖν ἐν τῷ καιρῷ τοῦ πάθους μὴ θρῆνον ποιεῖν τὴν χαρὰν προσέταττεν τοῦ κόσμου. Κἀμοῦ δὲ σήμερον πρὸς αὐτὸν μετατιθεμένης, μὴ πενθοσθὴν ἐμὴν ἐργάσησθε χαρμονήν· ἀλλὰ τὸ ἐμὸν σῶμα, καθὼς ἐγὼ τοῦτο σχηματίσω πρὸς τῇ κλίνῃ, κηδεύσατε πάντες. Δοκῶ γὰρ ἐκ τῶν χειρῶν αὐτῶν ἐνταφιάζεσθαι τοῦ Υἱοῦ μου, παρ' ἡμῶν τῶν ἐκείνου μαθητῶν κηδευομένη πιστῶς.	Remember his words, how at the time of his passion he ordered you not to make the joy of the world into lamentation. Today also as I am transferred to his side, do not make my rejoicing into sorrow but give funeral rites to my body, as I will arrange it on the bed. For I think I am being buried by the very hands of my Son, when I receive a funeral faithfully from you his disciples." (cf. 364B)	Dormition III (P 149 ftn. 10)
Perniola mentions in ftn. 6 that the falling asleep of Mary took place in Jerusalem at the house of St. John. And she was buried in Getsemani.			

393

| 368B | Μετὰ δὲ καὶ ἄλλων πολλῶν παρὰ Παύλου, καθὼς μαθεῖν ἠδυνήθημεν, πρὸς ἐπαίνων ἐντεύξεις τῇ Θεοτόκῳ προσαχθέντων, συντάσσεται πᾶσιν ἡ Παρθένος. Ἀναπίπτει τῷ ἐκστρωθέντι παρ' αὐτῆς κραβάτῳ· σχηματίζει τὸ ἄμωμον ἑαυτῆς ὡς ἠβουλήθη σῶμα· ἀφίησιν ὡς ἐν ὕπνῳ τὸ πνεῦμα. Μᾶλλον δὲ λέγειν, διίσταται τῆς σαρκὸς ἐν ἐγρηγόρσει, ἐλευθέραν φθορᾶς τὴν κατάλειψιν αὐτῆς ποιησαμένη. | And afterwards when many others besides Paul, as we have been able to learn, brought offerings of praise to the Theotokos, the Virgin bids farewell to all. She reclines on the cot which she has spread; she arranges her blameless body as she wished; she gives up her spirit as in sleep. Or to speak rather, she departs from the flesh in awakening, making her leave-taking free from corruption. | Dormition III (P 148 ftn. 10 and 18) |
| 369C/D | Καὶ ὁ μὲν ἁρπάσας αὐτό, πᾶσιν ἄβλεπτος· Θεὸς γὰρ ἦν ἀθεώρητος· ἡ δὲ σινδὼν ἐν νεφέλῃ κούφῃ ἐν τῇ σαρκικῶς προφητευομένῃ κούφῃ νεφέλῃ, ταῖς χερσὶ τότε τῶν ἀποστόλων, κούφως ἀνεμιζομένη κατεφάνη. Ἔγνωσαν οἱ μαθηταὶ τὴν πρὸς τὴν Μητέρα τοῦ Χριστοῦ σὺν ἀγγέλοις παρουσίαν· ὑφ' οὗ καὶ μεταστᾶσαν αὐτὴν πιστωθέντες, ἔδωκαν δόξαν τῷ Θεῷ ἐν αἰνέσει φωνῆς αὐτῶν, ταῦτα καὶ πρὸς τὸν λαὸν διεξελθόντες· Ἄνδρες Ἰσραηλῖται, τοῦτο νῦν γνωστὸν ὑμῖν ἐδείχθη πᾶσι περὶ Μαρίας τῆς κατὰ σάρκα μητρὸς τοῦ Χριστοῦ, ὡς ἅμα ἡμῖν καὶ ὑμῖν ἐπὶ τὸ μνῆμα τοῦτο νεκρὰ παραγενομένη, παρὰ τῶν ἡμετέρων ἀνελήφθη χειρῶν. Μηδεὶς οὖν δύσπιστος ἐν τούτῳ δειχθῇ. | And he who snatched it was unseen by all, for it was the invisible God; but the shroud in a light cloud, in the corporeally prophesied light cloud (cf. Isaiah 19.1), in the hands of the apostles then appeared lightly blown by the wind. The disciples recognized the arrival of Christ with angels to his mother. Being convinced that she was translated by him, they gave glory to God in praise of their voices, also speaking to the people as follows: "Men of Israel, this has now been made known to you all concerning Mary the mother of Christ according to the flesh, that to us and you together having arrived dead at this tomb, she was taken up from our hands. Let no one be shown doubtful in this matter. | Dormition III (P 149 ftn. 12 and 150 ftn. 14) |

369D and 372A	Μηδεὶς ἡμῖν ὡς ἐπὶ σώματος τοῦ Χριστοῦ κλοπὴν καὶ ἐν τῷ ταύτης λειψάνῳ ψευδῶς ἐπεγκαλείτω· ἀλλ' ἐὰν ἀκουσθῇ τοῦτο παρὰ τοῦ ἡγεμόνοςκαὶ τῶν ἀρχιερέων ὑμῶν, ἀμέριμνον τὴν ἀλήθειαν, καὶ μὴ τὸ ψεῦδος. ποιήσητε. Γίνεσθε μάρτυρες, ὧν ἐθεάσασθε. Γίνεσθε νέοι καὶ ὑμεῖς σαρκικοί τινες ἄγγελοι κατὰ τὸ μνῆμα σήμερον πορευθέντες. Πτερώσατε τὴν ἑαυτῶν ἐν τῇ ἀληθείᾳ γλῶσσαν. Εἴπατε καὶ ὑμεῖς· Ἴδε ὁ τόπος, ὅπου τέθαπται μὲν ἡ Παρθένος· μετετέθη δὲ ἡ ζωοτόκος Μαρία. Ἴδε καὶ ἡ σινδὼν χωρὶς τῆς ἔνδον σπαργανωθείσης ἐπιζητοῦσα τὴν ἐν αὐτῇ κατασφιγχθεῖσαν, ἣν ὡς ἄψυχον ἐσπαργάνου, καὶ ὡς ἐμψύχῳ νῦν ὑποστρωθῆναι ποθεῖ. Γίνεσθε καὶ ὑμεῖς γυναῖκες μυροφόροι τῆς μεταστάσης. Δράμετε, ἀπαγγείλατε τὴν ταύτης ἐκ τοῦ ζωοπαραδέκτου μνημείου μετάθεσιν.	Let no one accuse us falsely of theft as in the case of Christ's body, also in the case of her remains; but if this is heard from the governor and from your high priests, make the truth free from care and not falsehood. Become witnesses of what you have seen. You young people also become like angels in the body as you have gone today to the tomb. Give your tongue wings for the truth. Do you also say, 'Behold the place where the Virgin is buried, but Mary the life-bearer has been translated. Behold also the shroud without her who was wrapped in it, seeking her who was bound tightly in it, whom it wrapped as a lifeless [body] and now desires to be spread under as for a living [person]. You women also become myrrh-bearers for her translation. Run, report her transference from the life-receiving tomb.	Dormition III (P 149 ftn. 13 and 150 ftn. 15)
There are no references in the Sash Homily to Mary's Dormition or Assumption.			

References to Attraction/Bride/Bridal Chamber in Germanos I Patriarch of Constantinople (715-730)

PG 98 Location	Greek	English	Homily
292D	«Τίς αὕτη ἡ ἀναβαίνουσα ἀπὸ τῆς ἐρήμου, ὡς στελέχη καπνοῦ τεθυμιαμένη, σμύρναν καὶ λίβανον ἀπὸ πάντων κονιορτῶν μυρεψοῦ;»—«Δεῦρο ἀπὸ Λιβάνου, νύμφη μου, δεῦρο ἀπὸ Λιβάνου.»	"Who is that who comes up from the wilderness, perfumed with myrrh and frankincense, with all the fragrant powders of the merchants?" (Song of Songs 3.6)—"Come hither from Lebanon, my bride; come hither from Lebanon" (Song of Songs 4.8)	Presentation I
300D	ἐπίσπασαί σοι προσερειδομένην καὶ τῇ ὀσμῇ σου τεθελγμένην, ἣν ὡς κρίνον ἐξ ἀκανθῶν τῆς ἡμετέρας ἀναξιότητος ἐξελέξω· εὐχρωότατά σοι προσφερομένην ἐναγκάλισαι. Ἰδού σοι ταύτην παρατιθέμεθα καὶ ἑαυτοὺς ἀνατιθέμεθα.	Draw to yourself her who leans on you and is attracted by your fragrance. You chose her as a lily out of the brambles of our unworthiness. Embrace her who is brought to you with a most radiant complexion. Behold, to you we offer her [as our intercessor] and dedicate ourselves."	Presentation I
301A	Ὦ τῆς ἡμετέρας σωτηρίας αἴτιοι, τί ὑμᾶς προσείπω; Τί καλέσω; Ἐξίσταμαι βλέπων, ὁποῖον καρπὸν προσήξατε. Τοιοῦτος γὰρ ὅστις τῇ καθαρότητι θέλγει Θεὸν	"O causes of our salvation, what shall I say to you? What shall I call [you]? I am astonished seeing what kind of fruit you have brought forth, such a one as by her purity attracts	Presentation I

Gregory E. Roth

	ἐν αὐτῇ οἰκῆσαι. Οὐδὲ γὰρ πώποτέ τις γέγονεν ἢ γενήσεται τοιαύτη καλλονῇ διαλάμπουσα. Ὑμεῖς ὤφθητε οἱ ἐκ παραδείσου ἀφιγμένοι δύο διπλούμενοι ποταμοί, ὑπὲρ χρυσίον καὶ λίθον τίμιον φέροντες λαμπάδα, τὴν τῷ κάλλει τῆς ἑαυτῆς ἀμώμου παρθενίας καὶ ταῖς δροσιστικαῖς μαρμαρυγαῖς τὴν ἅπασαν γῆν καταυγάζουσαν.	God to dwell within her. For never yet has anyone existed or will anyone exist who shines forth in such beauty. You are seen as the two double rivers flowing out of paradise, (*cf.* Genesis 2.10-15) carrying a lamp more precious than gold and precious stones, who in the beauty of her blameless virginity and her dewy sparkling illuminates the whole earth.	
305C	ἢ ἐν τῇ τοῦ Κυρίου αὐλῇ ἤτοι τῷ ἁγίῳ αὐτοῦ ναῷ νυνὶ θεμελιουμένη, ἐν ᾗ ἡ ἀχειρότευκτος καὶ πεποικιλμένη παστὰς τοῦ νοητοῦ νυμφίου·	Right now you are being established in the court of the Lord, in his holy Temple, in which is located the decorated bridal chamber not made by hands of the bridegroom (*cf.* Psalm 19.5-6).	Presentation I
317B	Θεόνυμφε	bride of God,	Presentation II
321C	παρὰ τῆς θεοπνεύστου Γραφῆς μεμαθηκότες, πρὸς τὴν οὐράνιον νύμφην καὶ βασιλίδα καὶ Θεοτόκον	We have learned from the Holy Scriptures about this heavenly bride and queen, the Theotokos.	Annunciation
346C	ἀνθηροποιεῖ τὴν ἑαυτῆς κλίνην, ὡς ἐπὶ παστάδος παρθενεύοντος γάμου· τὴν ἕως τότε κατὰ πᾶσαν νύκτα διὰ τὸν πρὸς Χριστὸν καὶ Υἱόν, αὐτῆς ἐπιθυμίαν, τοῖς τῶν προσευχῶν θαλασσουμένην δάκρυσιν. «Ἐπὶ κοίτην γάρ μου, φησὶν ἡ Γραφή, ἐξεζήτησα, ὃν ἠγάπησεν ἡ ψυχή μου.»	she decks her bed with flowers, as for the chamber of the marriage of a virgin; [the bed] which until then every night (because of her desire for her Christ and Son) is inundated by the tears of her prayers. "For on my bed," says Scripture, "I have sought him whom my soul has loved" (Cant. 3.1 LXX).	Dormition III

398

References to Beauty in Germanos I Patriarch of Constantinople (715-730)

PG 98 Location	Greek	English	Homily
293D	τῷ πάσης ὑπεραρθῆναι καλλονῇ γλώσσης τε καὶ νοὸς ἐξεστηκότως, προάγει. Πέλαγος γὰρ ἀχανὲς τὰ ταύτης μεγαλεῖα, ὁ ἐξ αὐτῆς οὐράνιος γεννηθεὶς σταγὼν ἀνέδειξεν. Διὸ δὴ τοῦ χάριν καὶ ἄληπτος τῇ ἀπειρίᾳ ὁ ταύτης πλοῦτος πέφυκε,	Her beauty far surpasses the power of every tongue and mind. For her greatness is a vast sea, as the Heavenly drop born from her has shown. And therefore her richness is unlimited in its infinitude, and her wealth is inexhaustible.	Presentation I
297A	Δεῦτέ μοι, φησὶν, συγχαίρετε, αἵτινές τε καὶ ὅσοι τῇ γεννήσει συνειλεγμένοι, μειζόνως, ἄρτι τὴν ἐξ ἐμῶν σπλάγχνων ἀνατιθεμένη Κυρίῳ δῶρον θεοκαλλώπιστον ἡγιασμένον.	"Come with me, let us rejoice together, all women and men who rejoiced at her birth, even more now, as I dedicate to the Lord this divinely beautiful and holy gift recently received from my own womb.	Presentation I
297C	«Πᾶσα ἡ δόξα γὰρ, ἔφης, τῆς θυγατρὸς τοῦ βασιλέως ἔσωθεν ἐν κροσσωτοῖς χρυσοῖς,» περιβεβλημένη τῇ ἀμιάντῳ καὶ ἀσπίλῳ παρθενίᾳ, καὶ πεποικιλμένη τῇ ἀσυγκρίτῳ καλλονῇ, ὁμοιοτρόπως λελέξων·	"All glory is given to the daughter of the King who resides within [the temple] dressed in gold-fringed robes," of a pure and spotless virginity, and in the similar way you will have said, "embroidered with incomparable beauty" (Ps 44:14 LXX).	Presentation I

297C	δεῦρ' ἴθι, Δαυῒδ ἡωσφῶν· «Τίς αὕτη ἡ ἐκκύπτουσα ὡσεὶ ὄρθρος, καλὴ ὡς σελήνη, ἐκλεκτὴ ὡς ἥλιος; τί ὡραιώθησαν διαβήματά σου ἐν ὑποδήμασι;»	Come here David bringer of dawn's light[9]: "Who is this who shines out like the dawn, is as fair as the moon, and bright as the sun?" "How gracefully you walk in your sandals!" (Cant 7:2)	Presentation I
297D	—«Τί ὡραιώθης καὶ τί ἡδύνθης,» ἡ τὸν ἥλιον περιδυσομένη, καὶ καινὸν ὑπὸ τὸν ἥλιον προσάξουσα θέαμα!	"How beautiful and pleasant you are" (Cant 7:7) the one who shall be clothed in the Sun (Rev 12:1) and will bring forth a new wonder under the Sun! (cf. Ec. 1:9-10)	
300B	ὡραΐζεται δὲ ἡ αὐτοῦ εὐπρέπεια τῇ αὐτῆς εἰσόδῳ.	By her entry the temple's beauty is adorned.	Presentation I
301A	Οὐδὲ γὰρ πώποτέ τις γέγονεν ἢ γενήσεται τοιαύτη καλλονῇ διαλάμπουσα.	For never yet has anyone existed or will anyone exist who shines forth in such beauty.	Presentation I
301A	Ὑμεῖς ὤφθητε οἱ ἐκ παραδείσου ἀφιγμένοι δύο διπλούμενοι ποταμοί, ὑπὲρ χρυσίον καὶ λίθον τίμιον φέροντες λαμπάδα, τὴν τῷ κάλλει τῆς ἑαυτῆς ἀμώμου παρθενίας καὶ ταῖς δροσιστικαῖς μαρμαρυγαῖς τὴν ἅπασαν γῆν καταυγάζουσαν.	You are seen as the two double rivers flowing out of paradise, (cf. Genesis 2.10-15) carrying a lamp more precious than gold and precious stones, who in the beauty of her blameless virginity and her dewy sparkling illuminates the whole earth.	Presentation I
304A	ἧς τῇ καλλονῇ τῆς ὡραιότητος ἡδόμεναι θυγατέρες Ἰερουσαλὴμ αἶνον γεγηθυῖαι πλέκουσιν	Daughters of Jerusalem taking pleasure in the beauty of your comeliness joyously compose a hymn. The	Presentation I (P 118 ftns. 33 & 40)

---

[9]   ἡωσφῶν, attested only here

	καὶ βασιλεῖς τῆς γῆς μακαρίζουσιν· ἡ βάσις θεία γεγνωρισμένη καὶ θεοστήρικτος κλίμαξ δεδειγμένη τῷ πατριαρχικωτάτῳ Ἰακὼβ θυμηρέστατα. Καθέσθητι, ὦ Δέσποινα· καὶ πρέπει γάρ σοι τῇ βασιλίσσῃ καὶ ὑπὲρ πάσας τὰς βασιλείας τοῦ κόσμου δεδοξασμένῃ, ἐν τοιαύτῃ βαθμίδι ἐφέζεσθαι.	kings of the Earth call you blessed. Your ascent of the steps is recognized as divine and delightfully shown as a God-supported ladder to the great patriarch Jacob (*cf.* Genesis 28.12*ff*.). Sit down O Lady, for it is proper to you as the Queen glorified above all earthly kingdoms to be seated upon such steps.	
304B	Εὐπρεπές σοι τῷ Χερουβικωτάτῳ θρόνῳ ὁ ἡγιασμένος τόπος εἰς κατοικητήριον. Ἰδοὺ σοί, ὡς παντανάσσῃ, τὴν προκαθεδρίαν καταξίως ἔνειμα, ἀνάστησον δὴ καὶ αὐτὴ τοὺς καταραχθέντας. Καὶ νῦν οὖν μετὰ Δαυΐδ σοι προσφωνῶ· «Ἄκουσον, θύγατερ, καὶ ἴδε, καὶ κλῖνον τὸ οὖς σου, καὶ ἐπιλάθου τοῦ λαοῦ σου καὶ τοῦ οἴκου τοῦ πατρός σου, καὶ ἐπιθυμήσει ὁ βασιλεὺς τοῦ κάλλους σου.»	This holy place is a fitting dwelling for you who are the throne of the Cherubim. Behold, as Queen of all I have attributed, as it is fitting to you, the most honorable throne. Do you yourself raise up those who have been cast down. And now with David I cry unto you: 'Hear O daughter consider and incline your ear; forget not your people and your father's house; and the king will desire your beauty.' (Psalm 45.11 *ff.*)"	Presentation I
309A	τὴν τοῦ Θεοῦ κατοίκησιν ναοῦ εὐπρέπειαν ἀεὶ διατήρησον	Keep the dwelling-place of God always as the beauty of the temple.	Presentation I
Presentation II does not appear to have any references to beauty.			
	Χαῖρε, κεχαριτωμένη, τὸ πάγχρυσον καὶ παναμώμητον κάλλος καὶ τὸ ὑπερκείμενον καὶ ὄντως ὑπερθαύμαστον τοῦ Λόγου ἐνδιαίτημα.	*Hail, full of grace, the all-golden and all-blameless beauty and the exceptional and truly marvelous dwelling-place of the Word*	Annunciation

321C	Χαῖρε, κεχαριτωμένη, Χριστιανῶν ἁπάντων θαυμαστὸν καὶ εὐσυμπάθητον καταφύγιον, καὶ πάσης μεγαλουργοῦ καλλονῆς ὑψηλότερον θέαμα.	Hail full of grace, marvelous and sympathetic refuge of all Christians, and higher vision of the beauty of great achievements.	Annunciation
324A	Βλέπω σου, νεανίσκε. τῆς εὐμορφίας τὸ ἀξιογράφιστον κάλλος, καὶ τοῦ χαρακτῆρος τὴν αὐγηρὰν θεωρίαν· καὶ λόγους ἀκούω σου, οὓς οὐδέποτε ἀκήκοα, καὶ ἐν ὑποψίᾳ γίνομαι τάχα, ὅτι πλανῆσαί με παραγέγονας.	Young man, I see the beauty of your comely form which is worthy to be painted, and the radiant vision of your appearance, and I hear your words, which I have never heard before, and I am suspicious that you have come to lead me astray.	Annunciation
324A	Γνῶθι σαφῶς καὶ πιστώθητι, ὅτι μᾶλλον ἐγὼ ἐν ἐκπλήξει γέγονα θεασάμενος τὸ τοιοῦτόν σου θεογράφιστον κάλλος· καὶ βλέπων σε λοιπὸν, νομίζω δόξαν Κυρίου μου καταμανθάνειν.	Know truly and believe that I am more amazed at seeing your God-created beauty. Seeing you I know that I am examining closely the glory of my Lord.	Annunciation
336C	Οὐκ ἐπίσταμαι σαφῶς τὸ, ἐν ποίοις τόποις αὐλίζεται. Ἐπεὶ κατὰ ἀλήθειαν ἤθελον κἀγὼ αὐτὸν κατατυχεῖν· ἤθελον αὐτοῦ τὸ ἀξιοζωγράφιστον κάλλος θεάσασθαι, καὶ μετ' αὐτοῦ διαλεκτῆσαι·ὅτι εἶπέ μοι «Χαῖρε», καὶ ἄρτι λυποῦμαι.	I do not clearly understand in what place he dwells. I truly wished to go to him, to gaze upon his beauty which is worthy to be painted, and to have righteous dialogue with him. For, he said to me "Rejoice," and I am grieved just now.	Annunciation
340A	Χθὲς ἐξ ὑποψίας σφαλλόμενος, μέμψιν ἐπήνεγκα τῇ ὡραιότητί σου καὶ τῷ κάλλει σου· νῦν δὲ ἐξ ὕψους πληροφορίαν δεξάμενος, ἀπολογήσομαι ἅμα·	Yesterday I was thrown down by suspicion, shame I have brought to your beauty and your loveliness, but now receiving the fullness from on high, at once I shall give an account	Annunciation

	καὶ προσκυνήσω μετ' εὐλαβείας τὴν μεγαλοσύνην σου <u>καὶ εὐλογήσω τὸ ὄνομά σου</u> <εἰς τοὺς αἰῶνας, ὅτι ἠλέησε Κύριος τὸν λαὸν αὐτοῦ>.	and prostrate myself in reverence to your greatness and bless your name <unto the ages, for the Lord has had mercy on his people>.	
340D	Ἐπ' ἀληθείας γὰρ, καὶ τοὺς οὐρανοὺς ἐκαλλώπισας, καὶ τὴν γῆν ὑπερελάμπρυνας, Θεοτόκε.	For in truth, you beautified the heavens, and you illuminated the earth, O Theotokos.	Dormition I
345B	Σὺ, κατὰ τὸ γεγραμμένον, «ἐν καλλονῇ·» καὶ τὸ σῶμά σου τὸ παρθενικόν, ὅλον ἅγιον, ὅλον ἁγνὸν, ὅλον Θεοῦ κατοικητήριον· ὡς ἐκ τούτου λοιπὸν καὶ ἀλλότριον χοϊκῆς ἀναλύσεως. Ἐναλλαγὲν μὲν ὡς ἀνθρώπινον πρὸς ἄκραν ἀφθαρσίας ζωήν· σῶον δὲ τοῦτο καὶ ὑπερένδοξον, ζωοτελὲς καὶ ἀκοίμητον· καθ' ὅτιπερ οὐδὲ ἦν δυνατὸν παρὰ νεκροποιοῦ συνκλεισμοῦ τοῦτο κρατηθῆναι, ὡς σκεῦος ὑπάρχον θεηδόχον, καὶ ἔμψυχος ναὸς τῆς τοῦ Μονογενοῦς παναγίας θεότητος. Ἕνεκεν δὴ τούτων, μεθ' ἡμῶν σε, Θεοτόκε, πιστεύομεν περινοστεῖν.	You, as it is written, [are] "in beauty" (Cant 2.3 LXX) and your virginal body, altogether holy, altogether pure, altogether the residence of God; so because of this [it is] separated and alien from earthly dissolution. While remaining human it is changed to the sublime life of incorruptibility. This is safe and supremely glorious, life-accomplishing [its life ended] and unsleeping; as it was not possible for this to be controlled by death-dealing confinement, being a God-receiving vessel, and a living temple of the all-holy divinity of the Only-begotten One. Because of these things, we trust that you, O Theotokos, will return home with us.	Dormition I
Dormition II appears to have no references to beauty.			
Dormition III appears to have no references to beauty.			
Sash appears to have no references to beauty.			

References to the Childhood of Mary in Germanos I, Patriarch of Constantinople (715-730)

PG 98 Location	Greek	English	Homily
292C	ὑπεραναβαινούσης τῆς ἐξαρχούσης Θεόπαιδος	the preeminence of the excellent child of God	Presentation I
293A	παῖδα . . . χωροῦσαν	the child going	Presentation I
293A	Σήμερον γὰρ τριετίζουσα πρόεισι τῷ νομικῷ ναῷ ἀνατεθησομένη	Today, at three years of age, she goes towards her dedication in the temple of the law,	Presentation I
293B	Σήμερον βρέφος	Today a babe	Presentation I
293D	ἀπειροκάκῳ καὶ ἀδαήμονι ἡλικίᾳ	at a pure and innocent age	Presentation I
296B	τριετῆ χρόνον τετελεκυῖαν	the one who had reached three years of age	Presentation I
296D	Ἤδη μὲν οὖν ἀπογαλακτισθείσης αὐτῆς τῆς ἡμετέρας ζωῆς τροφοῦ	she who is the nourisher of our lives had been weaned	Presentation I
297C	ἐμὴ παῖς βασιλικώτατα	my regal child	Presentation I
300B	ἡ Θεόπαις,	the child of God	Presentation I
301A	τὴν παῖδα	the child	Presentation I
301C	παιδίον τῶν οὐρανῶν ἀνώτερον	child higher than the heavens	Presentation I
301C	βρέφος ὁρώμενον καὶ θεϊκὸν ἐργαστήριον νοούμενον	you who are seen as a child but are known as God's workshop	Presentation I
304B	ἡ παῖς	the child	Presentation I
304B	ἡ κόρη	the maiden	Presentation I
304C	τὸ βρέφος	the infant	Presentation I

308B	Χαίροις, ἡ τῇ σῇ γεννήσει στειρώσεως δεσμὰ λύσασα, καὶ ὀνειδισμὸν ἀτεκνίας λικμήσασα, καὶ νομικὴν κατάραν βυθίσασα, καὶ χάριτος εὐλογίαν ἀνθήσασα, καὶ τῇ πρὸς τὰ τῶν ἁγίων Ἅγια εἰσόδῳ εὐχῆς τελείωσιν γονικῆς καὶ θεμέλιον τῆς ἡμῶν ἀφέσεως καὶ χαρμονῆς συμπλήρωσιν τελειώσασα, ὡς χάριτος ἀρχὴν προαγαγοῦσα.	Hail, you who through your birth released the fetters of sterility, who scattered the reproach of childlessness, and sank the curse of the Law (cf. Galatians 3.13); and blossomed forth the grace of blessing—by entering the Holy of Holies you perfected the prayers of your parents and the foundation for forgiveness of our sins, fulfilling the perfection of harmony as the leader of the beginning of grace.	Presentation I
312A	Κόρην ἐξ ἐπαγγελίας, καὶ αὐτὴν τριετίζουσαν, εἰς τὸ τρίτον καταπέτασμα ὡς δῶρον ἄμωμον προσφερομένην, πρὸς τὸ ἐκεῖσε οἰκεῖν ἀπαραλείπτως, καὶ ὑπὸ τῶν πλουσίων τοῦ λαοῦ λιτανευομένην	A maiden from the promise, at the age of three years, is brought as a blameless gift within the third curtain, to live there continuously, and receives petitions from the wealthy men of the people (cf. Psalm 45.13).	Presentation II
312B	«Τί ἄρα ἔσται τὸ παιδίον τοῦτο;»	"What will this child be?" Lk 1.66	Presentation II
312D/ 313A	κόρην προσάγειν σκηνοβατεῖν εἰς τὰ ἄδυτα;	To bring a maiden to make her tent in the sanctuary?	Presentation II
312D	τὴν παῖδα	the child	Presentation II
312D	κόρην	a maiden	Presentation II
313C	τέκνον	child	Presentation II
313D	ἐμῆς παιδὸς	my child	Presentation II
316A	τὸ ἐμὸν τέκνον	my child	Presentation II
316A	τοῦτο	this [child]	Presentation II
316B	ἡ προσαγωγή σου	your offspring	Presentation II
316B	τὴν παῖδα	the child	Presentation II
316C	Ἡ δὲ παῖς σκιρτῶσα καὶ ἀγαλλομένη, καθάπερ ἐν θαλάμῳ, ἐν τῷ ναῷ τοῦ Θεοῦ ἐβάδιζε·	But the child skipping and rejoicing, as in a bridal chamber, walked in the Temple of God;	Presentation II

316C	τριετίζουσα μὲν τῷ χρόνῳ τῆς ἡλικίας, ὑπερτελὴς δὲ τῇ χάριτι τῇ θείᾳ, ὡς ἅτε προεγνωσμένη καὶ προωρισμένη καὶ ἐκλελεγμένη τῷ πάντων Θεῷ καὶ ταμίᾳ.	being three years old in her chronological age, but more than perfect in divine grace, as foreknown and predestined and chosen for the God and governor of all.	Presentation II
316C	Ἔμεινεν δὲ αὐτὴ εἰς τὰ τῶν ἁγίων ἐνδότερα Ἅγια, ἀμβροσίῳ τροφῇ δι' ἀγγέλου τρεφομένη, καὶ τοῦ θείου νέκταρος ποτιζομένη, μέχρι δευτέρας μεθηλικιώσεως·	She remained in the inner holy of holies, nourished with ambrosial food by an angel, and receiving drink of divine nectar, until her second advance in age-group.	Presentation II
324B	κόρην	a maiden	Annunciation
324C	Ἰωακεὶμ καὶ Ἄννα οἱ ἐμοὶ γονεῖς τυγχάνουσιν	Joachim and Anna are my parents	Annunciation
328B	παρθένον ἀπείρανδρον	an untried virgin	Annunciation
328B	κόρην ἀπειρόγαμον	an unmarried girl	Annunciation
329C	Χαρακτῆρα φέρουσα βασιλικόν, καὶ εἰς τὰ βασίλεια τῆς ἐμῆς Βηθλεὲμ τιθηνήσασα, καὶ εἰς <τὰ> ἅγια ἐκ παιδόθεν ἀμέμπτως διαπρέψασα· καὶ παρθένος λοιπὸν τυγχάνουσα, πῶς ἐγὼ μήτηρ ἀκούσω τοῦ παιδός μου;	I am of royal blood, and spent my earliest childhood in the royal house of Bethlehem, and my childhood I spent blamelessly in the temple; and being a virgin up to now, how can I be called the mother of my child?	Annunciation
332A	ὅτι ἐκ παιδόθεν ἐμίσησα τὸν ἀπὸ σαρκὸς ἐσπιλωμένον χιτῶνα, καὶ ἴχνος ἡδυπαθείας οὐκ ἔστιν ἐμοί.	From my childhood I have hated the spotted garment of the flesh, and no trace of enjoyment is in me.	Annunciation
336C	Ξενίσει σοι, οἶδα, τὰ λεγόμενα καὶ καταπλήττει σου τὸν νοῦν τῆς μυστικῆς κυοφορίας τὸ παράδοξον μυστήριον. Ἐγὼ δὲ τῆς ἐπενεχθείσης μοι συμφορᾶς αἴτιος οὐκ εἰμι, καθότι ἀπὸ βρέφους λατρεύειν εἴθισα τῷ Κυρίῳ μου τῷ ποιήσαντί με.	It is strange to you, I know. The paradoxical nature of my childbearing astounds your mind. I am not responsible for this condition which has been brought upon me. From infancy I have been accustomed to worship the Lord who made me.	Annunciation

There do not appear to be any direct references to either Mary's childhood or her youth in Dormition I, Dormition II, Dormition III nor the Sash.

References to the Citizenship of Human Beings/the Christian people in Germanos I, Patriarch of Constantinople (715-730)

PG 98 Location	Greek	English	Homily
305A	Χαίροις, τῇ τῶν βημάτων σου ῥυθμίσει καταπατήσασα τὸν δεινόν μοι ποδηγόν, κεχρηματικότα πρὸς τὴν παράβασιν σκολιογνώμονα καὶ μισόκαλον ὄφιν διάβολον·	Hail to you who by the rhythm of your footsteps trample down my terrible leader—that serpent with his crooked-minded, good-hating diabolical nature—who has counseled me toward transgression (cf. Genesis 3.1-13).	Presentation I (P Viventi 161 ftn. 5)
312B 312C	ἡμεῖς δὲ ὁ τοῦ Θεοῦ λαὸς ὁ περιούσιος, ἱερεῖς καὶ ἄρχοντες, κοσμικοί τε καὶ μονάζοντες, δοῦλοι καὶ ἐλεύθεροι, χειροτέχναι καὶ γηπόνοι, φυτοκόμοι καὶ ἁλιεῖς, νέοι καὶ πρεσβύται, ἄνδρες καὶ γυναῖκες· δεῦτε, προθύμως τῇ Θεοτόκῳ προσέλθωμεν, καὶ τὰ εἰς αὐτὴν προτελεσθέντα θεῖα μυστήρια [οἰκονομικῶς] ἐποπτεύσωμεν·	But we, the remnant of God's people (cf. 1 Peter 2.10), priests and rulers, secular and monastics, slaves and free, craftsmen and farmers, gatherers and fishermen, young and old, men and women: hither, let us eagerly approach the Theotokos, and let us watch the divine mysteries which were accomplished earlier in her.	Presentation II
321C	Χαῖρε, κεχαριτωμένη, Χριστιανῶν ἁπάντων θαυμαστὸν καὶ εὐσυμπάθητον καταφύγιον, καὶ πάσης μεγαλουργοῦ καλλονῆς ὑψηλότερον θέαμα.	Hail full of grace, marvelous and sympathetic refuge of all Christians, and higher vision of the beauty of great achievements.	Annunciation

329B	Χριστιανῶν ἁπάντων γενήσῃ κοινὸν ἱλαστήριον	You shall become the common propitiation of all Christians.	Annunciation
340C	Τῆς ἐνσάρκου σου μετὰ ἀνθρώπων συναναστροφῆς τοὺς ἐπαίνους ἐπανυμνήσω,	Shall I hymn the praises of your incarnate companionship with humanity	Dormition I
341A	Ἀλλὰ τῶν ἐλεεινῶν ἀνθρώπων πλάνῃ καὶ εἰδωλολατρείᾳ τότε διατελούντων, κνίσης τε θυσιῶν τὸν ἀέρα μολυνόντων, ἀφειδίασαν ἐκ τῆς τῶν ἀνθρώπων συνδιαγωγῆς λοιπὸν καὶ οἱ ἄγγελοι	But of the wretched men then living in error and idolatry, polluting the air with the smoke of sacrifices, for the rest even the angels ceased from companionship with men;	Dormition I
344A	ὅτιπερ διὰ τῆς σῆς ἀμώμου σαρκὸς οὐρανοπολίτης ὁ ἄνθρωπος ἀπετελέσθη	Because through your blameless flesh man has been made a citizen of heaven, and shepherds associated with angels.	Dormition I
344B	Ἐπὰν οὖν, παναγία Θεομῆτορ, ὁ οὐρανὸς, καὶ ἡ γῆ μᾶλλον εἰπεῖν, διὰ σοῦ κατεκομίσθη, πῶς ἔνδεκτον ὀρφανοὺς τῆς σῆς ἀναθεωρίας καταλεῖψαί σε τῇ μεταστάσει τοὺς ἀνθρώπους; Μὴ γένοιτο τοῦτο φρονεῖν ἡμᾶς! Ὥσπερ γὰρ ἐν τῷ κόσμῳ τούτῳ διάγουσα, οὐ ξένη τῶν οὐρανίων ὑπῆρχες διαιτημάτων, οὐδὲ μετα[τε]θεῖσα, τῆς σῆς ἀνθρώπων ἠλλοτριώθης τῷ πνεύματι συναναστροφῆς·	So since, O all-holy Mother of God, heaven, and what is more [the] earth, that through you was brought into a place of refuge, how is it acceptable for you to leave mankind orphaned of the sight of you at your translation? Far from us be it to think this! For as when you lived in this world, you were not a stranger to heavenly conversations, neither when you have been transferred have you alienated from mankind your spiritual counsel.	DormitionI (P Viventi 162 ftn. 7)
344D	Καὶ γὰρ, ὡς μετὰ τῶν ἀρχαιοτέρων ἡμῶν ἐν σαρκὶ συνεπολιτεύου, ὁμοίως καὶ μεθ' ἡμῶν τῷ πνεύματι συνοικεῖς· καὶ ἡ πολλή σου περὶ ἡμᾶς σκέπη, τὴν σὴν ἡμῶν χαρακτηρίζει συνομιλίαν.	For also, as you kept fellowship in the flesh with our ancestors, likewise also with us you dwell in the spirit. And your great oversight for us characterizes your companionship with us.	Dormition I

345A	Οὐ γὰρ ἀφῆκας, οὓς διέσωσας· κατέλιπας, οὓς συνήγαγες· ὅτι ζῇ σου τὸ πνεῦμα διὰ παντός, καὶ ἡ σὰρξ διαφθορὰν οὐχ ὑπέμεινε ταφῆς. Πάντας ἐπισκέπτῃ, καὶ ἡ ἐπισκοπή σου, Θεομῆτορ, ἐπὶ πάντας· ὥστε κἂν οἱ ὀφθαλμοὶ ἡμῶν κρατοῦνται τοῦ μὴ βλέπειν σε, παναγία, ἐν μέσῳ σὺ τῶν ἁπάντων ἐμφιλοχωρεῖς, ἐμφανίζουσα τοῖς ἀξίοις σου διαφόρως ἑαυτήν. Ἡ γὰρ σὰρξ οὐκ ἐμποδίζει τῇ δυνάμει καὶ ἐνεργείᾳ τοῦ πνεύματός σου· ὅπιπερ ὅπου θέλει πνεῖ σου τὸ πνεῦμα, ἐπειδὴ καθαρὸν τοῦτο καὶ ἄυλον· ἄφθαρτον καὶ ἀκηλίδωτον, καὶ τοῦ Πνεύματος τοῦ ἁγίου συνδιαιτικὸν πνεῦμα, καὶ τῆς Μονογενοῦς θεότητος ἐκλεκτόν.	You oversee all, O Mother of God, and your oversight is upon all, so that even if our eyes do not have the power to see you, all-holy one, you love to dwell in the midst of all, revealing yourself especially to those who are worthy of you. For the flesh does not hinder the power and activity of your spirit, just as wherever it wishes your spirit blows, since it is pure and immaterial; incorrupt and unstained, and a spirit which dwells together with the Holy Spirit, and the chosen one of the only-begotten divinity.	DormitionI (P Viventi 160 ftn. 1,162 ftn. 6, 164 ftn.12, 162 ftn. 7)
345B	Ὄντως γὰρ, ὄντως, καὶ πάλιν εὐχαριστικῶς ἐρῶ· οὐκ ἐχωρίσθης κἂν μετέστης τοῦ Χριστιανικοῦ γένους·	For truly, truly, and again I will say with thanksgiving: you were not separated from [us] the Christian family even when you departed.	Dormition I
345C/D	Μετέστης γοῦν τῶν ἐπιγείων, τοῦ δειχθῆναι τὸ τῆς φρικτῆς ἐνανθρωπήσεως βεβαιούμενον ἀφαντάστως μυστήριον· ἵνα σοῦ τὴν ἐκδημίαν τῶν προσκαίρων ὑπομεμενηκυίας, ὁ ἐκ σοῦ γεννηθεὶς Θεός, πιστευθῇ καὶ τέλειος προελθεῖν ἄνθρωπος, ἐξ ἀψευδοῦς Μητρὸς Υἱὸς, ὑποκειμένης νόμοις φυσικῶν ἀναγκασμάτων, ὅρου θείου κελεύσματι, καὶ χρόνου βιωτικοῦ παρακελεύσει	You departed from the earthly ones to show the mystery confirmed of his awesome assumption of humanity, so that when you had endured the exile from temporary [things], the God born from you would be believed to have come forth also a perfect man, the Son of the true Mother, subject to the laws of natural necessities, by the command of a divine decree, and by the order of biological time.	Dormition I (P Viventi 165 ftn. 13)

Gregory E. Roth

348C	Ἄρα οὖν, ὡς αἰωνίας σου τούτῳ καταπαύσεως οὔσης, πρὸς αὑτὸν ἀδιάφθορον προσελάβετό σε, πλησιοχώρως, ὡς εἴποι τις, τῶν σῶν λαλιῶν καὶ σπλάγχνων ἔχειν σε θέλων· διὸ καὶ ὅσα ζητεῖς παρ' αὑτοῦ, τεκνοπενθῷ ἐπιδίδωσι, καὶ ὅσαπερ αἰτεῖς ἐξ αὑτοῦ, θεοδυνάμως ἀποπληροῖ· ὁ ὢν εὐλογητὸς εἰς τοὺς αἰῶνας.	So since you are his eternal resting-place, he took you to himself free from corruption, wishing to have you nearby, as one might say, [with] your conversation and compassion. Therefore also whatever you seek from him, he gives with a child's affection, and whatever you seek from him, he fulfills with the power of God: who is blessed unto the ages. Amen.	Dormition II (P Viventi 164 ftn. 10)
348D	«Ἀγαλλιάσθωσαν καὶ εὐφρανθήτωσαν ἐπὶ σοὶ πάντες οἱ ζητοῦντές σε,» Θεοτόκε, «καὶ λεγέτωσαν διὰ παντός· Μεγαλυνθήτω ὁ Κύριος, οἱ ἀγαπῶντες» μεγαλύνειν κατὰ χρέως τὸ ὄνομά σου· ὅτι «τὸ στόμα» τῶν Χριστιανῶν «μελετήσει τὴν δικαιοσύνην σου» καὶ παρθενίαν σου· «ὅλην τὴν ἡμέραν τὸν ἔπαινον» τῆς ἁγιοσύνης τοῦ τόκου σου.	"Let all who seek you rejoice and be glad," O Theotokos, "and let them say always: 'Magnified be the Lord,' and those who love [you]" (Ps. 39.17 LXX) magnify your name as is needful, because "the mouth" of Christians "will meditate on your righteousness" (Ps. 34.28 LXX) and your virginity; all day long [they will meditate on] the praise of the holiness of your childbirth.	Dormition II
349A	Σὺ γὰρ εἶ τῆς ὄντως ἀληθινῆς Ζωῆς ἡ μήτηρ. Σὺ εἶ τῆς ἀναπλάσεως τοῦ Ἀδὰμ ἡ ζύμη. Σὺ εἶ τῶν ὀνειδισμῶν τῆς Εὔας ἡ ἐλευθερία. Ἐκείνη μήτηρ χοός, σὺ μήτηρ φωτός. Ἐκείνης ἡ μήτρα, φθορᾶς· ἡ δὲ σὴ γαστήρ, ἀφθαρσίας. Ἐκείνη θανάτου κατοίκησις, σὺ μετάστασις ἀπὸ θανάτου.	For you are the mother of the true Life. You leaven the new creation of Adam. You free Eve from reproach. She is the mother of earth; you are the mother of light. Her womb [is the source] of destruction; your belly [is the source] of imperishability. She is the dwelling-place of death; you are the removal from death.	Dormition II (P Viventi 161 ftn. 2)

352B	Ὅθεν καὶ ὁ Χριστιανὸς λαός σου, τὰ καθ' ἑαυτὸν ἀνακρίνων, πρὸς μὲν τὸν Θεὸν παρρησιαστικῶς ὑποστέλλεταί σοι τὰς δεήσεις προσφέρειν. Σὲ δυσωπεῖν ἀνενδοίαστος θαῤῥεῖ, παναγία, διὰ τὴν πεῖραν, καὶ τὰ πλήθη τῶν εἰς ἡμᾶς ἀγαθῶν σου, καὶ παραβιάσεσθαί σε πολλάκις ἐν ἱκεσίαις.	Therefore your Christian people examining their own [affairs], delegate you to bring their petitions to God with confident speech. They unhesitatingly make bold to entreat you, all-holy Lady, because of [their] experience and the multitude of your bounties towards us, and to constrain you often in supplications.	Dormition II
352B	τὴν τῶν ἀνθρώπων ὑπέρξενον ἐπιτυχίαν· τὴν ὑπόληψιν τοῦ γένους τῶν Χριστιανῶν· τὸ ὀχλούμενον τῶν ἁμαρτωλῶν προσφύγιον· τὴν καθ' ὥραν ἐν τῷ στόματι τῶν Χριστιανῶν φερομένην. Μόνον γὰρ εἰ θροηθῇ Χριστιανός, εἰ καὶ πρὸς λίθον τὸν ἑαυτοῦ προσκόψῃ πόδα, τὸ σὸν ἐπικαλεῖται πρὸς βοήθειαν ὄνομα.	You are the surpassingly strange good fortune of mankind. You are the support of the nation of Christians. You are the refuge importuned by sinners. You are carried from hour to hour in the mouth of Christians. For if one is merely called Christian, if he even strikes his foot against a stone (Ps. 90.12 LXX), he calls upon your name for help.	Dormition II
353B	Ἀλλὰ ἀρκεῖ σοι πρὸς ἔπαινον, ἀξιάγαστε, τὸ μὴ εὐπορεῖν ἡμᾶς ἐγκωμιάσαι τὰ σά. Ἔχεις ἐκ Θεοῦ τὸ μέγα πρὸς θρίαμβον ὕψος· διότι λαὸν αὐτῷ Χριστιανικὸν ἀπὸ σαρκὸς τῆς σῆς συνεστήσω, καὶ τὸ ὁμοιογενές σου, σύμμορφον τῆς θείας αὐτοῦ καὶ ὁμοιωτικῆς εἰκόνος ἀπειργάσω.	For you have from God the great sublime triumph; for which reason you have established a Christian people for him from your flesh, and related by birth to you, you have made conformable to his divinity and to his image which makes us like [him].	Dormition II (P Viventi 161 ftn. 4)
356A	Ἀλλ' ἡμῖν τοῖς Χριστιανοῖς καὶ Χριστιανικῇ Θεοτόκον σεβομένοις σε πίστει, παράτεινον τῆς ἀμεταθέτου σου προστασίας τὸ ἔλεος. Καὶ τὴν γὰρ κοίμησίν σου, Θεοτόκε, ζωὴν ἡγούμεθα δικαίως,	But to us Christians who venerate you with a Christian faith as Theotokos, stretch out the mercy of your unchangeable advocacy. For we rightly recognize your falling-asleep to be life, and we trust to	Dormition II

413

	καὶ σύνοικόν σε πνευματικῶς ἔχειν πεπιστεύκαμεν. Καὶ ὅταν θλίψις ἐγγὺς εἶ, ζητοῦντές σε λυτρούμεθα· καὶ ὅταν πάλιν χαρᾶς καιρός, σὺ εἶ ταύτης πρόξενος· καὶ ὅταν ἐν ὅλοις ὑπὸ σοῦ μεριμνώμεθα, μεθ' ἡμῶν σε διάγειν πιστοφορούμεθα. Ὃν γὰρ τρόπον ὁ διψῶν, πρὸς τὴν πηγὴν κατασπεύδει, οὕτω καὶ πᾶσα ψυχὴ πιστοτάτη πρὸς σὲ κατατρέχει, ἐμπλησθῆναι τῆς σῆς φλεγομένη βοηθείας. Καὶ πάλιν ὥσπερ τὸ τοῦ ἀέρος ἆσθμα ζωτικὴν τοῖς ἀνθρώποις ἐμπνέει τὴν ὄσφρησιν· οὕτω καὶ σὲ παντὸς ὀρθοδόξου Χριστιανοῦ ἐπὶ στόματος προφέρει πνοή.	have you as a spiritual house-mate. And when tribulation . . . you are near, seeking you we are ransomed. And when again it is time for joy, it is you who bring this. And when among all we are troubled, we trust that you are with us. For as the thirsty man hurries to the spring, so also every faithful soul runs to you, burning to be filled with your assistance. And again as the breath of air blows a life-giving aroma to mankind, so also the breath of every orthodox Christian carries you in the mouth.	
357A	Οὐκοῦν πίστει σε μεθ' ἡμῶν συνανάστροφον ἔχειν ὁμολογοῦμεν.	So in faith we confess that we have you as a companion with us.	Dormition II
357A	οὕτω καὶ σὲ μετελθοῦσαν συνδιάγωγον καὶ μετὰ τὴν ἐκδημίαν τοῦ σώματος πιστεύομεν ἀναθεωρεῖν	so also we believe that we will see you going with us as a leader even after our departure from the body	Dormition II
360D	Τὴν φθορὰν αὐτοῦ παρεᾷς· ἐπεὶ τοὺς ἐν τῷ κόσμῳ τῆς ἀντιλήψεως ὀρφανοὺς οὐκ ἀφήσεις·	Let its corruption go, since you will not leave those in the world orphaned of your protection;	Dormition III (P Viventi 164 ftn. 8)
361A	Ὅπου γὰρ ἐγώ, ἐκεῖ ζωὴ αἰώνιος, χαρὰ μὴ συγκρινομένη, κατοικία μὴ ἐξισουμένη, πολιτεία μὴ φθειρομένη.	For where I am, there is eternal life, joy incomparable, residence unequalled, commonwealth imperishable.	Dormition III
361C/D	Ἐγώ σε παρθένον ἀνέδειξα μητέρα· ἐγώ σε καὶ εὐφραινομένην ἐπὶ Τέκνῳ καταστήσω μητέρα.	I also will make you a mother rejoicing in her Child. I will show you to the world that is your	Dormition III (P Viventi 163 ftn. 9)

	Ἐγώ σοι τὸν κόσμον χρεώστην ἀναδείξω, καὶ μετερχομένης πλεῖον σοῦ τὸ ὄνομα καταδοξάσω. Ἐγώ σε τεῖχος κοσμικὸν οἰκοδομήσω, γέφυραν κλυδωνιζομένων, κιβωτὸνδιασωζομένων, βακτηρίαν χειραγωγουμένων, πρεσβείαν ἁμαρτανόντων, καὶ κλίμακα πρὸς οὐρανὸν τοὺς ἀνθρώπους ἀναβιβάζειν ἰσχύουσαν.	debtor, and I will glorify your name even more as you are translated. I will build you as a wall for the world, a bridge for those who are swamped, an ark for those who are being saved, a staff for those who are being led by the hand, an intercession for those who are sinning, and a ladder which has the power to raise mankind to heaven.	
373B	τί ἄν τις εἴποι περὶ τῆς θεοδοξάστου καὶ πανυμνήτου κόρης τῆς παναχράντου καὶ παναμώμου; Εἰ γὰρ αὕτη πόλις ἔμψυχος τοῦ βασιλέως ἐχρημάτισε Χριστοῦ, δικαίως ἄρα καὶ ὁ ταύτης πανάγιος ναός, οὗ καὶ τὰ Ἐγκαίνια σήμερον ἑορτάζομεν, πόλις δεδοξασμένη ἔστι τε καὶ ὀνομάζεται.	then what should one say about the God-glorified, ever-praised, all-pure and blameless maiden? If she bears the title of living city of the king, Christ, then justly also here most-holy temple, of which we celebrate today the festival, is and is called the glorified city.	Sash
373C	Πόλις οὐκ ἐπιγείῳ καὶ θνητῷ βασιλεῖ πολιτογραφοῦσα τοὺς ὑπὸ χεῖρα· ἀλλὰ τῷ ἐπουρανίῳ, τῷ εἰς ζωὴν αἰώνιον παραπέμποντι, καὶ βασιλείαν τὴν ἑαυτοῦ τοῖς αὐτῷ ἑπομένοις παρέχοντι.	A city not enrolling those under her hand in a mortal and earthly kingdom, but in one which is redolent with heavenly and eternal life, and she represents a kingdom in herself to those who are sworn to her.	Sash
373C	τὸ παλαιὸν καὶ διερρωγὸς τῆς ἁμαρτίας ἀποθέμενος ἔνδυμα, καὶ τὸ νέον τῆς εὐσεβείας περιβαλλόμενος, ἐν καινότητι ζωῆς πολιτεύεται. Τούτοις καὶ ἡ πανάμωμος εὐφραίνεται· οἷς ἀναρεταῖς, καὶ τῇ κατὰ Θεὸν εὐσεβεῖ καινιζόμενοι πολιτείᾳ,	The stripping off of the ancient bonds of sin; and the freshness of the enveloping pity, being a free citizen of the new life. (cf. 2 Cor. 4.17) And the Blameless one rejoices in these, who are pleasing, and in the godly pious, renewed citizenship,	Sash

References to the Conception, Birth and Childhood of Mary in Germanos I, Patriarach of Constantinople (715-730)

PG 98 Location	Greek	English	Homily
293A	Σήμερον γὰρ τριετίζουσα πρόεισι τῷ νομικῷ ναῷ ἀνατεθησομένη ἡ ναὸς ἀκηλίδωτος καὶ ὑπέρτατος μόνη χρηματίσασα τοῦ ἀρχιερέως καὶ τῶν ἁπάντων τελετάρχου Κυρίου, καὶ ἐν τῇ ἰδίᾳ μαρμαρυγῇ τῆς θεολαμποῦς αἴγλης, τὴν ἐν τῷ γράμματι ἀχλὺν διελοῦσα.	Today, at three years of age, she goes towards her dedication in the temple of the law, she who alone is called the stainless and greatest temple of the high priest and the Lord of all, and in whose bright light is the radiance of divine light which illuminates the darkness of the Law.	Presentation I (P—Immac 127 ftn 9)
293B	Σήμερον ὁ καινότατος καὶ καθαρώτατος ἀμόλυντος τόμος, οὐ χειρὶ γραφησόμενος, ἀλλὰ πνεύματι χρυσωθησόμενος, ταῖς κατὰ νόμον εὐλογίαις ἁγιαζομένη, χαριστήριον δῶρον προσάγεται.	Today a new, pure, unspoiled book which will not be written by hands, but written in gold by the spirit, hallowed with blessings according to the Law, she is brought forward as an acceptable gift.	Presentation I (P—Immac 127 ftn 11)
293C	Σήμερον τῷ ἱλαστηρίῳ ἀνατίθεται ἡ μόνη τοῖς τῶν βρότων ἐσφαλλομένοις διεξαχθεῖσιν ἀμπλακημάτων ἐπιρροαῖς, ἱλαστήριον καινόν τε καὶ θεοειδέστατον καθαρτικόν τε καὶ ἀχειρότευκτον χρηματίσασα.	Today she who alone is called the new, god-like, purifying and mercy seat, not made by hands, (cf. Hebrews 9.11) for mortals who have drowned in floods of sin is presented to the mercy seat of the temple.	Presentation I (P—Immac 128 ftn 16)

Gregory E. Roth

297A	Δεῦτέ μοι, φησὶν, συγχαίρετε, αἵτινές τε καὶ ὅσοι τῇ γεννήσει συνειλεγμένοι, μειζόνως, ἄρτι τὴν ἐξ ἐμῶν σπλάγχνων ἀνατιθεμένη Κυρίῳ δῶρον θεοκαλλώπιστον ἡγιασμένον.	"Come with me," she says, "let us rejoice together, all women and men who rejoiced at her birth, even more now, as I dedicate to the Lord this divinely beautiful and holy gift recently received from my own womb."	Presentation I (P—Immac 128 ftn 17)
300B	Εἰσάγεται μὲν οὖν οὕτως ἡ Θεόπαις, τοῖς κέρασιν ἵσταται, τῶν τε γονέων ἐπευξαμένων, τοῦ τε ἱερέως ἐπευλογήσοντος.	And thus the child of God is led in [and] takes her place by the horns, as her parents offer their vows, and the priest gives his blessing.	Presentation I (P—Immac 130 ftn 25)
300D	ἣν ὡς κρίνον ἐξ ἀκανθῶν τῆς ἡμετέρας ἀναξιότητος ἐξελέξω· εὐχρόωτάτά σοι προσφερομένην ἐναγκάλισαι. Ἰδού σοι ταύτην παρατιθέμεθα καὶ ἑαυτοὺς ἀνατιθέμεθα.	You chose her as a lily out of the brambles of our unworthiness. Embrace her who is brought to you with a most radiant complexion. Behold, to you we offer her [as our intercessor] and dedicate ourselves."	Presentation I (P—Immac 132 ftn 32)
301A	Ὦ τῆς ἡμετέρας σωτηρίας αἴτιοι, τί ὑμᾶς προσείπω; Τί καλέσω; Ἐξίσταμαι βλέπων, ὁποῖον καρπὸν προσήξατε. Τοιοῦτος γὰρ ὅστις τῇ καθαρότητι θέλγει Θεὸν ἐν αὐτῇ οἰκῆσαι. Οὐδὲ γὰρ πώποτέ τις γέγονεν ἢ γενήσεται τοιαύτη καλλονῇ διαλάμπουσα	"O causes of our salvation, what shall I say to you? What shall I call [you]? I am astonished seeing what kind of fruit you have brought forth, such a one as by her purity attracts God to dwell within her. For never yet has anyone existed or will anyone exist who shines forth in such beauty.	Presentation I (P—Immac 128 ftn 18)
304D	Χαίροις τοιγαροῦν τῇ τῆς Ἐδὲμ ἡμῖν θανατηφόρῳ καὶ ψυχοπύρῳ βρώσει γυμνωθεῖσιν, εὐκλεεῖ καὶ ἀχειροτεύκτῳ ἐνδύματι ἐν τῇ σῇ πρὸς τὰ τῶν ἁγίων Ἅγια εἰσδύσει σήμερον ἀλουργοειδῆ στολὴν ἤτοι θεοπερίβλητον ἄφεσιν ἐπαμφιάσασα, ἡ ἄφεσις τῶν παραπτωμάτων τοῖς βορβορώδεσιν ἡμῖν ἐκ Θεοῦ δοθεῖσα, Θεόνυμφε.	Therefore hail, forgiveness of transgressions given by God for us filthy ones, who are denuded by the death-dealing and soul-destroying food of Eden, as you put on the sea-purple robe which represents God-given forgiveness today for your entrance to the holy of holies in your glorious garment not made by hands (cf. Genesis 3.17), O bride of God.	Presentation I (P—Immac 128 ftn 19)

305A	Χαίροις, ἡ τῇ τῶν βημάτων σου ῥυθμίσει καταπατήσασα τὸν δεινόν μοι ποδηγόν, κεχρηματικότα πρὸς τὴν παράβασιν σκολιογνώμονα καὶ μισόκαλον ὄφιν διάβολον· καὶ συνοδεύουσαν ἐπιλαβομένη τὴν ὀλισθηρὰν φανεῖσαν φθαρτὴν οὐσίαν πρὸς τὴν ἄϋλον καὶ ἁγίαν ἀγήρω πάλιν σκηνήν.	Hail to you who by the rhythm of your footsteps trample down my terrible leader—that serpent with his crooked-minded, good-hating diabolical nature—who has counseled me toward transgression (*cf.* Genesis 3.1-13). But you controlling your changeable, visible, and corrupt nature continue to journey along toward the heavenly, holy and even eternal tent.	Presentation I (P—Immac 128 ftn 20)
305B	Χαίροις, ὁ τερπνότατος καὶ λογικὸς Θεοῦ παράδεισος, σήμερον πρὸς ἀνατολὰς τῆς αὐτοῦ θελήσεως φυτευόμενος δεξιᾷ παντοκράτορι, καὶ αὐτῷ τὸ εὐανθὲς κρίνον καὶ ἀμάραντον ῥόδον κυπρίζουσα, τοῖς πρὸς δυσμὰς θανάτου λοιμικὴν ψυχοφθόρον τε πικρίαν ἐκπιοῦσιν, ἐν ᾧ τὸ ζωοπάροχον ξύλον τῆς πρὸς ἀληθείας ἐπίγνωσιν ἐξανθεῖ, ἐξ οὗ οἱ γευσάμενοι ἀθανατίζονται.	Hail, delightful and rational paradise of God, which today is planted in the east by the omnipotent right hand of his will (*cf.* Genesis 2.8), who have blossomed forth the beautiful lily and the unfading rose for those who in the west have drunk the bitter soul-destroying plague of death, on whom the life-giving tree has sprouted forth to the intimate knowledge of the truth. Those who have tasted from it are made immortal.	Presentation I (P—Immac 128 ftn 22)

In 305B note the final line: "Those who have tasted from it are made immortal." This may express Germanos' understanding that Mary is the first of the saints who have achieved theosis.

305C	Χαίροις, τὸ τοῦ παμβασιλέως Θεοῦ ἱερότευκτον ἄχραντόν τε. καὶ καθαρώτατον παλάτιον, τὴν αὐτοῦ μεγαλειότητα περιβεβλημένη καὶ ξεναγοῦσά σου τῇ μυσταρχικῇ ἀπολαύσει ἅπαντας·	Hail, sacred, undefiled, most pure palace of the omnipotent God. You are wrapped in his grandeur and guide us all with your mystical joy.	Presentation I (P—Immac 127 ftn 12)

Perniola makes the claim on the evidence of three words: ἄχραντόν, καθαρώτατον, and ἱερότευκτον that Mary has been holy since the foundation of the temple.

308C	ἡ πάνχρυσος στάμνος, τὸν ἡδύτατον τῶν ψυχῶν ἡμῶν γλυκασμὸν ἤτοι Χριστὸν τὸ μάννα φέρουσα.	the all-gold container (cf. Exodus 16.33) who bore Christ, the manna, the sweet sweetness of our souls.	Presentation I (P—Immac 127 ftn 13)
312A	Κόρην ἐξ ἐπαγγελίας, καὶ αὐτὴν τριετίζουσαν, εἰς τὸ τρίτον καταπέτασμα ὡς δῶρον ἄμωμον προσφερομένην,	A maiden from the promise, at the age of three years, is brought as a blameless gift within the third curtain,	Presentation I I (P—Immac 127 ftn 14)
313B	ἵνα τί ἔθου με παραβολὴν ἐν τῷ γένει μου, καὶ κίνησιν κεφαλῆς ἐν τῇ φυλῇ μου; Ἵνα τί τῆς κατάρας τῶν σῶν προφητῶν μέτοχόν με ἀνέδειξας, δούς μοι μήτραν ἀτεκνοῦσαν, καὶ μασθοὺς ξηρούς; Ἵνα τί μου τὰ δῶρα ἀπρόσδεκτα ὡς ἀτέκνου ἐποίησας; Ἵνα τί μυκτηρισμόν με τοῖς γνωστοῖς, καὶ χλευασμὸν τοῖς ὑπὸ χεῖρα, καὶ τοῖς γείτοσιν ὄνειδος γενέσθαι κατέλιπες; Ἐπίβλεψον, Κύριε· εἰσάκουσον, Δέσποτα· σπλαγχνίσθητι, Ἅγιε. Ὁμοίωσόν με τοῖς πετεινοῖς τοῦ οὐρανοῦ, τοῖς θηρίοις τῆς γῆς, τοῖς τῆς θαλάσσης ἰχθύσιν· ὅτι καὶ αὐτὰ γόνιμά εἰσιν ἐνώπιόν σου, Κύριε. Μὴ χείρων φανείη τῶν ἀλόγων, Ὕψιστε, ἡ κατὰ σὴν ὁμοίωσιν καὶ εἰκόνα ὑπὸ σοῦ γεγονυῖα.	Why have you made me an example in my family, and a shaking of the head in my tribe? Why have you declared me a participant in the curse of your prophets, giving me a childless womb and dry breasts (cf. Hosea 9.14)? Why have you made my gifts unacceptable as of a childless [woman]? Why have you left me to become a cause of muttering for my acquaintances, and a mockery for those at hand, and a reproach for my neighbors? Look at [me], Lord; hear [me], Master; have compassion [on me], Holy One. Make me like the birds of heaven, the beasts of the earth, the fish of the sea: because they also are productive before you, Lord. May I not appear worse than the irrational animals, O Most High, I who have been made by you in your likeness and image (cf. Genesis 1.26).'	Presentation I I(P—Immac 130 ftn 26)
313C 313D	οὕτω τοίνυν ἐπικαμφθεὶς ὁ πρὸς οἶκτον ἕτοιμος καὶ φιλόψυχος Κύριος, ταῖς ἀμφοτέρων εὐχαῖς τὸν αὐτοῦ πέπομφεν ἄγγελον, τὴν τῆς ἐμῆς παιδὸς σύλληψιν ἡμῖν	thus you see the Lord who is ready for mercy and loves souls has bent down and sent an angel to the prayers of both of us, announcing to us the conception of my child. So	Presentation II

	προσαγγείλαντα. Αὐτίκα γοῦν ἡ φύσις πρὸς Θεοῦ κελευσθεῖσα, τὴν γονὴν εἰσεδέξατο· οὐ γὰρ πρὶν τῆς θείας χάριτος αὐτὴν τετόλμηκε δέξασθαι. Ἀλλ' ἐκείνης προεισελθούσης, οὕτως ἡ μύσασα μήτρα τὰς ἰδίας πύλας ἤνοιξε, καὶ τὴν ἐκ Θεοῦ παραθήκην ὑποδεξαμένη παρ' ἑαυτῇ κατέσχεν, ἄχρι Θεοῦ εὐδοκίᾳ τὸ ἐν αὐτῇ σπερμανθὲν εἰς φῶς ἐξῆλθεν.	therefore when [my] nature was bidden by God, it received the seed; for it did not dare to accept it before the divine grace. But when that [grace] preceded, then the closed womb opened its own gates, and receiving the deposit from God, held it in itself, until by the good will of God it brought forth to light that which had been sown in it.	

Perniola interprets this section 313B—D to indicate that Mary was conceived virginally. "E questo tanto più in quanto San Germano inclina a credere, come altrove abbiamo detto, che la concezione di Maria sia stata una concezione verginale. Subito infatti, egli scrive, al comando di Dio, la natura generò la prole, né ciò era stato possibile prima I della grazia divina; ma come essa per prima vi fece il suo ingresso, la matrice fino allora chiusa, aprì le sue porte, e ritenne presso di sé il dono ricevuto da Dio, fino a quando, per volere dello stesso Signore, quello che era stato concepito, venne alla luce. Non solo quindi la fecondità di Anna è frutto della grazia. di Dio, ma anche la Vergine che essa genera sarebbe un dono che Dio stesso affida alle sue viscere." 130 ftn 26. His claim: "E questo tanto più in quanto San Germano inclina a credere, come altrove abbiamo detto, che la concezione di Maria sia stata una concezione verginale," does not appear to be warranted within the text of Germanos' homilies. It is possible that Germanos held this position as a *theologumenon* (a non-binding belief that is a matter of opinion but not doctrine).

| 321A | Χαῖρε, κεχαριτωμένη, ἡ τοῦ μάννα στάμνος <ἡ> ὁλόχρυσος, καὶ σκηνὴ ὡς ἀληθῶς πορφυροποίητος, ἣν ὁ νέος Βεσελεὴλ χρυσοπρεπῶς κατεποίκιλεν. | Hail full of grace, [you are] the golden jar which contained the manna (*cf.* Hebrews 9.4), and [you are] the true royal tabernacle, which the new Bez'alel fittingly adorned in gold (*cf.* Exodus 31.2*ff.*). | Annunciation (P—Immac 127 ftn 30) |
| 336A | Μὴ γὰρ ἐκ τῆς φωνῆς συνέλαβες; ἐκ τοῦ αἰῶνος οὐκ ἠκούσθη, ὅτι ἀπὸ φωνῆς ῥημάτων ἐκυοφόρησε παρθένος ἀπείρανδρός ποτε· οὔτε οἱ πατέρες ἡμῶν ἀνήγγειλαν ἡμῖν ὅτι τοιοῦτον γέγονεν ἐν ταῖς ἀρχαίαις ἡμέραις. | You did not conceive by a voice, did you? Never has it been heard, that a virgin conceived by the sound of words without a man, nor did our fathers tell us that such an event occurred in the ancient days. | Annunciation |

345B	Σύ, κατὰ τὸ γεγραμμένον, «ἐν καλλονῇ·» καὶ τὸ σῶμά σου τὸ παρθενικόν, ὅλον ἅγιον, ὅλον ἁγνόν, ὅλον Θεοῦ κατοικητήριον· ὡς ἐκ τούτου λοιπὸν καὶ ἀλλότριον χοϊκῆς ἀναλύσεως.	You, as it is written, [are] "in beauty" (Cant 2.3 LXX) and your virginal body, altogether holy, altogether pure, altogether the residence of God; so because of this [it is] separated and alien from earthly dissolution.	Dormition I (P—Immac 131 ftn 27)
345C	Πῶς γὰρ εἶχε διάλυσις σαρκὸς πρὸς χοῦν καὶ κόνιν ἀνθυποστρέψαι σε, τὴν ἀπὸ θανάτου καταφθορᾶς, τὸν ἄνθρωπον, διὰ τῆς τοῦ Υἱοῦ σου λυτρωσαμένην σαρκώσεως;	For how could dissolution of the body to earth and dust recur in you who from the corruption of death ransomed mankind through the incarnation of your Son?	Dormition I (P—Immac 131 ftn 28)
357A	ἀνάπλασις γὰρ εἶ	for you are the re-fashioning	Dormition II (P—Immac 130 ftn 24)
357A	Ἐρρέτω θάνατος ἐπὶ σοί, Θεοτόκε, ζωὴν ὅτι τοῖς ἀνθρώποις προσήγαγες. Ἐρρέτω τάφος ἐπὶ σοί, ἐπειδήπερ ὕψους ἀκαταφράστου θεῖος ἐγένου θεμέλιος. Ἐρρέτω χοῦς ἐπὶ σοί· ἀνάπλασις γὰρ εἶ, ὅτι τοῖς ἐν ὕλῃ πηλοῦ διαφθαρεῖσι κεχρημάτικας, Δέσποινα. Οὐκοῦν πίστει σε μεθ' ἡμῶν συνανάστροφον ἔχειν ὁμολογοῦμεν.	Away with death for you, O Theotokos, because you have brought life to mankind! Away with the tomb for you, since you became the divine foundation of an impregnable fortress! Away with earth poured over you; for you are the re-fashioning, because you have been called Mistress of those who have perished in the substance of clay. So in faith we confess that we have you as a companion with us.	Dormition II (P—Immac 130 ftn 29)
364D	Ὥσπερ οὖν ἐκεῖ τὰ βαΐα τῶν φοινίκων νικητικὸν τὸν τοῦ Χριστοῦ προεμήνυον συμβολικῇ τῇ ὑποδείξει θάνατον, οὕτως καὶ τὸ ἐκ φοίνικος δοθὲν τῇ Θεοτόκῳ βραβεῖον, πληροφόρημα νίκης ὑπῆρχεν θανατοποιοῦ καταφθορᾶς.	So as there the branches of the palm-trees foretold the victorious death of Christ with a symbolic demonstration, so also the prize from a palm-tree given to the Theotokos was a fulfillment of victory over death-dealing corruption.	Dormition III (P—Immac 131 ftn 31)
Perniola does not quote, but paraphrases 364D. I have provided part of it.			

| 373A | καλῶν τοῦ Βασιλέως τοῦ μεγάλου πόλιν δὴ ταύτην οἶμαι σαφέστατα καὶ ἀναντιρρητικώτατα, τὴν ὄντως ἐκλελεγμένην, καὶ πασῶν ὑπερέχουσαν φάναι· οὐκ ὑπεροχῇ δομημάτων, καὶ ὕψει γεωλόφων ἐπαρμάτων· ἀλλὰ τὴν τῇ μεγαλοφυΐᾳ τῶν ἐνθέων ὑπερηρμένην ἀρετῶν, καὶ τῇ καθαρότητι ὑπερέχουσαν Μαρίαν τὴν ὑπέραγνον, καὶ ὑπεράμωμον Θεοτόκον. Ἐν ᾧ ὁ ὄντως ὢν Βασιλεὺς τῶν βασιλευόντων, καὶ Κύριος τῶν κυριευόντων κατεσκήνωσε· μᾶλλον δὲ, ἐν ᾗ πᾶν τὸ πλήρωμα τῆς θεότητος κατῴκησε σωματικῶς. | Truly and undebatably calling you "the city of the great king", the truly elected city and surpassing all other cities, not due to the height of the buildings nor the loftiness of the hills, but due to the greatness of the divine virtues, and by purity: Mary the most chaste and surpassingly unblemished Theotokos. (*cf.* Gal. 4.21) In whom the King of kings and the Lord of lords dwells, in whom all the fullness of divinity resided bodily. (*cf.* Col. 2.9) | Sash (P—Immac 128 ftn 15) |
| 373C/ 373D | Ἐγκαινίων δὲ, ὦ τίμιον καὶ σεπτόν, ἀκηκοότες, ἀκροατήριον, μὴ νεοκτίστοις οἰκοδομαῖς καὶ ἀρτιπαγέσι κατασκευαῖς τὸ τῶν Ἐγκαινίων ὑπολάβητε ὄνομα, ἀλλὰ τὸν ἐν πνεύματι καινισμόν, καθ' ὃν ὁ ἔσω ἡμῶν ἄνθρωπος, τὸ παλαιὸν καὶ διερρωγὸς τῆς ἁμαρτίας ἀποθέμενος ἔνδυμα, καὶ τὸ νέον τῆς εὐσεβείας περιβαλλόμενος, ἐν καινότητι ζωῆς πολιτεύεται. Τούτοις καὶ ἡ πανάμωμος εὐφραίνεται· οἷς ἀναρεταῖς, καὶ τῇ κατὰ Θεὸν εὐσεβεῖ καινιζόμενοι πολιτείᾳ, οὕτω καὶ τῶν ἁγνῶν τῆς ἁγνῆς ἁγνῶς Ἐγκαινίων κατατρυφήσωμεν· | But of the feast, worthy and august hearers, in this hall, it does not receive its name from newly constructed buildings nor from newly made buildings, but by that which is enriched by the Spirit. That which is inside of us humans. The stripping off of the ancient bonds of sin; and the freshness of the enveloping pity, being a free citizen of the new life. (*cf.* 2 Cor. 4.17) And the Blameless one rejoices in these, who are pleasing, and in the godly pious, renewed citizenship, and in this manner we shall celebrate in purity the purity of the purely pure feast, | Sash |

This passage appears to represent Germanos as holding the view that was held by Irenaeus concerning original sin and original guilt. Also see the separate article on the cosmology and anthropology.

References to the Cosmology and Mary in Germanos I, Patriarch of Constantinople (715-730)

PG 98 Location	Greek	English	Homily
293B	Σήμερον καὶ Ἄννα τὸν τῆς ἀτεκνίας ἐνδελεχισμόν, εὐτεκνίᾳ ἀμείψασα, ἀπλέτῳ χαρμονῇ ἔνθους γινομένη τοῖς πέρασι καρπὸν διακηρυκεύεται κεκτῆσθαι, στέρνοις ἐναγκαλισαμένη τὴν τῶν οὐρανῶν πλατυτέραν.	Today also Anna has exchanged the persistence of barrenness for fruitfulness, and becoming inspired by joy, proclaims to the ends of the earth that she has borne a child, embracing to her bosom the one who is wider than the heavens.	Presentation I
293D	Σήμερον ἡ τὸν τῶν ἁγίων Ἅγιον εἰσδεξομένη Πνεύματος ἁγιασμῷ, τοῖς τῶν ἁγίων Ἁγίοις ἁγιωτάτως καὶ εὐκλεῶς ἁγιασμῷ μείζονι, ἀπειροκάκῳ καὶ ἀδαήμονι ἡλικίᾳ, Χερουβὶμ δόξης ὑπεραρθεῖσα θαυμασιωτάτως ἐναποτίθεται.	Today she who will receive the Holy One of the Holy through the hallowing of the Spirit is placed in the holy of Holies at a pure and innocent age; and she who is marvelously exalted above the Cherubim, makes more holy the holy of Holies by her presence.	Presentation I
293D	Πέλαγος γὰρ ἀχανὲς τὰ ταύτης μεγαλεῖα, ὁ ἐξ αὐτῆς οὐράνιος γεννηθεὶς σταγὼν ἀνέδειξεν.	For her greatness is a vast sea, as the Heavenly drop born from her has shown.	Presentation I
297B	Δεῦρο δή μοι, καὶ ὁ τῶν προφητῶν θίασος τὸ ἐκλελεγμένον συνάθροισμα, ταῖς διὰ Πνεύματος Θεοῦ ὑμῖν ἐνηχημέναις ἀγλαοφανέσιν αἰνέσεσι καταρτίζοντες, τὸν ὕμνον κατασκευάζοιτε. Ἔνθα	Come with me also, company of the prophets, the assembly of the elect, ordering aright the resonating glorious hymns through the Holy Spirit of our God: let us sing a hymn. For there the word	Presentation I

	γὰρ προφητικῆς ἠχῆς δονακίζεται λόγος, ἐκεῖσε ἅπασα ἐναντιωτάτη δυσφημία ἐκνενευρισμένη γίνεται.	vibrates with prophetic sound, and thereby is severed all opposing evil speech.	
297C	δεῦρ' ἴθι, Δαυῒδ ἠωσφῶν· «Τίς αὕτη ἡ ἐκκύπτουσα ὡσεὶ ὄρθρος, καλὴ ὡς σελήνη, ἐκλεκτὴ ὡς ἥλιος; τί ὡραιώθησαν διαβήματά σου ἐν ὑποδήμασι;»	Come here David bringer of dawn's light[10]: "Who is this who shines out like the dawn, is as fair as the moon, and bright as the sun?" "How gracefully you walk in your sandals!" (Cant 7:2)	Presentation I
297D	—«Τί ὡραιώθης καὶ τί ἡδύνθης,» ἡ τὸν ἥλιον περιδυσομένη, καὶ καινὸν ὑπὸ τὸν ἥλιον προσάξουσα θέαμα!	"How beautiful and pleasant you are" (Cant 7:7) the one who shall be clothed in the Sun (Rev 12:1) and will bring forth a new wonder under the Sun! (*cf.* Ec. 1:9-10)	Presentation I
297D/ 300A	Οἱ προπάτορες τῆς ἀρᾶς ἀπολυθησόμενοι καὶ τῆς ἧς ἐξεβλήθητε τρυφῆς, τὴν οἴκησιν πάλιν ἀποκληρούμενοι· ἆρ' οὐχ τὴν αἰτίαν ὑμνήσετε τῆς σωτηρίας, ἀραρότοις ἐγκωμίοις καὶ μεγίσταις αἰνέσεσιν; ἢ καὶ μάλιστα ὑμῖν ἐστι κεκραγέναι καὶ με σὺν ὑμῖν καὶ πᾶσαν μετ' ἀμφοτέροις τὴν κτίσιν ἀγαλλιᾶσθαι.	Our ancestors who are about to be released from the curse and again inheriting the residence in paradise from which you were cast out: should you not hymn the cause of your salvation, with a fitting encomium and great praises? Indeed you especially ought to shout out, and I with you and with us both all creation [ought] to sing out in joy.	Presentation I
300B	σκιρτῶσι προπάτορες τὴν τῆς κατακρίσεως εἶρξιν ὑπεκφεύγοντες· τέρπονται οἱ προφῆται, καὶ σὺν αὐτοῖς ἅπασα ἡ ἐν χάριτι ἡλικία χαρμονικῶς προσκιρτᾷ.	The forefathers jump for joy, escaping the captivity of condemnation. The prophets are delighted, and with them all who are yet to come in this age of grace also leap for joy.	Presentation I

[10] ἠωσφῶν, attested only here

301A/ 301B	τὴν τῷ κάλλει τῆς ἑαυτῆς ἀμώμου παρθενίας καὶ ταῖς δροσιστικαῖς μαρμαρυγαῖς τὴν ἅπασαν γῆν καταυγάζουσαν. Ὑμεῖς ἀστέρες φαεινότατοι ἐγνωρίσθητε, τῷ στερεώματι ὥσπερ ἐμπεπαρμένοι,	who in the beauty of her blameless virginity and her dewy sparkling illuminates the whole earth. You have been made known as shining stars as if fixed in the firmament	Presentation I
301C	Ὑμετέρων ἡ χαρμονὴ κοσμικὴ γεγένηται· ὑμῶν τὸ κλέος ἅπασιν εὐφροσύνη ἐξήκουσται.	Your rejoicing has become that of the cosmos. Your renown is the universal joy of all men.	Presentation I
301C	Δεῦρο γοῦν μοι καὶ σύ, παιδίον τῶν οὐρανῶν ἀνώτερον.	Come to me, child, child higher than the heavens.	Presentation I
301D	Ἰδού σε στήριγμα βλέπω γενησομένην τῶν καταβεβηκότων πρὸς θάνατον.	Behold, I see you as one who will become a support for those who have descended to death.	Presentation I
304B	Εὐπρεπές σοι τῷ Χερουβικωτάτῳ θρόνῳ ὁ ἡγιασμένος τόπος εἰς κατοικητήριον.	This holy place is a fitting dwelling for you who are the throne of the Cherubim.	Presentation I
304B	Καὶ τῇ τῆς ἐπισιτήσεως ὑπηρεσίᾳ ἄγγελοι μετὰ δέους ἐλειτούργουν, καὶ ἐξ ἀΰλων ὑλικὴν τροφὴν ἢ ἄϋλον ἐσιτίζετο ἡ κόρη.	And angels did their duty of feeding with fear, and the maiden was fed by immaterial beings, whether with immaterial or material food	Presentation I
304C	οὕτω τε τὸ βρέφος ηὔξει καὶ ἐκραταιοῦτο· καὶ ἡ τῆς ἐν Ἐδὲμ ἡμῖν δεδομένης κατάρας ἅπασα ἐναντιότης ἠσθένει.	Thus the infant grew and was strengthened, and all the opposition which was given to us by the curse of Eden was weakened (cf. Genesis 3.16ff.).	Presentation I
304D	Χαίροις τοιγαροῦν τῇ τῆς Ἐδὲμ ἡμῖν θανατηφόρῳ καὶ ψυχοπύρῳ βρώσει γυμνωθεῖσιν, εὐκλεῖ καὶ ἀχειροτεύκτῳ ἐνδύματι ἐν τῇ σῇ πρὸς τὰ τῶν ἁγίων Ἅγια εἰσδύσει σήμερον ἀλουργοειδῆ στολὴν ἤτοι θεοπερίβλητον ἄφεσιν ἐπαμφιάσασα, ἡ ἄφεσις τῶν παραπτωμάτων τοῖς βορβορώδεσιν ἡμῖν ἐκ Θεοῦ δοθεῖσα, Θεόνυμφε.	Therefore hail, forgiveness of transgressions given by God for us filthy ones, who are denuded by the death-dealing and soul-destroying food of Eden, as you put on the sea-purple robe which represents God-given forgiveness today for your entrance to the holy of holies in your glorious garment not made by hands (cf. Genesis 3.17), O bride of God.	Presentation I

304D/ 305A	Χαίροις, ἡ τῇ ἐξάρξει σήμερον τῆς φαεινοτάτης καὶ σεβασμιοφόρου Πρόδου θίασον ἅπαντα προφητικὸν ἐπαγείρουσα, μουσικοῖς ὥσπερ ὀργάνοις εὐηχεστάτοις κυμβάλοις θεοφωνότατον ἀλαλαγμὸν ὑπανακρούοντας καὶ ἐν εὐφροσύνῃ ψυχαγωγῶς χορεύοντας.	Hail, you who today call together all the prophetic assembly for the beginning of your most brilliant and venerable Entrance, with well-tuned cymbals as with musical instruments striking up the divine-sounding strain and dancing in spiritual joy.	Presentation I
308B	Χαῖρε, κεχαριτωμένη Μαρία, ἡ τῶν ἁγίων ἁγιωτέρα, καὶ οὐρανῶν ὑψηλοτέρα, καὶ Χερουβὶμ ἐνδοξοτέρα, καὶ Σεραφὶμ τιμιωτέρα, καὶ ὑπὲρ πᾶσαν κτίσιν σεβασμιωτέρα· ἡ τῇ ἐνδόξῳ καὶ αἰγληφανεῖ σου Προόδῳ ἔλαιον ἡμῖν κομίζουσα, τὸν τοῦ νοητοῦ κατακλυσμοῦ λυτῆρα, τὸν σωτηριώδη ἡμῖν ὅρμον εὐαγγελιζομένη περιστερά· ἧς «αἱ πτέρυγες περιηργυρωμέναι καὶ τὰ μετάφρενα ἐν χλωρότητι χρυσίου,»	Hail, most blessed Mary (cf. Luke 1.28), the holiest of the holy ones, higher than the heavens, more glorious than the Cherubim and more honorable than the Seraphim, more blessed than all of creation. You are the dove who bears the olive branch to us in your glorious and splendid entry into the Temple announcing a saving refuge from the spiritual deluge (cf. Genesis 8.11). "The wings of a dove covered with silver, its pinions with green gold" (Ps. 67.14 LXX)	Presentation I
308C	Ἀλλ', ὦ πανάμωμε, καὶ πανύμνητε, καὶ πανσέβαστε, καὶ πάντων δημιουργημάτων ὑπερφερὲς Θεοῦ ἀνάθημα·	But O most blameless and all-laudable, most holy one, offering to God greater than all created things	Presentation I
316C	Ἔμεινεν δὲ αὐτὴ εἰς τὰ τῶν ἁγίων ἐνδότερα Ἅγια, ἀμβροσίῳ τροφῇ δι' ἀγγέλου τρεφομένη, καὶ τοῦ θείου νέκταρος ποτιζομένη, μέχρι δευτέρας μεθηλικιώσεως·	She remained in the inner holy of holies, nourished with ambrosial food by an angel, and receiving drink of divine nectar, until her second advance in age-group.	Presentation II

316D/ 317A	Ὑπῆρχε τοίνυν ἡ πανάχραντος ἐν τῷ οἴκῳ τοῦ τέκτονος Ἰωσήφ, τῷ ἀρχιτέκτονι Θεῷ τηρουμένη, ἕως τὸ πρὸ πάντων αἰώνων ἀπόκρυφον θεῖον μυστήριον ἐν αὐτῇ ἐτελέσθη, καὶ τοῖς βροτοῖς ὁ Θεὸς ἐξ αὐτῆς ὡμοιώθη.	So the all-pure one was in the house of Joseph the carpenter being protected, until the divine mystery hidden before all the ages (*cf.* Romans 16.25) was fulfilled in her, and from her God was made like mortals.	Presentation II
317B/C	Σὺ γὰρ μόνη Θεοτόκος, ὑψηλοτάτη ἐπὶ πᾶσαν τὴν γῆν· ἡμεῖς δέ σε, Θεόνυμφε, πίστει εὐλογοῦμεν, καὶ πόθῳ γεραίρομεν, καὶ φόβῳ προσκυνοῦμεν, ἀεί σε μεγαλύνοντες, καὶ σεπτῶς μακαρίζοντες.	For you alone are Theotokos, most sublime over all the earth; and we bless you in faith, bride of God, and with desire we honor you, and with fear we bow before you, always magnifying you, and solemnly calling you blessed (*cf.* Luke 1.49).	Presentation II
321B	Χαῖρε, κεχαριτωμένη, ψυχῆς ἀγαλλίαμα, καὶ ὅλου τοῦ κόσμου παγκόσμιον σέβασμα, καὶ ἁμαρτωλῶν ἁπάντων ἡ ὄντως ἀγαθὴ μεσιτεία.	Hail full of grace, exceeding great joy of the soul, and object of worship for the whole cosmos, and truly good mediator for all sinners.	Annunciation
321C	Ἄκουε, δεδοξασμένη· λόγους ἀποκρύφους τοῦ Ὑψίστου ἄκουε· «Ἰδοὺ συλλήψῃ ἐν γαστρί, καὶ τέξῃ υἱὸν καὶ καλέσεις τὸ ὄνομα αὐτοῦ Ἰησοῦν.» Ὁπλίζου λοιπὸν εἰς Χριστοῦ παρουσίαν· ἦλθον γὰρ εὐαγγελίσασθαί σοι τὰ προρρηθέντα, πρὸ καταβολῆς κόσμου.	Hear, most blessed one, hear the hidden words of the Most High. "Behold, you shall conceive in your womb, and you shall produce a son, and shall call him Jesus" (Luke 1.31). Prepare then for Christ's coming. For I have come to announce to you what has been decreed before the foundation of the cosmos.	Annunciation
324D	Ἡ <Ἤκουσας, ὅτι> ἐξ οἴκου καὶ πατριᾶς Δαβὶδ καταγομένη <τυγχάνω>, πῶς <οὖν> τοιούτοις φρικτοῖς καὶ ἐπουρανίοις ἐξυπηρετήσω μυστηρίοις; Καὶ πῶς Ἰησοῦν τὸν ἅγιον, τὸν ἐπὶ τῶν Χερουβὶμ καθεζόμενον, ἐγὼ πῶς ὑποδέξασθαι δυνήσομαι;	*<You have heard that>* I am of the House and the ancestry of David. How shall I assist in these awesome, heavenly mysteries? And how shall I be able to conceive the holy Jesus who sits upon the Cherubim?	Annunciation

Gregory E. Roth

325A	Ἵνα τί, καὶ διὰ τί, καὶ τίνος ἕνεκεν τὸν ἐμὸν εὐαγγελισμὸν ἐπὶ τοσοῦτον ἠπίστησας, δεδοξασμένη; καὶ μέχρι τίνος οὐ πειθαρχεῖς εἰς τὸν ἐξ οὐρανοῦ σοι πεμφθέντα ἄγγελον; Οὐκ εἰμὶ γὰρ ἐγὼ ὁ τὴν Εὔαν πλανήσας.	Why? For what purpose, for what reason, have you distrusted my good news, Glorified one? How long will you disobey the angel that was sent to you from heaven? I am not Eve's deceiver—far from it.	Annunciation
325B	Κἂν ἡ μορφή μου καταπλήττει σε, ἀλλ᾽ οἶδα ὅτι τὰ ῥήματα τοῦ στόματός μου <μεγάλης δόξης> πρόξενά σοι γενήσονται· καὶ μακαρίσει σε λοιπὸν ὁ οὐρανὸς καὶ ἡ γῆ.	Even though my voice and my form terrify you, I know that the words of my mouth shall become a harbinger <of ineffable joy> to you. And all heaven and earth shall bless you (cf. Luke 1.48).	Annunciation
325C	Λάβε δόματα παρ᾽ ἐμοῦ, καὶ ἀπόστα ἀπ᾽ ἐμοῦ, ὁ λαλῶν μοι· κἄν τε γὰρ ἄγγελος τυγχάνεις, κἂν ἄνθρωπος, μετὰ ἀληθείας τοῦτο οὐκ ἐπίσταμαι. Ἄγγελον θεωρῶ τῷ σχήματι, καὶ ἄνθρωπον κατανοῶ τῷ βλέμματι.	You who speak to me, receive [these] gifts from me and leave. Whether you are an angel or a man I do not truly know. I see the vestments of an angel, and in the glance I perceive a man.	Annunciation
325C	Μὴ γὰρ εἰς τὰ Ἅγια τῶν ἁγίων τυγχάνουσα, οὐχ ἑώρακάς με, εὐλογημένη; Ἑώρακάς με λοιπὸν καὶ τροφὴν ἐκ τῆς ἐμῆς πυρίνης ἐδέξω χειρός. Ἐγὼ γάρ εἰμι Γαβριὴλ ὁ διαπαντὸς παρεστηκὼς ἐνώπιον τῆς δόξης τοῦ Θεοῦ.	You saw me, didn't you, O blessed one, when you were in the Holy of Holies, and when you received nourishment from my fiery hands? I am Gabriel, who always stand before the glory of God.	Annunciation
328D	Σωτῆρα, ὡς λέγεις, ὅτι τέξομαι, λέξον μοι, νεανίσκε. Ξενίζει γὰρ ὡς ἀληθῶς, καὶ ἀγγέλων <τὰς> νοερὰς δυνάμεις, καὶ ἀρχαγγέλων τὰς φλογερὰς, καὶ πολυομμάτων ταξιαρχίας, τὰ σὰ εὐαγγέλια	Tell me, young man, what kind of savior, am I to bear? For truly your good news is strange even to the spiritual powers of angels, fiery might of archangels, and the commanders of the many-eyed [cherubim].	Annunciation

430

329B	οὐρανὸς γὰρ μέλλεις γενέσθαι, καὶ ναὸς θεοχώρητος, καὶ σκηνὴ Θεοῦ ἔμψυχος· ἑπτὰ στερεωμάτων εὐρυχωρότερός τε καὶ ὑψηλότερος καὶ θαυμασιώτερος.	You are about to become heaven, a God-containing tabernacle, a living temple of God, wider and higher and more wondrous than the seven firmaments.	Annunciation
329C	Ψηλαφήσας ὁ Ὕψιστος ὅλον τὸν κόσμον, καὶ μὴ εὑρὼν ὁμοίαν σου μητέρα, πάντως <ὡς οἶδεν> ἐκεῖνος, <καὶ> ὡς ἠθέλησεν, ὡς ηὐδόκησεν, ἐκ σοῦ τῆς ἡγιασμένης ἄνθρωπος διὰ φιλανθρωπίαν γενήσεται.	The Most High searched all the universe, and did not find a mother like you. Certainly, <as he knew,> as he wished, as he was pleased, from you, the holy one, he shall become man because of his love for mankind	Annunciation
329D	Ὦ παρθένε, χαρᾶς ἐπουρανίου πρόξενε· τερπνὸν καὶ θαυμαστὸν οἰκητήριον, καὶ τοῦ κόσμου παντὸς ἱλαστήριον, ἡ μόνη κατὰ ἀλήθειαν ἐν γυναιξὶν εὐλογημένη, ἑτοιμάζου λοιπὸν εἰς μυστικὴν Χριστοῦ παρουσίαν.	O Virgin, bringer of heavenly joy, joyful and marvelous dwelling place, and propitiation of the whole cosmos, the only truly blessed one among women (Luke 1.42), prepare yourself for the mystical coming of Christ.	Annunciation
332B	Βῆμα <φρικτὸν> καὶ κριτήριον ἀπαράλλακτον τοῦ μέλλοντος αἰῶνος εὐλαβήθητι, ὦ Ἰωσήφ, ὅπου καὶ ἄγγελοι τρέμουσι, οἱ μηδέποτε ἁμαρτήσαντες· περὶ δὲ τοῦ ἐπιγείου βασιλέως καὶ δικαστηρίου, ὅλως μή σοι μελέτω.	Fear, rather, the <terrible> court and the unchangeable judgment of the age to come, O Joseph, which even the angels fear who have never sinned. Do not be concerned at all for the earthly king and judgment.	Annunciation
337D	Φανήσεται τὸ σημεῖον ἐν τῷ οὐρανῷ· γέγραπται γὰρ ἐν τοῖς προφήταις· «Ἀνατελεῖ ἄστρον ἐξ Ἰακὼβ, καὶ ἀναστήσεται ἄνθρωπος ἐξ Ἰσραήλ, καὶ θραύσει τοὺς ἀρχηγοὺς Μωάβ.»	There will appear today in the heavens a sign, for so it is written in the prophets: "A star shall rise out of Jacob, and a man arise out of Israel, and shall crush the leaders of Moab (Numbers 24.17)."	Annunciation

Gregory E. Roth

340D	Τῶν ἐπιγείων ὅταν μετέστης, τῶν οὐρανίων προδήλως ἐπέβης· πλὴν οὔτε πρώην τῶν οὐρανίων ἠμοίρεις, οὔτε μετατεθεῖσα τῶν ἐπιγείων ἐξέστης· ἐπειδὴ, καὶ τῶν ἐν οὐρανοῖς ταγμάτων ὑψηλοτέρα κατέστης, καὶ τῶν ἐπὶ γῆς ποιημάτων ὑπερτέρα κατεφάνης. Ἐπ' ἀληθείας γὰρ, καὶ τοὺς οὐρανοὺς ἐκαλλώπισας, καὶ τὴν γῆν ὑπερελάμπρυνας, Θεοτόκε. Τοὺς μὲν οὐρανοὺς, ὅτιπερ ἅμα τοῦ στῆναι τὰ τῶν ἀνθρώπων γένη, ἄγγελοι τῆς τούτων ἐπιτροπεύειν προετάχθησαν ζωῆς· τοῦ ὁδηγεῖν, καὶ διοικεῖν, καὶ φυλάττειν αὐτοὺς, ἐν τῇ πρὸς Θεὸν ἀμεταθέτῳ πίστεως καρδίᾳ. «Ἔστησε γὰρ, φησὶν, ὅρια ἐθνῶν κατὰ ἀριθμὸν ἀγγέλων Θεοῦ.»	When you left earthly [places], you obviously entered the heavenly [places]; except earlier you were not lacking participation in the heavenly, nor did you depart from the earthly when you were transferred, since you were made more sublime than the ranks in heaven, and you were revealed as higher than the deeds of earth. For in truth, you beautified the heavens, and you illuminated the earth, O Theotokos. For when the heavens along with the generations of men were established, angels were assigned to tend their life; and to guide, and administer, and guard them, with an unchanging heart of faith towards God. "For he established," it is said, "bounds for the nations according to the number of the angels of God." (Deut. 32.8, Odes 2.8)	Dormition I
341A	Καὶ, «Παρεμβαλεῖ, φησὶν, ἄγγελος Κυρίου κύκλῳ τῶν φοβουμένων αὐτὸν, καὶ ῥύσεται αὐτούς.»	And it is said, "The angel of the Lord will encircle those who fear [the Lord] and will protect them." (Psalm 33.8 LXX)	Dormition I
341A 341B	Ἀλλὰ τῶν ἐλεεινῶν ἀνθρώπων πλάνῃ καὶ εἰδωλολατρείᾳ τότε διατελούντων, κνίσης τε θυσιῶν τὸν ἀέρα μολυνόντων, ἀφειδίασαν ἐκ τῆς τῶν ἀνθρώπων συνδιαγωγῆς λοιπὸν καὶ οἱ ἄγγελοι· ἀντανεῖλε δὲ παρ' αὐτῶν ὁ Θεὸς καὶ τὸ ἅγιον αὐτοῦ Πνεῦμα. Σοῦ	But of the wretched men then living in error and idolatry, polluting the air with the smoke of sacrifices, for the rest even the angels ceased from companionship with men; for God took away his holy Spirit from them in return. But when you gave birth in the last times to	Dormition I

432

	δὲ τεκούσης ἐπ᾽ ἐσχάτων τὸν «ἐν ἀρχῇ» Λόγον τοῦ Θεοῦ καὶ Πατρός, παρευθὺ τῆς σῆς κυήσεως, καὶ τῶν ἀγγέλων αἱ στρατιαί, ἀπὸ τῶν οὐρανῶν παρέκυψαν, τὸν ὑπὸ σοῦ γεγεννημένον ἀνυμνοῦντες Θεὸν, καὶ δόξαν ἐν τοῖς ὑψίστοις προστεθῆναι βοήσαντες, εἰρήνην ἐπὶ γῆς ἐκραύγασαν ἐπιφθάσαι· ὡς μηκέτι λοιπὸν ἔχθραν μεσοτοίχου μεταξὺ ἀγγέλων καὶ ἀνθρώπων, οὐρανοῦ τε καὶ γῆς, χρηματίζειν· ἀλλὰ σύμφωνον πολίτευμα, καὶ μίαν ἀντιφωνοῦσαν δοξο-λογίαν παρ᾽ ἀγγέλων καὶ ἀνθρώπων, τῷ ἑνὶ καὶ τριαδικῷ Θεῷ προσαναπέμπεσθαι παρ᾽ ἑκατέρων. Καὶ ὁ Πατὴρ δὲ τοῦ μονογενοῦς Υἱοῦ αὐτοῦ, μαρτυρῶν τῇ ἐκ σοῦ χωρὶς Πατρὸς σωματικῇ κυοφορίᾳ, εἰς αὐτὸν βοᾷ· «Ἐγὼ σήμερον γεγέννηκά σε.» Καὶ πάλιν· «Ἐκ γαστρὸς πρὸ ἑωσφόρου γεγέννηκά σε.»	him who "in the beginning' was the Word of God the Father (*cf.* John 1.1), at once upon your delivery even the armies of the angels bent down from the heavens, hymning the God who was born from you, and shouting that glory was attributed in the highest places and they cried out that peace had arrived on earth (*cf.* Luke 2.14). So no longer did they name enmity as a dividing wall between angels and men, heaven and earth, but a harmonious commonwealth and one antiphonal doxology from both angels and men, sent up to God one and trinity. And the Father of his only-begotten Son, bearing witness to his physical birth from you without a father, proclaims to him, "Today I have begotten you." (Psalm 2.7 LXX) And again, "From the womb before the morning star I have begotten you." (Psalm 109.3 LXX)	
344A	καὶ γαστέρα πάλιν, τὴν σὴν ἐσήμανε κοιλίαν, τοῦ δεῖξαι καὶ τὴν σαρκικὴν ἐκ σοῦ τοῦ Μονογενοῦς ἐπιδημίαν. Προεωσφόρον δὲ, τὴν πρὸ τοῦ αὔγους τότε δεδήλωκε νύκτα· ἑωσφόρον, τὴν ἡμέραν καλῶς ὑποτιθεμένη· ἐπειδὴ γὰρ ἐν νυκτὶ τὸ φῶς τοῖς ἐν σκότει καθημένοις ἐκύησας, προεωσφόρον τὴν ὥραν ἐκάλεσε τοῦ τόκου σου.	And again [Scripture] called your belly "womb", to show also the habitation of the Only-begotten from your flesh; but "before the morning star" has declared the night then before the dawning—morning star, you who well represent the day. Since in the night you bore light for those who sat in darkness (*cf.* Luke 1.79), [Scripture]	Dormition I

433

	Greek	English	
	«Ποιμένες γὰρ, φησὶν, ἦσαν ἐν τῇ χώρᾳ τῇ αὐτῇ ἀγραυλοῦντες, καὶ φυλάσσοντες φυλακὰς τῆς νυκτός.» Τοιαύτη ἡ προστεθεῖσα διὰ σοῦ τοῖς ἐπουρανίοις δόξα, Θεοτόκε. Μὴ γὰρ προσετέθη, οὐκ ἂν τὸ ἤδη δεδοξασμένον, Δόξαν ἐν ὑψίστοις, ἀνύμνουν οἱ ἄγγελοι, κατὰ τὸν καιρὸν, ἐπικαταλαβεῖν τῆς ἀφράστου σου κυοφορίας. Ποία δὲ καὶ τῶν ἐπιγείων ἡ ἔλλαμψις; ὅπιπερ διὰ τῆς σῆς ἀμώμου σαρκὸς οὐρανοπολίτης ὁ ἄνθρωπος ἀπετελέσθη, καὶ ποιμένες μετ᾽ ἀγγέλων ἐμίχθησαν.	called "before the morning star" the hour of your childbirth. For it says, "Shepherds were in the same place outdoors and keeping watch at night." (Luke 2.8) Such was glory shown to the heavenly ones through you, O Theotokos. If it had not been new—the angels would not be singing "Glory in the highest," in praise of your ineffable childbearing had it already been glorified. What kind of illumination is this also of earthlings? Because through your blameless flesh man has been made a citizen of heaven, and shepherds associated with angels.	
344B	Οἱ μὲν ἄγγελοι καταβατικοί . . . πρὸς τὴν ἄνω τοῦ Θεοῦ καὶ δεδοξασμένην ὑψωθέντες ἀξίαν· τουτέστι, τὴν ἄναρχον τοῦ Πατρὸς πρὸς τὸν Υἱὸν σοφισθέντες πρὸ τῶν αἰώνων γεννητικὴν, καὶ οὐ κτιστὴν ὁμοουσιότητα.	The angels descending . . . lifted up to the high and glorified worthiness of God; that is, having learned of the generative relation without beginning of the Father towards the Son before the ages, and not a created consubstantiality.	Dormition I
344C	ἐπειδὴ καὶ οὐρανὸς θεοχώρητος ἀνεδείχθης τοῦ ὑψίστου Θεοῦ, διὰ τὸν χωρητικὸν κόλπον σου πρὸς αὐτοῦ βασταγμοῦ· καὶ γῆ πάλιν αὐτῷ πνευματική, διὰ χωρητικὴν ὑπουργίαν ἐχρημάτισας τῆς σαρκός σου	For when you were proved to be a God-containing heaven of the most high God, since your bosom [was] able to carry Him, and again you were called a spiritual earth because of the [God-]containing service of your flesh.	Dormition I
352A	«Θυμὸν καὶ ὀργὴν καὶ θλίψιν, ἀποστολὴν δι᾽ ἀγγέλων πονηρῶν,» σῦ μεταβάλλεις	You repel "spirit and anger and tribulation, dispatched by evil angels" (Ps. 77.49 LXX).	Dormition II
352B	Τὴν τῶν ἀγγέλων ὑπὲρ ἔννοιαν θεωρίαν·	You are a vision beyond the understanding of the angels	Dormition II

353B	«Εὐλογημένον τοίνυν διὰ τοῦτο τὸ ὄνομά σου εἰς τοὺς αἰῶνας.» Πρὸ τοῦ ἡλίου τὸ φῶς σου. Ὑπερτέρα πάσης τῆς κτίσεως ἡ τιμή σου· πρὸ τῶν ἀγγέλων ἡ ὑπεροχή σου. «Ὑψηλοτέρα σὺ τοῦ οὐρανοῦ·» ἀλλὰ καὶ πλατυτέρα τοῦ οὐρανοῦ τῶν οὐρανῶν, καὶ τοῦ Γραφικῶς παρά τινος ἁγίου ἀντιφερομένου ἑβδόμου. Ὀγδοώτερε, καὶ εἰ ἔστι τις ἕτερος, καὶ ὑπερέκεινα τούτου λέγειν, οὐρανέ· εὐλογημένη σὺ ἐν γενεαῖς γενεῶν·	"Therefore your name is blessed because of this unto the ages" (Ps. 71.17 LXX). Before the sun [is/was] your light. Above all the creation is your honor. Before the angels is your greatness. "You [are] higher than the heaven" (Job 11.8) but also wider than the heaven of heavens, and than the holy seventh [heaven] which according to someone in Scripture distinguishes from it. You more than eighth heaven, and if it is possible to speak of any other beyond this: blessed are you to generations of generations;	Dormition II
356B	Ἄγγελοι ταῖς οὐρανίαις ἐγγαυριῶνται καταμοναῖς· ἡμεῖς τοῖς τῶν ἁγιωτάτων σου ναῶν εὐφραινόμεθα σχολασμοῖς.	Angels rejoice in the mansions of the heavens; we delight to spend time in your holy temples.	Dormition II
357A	καὶ πίστει τοὺς οὐρανούς, ὡς γέγραπται, κατηρτίσθαι νοοῦμεν·	In/by faith we know that the heavens have been fitted together, as it is written (Heb. 11.3; cf. Gen. 1.1);	Dormition II
357B	Οὐκ ἀμάρτυρος γὰρ ἡ μετάστασίς σου· οὐδὲ ψευδὴς ἡ κοίμησις. Ὁ οὐρανὸς τῶν ἐπὶ σοὶ τότε συνδραμόντων διηγεῖται δόξαν· ἡ γῆ, τὴν περὶ αὐτῶν παρίστησιν ἀλήθειαν· αἱ νεφέλαι, τὴν ἐξ αὐτῶν σοι διακονηθεῖσαν βοῶσι τιμήν· καὶ ἄγγελοι τὴν εἰς σὲ τότε γενομένην ἀπαγγέλλουσι δωροφορίαν· τὸ πῶς φημι κατὰ τὴν Ἰερουσαλὴμ οἱ ἀπόστολοι παρεγένοντο πρὸς σέ, καθάπερ καὶ Ἀμβακοὺμ ὁ προφήτης ἐκ μερῶν τῆς Ὀρεινῆς, ἐν ὥρᾳ μιᾷ διὰ νεφέλης ἁρπαγείς, καὶ ἀγγελικῆς δεξιᾶς ὑποληφθείς,	For your translation does not lack witness, nor is your dormition a deception. Heaven tells the glory (Ps. 19.1 LXX) of those who ran together for you then. Earth stands by the truth concerning them. The clouds cry out the honor which was furnished to you from them. And angels report the gift-giving which came to you then—I mean how the apostles came to your side in Jerusalem, as also Habakkuk the prophet from the part of the mountains in one hour snatched up by a cloud, and lifted up by an angelic right hand,	Dormition II

360B	Ὅταν πρὸς ἑαυτὸν Χριστὸς ὁ Θεὸς ἡμῶν τὴν Ζωοτόκον αὐτοῦ μετενεγκεῖν ἐβουλεύσατο Μητέρα, δι᾽ ἀγγέλου αὐτῇ καὶ πάλιν τοῦ συνήθους τὸ τῆς κοιμήσεως προμηνύει παραστατικόν· ὅπως μὴ καθὼς ἐν τοῖς λοιποῖς ἀνθρώποις αἰφνιδίως ὁ θάνατος ὑπερ-χόμενος, τάραχον καὶ αὐτῇ μετεκδημούσῃ ποιήσοι. Οἶδεν γὰρ ὁ τοῦ σώματος ἀπὸ ψυχῆς μερισμός, καὶ τῶν μεγάλων ἀνθρώπων περίλυπον ποιεῖν τὸ πνεῦμα.	When Christ our God planned to transfer his life-bearing Mother to his side, by an angel he announces to her the indication of her falling-asleep contrary to the usual; so that not as among the rest of mankind death coming invisibly should make distress for her also as she changes her habitation. For the separation of the body from the soul knows how to grieve the soul even of great men.	Dormition III
365B	Τούτων λαλουμένων, γίνεται τις ἄφνω βροντῆς βιαίας ἦχος, καὶ λαίλαψ ὑπογαίου νεφέλης ἐπιστασίας, ἐξ ἧς ὥσπερ τινὲς δροσόμματοι σταγόνες οἱ τοῦ Χριστοῦ μαθηταί, τῷ τῆς Παρθένου καθορμισθέντες ὁμοθυμαδὸν ἐπέστησαν οἴκῳ.	As these things were being said, there comes suddenly a forceful sound of thunder, and a storm cloud which hung low over the earth from which as if some dewy drops the disciples of Christ, landing at the Virgin's house stood together in a crowd.	Dormition III
368D	Κατεπλήττοντο τῇ ἄφνω ταύτης ἀποικίᾳ. Ἐξεθαμβοῦντο καὶ ἐπὶ τῇ τῶν ἀποστόλων ἐκ τῶν διασπορῶν ἐναέρῳ παρουσίᾳ. Διεφημίσθη γὰρ περὶ αὐτῶν ἐν ὅλῃ τῇ Ἱερουσαλήμ, ὡς ἂν ἔμβροντος καὶ λαιλαποειδὴς γεγονυῖα πρὸ ῥοπῆς ὁμίχλη, ὡς ὄμβρον αὐτοὺς καὶ δρόσον πνεύματος διασυρίζοντος, τῷ τῆς Παρθένου κατεστάλαξεν οἴκῳ.	They were thunderstruck by her sudden departure. They were amazed also at the aerial arrival of the apostles from their dispersion. For the rumor was spread about them in all Jerusalem, that a kind of cloud with lightning and storm coming before the decisive moment, as the spirit whistled	Dormition III
		through them like a rain and a dew, fell upon the house of the Virgin.	

No direct references to Germanos' cosmology is found in the Homily on the Sash.

References to Nicaean-Constantinopolitan Creed/theology in Germanos I Patriarch of Constantinople (715-730)

PG 98 Location	Greek	English	Homily
296C	ἡ γὰρ πάντων αἰτία καὶ τελεταρχικὴ θεότης, τρισὶν ἁγιασμοῖς, τρισὶν χαρακτῆρσιν, ἤτοι τρισὶν ὑποστάσεσιν, εἴπερ καὶ τρισὶ προσώποις ταυτολογεῖν δεῖ, ὁμοουσιώτατα ὡς τελείῳ ἀριθμῷ ἐν ἀσυγχύτῳ ἤτοι ἀγύρτῳ ἑνώσει, τοῦ ὑμνεῖσθαι ἡρετίσατο· οὔτε τῇ τοῦ ἐνδεοῦς πενίᾳ ἀτιμαζομένη, οὐδ' αὖ τῇ ὑπὲρ τούτων ἀριθμήσει πολυαρχαῖς φαντασιοσκοπουμένη	For the cause of all and the divine source of perfection has chosen to be praised in three blessings, in three characters, that is in three natures, and if indeed we need to say the same thing with "in three persons" in one essence, as a perfect number without confusion, a collective unity; neither is the deficient poverty dishonored, nor either is a vain fantasy indulged by a greater number with many origins.	Presentation I
341B 341C	Ὦ ῥήματα θεολογίας μεστά! Εἰ πρὸ γεννηθῆναι παρὰ σοῦ τῆς Παρθένου Μητρός, Υἱὸς οὗτος μονογενὴς τοῦ Θεοῦ, πῶς ὁ Πατήρ φησι πρὸς αὐτόν, «Ἐγὼ σήμερον γεγέννηκά σε;» Δῆλον ὅτι τὸ σήμερον, οὐχὶ τὴν τῆς θεότητος τοῦ Μονογενοῦς πρόσφατον παρίστησι ὕπαρξιν, ἀλλὰ τὴν πρὸς ἀνθρώπους σωματικὴν αὐτοῦ βεβαιοῖ παρουσίαν. Τὸ δέ, γεγέννηκά σε, τὸ τοῦ ἁγίου Πνεύματος ἐν τῷ Πατρὶ θεαρχικὸν ὁμοῦ καὶ συνεργητικὸν ἐμφαίνει	Oh sayings full of theology! If before being born from you, the Virgin Mother, this one was only-begotten Son of God, how does the Father say to him, "Today I have begotten you"? It is clear that "today" does not represent a new beginning of the divinity of the Only-begotten, but declares his corporeal presence among men. But the "I have begotten you" reveals the divinely-originate and	Dormition I

	συνούσιον. Ἐπειδὴ γὰρ οὐκ ἀλλότριον τὸ Πνεῦμα τοῦ Πατρός· εὐδοκίᾳ δὲ καὶ ἀποστολῇ τοῦ Πατρὸς ᾤκησεν ἐν σοὶ τῇ Παρθένῳ καὶ Μητρὶ, ἰδιοποιεῖται τὴν τοῦ παναγίου Πνεύματος ἐνέργειαν ὁ Πατήρ, ὅθεν τὴν ἐκ σοῦ σωματικὴν τοῦ Υἱοῦ αὐτοῦ πρόοδον καινοποιησάμενος μετὰ τοῦ Πνεύματος ὁ Πατὴρ, «Ἐγὼ, φησὶ τῷ Υἱῷ, σήμερον γεγέννηκά σε.» Καὶ τόδε, «Ἐκ γαστρὸς πρὸ ἑωσφόρου ἐγέννησά σε,» τῆς αὐτῆς ἔχεται πιστοφορίας τουτέστιν, ὅτι καὶ τὴν προαιώνιον τῆς θεότητος ἐν τῷ Μονογενεῖ πιστὸν μετὰ τοῦ Πατρὸς συναΐδιον οὐσίαν, καὶ τὴν ἔνσαρκον αὐτοῦ περὶ τὰ ἔσχατα τῶν καιρῶν ἐκ σοῦ τῆς Ἀειπαρθένου φυσικὴν καὶ ἀφάνταστον δείκνυσιν ἐνανθρώπησιν. Γαστέρα γὰρ προεωσφόρον, τὴν γεννητικὴν τοῦ προουρανίου καὶ ἐπιγείου Φωτὸς ὠνόμασεν ἡ Γραφὴ πρόοδον· τοῦ δειχθῆναι ὅτι πρὸ πάσης κτίσεως ὁρωμένης καὶ ἀοράτου, ὁ Μονογενὴς ὑπὸ τοῦ Πατρὸς ἀνάρχως, ἐκ Φωτὸς ἐγεννήθη Φῶς· καὶ γαστέρα πάλιν, τὴν σὴν ἐσήμανε κοιλίαν, τοῦ δεῖξαι καὶ τὴν σαρκικὴν ἐκ σοῦ τοῦ Μονογενοῦς ἐπιδημίαν. Προεωσφόρον δὲ, τὴν πρὸ τοῦ αὔγους τότε δεδήλωκε νύκτα· ἑωσφόρον, τὴν ἡμέραν καλῶς ὑποτιθεμένη	synergetic communion of the Holy Spirit in the Father. For since the Spirit is not alien to the Father, for by good will and sending of the Father he has come to dwell in you the Virgin and Mother, the Father makes his own the activity of the all-holy Spirit, whence the Father along with the Spirit making new the corporeal procession of the Son from you says, "Today I have begotten you." And this "From the womb before the morning star I begot you" relates to the same expression of faith, that also it reveals the preexisting essence of divinity in the Only-begotten shared with the coeternal essence of the Father, and his incarnate natural and non-imaginary entrance into humanity at the last times from you the Ever-virgin. For Scripture called "womb before the morning star" the generative procession of the Light which was before the heavens and appeared on earth: to show that before all visible and invisible creation the Only-begotten was born from the Father without beginning, Light was born from Light. And again [Scripture] called your belly "womb", to show also the habitation of the Only-begotten from your flesh; but "before the morning star" has declared the night then before the dawning—morning star, you who well represent the day.	

341D

344A

References to the Cult of Mary in Germanos I, Patriarch of Constantinople (715-730)

PG 98 Location	Greek	English	Homily
292C	Θυμηδίας μὲν πᾶσα θειοτάτη πανήγυρις ἑκάστοτε τελουμένη τοὺς θιασώτας ἐμπιπλᾷσι πνευματικῶς ἐκ θησαυρῶν καὶ θεορρύτων πηγῶν. Μεῖζον δὲ καὶ ὑπὲρ ἁπάσας λαμπροφορεῖται τελεταρχικῶς ψυχαγωγοῦσα ἡ ἀρτιύμνητος, ὅτῳ καὶ ὑπεραναβαινούσης τῆς ἐξαρχούσης Θεόπαιδος.	Every divine festival, whenever it is celebrated, spiritually fills those who are present from a treasury and divinely flowing spring. But even more and beyond other feasts does this recently hymned festival, brilliantly celebrated, attract the soul with holy joy and gives more joy in proportion to the preeminence of the excellent child of God.	Presentation I (P Cult 183 ftn. 15)
292C/D —293A	Συνδράμωμεν τῇ δρέψει τῶν περισπουδάστων ἀνθέων τοῦ οἰκείου τῆς θεομήτορος λειμῶνος.(292C) Εὐμυρίσωμεν ὡς ἐκ καλύκων ῥοδόχρουν αὐτῆς. καλλονὴν ἀναβαίνουσαν πλήρη θυμιαμάτων, ὡς Σολομῶντι ἐν τοῖς Ἄσμασιν φάσκοντι καλῶς ἐστίχισται· «Τίς αὕτη ἡ ἀναβαίνουσα ἀπὸ τῆς ἐρήμου, ὡς στελέχη καπνοῦ τεθυμιαμένη, σμύρναν καὶ λίβανον ἀπὸ πάντων κονιορτῶν μυρεψοῦ;»—«Δεῦρο ἀπὸ Λιβάνου, νύμφη μου, δεῦρο ἀπὸ Λιβάνου.» (292D)	Let us hasten to pick the precious flowers from the private meadow of the Mother of God. (292C) And let us be anointed with the perfume of her roses, as Solomon says in the beautiful verse of his Song: "Who is that who comes up from the wilderness, perfumed with myrrh and frankincense, with all the fragrant powders of the merchants?" (Song of Songs 3.6)—"Come hither from Lebanon,	Presentation I (P Cult 183 ftn. 16)

	Τοιγαροῦν σπουδαίως συναπέλθωμεν ἀλλήλους τῇ κοινωφελεῖ σωτηριώδει πανηγύρει τῆς Θεομήτορος προτρεπόμενοι,	my bride; come hither from Lebanon" (Song of Songs 4.8) (292D) So let us eagerly approach together this mutually beneficial, salvific feast of the Mother of God. (293A)	
304C	Horvath mentions this passage as illustrating the joy with which Germanos praises the Virgin Mary 291		Presentation I
304C	Ἀλλ' ἄγε δῆτα, φίλη Θεῷ πανήγυρις, ὁμοφώνως ὅσον τῇ ἡμετέρᾳ νηπιώδει ἐννοίᾳ ἡ ἰσχὺς ἔνεστι, τὸ Χαῖρε τῇ Παρθένῳ προσείπωμεν, οὐ τὴν αὐτῆς εὐφημῆσαι δυνάμενοι τέλειον ἑορτήν· ἀλλά γε· τὴν ἡμετέραν ἀσθένειαν παρηγοροῦντες ὅσον ἐφικτὸν, ἐπεὶ καὶ φίλον Θεῷ τὸ κατὰ δύναμιν.	But come now, assembly dear to God, whatever power is in our childish thoughts, with one voice let us proclaim the χαῖρε to the Virgin (cf. Luke 1.28), not being able adequately to hymn her perfect feast; but excusing our weakness as far as possible, since God is pleased with what is within our power.	Presentation I (H)
305D	Χαίροις, ἡ νέα Σιὼν, καὶ θεία Ἱερουσαλήμ, ἁγία «πόλις τοῦ μεγάλου ἄνακτος Θεοῦ, ἧς αὐτὸς Θεὸς ἐν ταῖς βάρεσι γινώσκεται,» καὶ βασιλεῖς ὑποκλίνων ἐν τῇ τῆς σῆς δόξης προσκυνήσει, καὶ κόσμον ἅπαντα ἐν ἀγαλλιάσει τὴν τῆς Προόδου σου πανήγυριν ἄγειν παρασκευάζων·	Hail, new Zion and holy Jerusalem, holy city of the great king—within his citadels God has shown himself a sure defense (cf. Psalm 47.3ff. LXX)—and [God] making kings subject to the veneration of your glory, and preparing all the world to celebrate in great joy the feast of your Entrance.	Presentation I (H)
308C —309A	Ἀλλ', ὦ πανάμωμε, καὶ πανύμνητε, καὶ πανσέβαστε, καὶ πάντων δημιουργημάτων ὑπερφερὲς Θεοῦ ἀνάθημα· ἀγεώργητε γῆ, ἀνήροτε ἄρουρα, εὐκληματοῦσα ἄμπελος, κρατὴρ εὐφραντικώτατε, κρήνη πηγάζουσα, Παρθένε γεννῶσα καὶ Μήτηρ ἀπείρανδρε, ἁγνείας κειμήλιον καὶ σεμνότητος	But O most blameless and all-laudable, most holy one, offering to God greater than all created things, untilled earth, unplowed field (cf. Ezekiel 19.10), well-pruned vineyard, most joyous wine bowl, gushing spring (cf. Ezekiel 17.6), virgin birth-giver and	Presentation I (P Cult 186 ftn.22)

ἐγκαλλώπισμα, ταῖς πρὸς τὸν σὸν, τὸν ἐκ σοῦ ἀπάτορα, Υἱόν τε καὶ Θεὸν πάντων δημιουργὸν εὐπροσδέκτοις καὶ μητροπειθέσι λιταῖς, τοὺς τῆς ἐκκλησιαστικῆς εὐταξίας οἴακας διέπουσα, εἰς ἀκύμαντον λιμένα ἤτοι ἀπόντιστον¹¹ ἐξ ἐπιρροίας αἱρέσεών τε καὶ σκανδάλων πηδαλιούχησον. (308C) Τοὺς ἱερεῖς τῇ δικαιοσύνῃ καὶ τῇ τῆς εὐκλεοῦς ἀμωμήτου εἰλικρινοῦς πίστεως ἀγαλλιάσει φωτεινοτάτως ἔνδυσον. Τοῖς ὑπὲρ πᾶσαν βαφὴν ἁλουργοειδῆ καὶ πάνχρυσον, ἢ μαργαρίτην, ἢ πολύτιμον λίθον διάδημά σε καὶ περιβόλαιον καὶ τῆς ἰδίας βασιλείας ἄσυλον κόσμον ὀρθοδόξοις ἄναξιν εἰληχόσιν, ἐν εἰρήνῃ καὶ εὐσταθείᾳ τὰ σκῆπτρα διέπουσα. Τὰ εἰς σὲ καὶ τὸν ἐκ σοῦ Θεὸν βλασφημοῦντα κακότεχνα βάρβαρα ἔθνη τοῖς τούτων ποσὶ στρωννύουσα ὑπόταξον. Τῷ ταῖς σαῖς ἐπικουρίαις ἀεὶ ἐπερειδομένῳ στρατῷ ἐν τῇ τοῦ πολέμου ὥρᾳ συνεπάμυνον· τό τε ὑπήκοον (308D) εὐηνίῳ εὐταξίας δουλείᾳ θεοπαραγγέλτως ἰέναι βεβαίωσον. Τὴν ὡς πύργον σε καὶ θεμέλιον κατέχουσαν τὴν σὴν πόλιν νικητικοῖς ἐπάθλοις καταστέφουσα, ἰσχὺν περιζώσασα φρούρησον· τὴν τοῦ Θεοῦ κατοίκησιν ναοῦ εὐπρέπειαν ἀεὶ διατήρησον· τοὺς σοὺς ὑμνητὰς ἐκ πάσης περιστάσεως καὶ ψυχικῶν	husbandless mother, treasure of purity and ornament of holiness, by your acceptable and motherly-persuasive petitions to your son, born from you without a father, and the God Creator of all, following the furrows of good ecclesiastical order, steer us from the floods of heresies and scandals to the calm and harbor where ships do not sink.12* (308C) Clothe the priests brilliantly with righteousness (cf. Psalm 131.16 LXX) and the joy of glorious blameless pure faith. [As for] those orthodox lords who have obtained you as a diadem and robe sea-purple and supremely golden dye, or pearl, or precious stone and the undefiled ornament of their own royalty, wielding their scepters in peace and stability; subject to them and spread under their feet the un-filial barbarian nations who blaspheme against you and the God [born] from you. (308D) Guard [them] in the hour of battle along with the army which always relies on your aid. Confirm [them] to go obediently by

---

¹¹ ἀπόντιστος here only—ἀκαταπόντιστος in Theodore the Studite and Nicholas Mysticus

	Greek	English	
	ἀλγηδόνων διαφύλαξον· τοῖς αἰχμαλώτοις τε ἀνάρρυσιν βραβεύουσα· ξενιζομένοις ἀστέγοις τε καὶ ἀπεριστάτοις, παραμυθία φάνηθι. Τῷ σύμπαντι κόσμῳ τὴν ἀντιληπτικήν σου χεῖρα ὄρεξον, ἵν' ἐν εὐφροσύνῃ τε καὶ ἀγαλλιάσει τὰς σὰς πανηγύρεις σὺν τῇ νῦν ἡμῖν ἑορταζομένῃ λαμπροτάτῃ τελετῇ διεξάγωμεν. Ἐν Χριστῷ Ἰησοῦ τῶν ἁπάντων Βασιλεῖ καὶ ἀληθινῷ Θεῷ ἡμῶν, ᾧ ἡ δόξα καὶ τὸ κράτος, ἅμα τῷ ἁγίῳ καὶ ζωαρχικῷ Πατρὶ, καὶ τῷ συναϊδίῳ καὶ ὁμοουσίῳ συνθρόνῳ Πνεύματι, νῦν καὶ ἀεὶ, καὶ εἰς τοὺς αἰῶνας τῶν αἰώνων. Ἀμήν.(309A)	God's command with the well-directed servitude of good order. Crowning with victorious trophies your city which holds you as tower and a foundation, protect [her], girding [her] with strength. Keep the dwelling-place of God always as the beauty of the temple. Preserve those who praise you from all misfortune and distress of soul. Providing rescue for the captives, appear as a succor to those who are strangers, homeless, and friendless. Stretch out your protectivehand for all the world, so that in joy and gladness we may celebrate your festival with the rites which we are now most gloriously performing. In Christ Jesus the King of all and our true God, to whom [be] glory and power, along with the holy Father, the source of life, and the coeternal Spirit, one in essence and sharing the throne, now and ever and to the ages of the ages. Amen (309A)	
312A	Δειξάτωσαν ἡμῖν οἱ κατ' αὐτῆς κινοῦντες τὰς γλώσσας, καὶ βλέποντες ὡς μὴ βλέποντες, ποῦ τοιαῦτα πώποτε κατεῖδον; Κόρην ἐξ ἐπαγγελίας, καὶ αὐτὴν τριετίζουσαν, εἰς τὸ τρίτον καταπέτασμα ὡς δῶρον ἄμωμον προσφερομένην, πρὸς τὸ ἐκεῖσε οἰκεῖν	Let them show us, those who wag their tongues against her, and who see as if not seeing, where they ever beheld such things? A maiden from the promise, at the age of three years, is brought as a blameless gift within the third	Presentation I (P Cult 181 ftn. 8)

ἀπαραλείπτως, καὶ ὑπὸ τῶν πλουσίων τοῦ λαοῦ λιτανευομένην· ὑπὸ παρθένων προπεμπομένην· μετὰ λαμπάδων προσαγομένην· ὑπὸ ἱερέων καὶ προφητῶν χερσὶν ὑπτίαις προσλαμβανομένην; Πῶς οὖν οὐκ ἠβουλήθησαν συνιέναι; Πῶς ὁρῶντες τὰ πρῶτα, τοῖς ἐσχάτοις ἠπίστησαν; Πῶς ξένα καὶ παρηλλαγμένα τὰ ἐπ' αὐτῇ προϊδόντες, τοῖς μετέπειτα γενομένοις ἀντέλεξαν; Οὐ γὰρ εἰκῆ, καὶ ὡς ἔτυχε, τὰ περὶ αὐτὴν πρῶτα γεγόνασιν· ἀλλὰ πάντα προοίμια τῶν ὑστάτων. (312A)
Εἰπάτωσαν γὰρ ἡμῖν οἱ παρ' ἑαυτοῖς σοφοὶ τὰ μάταια, πῶς καὶ ἑτέρων στείρων τεκουσῶν, οὐδεμιᾶς θυγάτριον εἰς τὰ τῶν ἁγίων ἀνατίθεται Ἅγια, καὶ ὑπὸ προφητῶν προσείληπται; Ἆρ' οὐκ εἶχον οἱ τοιαῦτα καὶ τηλικαῦτα εἰς αὐτὴν τότε θεωροῦντες εἰπεῖν, οἷα καὶ τούτων οἱ ὁμογνώμονες ὕστερον εἰς τὸν ἐκείνης υἱόν· «Τί ἄρα ἔσται τὸ παιδίον τοῦτο;» Πάνυ μὲν οὖν. Ἀλλ' οἱ μὲν ἀλλοτριόφρονες τὴν τῆς ἀπωλείας ὁδὸν ὁδευέτωσαν, καὶ τὸ ὑπ' αὐτῶν ὀρυχθέντι βαράθρῳ ἐμπιπτέτωσαν· ἡμεῖς δὲ ὁ τοῦ Θεοῦ λαὸς ὁ περιούσιος, ἱερεῖς καὶ ἄρχοντες, κοσμικοί τε καὶ μονάζοντες, δοῦλοι καὶ ἐλεύθεροι, χειροτέχναι καὶ γηπόνοι, φυτοκόμοι καὶ ἁλιεῖς, νέοι καὶ πρεσβύται, ἄνδρες καὶ γυναῖκες· (312B) δεῦτε, προθύμως τῇ

curtain, to live there continuously, and receives petitions from the wealthy men of the people (*cf.* Psalm 45.13). She is sent forth by virgins, brought forward with lamps, welcomed by priests and prophets with uplifted hands! How, when they see the beginning, did they disbelieve in the ending? How, when they had seen the strange and unusual [events] in her case, did they deny those which happened afterwards? For not at random, and as it chanced, did the first things happen concerning her; but all were preludes of the last things. (312A)
Let those who are vainly wise in their own sight tell us: How, when other barren women have given birth, is none of their daughters dedicated in the holy of holies and received by prophets? Could not those who then saw such great things [done] for her say, as also those of the same mind later [said] for her son: "What will this child be?"[13] Yes indeed. But let those of alien mind travel the road of perdition, and let them fall into the pit which they have dug.

---

[13] At Luke 1.66, these words are used about John the Baptist, not about Jesus.

Θεοτόκῳ προσέλθωμεν, καὶ τὰ εἰς αὐτὴν προτελεσθέντα θεῖα μυστήρια [οἰκονομικῶς] ἐποπτεύσωμεν· (312C)	But we, the remnant of God's people (cf. 1 Peter 2.10), priests and rulers, secular and monastics, slaves and free, craftsmen and farmers, gatherers and fishermen, young and old, men and women: hither, (312B) let us eagerly approach the Theotokos, and let us watch the divine mysteries which were accomplished earlier in her. (312C)	

Perniola quotes from part of this section 312A—C. It is clear that he is thinking of the whole section when he says: Il culto di Maria adunque è la via più breve per andare a Cristo, la via più sicura per raggiungere la salvezza. Solo gli 'ostinati precipitano miseramente nel baratro che essi stessi si scavano con la loro incredulità; i veri cristiani invece, « popolo prediletto di Dio, sacerdoti e principi, secolari e monaci, servi e liheri, artigiani e agricoltori, seminatori di piante e pescatori, giovani e vecchi, uomini e donne», tutti si accostano con fede alla Madre di Dio, e trovano in lei la loro salvezza. Ftn. 8 attributes the quotation to 312C.

317B/C	Σὺ γὰρ μόνη Θεοτόκος, ὑψηλοτάτη ἐπὶ πᾶσαν τὴν γῆν· ἡμεῖς δέ σε, Θεόνυμφε, πίστει εὐλογοῦμεν, καὶ πόθῳ γεραίρομεν, καὶ φόβῳ προσκυνοῦμεν, ἀεί σε μεγαλύνοντες, καὶ σεπτῶς μακαρίζοντες.	For you alone are Theotokos, most sublime over all the earth; and we bless you in faith, bride of God, and with desire we honor you, and with fear we bow before you, always magnifying you, and solemnly calling you blessed (cf. Luke 1.49).	Presentation II (H)

Much of the this section (317A-D and 320A-B), a set of petitions, can be seen as reasons for devotion to Mary. Horvath ascribes the passage as being 318C which is the Latin parallel. 291

317A/B	καὶ δὸς τοῖς τὴν σὴν ἑορτὴν τελοῦσιν, τὴν σὴν βοήθειαν, καὶ σκέπην, καὶ προστασίαν· ῥυομένη πάντοτε ταῖς σαῖς πρεσβείαις τούτους ἐκ πάσης ἀνάγκης καὶ κινδύνων, νόσων τε δεινῶν, καὶ συμφορῶν παντοίων, καὶ τῆς μελλούσης ἀπειλῆς δικαίας τοῦ Υἱοῦ σου.	and give to those who celebrate your feast your help, your protection, and your assistance, guarding always by your intercessions these people from every necessity and dangers, and dread diseases, and all kinds of misfortunes, and from the coming just threat of your Son.	Presentation II (H)

317C	Ἀλλ', ὦ μοι, Δέσποινα, μόνη τὸ ἐμὸν ἐκ Θεοῦ ψυχαγώγημα, τοῦ ἐν ἐμοὶ καύσωνος ἡ θεία δρόσος, τῆς ξηρανθείσης μου καρδίας ἡ θεόρρυτος ρανίς, τῆς ζοφερᾶς μου ψυχῆς ἡ τηλαυγεστάτη λαμπὰς, τῆς ἐμῆς πορείας ἡ ποδηγία,	But Oh me, Mistress, my only soul-leader from God, the divine dew of the burning in me, the moisture flowing from God for my parched heart, the bright-shining lamp of my darkened soul, the guide for my journey,	Presentation II (H)
325B	Κἂν ἡ μορφή μου καταπλήττει σε, <ἀλλ'> οἶδα ὅτι τὰ ρήματα τοῦ στόματός μου <μεγάλης δόξης> πρόξενά σοι γενήσονται· καὶ μακαρίσει σε λοιπὸν ὁ οὐρανὸς καὶ ἡ γῆ.	Even though my voice and my form terrify you, I know that the words of my mouth shall become a harbinger <of ineffable joy> to you. And all heaven and earth shall bless you (cf. Luke 1.48).	Annunciation (P Cult 180 ftn. 5)
329A	Ὑπὸ τὴν σὴν εὐσπλαγχνίαν καταφεύξεται πᾶν γένος ἀνθρώπων, καὶ πᾶσα γλῶσσα πηλίνη μακαρίσει σε· καὶ λαληθήσεται τὸ ὄνομά σου ἐν πάσῃ γενεᾷ, καὶ γενεᾷ, ὅτι διὰ [τοῦ] σοῦ Κύριος, τὸ φῶς τοῦ κόσμου, μέλλει τίκτεσθαι.	All the races of men shall take refuge under your compassion. And all tongues of clay shall bless you. And your name shall be spoken from generation to generation (cf. Luke 1.50), for through you, the Lord, the light of the world, is about to be born.	Annunciation (P Cult 180 ftn. 6)
340A	Ὁ χρεωστῶν, πάντοτε τὸν ἴδιον εὐεργέτην ἀνυμνεῖ. Ὁ σωζόμενος, οὐκ ἀγνοεῖ τοῦ οἰκείου Σωτῆρος τὴν σκέπην.	The debtor always praises his own benefactor. He who is being saved does not fail to recognize the protection of his own savior.	Dormition I (P Cult 180 ftn. 4)
340B	Ἐπίβλεψον ἐπὶ τὴν ταπείνωσιν τοῦ δούλου σου· ὕψωσον ταπεινοῦ στόμα, καὶ πεινῶντά με τὴν σὴν ἐπιθυμητῶς δοξολογίαν, τῶν σῶν ἔμπλησον τῆς ἐπιτυχίας ἀγαθῶν, ἵνα σου τῇ ἀντιλήψει τὸν νοῦν ποδηγούμενος, μὴ ἐντραπῶ μεγαλῦναί σε, Δέσποινα.	Regard the lowliness of your servant, lift up the mouth of the humble one, and fill me who hunger eagerly to sing your praise with the good things of your prosperity, so that with my mind led by your assistance I may not hesitate to magnify you, Mistress.	Dormition I (H) (P Cult 180 ftn. 4)

Gregory E. Roth

Germanos begins this homily (Dormition II) with proclaiming his debt. He also makes it clear that neither he nor any other encomiast is able to adequately give thanks or praise to the Theotokos. In the course of doing this he alludes to Mary's song at the Annunciation (Luke 1.46—55). It is the obligation of the debtor to praise the one to whom the debt is owed. Very quickly it becomes clear that Germanos' feels a great debt to Mary because of her work in the Incarnation. The whole of 340B expresses this. Horvath also mentions it as one of the reasons Germanos gives for devotion to Mary. 291			
Perniola rightly recognizes this anaphora as expressing a reason for the cult of Mary. He makes reference, however, only to 352C in ftn. 1, 179 and adds the rest in ftn. 2, 180.			
352C/D 353A	Σὲ τίς μὴ θαυμάσει τὴν ἀμετάθετον σκέπην, τὴν ἀμετάστατον καταφυγὴν, τὴν ἀκοίμητον πρεσβείαν, τὴν ἀδιάλειπτον σωτηρίαν, τὴν σταθερὰν βοήθειαν, τὴν ἀσάλευτον προστασίαν, τὸ ἀπόρθητον τεῖχος, τὸν θησαυρὸν τῶν ἀπολαύσεων, τὸν ἀνέγκλητον παράδεισον, τὸ ἀσφαλὲς ὀχύρωμα, τὸ κραταιὸν περιχαράκωμα, τὸν ἰσχυρὸν τῆς ἀντιλήψεως πύργον, τὸν λιμένα τῶν χειμαζομένων, τὴν γαλήνην τῶν τεταραγμένων, τὴν τῶν ἁμαρτωλῶν ἐγγυητὴν, τὴν τῶν ἀπεγνωσμένων προσαγωγὴν, τὴν τῶν ἐξορισθέντων ἀνάληψιν, τὴν τῶν ἐκδιωχθέντων ὑποστροφήν, τὴν τῶν ἀλλοτριωθέντων οἰκείωσιν, τὴν τῶν κατακεκριμένων παράθεσιν, τὴν τῶν καθηρημένων εὐλογίαν, τὴν δρόσον τῆς ψυχικῆς αὐχμηρίας, τὴν σταγόνα τῆς ἐκτακείσης βοτάνης. «Τὰ γὰρ ὀστᾶ ἡμῶν, ὡς γέγραπται, διὰ σοῦ καθάπερ βοτάνην ἀνατελεῖ·» τὴν τοῦ ἀμνοῦ καὶ ποιμένος μητέρα, καὶ πάντων τῶν ἀγαθῶν γνωριζομένην πρόξενον.	Who will not be amazed at your unchanging protection, your immovable refuge, your unsleeping intercession, your unceasing salvation, your secure assistance, your unshakable advocacy, your impregnable wall, your storehouse of enjoyment, your blameless paradise, your safe stronghold, your mighty entrenchment, your strong tower of protection, your harbor for the storm-tossed, your calm for those in turmoil, your surety for sinners, access for the hopeless, restoration of the banished, return of the exiles, reconciliation of those alienated, reunion of those condemned, blessing of those convicted, dew for the soul's drought, drop of water for the withering plant ("for our bones," as it is written, "through you rise up like a plant" (Isaiah 66.14 LXX)), the mother of the lamb and the shepherd, and the one recognized as bringer of all good things.	Dormition II (P Cult 179 ftn. 1 and 180 ftn. 2)

353B/ C-356A	Horvath points to this passage as one of the reason Germanos gives as a reason for devotion to Mary 290 Perniola also refers to 353C—356A ftn. 9, 181 and ftn. 12, 182. Where he adds 356B.		Dormition II (H)
	τὸν κόσμον τοῦτον ἔθνη, καινῷ δεκτῷ καὶ αὐτὰ μακαριοῦσί σε, Παρθένε. Ὅταν γὰρ ὁ ἐκ σοῦ γεννηθεὶς ἥξει «κρῖναι τὴν οἰκουμένην ἐν δικαιοσύνῃ, ὄψονται καὶ κόψονται,» οἱ μὴ Θεοτόκον σε πιστῶς ὁμολογῆσαι θελήσαντες· καὶ τότε γνώσονται, (356A) ποίου θησαυροῦ ἑαυτοὺς κακοβούλως ἐζημίωσαν. Ἀλλ᾽ ἡμῖν τοῖς Χριστιανοῖς καὶ Χριστιανικῇ Θεοτόκον σεβομένοις σε πίστει, παράτεινον τῆς ἀμεταθέτου σου προστασίας τὸ ἔλεος. Καὶ τὴν γὰρ κοίμησίν σου, Θεοτόκε, ζωὴν ἡγούμεθα δικαίως, καὶ σύνοικόν σε πνευματικῶς ἔχειν πεπιστεύκαμεν. Καὶ ὅταν θλίψις ἐγγὺς εἶ, ζητοῦντές σε λυτρούμεθα· καὶ ὅταν πάλιν χαρᾶς καιρὸς, σὺ εἶ ταύτης πρόξενος· καὶ ὅταν ἐν ὅλοις ὑπὸ σοῦ μεριμνώμεθα, μεθ᾽ ἡμῶν σε διάγειν πιστοφορούμεθα. Ὃν γὰρ τρόπον ὁ διψῶν, πρὸς τὴν πηγὴν κατασπεύδει, οὕτω καὶ πᾶσα ψυχὴ πιστοτάτη πρὸς σὲ κατατρέχει, ἐμπλησθῆναι τῆς σῆς φλεγομένη βοηθείας.	blessed are you to generations of generations; (353C) but also in you have all the tribes of the earth been blessed (cf. Gen. 12.3 etc.). For there is no place where you are not glorified, nor tribe, from which fruit has not sprouted from you for God; so that even the nations which have not known you in this world, at an acceptable time (Isaiah 49.8; cf. 2 Cor. 6.2) will call you blessed, O Virgin. For when he who is born from you will come "to judge the inhabited world in righteousness" (Ps. 97.9 LXX), "they will see and beat their breasts" (Zach. 12.10 LXX) those who did not wish to confess you in faith as Theotokos. And then they will know,(356A) of what a treasure they have deprived themselves by their evil counsel. But to us Christians who venerate you with a Christian faith as Theotokos, stretch out the mercy of your unchangeable advocacy. For we rightly recognize your falling-asleep to be life, and we trust to have you as a spiritual house-mate. And when tribulation . . . you are near, seeking you we are ransomed. And when again it is time for joy, it is you who bring this. And when among all we are troubled, we trust that you are with us. For as the thirsty man	Dormition II (H) (P Cult 181 ftn.9) and)(P Cult 181 ftn.12 for 356A)

	Καὶ πάλιν ὥσπερ τὸ τοῦ ἀέρος ἆσθμα ζωτικὴν τοῖς ἀνθρώποις ἐμπνέει τὴν ὄσφρησιν· οὕτω καὶ σὲ παντὸς ὀρθοδόξου Χριστιανοῦ ἐπὶ στόματος προφέρει πνοή.	hurries to the spring, so also every faithful soul runs to you, burning to be filled with your assistance. And again as the breath of air blows a life-giving aroma to mankind, so also the breath of every orthodox Christian carries you in the mouth.	
356B	Ἄγγελοι ταῖς οὐρανίων ἐγγαυριῶνται καταμοναῖς· ἡμεῖς τοῖς τῶν ἁγιωτάτων σου ναῶν εὐφραινόμεθα σχολασμοῖς. Εἰ γὰρ ὁ Σολομώντειος ναός, πάλαι τὸν οὐρανὸν ἐπὶ τῆς γῆς ἐσκιογράφει, πόσῳ μᾶλλον ἐμψύχου σοῦ ναοῦ γεγονυίας τοῦ Χριστοῦ, μὴ καὶ τὰς Ἐκκλησίας τὰς σὰς, ὡς ἐπιγείους οὐρανοὺς δικαίως ἔστιν ἀνακομπάζειν; ἀστέρες λαμπηδογλωσσοῦσιν ἐν τῷ στερεώματι τοῦ οὐρανοῦ·	Angels rejoice in the mansions of the heavens; we delight to spend time in your holy temples. For if the temple of Solomon formerly made a shadow of heaven on earth, how much more when you have become a living temple of Christ, is it not right to adorn your churches as earthly heavens? Stars speak brilliantly in the firmament of heaven.	Dormition II (P Cult 183 ftn. 13)
357A	Οὐκοῦν πίστει σε μεθ' ἡμῶν συνανάστροφον ἔχειν ὁμολογοῦμεν. Εἰ μὴ γὰρ ἐν τούτῳ παρηγορούμεθα, ἐξέλιπεν ἂν τῇ ἐπιθυμίᾳ τῇ πρὸς σὲ, τὸ ἡμέτερον πνεῦμα· καὶ πίστει τοὺς οὐρανοὺς, ὡς γέγραπται, κατηρτίσθαι νοοῦμεν· οὕτω καὶ σὲ μετελθοῦσαν συνδιάγωγον καὶ μετὰ τὴν ἐκδημίαν τοῦ σώματος πιστεύομεν ἀναθεωρεῖν. Οὐ γὰρ ὀδύνη τοσαύτη τῇ ψυχῇ, τῆς σαρκὸς ὅταν ἀποσπασθῇ, ὅσον ὀδυνηρότερον σοῦ στερηθῆναι, πανάχραντε. Ὅθεν κατὰ τὸ γεγραμμένον	So in faith we confess that we have you as a companion with us. For if we were not comforted by this, our spirit would have failed in our desire for you. By faith we know that the heavens have been fitted together, as it is written (Heb. 11.3; cf. Gen. 1.1); so also we believe that we will see you going with us as a leader even after our departure from the body. For it is not such a pain for the soul, when it is drawn out of the flesh, as it is more painful to be deprived of you, all-pure one. For this reason it is written, "Even if my body sleeps, my heart wakes" (Cant. 5.2 LXX).	Dormition II (P Cult 183 ftn. 14)

	, «Κἂν τὸ σῶμά σου καθεύδει, ἡ καρδία σου ἀγρυπνεῖ.»		

On pages 181 and 182 ftns 12 and 13 are reversed in Perniola's text.

361D	Ἐγώ σοι τὸν κόσμον χρεώστην ἀναδείξω	I will show you to the world that is your debtor	Dormition III (H)
372C	Πρὸς τίνα γὰρ ἄλλον ἀπελευσόμεθα; Ῥήματα ζωῆς ἔχεις τὰ πρὸς τὸν Θεὸν ὑπὲρ ἡμῶν τῆς σῆς παραθέσεως ἱκετεύματα. Σὺ γὰρ εἶ ἡ πάντοτε ποιήσασα, καὶ ποιεῖν μὴ ἐνδιδοῦσα μεγαλεῖα μεθ' ἡμῶν· καὶ ἅγιον τὸ ὄνομά σου τὸ ἐξ ἀγγέλων καὶ ἀνθρώπων μακαριζόμενον ἐν πάσαις γενεαῖς γενεῶν, ἀπὸ τοῦ νῦν, καὶ ἕως τοῦ αἰῶνος τῶν αἰώνων. Ἀμήν.	For to whom else shall we flee? You have the words of life which are supplications of your intercession on our behalf before God. For you are the one who always does, and never ceases to do great things with us, and holy is your name which is called blessed by angels and men in all generations of generations (Luke 1.48-50), from now and unto the age of ages. Amen.	Dormition III (P Cult 186 ftn. 23)
373C	Πόλις οὐκ ἐπιγείῳ καὶ θνητῷ βασιλεῖ πολιτογραφοῦσα τοὺς ὑπὸ χεῖρα· ἀλλὰ τῷ ἐπουρανίῳ, τῷ εἰς ζωὴν αἰώνιον παραπέμποντι, καὶ βασιλείαν τὴν ἑαυτοῦ τοῖς αὐτῷ ἑπομένοις παρέχοντι.	A city not enrolling her subjects under a mortal and earthly king, but under a heavenly [king] who escorts them to eternal life, and provides his kingdom to those who follow him.	Sash (P Cult 181 ftn.7)
373C —376A	Ἐγκαινίων δέ, ὦ τίμιον καὶ σεπτὸν, ἀκηκοότες, ἀκροατήριον, μὴ νεοκτίστοις οἰκοδομαῖς καὶ ἀρτιπαγέσι κατασκευαῖς τὸ τῶν Ἐγκαινίων ὑπολάβητε ὄνομα, ἀλλὰ τὸν ἐν πνεύματι καινισμὸν, καθ' ὃν ὁ ἔσω ἡμῶν ἄνθρωπος, τὸ παλαιὸν καὶ διερρωγὸς τῆς ἁμαρτίας ἀποθέμενος ἔνδυμα, καὶ τὸ νέον τῆς εὐσεβείας περιβαλλόμενος, ἐν καινότητι ζωῆς	But of the feast, worthy and august hearers, in this hall, it does not receive its name from newly constructed buildings nor from newly made buildings, but by that which is enriched by the Spirit. That which is inside of us humans. The stripping off of the ancient bonds of sin; and the freshness of the enveloping pity, being a free citizen of the new life. (cf. 2 Cor. 4.17) And the Blameless one rejoices in these, who are pleasing, and in the godly pious, renewed	Sash (P Cult 184 ftn. 17)

	πολιτεύεται. Τούτοις καὶ ἡ πανάμωμος εὐφραίνεται· οἷς ἀνάρετaῖς, καὶ τῇ κατὰ Θεὸν εὐσεβεῖ καινιζόμενοι πολιτείᾳ, οὕτω καὶ τῶν ἁγνῶν τῆς ἁγνῆς ἁγνῶς Ἐγκαινίων κατατρυφήσωμεν· καὶ ὡς αὐτῇ παρούσῃ μέλλοντες προσιέναι, οὕτω τῷ ταύτης σεβασμίῳ ναῷ προσερχόμενοι, πάντα ῥυθμίσωμεν, καὶ πάντα πρὸς τὸ κρεῖττον μεταβαλλώμεθα· πρᾶξίν τε καὶ λόγον, καὶ θεωρίαν. Μηδὲν ἔστω ἡμῶν τῆς ἡμέρας ἀνάξιον· μὴ βῆμα ποδός, μὴ γέλως ὀδόντων, τὸ δὴ λεγόμενον· μὴ στολισμὸς ἐσθῆτος πρὸς τὸ ἀπρεπὲς ἐκτρεπέσθωσαν.	citizenship, and in this manner we shall celebrate in purity the purity of the purely pure feast, and as we are about to approach this event, in like manner, we come to this holy temple, we shall bring into order all things, and we shall transform all things to the better, in act and in word and thought. Let nothing of us be unworthy of today, neither the walking of the feet, not laughing[14], nor word; do not be turned aside by unsuitable clothing.	
376B	Συνεκλάμπει γὰρ ταύτῃ καὶ ἡ τιμίας καὶ σεβασμίας αὐτῆς ζώνης κατάθεσις καὶ προσκύνησις· καὶ τῶν πανακράντων τοῦ ταύτης Υἱοῦ σπαργάνων τῶν τιμιωτάτων. Ζώνης ἐκείνης, ἣ τὸν πανάγιον ἐκεῖνο περιέσφιγγε σῶμα, καὶ τὸν ἐν κοιλίᾳ κρυπτόμενον Θεὸν περιέβαλλε. Ζώνης ἐκείνης, ἥτις	For in this city is shown forth both the disposition and veneration of the holy, honorable sash of the Theotokos and the all holy and most worthy[15] swaddling clothes of her Son. That Sash, which wrapped around her body, and surrounded in the womb the hidden God. That Sash, which beautifully adorned the container of God, and most holy.	Sash (P Cult 184 ftn 18)

---

[14] Mary Cunningham mentions that this is a strange Greek expression: μὴ γέλως ὀδόντων whose meaning is presumably to laugh showing the teeth. Cunningham, Wider, 248 ftn 3.

[15] Mary Cunningham emends the word πανακράντων to παναχράντων. The former does not appear in either a search of the *TLG* or Lampe (except in this passage of Germanos). Ἄκραντος does appear in *LSJ*, in Pindar, etc. However the meaning is "unfulfilled," "fruitless," "idle," which would be inappropriate here. The adjective πανάχραντος is a regular epithet of the Theotokos.

	τὴν τοῦ Θεοῦ κιβωτὸν ὡραίως κατεκόσμει, καὶ σεμνοτάτως. Ζώνης ἐκείνης, ἣ πολλάκις ἐκ τῶν ἀχράντων τῆς παναχράντου τοῦ γάλακτος κατεπιαίνετο σταλαγμῶν, Καὶ μήτις ἀπεικὸς εἶναι ἡγήσαιτο τοῦτο τῶν μεμψιμοίρων, ὡς ἐμψύχοις διαλεξόμεθα, καὶ τὴν εὐφημίαν προσοίσομεν.	That sash, that was enriched by the all-pure drips of milk of the most-pure one. And let no one of the grumblers, (cf. Judges 16) think it unreasonable that we shall speak as having life, and we shall offer the praises.	
376B/C	Εἰ γὰρ ἀγγεῖον μύρῳ προσομιλῆσαν κἂν πρὸς βραχὺ, καὶ τούτου κενωθέντος οἶδε μέχρι πολλοῦ τὴν εὐωδίαν διαφυλάττειν, τί ἂν τις εἴποι περὶ τῆς, τὸ ὄντως ἀκένωτον ἐκεῖνο καὶ θεῖον μύρον, τὸ καθαρώτατον λέγω τῆς Θεοτόκου σῶμα καὶ παναμώμητον, περιειλησάσης ζώνης, καὶ συμπλακείσης μέχρι πολλοῦ; Οὐκ εἰς αἰῶνα τὴν εὐωδίαν τὴν ἰαμάτων παραφυλάξειε, καὶ τοῖς πίστει καὶ πόθῳ προσιοῦσιν ἐμπλήσειεν; Εὐωδίαν, οὐχὶ θηλυτικήν τινα καὶ ἀπόβλητον, ἀλλὰ θείαν καὶ πανσεβάσμιον· παθῶν ψυχῆς τε καὶ σώματος θερμοτάτην ἐλάτειρα.	For if a vessel contains an unguent for only a short time and then is emptied yet the odor of the unguent remains for a long time. This being true, what might one say about the Sash, and that truly un-emptied and holy myrrh—I mean the true and blameless body of the Theotokos, and the Sash that was tied about her middle, embracing her for a long time? Would not the fabric preserve the odor for a long time, and would not those who draw near with faith and love be filled? A sweet smell, not like that of women's perfume, but a divine and august fragrance, driving away the passions of the soul and body.	Sash (P Cult 184 ftn. 19)
376D— 377B/C	Perniola mentions this long anaphora on the Sash in which are contained references to the cult. Germanos mentions a personal experience in this part. "Oh Sash, you both bound up and restrained the weakness of our nature and hobble both our seen and unseen enemies! For such things happen to me being pierced by the all holy One and being carried away by the force of my words, I have forgotten about the winding sheet." This section also contain reference to the swaddling clothes which Germanos seems to have forgotten until this point. (376D) Sash (Cult 185 ftn. 21)		

Gregory E. Roth

380A	Ὡς γὰρ τὸ σῶμα ἡμῶν ζωτικῆς ἐνεργείας τὸ ἀναπνεῖν τεκμήριον κέκτηται, οὕτω καὶ τὸ σὸν πανάγιον ὄνομα ἀδιαλείπτως ἐν τοῖς τῶν σῶν δούλων ἅγιον ὄνομα ἀδιαλείπτως ἐν τοῖς τῶν σῶν δούλων στόμασι προφερόμενον ἐν παντὶ καιρῷ καὶ τόπῳ καὶ τρόπῳ, ζωῆς καὶ θυμηδίας καὶ βοηθείας οὐχὶ τεκμήριον, ἀλλὰ πρόξενον γίνεται. Σκέποις ἡμᾶς πτέρυξι τῆς σῆς ἀγαθότητος. Φρουρήσῃς ἡμᾶς ταῖς μεσιτείαις σου. Παράσχοις ἡμῖν τὴν αἰώνιον ζωήν, Χριστιανῶν ἐλπὶς ἀκαταίσχυντε.	The breath and the life of Christians, for just as our bodies have breath as a sign of its living energy, so also your all holy name continually being carried forth on the lips of your servant in all times and places and points, not [only] a sure sign of life, wellbeing and aid, but a defender. Shelter us under the wings of your great goodness. (*cf.* Ps. 17.8) Guard us through your intercession. Supply to us life eternal, a reliable hope of Christians.	Sash (P Cult 182 ftn. 11)
380C	Τίς οὕτω τοῦ τῶν ἀνθρώπων γένους μετὰ τὸν σὸν Υἱὸν ὡς σὺ προνοεῖται; Τίς οὕτως ἀντιληπτικῶς τῶν ἡμετέρων προΐσταται θλίψεων;	Who then, but you after your Son, would take thought of the race of men? Who then defends us by taking our part in tribulation?	Sash (P Cult 182 ftn. 10)
381B/C	Σὺ τὰς τοῦ πονηροῦ κατὰ τῶν σῶν δούλων ἐπαναστάσεις, τῇ κλήσει σου μόνῃ τῇ παναγίᾳ ἀποδιώκουσα διασώζεις. Σὺ τοὺς ἐπικαλουμένους σε ἐκ πάσης ἀνάγκης, ἐκ παντοίων πειρασμῶν προφθάνουσα ἐκλυτροῦσαι, πανάμωμε. Ὅθεν καὶ τῷ σῷ ναῷ σπουδαίως προστρέχομεν· καὶ ἐν αὐτῷ ἑστῶτες, ἐν οὐρανῷ ἑστάναι νομίζομεν. Ἐν τούτῳ δοξολογοῦντές σε, ἀγγέλοις συγχορεύειν	You continue to protect your servants from the host of evil, you continue to preserve those who flee only to your holy name. You continue to anticipate ransoming those who call upon you in all needs, and all sorts of temptation, Oh all blameless one. For which reason we speedily flee to your temple; and standing in it we know ourselves to be in heaven We praise you in it joining with the choir of the angels. For what race of men is well off without being Christians	Sash (P Cult 185 ftn. 20)

452

ἡγούμεθα. Ποῖον γὰρ γένος ἀνθρώπων πάρεξ Χριστιανῶν τοιαύτης εὐπόρησε δόξης, τοιαύτης ἐπέτυχεν ἀντιλήψεως, τοιαύτης προστασίας πεπλούτηκε; Τίς πιστῶς τῇ τιμίᾳ σου ζώνῃ προσατενίσας, Θεοτόκε, οὐκ εὐθὺς θυμηδίας ἐμπίπλαται; Τίς θερμῶς ταύτῃ προσπεσών, κενὸς τῆς συμφερούσης αἰτήσεως ἐξελήλυθε; Τίς τὸν σὸν χαρακτῆρα ἐνοπτριζόμενος, οὐκ αὐτίκα πάσης θλίψεως ἐπιλέλησται;	and having such a defense and advocacy? Who gazing in faith, when he has gazed at your worthy Sash, Theotokos, is not filled with delight? Who fervently falling down before it, vainly lifts up offerings of praise? Who contemplating your character[16], does not forget immediately all his tribulation?	

---

[16]   Mary Cunningham translates this phrase as referring to an image of the Virgin or the Sash. It is a difficult passage. See Cunningham, Wider 254 ftn. 16.

References to Debt to Mary in Germanos I, Patriarch of Constantinople (715-730)

PG 98 Location	Greek	English	Homily
340A	Ὁ χρεωστῶν, πάντοτε τὸν ἴδιον εὐεργέτην ἀνυμνεῖ. Ὁ σωζόμενος, οὐκ ἀγνοεῖ τοῦ οἰκείου Σωτῆρος τὴν σκέπην.	The debtor always praises his own benefactor. He who is being saved does not fail to recognize the protection of his own savior.	Dormition I
352C	Ἐπὰν γὰρ πολλὰ χρεωστῶν οὐδὲν ἀνταποδίδωσί σοι, πληθύνει τὴν εὐχαριστίαν, ὡς σὺ τὴν προστασίαν.	For although he is greatly in your debt he gives you nothing in return, he multiplies thanksgiving, [just] as you [multiply] your advocacy.	Dormition II
361D	Ἐγώ σοι τὸν κόσμον χρεώστην ἀναδείξω, καὶ μετερχομένης πλεῖον σοῦ τὸ ὄνομα καταδοξάσω.	I will show you to the world that is your debtor, and I will glorify your name even more as you are translated.	Dormition III
While there are references to the unworthiness of Germanos himself and those who attempt to praise Mary found in the Homilies on the Presentation and the Sash none makes specific reference to the debt owned to Mary.			

References to the Dormition of Mary in Germanos I, Patriarch of Constantinople (715-730)

PG 98 Location	Greek	English	Homily
340C	τῆς νῦν ὑποθέσεως, τῆς τιμίας καὶ ἐνδόξου σου, Θεομῆτορ, μεταστάσεως, ἀπάρξηται τὸν ὕμνον.	let it begin the hymn of the present topic, your honorable and glorious translation.	Dormition I
345B	Σὺ, κατὰ τὸ γεγραμμένον, «ἐν καλλονῇ·» καὶ τὸ σῶμά σου τὸ παρθενικὸν, ὅλον ἅγιον, ὅλον ἁγνὸν, ὅλον Θεοῦ κατοικητήριον· ὡς ἐκ τούτου λοιπὸν καὶ ἀλλότριον χοϊκῆς ἀναλύσεως. Ἐναλλαγὲν μὲν ὡς ἀνθρώπινον πρὸς ἄκραν ἀφθαρσίας ζωήν· σῶον δὲ τοῦτο καὶ ὑπερένδοξον, ζωοτελὲς καὶ ἀκοίμητον· καθ' ὅτιπερ οὐδὲ ἦν δυνατὸν παρὰ νεκροποιοῦ συνκλεισμοῦ τοῦτο κρατηθῆναι, ὡς σκεῦος ὑπάρχον θεηδόχον, καὶ ἔμψυχος ναὸς τῆς τοῦ Μονογενοῦς παναγίας θεότητος. Ἕνεκεν δὴ τούτων, μεθ' ἡμῶν σε, Θεοτόκε, πιστεύομεν περινοστεῖν.	You, as it is written, [are] "in beauty" (Cant 2.3 LXX) and your virginal body, altogether holy, altogether pure, altogether the residence of God; so because of this [it is] separated and alien from earthly dissolution. While remaining human it is changed to the sublime life of incorruptibility. This is safe and supremely glorious, life-accomplishing [it's life ended] and unsleeping; as it was not possible for this to be controlled by death-dealing confinement, being a God-receiving vessel, and a living temple of the all-holy divinity of the Only-begotten One. Because of these things, we trust that you, O Theotokos, will return home with us.	
345C	Πῶς γὰρ εἶχε διάλυσις σαρκὸς πρὸς χοῦν καὶ κόνιν ἀνθυποστρέψαι σε, τὴν ἀπὸ θανάτου καταφθορᾶς, τὸν ἄνθρωπον, διὰ τῆς τοῦ Υἱοῦ σου λυτρωσαμένην σαρκώσεως;	For how could dissolution of the body to earth and dust recur in you who from the corruption of death ransomed mankind through the incarnation of your Son?	Dormition I

345D	τὸ σὸν τῆς κοιμήσεως ζωοπαράδεκτον μνῆμα	the memorial of your life-receiving dormition	Dormition I
348A	θεοχώρητον οὖσαν ἀγγεῖον	a God-containing vessel	Dormition I
348A	καὶ καθάπερ ὕπνον τὴν κοίμησιν ὑπολαβεῖν	to experience death simply as sleep	Dormition I
348A	τὴν μετάστασιν ὡς Μητέρα τῆς Ζωῆς	translation like arising as Mother of Life.	Dormition I
348B	Οἶκος γὰρ αὐτῷ καταπαύσεως σὺ γέγονας σωματικός, Θεοτόκε, καὶ τόπος ἀναπαύσεως αὐτὸς χρηματίζει μεταστάσει, πανύμνητε. «Αὕτη γὰρ, φησὶν, ἡ κατάπαυσίς μου εἰς αἰῶνα αἰῶνος·» τουτέστιν, Ἡ ἐκ σοῦ περιβληθεῖσα τούτῳ, Θεοτόκε, σάρξ· μεθ’ ἧς οὐ μόνον εἰς τὸν παρόντα τοῦτον αἰῶνα ἐπιφανεὶς ὁ Χριστὸς ἐπιστεύθη, ἀλλὰ καὶ κατὰ τὸν μέλλοντα αἰῶνα, σὺν τῇ τοιαύτῃ σου σαρκὶ, ἐρχόμενος κρῖναι ζῶντας καὶ νεκροὺς ἐμφανισθήσεται. Ἄρα οὖν, ὡς αἰωνίας σου τούτῳ καταπαύσεως οὔσης, πρὸς αὐτὸν ἀδιάφθορον προσελάβετό σε,	For you have become a corporeal house of rest for him, O Theotokos, and you are called the very place of repose by your translation, all-praised one. "For this is my rest," he/it says, "unto the age of the age;" (Psalm 131.14 LXX) that is, the flesh put on by him from you, O Theotokos—with which we believe that Christ has appeared not only for this present age, but also will be revealed in the coming age, with such flesh from you, coming to judge the living and the dead. So since you are his eternal resting-place, he took you to himself free from corruption,	Dormition I
349A	μετάστασις ἀπὸ θανάτου	you are the removal from death	Dormition II
349B	καὶ πρὸς τὴν ζωὴν ἐπανῆλθες	and passed over to life	Dormition II
356A	Καὶ τὴν γὰρ κοίμησίν σου, Θεοτόκε, ζωὴν ἡγούμεθα δικαίως	For we rightly recognize your falling-asleep to be life, O Theotokos	Dormition II
357A	Ἐρρέτω τάφος ἐπὶ σοί,	Away with the tomb for you	Dormition II
357B	Καὶ κἂν τὸ ἀπαραίτητον τοῦ θανάτου, τῇ ἀνθρωπίνῃ παρεδέξω φύσει	even though you have received the inevitability of death due to your human nature,	Dormition II
357B	Οὐκ ἀμάρτυρος γὰρ ἡ μετάστασίς σου· οὐδὲ ψευδὴς ἡ κοίμησις	For your translation does not lack witness, nor is your dormition a deception	Dormition II

357C	καὶ τούτου χάριν, τὸ θεηδόχον σου σῶμα, παρὰ νεκροποιοῦ καταφθορᾶς, ἔπρεπεν ὄντως μὴ συγκλεισθῆναι·	And for the sake of this, it was truly fitting that your God-receiving body should not be shut in by deathly corruption,	Dormition II
357D	ἀλλὰ καὶ τὸν τάφον ὡς ἀνθρώπινον ὑποδέξασθαι τὸ ἴδιον φύραμα· καὶ σοῦ ζωοτελῶς πρὸς τὰ οὐράνια, τῆς οἰκείας μεταστάσης ζωῆς	but that the tomb received its own mixture as human, and with a living conclusion of your own life transferring to the heavenly places.	Dormition II
360A	Καὶ ἡ περὶ τῆς σωματικῆς κοιμήσεως τῆς Ζωοτόκου καὶ ἀειπαρθένου Μαρίας διήγησις	And the exposition concerning the corporeal falling-asleep of the life-bearing and ever-virgin Mary	Dormition III
360B	τῆς ἀειμνήστου μεταστάσεως αὐτῆς	her ever-memorable translation.	Dormition III
360B	τὸ τῆς κοιμήσεως προμηνύει παραστατικόν	her falling-asleep contrary to the usual	Dormition III
360C	Ὁρῶντα γὰρ τὴν σὴν πρὸς ἐμὲ τιμητικὴν . . . μετάθεσιν	As I see your honorable transfer towards me	Dormition III
361B	μεταβαινούσης σου τοῦ βίου	when you pass over from life	Dormition III
361D	καὶ μετερχομένης πλεῖον σοῦ τὸ ὄνομα καταδοξάσω	I will glorify your name even more as you are translated	Dormition III
364A	Προσανακλήθητι, καὶ μόνον ἐν σχήματι τῷ Γεθσημανῆ τοῦ μνήματος χωρίῳ	Be summoned upwards, and only in appearance [be summoned] to Gethsemane the place of the tomb	Dormition III
364A	καθὼς ἐγὼ πρὸ τοῦ παθεῖν με δι᾽ ἀνθρωπίνην προσευχὴν ἐκεῖσε τὰ γόνατα. Σοῦ γὰρ προτυπούμενος τὴν κοίμησιν, ἔκλινα κἀγὼ πρὸς τὸ τοιοῦτον χωρίον τὰ ἐμὰ τοῦ ἐκ σοῦ σώματος γόνατα. Ὡς οὖν ἐγὼ μετὰ τὴν τότε γονυκλισίαν πρὸς τὸν ζωοποιὸν ἐξῆλθον καὶ ἑκούσιον τοῦ σταυροῦ μου θάνατον, καὶ σὺ μετὰ τὴν κατάθεσιν τοῦ σοῦ λειψάνου πρὸς ζωὴν παραχρῆμα μετατεθήσῃ	as I before I suffered set down my knees there in a human prayer. For prefiguring your dormition, I myself also bent the knees of my body towards such a place. So as I after the kneeling at that time went forth to my life-giving and willing death on the cross, you also after the laying-down of your remains will immediately be transferred to life.	Dormition III

364B	ἐπὶ τιμῇ τῆς ἐξόδου σου, πανάχραντε	for the honor of your departure, all-pure one	Dormition III
364C	Ἑτοιμάζει προθύμως τὰ πρὸς τὴν ἔξοδον	She eagerly prepares [the necessities] for her departure	Dormition III
364C	Δημοσιεύει τὴν μετάστασιν	She makes public announcement of her translation	Dormition III
364C	μετερχομένην	going over	Dormition III
365C	μεταστάσει	translation	Dormition III
365D	μετατιθεμένης	transferred	Dormition III
368B	μετατεθῆναί	transferred	Dormition III
368B	διίσταται τῆς σαρκὸς ἐν ἐγρηγόρσει	she departs from the flesh in awakening	Dormition III
368B	ἐλευθέραν φθορᾶς τὴν κατάλειψιν αὐτῆς ποιησαμένη	making her leave-taking free from corruption	Dormition III
368D	ἀποικίᾳ	departure	Dormition III
369C	ὑφ' οὗ καὶ μεταστᾶσαν αὐτὴν πιστωθέντες	Being convinced that she was translated by him	Dormition III
369D 372A	Ἴδε ὁ τόπος, ὅπου τέθαπται μὲν ἡ Παρθένος· μετετέθη δὲ ἡ ζωοτόκος Μαρία. Ἴδε καὶ ἡ σινδὼν χωρὶς τῆς ἔνδον σπαργαν-ωθείσης ἐπιζητοῦσα τὴν ἐν αὐτῇ κατασφιγχθεῖσαν, ἣν ὡς ἄψυχον ἐσπαργάνου, καὶ ὡς ἐμψύχῳ νῦν ὑποστρωθῆναι ποθεῖ.	Behold the place where the Virgin is buried, but Mary the life-bearer has been translated. Behold also the shroud without her who was wrapped in it, seeking her who was bound tightly in it, whom it wrapped as a lifeless [body] and now desires to be spread under as for a living [person].	Dormition III
372A	καὶ μετατεθεῖσαν	and transferred	Dormition III
372B	γέγονεν ἀφανής	at this became invisible	Dormition III
372B	τὸ μνῆμα κενὸν ἀφῆκεν	she left the tomb empty	Dormition III

References to Mary as Empress or Queen in Germanos I, Patriarch of Constantinople (715-730)

PG 98 Location	Greek	English	Homily
297C	ἐμὴ παῖς βασιλικώτατα	my regal child	Presentation I
304A	Καθέσθητι, ὦ Δέσποινα· καὶ πρέπει γάρ σοι τῇ βασιλίσσῃ καὶ ὑπὲρ πάσας τὰς βασιλείας τοῦ κόσμου δεδοξασμένη, ἐν τοιαύτῃ βαθμίδι ἐφέζεσθαι.	Sit down O Lady, for it is proper to you as the Queen glorified above all earthly kingdoms to be seated upon such steps.	Presentation I
304A	Εὐπρεπές σοι τῷ Χερουβικωτάτῳ θρόνῳ ὁ ἡγιασμένος τόπος εἰς κατοικητήριον.	This holy place is a fitting dwelling for you who are the throne of the Cherubim.	Presentation I
304B	ὡς παντανάσσῃ	Queen of all	Presentation I
309B	ἰδοὺ πρόοδος τῆς ἀμωμήτου νύμφης· ἰδοὺ προπομπὴ πρώτη τῆς βασιλίδος· ἰδοὺ σήμαντρον ἀκριβὲς τῆς ἐσομένης περὶ αὐτὴν δόξης·	Behold, the arrival of the blameless bride (cf. 2 Peter 3.14). Behold, the first procession of the queen. Behold, an accurate sign of the glory which will surround her.	Presentation II
316C	δεῦρο, Δέσποινα τῶν γηγενῶν ἁπάντων· εἴσελθε εἰς τὴν δόξαν τοῦ Κυρίου σου· τέως μὲν, εἰς τὴν κάτω καὶ πατουμένην, μετ' οὐ πολὺ δὲ, εἰς τὴν ἄνω καὶ ἄβατον ἀνθρώποις.	Come here, mistress of all born on earth. Enter into the glory of your Lord: for now, into [the glory] here below where men walk, but after a short time, into the [glory] above which is inaccessible to human beings."	Presentation II

321A	σκηνὴ ὡς ἀληθῶς πορφυροποίητος	the true royal tabernacle	Annunciation
321C	τὴν οὐράνιον νύμφην καὶ βασιλίδα καὶ Θεοτόκον	heavenly bride and queen, the Theotokos	Annunciation
324B	Τάχα δὲ καὶ ἣν κατέχεις πορφύραν, προμηνύει τὸ βασιλικὸν ἀξίωμα	Perhaps even that purple thread you are holding foretells your royal status	Annunciation
325A	Θρόνος θεοβάστακτος, καὶ βασιλικὴ καθέδρα τοῦ ἐπουρανίου Βασιλέως κληθήσῃ, καθότι Βασίλισσα καὶ Δέσποινα, καὶ βασιλέως ἐπιγείου θυγάτηρ τυγχάνεις, καὶ χαρακτῆρα ἔχεις βασιλικόν	You shall be called the throne which bears God, the royal seat of the heavenly King. As you are Queen and Virgin, and a daughter of [David] the earthly king, so you have a royal character.	Annunciation
325A	βασιλικὴ καθέδρα τοῦ ἐπουρανίου Βασιλέως κληθήσῃ	the royal seat of the heavenly King	Annunciation
325A	Θρόνος Ὑψίστου ἐγὼ πῶς γενήσομαι, ἑρμήνευσόν μοι, ὁ λαλῶν μοι· καὶ πῶς τὸ ὑπὲρ ἥλιον φῶς ἐκεῖνο τὸ ἀψηλάφητον ψηλαφήσει σὰρξ πηλίνη; Ἀμήχανα κηρύττεις, νεανίσκε, εὐαγγέλια.	How shall I become the throne of the Most High? Answer me, you who are speaking to me! How can flesh made of clay touch the unapproachable light which is brighter than the Sun? You are proclaiming impossible news, young man.	Annunciation
325A	χαρακτῆρα ἔχεις βασιλικόν	so you have a royal character.	Annunciation
328A	Ξενίζομαι, δεδοξασμένη, ὅτι ἀκμὴν διστάζεις με τὸν ἐκ τοσούτων ὑψωμάτων εἰς σὲ παραγενόμενον. Ἐμὲ γὰρ ἔξεστι μᾶλλον εὐλαβεῖσθαί σε ὡς Μητέρα Κυρίου μου μέλλουσαν ἔσεσθαι, καὶ τρέμειν σου τὸ βασιλικὸν ἀξίωμα.	I cannot comprehend, O holy one, that you are doubtful about me who come to you from on high. Rather, I should be cautious concerning you as you are about to become the mother of my Lord, and I should tremble in your royal presence.	Annunciation

328A	Ὅλη διόλου καθαρὰ καὶ ἄμεμπτος τυγχάνουσα, θαυμάζω πῶς ἐπὶ τοσοῦτον τοῖς ἐμοῖς ἠπίστησας ῥήμασιν, ἡ κεχαριτωμένη. Ἰδοὺ <γὰρ> ὁ Βασιλεὺς τῆς δόξης, ὡς λογίζομαι, ἔτι λαλοῦντός μου, ἐν σοὶ τῇ βασιλίδι ἐνῴκησεν.	You have been entirely pure and blameless. I am amazed that you have so much distrusted my words, O full of grace. Behold even as I speak, I think that the King of Glory has made his residence in you, O Queen.	Annunciation
329C	Χαρακτῆρα φέρουσα βασιλικόν, καὶ εἰς τὰ βασίλεια τῆς ἐμῆς Βηθλεὲμ τιθηνήσασα, καὶ εἰς ἅγια ἐκ παιδόθεν ἀμέμπτως διαπρέψασα· καὶ παρθένος λοιπὸν τυγχάνουσα, πῶς ἐγὼ μήτηρ ἀκούσω τοῦ παιδός μου;	I am of royal blood, and spent my earliest childhood in the royal house of Bethlehem, and my childhood I spent blamelessly in the temple; and being a virgin up to now, how can I be called the mother of my child?	Annunciation
336B	οὐχ ὡς βασιλίδι τινὶ διαλεγόμενος·	You do not converse with me like a queen	Annunciation
340B	Δέσποινα	Mistress	Dormition I
357A	Ἐρρέτω χοῦς ἐπὶ σοί· ἀνάπλασις γὰρ εἶ, ὅτι τοῖς ἐν ὕλῃ πηλοῦ διαφθαρεῖσι κεχρημάτικας, Δέσποινα.	Away with earth poured over you; for you are the re-fashion-ing, because you have been called Mistress of those who have perished in the substance of clay	Dormition II
372B	καὶ τὸν παράδεισον τῆς ἰδίας ἐγέμισε δόξης, καὶ τῆς οὐρανίου ζωῆς τὴν κατάπαυσιν ἔχει· καὶ μετὰ τῆς τοῦ Θεοῦ τρυφῆς συγκάτοικος ὑπάρχει.	and she filled paradise with her own glory, and she has the rest of eternal life, and she is a companion of the luxury of God."	Dormition III
381D/ 384A	Ἔπιδε ἐξ ἁγίου κατοικητηρίου σου τούτου τὸ περιεστώς σοι πιστότατον ἄθροισμα, τὸ σὲ Κυρίαν καὶ προστάτιν καὶ Δέσποιναν ἔχειν κατα-πλουτῆσαν,	Behold the most faithful gathering which surrounds you from this your holy dwelling, which is rich in having you as Lady, patroness and Mistress	Sash

References to Heaven and Earth in Germanos I, Patriarch of Constantinople (715-730)

PG 98 Location	Greek	English	Homily
325B	Κἂν ἡ μορφή μου καταπλήττει σε, ἀλλ᾽ οἶδα ὅτι τὰ ῥήματα τοῦ στόματός μου μεγάλης δόξης πρόξενά σοι γενήσονται· καὶ μακαρίσει σε λοιπὸν ὁ οὐρανὸς καὶ ἡ γῆ.	Even though my voice and my form terrify you, I know that the words of my mouth shall become a harbinger of ineffable joy to you. And all heaven and earth shall bless you (*cf.* Luke 1.48).	Annunciation
340D	Τῶν ἐπιγείων ὅταν μετέστης, τῶν οὐρανίων προδήλως ἐπέβης· πλὴν οὔτε πρώην τῶν οὐρανίων ἡμοίρεις, οὔτε μετατεθεῖσα τῶν ἐπιγείων ἐξέστης· ἐπειδὴ, καὶ τῶν ἐν οὐρανοῖς ταγμάτων ὑψηλοτέρα κατέστης, καὶ τῶν ἐπὶ γῆς ποιημάτων ὑπερτέρα κατεφάνης. Ἐπ᾽ ἀληθείας γὰρ, καὶ τοὺς οὐρανοὺς ἐκαλλώπισας, καὶ τὴν γῆν ὑπερελάμπρυνας, Θεοτόκε. Τοὺς μὲν οὐρανοὺς, ὅπιπερ ἅμα τοῦ στῆναι τὰ τῶν ἀνθρώπων γένη, ἄγγελοι τῆς τούτων ἐπιτροπεύειν προετάχθησαν ζωῆς· τοῦ ὁδηγεῖν, καὶ διοικεῖν, καὶ φυλάττειν αὐτοὺς, ἐν τῇ πρὸς Θεὸν	When you left earthly [places], you obviously entered the heavenly [places]; except earlier you were not lacking participation in the heavenly, nor did you depart from the earthly when you were transferred, since you were made more sublime than the ranks in heaven, and you were revealed as higher than the deeds of earth. For in truth, you beautified the heavens, and you illuminated the earth, O Theotokos. For when the heavens along with the generations of men were established, angels were assigned to tend their life; and to guide, and administer, and	Dormition I

	ἀμεταθέτῳ πίστεως καρδίᾳ. «Ἔστησε γὰρ, φησὶν, ὅρια ἐθνῶν κατὰ ἀριθμὸν ἀγγέλων Θεοῦ.»	guard them, with an unchanging heart of faith towards God. "For he established," it is said, "bounds for the nations according to the number of the angels of God." (Deut. 32.8, Odes 2.8)	
341D	Γαστέρα γὰρ προεωσφόρον, τὴν γεννητικὴν τοῦ προουρανίου καὶ ἐπιγείου Φωτὸς ὠνόμασεν ἡ Γραφὴ πρόοδον· τοῦ δειχθῆναι ὅτι πρὸ πάσης κτίσεως ὁρωμένης καὶ ἀοράτου, ὁ Μονογενὴς ὑπὸ τοῦ Πατρὸς ἀνάρχως, ἐκ Φωτὸς ἐγεννήθη Φῶς·	For Scripture called "womb before the morning star" the generative procession of the Light which was before the heavens and appeared on earth: to show that before all visible and invisible creation the Only-begotten was born from the Father without beginning, Light was born from Light.	Dormition I
344B	Ἐπὰν οὖν, παναγία Θεομῆτορ, ὁ οὐρανὸς, καὶ ἡ γῆ μᾶλλον εἰπεῖν, διὰ σοῦ κατεκομίσθη,	So since, O all-holy Mother of God, heaven, and what is more [the] earth, that through you was brought into a place of refuge,	Dormition I
344C	ἐπειδὴ καὶ οὐρανὸς θεοχώρητος ἀνεδείχθης τοῦ ὑψίστου Θεοῦ, διὰ τὸν χωρητικὸν κόλπον σου πρὸς αὐτοῦ βασταγμοῦ· καὶ γῆ πάλιν αὐτῷ πνευματική, διὰ χωρητικὴν ὑπουργίαν ἐχρημάτισας τῆς σαρκός σου	For when you were proved to be a God-containing heaven of the most high God, since your bosom [was] able to carry(ing) Him, and again you were called a spiritual earth because of the [God-] containing service of your flesh.	Dormition I
356B	Ποῖον γὰρ γένος ἀνθρώπων, πάρεξ εἰπεῖν Χριστιανῶν, τοιαύτης ἐπέτυχε δόξης, τοιαύτης εὐπόρησεν ὑπολήψεως; Ἄγγελοι ταῖς οὐρανίων ἐγγαυριῶνται καταμοναῖς· ἡμεῖς τοῖς τῶν ἁγιωτάτων σου	For what race of men, not to speak [only] of Christians, has obtained such glory, has abounded in such support? Angels rejoice in the mansions of the heavens; we delight to spend time in your	Dormition II

	ναῶν εὐφραινόμεθα σχολασμοῖς. Εἰ γὰρ ὁ Σολομώντειος ναός, πάλαι τὸν οὐρανὸν ἐπὶ τῆς γῆς ἐσκιογράφει, πόσῳ μᾶλλον ἐμψύχου σοῦ ναοῦ γεγονυίας τοῦ Χριστοῦ, μὴ καὶ τὰς Ἐκκλησίας τὰς σὰς, ὡς ἐπιγείους οὐρανοὺς δικαίως ἔστιν ἀνακομπάζειν; ἀστέρες λαμπηδογλωσσοῦσιν ἐν τῷ στερεώματι τοῦ οὐρανοῦ·	holy temples. For if the temple of Solomon formerly made a shadow of heaven on earth, how much more when you have become a living temple of Christ, is it not right to adorn your churches as earthly heavens? Stars speak brilliantly in the firmament of heaven.	
360C	Καθὼς οὖν τὴν γῆν καὶ τοὺς ἐν τῇ γῇ χαρᾶς ἐπλήρωσας, κεχαριτωμένη, χαροποίησον καὶ τὰ οὐράνια πάλιν.	So as you filled the earth and those on the earth with joy, O blessed one, now make the heavenly places also joyous.	Dormition III
No references found in the Sash			

References to History in Germanos I
Patriarch of Constantinople
(715-730)

PG 98 Location	Greek	English	Homily
361D/ 364A	ἄφες τὴν κάτω Ἰερουσαλήμ· ἀνάδραμε πρὸς τὴν οὐράνιον πόλιν, ὅτι τῆς κάτω Ἰερουσαλὴμ μεγαλυνθήσεται μετὰ μικρὸν «ὁ κοπετός, ὡς κοπετός, κατὰ τὸ γεγραμμένον, ῥοῶνος ἐκκοπτομένου ἐν πεδίῳ.»	Run up to the heavenly city, because the Jerusalem below [troubles] will be magnified in a short time: "The noise, like the noise," as it is written, "of a pomegranate-orchard being cut down on the plain"	Dormition III
373B	Εἰ γὰρ οἷς τὰ ὀνόματα ἐπὶ τῶν γαιῶν ἐπικέκληνται, εἰς μακρὸν τὴν μνήμην τῆς κλήσεως διασώζουσιν· ἄλλων δὲ ὧν οὐδὲ διὰ χειλέων δίκαιον τὰ ὀνόματα φέρειν, στῆλαι καὶ τεμένη, καὶ εἴδωλα μέχρι καὶ τῆς σήμερον, εἰ καὶ τῇ φήμῃ μόνῃ· ἀλλ' οὖν ὑπερεκτέτανται, καὶ ὡς αὐτοὶ περιόντες, τοῖς τῶν ἀφελεστέρων ὠσὶ διεκωδωνίσθησαν, τί ἄν τις εἴποι περὶ τῆς θεοδοξάστου καὶ πανυμνήτου κόρης τῆς παναχράντου καὶ παναμώμου;	For if those whose names are not longer upon the Earth, are remembered in invocations for a long time, that is those whose names it is not right for us to remember, to whom are build stile and temples, and idols even up to today; if only by reputations; then others remain, as if they were still around, they have hung on the ears of the simpler folk, then what should one say about the God-glorified, ever-praised, all-pure and blameless maiden?	Sash

References to Iconography in Germanos I, Patriarch of Constantinople (715-730)

PG 98 Location	Greek	English	Homily
305B	πηγὴ ἡ θεόβρυτος, ἀφ' ἧς οἱ τῆς θεογνωσίας ποταμοὶ τὸ διειδέστατον καὶ ἀγλαοφανὲς τῆς ὀρθοδοξίας ὕδωρ διαρρέοντες, ἵλην τὴν τῶν αἱρέσεων ἐκμειοῦσιν.	A fountain pouring out God, from which the rivers of divine knowledge pour out the bright clear water of orthodoxy and drown out the company of the heretics.	Presentation I
324A	Βλέπω σου, νεανίσκε. τῆς εὐμορφίας τὸ ἀξιογράφιστον κάλλος, καὶ τοῦ χαρακτῆρος τὴν αὐγηρὰν θεωρίαν· καὶ λόγους ἀκούω σου, οὓς οὐδέποτε ἀκήκοα, καὶ ἐν ὑποψίᾳ γίνομαι τάχα, ὅτι πλανῆσαί με παραγέγονας.	Young man, I see the beauty of your comely form which is worthy to be painted, and the radiant vision of your appearance, and I hear your words, which I have never heard before, and I am suspicious that you have come to lead me astray.	Annunciation
336C	Οὐκ ἐπίσταμαι σαφῶς τὸ, ἐν ποίοις τόποις αὐλίζεται. Ἐπεὶ κατὰ ἀλήθειαν ἤθελον κἀγὼ αὐτὸν κατατυχεῖν· ἤθελον αὐτοῦ τὸ ἀξιοζωγράφιστον κάλλος θεάσασθαι, καὶ μετ' αὐτοῦ διαλεκτῆσαι·ὅτι εἶπέ μοι «Χαῖρε», καὶ ἄρτι λυποῦμαι.	I do not clearly understand in what place he dwells. I truly wished to go to him, to gaze upon his beauty which is worthy to be painted, and to have righteous dialogue with him. For, he said to me "Rejoice," and I am grieved just now.	Annunciation

356C	αἱ σωματικαί σου, Θεομῆτορ, τῶν εἰκόνων χρωματουργίαι, τὴν ἐπίδοσιν τῶν σῶν ἡμῖν ἀναστράπτουσι δωρεῶν.	The material painting [color] of your images [icons], Mother of God, illuminates the giving of your gifts to us	Dormition II
381C	Τίς τὸν σὸν χαρακτῆρα ἐνοπτριζόμενος, οὐκ αὐτίκα πάσης θλίψεως ἐπιλέλησται;	Who contemplating your character[17], does not forget immediately all his tribulation?	Sash

---

[17]   Mary Cunningham translates this phrase as referring to an image of the Virgin or the Sash. It is a difficult passage. See, Cunningham, Wider 254 ftn. 16.

References to the Incarnation in Germanos I, Patriarch of Constantinople (715-730)

PG 98 Location	Greek	English	Homily
293A	ἡ ναὸς ἀκηλίδωτος καὶ ὑπέρτατος μόνη χρηματίσασα τοῦ ἀρχιερέως καὶ τῶν ἀπάντων τελετάρχου Κυρίου	she who alone is called the stainless and greatest temple of the high priest and the Lord of all	Presentation I
293B	Σήμερον καὶ Ἄννα τὸν τῆς ἀτεκνίας ἐνδελεχισμὸν, εὐτεκνίᾳ ἀμείψασα, ἀπλέτῳ χαρμονῇ ἔνθους γινομένη τοῖς πέρασι καρπὸν διακηρυκεύεται κεκτῆσθαι, στέρνοις ἐναγκαλισαμένη τὴν τῶν οὐρανῶν πλατυτέραν.	Today also Anna has exchanged the persistence of barrenness for fruitfulness, and becoming inspired by joy, proclaims to the ends of the earth that she has borne a child, embracing to her bosom the one who is wider than the heavens.	Presentation I
293C/D	Σήμερον ἡ τὸν τῶν ἁγίων Ἅγιον εἰσδεξομένη Πνεύματος ἁγιασμῷ, τοῖς τῶν ἁγίων Ἁγίοις ἁγιωτάτως καὶ εὐκλεῶς ἁγιασμῷ μείζονι, ἀπειροκάκῳ καὶ ἀδαήμονι ἡλικίᾳ, Χερουβὶμ δόξης ὑπεραρθεῖσα θαυμασιωτάτως ἐναποτίθεται.	Today she who will receive the Holy One of the Holy through the hallowing of the Spirit is placed in the holy of Holies at a pure and innocent age; and she who is marvelously exalted above the Cherubim, makes more holy the holy of Holies by her presence.	Presentation I
293D	Πέλαγος γὰρ ἀχανὲς τὰ ταύτης μεγαλεῖα, ὁ ἐξ αὐτῆς οὐράνιος γεννηθεὶς σταγὼν ἀνέδειξεν.	For her greatness is a vast sea, as the Heavenly drop born from her has shown.	

296D	Ἐπεὶ γοῦν αὐτῆς γε τῆς παναγίας καὶ ὑπεραρχίου Τριάδος ὁ εἷς, τῇ ταύτης τῆς παρθενομήτορος κόρης γαστρί, Πατρικῇ εὐδοκίᾳ, ἰδιοθελῶς, τοῦ τε παναγίου Πνεύματος ἐπισκιάσει χωρηθῆναι ἠπείγετο	When, at last, the One, All-Holy, unoriginate Trinity, deigned to be contained in the belly of the Virgin Mother, through good will of the Father and of the Son and by the overshadowing of the Holy Spirit	Presentation I
300C	Δέδεξο τὴν δεδεξομένην τὸ ἄϋλον καὶ ἀκατάληπτον πῦρ· δέδεξο τὴν δοχεῖον χρηματίσουσαν τοῦ Υἱοῦ καὶ Λόγου τοῦ Πατρὸς καὶ μόνου Θεοῦ·	"Receive her who will receive the immaterial and uncontainable fire. Receive her who will be called the container of the Son and Word of the only God and Father.	Presentation I
301A	Ἐξίσταμαι βλέπων, ὁποῖον καρπὸν προσήξατε. Τοιοῦτος γὰρ ὅστις τῇ καθαρότητι θέλει Θεὸν ἐν αὐτῇ οἰκῆσαι. Οὐδὲ γὰρ πώποτέ τις γέγονεν ἢ γενήσεται τοιαύτη καλλονῇ διαλάμπουσα.	I am astonished seeing what kind of fruit you have brought forth, such a one as by her purity attracts God to dwell within her. For never yet has anyone existed or will anyone exist who shines forth in such beauty.	Presentation I
305C	ἐφ' ᾗ τὸ πλανηθὲν ἐπιστρέψαι βουληθείς, ὁ Λόγος τὴν σάρκα νενύμφευται, τοὺς ἤδη οἰκείᾳ βουλήσει διενηνεγμένους καταλλάσσων.	Through you, the Word which was married to the flesh willingly wished to reconcile those wanderers (cf. Romans 5.10) who through their own private will had been separated.	Presentation I
316D/ 317A	Ὑπῆρχε τοίνυν ἡ πανάχραντος ἐν τῷ οἴκῳ τοῦ τέκτονος Ἰωσήφ, τῷ ἀρχιτέκτονι Θεῷ τηρουμένη, ἕως τὸ πρὸ πάντων αἰώνων ἀπόκρυφον θεῖον μυστήριον ἐν αὐτῇ ἐτελέσθη, καὶ τοῖς βροτοῖς ὁ Θεὸς ἐξ αὐτῆς ὡμοιώθη.	So the all-pure one was in the house of Joseph the carpenter being protected, until the divine mystery hidden before all the ages (cf. Romans 16.25) was fulfilled in her, and from her God was made like mortals.	Presentation II

317A	Ἄπιθι τοιγαροῦν, ὦ Δέσποινα Θεομῆτορ, ἄπιθι πρὸς τὴν σὴν κληρουχίαν, καὶ βάδιζε εἰς τὰς αὐλὰς τοῦ Κυρίου, σκιρτῶσα καὶ χαίρουσα, τρεφομένη καὶ θάλλουσα, προσδεχομένη ἡμέραν ἐξ ἡμέρας τὴν ἐν σοὶ τοῦ παναγίου Πνεύματος ἔλευσιν, καὶ τῆς δυνάμεως τοῦ Ὑψίστου τὴν ἐπισκίασιν, καὶ τοῦ Υἱοῦ σου τὴν σύλληψιν, ὡς Γαβριὴλ σοι προσφωνήσει·	Therefore go, Lady and Mother of God, go to your inheritance, and walk in the halls of the Lord, skipping and rejoicing, nourished and flourishing, awaiting from day to day the coming of the Holy Spirit in you, and the overshadowing of the power of the Most High (*cf.* Luke 1.26), and the conception of your Son, as Gabriel will address you;	Presentation II
321D	Βουλὴν ἀρχαίαν πληρῶσαι βουλόμενος, καὶ ἐλεῆσαι τὸν πλανηθέντα ἄνθρωπον, ἄνθρωπος [γενόμενος] ὁ φιλάνθρωπος, φιλανθρωπίας ἀγαθότητι γενέσθαι ηὐδόκησεν· καὶ τί λοιπὸν τὸν ἐμὸν οὐ προσδέχῃ ἀσπασμόν, ἡ κεχαριτωμένη;	The Lover of mankind, wishing to fulfill His ancient plan, and having mercy on mankind's wandering, was pleased in his goodness and love for man to become man. Why do you not accept my greeting, O blessed one?	Annunciation
341B	Εἰ πρὸ γεννηθῆναι παρὰ σοῦ τῆς Παρθένου Μητρός, Υἱὸς οὗτος μονογενὴς τοῦ Θεοῦ, πῶς ὁ Πατήρ φησι πρὸς αὐτόν, «Ἐγὼ σήμερον γεγέννηκά σε;» Δῆλον ὅτι τὸ σήμερον, οὐχὶ τὴν τῆς θεότητος τοῦ Μονογενοῦς πρόσφατον παρίστησι ὕπαρξιν, ἀλλὰ τὴν πρὸς ἀνθρώπους σωματικὴν αὐτοῦ βεβαιοῖ παρουσίαν	If before being born from you, the Virgin Mother, this one was only-begotten Son of God, how does the Father say to him, "Today I have begotten you"? It is clear that "today" does not represent a new beginning of the divinity of the Only-begotten, but declares his corporeal presence among men.	Dormition I
341C	Ἐπειδὴ γὰρ οὐκ ἀλλότριον τὸ Πνεῦμα τοῦ Πατρός· εὐδοκίᾳ δὲ καὶ ἀποστολῇ τοῦ Πατρὸς ᾤκησεν ἐν σοὶ τῇ Παρθένῳ καὶ Μητρὶ	For since the Spirit is not alien to the Father, for by good will and sending of the Father he has come to dwell in you the Virgin and Mother,	Dormition I

344C	ἐπειδὴ καὶ οὐρανὸς θεοχώρητος ἀνεδείχθης τοῦ ὑψίστου Θεοῦ	For when you were proved to be a God-containing heaven of the most high God	Dormition I
345B	ὅλον Θεοῦ κατοικητήριον	altogether the residence of God	Dormition I
345C	διὰ τῆς τοῦ Υἱοῦ σου λυτρωσαμένην σαρκώσεως	through the incarnation of your Son	Dormition I
345C	τῆς φρικτῆς ἐνανθρωπήσεως	of his awesome assumption of humanity	Dormition I
348A	Ἐπειδὴ γὰρ ὁ κενωθεὶς ἐν σοὶ, Θεὸς ἦν ἀπ' ἀρχῆς,	For since he who emptied himself in you was God from the beginning and Life before the ages	Dormition I
348B	Ἡ ἐκ σοῦ περιβληθεῖσα τούτῳ, Θεοτόκε, σάρξ· μεθ' ἧς οὐ μόνον εἰς τὸν παρόντα τοῦτον αἰῶνα ἐπιφανεὶς ὁ Χριστὸς ἐπιστεύθη, ἀλλὰ καὶ κατὰ τὸν μέλλοντα αἰῶνα, σὺν τῇ τοιαύτῃ σου σαρκὶ,	the flesh put on by him from you, O Theotokos—with which we believe that Christ has appeared not only for this present age, but also will be revealed in the coming age, with such flesh from you	Dormition I
349A	ἐκ παρθένου σαρκωθεὶς	he who was incarnate of a virgin	Dormition II
349B	Τότε γὰρ πνευματικὸς ὁ ἄνθρωπος, ὅταν σὺ, Θεοτόκε, Πνεύματος ἁγίου κατοικητήριον ἐγένου	For then is a man spiritual, when you, O Theotokos, became the dwelling-place of the Holy Spirit.	Dormition II
353B	διότι λαὸν αὐτῷ Χριστιανικὸν ἀπὸ σαρκὸς τῆς σῆς συνεστήσω	for which reason you have established a Christian people for him from your flesh	Dormition II
356C	Διὰ τοῦτο μακάριος κἂν ἁμαρτωλὸς ὁ ἄνθρωπος, ὅτιπερ συγγενῆ σε κατ' οὐσίαν κτησάμενος εὑρέθη, καὶ θείας φύσεως διὰ σοῦ κοινωνὸς	Because of this man is blessed even if he is a sinner, since he has been found to have you as a relative in essence, and through you he is a partaker of the divine nature.	Dormition II

357C	καὶ τούτου χάριν, τὸ θεηδόχον σου σῶμα, παρὰ νεκροποιοῦ καταφθορᾶς, ἔπρεπεν ὄντως μὴ συγκλεισθῆναι· ἀλλὰ καὶ τὸν τάφον ὡς ἀνθρώπινον ὑποδέξασθαι τὸ ἴδιον φύραμα· καὶ σοῦ ζωοτελῶς πρὸς τὰ οὐράνια, τῆς οἰκείας μεταστάσης ζωῆς	And for the sake of this, it was truly fitting that your God-receiving body should not be shut in by deathly corruption, but that the tomb received its own mixture as human, and with a living conclusion of your own life transferring to the heavenly places.	Dormition II
357D			

The following reference to the Incarnation comes as a reason why Mary did not suffer death in the way other humans do. It is in a section where Germanos uses the hardening of the bones at death and compares the norm with Mary's death. It is a reference to Proverbs 15.30 and Psalm 54.22 LXX.

360B	διότι τῇ ἀναστάσει τοῦ ὑπ' αὐτῆς γεννηθέντος ἡπαλύνθησαν ὑπὲρ ἔλαιον τῇ ἀφθαρσίᾳ.	by the resurrection of him who was born from her they [the bones] were softened by incorruption more than with oil	Dormition III
360C	ὡς μὴ προεγνωκυῖα τὴν ἰδίαν ἔξοδον, ἡ τὸν γνώστην τῶν ὅλων τεκοῦσα Θεὸ	as not knowing in advance her own departure (she who bore the God who knows all)	Dormition III
361B	Ἐμοὶ τὸ σῶμά σου πίστευσον, ὅτι κἀγὼ τῇ κοιλίᾳ σου τὴνἐμὴν παρεκατεθέμην θεότητα	Entrust your body to me, because I also deposited my godhead in your belly	Dormition III
361C	Οὐ καυχήσεται θάνατος ἐπί σοί· Ζωὴν γὰρ ἐκύησας	Death will not boast over you, for you gave birth to Life	Dormition III
361C	Σκεῦος ἐμὸν ἐγένου· οὐ ῥαγώσει τοῦτο σύντριμμα θανατοφθόρου καταπτώσεως	You became my vessel; the fracture of death-corrupting fall will not break this	Dormition III
364A	οὐ συλληφθησόμενος πάλιν ὑπὸ σοῦ, ὡς ἐφ' ἅπαξ οἰκήσας ἐν σοί,	not in order to be conceived again by you (as once and for all I have dwelt in you)	Dormition III
364C	ὡς καὶ ὁ ὑπ' αὐτῆς γεννηθεὶς ἐνίκησεν τὸν ᾅδην, Χριστός	as also the Christ who received birth from her conquered Hades.	Dormition III

365A	Υἱὸς μὲν σαρκὶ γεννηθεὶς ὑπ' ἐμοῦ· Πατὴρ δὲ καὶ Κτίστης καὶ Θεὸς τῆς ἰδίας οὗτος μητρός.	He is a Son given birth in the flesh by me, but Father and Creator and God of his own mother	Dormition III
368A	τὴν σῶμα τῷ ἀσωμάτῳ χορηγήσασαν ἐν περιβολῇ	since you provided a body to the bodiless One in which he covered himself	Dormition III
368A	Ἐγώ σε τοῖς ἔθνεσιν ἕως χθὲς, Θεὸν σαρκικῶς ἐκήρυττον γεγεννηκέναι·	I was proclaiming you to the gentiles until yesterday, that you had borne God in the flesh	Dormition III
369B	οἱ τὸν Υἱὸν διὰ τῆς μητρὸς, τὴν μητέρα διὰ τὸν Υἱὸν ὑπερτίμως σεβασθέντες· οἱ διὰ τὸν ἔνσαρκον γεγονότα Θεὸν, τῇ χορηγῷ τῆς σαρκὸς αὐτοῦ, γνησίως τότε δεδουλευκότες Μητρί	those how venerated with great honor the Son through his mother and the mother because of the Son, who because of God who became incarnate, nobly gave service to the mother who provided his flesh.	Dormition III
369C 369D	Ἄνδρες Ἰσραηλῖται, τοῦτο νῦν γνωστὸν ὑμῖν ἐδείχθη πᾶσι περὶ Μαρίας τῆς κατὰ σάρκα μητρὸς τοῦ Χριστοῦ, ὡς ἅμα ἡμῖν καὶ ὑμῖν ἐπὶ τὸ μνῆμα τοῦτο νεκρὰ παραγενομένη, παρὰ τῶν ἡμετέρων ἀνελήφθη χειρῶν	"Men of Israel, this has now been made known to you all concerning Mary the mother of Christ according to the flesh, that to us and you together having arrived dead at this tomb, she was taken up from our hands	Dormition III
376A	τοῦ Θεοῦ κατὰ σάρκα Μητρὸς	God's most pure mother according to the flesh	Sash

References to the Intercession of Mary in Germanos I, Patriarch of Constantinople (715-730)

PG 98 Location	Greek	English	Homily
300D	Ἰδού σοι ταύτην παρατιθέμεθα καὶ ἑαυτοὺς ἀνατιθέμεθα.	Behold, to you we offer her [as our intercessor] and dedicate ourselves."	Presentation I
308C	Υἱόν τε καὶ Θεὸν πάντων δημιουργὸν εὐπροσδέκτοις καὶ μητροπειθέσι λιταῖς,	by your acceptable and motherly-persuasive petitions to your son,	Presentation I
317A/ B/C	Ἄπιθι τοιγαροῦν, ὦ Δέσποινα Θεομῆτορ, ἄπιθι πρὸς τὴν σὴν κληρουχίαν, καὶ βάδιζε εἰς τὰς αὐλὰς τοῦ Κυρίου, σκιρτῶσα καὶ χαίρουσα, τρεφομένη καὶ θάλλουσα, προσδεχομένη ἡμέραν ἐξ ἡμέρας τὴν ἐν σοὶ τοῦ παναγίου Πνεύματος ἔλευσιν, καὶ τῆς δυνάμεως τοῦ Ὑψίστου τὴν ἐπισκίασιν, καὶ τοῦ Υἱοῦ σου τὴν σύλληψιν, ὡς Γαβριὴλ σοι προσφωνήσει· καὶ δὸς τοῖς τὴν σὴν ἑορτὴν τελοῦσιν, τὴν σὴν βοήθειαν, καὶ σκέπην, καὶ προστασίαν· ῥυομένη πάντοτε ταῖς σαῖς πρεσβείαις τούτους ἐκ πάσης ἀνάγκης καὶ κινδύνων, νόσων τε δεινῶν, καὶ συμφορῶν παντοίων, καὶ τῆς μελλούσης ἀπειλῆς δικαίας τοῦ Υἱοῦ σου.	Therefore go, Lady and Mother of God, go to your inheritance, and walk in the halls of the Lord, skipping and rejoicing, nourished and flourishing, awaiting from day to day the coming of the Holy Spirit in you, and the overshadowing of the power of the Most High (*cf.* Luke 1.26), and the conception of your Son, as Gabriel will address you; and give to those who celebrate your feast your help, your protection, and your assistance, guarding always by your intercessions these people from every necessity and dangers, and dread diseases, and all kinds of misfortunes, and from the coming just threat of your Son. Set them,	Presentation II (P Grazie 168 ftn. 3)

	Τάξον δὲ αὐτοὺς, ὡς τοῦ Δεσπότου μήτηρ, ἐν τόπῳ τρυφῆς, ἔνθα φῶς καὶ εἰρήνη, καὶ τῶν ὀρεκτῶν ἡ ἀκροτάτη δόσις· «Καὶ γενηθήτω ἄλαλα τὰ χείλη τὰ δόλια, τὰ λαλοῦντα κατὰ σοῦ τῆς δικαίας, ἀνομίαν ἐν ὑπερηφανείᾳ καὶ ἐξουδενώσει·» καὶ ἐξουδενωθήτω ἐν τῇ πόλει σου ἡ τούτων εἰκών· αἰσχυνθήτωσαν, καὶ ἐκλιπέτωσαν, καὶ ἀπολέσθωσαν, καὶ γνώτωσαν ὅτι ὄνομά σοι Δέσποινα. Σὺ γὰρ μόνη Θεοτόκος, ὑψηλοτάτη ἐπὶ πᾶσαν τὴν γῆν· ἡμεῖς δέ σε, Θεόνυμφε, πίστει εὐλογοῦμεν, καὶ πόθῳ γεραίρομεν, καὶ φόβῳ προσκυνοῦμεν, ἀεί σε μεγαλύνοντες, καὶ σεπτῶς μακαρίζοντες.	as you are the mother of the Master, in a place of comfort, where [there are] light and peace, and the ultimate giving of things desired. "And may the deceitful lips be mute, those which speak lawlessness in arrogance and contempt against you the righteous woman" (cf. Psalm 31.19). And let the image of these [people] be brought to naught in your city. Let them be put to shame, and let them die out, and let them perish, and let them know that your name is Mistress (cf. Psalm 83.17-18). For you alone are Theotokos, most sublime over all the earth; and we bless you in faith, bride of God, and with desire we honor you, and with fear we bow before you, always magnifying you, and solemnly calling you blessed (cf. Luke 1.49).	
317C/D 320A	Ἀλλ', ὦ μοι, Δέσποινα, μόνη τὸ ἐμὸν ἐκ Θεοῦ ψυχαγώγημα, τοῦ ἐν ἐμοὶ καύσωνος ἡ θεία δρόσος, τῆς ξηρανθείσης μου καρδίας ἡ θεόρρυτος ῥανίς, τῆς ζοφερᾶς μου ψυχῆς ἡ τηλαυγεστάτη λαμπάς, τῆς ἐμῆς πορείας ἡ ποδηγία, τῆς ἀσθενείας μου ἡ δύναμις, τῆς γυμνώσεως ἡ ἀμφίασις, τῆς πτωχείας ὁ πλοῦτος, τὸ τῶν ἀνιάτων τραυμάτων τὸ ἴαμα, ἡ τῶν δακρύων ἀναίρεσις, τῶν στεναγμῶν ἡ κατάπαυσις, τῶν συμφορῶν ἡ μεταποίησις, τῶν ὀδυνῶν ὁ κουφισμός, τῶν δεσμῶν ἡ λύσις, τῆς	But Oh me, Mistress, my only soul-leader from God, the divine dew of the burning in me, the moisture flowing from God for my parched heart, the bright-shining lamp of my darkened soul, the guide for my journey, the power for my weakness, the clothing of my nakedness, the wealth of my poverty, the healing of my incurable wounds, the removal of tears, the cessation of groaning, the reversal of misfortunes, the lightening of pains, the release of fetters, the hope of my salvation, hear my prayers: have pity on my	Presentation II (P Grazie 168 ftn. 4)

	σωτηρίας μου ἡ ἐλπίς, εἰσάκουσόν μου τῶν προσευχῶν· οἴκτειρόν μου τοὺς στεναγμούς, καὶ πρόσδεξαί μου τοὺς ὀδυρμούς. Ἐλέησόν με ἐπικαμφθεῖσα τοῖς δάκρυσι τοῖς ἐμοῖς, σπλαγχνίσθητι ἐπ' ἐμοὶ ὡς μήτηρ τοῦ φιλανθρώπου Θεοῦ.	groaning, and accept my lamentations. Have mercy on me, bending down to my tears.	
317B-D/ 320A-B	Beginning with 317A there follows a long prayer in which Germanos expresses his faith in the Intercession of the Virgin Mary		Presentation II
Mary's dwelling with both God and man is a necessary condition for her role as Mediatrix. See, Horvath 289-90 *cf* 356A.			
317D 320A/B	Ἐλέησόν με ἐπικαμφθεῖσα τοῖς δάκρυσι τοῖς ἐμοῖς, σπλαγχνίσθητι ἐπ' ἐμοὶ ὡς μήτηρ τοῦ φιλανθρώπου Θεοῦ. Ἐπίβλεψον καὶ κατάνευσον πρὸς τὴν ἐμὴν ἱκεσίαν, ἐκπλήρωσόν μου τὸ ἐκδιψώμενον καταθύμιον, καὶ σύναψόν με τῇ ἐμῇ συγγόνῳ καὶ συνδούλῃ ἐν τῇ γῇ τῶν πραέων, ἐν σκηναῖς τῶν δικαίων, καὶ χορῷ τῶν ἁγίων· καὶ ἀξίωσόν με, ἡ πάντων προστασία καὶ χαρά, καὶ φαιδρὰ θυμηδία, συνευφρανθῆναι ταύτῃ, δέομαί σου, ἐν τῇ χαρᾷ ἐκείνῃ τῇ ὄντως ἀνεκφράστῳ τοῦ ἐκ σοῦ γεννηθέντος Θεοῦ καὶ	Have compassion on me, as mother of the God who loves mankind. Look down and assent to my supplication, fill up my thirsty desire, and join me to my relative and fellow servant[18] in the land of the meek, in the tents of the just (*cf.* Psalm 118.15), in the choir of the saints (*cf.* Psalm 116.9); and make me worthy, I beg you, O protection and joy of all and brilliant gladness of heart, to rejoice along with her[19], in your truly ineffable joy, [because] of the God and King who was born from you,	Presentation II (P Grazie 169 ftn. 5)

---

[18] We do not know who this relative of Germanos was, but it must have been a woman who followed a life of service to God. Georges Gharib and Luigi Gambero. *Testi Mariani Del Primo Millennio*. Roma: Città Nuova Editrice, 1989. 336 nt. 8. While we do not know the name of Germanos' relative this passage is redolent of the final prayers in the Orthodox funeral and memorial service and should be read as one who is familiar with them as Germanos' auditors would have been.

[19] This is a reference to Germanos' relative.

	Βασιλέως, καὶ τῷ νυμφῶνι αὐτοῦ τῷ ἀφθάρτῳ, καὶ τρυφῇ τῇ ἀλήκτῳ καὶ ἀκορέστῳ, καὶ ἐν τῇ ἀνεσπέρῳ καὶ ἀπεράντῳ βασιλείᾳ. Ναί, Δέσποινα· ναὶ, τὸ ἐμὸν καταφύγιον, ἡ ζωὴ καὶ ἡ ἀντίληψις, τὸ ὅπλον καὶ τὸ καύχημα, ἡ ἐλπίς μου καὶ τὸ σθένος μου. Δός μοι σὺν αὐτῇ ἀπολαῦσαι τῶν τοῦ Υἱοῦ σου ἀνεκδιηγήτων καὶ ἀκαταλήπτων δωρεῶν ἐν τῇ ἐπουρανίῳ διαμονῇ. Ἔχεις γάρ, οἶδα, σύνδρομον τῇ θελήσει τὸ δύνασθαι, ὡς τοῦ Ὑψίστου μήτηρ· καὶ διὰ τοῦτο τολμῶ. Μὴ οὖν ἀποστερηθείην, πανάχραντε Κυρία, τῆς ἐμῆς προσδοκίας· ἀλλὰ τύχοιμι ταύτης, Θεόνυμφε, ἡ τὴν τῶν ὅλων προσδοκίαν ὑπὲρ λόγον τεκοῦσα, τὸν Κύριον ἡμῶν Ἰησοῦν Χριστόν, τὸν ἀληθινὸν Θεὸν καὶ Δεσπότην· ᾧ πρέπει πᾶσα δόξα, τιμή, καὶ προσκύ-νησις, σὺν τῷ ἀνάρχῳ Πατρί, καὶ τῷ ζωοποιῷ Πνεύματι, νῦν καὶ ἀεὶ, καὶ εἰς τοὺς αἰῶνας τῶν αἰώνων. Ἀμήν.	and in his imperishable bridal-chamber, and in the unceasing and insatiable delight, and in the kingdom which has no evening and no limit. Yes, Mistress; yes, my refuge, my life and my support, my armor and my boast, my hope and my strength. Grant me with her to enjoy the inexpressible and unceasing gifts in the heavenly mansion. For as the mother of the Most High you have, I know, the power which runs along with the will; and because of this I am bold. Therefore may I not be deprived, all-undefiled Lady, of my expectation (*cf.* Galatians 6.4); but may I obtain this, Bride of God, you who gave birth beyond words to the expectation of all, our Lord Jesus Christ, the true God and Master: to whom is due all glory, honor, and veneration, with the Father who has no beginning, and the life-giving Spirit, now and ever, and to the ages of ages. Amen.	
321B	Χαῖρε, κεχαριτωμένη, ψυχῆς ἀγαλλίαμα, καὶ ὅλου τοῦ κόσμου παγκόσμιον σέβασμα, καὶ ἁμαρτωλῶν ἁπάντων ἡ ὄντως ἀγαθὴ μεσιτεία	Hail full of grace, exceeding great joy of the soul, and object of worship for the whole cosmos, and truly good mediator for all sinners.	Annunciation
329B	Χριστιανῶν ἁπάντων γενήσῃ κοινὸν ἱλαστήριον· καὶ διὰ τοῦτο πάλιν, ἐπιφθέγγομαί σοι τὴν πρέπουσαν φωνήν, «<Χαῖρε,> Κεχαριτωμένη·	You shall become the common propitiation of all Christians. And therefore again I salute you as is fitting, "<*Hail*> O full of grace, the Lord	Annunciation

	ὁ Κύριος μετὰ σοῦ· εὐλογημένη σὺ ἐν γυναιξὶ, καὶ εὐλογημένος ὁ καρπὸς τῆς κοιλίας σου.»	is with you, blessed are you among women, blessed is the fruit of your womb" (Luke 1.38).	
344C	σύνοικος ἦσθα διὰ παντὸς τοῦ Θεοῦ	you were always a dweller with God	Dormition I

Perniola views the following part of the First Homily on the Dormition to be the height of Germanos' Mariology: Nello svolgimento di una dottrin a così delicata e consolante, San Germano tocca la nota più bella e più alta di tutta la sua mariologia; logico e deduttivo nel suo ragionamento, pone l'intercessione di Maria a nostro favore in relazione con la sua assunzione al cielo, come un effetto alla propria causa. La Vergine infatti pur dimorando in cielo, abita tuttavi a in mezzo agli uomini, e si manifesta in diverse maniere a chi. ne è degno, poichè la sua carne non è di impedimento alta potente energia del suo spirito, il quale dove vuole, spira, essendo immateriale. 167

| 344D/ 345A | Καὶ γὰρ, ὡς μετὰ τῶν ἀρχαιοτέρων ἡμῶν ἐν σαρκὶ συνεπολιτεύου, ὁμοίως καὶ μεθ' ἡμῶν τῷ πνεύματι συνοικεῖς· καὶ ἡ πολλή σου περὶ ἡμᾶς σκέπη, τὴν σὴν ἡμῶν χαρακτηρίζει συνομιλίαν. Καὶ τῆς φωνῆς σου πάντες ἀκούομεν· καὶ ἡ φωνὴ τῶν ὅλων πρὸς τὰ σὰ τῆς ἀκροάσεως ὦτα· καὶ γινωσκόμενοι παρὰ σοῦ διὰ τῆς ἀντιλήψεως, ἐπιγινώσκομέν σου προστατικὴν ἀεὶ τὴν ἀντίληψιν. Κωλυτικὸν γὰρ οὐδέν, μερισμὸν λέγω ψυχῆς καὶ σώματος, μεταξὺ τῆς σῆς καὶ τῶν σῶν δούλων διαγνώσεως. Οὐ γὰρ ἀφῆκας, οὓς διέσωσας· κατέλιπας, οὓς συνήγαγες· ὅτι ζῇ σου τὸ πνεῦμα διὰ παντὸς, καὶ ἡ σάρξ διαφθορὰν οὐχ ὑπέμεινε ταφῆς. Πάντας ἐπισκέπτῃ, καὶ ἡ ἐπισκοπή σου, Θεομῆτορ, ἐπὶ πάντας· ὥστε κἂν οἱ ὀφθαλμοὶ ἡμῶν κρατοῦνται τοῦ μὴ βλέπειν σε, | For also, as you kept fellowship in the flesh with our ancestors, likewise also with us you dwell in the spirit. And your great oversight for us characterizes your companionship with us. And we all hear your voice, and the voice of all [comes] to your ears of hearing, and being known by you through your support, we recognize always your protective support. For there is no barrier—I mean not even due to the separation of the soul and body—for you recognize your servants. For you did not abandon those whom you saved, you [did not] leave those whom you gathered together; because your spirit lives always, and your flesh did not endure the corruption of the grave. You oversee all, O Mother of God, and your oversight is upon all, so that even | Dormition I (P Grazie 168 ftn. 1) |

	παναγία, ἐν μέσῳ σὺ τῶν ἁπάντων ἐμφιλοχωρεῖς, ἐμφανίζουσα τοῖς ἀξίοις σου διαφόρως ἑαυτήν. Ἡ γὰρ σὰρξ οὐκ ἐμποδίζει τῇ δυνάμει καὶ ἐνεργείᾳ τοῦ πνεύματός σου· ὅτιπερ ὅπου θέλει πνεῖ σου τὸ πνεῦμα, ἐπειδὴ καθαρὸν τοῦτο καὶ ἄϋλον· ἄφθαρτον καὶ ἀκηλίδωτον, καὶ τοῦ Πνεύματος τοῦ ἁγίου συνδιαιτικὸν πνεῦμα, καὶ τῆς Μονογενοῦς θεότητος ἐκλεκτόν.	if our eyes do not have the power to see you, all-holy one, you love to dwell in the midst of all, revealing yourself especially to those who are worthy of you. For the flesh does not hinder the power and activity of your spirit, just as wherever it wishes your spirit blows, since it is pure and immaterial; incorrupt and unstained, and a spirit which dwells together with the Holy Spirit, and the chosen one of the only-begotten divinity.	
348C	διὸ καὶ ὅσα ζητεῖς παρ' αὐτοῦ, τεκνοπενθῷ ἐπιδίδωσι, καὶ ὅσαπερ αἰτεῖς ἐξ αὐτοῦ, θεοδυνάμως ἀποπληροῖ· ὁ ὢν εὐλογητὸς εἰς τοὺς αἰῶνας. Ἀμήν.	Therefore also whatever you seek from him, he gives with a child's affection, and whatever you seek from him, he fulfills with the power of God: who is blessed unto the ages.	Dormition I (P Grazie 170 ftn. 7)
349A	Δυνατὴ τοιγαροῦν πρὸς σωτηρίαν ἡ βοήθειά σου, Θεοτόκε, καὶ μὴ χρήζουσά τινος ἑτέρου πρὸς τὸν Θεὸν παραθέτου.	Therefore your aid is powerful for salvation, O Theotokos, even needing no other advocate with God.	Dormition II (P Grazie 170 ftn. 6)
349B	διότι καὶ ἡ προστασία σου ζῶσα, καὶ ἡ πρεσβεία σου ζωή, καὶ ἡ σκέπη σου διηνεκής	because your advocacy is living, and your intercession is life, and your protection is ceaseless	Dormition II
349B	εἰ μὴ διὰ σοῦ, παναγία	if not through you, all-holy [lady].	Dormition II
349B/C	Ἐκείνη ὡς γῆ οὖσα εἰς γῆν παρῆλθε· σὺ δὲ Ζωὴν ἡμῖν ἔτεκες, καὶ πρὸς τὴν ζωὴν ἐπανῆλθες, καὶ Ζωὴν τοῖς ἀνθρώποις, καὶ μετὰ θάνατον, προξενεῖν κατίσχυσας. «Οὐκ ἔστι τῆς ἀντιλήψεώς σου κόρος,» οὐδὲ τῆς ζωοκοιμήτου	She, as being earth, passed into earth; but you bore Life for us, and passed over to life, and obtained the power to mediate life to mankind, even after death. "There is no end of your succor" nor is there any danger,	Dormition II (P Grazie 171 ftn. 8)

	σου μεταθέσεως ἐπιζήμιος, ὡς εἰπεῖν, ὑποτρέχουσα τοῖς ἀνθρώποις αἴσθησις· διότι καὶ ἡ προστασία σου ζῶσα, καὶ ἡ πρεσβεία σου ζωή, καὶ ἡ σκέπη σου διηνεκής. Εἰ μὴ γὰρ σὺ προηγοῦ, οὐδεὶς πνευματικὸς ἀπετελεῖτο· οὐδεὶς ἐν Πνεύματι τὸν Θεὸν προσεκύνει. Τότε γὰρ πνευματικὸς ὁ ἄνθρωπος, ὅταν σύ, Θεοτόκε, Πνεύματος ἁγίου κατοικητήριον ἐγένου. Οὐδεὶς θεογνωσίας ἀνάμεστος, εἰ μὴ διὰ σοῦ, παναγία· οὐδεὶς ὁ σωζόμενος, εἰ μὴ διὰ σοῦ, Θεοτόκε· οὐδεὶς κινδύνων ἐλεύθερος, εἰ μὴ διὰ σοῦ, Παρθενομῆτορ· οὐδεὶς ὁ λελυτρωμένος, εἰ μὴ διὰ σοῦ, Θεομῆτορ· οὐδεὶς ὁ ἐλεούμενος δῶρον, εἰ μὴ διὰ σοῦ, Θεοχώρητε.	so to speak, nor should we humans perceive any when your transfer in living sleep comes into human [awareness], because your advocacy is living, and your intercession is life, and your protection is ceaseless. For if you were not guiding, no one would be made fully spiritual; no one would be worshipping God in spirit (John 4.24). For then is a man fully spiritual, when you, O Theotokos, became the dwelling-place of the Holy Spirit. No one is filled with divine knowledge, if not through you, all-holy [lady]. No one is saved, if not through you, Theotokos. No one is free from dangers, if not through you, Virgin Mother. No one is redeemed, if not through you, Mother of God. No one receives the gift of mercy, if not through you, Theochoretos.	
349C (352A)	Τίς γὰρ τῶν ἁμαρτωλῶν ἐπὶ τοσοῦτον ὑπερμαχεῖ; Τίς τῶν ἀδιορθώτων κατὰ τοσοῦτον [ἀντιφωνητικῶς] ὑπεραπο-λογεῖται; Πᾶς γὰρ τῶν δυναμένων ἔσθ' ὅτε καὶ βοηθεῖν, τῆς παραβολικῆς συκῆς τὴν ἐκτομὴν ἐν ἡμῖν εὐλαβούμενος, ἀνεβάλλετο τὴν ὑπὲρ ἡμῶν ἱκεσίαν τῷ Θεῷ προσαναπέμψαι· ἵνα μὴ τῆς ἀποφάσεως διὰ τὸ ἄκαρπον τῆς ὑποσχέσεως δοθείσης,	For who among sinners can prevail to such an extent? Who among those not made upright can speak so strongly in his defense? For everyone who is sometimes able to assist, being wary of the cutting-down of the fig tree in the parable (Luke 13.6ff.), deferred sending up his supplication to God on our behalf; lest if rejection was given	Dormition II (P Grazie 171 ftn. 9 and 168 ftn. 2)

	ἄδεκτος ἡ ἀντιφώνησις ὀφθῇ. Σὺ δὲ, μητρῴαν ἔχουσα πρὸς τὸν Θεὸν τὴν ἰσχὺν, καὶ τοῖς καθ' ὑπεροχὴν ἁμαρτάνουσι, καθ' ὑπερβολὴν τὴν συγχώρησιν ἐξανύεις. Οὐδὲ γὰρ ἐνδέχεταί σέ ποτε παρακουσθῆναι, ἐπειδὴ πειθαρχεῖ σοι κατὰ πάντα καὶ διὰ πάντα, καὶ ἐν πᾶσιν ὁ Θεὸς, ὡς ἀληθινῇ αὐτοῦ καὶ ἀχράντῳ Μητρί.	because of the fruitlessness of the promise, the answer seem unacceptable. But you, having a mother's power with God, accomplish succor in surpassing degree even for those extremely sinful. For it is not possible for your voice ever to be disregarded, since God is obedient to you in every way and for every reason and in every situation, as you are his true and pure Mother.	
352A	Σὺ δὲ, μητρῴαν ἔχουσα πρὸς τὸν Θεὸν τὴν ἰσχὺν, καὶ τοῖς καθ' ὑπεροχὴν ἁμαρτάνουσι, καθ' ὑπερβολὴν τὴν συγχώρησιν ἐξανύεις	But you, having a mother's power with God, accomplish succor in surpassing degree even for those extremely sinful.	Dormition II (P Grazie 172 ftn. 11)
352A	Οὐδὲ γὰρ ἐνδέχεταί σέ ποτε παρακουσθῆναι, ἐπειδὴ πειθαρχεῖ σοι κατὰ πάντα καὶ διὰ πάντα, καὶ ἐν πᾶσιν ὁ Θεὸς, ὡς ἀληθινῇ αὐτοῦ καὶ ἀχράντῳ Μητρί	For it is not possible for your voice ever to be disregarded, since God is obedient to you in every way and for every reason and in every situation, as you are his true and pure Mother	Dormition II
352A	Ὅθεν ὁ θλιβόμενος, εὐλόγως πρὸς σὲ καταφεύγει· ὁ ἀσθενῶν, σοὶ προσκολλᾶται· ὁ πολεμούμενος, σὲ τοῖς ἐχθροῖς ἀνθοπλίζει.	Therefore he who suffers tribulation takes blessed refuge with you; he who is sick, clings to you; he who wages war, takes you as armor against his enemies	Dormition II
352A/ 353A	«Θυμὸν καὶ ὀργὴν καὶ θλίψιν, ἀποστολὴ δι' ἀγγέλων πονηρῶν,» σὺ μεταβάλλεις. Ἀπειλὴν δικαίαν καὶ ψῆφον ἀξιοπαθοῦς καταδίκης σὺ μεταστρέφεις, ἀγαπῶσα μεγάλως τὸν ἐπικεκλημένον τῷ ὀνόματι τοῦ Υἱοῦ σου λαόν. Ὅθεν καὶ ὁ Χριστιανὸς λαός	You repel "spirit and anger and tribulation, dispatched by evil angels" (Ps. 77.49 LXX). You turn back just threats and the verdict of deserved punishment, loving greatly the people who are called by the name of your Son. Therefore your Christian people examining their own [affairs], delegate you	Dormition II (P Grazie 172 ftn. 10)

σου, τὰ καθ' ἑαυτὸν ἀνακρίνων, πρὸς μὲν τὸν Θεὸν παρρησιαστικῶς ὑποστέλλεταί σοι τὰς δεήσεις προσφέρειν. Σὲ δυσωπεῖν ἀνενδοιάστος θαρρεῖ, παναγία, διὰ τὴν πεῖραν, καὶ τὰ πλήθη τῶν εἰς ἡμᾶς ἀγαθῶν σου, καὶ παραβιάσεσθαί σε πολλάκις ἐν ἱκεσίαις. Ἀνθ' ὧν τίς σε μὴ μακαρίσει; Τὴν τῶν ἀγγέλων ὑπὲρ ἔννοιαν θεωρίαν· τὴν τῶν ἀνθρώπων ὑπέρξενον ἐπιτυχίαν· τὴν ὑπόληψιν τοῦ γένους τῶν Χριστιανῶν· τὸ ὀχλούμενον τῶν ἁμαρτωλῶν προσφύγιον· τὴν καθ' ὥραν ἐν τῷ στόματι τῶν Χριστιανῶν φερομένην. Μόνον γὰρ εἰ θροηθῇ Χριστιανός, εἰ καὶ πρὸς λίθον τὸν ἑαυτοῦ προσκόψῃ πόδα, τὸ σὸν ἐπικαλεῖται πρὸς βοήθειαν ὄνομα. Σὲ τοιγαροῦν τις δοξάζων, ἀπαύστως οὐ μὴ δοξάζεται. Δοξάζειν σε, μᾶλλον ἐὰν ἀκόρως ἐνάρξηται. Ἀδύνατον γὰρ ἐπαξίως ἀνυμνῆσαί σε. Τὸ διὰ παντὸς μεγαλύνειν σε ποθεῖ, διὰ τοῦ διηνεκῶς δοξολογεῖν σε, παραψυχὴν τοῦ χρέους ἀναλαμβάνων. Ἐπὰν γὰρ πολλὰ χρεωστῶν οὐδὲν ἀνταποδίδωσί σοι, πληθύνει τὴν εὐχαριστίαν, ὡς σὺ τὴν προστασίαν. Ἐπειδὴ πανάγαθον δώρημα τέλος μὴ δεχόμενον, τὴν εὐχαριστίαν ὡς ἐν ἀρχῇ, ἀεὶ τὸ ἀγαθὸν ποιοῦντι προσάγει. Σὲ τίς μὴ	to bring their petitions to God with confident speech. They unhesitatingly make bold to entreat you, all-holy Lady, because of [their] experience and the multitude of your bounties towards us, and to constrain you often in supplications. In return who will not bless you (*cf.* Luke 1.48)? You are a vision beyond the understanding of the angels. You are the surpassingly strange good fortune of mankind. You are the support of the nation of Christians. You are the refuge importuned by sinners. You are carried from hour to hour in the mouth of Christians. For if one is merely called Christian, if he even strikes his foot against a stone (Ps. 90.12 LXX), he calls upon your name for help. Therefore anyone who glorifies does not consider unceasingly. To glorify you, rather even if he begins insatiably. For it is impossible to praise you as you deserve. [He] desires to magnify you always, because he speaks your praise unceasingly, taking consolation from this need. [For anyone who glorifies you must consider that he should do it without ceasing. And even though he begins with much zeal he will find it impossible to rightly glorify you as you deserve.] For although he is greatly in your debt he gives you nothing in return,

θαυμάσει τὴν ἀμετάθετον σκέπην, τὴν ἀμετάστατον καταφυγήν, τὴν ἀκοίμητον πρεσβείαν, τὸν ἀνέγκλητον παράδεισον, τὸ ἀσφαλὲς ὀχύρωμα, τὸ κραταιὸν περιχαράκωμα, τὸν ἰσχυρὸν τῆς ἀντιλήψεως πύργον, τὸν λιμένα τῶν χειμαζομένων, τὴν γαλήνην τῶν τεταραγμένων, τὴν τῶν ἁμαρτωλῶν ἐγγυητήν, τὴν τῶν ἀπεγνωσμένων προσαγωγήν, τὴν τῶν ἐξορισθέντων ἀνάληψιν, τὴν τῶν ἐκδιωχθέντων ὑποστροφήν, τὴν τῶν ἀλλοτριωθέντων οἰκείωσιν, τὴν τῶν κατακεκριμένων παράθεσιν, τὴν τῶν καθῃρημένων εὐλογίαν, τὴν δρόσον τῆς ψυχικῆς αὐχμηρίας, τὴν σταγόνα τῆς ἐκτακείσης βοτάνης. «Τὰ γὰρ ὀστᾶ ἡμῶν, ὡς γέγραπται, διὰ σοῦ καθάπερ βοτάνην ἀνατελεῖ·» τὴν τοῦ ἀμνοῦ καὶ ποιμένος μητέρα, καὶ πάντων τῶν ἀγαθῶν γνωριζομένην πρόξενον. Ὅσα τὰ σά, παράδοξα, «ἀληθινά, δεδικαιωμένα ἐπὶ τὸ αὐτό, ἐπιθυμήματά τε πάντα καὶ γλυκύτερα ὑπὲρ μέλι καὶ κηρίον. Καὶ γὰρ οἱ δοῦλοί σου ποθοῦμεν αὐτά, ἐν τῷ ποθεῖν αὐτά, ἀντάμειψις ἐκ σοῦ πολλή.»—«Τὰ ἐλέη σου τίς συνήσει;»	he multiplies thanksgiving, [just] as you [multiply] your advocacy. Since he brings to the one who always does good thanksgiving as at the beginning, an all-good gift having no end. Who will not be amazed at your unchanging protection, your immovable refuge, your unsleeping intercession, your unceasing salvation, your secure assistance, your unshakable advocacy, your impregnable wall, your storehouse of enjoyment, your blameless paradise, your safe stronghold, your mighty entrenchment, your strong tower of protection, your harbor for the storm-tossed, your calm for those in turmoil, your surety for sinners, access for the hopeless, restoration of the banished, return of the exiles, reconciliation of those alienated, reunion of those condemned, blessing of those convicted, dew for the soul's drought, drop of water for the withering plant ("for our bones," as it is written, "through you rise up like a plant" (Isaiah 66.14 LXX)), the mother of the lamb and the shepherd, and the one recognized as bringer of all good things. Whatever is yours, is paradoxical, "true, and all together made righteous, all desirable and sweeter than honey and honeycomb; for your servants desire them, in desiring them, great reward [is obtained] from you" (Ps. 18.10-12 LXX). "Who will understand your mercies?" (Ps. 106.43 LXX)	

352B	Ὅθεν καὶ ὁ Χριστιανὸς λαός σου, τὰ καθ᾽ ἑαυτὸν ἀνακρίνων, πρὸς μὲν τὸν Θεὸν παρρησιαστικῶς ὑποστέλλεταί σοι τὰς δεήσεις προσφέρειν.	Therefore your Christian people examining their own [affairs], delegates you to bring their petitions to God with confident speech.	Dormition II
352B	Σὲ δυσωπεῖν ἀνενδοίαστος θαρρεῖ, παναγία, διὰ τὴν πεῖραν, καὶ τὰ πλήθη τῶν εἰς ἡμᾶς ἀγαθῶν σου, καὶ παραβιάσεσθαί σε πολλάκις ἐν ἱκεσίαις.	They unhesitatingly make bold to entreat you, all-holy Lady, because of [their] experience and the multitude of your bounties towards us, and to constrain you often in supplications.	Dormition II
352C	Ἐπὰν γὰρ πολλὰ χρεωστῶν οὐδὲν ἀνταποδίδωσί σοι, πληθύνει τὴν εὐχαριστίαν, ὡς σὺ τὴν προστασίαν.	For although he is greatly in your debt he gives you nothing in return, he multiplies thanksgiving, [just] as you [multiply] your advocacy.	Dormition II
353B	Ἔχεις ἐκ Θεοῦ τὸ μέγα πρὸς θρίαμβον ὕψος· διότι λαὸν αὐτῷ Χριστιανικὸν ἀπὸ σαρκὸς τῆς σῆς συνεστήσω	For you have from God the great sublime triumph; for which reason you have established a Christian people for him from your flesh,	Dormition II
356A	καὶ σύνοικόν σε πνευματικῶς ἔχειν πεπιστεύκαμεν	we trust to have you as a spiritual house-mate.	Dormition II
356C	Διὰ τοῦτο μακάριος κἂν ἁμαρτωλὸς ὁ ἄνθρωπος, ὅτιπερ συγγενὴ σε κατ᾽ οὐσίαν κτησάμενος εὑρέθη, καὶ θείας φύσεως διὰ σοῦ κοινωνὸς	Because of this man is blessed even if he is a sinner, since he has been found to have you as a relative in essence, and through you he is a partaker of the divine nature.	Dormition II (P Grazie 172 ftn. 11)
357D	ἀχώριστον δὲ τῆς τῶν ἀνθρώπων συναναστροφῆς εὑρεθῆναι τὸ πνεῦμά σου	the finding of your spirit is inseparable from the companionship with mankind	Dormition II
360D	ἐπεὶ τοὺς ἐν τῷ κόσμῳ τῆς ἀντιλήψεως ὀρφανοὺς οὐκ ἀφήσεις· ἀλλ᾽ ὥσπερ ἐγὼ μὴ ὢν ἐκ τοῦ κόσμου, ἐπιβλέπω καὶ διοικῶ τοὺς ἐν τῷ	since you will not leave those in the world orphaned of your protection; but as I, although I am not in the world, oversee and care for	Dormition III

Gregory E. Roth

	κόσμῳ· οὕτως καὶ ἡ σὴ προστασία οὐκ ἀφαιρεθήσεται μέχρι συντελείας ἐκ τῶν τοῦ κόσμου.	those in the world, so also your advocacy will not be taken away from those in the world until the end.	
361D	πρεσβείαν ἁμαρτανόντων	an intercession for those who are sinning	Dormition III
361D	γέφυραν κλυδωνιζομένων	a bridge for those who are swamped	Dormition III
365B/C	Διότι μὲν ἐν τῇ τοῦ κόσμου τούτου παροικίᾳ σὲ, Θεομῆτορ, σύνοικον ἔχοντες, καὶ ὡς αὐτὸν τὸν Χριστὸν θεωροῦντές σε παρεμυθούμεθα βλέποντες, ἀδολεσχοῦμεν ἐπὶ τῇ σῇ μεταστάσει. Ἐπεὶ δὲ καὶ θεϊκῇ ἐξουσίᾳ, καὶ σαρκικῇ πρὸς μητέρα προσπαθείᾳ, πρὸς τὸν Θεὸν ἐπεζητήθης ἀναλῦσαι, χαίρομεν τῷ ἐπὶ σοὶ πρεπόντως ἐκπληρουμένῳ,	"Because having you as a companion in the sojourn of this world, O Mother of God, and seeing you like Christ himself we are consoled when we behold [you], we meditate on your translation. But since by divine authority and fleshly attachment to a mother, you have been asked to return to God, we rejoice at what is being accomplished fittingly for you, and turning	Dormition III (P Grazie 168 ftn. 2)
	καὶ συμφερόντως ἐκβησομένῳ. Καὶ γὰρ πληροφορίαν ζωῆς αἰωνίου καὶ ἡμεῖς ἐπὶ σοὶ προσλαμβάνομεν, καὶ μεσῖτίν σε πρὸς Θεὸν μεθισταμένην κεκτήμεθα. Οὐδὲ γὰρ καὶ ἥρμοζεν τὴν Μητέρα τοῦ Θεοῦ ἐν μέσῳ γενεᾶς σκολιᾶς καὶ διεστραμμένης διάγειν, ἀλλ᾽ ἐν σκηναῖς οὐρανίων καὶ ἀφθάρτων διατριβῶν μετελθεῖν.	out advantageously. For we also acquire fulfillment of eternal life in addition to you, and we have obtained you as an intercessor who is being translated to God's side. For it was not suitable for the Mother of God to live in the midst of a crooked and perverted generation (Philippians 2.15), but to pass over to the tents of the heavenly and imperishable dwellings."	
368B	ἀπάρτι καὶ πρὸς αὐτὸν μετατεθῆναί σε διδάξω τοῦ γνωσθῆναι αὐτοῖς ἔθνεσιν τὸ σωτήριον αὐτῶν ἐν τῇ σῇ κραταιοῦσθαι πρεσβείᾳ· ὅπως ἔχειν καὶ αὐτὰ προστασίαν πρὸς τὸν Θεὸν ἀμετάθετον	From now on I will also teach that you have been transferred to his side so that it may be made known to the very gentiles that their salvation is strengthened by your intercession and that they have immovable assistance with God."	Dormition III

490

372D	Μέμνησο Χριστιανῶν τῶν σῶν δούλων. Παράθου καὶ πάντων δεήσεις, τὰς ὅλων ἐλπίδας. Τὴν πίστιν στερέωσον· τὰς Ἐκκλησίας ἕνωσον· τὴν βασιλείαν τροπαιο-φόρησον· τῷ στρατῷ συμπολέμησον· τὸν κόσμον εἰρήνευσον, καὶ πάντας κινδύνων καὶ πειρασμῶν λυτρουμένη, ἀκατάκριτον ἑκάστῳ τὴν ἡμέραν τῆς ἀνταποδόσεως παρασχεθῆναι δυσώπησον. Πρὸς τίνα γὰρ ἄλλον ἀπελευσόμεθα; Ῥήματα ζωῆς ἔχεις τὰ πρὸς τὸν Θεὸν ὑπὲρ ἡμῶν τῆς σῆς παραθέσεως ἱκετεύματα. Σὺ γὰρ εἶ ἡ πάντοτε ποιήσασα, καὶ ποιεῖν μὴ ἐνδιδοῦσα μεγαλεῖα μεθ' ἡμῶν· καὶ ἅγιον τὸ ὄνομά σου τὸ ἐξ ἀγγέλων καὶ ἀνθρώπων μακαριζόμενον ἐν πάσαις γενεαῖς γενεῶν, ἀπὸ τοῦ νῦν, καὶ ἕως τοῦ αἰῶνος τῶν αἰώνων. Ἀμήν.	Remember your Christian servants. Present the prayers of all, the hopes of all. Confirm our faith. Unite the churches. Give victory to the empire. Fight alongside the army. Bring peace to the world, and ransoming all from dangers and temptations, vouchsafe to provide for each the day of reckoning without condemnation. For to whom else shall we flee? You have the words of life which are supplications of your intercession on our behalf before God. For you are the one who always does, and never ceases to do great things with us, and holy is your name which is called blessed by angels and men in all generations of generations, from now and unto the age of ages. Amen.	Dormition III
377C (381B)	Ὦ ζώνη φαιδρά, ἡ τῆς τοῦ ἀφθάρτου Θεοῦ Μητρὸς τὸ ὑπέρσεμνον σῶμα σεμνοπρεπῶς προσεγγίσασα, κἀκεῖθεν τὴν ἀφθαρσίαν ἀμφιασαμένη, ἀπαρασάλευτος καὶ ἄφθαρτος μένουσα, ὡς εἰς ἡμᾶς τις λόγος τῆς ἀληθείας κατελήλυθεν! Ἀλλὰ τί καὶ τῶν ἀδυνάτων ἐπιχειροῦμεν, καὶ ὑπὲρ	Oh radiant Sash, which honorably surrounded the very venerable body of the Mother of the incorruptible God, and thence is surrounded by incorruption, and continued to remain intact and incorruptible, and this true tradition has come down to us[20].But we are attempting the impossible, and are urging ourselves	Sash (P Grazie 174 ftn. 12)

---

[20] See also Cunningham, Wider 251 ftn. 10.

τὰ ἐσκαμμένα πηδᾶν ἐπειγόμεθα· τῆς ἐκ τῶν λόγων τιμῆς ταῦτα τιμᾶν κατ' ἀξίαν πειρώμενοι, ὅπερ καὶ ἀγγέλοις ἀδύνατον. Πλὴν, ὦ τιμία τῆς ὑπερτίμου τοῦ Θεοῦ Μητρὸς ζώνη, περίζωσον τὰς ὀσφῦς ἡμῶν ἀλήθειαν, δικαιοσύνην τε καὶ πραότητα. Τῆς ἀϊδίου καὶ μακαρίας ζωῆς ποίησον κληρονόμους, καὶ τὴν ἐπίκηρον ἡμῶν ταύτην ζωήν, ἐχθρῶν ἀοράτων τε καὶ ὁρατῶν, ἀνεπιβούλευτον διατήρησον. Τὴν πίστιν ἐν εἰρήνῃ ἀσάλευτον διαφύλαξον. Τὴν σὴν κληρονομίαν, τὸν σὸν λαὸν, ὦ πανάχραντε τῆς παναχράντου ζώνη, ὀρθοὺς τῇ πίστει, σώους τῷ κατὰ Θεὸν βίῳ, ἀβλαβεῖς τῆς οἱασοῦν ἐπηρείας διάσωζε. Ἔχοιμέν σε ἰσχὺν καὶ βοήθειαν, τεῖχος καὶ προπύργιον λιμένα καὶ καταφυγὴν σωτήριον. Σὺ δέ μοι, ὦ πάναγνε, καὶ πανάγαθε, καὶ πολυεύσπλαγχνε Δέσποινα, τὸ τῶν Χριστιανῶν παραμύθιον, τὸ τῶν θλιβομένων θερμότατον παρηγόρημα, τὸ τῶν ἁμαρτανόντων ἑτοιμότατον καταφύγιον, μὴ ἐγκαταλίπῃς ἡμᾶς	on beyond, to leap over the trench, and we are attempting to honor [the swaddling clothes and the sash] worthily in words, which is impossible even to the angels. What's more, Oh honorable Sash of the all honorable Mother[21], surround with truth our loins, with righteousness and meekness. Makes inheritors of eternal and blessed life, (cf. Titus 3.7) and unassailed by enemies both visible and invisible. And guard our faith unshaken. Oh all pure Sash of the all pure One, guard unharmed from any kind of insult your inheritance, your people in upright faith, and save (them) through the godly life. May we have you as strength and aid, a wall and a tower a harbor and a safe refuge[22]. But you are to me, Oh most pure, all good and most compassionate Lady, the correction of Christians, the warmest encouragement of the afflicted, the ready refuge of sinners, do not forsake us orphans of your aid. For if by you we should be forsaken, then to whom shall we flee? And what shall	

---

[21] The phrase: ὦ τιμία τῆς ὑπερτίμου τοῦ Θεοῦ Μητρὸς ζώνη demonstrates the difficulty of translation from Greek to English. Mary Cunningham points it out as an instance of metaclisis, a rhetorical device that is seldom used in English. See Cunningham, *Wider* 252 ftn. 12.

[22] This phrase is a familiar petition in the litanies of the Orthodox Church.

ὀρφανοὺς τῆς σῆς ἀντιλήψεως. Εἰ γὰρ ὑπὸ σοῦ ἐγκαταλειφθείημεν, ποῦ ἄρα καὶ προσδραμούμεθα. Τί δὲ ἄρα καὶ γενησόμεθα, ὦ παναγία Θεοτόκε; ἡ τῶν Χριστιανῶν πνοὴ καὶ ζωή. Ὡς γὰρ τὸ σῶμα ἡμῶν ζωτικῆς ἐνεργείας τὸ ἀναπνεῖν τεκμήριον κέκτηται, οὕτω καὶ τὸ σὸν πανάγιον ὄνομα ἀδιαλείπτως ἐν τοῖς τῶν σῶν δούλων ἅγιον ὄνομα ἀδιαλείπτως ἐν τοῖς τῶν σῶν δούλων στόμασι προφερόμενον ἐν παντὶ καιρῷ καὶ τόπῳ καὶ τρόπῳ, ζωῆς καὶ θυμηδίας καὶ βοηθείας οὐχὶ τεκμήριον, ἀλλὰ πρόξενον γίνεται. Σκέποις ἡμᾶς πτέρυξι τῆς σῆς ἀγαθότητος. Φρουρήσῃς ἡμᾶς ταῖς μεσιτείαις σου. Παράσχοις ἡμῖν τὴν αἰώνιον ζωήν, Χριστιανῶν ἐλπὶς ἀκαταίσχυντε. Ἡμεῖς γὰρ οἱ πτωχοὶ θείων ἔργων καὶ τρόπων, τὸν διὰ σοῦ παρασχεθέντα ἡμῖν τῆς χρηστότητος πλοῦτον θεασάμενοι, εἴπωμεν· «Τοῦ ἐλέους Κυρίου πλήρης ἡ γῆ.» Ἡμεῖς ἐν τῷ πλήθει τῶν ἁμαρτιῶν ἐκ Θεοῦ δεδιωγμένοι, ἐζητήσαμεν διὰ σοῦ τὸν Θεόν, καὶ εὕρομεν· καὶ εὑρόντες ἐσώθημεν. Δυνατὴ τοιγαροῦν πρὸς σωτηρίαν ἡ βοήθειά σου, Θεοτόκε, καὶ μὴ χρῄζουσά τινος

we become, Oh all holy Theotokos? The breath and the life of Christians, for just as our bodies have breath as a sign of its living energy, so also your all holy name continually being carried forth on the lips of your servant in all times and places and points, not [only] a sure sign of life, wellbeing and aid, but a defender. Shelter us under the wings of your great goodness. (cf. Ps. 17.8) Guard us through your intercession. Supply to us life eternal, a reliable hope of Christians. For we are beggars, impoverished in the way of life and works of God, which we have seen through your kindness to us (cf. Ps. 31.9) the rich one, Let us say: "The mercy of the Lord fills the earth"[23] (Ps 33.5) We had been driven away from God in the multitude of our sins, but through you we sought after God and found Him. Therefore certainly your help is a power for salvation, Oh Theotokos, and no other help is needed to (find) God. This we know, and have experienced in many requests and your warm response, ungrudgingly we have received the answers to our petitions, and we flee to you, your people, your inheritance, your flock, (cf. Luke. 12.32)

---

[23] Ps. 32:5

493

ἑτέρου πρὸς Θεὸν μεσίτου. Τοῦτο καὶ ἡμεῖς ἐπιστάμενοι, οὐ μὴν ἀλλὰ καὶ πείρᾳ μαθόντες ἐξ ὧν πολλάκις αἰτοῦντές σε τὴν θερμοτάτην ἡμῶν ἀντίληψιν, ἀφθόνως τὰς τῶν αἰτήσεων παροχὰς λαμβάνομεν, καὶ τανῦν σοὶ προσφεύγομεν, ὁ σὸς λαός, ἡ σὴ κληρονομία, τὸ σὸν ποίμνιον, τὸ τῇ τοῦ σοῦ Υἱοῦ κλήσει κατακαλλυνόμενον. Οὐκ ἔστιν ὄντως τῆς σῆς μεγαλειότητος πέρας· οὐκ ἔστι τῆς σῆς ἀντιλήψεως κόρος. Οὐκ ἔστι τῶν σῶν εὐεργεσιῶν ἀριθμός. Οὐδεὶς γὰρ ὁ σωζόμενος εἰ μὴ διὰ σοῦ, παναγία. Οὐδεὶς ὁ τῶν δεινῶν λυτρούμενος, εἰ μὴ διὰ σοῦ, πανάμωμε. Οὐδεὶς ὁ συγχωρούμενος δῶρον εἰ μὴ διὰ σοῦ, πάναγνε. Οὐδεὶς ὁ ἐλεούμενος χάριτι, εἰ μὴ διὰ σοῦ, πάνσεμνε. Ἀνθ᾽ ὧν, τίς σε μὴ μακαρίσει; τίς μὴ μεγαλυνεῖ; εἰ καὶ μὴ κατ᾽ ἀξίαν, ἀλλ᾽ οὖν προθυμότατα· σὲ τὴν δεδοξασμένην· σὲ τὴν	the one (flock) which is becoming beautiful by the call of your Son. There is truly no end to your magnificence;[24] and there are no boundaries to your help. Your good works are innumerable. For no one is saved except through you, Oh holy one. (cf. Acts 4.12) No one is ransomed from bad things, except through you, all blameless one, no one receives gifts except through you, all holy one. No one receives grace except through you all venerable one.[25] Wherefore, who would not praise you? (Luke. 1.48 ff) Who would not magnify you? If not worthily, at least heartily, Oh glorious one, Oh blessed one, Oh you who received magnification from your Son and your God as great and wondrous, wherefore all generations shall praise you. Who then, but you after your Son, would take thought of the race of men? Who then defends us by taking our part in tribulation? Who then

[24]   Horvath comments that "The Marian devotion of Germanus I, Patriarch of Constantinople from 715-730 (born c. 634, d. 733), resembles that of St Bernard of Clairvaux. His praises and eulogies of Mary have almost no limit." "Germanos of Constantinople and the Cult of the Virgin Mary, Mother of God, Mediatrix of All Men". *De cultu mariano saeculis VI-XI;* acta Congressus Mariologici Mariani Internationalis in Croatia anno 1971 celebrati. 1972. Pontificia Academia Mariana Internationalis. 285.

[25]   Mary Cunningham comments on this passage "Germanos seems to go further in this homily than do other preachers in extolling Mary's central role in obtaining God's mercy for humankind." See Cunningham, *Wider* 253 ftn. 14. However, one must read this homily not in parts but as a whole. See, a few line later, the reason: "Oh you who received magnification from your Son and your God as great and wondrous". And elsewhere where Mary's role in the Incarnation is clearly tied to her role as Mediatrix. See also 380B where εἰ μὴ διὰ σοῦ is repeated in the anaphora so that it becomes clear that Germanos views Mary as a necessary agent "through" whom salvation comes.

μεμακαρισμένην· σὲ τὴν
μεγαλεῖα σχοῦσαν παρ'
αὐτοῦ τοῦ σμένην· σὲ
τὴν μεγαλεῖα σχοῦσαν
παρ' αὐτοῦ τοῦ σοῦ Υἱοῦ
καὶ Θεοῦ ὡς μεγάλα
καὶ θαυμαστά· ὅθεν
σε καὶ γενεαὶ πᾶσαι
γεραίρουσιν.
Τίς οὕτω τοῦ τῶν
ἀνθρώπων γένους μετὰ
τὸν σὸν Υἱὸν ὡς σὺ
προνοεῖται; Τίς οὕτως
ἀντιληπτικῶς τῶν
ἡμετέρων προΐσταται
θλίψεων; Τίς οὕτως
ὀξέως προφθάνων ῥύεται
τῶν ὑπερχομένων ἡμῖν
πειρασμῶν.
Τίς τοσοῦτον, τῶν
ἁμαρτωλῶν ἱκεσίαις
ὑπερμαχεῖ; Τίς τῶν
ἀδιορθώτων κατὰ
τοσοῦτον ἀντιφωνητικῶς
ὑπεραπολογεῖται; Σὺ
γὰρ μὴ
τρῴαν ἔχουσα πρὸς τὸν
σὸν Υἱὸν τὴν παρρησίαν
καὶ τὴν ἰσχὺν, ἡμᾶς
τοὺς ταῖς ἁμαρτίαις
κατακεκριμένους, καὶ
μὴ τολμῶντας μηδὲ
τὸ ὕψος ἐμβλέψαι τοῦ
οὐρανοῦ, σαῖς ἐντεύξεσι
καὶ σαῖς μεσιτείαις καὶ
σῴζεις, καὶ τῆς αἰωνίου
λυτροῦσαι κολάσεως.
Ὅθεν ὁ θλιβόμενος
πρὸς σὲ καταφεύγει·
ὁ ἀδικούμενος ἐπὶ σὲ
προστρέχει· ὁ τοῖς δεινοῖς
συνεχόμενος, τὴν σὴν
ἐπικαλεῖται βοήθειαν.
Ὅλα τὰ σά, Θεοτόκε,
παράδοξα, ὅλα ὑπὲρ
φύσιν, ὅλα ὑπὲρ λόγον
καὶ δύναμιν. Διὰ τοῦτο καὶ
ἡ προστασία σου,

going swiftly before us
delivers us from overtaking
temptations? Who then
through prayer fights on
behalf of us sinners? Who
then defends so out spoken
those who have little hope
of amendment of life? For
you having a maternal
freedom of speech and
strength towards your
Son, we having been
condemned by our sins,
and not daring to look
to the heights of heaven,
you have saved by your
petitions and intercessions
and you redeem from
eternal punishment.(*cf.* Ps.
32.7) On which account
the affected ones flee to
you, the wrongdoer runs to
you; the one constrained
by fears, appeals for
your help. All your own,
Theotokos (Luke. 5.26),
paradox, all above nature,
all beyond words and
power. Through which
also is your protection that
is beyond understanding.
For you have reconciled
and established the
estranged, the one who
have given up, those who
had become enemies by
your birth-giving you
have made children and
an inheritance. (*cf.* Rm.
8.17) You have extended
your hand of aid to those
who have been plunged
into the sea of every kind
of sin, rescuing them from
the waves. You continue
to protect your servants
from the host of evil, you
continue to preserve those

ὑπὲρ ἔννοιαν. Τοὺς γὰρ ἀπωσμένους, τοὺς ἐκδεδιωγμένους, τοὺς ἐκπεπολεμωμένους, τῷ σῷ τόκῳ κατήλλαξας καὶ ᾠκείωσας· καὶ υἱοὺς καὶ κληρονόμους πεποίηκας. Σὺ τοὺς καθ᾽ ἑκάστην ταῖς ἁμαρτίαις καταποντιζο-μένους, χεῖρας βοηθείας ἐκτείνουσα, ἐξέλκεις τοῦ κλύδωνος. Σὺ τὰς τοῦ πονηροῦ κατὰ τῶν σῶν δούλων ἐπαναστάσεις, τῇ κλήσει σου μόνῃ τῇ παναγίᾳ ἀποδιώκουσα διασώζεις. Σὺ τοὺς ἐπικαλουμένους σε ἐκ πάσης ἀνάγκης, ἐκ παντοίων πειρασμῶν προφθάνουσα ἐκλυτροῦσαι, πανάμωμε. Ὅθεν καὶ τῷ σῷ ναῷ σπουδαίως προστρέχομεν· καὶ ἐν αὐτῷ ἑστῶτες, ἐν οὐρανῷ ἑστάναι νομίζομεν. Ἐν τούτῳ δοξολογοῦντές σε, ἀγγέλοις συγχορεύειν ἡγούμεθα. Ποῖον γὰρ γένος ἀνθρώπων πάρεξ Χριστιανῶν τοιαύτης εὐπόρησε δόξης, τοιαύτης ἐπέτυχεν ἀντιλήψεως, τοιαύτης προστασίας πεπλούτηκε; Τίς πιστῶς τῇ τιμίᾳ σου ζώνῃ προσατενίσας, Θεοτόκε, οὐκ εὐθὺς θυμηδίας ἐμπίπλαται; Τίς θερμῶς ταύτῃ προσπεσών, κενὸς τῆς συμφερούσης αἰτήσεως ἐξελήλυθε; Τίς τὸν σὸν χαρακτῆρα ἐνοπτριζόμενος, οὐκ αὐτίκα πάσης θλίψεως ἐπιλέληται;

who flee only to your holy name. You continue to anticipate ransoming those who call upon you in all needs, and all sorts of temptation, Oh all blameless one. For which reason we speedily flee to your temple; and standing in it we know ourselves to be in heaven. We praise you in it joining with the choir of the angels. For what race of men is well off without being Christians and having such a defense and advocacy? Who gazing in faith, when he has gazed at your worthy Sash, Theotokos, is not filled with delight? Who fervently falling down before it, vainly lifts up offerings of praise? Who contemplating your character, does not forget immediately all his tribulation?

| 381D/ 384A | Ἔπιδε ἐξ ἁγίου κατοικητηρίου σου τούτου τὸ περιεστώς σοι πιστότατον ἄθροισμα, τὸ σὲ Κυρίαν καὶ προστάτιν καὶ Δέσποιναν ἔχειν καταπλουτῆσαν, τὸ σὲ ἐκ ψυχῆς ὑμνῆσαι συνεληλυθὸς, Θεοτόκε, καὶ ἐπισκοπῇ σου θείᾳ ἐπισκεψαμένη, πάσης ἐξέλου τούτους συμφορᾶς τε καὶ θλίψεως· παντοίας νόσου, παντοίας βλάβης, παντοίας ἐξάρπασον ἐπηρείας· πάσης χαρᾶς, πάσης ἰάσεως, πάσης χάριτος ἔμπλησον· καὶ ἐν τῇ τοῦ σοῦ Υἱοῦ ἐλεύσει τοῦ φιλανθρώπου Θεοῦ ἡμῶν, ὅτε κριθῆναι πάντες παραστησόμεθα, τῇ κραταιᾷ σου χειρὶ, ὡς μητρῴαν ἔχουσα παρρησίαν τε καὶ ἰσχὺν, τοῦ αἰωνίου ἡμᾶς ἐξαγαγοῦσα πυρὸς, τῶν αἰωνίων ἐπιτυχεῖν ἀξίωσον ἀγαθῶν· χάριτι καὶ φιλανθρωπίᾳ τοῦ ἐκ σοῦ τεχθέντος Κυρίου ἡμῶν Ἰησοῦ Χριστοῦ· ᾧ ἡ δόξα καὶ τὸ κράτος, νῦν καὶ εἰς τοὺς αἰῶνας τῶν αἰώνων. Ἀμήν. | Behold the most faithful gathering which surrounds you from this your holy dwelling, which is rich in having you as Lady, patroness and Mistress, which has come together to sing hymns from a soul, Theotokos, and is looked after by your holy oversight, take these people out of all misfortune and tribulation, all disease, all harm, all contumely rescue. All joy, all health, all grace fill (these people) in the coming of your Son, our man loving God, when we shall be judged, by your strong hand, having motherly boldness and strength and having received us from eternal fire, make us worthy to attain eternal good things, by the grace and love of your Son Jesus Christ to whom be glory and might unto the ages of ages. Amen. | Sash (P 176 ftn. 13) |

References to the Liturgy in Germanos I, Patriarch of Constantinople (715-730)

PG 98 Location	Greek	English	Homily
292A	Θυμηδίας μὲν πᾶσα θειοτάτη πανήγυρις ἑκάστοτε τελουμένη τοὺς θιασώτας ἐμπιπλᾷσι πνευματικῶς ἐκ θησαυρῶν καὶ θεορρύτων πηγῶν. Μεῖζον δὲ καὶ ὑπὲρ ἁπάσας λαμπροφορεῖται τελεταρχικῶς ψυχαγωγοῦσα ἡ ἀρτιύμνητος, ὅτῳ καὶ ὑπεραναβαινούσης τῆς ἐξαρχούσης Θεόπαιδος. Καὶ γὰρ αὐτῆς ἱερουργικωτάτη περίεισιν ἐτήσιος πανδαισία	Every divine festival, whenever it is celebrated, spiritually fills those who are present from a treasury and divinely flowing spring. But even more and beyond other feasts does the recently hymned festival, brilliantly celebrated, attract the soul with holy joy and gives more joy in proportion to the preeminence of the excellent child of God. For the annual observation of this feast is coming,	Presentation I
296B	Καὶ ταύτην μὲν οἱ οἰκεῖοι γεννήτορες, τριετῆ χρόνον τετελεκυῖαν, Θεῷ ἀναφέρουσιν. Ἀλλ' ὡς μέγιστος ὁ τρισάριθμος καὶ λίαν τιμώμενος καὶ παντί που πάσης βεβαιώσεως αἴτιος· τρισὶ μὲν λίθοις Δαυῒδ σφενδονῶν τὸν ἀλάστορα Γολιάθ· τρισὶ δὲ περιόδῳ ὁ Θεσβίτης Ἠλιοῦ, ὡς οὐρανίου πυρὸς ἐν ὕδατι φλέγοντος ἐπέρχεται φλόξ, πιστεύειν	And her own parents presented to God the one who had reached three years of age. But how great is the three-fold number and exceedingly honored and for everyone a cause of all security! With three stones David slew the infamous Goliath (cf. 1 Samuel 17.40ff.), and Elijah the Tishbite, as by three circuits he brought thus the flame of fire onto water (cf. 1 Kings	Presentation I

	παρασκευάζει· ἰσομέτροις δ' ἡμέραις Ἰωνᾶς ἁλιπλόου θηρὸς στέρνοις περιφερόμενος, τοῦ τὸ μέγα κῆτος Θεοῦ χειρισαμένου τύπος γνωρίζεται· τοσαυτάριθμοι δὲ παῖδες κάμινον πατοῦντες καὶ δρόσῳ οὐρανίῳ πιαινόμενοι εὐψύχως περιπολεύουσι· τρισὶ δὲ περικυκλουμένῃ ἐνιαυτῶν περιόδῳ τῷ δεκατοῦσθαι Ἰησοῦς ὁ ἐμὸς Κύριος, τοῦ τῆς παραβάσεώς με μολυσμοῦ ἀποκαθαίρει·	18.34*ff.*), prepares [men] to believe. And for an equal number of days Jonah was carried about in the breast of the beast covered with water (*cf.* Jonah 2.1*ff.*). He is declared an image of God who managed the whale. And in like time the children boldly walked about in the furnace nourished by the heavenly dew (*cf.* Daniel 3.49*ff.*). And my Lord Jesus' ministry was for a period of three encircling years, cleansing me from the stain of my transgression	
297D	Πάρεσο, μεγαλόφωνος Ἰεζεκιήλ, τὴν κεφαλίδα θεόθεν κατίσχων τοῦ ζωοποιοῦ Πνεύματος καὶ κεκράζων τὴν εὐφημίαν τῇ ἀνατολοβλέπτῳ καὶ θεοπαρόδῳ ἐσφραγισμένῃ πύλῃ, καὶ εἴτις ἄλλος κατ' ἄμφω τοῦ ἱερολέκτου τάγματος, ἤτοι ὁ τῶν βλεπόντων ἐπίλοιπος ἅπας χορὸς, ἀναφωνεῖτε, προφητευθέντων δεδορκότες τὴν ἔκβασιν ἰοῦσαν.	Come, loud-voiced Ezekiel, holding the divine scroll of the life-creating Spirit and crying your holy words to the eastward oriented and sealed gate (Ezekiel 44:1) which only God goes through; and anyone else in holy orders, or all the rest of the choir of spectators, raise your voices, having seen accomplishment of thing that have been prophesied.	Presentation I
300B	Εἰσάγεται μὲν οὖν οὕτως ἡ Θεόπαις, τοῖς κέρασιν ἵσταται, τῶν τε γονέων ἐπευξαμένων, τοῦ τε ἱερέως ἐπευλογήσοντος.	And thus the child of God is led in [and] takes her place by the horns, as her parents offer their vows, and the priest gives his blessing.	Presentation I

304A	Πλησίασον τῇ τραπέζῃ προσκυνήσουσα, περὶ ἧς ἐν συμβόλοις πλείοσι λέλεκται τράπεζαν κεχρηματικέναι σε λογικωτάτην καὶ ἀμόλυντον. Ὅδευσον διὰ τῆς ἐπαύλεως τοῦ ὅλου θυσιαστηρίου, ὡς ὀσμὴν θυμιάματος ἐκπνέουσα, καὶ ὑπὲρ μύρον τοῖς ὀσφραινομένοις γεγενημένη ἡ καλῶς τῆς θεολέκτου γλώσσης καὶ πνευματεμφόρου τοῦ προφήτου πύριον ἐξηχημένη.	Approach in order to venerate the table, you who are called the living, undefiled table, which has been spoken of in many symbols. Make your way through the courts of the whole sanctuary breathing out as an odor of incense (*cf.* Exodus 30.1*ff.*). You have become more fragrant than myrrh, you who have been proclaimed by the God-chosen tongue of the spirit-filled prophet to be a censer.	Presentation I
304C	Ὑπερβέβηκε μὲν γὰρ οὖν ἅπασαν ἔννοιαν ἡ μόνη παρθένος καὶ μήτηρ γνωρισθεῖσα, καὶ δῆλον τὸ αἴτιον. Τίς γὰρ παρθένος ἔτεκεν, ἢ τεκοῦσα ἄσυλον τὴν παρθενίαν τετήρηκεν, εἰ μὴ σὺ μόνη, ἡ ἀπεριτρέπτως ἡμῖν σαρκὶ Θεὸν κυήσασα, πανολβιακόρη;	For the only [woman] known as virgin and mother has surpassed all thought, and the cause is clear. For what virgin has given birth, or after giving birth has preserved her virginity undefiled, except you alone, who truly bore God in the flesh for us, all-blessed maiden?	Presentation I
308D	Τοὺς ἱερεῖς τῇ δικαιοσύνῃ καὶ τῇ τῆς εὐκλεοῦς ἀμωμήτου εἰλικρινοῦς	Clothe the priests brilliantly with righteousness (*cf.* Psalm 131.16 LXX)	Presentation I
	πίστεως ἀγαλλιάσει φωτεινοτάτως ἔνδυσον.	and the joy of glorious blameless pure faith.	
340C	θριάμβων παρακατιών	triumphal songs/rites in narrative	Dormition I
What follows is a rudimentory hymn to the Theotokios much like "More Honorable than the Cherubim . . . "			
353B	«Εὐλογημένον τοίνυν διὰ τοῦτο τὸ ὄνομά σου εἰς τοὺς αἰῶνας.»	"Therefore your name is blessed because of this unto the ages"	Dormition II
353B	Πρὸ τοῦ ἡλίου τὸ φῶς σου	Before the sun [is/was] your light.	Dormition II

353B	Ὑπερτέρα πάσης τῆς κτίσεως ἡ τιμή σου	Above all the creation is your honor	Dormition II
353B	πρὸ τῶν ἀγγέλων ἡ ὑπεροχή σου	Before the angels is your greatness.	Dormition II
353B	«Ὑψηλοτέρα σὺ τοῦ οὐρανοῦ·» ἀλλὰ καὶ πλατυτέρα τοῦ οὐρανοῦ τῶν οὐρανῶν	"You [are] higher than the heaven" but also wider than the heaven of heavens,	Dormition II
	Ἄγγελοι ταῖς οὐρανίων ἐγγαυριῶνται καταμοναῖς· ἡμεῖς τοῖς τῶν ἁγιωτάτων σου ναῶν εὐφραινόμεθα σχολασμοῖς. Εἰ γὰρ ὁ Σολομώντειος ναὸς, πάλαι τὸν οὐρανὸν ἐπὶ τῆς γῆς ἐσκιογράφει, πόσῳ μᾶλλον ἐμψύχου σοῦ ναοῦ γεγονυίας τοῦ Χριστοῦ, μὴ καὶ τὰς Ἐκκλησίας τὰς σὰς, ὡς ἐπιγείους οὐρανοὺς δικαίως ἔστιν ἀνακομπάζειν; ἀστέρες λαμπηδογλωσσοῦσιν ἐν τῷ στερεώματι τοῦ οὐρανοῦ·	Angels rejoice in the mansions of the heavens; we delight to spend time in your holy temples. For if the temple of Solomon formerly made a shadow of heaven on earth, how much more when you have become a living temple of Christ, is it not right to adorn your churches as earthly heavens? Stars speak brilliantly in the firmament of heaven.	Dormition II

These phrases illustrate the liturgical and icongraphic conscience of Germanos. His thought was to influence much of Orthodox iconographic and liturgical development.

364A	πρὸς τὸν ζωοποιὸν ἐξῆλθον καὶ ἑκούσιον τοῦ σταυροῦ μου θάνατον	at that time went forth to my life-giving and willing death on the cross	Dormition III
368A	βαθμικῇ	High Place	Dormition III

No references appear in the Homily on the Sash

Reference to Mary and Eve in the Creation Story in Germanos I, Patriarch of Constantinople (715-730)

PG 98 Location	Greek	English	Homily
300A	Οἱ προπάτορες τῆς ἀρᾶς ἀπολυθησόμενοι καὶ τῆς ἧς ἐξεβλήθητε τρυφῆς, τὴν οἴκησιν πάλιν ἀποκληρούμενοι· ἆρ' οὐχ τὴν αἰτίαν ὑμνήσετε τῆς σωτηρίας, ἀραρότοις ἐγκωμίοις καὶ μεγίσταις αἰνέσεσιν; ἢ καὶ μάλιστα ὑμῖν ἐστι κεκραγέναι καὶ με σὺν ὑμῖν καὶ πᾶσαν μετ' ἀμφοτέροις τὴν κτίσιν ἀγαλλιᾶσθαι.	Our ancestors who are about to be released from the curse and again inheriting the residence in paradise from which you were cast out: should you not hymn the cause of your salvation, with a fitting encomium and great praises? Indeed you especially ought to shout out, and I with you and with us both all creation [ought] to sing out in joy.	Presentation I
300B	σκιρτῶσι προπάτορες τὴν τῆς κατακρίσεως εἶρξιν ὑπεκφεύγοντες	The forefathers jump for joy, escaping the captivity of condemnation.	Presentation I
300C	Πάλιν οἱ γεννήτορες βοῶσιν τῷ ἱερεῖ	Once again, the forefathers call to the priest:	Presentation I
300C	περίπτυξαι τὴν περισκέπουσαν ἡμῶν τὴν ἐν Ἐδὲμ γυμνωθεῖσαν φύσιν·	Enfold her who covers our nature which was stripped bare in Eden.	Presentation I

304D	Χαίροις τοιγαροῦν τῇ τῆς Ἐδὲμ ἡμῖν θανατηφόρῳ καὶ ψυχοπύρῳ βρώσει γυμνωθεῖσιν,	Therefore hail, forgiveness of transgressions given by God for us filthy ones, who are denuded by the death-dealing and soul-destroying food of Eden,	Presentation I
305A	Χαίροις, ἡ τῇ τῶν βημάτων σου ῥυθμίσει καταπατήσασα τὸν δεινόν μοι ποδηγὸν, κεχρηματικότα πρὸς τὴν παράβασιν σκολιογνώμονα καὶ μισόκαλον ὄφιν διάβολον	Hail to you who by the rhythm of your footsteps trample down my terrible leader—that serpent with his crooked-minded, good-hating diabolical nature—who has counseled me toward transgression (cf. Genesis 3.1-13).	Presentation I
Note in 305A Germanos attributes his own failing to the influence of the snake placing himself along side of Adam and Eve.			
316D	καὶ κατακληροῦται Ἰωσὴφ ὁ δίκαιος, καὶ τὴν ἁγίαν ταύτην Παρθένον οἰκονομικῶς ἐκ τοῦ ναοῦ τοῦ Θεοῦ καὶ τῶν αὐτοῦ ἱερέων παραλαμβάνει, πρὸς δελεασμὸν τοῦ ἀρχεκάκου ὄφεως· ἵνα μὴ ὡς παρθένῳ προσβάλῃ τῇ ἀκηράτῳ κόρῃ, ἀλλ' ὡς ἅτε μεμνηστευμένην ταύτην παραδράμῃ.	And then by the assent of God and the counsel of the priests a lot is drawn concerning her, and Joseph the just is allotted, and receives this holy Virgin according to the dispensation from the Temple of God and his priests, to ensnare the serpent who originated evil, so that he should not attack the undefiled maiden as a virgin, but as a betrothed woman he should pass her by.	Presentation II

324B	Δέδοικα καὶ τρέμω σου τοὺς τοιούτους λόγους· καὶ ὑπολαμβάνω, ὡς ἄλλην Εὔαν πλανῆσαί με παραγέγονας. Ἐγὼ δὲ οὐκ εἰμὶ κατ' ἐκείνην. Πῶς δὲ καὶ ἀσπάζεσαι κόρην, ἣν οὐδέποτε ἐθεάσω;	I am afraid and I tremble at your words. I suspect that you have come to deceive me like another Eve. I am nothing like her. What a greeting you bring to a maiden whom you have never seen before!	Annunciation
325A	Ἵνα τί, καὶ διὰ τί, καὶ τίνος ἕνεκεν τὸν ἐμὸν εὐαγγελισμὸν ἐπὶ τοσοῦτον ἠπίστησας, δεδοξασμένη; καὶ μέχρι τίνος οὐ πειθαρχεῖς εἰς τὸν ἐξ οὐρανοῦ σοι πεμφθέντα ἄγγελον; Οὐκ εἰμὶ γὰρ ἐγὼ ὁ τὴν Εὔαν πλανήσας.	Why? For what purpose, for what reason, have you distrusted my good news, Glorified one? How long will you disobey the angel that was sent to you from heaven? I am not Eve's deceiver—far from it.	Annunciation
336B	Νῦν λέξω, Μαρία, ὅτι τοῖς ἴχνεσιν Εὔας σῆς μητρὸς ἐξηκολούθησας.	Now I will say, Mary, that you have followed the path of your mother Eve	Annunciation
349A	Σὺ εἶ τῆς ἀναπλάσεως τοῦ Ἀδὰμ ἡ ζύμη. Σὺ εἶ τῶν ὀνειδισμῶν τῆς Εὔας ἡ ἐλευθερία	You leaven the new creation of Adam. You free Eve from reproach	Dormition II
349A	Ἐκείνη μήτηρ χοός, σὺ μήτηρ φωτός	She is the mother of earth; you are the mother of light	Dormition II
349A	Ἐκείνης ἡ μήτρα, φθορᾶς· ἡ δὲ σὴ γαστήρ, ἀφθαρσίας	Her womb [is the source] of destruction; your belly [is the source] of imperishability	Dormition II
349A	Ἐκείνη θανάτου κατοίκησις, σὺ μετάστασις ἀπὸ θανάτου.	She is the dwelling-place of death; you are the removal from death	Dormition II

505

349A	Ἐκείνη βλεφάρων καταχθονισμός, σὺ γρηγορούντων ὀφθαλμῶν ἀκοίμητος δόξα	She brings eyelids down to earth; you are the unsleeping glory of wakeful eyes	Dormition II
349A	Ἐκείνης τὰ τέκνα, λύπη· ὁ δὲ σὸς Υἱός, παγγενὴς χαρά	Her children are grief; but your Son is universal joy.	Dormition II
349B	Ἐκείνη ὡς γῆ οὖσα εἰς γῆν παρῆλθε· σὺ δὲ Ζωὴν ἡμῖν ἔτεκες, καὶ πρὸς τὴν ζωὴν ἐπανῆλθες, καὶ Ζωὴν τοῖς ἀνθρώποις, καὶ μετὰ θάνατον, προξενεῖν κατίσχυσα	She, as being earth, passed into earth; but you bore Life for us, and passed over to life, and obtained the power to mediate life to mankind, even after death	Dormition II
361C	Οὐ καυχήσεται θάνατος ἐπὶ σοί· Ζωὴν γὰρ ἐκύησας. Σκεῦος ἐμὸν ἐγένου· οὐ ῥαγώσει τοῦτο σύντριμμα θανατοφθόρου καταπτώσεως.	Death will not boast over you, for you gave birth to Life. You became my vessel; the fracture of death-corrupting fall will not break this.	Dormition III
361D	Ἄνοιξον σὺ τὸν παράδεισον, ὃν ἡ συγγενής σου καὶ ὁμοφυής ἀπέκλεισεν Εὖα	Do you open paradise, which your relative and tribeswoman Eve closed	Dormition III
Eve is not mentioned by name in the Homily on the Sash			

References to the Motherhood of Mary in Germanos I, Patriarch of Constantinople (715-730)

PG 98 Location	Greek	English	Homily
292A	Θεομήτορος	the Mother of God	Presentation I
293A	Μαρίαν τὴν πάναγνον καὶ Θεομήτορα	Mary the all-holy Mother of God	Presentation I (P 117 ftn. 27)
296D	παρθενομήτορος	of the Virgin Mother	Presentation I
296D	Ἤδη μὲν οὖν ἀπογαλακτισθείσης αὐτῆς τῆς ἡμετέρας ζωῆς τροφοῦ	she who is the nourisher of our lives had been weaned	Presentation I
300B	τὴν Θεομήτορα	the Mother of God	Presentation I
300C	Δέδεξο τὴν δεδεξομένην τὸ ἄϋλον καὶ ἀκατάληπτον πῦρ· δέδεξο τὴν δοχεῖον χρηματίσουσαν τοῦ Υἱοῦ καὶ Λόγου τοῦ Πατρὸς καὶ μόνου Θεοῦ·	"Receive her who will receive the immaterial and uncontainable fire. Receive her who will be called the container of the Son and Word of the only God and Father.	Presentation I (H 286 ftn. 10)
301B	Ὑμεῖς ὡράθητε ὑπὲρ τὸν πάλαι χαλκευθέντα χρυσὸν πρὸς τὸ τῆς κιβωτοῦ κάλυμμα τὴν τῆς νέας διαθήκης, τοῦ ἐν σταυρῷ ἡμῖν ἄφεσιν ὑπογράψαντος νοητήν τε καὶ θείαν κιβωτὸν περικαλύπτοντες.	You appeared to cover the mystical and holy Ark of the new covenant of Him who on the Cross wrote the forgiveness of our sin, [forming] a covering which far surpasses the one which long ago was wrought of gold to cover the Ark (cf. Exodus 25.10).	Presentation I (P 118 ftn. 31)
Horvath lists the words below in the next two rows as types of divine motherhood in Mary.			
304A	βασίλισσα	Queen	Presentation I (H 286 ftn. 15) (P 118 ftns. 33 & 40

304A— 305BC	Palace, temple, city, bridal chamber, rational sacrifice, table	παλάτιον, ναός, πόλις, παστὰς τοῦ νοητοῦ, λογικώτατον θυσιαστήριον, τράπεζα	Presentation I (H 286 ftn. 11) (P 116 ftn. 22)
304C	ἡ μόνη παρθένος καὶ μήτηρ γνωρισθεῖσα	the only [woman] known as virgin and mother	Presentation I
304C/D	Ὑπερβέβηκε μὲν γὰρ οὖν ἅπασαν ἔννοιαν ἡ μόνη παρθένος καὶ μήτηρ γνωρισθεῖσα, καὶ δῆλον τὸ αἴτιον. Τίς γὰρ παρθένος ἔτεκεν, ἢ τεκοῦσα ἄσυλον τὴν παρθενίαν τετήρηκεν, εἰ μὴ σὺ μόνη, ἡ ἀπεριτρέπτως ἡμῖν σαρκὶ Θεὸν κυήσασα, πανολβιακόρη; Χαίροις τοιγαροῦν τῇ τῆς Ἐδὲμ ἡμῖν θανατηφόρῳ καὶ ψυχοπύρῳ βρώσει γυμνωθεῖσιν, εὐκλεεῖ καὶ ἀχειροτεύκτῳ ἐνδύματι ἐν τῇ σῇ πρὸς τὰ τῶν ἁγίων Ἅγια εἰσδύσει σήμερον ἀλουργοειδῆ στολὴν ἤτοι θεοπερίβλητον ἄφεσιν ἐπαμφιάσασα, ἡ ἄφεσις τῶν παραπτωμάτων τοῖς βορβορώδεσιν ἡμῖν ἐκ Θεοῦ δοθεῖσα, Θεόνυμφε.	For the only [woman] known as virgin and mother has surpassed all thought, and the cause is clear. For what virgin has given birth, or after giving birth has preserved her virginity undefiled, except you alone, who truly bore God in the flesh for us, all-blessed maiden? Therefore hail, forgiveness of transgressions given by God for us filthy ones, who are denuded by the death-dealing and soul-destroying food of Eden, as you put on the sea-purple robe which represents God-given forgiveness today for your entrance to the holy of holies in your glorious garment not made by hands (cf. Genesis 3.17), O bride of God.	Presentation I (P 116 ftn. 22)
305B/C	Χαίροις, ἡ νοητικὴν θείαν δρόσον ἡμῖν ἐπιστάζουσα φωτεινὴ νεφέλη, ἡ τῇ τῶν Ἁγίων ἁγίᾳ σήμερον ὑπεισδύσει τοῖς ἐν σκιᾷ θανάτου κατεχομένοις παμφαίνοντα ἥλιον ἐξανατείλασα· πηγὴ ἡ θεόβρυτος, ἀφ᾽ ἧς οἱ τῆς θεογνωσίας ποταμοὶ τὸ διειδέστατον καὶ ἀγλαοφανὲς τῆς ὀρθοδοξίας ὕδωρ	Hail, bright cloud (cf. Exodus 19.16) who continues to drop divine spiritual dew upon us (cf. Exodus 16.13), you who today by your holy entrance into the Holy of Holies have made to shine the all-brilliant Sun upon those who remain in the shadow of death. A fountain pouring out God, from which the rivers of divine knowledge pour	Presentation I(P 118 ftns. 34, 37, 38 & 39)

	διαρρέοντες, ἴλην τὴν τῶν αἱρέσεων ἐκμειοῦσιν.	out the bright clear water of orthodoxy and drown out the company of the heretics.	
	ΙΕ′. Χαίροις, ὁ τερπνότατος καὶ λογικὸς Θεοῦ παράδεισος, σήμερον πρὸς ἀνατολὰς τῆς αὐτοῦ θελήσεως φυτευόμενος δεξιᾷ παντοκράτορι, καὶ αὐτῷ τὸ εὐανθὲς κρίνον καὶ ἀμάραντον ῥόδον κυπρίζουσα, τοῖς πρὸς δυσμὰς θανάτου λοιμικὴν ψυχοφθόρον τε πικρίαν ἐκπιοῦσιν, ἐν ᾧ τὸ ζωοπάροχον ξύλον τῆς πρὸς ἀληθείας ἐπίγνωσιν ἐξανθεῖ, ἐξ οὗ οἱ γευσάμενοι ἀθανατίζονται. Χαίροις, τὸ τοῦ παμβασιλέως Θεοῦ ἱερότευκτον ἄχραντόν τε. καὶ καθαρώτατον παλάτιον, τὴν αὐτοῦ μεγαλειότητα περιβεβλημένη καὶ ξεναγοῦσά σου τῇ μυσταρχικῇ ἀπολαύσει ἅπαντας· ἢ ἐν τῇ τοῦ Κυρίου αὐλῇ ἤτοι τῷ ἁγίῳ αὐτοῦ ναῷ νυνὶ θεμελιουμένη, ἐν ᾗ ἡ ἀχειρότευκτος καὶ πεποικιλμένη παστὰς τοῦ νοητοῦ νυμφίου· ἐφ' ᾗ τὸ πλανηθὲν ἐπιστρέψαι βουληθείς, ὁ Λόγος τὴν σάρκα νενύμφευται, τοὺς ἤδη οἰκείᾳ βουλήσει διενηνεγμένους καταλλάσσων.	Hail, delightful and rational paradise of God, which today is planted in the east by the omnipotent right hand of his will (*cf.* Genesis 2.8), who have blossomed forth the beautiful lily and the unfading rose for those who in the west have drunk the bitter soul-destroying plague of death, on whom the life-giving tree has sprouted forth to the intimate knowledge of the truth. Those who have tasted from it are made immortal. Hail, sacred, undefiled, most pure palace of the omnipotent God. You are wrapped in his grandeur and guide us all with your mystical joy. Right now you are being established in the court of the Lord, in his holy Temple, in which is located the decorated bridal chamber not made by hands of the bridegroom (*cf.* Psalm 19.5-6). Through you, the Word which was married to the flesh willingly wished to reconcile those wanderers (*cf.* Romans 5.10) who through their own private will had been separated	
308A	πιότατον καὶ κατάσκιον ὄρος· ἐν ᾧ ὁ λογικὸς ἀμνὸς ἐκτραφεὶς	O fertile (Ps. 67.15-17) shady mountain (Hab 3.3) in whom the rational lamb has been nourished,	Presentation I

308A	Χαίροις, ὁ τοῦ Θεοῦ ἅγιος θρόνος, ἡ θεῖον ἀνάθημα, ἡ δόξης οἶκος, ἡ περικαλλὲς ἀγλάϊσμα, καὶ ἐκλεκτὸν κειμήλιον, καὶ παγκόσμιον ἱλαστήριον, «καὶ Θεοῦ δόξαν διηγούμενος οὐρανός.» Ἀνατολὴ ἄδυτον λαμπτῆρα ἀνατέλλουσα· οὗ «ἀπ' ἄκρου τοῦ οὐρανοῦ ἡ ἔξοδος καὶ τῆς θέρμης,» ἤτοι τῆς διοικητικῆς προνοίας, «ἔκτοθεν οὐδεὶς τῶν πώποτε γινομένων.»	Hail, holy throne of God, the divine gift, house of glory, the most beautiful splendor and elect treasure and universal propitiation, and "heaven declaring the glory of God," (Psalm 18.2 LXX) the Orient who has raised the unapproachable radiant one, who sends forth from the highest heaven his warmth (Psalm 18.7LXX)—that is to say his managing forethought—from which no one ever can hide.	Presentation I (P 118 ftns. 34 & 43
308C	ἡ πάνχρυσος στάμνος	the all-gold container	Presentation I (P 118 ftn 31)
308C	Παρθένε γεννῶσα καὶ Μήτηρ ἀπείρανδρε	virgin birth-giver and husbandless mother	Presentation I (P 118 ftn. 37)
309B	τῆς Μητρὸς τοῦ Κυρίου	the Mother of the Lord	Presentation II
312C	τῇ Θεοτόκῳ	the Theotokos	Presentation II
316C	Ἡ δὲ παῖς σκιρτῶσα καὶ ἀγαλλομένη, καθάπερ ἐν θαλάμῳ, ἐν τῷ ναῷ τοῦ Θεοῦ ἐβάδιζε· τριετίζουσα μὲν τῷ χρόνῳ τῆς ἡλικίας, ὑπερτελὴς δὲ τῇ χάριτι τῇ θεία, ὡς ἅτε προεγνωσμένη καὶ προωρισμένη καὶ ἐκλελεγμένη τῷ πάντων Θεῷ καὶ ταμίᾳ.	But the child skipping and rejoicing, as in a bridal chamber, walked in the Temple of God; being three years old in her chronological age, but more than perfect in divine grace, as foreknown and predestined and chosen for the God and governor of all.	Presentation II (P 114 ftn. 19)
317A	καὶ τοῖς βροτοῖς ὁ Θεὸς ἐξ αὐτῆς ὡμοιώθη	and from her God was made like mortals	Presentation II (P 115 ftn. 20)
317A	Δέσποινα Θεομῆτορ	Lady and Mother of God	Presentation II (P 115 ftn. 20)
317B	Σὺ γὰρ μόνη Θεοτόκος	For you alone are Theotokos	Presentation II
320A	ὡς μήτηρ τοῦ φιλανθρώπου Θεοῦ	mother of the God who loves mankind	Presentation II
320B	Θεόνυμφε, ἡ τὴν τῶν ὅλων προσδοκίαν ὑπὲρ λόγον τεκοῦσα	Bride of God, you who gave birth beyond words to the expectation of all	Presentation II

321A	ἡ τοῦ μάννα στάμνος ὁλόχρυσος	the golden jar which contained the manna	Annunciation (P 119 ftn. 45)
321B	ὁ ναὸς ὁ ἔμψυχος τῆς μεγαλοπρεποῦς δόξης	the living temple of the majestic glory	Annunciation
321B	ἡ ζωὴν φέρουσα, καὶ τρέφουσα τὸν τρέφοντα· καὶ γάλα ποτίζουσα, τὸν ἐκ πέτρας μέλι πάλαι πηγάσαντα	[you are] the carrier of life, nourisher of the nourisher, the one who gives milk to him who caused honey to spring from rocks long ago	Annunciation (P 112 ftn. 7)
321B	Χαῖρε, κεχαριτωμένη, ἡ φιλάνθρωπον Δεσπότην ὑπὲρ κοινῆς τοῦ γένους τῶν ἀνθρώπων κυοφορήσασα σωτηρίας.	Hail full of grace, who for the sake of the salvation of all human kind bore the Master who loves mankind	Annunciation
321C	Ἄκουε, δεδοξασμένη· λόγους ἀποκρύφους τοῦ Ὑψίστου ἄκουε· «Ἰδοὺ συλλήψῃ ἐν γαστρί, καὶ τέξῃ υἱὸν καὶ καλέσεις τὸ ὄνομα αὐτοῦ Ἰησοῦν.» Ὁπλίζου λοιπὸν εἰς Χριστοῦ παρουσίαν· ἦλθον γὰρ εὐαγγελίσασθαί σοι τὰ προρρηθέντα, πρὸ καταβολῆς κόσμου.	Hear, most blessed one, hear the hidden words of the Most High. "Behold, you shall conceive in your womb, and you shall produce a son, and shall call him Jesus" (Luke 1.31). Prepare then for Christ's coming. For I have come to announce to you what has been decreed before the foundation of the cosmos.	Annunciation
324A	Γνῶθι σαφῶς καὶ πιστώθητι, ὅτι μᾶλλον ἐγὼ ἐν ἐκπλήξει γέγονα θεασάμενος τὸ τοιοῦτόν σου θεογράφιστον κάλλος· καὶ βλέπων σε λοιπόν, νομίζω δόξαν Κυρίου μου καταμανθάνειν.	Know truly and believe that I am more amazed at seeing your God-created beauty. Seeing you I know that I am examining closely the glory of my Lord.	Annunciation (P 116 ftn. 23)
324B	Εὐαγγελίζομαί σοι χαρᾶς εὐαγγέλια· εὐαγγελίζομαί σοι τόκον ἀνεννόητον· εὐαγγελίζομαί σοι παρουσίαν ὑψηλοῦ Βασιλέως ἀνεκδιήγητον. Τάχα δὲ καὶ ἣν κατέχεις πορφύραν, προμηνύει τὸ βασιλικὸν ἀξίωμα.	I proclaim to you good news of joy. I proclaim to you unimaginable birth. I proclaim to you the inexplicable coming of the Most High. Perhaps even that purple thread you are holding foretells your royal status	Annunciation

325A	Θρόνος θεοβάστακτος	the throne which bears God	Annunciation
325A	βασιλικὴ καθέδρα τοῦ ἐπουρανίου Βασιλέως κληθήσῃ	the royal seat of the heavenly King	Annunciation
328A	σε ὡς Μητέρα Κυρίου μου μέλλουσαν ἔσεσθαι	as you are about to become the mother of my Lord	Annunciation
328B	«Πνεῦμα ἅγιον ἐπελεύσεται ἐπὶ σέ, καὶ δύναμις Ὑψίστου ἐπισκιάσει σοι· διὸ καὶ τὸ γεννώμενον ἅγιον, κληθήσεται Υἱὸς Θεοῦ. Μὴ φοβοῦ, Μαριάμ· εὗρες γὰρ χάριν παρὰ τῷ Θεῷ.»	"The Holy Spirit will come upon you, and the power of the Most High will overshadow you, and therefore the holy one who is born of you shall be called the Son of God. Fear not Mary, you have found favor with God" (Luke 1.35 and 1.30).	Annunciation
328C	Σωτῆρα τέξεις τὸν Κύριον, τὸν ἕνα τῆς ζωαρχικῆς Τριάδος, καὶ χαρὰν τῷ κόσμῳ προξενήσεις ἀνεκλάλητον, ἣν οὐδεὶς οὐδέποτε ἀγγέλων ἢ ἀνθρώπων προεξένησεν· καὶ ἔσται τὸ ὄνομά σου εὐλογημένον.	You shall bear the Lord, the Savior, who is one of the life-beginning Trinity. You shall bring unexpected joy to the world, which neither angels nor men have ever brought; and your name shall be called blessed.	Annunciation
328D	Τέρψις καὶ διόλου γλυκασμός ἐστι τὰ ῥήματά σου, δεδοξασμένη· καὶ διὰ τοῦτό σοι λέξω· ὅτι οὐκ ἐκ θελήματος σαρκός, ἀλλ᾽ ἐκ θελήματος Θεοῦ, καὶ ἐξ ἐπιφοιτήσεως τοῦ ἁγίου Πνεύματος, ἡ σὴ κυοφορία γενήσεται	At all times your words are sweet and joyous, O blessed one. It is because of this that I will say to you, your pregnancy is due not to the will of the flesh but to the will of God and the descent of the Holy Spirit (*cf.* John 1.13).	Annunciation
329A	Τίς πληροφορήσει τὸν Ἰωσήφ, ὅτι οὐκ ἐκ θελήματος ἀνδρὸς <σαρκός>, ἀλλ᾽ ἐξ ἐπιφοιτήσεως τοῦ ἁγίου Πνεύματος ἐγὼ συλλήψομαι; καθότι ἐκ τοῦ αἰῶνος οὐκ ἠκούσθη ὅτι παρθένος ἀπείρανδρος βρέφος τέτοκεν.	Who will persuade Joseph that I shall conceive not by the will of man, but by the descent of the Holy Spirit? For it has never at any time been heard that a virgin has given birth to a child without a man.	Annunciation

329A	Ἡλίκη <Ὑλική>²⁶ τυγχάνουσα, καὶ ἐκ γῆς τὴν γέννησιν <γένεσιν> ἔχουσα, πῶς καταφύγῃ ἀνθρώπων γένος εἰς ἐμέ; καὶ πῶς Χριστόν, τὸ φῶς τοῦ κόσμου ἐναγκαλίσομαι; καὶ πῶς ὁ ἥλιος ἐκεῖνος ὁ ἄδυτος, ὑπὸ τῆς νοητῆς σελήνης βασταχθήσεται; <πῶς τὸ φῶς τοῦ κόσμου ἐναγκαλίσομαι Χριστόν; ἢ πῶς ὁ ἥλιος ἐκεῖνος ὁ ἄδυτος ὑπὸ τὴν σελήνην βασταχθήσεται; ἢ πῶς ἀνθρώπων γένος εἰς ἐμὲ καταφεύξεται;>	How shall the race of men flee to me who am matter and drawn from the earth? And how shall I embrace Christ the Light of the World? And how shall that unsetting Sun be born by the spiritual moon? <Or how will the race of men take refuge with me?>	Annunciation
329B	Φαιδρὸν ἀνάλαβε βλέμμα, δεδοξασμένη· οὐρανὸς γὰρ μέλλεις γενέσθαι, καὶ ναὸς θεοχώρητος, καὶ σκηνὴ Θεοῦ ἔμψυχος· ἑπτὰ στερεωμάτων εὐρυχωρότερός τε καὶ ὑψηλότερος καὶ θαυμασιώτερος.	Put on a joyful countenance, O blessed one. You are about to become heaven, a God-containing tabernacle, a living temple of God, wider and higher and more wondrous than the seven firmaments.	Annunciation
329B	Φρίττω τοῦ παραδόξου τῆς ξένης μου λοχείας τὰ ἐγκαίνια· εὐλαβοῦμαι δὲ καὶ τὸν Ἰωσήφ, καὶ τί λοιπὸν συμβήσεται <μοι> οὐκ οἶδα. Συμφέρει μοι οὖν, εἰς οἶκον Ζαχαρίου ἀπελθεῖν, πρὸς τὴν ἐμὴν συγγενίδα	I shiver at the beginning of the paradox of my unusual childbearing. I am concerned about Joseph and I do not know what will happen. But it is good for me to go to the house of Zacharias, to see my kinswoman.	Annunciation

---

²⁶ The acrostic requires the reading ὑλική.

513

329B	Χριστιανῶν ἀπάντων γενήσῃ κοινὸν ἱλαστήριον· καὶ διὰ τοῦτο πάλιν, ἐπιφθέγγομαί σοι τὴν πρέπουσαν φωνήν, «<Χαῖρε,> Κεχαριτωμένη· ὁ Κύριος μετὰ σοῦ· εὐλογημένη σὺ ἐν γυναιξί, καὶ εὐλογημένος ὁ καρπὸς τῆς κοιλίας σου.»	You shall become the common propitiation of all Christians. And therefore again I salute you as is fitting, "<Hail> O full of grace, the Lord is with you, blessed are you among women, blessed is the fruit of your womb" (Luke 1.38).	Annunciation
329C	Χαρακτῆρα φέρουσα βασιλικὸν, καὶ εἰς τὰ βασίλεια τῆς ἐμῆς Βηθλεὲμ τιθηνήσασα, καὶ εἰς ἅγια ἐκ παιδόθεν ἀμέμπτως διαπρέψασα· καὶ παρθένος λοιπὸν τυγχάνουσα, πῶς ἐγὼ μήτηρ ἀκούσω τοῦ παιδός μου;	I am of royal blood, and spent my earliest childhood in the royal house of Bethlehem, and my childhood I spent blamelessly in the temple; and being a virgin up to now, how can I be called the mother of my child?	Annunciation (P 112 ftn. 6
329D	Ὦ παρθένε, χαρᾶς ἐπουρανίου πρόξενε· τερπνὸν καὶ θαυμαστὸν οἰκητήριον, καὶ τοῦ κόσμου παντὸς ἱλαστήριον, ἡ μόνη κατὰ ἀλήθειαν ἐν γυναιξὶν εὐλογημένη, ἑτοιμάζου λοιπὸν εἰς μυστικὴν Χριστοῦ παρουσίαν.	O Virgin, bringer of heavenly joy, joyful and marvelous dwelling place, and propitiation of the whole cosmos, the only truly blessed one among women (Luke 1.42), prepare yourself for the mystical coming of Christ.	Annunciation
332A	μητέρα παρ' ἐλπίδα καὶ οὐ παρθένον τυγχάνουσαν;	a mother contrary to expectation and not a virgin?	Annunciation (P 113 ftn. 15)
333C	Θλίψεως ἡμέρα κατέλαβέ με, καὶ μέμψις ἐξ ὑποψίας ἐπῆλθέν μοι· καὶ ἐξέτασις μνήστορός μου κατεπείγει με· καὶ κυοφόρησις παιδός μου κατηγορεῖ με· καὶ ὁ τὸ «Χαῖρε» μοί λέξας ἄγγελος τάχα ἀπεκρύβη· καὶ τί λοιπὸν λογίσομαι, οὐκ οἶδα.	The day of affliction fell upon me, and blame and suspicion came upon me; and the scrutiny of my betrothed was placed firmly on me; and my pregnancy accused me, and the Angel who cried "Hail" is quickly hidden, and what else I may say I do not know.	Annunciation

333D	Κρύψω λοιπὸν ἐμαυτήν, εἰς ἓν τῶν σπηλαίων τῆς ἐμῆς Βηθλεέμ, καὶ εἰσδέξομαι νενομισμένον καιρὸν ἐμῆς κυοφορίας· καὶ μάθω τίς ὁ ἐξ ἐμοῦ μέλλων τίκτεσθαι. Λογίζομαι γὰρ ὅτι <ἴσως> ὁ Θεὸς ἐπόψεται <ἐπίδοι> τὴν ταπείνωσίν <τῇ ταπεινώσει> μου.	I shall hide myself in one of my caves in my town of Bethlehem. I shall await the appropriate time of my birth-giving. May I learn who this is to whom I am about to give birth, for I reckon that the Lord will regard my lowliness (*cf.* Luke 1.48).	Annunciation
336A	Μὴ γὰρ οὐ γέγραπται ἐν τοῖς προφήταις, «Ὅτι Παρθένος ἐν γαστρὶ λήψεται, καὶ παιδίον ἡμῖν τεχθήσεται;» Μὴ <γὰρ> ἔχεις εἰπεῖν ὅτι οἱ προφῆται ψεύδονται; σφάλλῃ λοιπόν, ὦ Ἰωσήφ, ἐπὶ πολὺ μαινόμενος.	Is it not written in the Scriptures, "That a virgin shall conceive, and shall bear a child to us" (*cf.* Isaiah 7.14)? You cannot say that the prophets lie, can you? You are mistaken, O Joseph, you are out of your mind about many things.	Annunciation
336B	Ξενίσει ὁ τόκος, ὡς ἐμοὶ δοκεῖ, οὐ μόνον ἐμοί, ἀλλὰ καὶ ἀγγέλους καὶ ἀνθρώπους, καὶ οὐκ ἂν πιστεύσωσι. Τίς ποτε ἀκηκόεεν, ὅτι παρθένος βρέφος τέτοκεν, καὶ μάλιστα ἀπείρανδρος τυγχάνουσα;	Your motherhood is strange, as it seem to me, and not only to me but also to angels and men, and they would not believe this. Who has ever heard that a virgin has borne an infant, and especially without a man?	Annunciation
336C	Ξενίσει σοι, οἶδα, τὰ λεγόμενα καὶ καταπλήττει σου τὸν νοῦν τῆς μυστικῆς κυοφορίας τὸ παράδοξον μυστήριον. Ἐγὼ δὲ τῆς ἐπενεχθείσης μοι συμφορᾶς αἴτιος οὐκ εἰμι,	It is strange to you, I know. The paradoxical nature of my childbearing astounds your mind. I am not responsible for this condition which has been brought upon me.	Annunciation
336D	Πίστευε προφήταις Θεοῦ, καὶ μὴ ἐπὶ τοσοῦτον τῇ περισσοτέρᾳ λύπῃ κατατήξῃς ἑαυτόν· εὑρήσεις γὰρ ἐν αὐτοῖς γεγραμμένα· «Ἰδοὺ ἡ παρθένος ἐν γαστρὶ ἕξει, καὶ τέξεται υἱόν, καὶ καλέσουσι τὸ ὄνομα αὐτοῦ Ἐμμανουήλ.»	Believe the prophets of God, and concerning this matter do not allow yourself to sink into greater pain. For you shall find it written in them, "Behold, a virgin shall conceive and bring forth a son, and they shall call his name Emmanuel. (Matthew 1.23)"	Annunciation

337B	Συντηρήσω ἄρα τοὺς λόγους σου ἐν τῇ καρδίᾳ μου, καὶ στέρξω μικρὸν λοιπὸν ἔτι ἐν τῷ οἴκῳ σου· καὶ ἐκδέξομαι καιρὸν ἀπογραφῆς καὶ ἡμέραν κυοφορίας μου, μέχρις ἂν καὶ φόρους τελέσωμεν Αὐγούστῳ Καίσαρι, Αὐγούστῳ Ῥωμαίων τῷ νῦν βασιλεύοντι.	I shall guard your words in my heart, and I shall be content in your house a little longer, and I shall await the time of enrollment and the day of my giving birth, until we shall bring the tribute to Caesar Augustus, the Emperor who now rules the Romans.	Annunciation
337B	Τάχα ἄγγελος ἦν ὁ φανείς μοι καθ' ὕπνον, καὶ λέξας μοι· «Ἰωσὴφ υἱὸς Δαβίδ, μὴ φοβηθῇς παραλαβεῖν Μαριὰμ τὴν γυναῖκά σου· τὸ γὰρ ἐν αὐτῇ γεννηθὲν, ἐκ Πνεύματός ἐστιν	Perhaps it was an angel who appeared to me in a dream, and said to me: "Joseph, son of David, fear not to take Mary to you as a wife, for that which shall come of her, is of the Holy Spirit, and she shall produce a son and you shall call his	Annunciation
	ἁγίου· τέξεται δὲ υἱόν, καὶ καλέσεις τὸ ὄνομα αὐτοῦ Ἰησοῦν.»	name Jesus (Matthew 1.20*ff.*).''	
337C	Ὑποδείξει μοι πάντως φανείς μοι καὶ τὸν τόπον καὶ τὸ σπήλαιον· σὺ δὲ, Μαρία, τὰ σπάργανα ἑτοίμασον. Κἄν τε προφήτης, κἄν τε βασιλεὺς ὑπάρχει <ὑπάρχῃ> ὁ μέλλων τίκτεσθαι, ἡμεῖς οὐκ οἴδαμεν, «ὅτι Ναζωραῖος κληθήσεται.»	Surely he will appear and show me the place and the cave. But you, Mary, prepare the swaddling clothes. Whether a prophet or a king is the one about to be born, we do not know, "for he shall be called a Nazarene (Matthew 2.23)."	Annunciation
337C	Ὑπολαμβάνω ὅτι βασιλεὺς κληθήσεται ὁ μέλλων τίκτεσθαι· γέγραπται γὰρ ἐν τοῖς προφήταις· «Χαῖρε σφόδρα, θύγατερ Σιών· κήρυσσε, θύγατερ Ἰερουσαλήμ· ἰδοὺ ὁ βασιλεύς σου ἔρχεταί σοι δίκαιος καὶ σώζων.»	I suspect that the one who is about to be born shall be called a king. For it is written in the prophets: "Rejoice greatly, O daughter of Zion. Shout aloud, O daughter of Jerusalem. Lo your King comes to you, righteous and saving (Zachariah 9.9)."[27]	Annunciation

---

[27] Text from Zachariah 9.9. This is only the first half of the LXX.

337C	Φανερώσει μοι λοιπὸν ὁ καθ' ὕπνον χρηματίσας μοι, καὶ τὰ μέλλοντα ἡμῖν μετὰ ταῦτα συμβαίνειν. Ἐγὼ καὶ τὸν Ἡρώδην εὐλαβοῦμαι, ὅτι ποτέ τινος μηνύσαντος, ποιήσει ζήτησιν τοῦ παρ' ἡμῖν τικτομένου παιδός.	He who appeared to me in the dream shall reveal those things which are about to happen to us. I shall be cautious of Herod, for if some one should give away the secret, he will seek to know about the birth of the child.	Annunciation
340A	Χρυσός, ὡς ἐμοὶ < δοκεῖ > <καὶ σμύρνα καὶ λίβανος>, προσενεχθήσεται τῷ	Gold as it seems to me, <and myrrh and incense>, shall be brought to the one about	Annunciation
	μέλλοντι τίκτεσθαι <ὡς Βασιλεῖ καὶ Θεῷ καὶ Ἀνθρώπῳ>· καθὼς φησιν ὁ προφήτης καὶ βασιλεὺς Δαβίδ, 'ὅτι «Ζήσεται καὶ δοθήσεται αὐτῷ ἐκ τοῦ χρυσίου τῆς Αραβίας».	to be born (cf. Matthew 2.11) as the prophet and king David said, for "He shall live and the gold of Arabia shall be given to him (Psalm 72.19)."	
340A	Ψηλαφήσωμεν λοιπόν, εἰ βούλει <καὶ> τόπον ἀψηλάφητον, καθότι καιρὸς ὑπέστι τῆς γεννήσεως, χρήζομεν γὰρ κατὰ τὴν ὁδον καὶ ὑποζύγιον · ἰδοῦ γὰρ βλέπω σε πάνυ στυγνάζουσαν, καὶ νομίζω ὅτι τεκεῖν ἐπείγεσαι.	Henceforth, let us feel our way. If you wish an untouched place, as the time comes for the birth, for we shall have need of a beast of burden to go there. For behold I see you extremely gloomy, and I know that you are about to give birth.	Annunciation
340B	δέσπινα	lady	Dormition I (H 286 ftn. 14
340C	τῆς τιμίας καὶ ἐνδόξου σου, Θεομῆτορ, μεταστάσεως,	your honorable and glorious translation, O Mother of God.	Dormition I
341B	τῆς Παρθένου Μητρός	the Virgin Mother	Dormition I (P 113 ftn. 12)
341C	τῇ Παρθένῳ καὶ Μητρὶ	the Virgin and Mother	Dormition I
344A	καὶ γαστέρα πάλιν, τὴν σὴν ἐσήμανε κοιλίαν, τοῦ δεῖξαι καὶ τὴν σαρκικὴν ἐκ σοῦ τοῦ Μονογενοῦς ἐπιδημίαν	And again [Scripture] called your belly "womb", to show also the habitation of the Only-begotten from your flesh	Dormition I
344B	παναγία Θεομῆτορ	O all-holy Mother of God	Dormition I

Gregory E. Roth

344C	ἐπειδὴ καὶ οὐρανὸς θεοχώρητος ἀνεδείχθης τοῦ ὑψίστου Θεοῦ	a God-containing heaven of the most high God	Dormition I (H 286 ftn. 13) (P 119 ftn. 44)
344C	διὰ τὸν χωρητικὸν κόλπον σου πρὸς αὐτοῦ βασταγμοῦ	since your bosom [was] able to carry(ing) Him	Dormition I (P 119 ftn. 44)
344C	τὴν Μητέρα τῆς ζωῆς	the Mother of life	Dormition I
345B	ὡς σκεῦος ὑπάρχον θεηδόχον	being a God-receiving vessel	Dormition I
345B	καὶ ἔμψυχος ναὸς τῆς τοῦ Μονογενοῦς παναγίας θεότητος	a living temple of the all-holy divinity of the Only-begotten One	Dormition I
348A	θεοχώρητον . . . ἀγγεῖον	God-containing vessel	Dormition I (H 286 n.12).
348A	σύνοικον ἔδει τῆς Ζωῆς	companion with Life	Dormition I
348A	ὡς ἐγρήγορσιν ὑποστῆναι τὴν μετάστασιν ὡς Μητέρα τῆς Ζωῆς	through this translation arise as Mother of Life	Dormition I
348D	«ὅλην τὴν ἡμέραν τὸν ἔπαινον» τῆς ἁγιοσύνης τοῦ τόκου σου.	all day long [they will meditate on] the praise of the holiness of your childbirth	Dormition II
349A	Σὺ γὰρ εἶ τῆς ὄντως ἀληθινῆς Ζωῆς ἡ μήτηρ	For you are the mother of the true Life	Dormition II
349A	Ἐκείνη μήτηρ χοός, σὺ μήτηρ φωτός	She is the mother of earth; you are the mother of light	Dormition II
349A	Ἐκείνης ἡ μήτρα, φθορᾶς· ἡ δὲ σὴ γαστήρ, ἀφθαρσίας	Her womb [is the source] of destruction; your belly [is the source] of imperishability	Dormition II
349A	Ἐκείνης τὰ τέκνα, λύπη· ὁ δὲ σὸς Υἱὸς, παγγενὴς χαρά	Her children are grief; but your Son is universal joy.	Dormition II
349B	εἰ μὴ διὰ σοῦ, Παρθενομῆτορ	if not through you, Virgin Mother	Dormition II
352A	Οὐδὲ γὰρ ἐνδέχεταί σέ ποτε παρακουσθῆναι, ἐπειδὴ πειθαρχεῖ σοι κατὰ πάντα καὶ διὰ πάντα, καὶ ἐν πᾶσιν ὁ Θεός, ὡς ἀληθῆ αὐτοῦ καὶ ἀχράντῳ Μητρί	For it is not possible for your voice ever to be disregarded, since God is obedient to you in every way and for every reason and in every situation, as you are his true and pure Mother	Dormition II

518

353A	τὴν τοῦ ἀμνοῦ καὶ ποιμένος μητέρα	the mother of the lamb and the shepherd	Dormition II
356C	Θεομῆτορ	Mother of God	Dormition II
360B	τὴν Ζωοτόκον αὐτοῦ. Μητέρα	his life-bearing Mother	Dormition III
361A	ἀχώριστος μήτηρ	mother inseparable	Dormition III
361C	Ἔρχου προθύμως πρὸς τὸν ὑπὸ σοῦ γεγεννημένον. Εὔφρᾶναί σεβούλομαι τεκνοχρέως· ἀποδοῦναί σοι τὰ τῆς μητρικῆς κοιλίας ἐνοίκια· τῆς γαλακτοτροφίας τὸν μισθόν· τῆς ἀνατροφῆς τὴν ἀντάμειψιν· τοῖς σπλάγχνοις σου τὴν πληροφορίαν	Come willingly to the one who was borne by you. I want to make you joyful as a child should, to pay back to you the rent of the maternal womb, the wages of wet-nursing, the exchange for upbringing, the fulfillment for your affection	Dormition III (P 113 ftn. 14)
361C	οὐκ ἀντιπερισπάσαι γὰρ οἶδα πρὸς ἑτέρου τέκνου διάθεσιν. Ἐγώ σε παρθένον ἀνέδειξα μητέρα· ἐγώ σε καὶ εὐφραινομένην ἐπὶ Τέκνῳ καταστήσω μητέρα	Since you obtained me as your only-begotten Son, O mother, prefer rather to live with me; for I know you have no other child. I showed/proved you to be a virgin mother	Dormition III
364B	ἡ Θεομήτωρ	Mother of God	Dormition III
364C	Ἦν δὲ τὸ βραβεῖον, φοίνικος κλάδος, σύμβολον νίκης κατὰ θανάτου, καὶ ζωῆς ἀμαράντου προεκτύπωμα· τοῦ πιστωθῆναι μετερχομένην, ὅτι κατα-δυναστεύσειεν τῆς φθορᾶς, ὡς καὶ ὁ ὑπ᾽ αὐτῆς γεννηθεὶς ἐνίκησεν τὸν ᾅδην, Χριστός	she shows the prize which was given to her. The prize was a branch, a symbol of victory over death, and a prefiguration of unwithering life, to confirm that she is going over, that she may prevail over corruption, as also the Christ who received birth from her conquered Hades	Dormition III
365A	Εἰ οὖν ὑμεῖς γονεῖς ὄντες ἐκ φθαρτῶν καὶ ἐκ ῥύπου συναφείας παίδων, οὐ καρτερεῖτε τούτων πρὸς ῥοπὴν χωρισθῆναι, πῶς ἐγὼ Θεὸν Υἱὸν κεκτημένη, καὶ σπλάγχνα μονομερῆ πρὸς	So if you being parents from perishable children and the union of pollution, will not refuse to be separated from these for an instance, how shall I who have obtained God as a Son and maintain my	

	αὐτὸν ἐπέχουσα, διότι χωρὶς ἀνδρὸς αὐτὸν ἀφθάρτως καὶ παρθενικῶς ἐκύησα, μὴ μεῖζον ὑμῶν νενίκημαι παρὰ τῶν σπλάγχνων;	affection singly for him, because without a husband I bore him incorruptibly and virginally, how shall I not be overcome more than you by my affection?	
365B	Ἐπεὶ δὲ καὶ θεϊκῇ ἐξουσίᾳ, καὶ σαρκικῇ πρὸς μητέρα προσπαθείᾳ, πρὸς τὸν Θεὸν ἐπεζητήθης ἀναλῦσαι	since by divine authority and fleshly attachment to a mother, you have been asked to return to God	Dormition III
365C	Οὐδὲ γὰρ καὶ ἥρμοζεν τὴν Μητέρα τοῦ Θεοῦ ἐν μέσῳ γενεᾶς σκολιᾶς καὶ διεστραμ-μένης διάγειν, ἀλλ' ἐν σκηναῖς οὐρανίων καὶ ἀφθάρτων διατριβῶν μετελθεῖν	For it was not suitable for the Mother of God to live in the midst of a crooked and perverted generation, but to pass over to the tents of the heavenly and imperishable dwellings. (Philippians 2.15)	Dormition III
368A	Χαῖρε, Μῆτερ τῆς ζωῆς, καὶ τοῦ ἐμοῦ κηρύγματος ἡ ὑπόληψις	"Rejoice, Mother of life, and subject of my proclamation.	Dormition III
369B	οἱ τὸν Υἱὸν διὰ τῆς μητρός, τὴν μητέρα διὰ τὸν Υἱὸν ὑπερτίμως σεβασθέντες· οἱ διὰ τὸν ἔνσαρκον γεγονότα Θεόν, τῇ χορηγῷ τῆς σαρκὸς αὐτοῦ, γνησίως τότε δεδουλευκότες Μητρί	those how venerated with great honor the Son through his mother and the mother because of the Son, who because of God who became incarnate, nobly gave service to the mother who provided his flesh.	Dormition III
369C 369D	Ἄνδρες Ἰσραηλῖται, τοῦτο νῦν γνωστὸν ὑμῖν ἐδείχθη πᾶσι περὶ Μαρίας τῆς κατὰ σάρκα μητρὸς τοῦ Χριστοῦ, ὡς ἅμα ἡμῖν καὶ ὑμῖν ἐπὶ τὸ μνῆμα τοῦτο νεκρὰ παραγενομένη, παρὰ τῶν ἡμετέρων ἀνελήφθη χειρῶν	"Men of Israel, this has now been made known to you all concerning Mary the mother of Christ according to the flesh, that to us and you together having arrived dead at this tomb, she was taken up from our hands	Dormition III
372B	τῆς Θεομήτορος	the mother of God	Dormition III

376B	Ζώνης ἐκείνης, ἣ τὸν πανάγιον ἐκεῖνο περιέσφιγγε σῶμα, καὶ τὸν ἐν κοιλίᾳ κρυπτόμενον Θεὸν περιέβαλλε. Ζώνης ἐκείνης, ἥτις τὴν τοῦ Θεοῦ κιβωτὸν ὡραίως κατεκόσμει, καὶ σεμνοτάτως.	That Sash, which wrapped around her body, and surrounded in the womb the hidden God. That Sash, which beautifully adorned the container of God, and most holy.	Sash (P 112 ftn. 9)
376D	Μητρὸς	Mother	Sash
377A	τῇ Μητρὶ	Mother	Sash (P 112 ftn. 10)
377A	τὴν τεκοῦσαν	Mother	Sash
377C	ἡ τῆς τοῦ ἀφθάρτου Θεοῦ Μητρὸς Μητρὸς τὸ ὑπέρσεμνον σῶμα σεμνοπρεπῶς προσεγγίσασα	surrounded the very venerable body of the Mother of the incorruptible God	Sash
381A	Σὺ γὰρ μητρῴαν ἔχουσα πρὸς τὸν σὸν Υἱὸν τὴν παρρησίαν καὶ τὴν ἰσχὺν	a maternal freedom of speech and strength towards your Son	Sash
384A	ὡς μητρῴαν ἔχουσα παρρησίαν τε καὶ ἰσχὺν	having motherly boldness and strength	Sash

521

References to the Nativity of Jesus in Germanos I, Patriarch of Constantinople (715-730)

PG 98 Location	Greek	English	Homily
300C	κράτησον τὴν ἐν τῷ ἰδίῳ τόκῳ τὴν καθ' ἡμῶν δειλίαν φερομένην θανάτου ἰσχὺν καὶ ᾅδου τυραννίδα κρατήσουσαν	Possess her, who endures fear like ours in her own childbearing and will be victorious over the power of death and the tyranny of hell	Presentation I
324B	Δέξαι ἀγγελίας χαρὰν ἀξιάκουστον, καὶ ἐγκώμιον τό σοι πρεπωδέστατον· ὁ γὰρ «ἐκ σοῦ τικτόμενος, Υἱὸς Ὑψίστου κληθήσεται,» καὶ Υἱός ὑπὸ σου τῆς ἡγιασμένης ὑπερβολῇ χρηστότητος βασταχθήσεται.	Accept this joyful message which is worthy of being heard, along with the song of praise which is due to you. For "the one who is borne of you, shall be called the son of the Most High" (Luke 1.35), and your son shall be born in the height of hallowed goodness.	Annunciation
325D	Νῦν ἠρξάμην λαλεῖν· Πλήρης εἰμὶ ῥημάτων αἰωνίων <οὐρανίων>· λέξω σοι λοιπόν, ὅτι ὁ Κύριος μετὰ σοῦ μέλλει τίκτεσθαι, Βασιλεὺς βασιλέων, «καὶ βασιλεύει ἐπὶ τὸν οἶκον Ἰακώβ, καὶ τῆς βασιλείας αὐτοῦ οὐκ ἔσται τέλος.»	Now I have begun to speak. I am full of eternal words; and for the rest I shall tell you that the Lord who is about to be born of you, is the King of kings, and "will rule over the House of Jacob forever and of his kingdom there shall be no end" (Luke 1.35).	Annunciation

523

328B	«Πνεῦμα ἅγιον ἐπελεύσεται ἐπὶ σέ, καὶ δύναμις Ὑψίστου ἐπισκιάσει σοι· διὸ καὶ τὸ γεννώμενον ἅγιον, κληθήσεται Υἱὸς Θεοῦ. Μὴ φοβοῦ, Μαριάμ· εὗρες γὰρ χάριν παρὰ τῷ Θεῷ.»	"The Holy Spirit will come upon you, and the power of the Most High will overshadow you, and therefore the holy one who is born of you shall be called the Son of God. Fear not Mary, you have found favor with God" (Luke 1.35 and 1.30).	Annunciation
337B	Συντηρήσω ἄρα τοὺς λόγους σου ἐν τῇ καρδίᾳ μου, καὶ στέρξω μικρὸν λοιπὸν ἔτι ἐν τῷ οἴκω σου· καὶ ἐκδέξομαι καιρὸν ἀπογραφῆς καὶ ἡμέραν κυοφορίας μου, μέχρις ἂν καὶ φόρους τελέσωμεν Αὐγούστω Καίσαρι, Αὐγούστω Ῥωμαίων τῷ νῦν βασιλεύοντι.	I shall guard your words in my heart, and I shall be content in your house a little longer, and I shall await the time of enrollment and the day of my giving birth, until we shall bring the tribute to Caesar Augustus, the Emperor who now rules the Romans.	Annunciation
337B	Τάχα ἄγγελος ἦν ὁ φανείς μοι καθ' ὕπνον, καὶ λέξας μοι· «Ἰωσὴφ υἱὸς Δαβὶδ, μὴ φοβηθῇς παραλαβεῖν Μαριὰμ τὴν γυναῖκά σου· τὸ γὰρ ἐν αὐτῇ γεννηθὲν, ἐκ Πνεύματός ἐστιν ἁγίου· τέξεται δὲ υἱόν, καὶ καλέσεις τὸ ὄνομα αὐτοῦ Ἰησοῦν.»	Perhaps it was an angel who appeared to me in a dream, and said to me: "Joseph, son of David, fear not to take Mary to you as a wife, for that which shall come of her, is of the Holy Spirit, and she shall produce a son and you shall call his name Jesus (Matthew 1.20*ff.*)."	Annunciation
337C	Ὑποδείξει μοι πάντως φανείς μοι καὶ τὸν τόπον καὶ τὸ σπήλαιον· σὺ δὲ, Μαρία, τὰ σπάργανα ἑτοίμασον. Κἄν τε προφήτης, κἄν τε βασιλεὺς ὑπάρχη ὁ μέλλων τίκτεσθαι, ἡμεῖς οὐκ οἴδαμεν, «ὅτι Ναζωραῖος κληθήσεται.»	Surely he will appear and show me the place and the cave. But you, Mary, prepare the swaddling clothes. Whether a prophet or a king is the one about to be born, we do not know, "for he shall be called a Nazarene (Matthew 2.23)."	Annunciation

337C	Ὑπολαμβάνω ὅτι βασιλεὺς κληθήσεται ὁ μέλλων τίκτεσθαι· γέγραπται γὰρ ἐν τοῖς προφήταις· «Χαῖρε σφόδρα, θύγατερ Σιών· κήρυσσε, θύγατερ Ἱερουσαλήμ· ἰδοὺ ὁ βασιλεύς σου ἔρχεταί σοι δίκαιος καὶ σώζων.»	I suspect that the one who is about to be born shall be called a king. For it is written in the prophets: "Rejoice greatly, O daughter of Zion. Shout aloud, O daughter of Jerusalem. Lo your King comes to you, righteous and saving (Zachariah 9.9)."[28]	Annunciation
337C	Φανερώσει μοι λοιπὸν ὁ καθ᾽ ὕπνον χρηματίσας μοι, καὶ τὰ μέλλοντα ἡμῖν μετὰ ταῦτα συμβαίνειν. Ἐγὼ καὶ τὸν Ἡρώδην εὐλαβοῦμαι ὅτι ποτέ τινος μηνύσαντος, ποιήσει ζήτησιν τοῦ παρ᾽ ἡμῖν τικτομένου παιδός.	He who appeared to me in the dream shall reveal those things which are about to happen to us. I shall be cautious of Herod, for if some one should give away the secret, he will seek to know about the birth of the child.	Annunciation
340A	Χρυσός, ὡς ἐμοὶ < δοκεί > <καὶ σμύρνα καὶ λίβανος>, προσενεχθήσεται τῷ μέλλοντι τίκτεσθαι <ὡς Βασιλεῖ καὶ Θεῷ καὶ Ἀνθρώπῳ>· καθὼς φήσιν ὁ προφήτης καὶ βασιλεὺς Δαβίδ, ὅτι «Ζήσεται καὶ δοθήσεται αὐτῷ ἐκ τοῦ χρυσίου τῆς Ἀραβίας».	Gold as it seems to me, <and myrrh and incense>, shall be brought to the one about to be born (cf. Matthew 2.11) as the prophet and king David said, for "He shall live and the gold of Arabia shall be given to him (Psalm 72.19)."	Annunciation
340A	Ψηλαφήσωμεν λοιπόν, εἰ βούλει τόπον ἀψηλάφητον, καθότι καιρὸς ὑπέστι τῆς γεννήσεως, χρήζομεν γὰρ κατὰ τὴν ὁδὸν καὶ ὑποζύγιον · ἰδοὺ γὰρ βλέπω σε πάνυ στυγνάζουσαν, καὶ νομίζω ὅτι τεκεῖν ἐπείγεσαι.	Henceforth, let us feel our way. If you wish an untouched place, as the time comes for the birth, for we shall have need of a beast of burden to go there. For behold I see you extremely gloomy, and I know that you are about to give birth.	Annunciation

---

[28]   Text from Zachariah 9.9. This is only the first half of the LXX.

Gregory E. Roth

344A	καὶ γαστέρα πάλιν, τὴν σὴν ἐσήμανε κοιλίαν, τοῦ δεῖξαι καὶ τὴν σαρκικὴν ἐκ σοῦ τοῦ Μονογενοῦς ἐπιδημίαν. Προεωσφόρον δέ, τὴν πρὸ τοῦ αὔγους τότε δεδήλωκε νύκτα· ἑωσφόρον, τὴν ἡμέραν καλῶς ὑποτιθεμένη· ἐπειδὴ γὰρ ἐν νυκτὶ τὸ φῶς τοῖς ἐν σκότει καθημένοις ἐκύησας, προεωσφόρον τὴν ὥραν ἐκάλεσε τοῦ τόκου σου. «Ποιμένες γὰρ, φησὶν, ἦσαν ἐν τῇ χώρᾳ τῇ αὐτῇ ἀγραυλοῦντες, καὶ φυλάσσοντες φυλακὰς τῆς νυκτός.» Τοιαύτη ἡ προστεθεῖσα διὰ σοῦ τοῖς ἐπουρανίοις δόξα, Θεοτόκε. Μὴ γὰρ προσετέθη, οὐκ ἂν τὸ ἤδη δεδοξασμένον, Δόξαν ἐν ὑψίστοις, ἀνύμνουν οἱ ἄγγελοι, κατὰ τὸν καιρόν, ἐπικαταλαβεῖν τῆς ἀφράστου σου	And again [Scripture] called your belly "womb", to show also the habitation of the Only-begotten from your flesh; but "before the morning star" has declared the night then before the dawning—morning star, you who well represent the day. Since in the night you bore light for those who sat in darkness (cf. Luke 1.79), [Scripture] called "before the morning star" the hour of your childbirth. For it says, "Shepherds were in the same place outdoors and keeping watch at night." (Luke 2.8) Such was glory shown to the heavenly ones through you, O Theotokos. If it had not been new—the angels would not be singing "Glory in the highest," in praise of your ineffable childbearing had it	Dormition I
	κυοφορίας. Ποία δὲ καὶ τῶν ἐπιγείων ἡ ἔλλαμψις; ὅτιπερ διὰ τῆς σῆς ἀμώμου σαρκὸς οὐρανοπολίτης ὁ ἄνθρωπος ἀπετελέσθη, καὶ ποιμένες μετ' ἀγγέλων ἐμίχθησαν.	already been glorified. What kind of illumination is this also of earthlings? Because through your blameless flesh man has been made a citizen of heaven, and shepherds associated with angels.	
361C	Ἔρχου προθύμως πρὸς τὸν ὑπὸ σοῦ γεγεννημένον.	Come willingly to the one who was borne by you.	Dormition III
No references appear in the Sash			

526

References to Mary and Paradox in the Homilies of Germanos I, Patriarch of Constantinople (715-730)

PG 98 Location	Greek	English	Homily
296A	Ἐν τῷ κατοίκτρῳ γὰρ τὸ μυστήριον ὑπερβλύζει καὶ βλαστάνον ὑπερανίσταται καὶ ἀΰλους νόας, μὴ ὅτι γε ἐνύλους, τῆς πανολβίου καὶ πανάγνου κόρης!	For the mystery overflows and the plant grows taller even than the incorporeal minds, not to mention the incarnate minds, in the compassion of the all-rich and pure maiden!	Presentation I (P 116 ftn. 21) (H 286 ftn. 8)
309C	Τίς ἔγνω τοιοῦτον πώποτε; Τίς εἶδεν, ἢ τίς ἤκουσε τῶν νῦν ἢ τῶν πάλαι, θῆλυ προσαγόμενον εἰς τὰ τῶν ἁγίων ἐνδότερα Ἅγια, τὰ μικροῦ δεῖν καὶ ἀνδράσιν ἀπρόσιτα, ἐν αὐτοῖς κατοικεῖν καὶ ἐνδιατρέφεσθαι; Ἆρ' οὐκ ἀπόδειξις ἐναργὴς τοῦτο τῆς ἐπ' αὐτῇ γενησομένης ξένης εἰς ὕστερον μεγαλουργίας; Ἆρ' οὐ σημεῖον ἐμφανές; Ἆρ' οὐ τεκμήριον εὔδηλον;	Who ever knew such a thing? Who saw, or who heard, of men now or men of old, that a female was led into the inner holy places of the holy places, which are barely accessible even to men, to live in them and to pass her time in them? Is this not a clear demonstration of the strange miracle to be done for her later? Is it not an evident sign? Is it not an obvious testimony?	Presentation II
324D	Ἡνίκα τελεσθῶσιν οἱ λόγοι μου εἰς τὸν καιρὸν αὐτῶν, τότε συνήσεις τοῦ ἀκαταλήπτου μυστηρίου τὴν δύναμιν. Τότε γνώσῃ τῶν ἐμῶν ῥημάτων τὴν ἔκβασιν.	When my words shall come to pass in their own time, then you will understand the power of this incomprehensible mystery. Then you will know the result of my words and the ineffable condescension of the Most High.	Annunciation

Gregory E. Roth

328B	τοῦτόν σου τὸν παράδοξον εὐαγγελισμόν	this paradoxical good news?	Annunciation
328C	Ῥίψον τὴν ἄπιστον γνώμην, Παρθένε. Ἰδοὺ γὰρ, ὡς ἐμοὶ δοκεῖ, ἐτελέσθησαν οἱ λόγοι μου· καὶ ἡ κοιλία σου ὄγκον βαστάζει· καὶ εἰ μὴ βούλει, «Οὐκ ἀδυνατήσει παρὰ τῷ Θεῷ πᾶν ῥῆμα.»	Cast away your unbelief, Virgin. For behold, as it seems to me, my words have been accomplished, a lump is rising in your belly. Even if you do not wish it, "with God nothing is impossible" (Luke 1:37).	Annunciation
328D	Σωτῆρα, ὡς λέγεις, ὅτι τέξομαι, λέξον μοι, νεανίσκε. Ξενίζει γὰρ ὡς ἀληθῶς, καὶ ἀγγέλων <τὰς> νοερὰς δυνάμεις, καὶ ἀρχαγγέλων τὰς φλογερὰς, καὶ πολυομμάτων ταξιαρχίας, τὰ σὰ εὐαγγέλια	Tell me, young man, what kind of savior, am I to bear? For truly your good news is strange even to the spiritual powers of angels, fiery might of archangels, and the commanders of the many-eyed [cherubim].	Annunciation
329B	Φαιδρὸν ἀνάλαβε βλέμμα, δεδοξασμένη· οὐρανὸς γὰρ μέλλεις γενέσθαι, καὶ ναὸς θεοχώρητος, καὶ σκηνὴ Θεοῦ ἔμψυχος· ἑπτὰ στερεωμάτων εὐρυχωρότερός τε καὶ ὑψηλότερος καὶ θαυμασιώτερος.	Put on a joyful countenance, O blessed one. You are about to become heaven, a God-containing tabernacle, a living temple of God, wider and higher and more wondrous than the seven firmaments.	Annunciation
329B	Φρίττω τοῦ παραδόξου τῆς ξένης μου λοχείας τὰ ἐγκαίνια	I shiver at the beginning of the paradox of my unusual childbearing.	Annunciation
336B	Ξενίσει ὁ τόκος, ὡς ἐμοὶ δοκεῖ, οὐ μόνον ἐμοί, ἀλλὰ καὶ ἀγγέλους καὶ ἀνθρώπους, καὶ οὐκ ἂν πιστεύσωσι. Τίς ποτε ἀκηκόεεν, ὅτι παρθένος βρέφος τέτοκεν, καὶ μάλιστα ἀπείρανδρος τυγχάνουσα;	Your motherhood is strange, as it seem to me, and not only to me but also to angels and men, and they would not believe this. Who has ever heard that a virgin has borne an infant, and especially without a man?	Annunciation

336C	τὰ λεγόμενα καὶ καταπλήττει σου τὸν νοῦν τῆς μυστικῆς κυοφορίας τὸ παράδοξον μυστήριον.	The paradoxical nature of my childbearing astounds your mind.	Annunciation
340B	τὰ τῶν παραδόξων κεκτημένην θαυμάσια	you who have obtained marvels of paradoxical gifts	Dormition I
352B	Τὴν τῶν ἀγγέλων ὑπὲρ ἔννοιαν θεωρίαν·	You are a vision beyond the understanding of the angels.	Dormition II
352B	τὴν τῶν ἀνθρώπων ὑπέρξενον ἐπιτυχίαν·	You are the surpassingly strange good fortune of mankind.	Dormition II
353A	Ὅσα τὰ σά, παράδοξα, «ἀληθινά, δεδικαιωμένα ἐπὶ τὸ αὐτό, ἐπιθυμήματά τε πάντα καὶ γλυκύτερα ὑπὲρ μέλι καὶ κηρίον. Καὶ γὰρ οἱ δοῦλοί σου ποθοῦμεν αὐτά, ἐν τῷ ποθεῖν αὐτά, ἀντάμειψις ἐκ σοῦ πολλή.»	Whatever is yours, is paradoxical, "true, and all together made righteous all desirable and sweeter than honey and honeycomb; for your servants desire them, in desiring them, great reward [is obtained] from you" (Ps. 18.10-12 LXX).	Dormition II
365A	Υἱὸς μὲν σαρκὶ γεννηθεὶς ὑπ' ἐμοῦ· Πατὴρ δὲ καὶ Κτίστης καὶ Θεὸς τῆς ἰδίας οὗτος μητρός.	He is a Son given birth in the flesh by me, but Father and Creator and God of his own mother.	Dormition III
381A	Ὅλα τὰ σά, Θεοτόκε, παράδοξα, ὅλα ὑπὲρ φύσιν, ὅλα ὑπὲρ λόγον καὶ δύναμιν. Διὰ τοῦτο καὶ ἡ προστασία σου, ὑπὲρ ἔννοιαν.	All your own, Theotokos (Luke. 5.26), is paradox, all above nature, all beyond words and power. Therefore also your protection is beyond understanding.	Sash

References to the Parallel Events in the lives of Mary and Jesus in Germanos I, Patriarch of Constantinople (715-730)

PG 98 Location	Greek	English	Homily
293C	Σήμερον τῷ ἱλαστηρίῳ ἀνατίθεται ἡ μόνη τοῖς τῶν βρότων ἐσφαλλομένοις διεξαχθεῖσιν ἀμπλακημάτων ἐπιρροαῖς, ἱλαστήριον καινόν τε καὶ θεοειδέστατον καθαρτικόν τε καὶ ἀχειρότευκτον χρηματίσασα.	Today she who alone is called the new, god-like, purifying and mercy seat, not made by hands, (*cf.* Hebrews 9.11) for mortals who have drowned in floods of sin is presented to the mercy seat of the temple.	Presentation I (P Somiglianza 196 ftn. 16)
293D 296A	Πέλαγος γὰρ ἀχανὲς τὰ ταύτης μεγαλεῖα, ὁ ἐξ αὐτῆς οὐράνιος γεννηθεὶς σταγὼν ἀνέδειξεν. Διὸ δὴ τοῦ χάριν καὶ ἄληπτος τῇ ἀπειρίᾳ ὁ ταύτης πλοῦτος πέφυκε, καὶ ἡ αὐτῆς τρυφὴ ἀδάπανος·	For her greatness is a vast sea, as the Heavenly drop born from her has shown. And therefore her richness is unlimited in its infinitude, and her wealth is inexhaustible.	Presentation I (P Somiglianza 191 ftn. 3)
	Perniola claims that the above quote from 293D confirms that Mary was also conceived Immaculately. Ed è ancora questa singolare dignità che unisce intimamente la madre al figlio, Gesù a Maria, nella vita e nella morte, nella gloria e nell'amore dei cristiani. Alla concezione verginale di Cristo corrisponde quella immacolata di Maria; Cristo è la nostra vita, e Maria è detta ugualmente «nutrice della nostra vita» (cf. 296D below)		
296D	Ἐπεὶ γοῦν αὐτῆς γε τῆς παναγίας καὶ ὑπεραρχίου Τριάδος ὁ εἷς, τῇ ταύτης τῆς παρθενομήτορος κόρης γαστρὶ, Πατρικῇ εὐδοκίᾳ, ἰδιοθελῶς, τοῦ	When, at last, the One, All-Holy, unoriginate Trinity, deigned to be contained in the belly of the Virgin Mother, through good will of the Father and of the Son	Presentation I

	τε παναγίου Πνεύματος ἐπισκιάσει χωρηθῆναι ἠπείγετο· ἔδει δὲ καὶ ταύτην τῷ αὐτῷ τοῦ ἀριθμοῦ δεδοξασμένην κλέει ἱερουργεῖσθαι λαμπρότατα· τοῦ χάριν καὶ ἐνιαυτῶν τριῶν τῷ ναῷ προσάγεται, βεβαίως τὰ πάντα καὶ ἀσφαλῶς ᾠκονομηκότος τοῦ ταύτης πλαστουργοῦ τε καὶ τέκους.	and by the overshadowing of the Holy Spirit, then it was necessary for her who had been glorified by the same number to be most brilliantly consecrated, and because of this she is brought into the temple at three years of age. Her Fashioner and Son puts all things finally and surely in order.	
296D	Ἤδη μὲν οὖν ἀπογαλακτισθείσης αὐτῆς τῆς ἡμετέρας ζωῆς τροφοῦ, οἱ ταύτης τοκεῖ, τὴν, ἣν ὑπέσχοντο, προθεσμίαν τελειοῦσι.	When she who is the nourisher of our lives had been weaned, her parents fulfill the commitment which they had promised.	Presentation I (P Somiglianza 191 ftn. 4)
300C	εἰσάγαγε τῷ θυσιαστηρίῳ τὴν εἰς τὴν ἀρχαίαν νομὴν ἡμᾶς τοῦ παραδείσου εἰσοικίσουσαν·	Lead into the sanctuary her who will restore us to the ancient pasture of paradise.	Presentation I
301A	Τοιγαροῦν ὁ Ζαχαρίας τὴν παῖδα δεδεγμένος, πρῶτα τοῖς γονεῦσιν εἰκότως προσφθέγγεται· Ὦ τῆς ἡμετέρας σωτηρίας αἴτιοι, τί ὑμᾶς προσείπω; Τί καλέσω; Ἐξίσταμαι	So then Zacharias having received the child, probably first addresses the parents saying: "O causes of our salvation, what shall I say to you? What shall I call [you]? I am astonished seeing	Presentation I (P Somiglianza 191 ftn. 5) and Presentation I (P Somiglianza 193 ftn. 18)
	βλέπων, ὁποῖον καρπὸν προσήξατε. Τοιοῦτος γὰρ ὅστις τῇ καθαρότητι θέλγει Θεὸν ἐν αὐτῇ οἰκῆσαι. Οὐδὲ γὰρ πώποτέ τις γέγονεν ἢ γενήσεται τοιαύτη καλλονῇ διαλάμπουσα.	what kind of fruit you have brought forth, such a one as by her purity attracts God to dwell within her. For never yet has anyone existed or will anyone exist who shines forth in such beauty.	

In ftn. 5 Perniola claims that «l'autrice della nostra salvezza» appears in 300A. It does not appear there and the closest term is addressed to the Theotokos' parents by Zacharias and is found in 301A.
Ὦ τῆς ἡμετέρας σωτηρίας αἴτιοι is clearly an address to the parents of the Theotokos.

301C	Μακάριοι μασθοὶ οἷς ἐτιθηνήθη, καὶ γαστὴρ ἣ βεβάστακται	Fortunate are the breasts by which she was nursed and the womb that carried her (*cf.* Luke 11.27).	Presentation I
301D	Εἴσελθε τοῖς τοῦ βήματος προθύροις, ἡ τὰ τοῦ θανάτου πρόθυρα συνθλῶσα.	Come into the entry doors of the Bema, you who destroy the doors of death.	Presentation I
312B	«Τί ἄρα ἔσται τὸ παιδίον τοῦτο;»	"What will this child be?"	Presentation II
312C/D	Οὐδὲν ὁ προφήτης ἐφθέγξατο τοιοῦτον· ἀλλ' ὡς προειδὼς τὸ ἐσόμενον· ἐπεὶ προφήτης ἦν· πάντως προσδεχόμενος ταύτην, καὶ προσμένων, οἷον ὁ μετ' αὐτὸν Συμεὼν τὸν ἐκείνης υἱόν, δέχεται ταύτην προθύμως.	The prophet uttered nothing of this sort, but as if foreseeing what would be, since he was a prophet, assuredly accepting her, and waiting, as after him Simeon [awaited] her son, he receives her willingly (*cf.* Luke 2.25*ff*)	Presentation II
313C/D	οὕτω τοίνυν ἐπικαμφθεὶς ὁ πρὸς οἶκτον ἕτοιμος καὶ φιλόψυχος Κύριος, ταῖς ἀμφοτέρων εὐχαῖς τὸν αὐτοῦ πέπομφεν ἄγγελον, τὴν τῆς ἐμῆς παιδὸς σύλληψιν ἡμῖν προσαγγείλαντα. Αὐτίκα γοῦν ἡ φύσις πρὸς Θεοῦ κελευσθεῖσα, τὴν γονὴν εἰσεδέξατο· οὐ γὰρ πρὶν τῆς θείας χάριτος αὐτὴν τετόλμηκε δέξασθαι. Ἀλλ' ἐκείνης προεισελθούσης, οὕτως ἡ μύσασα μήτρα τὰς ἰδίας πύλας ἤνοιξε, καὶ τὴν ἐκ Θεοῦ παραθήκην ὑποδεξαμένη παρ' ἑαυτῇ κατέσχεν, ἄχρι Θεοῦ εὐδοκίᾳ τὸ ἐν αὐτῇ σπερμανθὲν εἰς φῶς ἐξῆλθεν.	thus you see the Lord who is ready for mercy and loves souls has bent down and sent an angel to the prayers of both of us, announcing to us the conception of my child. So therefore when [my] nature was bidden by God, it received the seed; for it did not dare to accept it before the divine grace. But when that [grace] preceded, then the closed womb opened its own gates, and receiving the deposit from God, held it in itself, until by the good will of God it brought forth to light that which had been sown in it.	Presentation II

321A	Χαῖρε, κεχαριτωμένη, ἡ τοῦ μάννα στάμνος <ἡ> ὁλόχρυσος, καὶ σκηνὴ ὡς ἀληθῶς πορφυροποίητος, ἣν ὁ νέος Βεσελεὴλ χρυσοπρεπῶς κατεποίκιλεν.	Hail full of grace, [you are] the golden jar which contained the manna (*cf.* Hebrews 9.4), and [you are] the true royal tabernacle, which the new Bez'alel fittingly adorned in gold (*cf.* Exodus 31.2*ff.*).	Annunciation (P Somiglianza 193 ftn. 17)
324A	Perniola combines the conversation between Jesus and Philip found in Jn 14.8—9 (cf ftn. 19 193) with Mary's comment concerning the beauty of the Angel. From this he draws a parallel between Jesus and Mary. «Chi vede me, aveva detto Gesù a Filippo che lo richiedeva di mostrare loro il Padre, chi vede me, vede il Padre mio»; ed a noi potrebbe ripetere: Chi vede me, vede la madre mia, vede Maria. In quanto Dio, egli era l'immagine viven te e sostanziale del Padre, ma in quanto uomo ripeteva in sè le fattezze di Maria. E già l'angelo, entrando nella casetta di Nazaret, e mirandola in volto, ci dice San Germano, era rimasto stupefatto nel contemplare la sua bellezza che aveva del divino, e gli era sembrato di trovarsi dinnanzi alla gloria del suo Signore;		Annunciation (P Somiglianza 193 ftn. 20)
345D	σοῦ, τῆς ὡς μιᾶς τῶν καθ' ἡμᾶς τυγχανούσης σωμάτων, καὶ διὰ τοῦτο μὴ τοῦ κοινοῦ τῶν ἀνθρώπων θανάτου δυνηθείσης ἐκφυγεῖν τὸ συνάντημα· ὃν τρόπον καὶ ὁ σὸς Υἱὸς καὶ πάντων Θεὸς, καὶ αὐτὸς, ὅσον εἰπεῖν, διὰ τὸν παντὸς ἀποθνήσκοντα τοῦ γένους ἡμῶν ἄνθρωπον, τοῦ ὁμοίου σαρκικῶς «ἀπεγεύσατο θανάτου»· παραδοξάσας δηλαδή, κατὰ τὸν ἴδιον αὐτοῦ καὶ ζωοποιὸν τάφον, καὶ τὸ σὸν τῆς κοιμήσεως ζωοπαράδεκτον μνῆμα· ὥστε ἀμφοτέρων	You, as one who happens [to have] a body like ours, and because of this not being able to escape the encounter with the common death of mankind, in the same way as your Son and the God of all himself, so to speak, because of his humanity, [like] all of our race, "tasted" of a similar "death in the flesh"(Heb. 2.9): obviously glorifying, along with his own unique and life-creating burial, also the memorial of your life-receiving	Dormition I (P Somiglianza 192 ftn. 13)

	σώματα μὲν ἀφαντάστως ὑπο—δεξαμένων, διαφθορὰν δὲ μηδαμῶς ἐνεργησάντων.	dormition, so that the both [graves] received bodies not in appearance only, but did not at all cause corruption.	
348A/ B/C	Ἐπειδὴ γὰρ ὁ κενωθεὶς ἐν σοί, Θεὸς ἦν ἀπ' ἀρχῆς, καὶ ζωὴ προαιώνιος, καὶ τὴν Μητέρα τῆς Ζωῆς σύνοικον ἔδει τῆς Ζωῆς γεγονέναι, καὶ καθάπερ ὕπνον τὴν κοίμησιν ὑπολαβεῖν, καὶ ὡς ἐγρήγορσιν ὑποστῆναι τὴν μετάστασιν ὡς Μητέρα τῆς Ζωῆς. Ὥσπερ γὰρ τέκνον τὴν ἰδίαν ζητεῖ καὶ ποθεῖ μητέρα, καὶ μήτηρ συνδιάγειν τῷ τέκνῳ φιλεῖ, οὕτως καὶ σὲ φιλότεκνα σπλάγχνα πρὸς τὸν Υἱόν σου καὶ Θεὸν κεκτημένην, ἥρμοσεν πρὸς αὐτὸν ἐπανελθεῖν· καὶ τὸν Θεὸν δέ, μητροφιλῆ διακρατοῦντα πρὸς σὲ στοργήν, συνδίαιτόν σοι τὴν ἑαυτοῦ καὶ πάντως ἔπρεπε καταστῆναι συνομιλίαν. Τούτῳ δὲ τρόπῳ τὴν ἀποβίωσιν τῶν περαινομένων πεπονθυῖα, πρὸς τὰς ἀφθάρτους τῶν αἰωνίων μετῴκησας διατριβάς, ὅπου Θεὸς ἐναυλίζεται, μεθ' οὗ καὶ σὺ συνδιάγωγος οὖσα, Θεοτόκε, οὐκ ἀποχωρίζῃ τῆς τούτου συναναστροφῆς. Οἶκος γὰρ αὐτῷ καταπαύσεως	For since he who emptied himself in you was God from the beginning and Life before the ages, and it was necessary for the Mother of Life to become a companion with Life, and to experience death simply as sleep, and through this translation arise as Mother of Life. For just as a child seeks and desires its own mother, and a mother loves to spend time with her child, so also it suited you who have acquired a child-loving compassion for your Son and God to ascend to him; and also it undoubtedly befitted the God who has mother-loving affection for you to establish for you his companionship and fellowship. In this manner having endured the departure from this passing life, you have moved to the imperishable haunts of the eternal ones, where God dwells, with whom you also being a companion, O Theotokos, do not separate yourself from the activity of this	Dormition I (P Somiglianza 192 ftn. 6)

	σὺ γέγονας σωματικός, Θεοτόκε, καὶ τόπος ἀναπαύσεως αὐτὸς χρηματίζει μεταστάσει, πανύμνητε. «Αὕτη γὰρ, φησὶν, ἡ κατάπαυσίς μου εἰς αἰῶνα αἰῶνος·» τουτέστιν, Ἡ ἐκ σοῦ περιβληθεῖσα τούτῳ, Θεοτόκε, σάρξ· μεθ᾽ ἧς οὐ μόνον εἰς τὸν παρόντα τοῦτον αἰῶνα ἐπιφανεὶς ὁ Χριστὸς ἐπιστεύθη, ἀλλὰ καὶ κατὰ τὸν μέλλοντα αἰῶνα, σὺν τῇ τοιαύτῃ σου σαρκί, ἐρχόμενος κρῖναι ζῶντας καὶ νεκροὺς ἐμφανισθήσεται. πλησιοχώρως, ὡς εἴποι τις, τῶν σῶν λαλιῶν καὶ σπλάγχνων ἔχειν σε θέλων· διὸ καὶ ὅσα ζητεῖς παρ᾽ αὐτοῦ, τεκνοπενθῷ ἐπιδίδωσι, καὶ ὅσαπερ αἰτεῖς ἐξ αὐτοῦ, θεοδυνάμως ἀποπληροῖ· ὁ ὢν εὐλογητὸς εἰς τοὺς αἰῶνας. Ἀμήν	[world]. For you have become a corporeal house of rest for him, O Theotokos, and you are called the very place of repose by your translation, all-praised one. "For this is my rest," he/it says, "unto the age of the age;" (Psalm 131.14 LXX) that is, the flesh put on by him from you, O Theotokos—with which we believe that Christ has appeared not only for this present age, but also will be revealed in the coming age, with such flesh from you, coming to judge the living and the dead. So since you are his eternal resting-place, he took you to himself free from corruption wishing to have you nearby, as one might say, [with] your conversation and compassion. Therefore also whatever you seek from him, he gives with a child's affection, and whatever you seek from him, he fulfills with the power of God: who is blessed unto the ages. Amen.	
360D	Διὰ πάντων γὰρ ἔχεις τὸ κεχαριτωμένον τῆς προσηγορίας ἀξίωμα. Ὡς ὅταν σὺ μέλλουσα συλλαμβάνειν με, χαίρειν ἐμηνύθης, χαῖρε καὶ ἄρτι προσλαμβάνεσθαι ζητουμένη παρ᾽ ἐμοῦ. Μὴ ταραχθῇς	You rightly possess the title "full of grace" in every way. As when you, being about to conceive me, were addressed with "hail," hail also as I seek to receive you at my side. Do not be disturbed as	Dormition III (P Somiglianza 192 ftn. 7)

	ἐγκαταλιποῦσα τὸν φθειρόμενον σὺν ταῖς ἐπιθυμίαις αὐτοῦ κόσμον. Τὴν φθορὰν αὐτοῦ παρεᾷς· ἐπεὶ τοὺς ἐν τῷ κόσμῳ τῆς ἀντιλήψεως ὀρφανοὺς οὐκ ἀφήσεις· ἀλλ' ὥσπερ ἐγὼ μὴ ὢν ἐκ τοῦ κόσμου, ἐπιβλέπω καὶ διοικῶ τοὺς ἐν τῷ κόσμῳ· οὕτως καὶ ἡ σὴ προστασία οὐκ ἀφαιρεθήσεται μέχρι συντελείας ἐκ τῶν τοῦ κόσμου.	you leave the world which perishes along with its desires. Let its corruption go, since you will not leave those in the world orphaned of your protection; but just as I, although I am not in the world, oversee and care for those in the world, so also your advocacy will not be taken away from those in the world until the end.	
361A	Ὅπου τοίνυν ἐγώ, καὶ σὺ μέλλεις ὑπάρχειν, ἀχώριστος μήτηρ, ἐν ἀδιαζεύκτῳ Υἱῷ	So where I am, there you also will be, mother inseparable, with your inseparable Son.	Dormition III (P Somiglianza 190 ftn. 8)
361D	Ἐγώ σοι τὸν κόσμον χρεώστην ἀναδείξω, καὶ μετερχομένης πλεῖόν σου τὸ ὄνομα καταδοξάσω.	I will show you to the world that is your debtor, and I will glorify your name even more as you are translated.	Dormition III (P Somiglianza 190 ftn. 2)
364A	Θὲς ἐν τῷ Γεθσημανῆ χωρίῳ τεθαρρηκότως τὸ σῶμά σου, καθὼς ἐγὼ πρὸ τοῦ παθεῖν με δι' ἀνθρωπίνην προσευχὴν ἐκεῖσε τὰ γόνατα. Σοῦ γὰρ προτυπούμενος τὴν κοίμησιν, ἔκλινα κἀγὼ πρὸς τὸ τοιοῦτον χωρίον τὰ ἐμὰ τοῦ ἐκ σοῦ σώματος γόνατα. Ὡς οὖν ἐγὼ μετὰ τὴν τότε γονυκλισίαν πρὸς τὸν ζωοποιὸν ἐξῆλθον καὶ ἑκούσιον τοῦ σταυροῦ μου θάνατον, καὶ σὺ μετὰ τὴν κατάθεσιν τοῦ σοῦ λειψάνου πρὸς ζωὴν παραχρῆμα μετατεθήσῃ	Set down your body in the place of Gethsemane with good cheer, as I before I suffered set down my knees there in a human prayer. For prefiguring your dormition, I myself also bent the knees of my body towards such a place. So as I after the kneeling at that time went forth to my life-giving and willing death on the cross, you also after the laying-down of your remains will immediately be transferred to life.	Dormition III (P Somiglianza 192 ftn. 10)

| 364C/D | Δημοσιεύει τὴν μετάστασιν, δηλοποιεῖ τὰ παρ' ἀγγέλου πρὸς αὐτὴν δηλωθέντα·δεικνύει καὶ τὸ δοθὲν αὐτῇ βραβεῖον. Ἦν δὲ τὸ βραβεῖον, φοίνικος κλάδος, σύμβολον νίκης κατὰ θανάτου, καὶ ζωῆς ἀμαράντου προεκτύπωμα· τοῦ πιστωθῆναι μετερχομένην, ὅτι καταδυναστεύσειεν τῆς φθορᾶς, ὡς καὶ ὁ ὑπ' αὐτῆς γεννηθεὶς ἐνίκησεν τὸν ᾅδην, Χριστός. Τοιοῦτον τὸ βραβεῖον τοῦ φοίνικος, ἐν ᾧ καὶ οἱ θεοφιλεῖς τῶν Ἑβραίων παῖδες ἐπὶ τὸ πάθος ἐγγίζοντι τῷ Χριστῷ, ὡς νικητῇ τούτῳ μέλλοντι γίνεσθαι τοῦ θανάτου, δοξολογητικῶς ἐπέσεισαν, κράζοντες· «Ὡσαννὰ ἐν τοῖς ὑψίστοις·» τουτέστι, Σῶσον δή, ὁ ἐν ὑψίστοις. Τὸ γὰρ Ὡσαννὰ παρ' Ἑβραίοις σῶσον δὴ μεθερμηνεύεται. Ὥσπερ οὖν ἐκεῖ τὰ βαΐα τῶν φοινίκων νικητικὸν τὸν τοῦ Χριστοῦ προεμήνυον συμβολικῇ τῇ ὑποδείξει θάνατον, οὕτως καὶ τὸ ἐκ φοίνικος δοθὲν τῇ Θεοτόκῳ βραβεῖον, πληροφόρημα νίκης ὑπῆρχεν θανατοποιοῦ καταφθορᾶς. | She makes public announcement of her translation, she reveals what has been revealed to her by the angel; she shows the prize which was given to her. The prize was a branch, a symbol of victory over death, and a pre-figuration of un-withering life, to confirm that she is going over, that she may prevail over corruption, as also the Christ who received birth from her conquered Hades. Such a prize/branch of a palm-tree, in/ with which also the god-loving children of the Hebrews, when Christ was approaching his passion, as to this one about to become a victor over death, shook with songs of praise, crying out, "Hosanna in the highest;" that is, "Save indeed, [you who are] in the highest." For "Hosanna" among the Hebrews is interpreted as "Save indeed." So as there the branches of the palm-trees foretold the victorious death of Christ with a symbolic demonstration, so also the prize from a palm-tree given to the Theotokos was a fulfillment of victory over death-dealing corruption. | Dormition III (P Somiglianza 192 ftn. 11) |

365B/C	Καὶ ἰδόντες αὐτήν, προσεκύνησαν ταύτῃ φιλοφρόνως, καὶ τὴνεῖδησιν τῆς ἀφίξεως ἐξ αὐτῆς μεμαθηκότες, τοιαῦτα πρὸς αὐτὴν διεξῆλθον· Διότι μὲν ἐν τῇ τοῦ κόσμου τούτου παροικίᾳ σέ, Θεομῆτορ, σύνοικον ἔχοντες, καὶ ὡς αὐτὸν τὸν Χριστὸν θεωροῦντές σε παρεμυθούμεθα βλέποντες, ἀδολεσχοῦμεν ἐπὶ τῇ σῇ μεταστάσει.	And when they saw her, they bowed before her lovingly, and when they learned the form of the arrival from her, they narrated the following to her: "Because having you as a companion in the sojourn of this world, O Mother of God, and seeing you like Christ himself we are consoled when we behold [you], we meditate on your translation	Dormition III (P Somiglianza 193 ftn. 21)
368A/B	ῥίπτει Παῦλος ἑαυτὸν εἰς τοὺς θεοβαστάκτους αὐτῆς πόδας, καὶ μαθὼν ἐφ' ᾧ καὶ αὐτὸς παραγέγονεν, σὺν μεγάλῳ καὶ ἐνδακρύῳ στεναγμῷ ἀνοίξας τὸ ἔτοιμον καὶ διδασκαλικὸν αὐτοῦ στόμα, ἐγκωμιάζει μεγάλως τὴν Παρθένον, ἐξ ὧν ὀλίγα ταῦτα· Χαῖρε, Μῆτερ τῆς ζωῆς, καὶ τοῦ ἐμοῦ κηρύγματος ἡ ὑπόληψις. Χαῖρε, τῆς ἐμῆς ψυχαγωγίας ἡ ἐπιτυχία. Εἰ γὰρ καὶ τὸν Χριστὸν σαρκὶ μὴ τεθέαμαι, σὲ βλέπων ἐν σώματι, τὸν Χριστὸν θεωρεῖν παρηγορούμην, τὴν σῶμα τῷ ἀσωμάτῳ χορηγήσασαν ἐν περιβολῇ. Τὸν οὖν εἰς Χριστὸν πόθον τῷ σῷ προανεπληρούμην προσώπῳ. Ἐγώ σε τοῖς ἔθνεσιν ἕως χθές, Θεὸν σαρκικῶς ἐκήρυττον γεγεννηκέναι· ἀπάρτι καὶ πρὸς αὐτὸν	Paul throws himself at her feet which carried God, and learning for what purpose he himself had arrived, with great and tearful groaning opening his ready and didactic mouth, he makes a great encomium for the Virgin, of which these are a few [words]: "Rejoice, Mother of life, and subject of my proclamation. Rejoice, the accomplishment of my soul's journey. For even if I have not beheld Christ in the flesh, seeing you in the body, I have the consolation of contemplating Christ, since you provided a body to the bodiless One in which he covered himself. So we satisfy our desire for Christ with your person/ face. I was proclaiming you to the gentiles until yesterday, that you had	Dormition III (P Somiglianza 193 ftn.22)

	μετατεθῆναί σε διδάξω τοῦ γνωσθῆναι αὐτοῖς ἔθνεσιν τὸ σωτήριον αὐτῶν ἐν τῇ σῇ κραταιοῦσθαι πρεσβείᾳ· ὅπως ἔχειν καὶ αὐτὰ προστασίαν πρὸς τὸν Θεὸν ἀμετάθετον.	borne God in the flesh. From now on I will also teach that you have been transferred to his side so that it may be made known to the very gentiles" that their salvation is strengthened by your intercession and that they have immovable assistance with God.	
372A

372B | ἐν σοὶ δὲ τῇ Γεθσημανῇ πάντες, οἵ τε μαθηταὶ τοῦ Σωτῆρος ἡμεῖς καὶ ὁ σωρευθεὶς ἐν ταύτῃ τῇ κηδείᾳ τῆς ἀειπαρθένου Μαρίας [ὄχλος] τὴν ταφεῖσαν ἐν τῷ μνημείῳ τεθεῖσαν καὶ μετατεθεῖσαν ἴδομεν. Ἥ τις χωρὶς πάσης ἀντιλογίας πρὸ τοῦ συγκλεισθῆναι τῷ λίθῳ τοῦ μνήματος, ταύτῃ γέγονεν ἀφανής· ἵνα μὴ σφραγίδων δίχα καὶ φυλάκων χωρὶς κατατεθεῖσα, εὔκαιρον ἀφορμὴν περὶ κλοπῆς τοῖς ἀπιστοῦσιν ἐμποιήσῃ. Ἀλλ' ἰδοὺ ὑμνουμένη καὶ τῷ τάφῳ κατακενουμένη, καὶ τὸ μνῆμα κενὸν ἀφῆκεν· καὶ τὸν παράδεισον τῆς ἰδίας ἐγέμισε δόξης, καὶ τῆς οὐρανίου ζωῆς τὴν κατάπαυσιν ἔχει· καὶ μετὰ τῆς τοῦ Θεοῦ τρυφῆς συγκάτοικος ὑπάρχει. | And you Gethsemane, blessed place, which has found glory like Joseph's garden. There Peter and John, running and finding the linen clothes and the handkerchief, believed that Christ had risen. But in you Gethsemane all saw, both we the disciples of the Savior and [the crowd] which was gathered in this funeral of the ever-virgin Mary, her who was buried, laid in the tomb, and transferred. She who without any dispute before the tomb was shut with a stone, at this became invisible, so that not having been laid down without seals and apart from guards she might make a favorable opportunity [to allege] theft for the unbelievers. But behold as she was being hymned [in procession] came to the tomb which she left empty; and she filled paradise with her own glory, and she has the rest of eternal life, and she is a companion of the luxury of God." | Dormition III (P Somiglianza 192 ftn. 12) |

| 376D— 377D | Ὦ ζώνη, ἡ τὴν τῆς ζωῆς πηγὴν περιζώσασα, καὶ ζωὴν παρέχουσα τοῖς σὲ τιμῶσιν αἰώνιον! Ὦ ζώνη, ἡ τὰς τῶν σοὶ προστρεχόντων ὀσφύας, νέκρωσιν μὲν κατὰ παθῶν δωρουμένη, ἀνδρίαν δὲ πρὸς πρᾶξιν ἀρετῶν καὶ ἐνέργειαν! Ὦ ζώνη, ἡ τὸ ἀσθενὲς τῆς ἡμετέρας φύσεως ἀναστέλλουσά τε καὶ περισφίγγουσα· καὶ τοὺς ἀοράτους τε καὶ ὁρατοὺς ἐχθροὺς ἡμῶν συμποδίζουσα! Ἀλλ' οἷα γάρ μοι συμβέβηκε, τῷ πόθῳ τῆς πανάγνου νυττόμενον, καὶ τῇ τοῦ λόγου ῥύμῃ κατεπαγόμενον, τῶν σπαργάνων ἐπιλαθέσθαι. Καὶ οὐ θαυμαστόν· Μητρὸς γὰρ δοξαζομένης, ὅδε φιλομήτωρ. Υἱὸς εὐφραίνεται. Ἀλλὰ καὶ νόμῳ ὑπείκοντες φύσεως, εἰ καὶ ὑπὲρ φύσιν τὰ πράγματα, τῇ Μητρὶ πρῶτον τὸ γέρας ἀφοσιώσομεν. Καὶ οὐκ ἀπώσεται Κύριος πάντως, ὁ ὑπεράγαθος. Ὡς γὰρ ἀψευδῶς ἄνθρωπος ἐξ αὐτῆς προελθεῖν εὐδόκησε, καὶ Υἱὸς αὐτῆς κληθῆναι ἠξίωσεν, ἀποδέξεται τὴν τόλμαν ὡς κατὰ ἄνθρωπον γεγονυῖαν ὁ πολυεύσπλαγχνος. Πλὴν σπαργάνων μνησθείς, πάλιν πρὸς τὴν τεκοῦσαν | Oh Sash, you have girded about the well of Life, and offer life to those who honor you, in fact eternal life![29] Oh Sash, you give to the loins of those who turn to you mortification on the one hand, and on the other hand, manliness and energy in the practice of virtue! Oh Sash, you both bound up and restrained the weakness of our nature and hobble both our seen and unseen enemies! For such things happen to me being pierced by the all holy One and being carried away by the force of my words, I have forgotten about the winding sheet. And it is no wonder! A mother loving Son rejoices in His Mother being glorified. But yielding to the law of our nature, even if the matter is beyond our nature, as is fitting we honor first the Mother. For the Lord surely will not reject the all holy One. For he deigned as is fitting we honor first the Mother. For the Lord surely will not reject the all holy One. For he deigned to come forth from her as truly human, and he deigned | Zone (P Somiglianza 189 ftn. 1) |

---

[29]   The Greek phrase: Ὦ ζώνη, ἡ τὴν τῆς ζωῆς πηγὴν περιζώσασα, καὶ ζωὴν παρέχουσα τοῖς σὲ τιμῶσιν αἰώνιον! does play on the words "ζώνη" and "ζωῆς" as Mary Cunningham points out. See, Cunningham, Wider 250 ftn. 8. Much is lost in translation here and elsewhere in Germanos' homilies.

ἀνάγομαι. Αὕτη γὰρ ταῦτα ταῖς ἁγναῖς αὐτῆς χερσὶ κατεσκεύασεν. Αὕτη βρεφοπρεπῶς τὸν μέγαν Κύριον χερσὶ μητρῴαις ἐν τούτοις ἐνείλιττεν. Αὕτη σὺν τούτοις τοῦτον ἐγκόλπιον φέρουσα, ἐγαλούχει, τὸν πάσῃ φύσει πνοὴν καὶ τροφὴν παρεχόμενον. Ἀλλ' ὦ σπάργανα, τὸν ἐλευθερωτὴν Κύριον ἐνειλήσαντα, καὶ τῶν ἡμετέρων παραπτωμάτων σειρὰς διαλύσαντα! Ὦ σπάργανα, τὰ τὸν κραταιὸν Κύριον περισφίγξαντα, καὶ τὴν τοῦ γένους ἡμῶν ἀσθένειαν ἀναρρώσαντα! Ὦ σπάργανα, πιστοὺς μὲν φρουροῦντά τε καὶ περιφυλάττοντα· τοὺς ἐναντίους δὲ δεσμοῦντα, καὶ καταβάλλοντα! Ἀλλ' ὦ σπάργανα καὶ ζώνη σεπτή! νέμοιτέ μοι τὸν ἁγιασμὸν, τὴν ῥῶσιν, τὸν ἱλασμὸν, παναγία Θεοτόκε; ἡ τῶν Χριστιανῶν πνοὴ καὶ ζωή. τὴν ὑγίειαν· ἐμοί τε, καὶ τοῖς πόθῳ τῷδε προσιοῦσι καὶ προσκυνοῦσι σεπτῷ σου ναῷ. Ὦ ζώνη σεπτή, ἡ τὴν σὴν πόλιν περικυκλοῦσα καὶ περιέπουσα, καὶ Βαρβαρικῆς ἐπιδρομῆς ἀνεπιβούλευτον	to be called her Son. The all compassionate One will accept our human boldness. But having mentioned the swaddling clothes, again I return to the Mother. For she prepared them with her hands. And she wrapped the great Lord, who was a child in these swaddling clothes. And carrying him on her lap she gave him milk, He who granted breath and substance to every kind of being. But Oh swaddling clothes, you bound the most free Lord, and you let loose [the] cords of our transgressions![30] (*cf.* Prov. 5.22) Oh swaddling clothes, you bound tightly the mighty Lord, and you strengthened the weakness of our race! Oh swaddling clothes, you guarded and infolded faith, and you fettered the enemy and overthrew him! And Oh swaddling clothes and venerable Sash! Grant me sanctification, strength, propitiation and health to me and to those who draw near in love and venerate your holy temple. Oh venerable Sash, that surrounds and	

---

30 Germanos all but forgets the swaddling clothes. See, Cunningham, Wider 251 ftn. 9.

διασώζουσα! Ὦ ζώνη τιμία, ἡ τὸν Θεὸν Λόγον ἐγγάστριον ὄντα περιειλήσασα, καὶ τὴν τῶν ἰάσεων εὐλογίαν ἐκεῖθεν πλουτήσασα, καὶ ἡμῖν ἀντιπέμπουσα! Ὦ ζώνη φαιδρὰ, ἡ τῆς τοῦ ἀφθάρτου Θεοῦ Μητρὸς τὸ ὑπέρσεμνον σῶμα σεμνοπρεπῶς προσεγγίσασα, κἀκεῖθεν τὴν ἀφθαρσίαν ἀμφιασαμένη, ἀπαρασάλευτος καὶ ἄφθαρτος μένουσα, ὡς εἰς ἡμᾶς τις λόγος τῆς ἀληθείας κατελήλυθεν! Ἀλλὰ τί καὶ τῶν ἀδυνάτων ἐπιχειροῦμεν, καὶ ὑπὲρ τὰ ἐσκαμμένα πηδᾶν ἐπειγόμεθα· τῆς ἐκ τῶν λόγων τιμῆς ταῦτα τιμᾶν κατ᾽ ἀξίαν πειρώμενοι, ὅπερ καὶ ἀγγέλοις ἀδύνατον. Πλήν, ὦ τιμία τῆς ὑπερτίμου τοῦ Θεοῦ Μητρὸς ζώνη, περίζωσον τὰς ὀσφῦς ἡμῶν ἀλήθειαν, δικαιοσύνην τε καὶ πραότητα. Τῆς ἀϊδίου καὶ μακαρίας ζωῆς ποίησον κληρονόμους, καὶ τὴν ἐπίκηρον ἡμῶν ταύτην ζωήν, ἐχθρῶν ἀοράτων τε καὶ ὁρατῶν, ἀνεπιβούλευτον	cares for your city, and without plotting kept it safe from the attacks of barbarians.[31] Oh radiant Sash, which honorably surrounded the very venerable body of the Mother of the incorruptible God, and thence is surrounded by incorruption, and continued to remain intact and incorruptible, and this true tradition has come down to us[32]. But we are attempting the impossible, and are urging ourselves on beyond, to leap over the trench, and we are attempting to honor [the swaddling clothes and the sash] worthily in words, which is impossible even to the angels. What's more, Oh honorable Sash of the all honorable Mother[33], surround with truth our loins, with righteousness and meekness. Makes inheritors of eternal and blessed life, (*cf.* Titus 3.7) and unassailed by enemies both visible and invisible. And guard our faith unshaken. Oh all pure	

---

[31]   Constantinople was besieged numerous times in its history. In Germanos time the most see especially the Arab siege in 714. For an interesting study of the walls of Constantinople see, Stephen R.Turnbull, and Peter Dennis. The Walls of Constantinople Ad 324-1453. Fortress. Oxford: Osprey Publishing, 2004 48

[32]   See also Cunningham, *Wider* 251 ftn. 10.

[33]   The phrase: ὦ τιμία τῆς ὑπερτίμου τοῦ Θεοῦ Μητρὸς ζώνη demonstrates the difficulty of translation from Greek to English. Mary Cunningham points it out as an instance of metaclisis a rhetorical device that is seldom used in English. See, Cunningham, Wider 252 ftn. 12.

διατήρησον. Τὴν πίστιν ἐν εἰρήνῃ ἀσάλευτον διαφύλαξον. Τὴν σὴν κληρονομίαν, τὸν σὸν λαὸν, ὦ πανάχραντε τῆς παναχράντου ζώνῃ, ὀρθοὺς τῇ πίστει, σώους τῷ κατὰ Θεὸν βίῳ, ἀβλαβεῖς τῆς οἱασοῦν ἐπηρείας διάσωζε. Ἔχοιμέν σε ἰσχὺν καὶ βοήθειαν, τεῖχος καὶ προπύργιον λιμένα καὶ καταφυγὴν σωτήριον. Σὺ δέ μοι, ὦ πάναγνε, καὶ πανάγαθε, καὶ πολυεύσπλαγχνε Δέσποινα, τὸ τῶν Χριστιανῶν παραμύθιον, τὸ τῶν θλιβομένων θερμότατον παρηγόρημα, τὸ τῶν ἁμαρτανόντων ἑτοιμότατον καταφύγιον, μὴ ἐγκαταλίπῃς ἡμᾶς ὀρφανοὺς τῆς σῆς ἀντιλήψεως. Εἰ γὰρ ὑπὸ σοῦ ἐγκαταλειφθείημεν, ποῦ ἄρα καὶ προσδραμούμεθα. Τί δὲ ἄρα καὶ γενησόμεθα, ὦ	Sash of the all pure One, guard unharmed from any kind of insult your inheritance, your people in upright faith, and save (them) through the godly life. May we have you as strength and aid, a wall and a tower a harbor and a safe refuge[34]. But you are to me, Oh most pure, all good and most compassionate Lady, the correction of Christians, the warmest encouragement of the afflicted, the ready refuge of sinners, do not forsake us orphans of your aid[35]. For if by you we should be forsaken, then to whom shall we flee? And what shall we become, Oh all holy Theotokos? The breath and the life of Christians.	

---

[34]   This phrase is a familiar petition in the litanies of the Orthodox Church.
[35]   See, Dormition I, 344B; Dormition III 360D, 364A for references to being orphaned.

References to the Power of Mary in Germanos I Patriarch of Constantinople (715-730)

PG 98 Location	Greek	English	Homily
293A	Τοιγαροῦν σπουδαίως συναπέλθωμεν ἀλλήλους τῇ κοινωφελεῖ σωτηριώδει πανηγύρει τῆς Θεομήτορος προτρεπόμενοι, καὶ τοῖς ἀδύτοις προκύψαντες εἰσβλέψωμεν παῖδα τὴν πρὸς τὸ δεύτερον καταπέτασμα χωροῦσαν, Μαρίαν τὴν πάναγνον καὶ Θεομήτορα, τὴν ἀκαρπίας στείρωσιν διαλύσασαν, καὶ νομικοῦ γράμματος σκιὰν τῇ τοῦ τόκου χάριτι διελάσασαν. Β΄. Σήμερον γὰρ τριετίζουσα πρόεισι τῷ νομικῷ ναῷ ἀνατεθησομένη ἡ ναὸς ἀκηλίδωτος καὶ ὑπέρτατος μόνη χρηματίσασα τοῦ ἀρχιερέως καὶ τῶν ἁπάντων τελετάρχου Κυρίου, καὶ ἐν τῇ ἰδίᾳ μαρμαρυγῇ τῆς θεολαμποῦς αἴγλης, τὴν ἐν τῷ γράμματι ἀχλὺν διελοῦσα.	So let us eagerly approach together this mutually beneficial, salvific feast of the Mother of God. And bowing before the unapproachable place [the holy of Holies] let us watch the child going toward the second veil, Mary the all-holy Mother of God who put an end to unfruitful sterility, and exchanged the mere shadow of the letter of the law (*cf.* Hebrews 10.1*ff*) through the grace of her birth-giving.[36] 2—Today, at three years of age, she goes towards her dedication in the temple of the law, she who alone is called the stainless and greatest temple of the high priest and the Lord of all, and in whose bright light is the radiance of divine light which illuminates the darkness of the Law.	Presentation I (P Prodigio 117 ftn. 27

---

[36] This is the first reference in this homily to the place of the Virgin as the instrument of the Incarnation.

293B	Σήμερον τῷ ἱερεῖ βρέφος ἀποδίδοται, ἡ τὸν δι' ἡμᾶς βρεφωθέντα σαρκὶ μόνον Ἀρχιερέα Θεὸν τεσσαρακονθήμερον ἀναθησομένη οἰκείαις ὠλέναις τὸν ἄσχετον κατέχουσα, ὑπὲρ πᾶσαν βρότειον ἔννοιαν. Σήμερον ὁ καινότατος καὶ καθαρώτατος ἀμόλυντος τόμος, οὐ χειρὶ γραφησόμενος, ἀλλὰ πνεύματι χρυσωθησόμενος, ταῖς κατὰ νόμον εὐλογίαις ἁγιαζομένη, χαριστήριον δῶρον προσάγεται.	Today a babe is handed over to a priest, the one who will dedicate the only high-priestly God made flesh as a child at forty days for us, having received in his welcoming arms (*cf.* Luke 1.22*ff.*) the uncontainable One who is beyond all human knowing.[37] Today a new, pure, unspoiled book which will not be written by hands, but written in gold by the spirit, hallowed with blessings according to the Law, she is brought forward as an acceptable gift.	Presentation I (P Prodigio 112 ftn. 8; 118 ftn. 30 and 118 ftn. 36)
293C	Σήμερον ἡ τοῦ θείου ναοῦ πύλη διαπετασθεῖσα, τὴν ἀνατολόβλεπτον καὶ ἐσφραγισμένην τοῦ Ἐμμανουὴλ πύλην εἰσιοῦσαν δέχεται.	Today the gate of God's temple is opened to receive the entry of the eastward looking, sealed gate of Emmanuel (*cf.* Ezekiel 44.1-3).	Presentation I (P Prodigio 118 ftn. 35)
293C (—304A)	Σήμερον ἡ ἱερὰ τοῦ ναοῦ τράπεζα λαμπρύνεσθαι ἄρχεται, πρὸς ἀναιμάκτους θυσίας τὴν μεταβίβασιν μετηλλαχυῖα τῇ τῆς οὐρανίου καὶ ψυχοτρόφου ἄρτου τραπέζης θείας προσκυνήσεως μεθέξει καὶ γλυκυτάτῳ ἀσπασμῷ.	Today the sacred Table of the temple joyfully meets and participates in the true divine table of the heavenly soul-feeding bread and by changing to the worship of the bloodless sacrifice begins to shine.	Presentation I (P Prodigio 117 ftn. 28)

---

[37]   This is a reference to the Presentation in the Temple of Christ. Germanos makes reference to that event to set the events of the Presentation of the Theotokos in the context of her role in the Incarnation. Mary and Joseph present Jesus to Simeon as Mary was presented to Zacharias by Joachim and Anna. Both presentations were necessary parts of salvation history.

293D—296A	τοῦ αἴνους τῷ πάσης ὑπεραρθῆναι καλλονῇ γλώσσης τε καὶ νοὸς ἐξεστηκότως, προάγει. Πέλαγος γὰρ ἀχανὲς τὰ ταύτης μεγαλεῖα, ὁ ἐξ αὐτῆς οὐράνιος γεννηθεὶς σταγὼν ἀνέδειξεν. Διὸ δὴ τοῦ χάριν καὶ ἄληπτος τῇ ἀπειρίᾳ ὁ ταύτης πλοῦτος πέφυκε, καὶ ἡ αὐτῆς τρυφὴ ἀδάπανος· πᾶσι μὲν γὰρ ἐν ἅπασι κορέννυσθαι ἔνεστιν. Ἐν δὲ τοῖς ταύτης ἐφυμνείοις τε καὶ πανηγύρεσιν ἀκόρεστος ἡ πανδαισία τῇ ἡδύτητι πέλει . . . Ἐν τῷ κατοίκτρῳ γὰρ τὸ μυστήριον ὑπερβλύζει καὶ βλαστάνον ὑπερανίσταται καὶ ἀΰλους νόας, μὴ ὅτι γε ἐνύλους, τῆς πανολβίου καὶ παναγνοῦ κόρης!	Her beauty far surpasses the power of every tongue and mind. For her greatness is a vast sea, as the Heavenly drop born from her has shown. And therefore her richness is unlimited in its infinitude, and her wealth is inexhaustible. For while it is possible for everyone in everything else to be sated, it is not possible in this feasting to give too much sweetness in her hymns and festivals. . . . For the mystery overflows and the plant grows taller even than the incorporeal minds, not to mention the incarnate minds, in the compassion of the all-rich and pure maiden!	Presentation I (P Prodigio 116 ftn. 21)
297D	Σήμερον ἡ τοῦ θείου ναοῦ πύλη διαπετασθεῖσα, τὴν ἀνατολόβλεπτον καὶ ἐσφραγισμένην τοῦ Ἐμμανουὴλ πύλην εἰσιοῦσαν δέχεται.	Today the gate of God's temple is opened to receive the entry of the eastward looking, sealed gate of Emmanuel (cf. Ezekiel 44.1-3).	Presentation I (P Prodigio 118 ftn. 35)
300D	Ἴδε, Κύριε, ἴδε· ἣν δέδωκας, λάβε· ἣν παρέσχες, εἴσδεξαι· ἣν ἡμῖν διαλύουσαν στείρωσιν ἔνειμας, δέχου· δι' αὐτῆς καὶ νόμου ἀπαιδίαν κατακρίνων, ἐλυτρώσω ἡμᾶς ἐνδελεχισμοῦ δεινοτάτου δι' αὐτῆς· ταύτην καλῶς ἡμᾶς διοικήσασαν ἀπολάμβανε,	"Behold, Lord, accept her whom you gave. Receive her whom you provided. Accept her whom you assigned to destroy our barenness, overcoming through her the barrenness of the Law, you have ransomed us through her from the terrible persistence [daily repetition of temple	Presentation I (P Prodigio 114 ftn. 18)

	ἣν ἡρετίσω, καὶ προώρισας, καὶ ἡγίασας, ἐπίσπασαί σοι προσερειδομένην καὶ τῇ ὀσμῇ σου τεθελγμένην, ἣν ὡς κρίνον ἐξ ἀκανθῶν τῆς ἡμετέρας ἀναξιότητο ἐξελέξω· εὐχρωώτατά σοι προσφερομένην ἐναγκάλισαι. Ἰδού σοι ταύτην παρατιθέμεθα καὶ ἑαυτοὺς ἀνατιθέμεθα.	sacrifices?]. House her who so well has housed us, her whom you have chosen, and have foreseen, and have blessed. Draw to yourself her who leans on you and is attracted by your fragrance. You chose her as a lily out of the brambles of our unworthiness. Embrace her who is brought to you with a most radiant complexion. Behold, to you we offer her [as our intercessor] and dedicate ourselves."	
301A	Ὑμεῖς ὤφθητε οἱ ἐκ παραδείσου ἀφιγμένοι δύο διπλούμενοι ποταμοί, ὑπὲρ χρυσίον καὶ λίθον τίμιον φέροντες λαμπάδα, τὴν τῷ κάλλει τῆς ἑαυτῆς ἀμώμου παρθενίας καὶ ταῖς δροσιστικαῖς μαρμαρυγαῖς τὴν ἅπασαν γῆν καταυγάζουσαν.	You are seen as the two double rivers flowing out of paradise, (cf. Genesis 2.10-15) carrying a lamp more precious than gold and precious stones, who in the beauty of her blameless virginity and her dewy sparkling illuminates the whole earth.	Presentation I (P Prodigio 118 ftn. 31)
Perniola lists this as from 301C but it appears in 301A and not at all in 308C as ftn. 31 suggests.			
301B	Ὑμεῖς τὰ τῆς νέας διαθήκης νοητοῦ ναοῦ ἐκλαμπρότατα κέρατα ἐγνωρίσθητε, ἐν τοῖς σφῶν στέρνοις κατίσχοντες τὸ τοῦ ἱεροῦ σφαγίου ἡγιασμένον καὶ θεεγκαίνιστον λογικώτατον θυσιαστήριον. Ὑμεῖς ὡράθητε ὑπὲρ τὸν πάλαι χαλκευθέντα χρυσὸν πρὸς τὸ τῆς κιβωτοῦ κάλυμμα τὴν τῆς νέας διαθήκης, τοῦ ἐν σταυρῷ ἡμῖν ἄφεσιν	You have been made known as the shining horns of the new righteous, spiritual temple, holding in your breasts the holy, God-acknowledged, rational altar of the sacred victim. You appeared to cover the mystical and holy Ark of the new covenant of Him who on the Cross wrote the forgiveness of our sin, [forming] a covering	Presentation I (P Prodigio 118 ftn. 29 and 118 ftn. 31)

	ὑπογράψαντος νοητήν τε καὶ θείαν κιβωτὸν περικαλύπτοντες.	which far surpasses the one which long ago was wrought of gold to cover the Ark (cf. Exodus 25.10).	
304A	Πλησίασον τῇ τραπέζῃ προσκυνήσουσα, περὶ ἧς ἐν συμβόλοις πλείοσι λέλεκται τράπεζαν κεχρηματικέναι σε λογικωτάτην καὶ ἀμόλυντον. Ὅδευσον διὰ τῆς ἐπαύλεως τοῦ ὅλου θυσιαστηρίου, ὡς ὀσμὴν θυμιάματος ἐκπνέουσα, καὶ ὑπὲρ μύρον τοῖς ὀσφραινομένοις γεγενημένη ἡ καλῶς τῆς θεολέκτου γλώσσης καὶ πνευματεμφόρου τοῦ προφήτου πύριον ἐξηχημένη. Ἀνάβηθι, ἀνάβηθι ἐπὶ βαθμίδα ἱεροῦ δόμου· ἧς τῇ καλλονῇ τῆς ὡραιότητος ἡδόμεναι θυγατέρες Ἰερουσαλὴμ αἶνον γεγηθυῖαι πλέκουσιν καὶ βασιλεῖς τῆς γῆς μακαρίζουσιν· ἡ βάσις θεία γεγνωρισμένη καὶ θεοστήρικτος κλίμαξ δεδειγμένη τῷ πατριαρχικωτάτῳ Ἰακὼβ θυμηρέστατα. Καθέσθητι, ὦ Δέσποινα· καὶ πρέπει γάρ σοι τῇ βασιλίσσῃ καὶ ὑπὲρ πάσας τὰς βασιλείας τοῦ κόσμου δεδοξασμένῃ, ἐν τοιαύτῃ βαθμίδι ἐφέζεσθαι	Approach in order to venerate the table, you who are called the living, undefiled table, which has been spoken of in many symbols. Make your way through the courts of the whole sanctuary breathing out as an odor of incense (cf. Exodus 30.1ff.). You have become more fragrant than myrrh, you who have been proclaimed by the God-chosen tongue of the spirit-filled prophet to be a censer. Go up, go up to the steps of the holy house. Daughters of Jerusalem taking pleasure in the beauty of your comeliness joyously compose a hymn. The kings of the Earth call you blessed. Your ascent of the steps is recognized as divine and delightfully shown as a God-supported ladder to the great patriarch Jacob (cf. Genesis 28.12ff.). Sit down O Lady, for it is proper to you as the Queen glorified above all earthly kingdoms to be seated upon such steps.	Presentation I (P Prodigio 118 ftn. 32; ftn. 33 and ftn. 40)
304C	Τίς γὰρ παρθένος ἔτεκεν, ἢ τεκοῦσα ἄσυλον τὴν παρθενίαν τετήρηκεν, εἰ μὴ σὺ	For what virgin has given birth, or after giving birth has preserved her virginity	Presentation I (P Prodigio 116 ftn. 22)

	μόνη, ἡ ἀπεριτρέπτως ἡμῖν σαρκὶ Θεὸν κυήσασα, πανολβία κόρη;	undefiled, except you alone, who truly bore God in the flesh for us, all-blessed maiden?	
305B	Χαίροις, ἡ νοητικὴν θείαν δρόσον ἡμῖν ἐπιστάζουσα φωτεινὴ νεφέλη, . . . πηγὴ ἡ θεόβρυτος, ἀφ' ἧς οἱ τῆς θεογνωσίας ποταμοὶ τὸ διειδέστατον καὶ ἀγλαοφανὲς τῆς ὀρθοδοξίας ὕδωρ διαρρέοντες, ἴλην τὴν τῶν αἱρέσεων ἐκμειοῦσιν.	Hail, bright cloud (cf. Exodus 19.16) who continues to drop divine spiritual dew upon us (cf. Exodus 16.13), . . . A fountain pouring out God, from which the rivers of divine knowledge pour out the bright clear water of orthodoxy and drown out the company of the heretics.	Presentation I (P Prodigio 118 ftn. 39, 41 and 42)
305B/C	Χαίροις, ὁ τερπνότατος καὶ λογικὸς Θεοῦ παράδεισος, σήμερον πρὸς ἀνατολὰς τῆς αὐτοῦ θελήσεως φυτευόμενος δεξιᾷ παντοκράτορι, καὶ αὐτῷ τὸ εὐανθὲς κρίνον καὶ ἀμάραντον ῥόδον κυπρίζουσα, τοῖς πρὸς δυσμὰς θανάτου λοιμικὴν ψυχοφθόρον τε πικρίαν ἐκπιοῦσιν, ἐν ᾧ τὸ ζωοπάροχον ξύλον τῆς πρὸς ἀληθείας ἐπίγνωσιν ἐξανθεῖ, ἐξ οὗ οἱ γευσάμενοι ἀθανατίζονται.	Hail, delightful and rational paradise of God, which today is planted in the east by the omnipotent right hand of his will (cf. Genesis 2.8), who have blossomed forth the beautiful lily and the unfading rose for those who in the west have drunk the bitter soul-destroying plague of death, on whom the life-giving tree has sprouted forth to the intimate knowledge of the truth. Those who have tasted from it are made immortal.	Presentation I (P Prodigio 118 ftn. 39)
305C	Χαίροις, τὸ τοῦ παμβασιλέως Θεοῦ ἱερότευκτον ἄχραντόν τε. καὶ καθαρώτατον παλάτιον, τὴν αὐτοῦ μεγαλειότητα περιβεβλημένη καὶ ξεναγοῦσά σου τῇ μυσταρχικῇ ἀπολαύσει ἅπαντας·	Hail, sacred, undefiled, most pure palace of the omnipotent God. You are wrapped in his grandeur and guide us all with your mystical joy.	Presentation I (P Prodigio 118 ftn. 37)

305C	ἐφ' ᾗ τὸ πλανηθὲν ἐπιστρέψαι βουληθείς, ὁ Λόγος τὴν σάρκα νενύμφευται, τοὺς ἤδη οἰκείᾳ βουλήσει διενηνεγμένους καταλλάσσων.	Through you, the Word which was married to the flesh willingly wished to reconcile those wanderers (cf. Romans 5.10) who through their own private will had been separated.	Presentation I (P Prodigio 118 ftn. 38)
305A & 308D	ἡ ὄντως χρυσοειδὴς καὶ φωτεινή . . . ἑπτάφωτος λυχνία τῷ ἀδύτῳ φωτὶ ὑφαπτομένη καὶ τῷ τῆς ἁγνείας ἐλαίῳ πιαινομένη, καὶ τοῖς ἐν ζόφῳ πταισμάτων ἀχλύϊ τυφλώττουσι αἴγλης ἀνατολὴν πιστουμένη.	Truly golden and brilliant . . . You the seven-lighted lamp stand (cf. Exodus 25.31) enkindled by the unapproachable Light and filled by the oil of purity, and giving the rising of its gleam to the blind in the darkness of sin.	Presentation I (P Prodigio 118 ftn. 34)
308A	Χαίροις, τὸ ἐκ τοῦ Θεοῦ πιότατον καὶ κατάσκιον ὄρος· ἐν ᾧ ὁ λογικὸς ἀμνὸς ἐκτραφεὶς τὰς ἡμῶν ἁμαρτίας καὶ τὰς νόσους ἐβάστασεν· ἐξ οὗ ὁ ἀχειρότμητος λίθος κυλισθείς, βωμοὺς εἰδωλικοὺς συνέθλασεν, καὶ «εἰς κεφαλὴν γωνίας ἐν ὀφθαλμοῖς ἡμῶν θαυμαστούμενος γέγονεν.»	Hail, O fertile (Ps. 67.15-17 LXX) shady mountain (Hab. 3.3) in whom the rational lamb has been nourished, he who has set aside our sins, from whom the stone not made by hands was quarried (Dan. 2.34), he who has crushed the sacrificial idols and "the head of the cornerstone has become marvelous in our eyes" (Ps. 117.22, 23).	Presentation I (P Prodigio 118 ftn. 43)
308B	ἡ τῇ ἐνδόξῳ καὶ αἰγληφανεῖ σου Προόδῳ ἔλαιον ἡμῖν κομίζουσα, τὸν τοῦ νοητοῦ κατακλυσμοῦ λυτῆρα, τὸν σωτηριώδη ἡμῖν ὅρμον εὐαγγελιζομένη περιστερά·	You are the dove who bears the olive branch to us in your glorious and splendid entry into the Temple announcing a saving refuge from the spiritual deluge (cf. Genesis 8.11).	Presentation I (P Prodigio 119 ftn. 48)

316C	Ἡ δὲ παῖς σκιρτῶσα καὶ ἀγαλλομένη, καθάπερ ἐν θαλάμῳ, ἐν τῷ ναῷ τοῦ Θεοῦ ἐβάδιζε· τριετίζουσα μὲν τῷ χρόνῳ τῆς ἡλικίας, ὑπερτελὴς δὲ τῇ χάριτι τῇ θείᾳ, ὡς ἅτε προεγνωσμένη καὶ προωρισμένη καὶ ἐκλελεγμένη τῷ πάντων Θεῷ καὶ ταμίᾳ.	But the child skipping and rejoicing, as in a bridal chamber, walked in the Temple of God; being three years old in her chronological age, but more than perfect in divine grace, as foreknown and predestined and chosen for the God and governor of all.	Presentation II(P Prodigio 114 ftn. 19)
316C/D —317A	καὶ τότε νεύματι Θεοῦ, καὶ βουλῇ ἱερέων δίδοται περὶ αὐτῆς κλῆρος, καὶ κατακληροῦται Ἰωσὴφ ὁ δίκαιος, καὶ τὴν ἁγίαν ταύτην Παρθένον οἰκονομικῶς ἐκ τοῦ ναοῦ τοῦ Θεοῦ καὶ τῶν αὐτοῦ ἱερέων παραλαμβάνει, πρὸς δελεασμὸν τοῦ ἀρχεκάκου ὄφεως· ἵνα μὴ ὡς παρθένῳ προσβάλῃ τῇ ἀκηράτῳ κόρῃ, ἀλλ' ὡς ἅτε μεμνηστευμένην ταύτην παραδράμῃ. Ὑπῆρχε τοίνυν ἡ πανάχραντος ἐν τῷ οἴκῳ τοῦ τέκτονος Ἰωσήφ, τῷ ἀρχιτέκτονι Θεῷ τηρουμένη, ἕως τὸ πρὸ πάντων αἰώνων ἀπόκρυφον θεῖον μυστήριον ἐν αὐτῇ ἐτελέσθη, καὶ τοῖς βροτοῖς ὁ Θεὸς ἐξ αὐτῆς ὡμοιώθη.	And then by the assent of God and the counsel of the priests a lot is drawn concerning her, and Joseph the just is allotted, and receives this holy Virgin according to the dispensation from the Temple of God and his priests, to ensnare the serpent who originated evil, so that he should not attack the undefiled maiden as a virgin, but as a betrothed woman he should pass her by. So the all-pure one was in the house of Joseph the carpenter being protected, until the divine mystery hidden before all the ages (*cf.* Romans 16.25) was fulfilled in her, and from her God was made like mortals.	Presentation II(P Prodigio 115 ftn. 20
321A	Χαῖρε, κεχαριτωμένη, ὁ θρόνος ὁ ὑψηλὸς καὶ ἐπηρμένος τοῦ τῶν ὅλων ποιητοῦ, καὶ λυτρωτοῦ, καὶ πάντα χειρὶ περιέποντος, ὅσα ἐν οὐρανῷ, καὶ ὅσα ἐπὶ τῆς γῆς.	Hail full of grace, [you are] the lofty high throne of the Maker of all, the redeemer, the administrator of all things in heaven and on earth.	Annunciation (P Prodigio 119 ftn. 45)

321B	Χαῖρε, κεχαριτωμένη, ἡ ζωὴν φέρουσα, καὶ τρέφουσα τὸν τρέφοντα· καὶ γάλα ποτίζουσα, τὸν ἐκ πέτρας μέλι πάλαι πηγάσαντα.	Hail full of grace, [you are] the carrier of life, nourisher of the nourisher, the one who gives milk to him who caused honey to spring from rocks long ago (*cf.* Deuteronomy 32.13).	Annunciation (P Prodigio 112 ftn. 7)
324A	Γνῶθι σαφῶς καὶ πιστώθητι, ὅτι μᾶλλον ἐγὼ ἐν ἐκπλήξει γέγονα θεασάμενος τὸ τοιοῦτόν σου θεογράφιστον κάλλος· καὶ βλέπων σε λοιπὸν, νομίζω δόξαν Κυρίου μου καταμανθάνειν	Know truly and believe that I am more amazed at seeing your God-created beauty. Seeing you I know that I am examining closely the glory of my Lord.	Annunciation (P Prodigio 116 ftn. 23)
325D	Νῦν ἠρξάμην λαλεῖν· Πλήρης εἰμὶ ῥημάτων αἰωνίων· λέξω σοι λοιπὸν, ὅτι ὁ Κύριος μετὰ σοῦ μέλλει τίκτεσθαι, Βασιλεὺς βασιλέων, «καὶ βασιλεύει ἐπὶ τὸν οἶκον Ἰακὼβ, καὶ τῆς βασιλείας αὐτοῦ οὐκ ἔσται τέλος.»	Now I have begun to speak. I am full of eternal words; and for the rest I shall tell you that the Lord who is about to be born of you, is the King of kings, and "will rule over the House of Jacob forever and of his kingdom there shall be no end" (Luke 1.35).	Annunciation (P Prodigio 112 ftn. 3)
328C	Σωτῆρα τέξεις τὸν Κύριον, τὸν ἕνα τῆς ζωαρχικῆς Τριάδος, καὶ χαρὰν τῷ κόσμῳ προξενήσεις ἀνεκλάλητον, ἣν οὐδεὶς οὐδέποτε ἀγγέλων ἢ ἀνθρώπων προεξένησεν· καὶ ἔσται τὸ ὄνομά σου εὐλογημένον.	You shall bear the Lord, the Savior, who is one of the life-beginning Trinity. You shall bring unexpected joy to the world, which neither angels nor men have ever brought; and your name shall be called blessed.	Annunciation (P Prodigio 112 ftn. 4)
329A	Ὑπὸ τὴν σὴν εὐσπλαγχνίαν καταφεύξεται πᾶν γένος ἀνθρώπων, καὶ πᾶσα γλῶσσα πηλίνη μακαρίσει σε· καὶ λαληθήσεται τὸ ὄνομά σου ἐν πάσῃ γενεᾷ,	All the races of men shall take refuge under your compassion. And all tongues of clay shall bless you. And your name shall be spoken	Annunciation (P Prodigio 112 ftn. 5)

	καὶ γενεᾷ, ὅτι διὰ [τοῦ] σοῦ Κύριος, τὸ φῶς τοῦ κόσμου, μέλλει τίκτεσθαι.	from generation to generation (*cf.* Luke 1.50), for through you, the Lord, the light of the world, is about to be born.	
329C	Ψηλαφήσας ὁ Ὕψιστος ὅλον τὸν κόσμον, καὶ μὴ εὑρὼν ὁμοίαν σου μητέρα, πάντως <ὡς οἶδεν> ἐκεῖνος; <καὶ> ὡς ἠθέλησεν, ὡς ηὐδόκησεν, ἐκ σοῦ τῆς ἡγιασμένης ἄνθρωπος διὰ φιλανθρωπίαν γενήσεται.	The Most High searched all the universe, and did not find a mother like you. Certainly, <*as he knew,*> as he wished, as he was pleased, from you, the holy one, he shall become man because of his love for mankind.	Annunciation (P Prodigio 112 ftn. 6)
332A	Ἄσπιλόν σε παρέλαβον ἐξ οἴκου Κυρίου, καὶ παρθένον ἀμόλυντον κατέλιπόν σε ἐν τῷ οἴκῳ μου· καὶ τί τοῦτο ὃ νῦν ὁρῶ, μητέρα παρ᾽ ἐλπίδα καὶ οὐ παρθένον τυγχάνουσαν; εἰπέ μοι, Μαρία· τὸ ἀληθὲς ἐν τάχει λέγε μοι.	Undefiled, I received you from the house of the Lord, and an undefiled virgin I kept you in my house. And what is this which I now see, a mother contrary to expectation and not a virgin? Speak to me, Mary. Quickly, tell me the truth.	Annunciation (P Prodigio 113 ftn. 15)
341A/B	Καὶ, «Παρεμβαλεῖ, φησίν, ἄγγελος Κυρίου κύκλῳ τῶν φοβουμένων αὐτὸν, καὶ ῥύσεται αὐτούς.» Ἀλλὰ τῶν ἐλεεινῶν ἀνθρώπων πλάνῃ καὶ εἰδωλολατρείᾳ τότε διατελούντων, κνίσης τε θυσιῶν τὸν ἀέρα μολυνόντων, ἀφειδίασαν ἐκ τῆς τῶν ἀνθρώπων συνδιαγωγῆς λοιπὸν καὶ οἱ ἄγγελοι· ἀντανεῖλε δὲ παρ᾽ αὐτῶν ὁ Θεὸς καὶ τὸ ἅγιον αὐτοῦ Πνεῦμα. Σοῦ δὲ τεκούσης ἐπ᾽ ἐσχάτων τὸν «ἐν ἀρχῇ» Λόγον τοῦ Θεοῦ καὶ Πατρὸς, παρευθὺ τῆς	And it is said, "The angel of the Lord will encircle those who fear [the Lord] and will protect them." (Psalm 33.8 LXX) But of the wretched men then living in error and idolatry, polluting the air with the smoke of sacrifices, for the rest even the angels ceased from companionship with men; for God took away his holy Spirit from them in return. But when you gave birth in the last times to him who "in the beginning' was the Word of God	Dormition I (P Prodigio 113 ftn. 12)

σῆς κυήσεως, καὶ τῶν ἀγγέλων αἱ στρατιαί, ἀπὸ τῶν οὐρανῶν παρέκυψαν, τὸν ὑπὸ σοῦ γεγεννημένον ἀνυμνοῦντες Θεὸν, καὶ δόξαν ἐν τοῖς ὑψίστοις προστεθῆναι βοήσαντες, εἰρήνην ἐπὶ γῆς ἐκραύγασαν ἐπιφθάσαι· ὡς μηκέτι λοιπὸν ἔχθραν μεσοτοίχου μεταξὺ ἀγγέλων καὶ ἀνθρώπων, οὐρανοῦ τε καὶ γῆς, χρηματίζειν· ἀλλὰ σύμφωνον πολίτευμα, καὶ μίαν ἀντιφωνοῦσαν δοξο-λογίαν παρ᾽ ἀγγέλων καὶ ἀνθρώπων, τῷ ἑνὶ καὶ τριαδικῷ Θεῷ προσαναπέμπεσθαι παρ᾽ ἑκατέρων. Καὶ ὁ Πατὴρ δὲ τοῦ μονογενοῦς Υἱοῦ αὐτοῦ, μαρτυρῶν τῇ ἐκ σοῦ χωρὶς Πατρὸς σωματικῇ κυοφορίᾳ, εἰς αὐτὸν βοᾷ· «Ἐγὼ σήμερον γεγέννηκά σε.» Καὶ πάλιν· «Ἐκ γαστρὸς πρὸ ἑωσφόρου γεγέννηκά σε.» Ὦ ῥήματα θεολογίας μεστά! Εἰ πρὸ γεννηθῆναι παρὰ σοῦ τῆς Παρθένου Μητρὸς, Υἱὸς οὗτος μονογενὴς τοῦ Θεοῦ, πῶς ὁ Πατήρ φησι πρὸς αὐτόν, «Ἐγὼ σήμερον γεγέννηκά σε;» Δῆλον ὅτι τὸ σήμερον, οὐχὶ τὴν τῆς θεότητος τοῦ Μονογενοῦς πρόσφατον παρίστησι ὕπαρξιν, ἀλλὰ τὴν πρὸς ἀνθρώπους σωματικὴν αὐτοῦ βεβαιοῖ παρουσίαν.

the Father (cf. John 1.1), at once upon your delivery even the armies of the angels bent down from the heavens, hymning the God who was born from you, and shouting that glory was attributed in the highest places and they cried out that peace had arrived on earth (cf. Luke 2.14). So no longer did they name enmity as a dividing wall between angels and men, heaven and earth, but a harmonious commonwealth and one antiphonal doxology from both angels and men, sent up to God one and trinity. And the Father of his only-begotten Son, bearing witness to his physical birth from you without a father, proclaims to him, "Today I have begotten you." (Psalm 2.7 LXX) And again, "From the womb before the morning star I have begotten you." (Psalm 109.3 LXX) Oh sayings full of theology! If before being born from you, the Virgin Mother, this one was only-begotten Son of God, how does the Father say to him, "Today I have begotten you"? It is clear that "today" does not represent a new beginning of the divinity of the Only-begotten, but declares his corporeal presence among men.

344C	ἐπειδὴ καὶ οὐρανὸς θεοχώρητος ἀνεδείχθης τοῦ ὑψίστου Θεοῦ, διὰ τὸν χωρητικὸν κόλπον σου πρὸς αὐτοῦ βασταγμοῦ· καὶ γῆ πάλιν αὐτῷ πνευματικὴ, διὰ χωρητικὴν ὑπουργίαν ἐχρημάτισας τῆς σαρκός σου.	For when you were proved to be a God-containing heaven of the most high God, since your bosom [was] able to carry(ing) Him, and again you were called a spiritual earth because of the [God-] containing service of your flesh.	Dormition I (P Prodigio 119 ftn. 44)
361C	Ἐγώ σε παρθένον ἀνέδειξα μητέρα· ἐγώ σε καὶ εὐφραινομένην ἐπὶ Τέκνῳ καταστήσω μητέρα.	I showed/proved you to be a virgin mother; I also will make you a mother rejoicing in her Child.	Dormition III (P Prodigio 113 ftn. 14)
376B	Ζώνης ἐκείνης, ἣ τὸν πανάγιον ἐκεῖνο περιέσφιγγε σῶμα, καὶ τὸν ἐν κοιλίᾳ κρυπτόμενον Θεὸν περιέβαλλε. Ζώνης ἐκείνης, ἥτις τὴν τοῦ Θεοῦ κιβωτὸν ὡραίως κατεκόσμει, καὶ σεμνοτάτως.	That Sash, which wrapped around her body, and surrounded in the womb the hidden God. That Sash, which beautifully adorned the container of God, and most holy.	Sash (P Prodigio 11 ftn. 9)
377A	Αὕτη γὰρ ταῦτα ταῖς ἀγναῖς αὐτῆς χερσὶ κατεσκεύασεν. Αὕτη βρεφοπρεπῶς τὸν μέγαν Κύριον χερσὶ μητρῴαις ἐν τούτοις ἐνείλιπτεν. Αὕτη σὺν τούτοις τοῦτον ἐγκόλπιον φέρουσα, ἐγαλούχει, τὸν πάσῃ φύσει πνοὴν καὶ τροφὴν παρεχόμενον.	For she prepared them with her hands. And she wrapped the great Lord, who was a child in these swaddling clothes. And carrying him on her lap she gave him milk, He who granted breath and substance to every kind of being.	Sash (P Prodigio 11 ftn. 10)
377B	Ἀλλ' ὦ σπάργανα, τὸν ἐλευθερωτὴν Κύριον ἐνειλήσαντα, καὶ τῶν ἡμετέρων παραπτωμάτων σειρὰς διαλύσαντα!	But Oh swaddling clothes, you bound the most free Lord, and you let loose [the] cords of our transgressions![38] (cf. Prov. 5.22)	Sash (P Prodigio 112 ftn. 11)

---

[38] Germanos all but forgets the swaddling clothes. See Cunningham, Wider 251 ftn. 9.

References to the Protection of Mary in Germanos I, Patriarch of Constantinople (715-730)

PG 98 Location	Greek	English	Homily
309A	Τὴν ὡς πύργον σε καὶ θεμέλιον κατέχουσαν τὴν σὴν πόλιν νικητικοῖς ἐπάθλοις καταστέφουσα, ἰσχὺν περιζώσασα φρούρησον·	Crowning with victorious trophies your city which holds you as tower and a foundation, protect [her], girding [her] with strength.	Presentation I
309A	τοὺς σοὺς ὑμνητὰς ἐκ πάσης περιστάσεως καὶ ψυχικῶν ἀλγηδόνων διαφύλαξον· τοῖς αἰχμαλώτοις τε ἀνάρρυσιν βραβεύουσα· ξενιζομένοις ἀστέγοις τε καὶ ἀπεριστάτοις, παραμυθία φάνηθι. Τῷ σύμπαντι κόσμῳ τὴν ἀντιληπτικήν σου χεῖρα ὄρεξον, ἵν' ἐν εὐφροσύνῃ τε καὶ ἀγαλλιάσει τὰς σὰς πανηγύρεις σὺν τῇ νῦν ἡμῖν ἑορταζομένῃ λαμπροτάτῃ τελετῇ διεξάγωμεν.	Preserve those who praise you from all misfortune and distress of soul. Providing rescue for the captives, appear as a succor to those who are strangers, homeless, and friendless. Stretch out your protective hand for all the world, so that in joy and gladness we may celebrate your festival with the rites which we are now most gloriously performing.	Presentation I
317B	καὶ δὸς τοῖς τὴν σὴν ἑορτὴν τελοῦσιν, τὴν σὴν βοήθειαν, καὶ σκέπην, καὶ προστασίαν· ῥυομένη πάντοτε ταῖς σαῖς πρεσβείαις τούτους ἐκ πάσης ἀνάγκης καὶ κινδύνων, νόσων τε δεινῶν, καὶ συμφορῶν παντοίων, καὶ τῆς μελλούσης ἀπειλῆς δικαίας τοῦ Υἱοῦ σου.	and give to those who celebrate your feast your help, your protection, and your assistance, guarding always by your intercessions these people from every necessity and dangers, and dread diseases, and all kinds of misfortunes, and from the coming just threat of your Son.	Presentation II

557

320A	ἡ πάντων προστασία καὶ χαρά,	O protection and joy of all	Presentation II
321B	Χαῖρε, κεχαριτωμένη, θύρα θλιβομένων, καὶ προστασία φοβερά, τῶν εἰλικρινεῖ καρδίᾳ Θεοτόκον ὁμολογούντων σε.	Hail full of grace, gate for the afflicted, formidable guardian of those who with pure hearts confess you to be the Theotokos	Annunciation
321C	Χαῖρε, κεχαριτωμένη, Χριστιανῶν ἁπάντων θαυμαστὸν καὶ εὐσυμπάθητον καταφύγιον, καὶ πάσης μεγαλουργοῦ καλλονῆς ὑψηλότερον θέαμα,	Hail full of grace, marvelous and sympathetic refuge of all Christians, and vision higher than any beauty of great achievements.	Annunciation
340A	Ὁ χρεωστῶν, πάντοτε τὸν ἴδιον εὐεργέτην ἀνυμνεῖ. Ὁ σωζόμενος, οὐκ ἀγνοεῖ τοῦ οἰκείου Σωτῆρος τὴν σκέπην.	The debtor always praises his own benefactor. He who is being saved does not fail to recognize the protection of his own savior.	Dormition I
344D/ 345A	καὶ ἡ πολλή σου περὶ ἡμᾶς σκέπη, τὴν σὴν ἡμῶν χαρακτηρίζει συνομιλίαν. Καὶ τῆς φωνῆς σου πάντες ἀκούομεν· καὶ ἡ φωνὴ τῶν ὅλων πρὸς τὰ σὰ τῆς ἀκροάσεως ὦτα· καὶ γινωσκόμενοι παρὰ σοῦ διὰ τῆς ἀντιλήψεως, ἐπιγινώσκομέν σου προστατικὴν ἀεὶ τὴν ἀντίληψιν	And your great oversight for us characterizes your companionship with us. And we all hear your voice, and the voice of all [comes] to your ears of hearing, and being known by you through your support, we recognize always your protective support.	Dormition I
352C/D 353A	Σὲ τίς μὴ θαυμάσει τὴν ἀμετάθετον σκέπην, τὴν ἀμετάστατον καταφυγήν, τὴν ἀκοίμητον πρεσβείαν, τὴν ἀδιάλειπτον σωτηρίαν, τὴν σταθερὰν βοήθειαν, τὴν ἀσάλευτον προστασίαν, τὸ ἀπόρθητον τεῖχος, τὸν θησαυρὸν τῶν ἀπολαύσεων, τὸν ἀνέγκλητον παράδεισον,	Who will not be amazed at your unchanging protection, your immovable refuge, your unsleeping intercession, your unceasing salvation, your secure assistance, your unshakable advocacy, your impregnable wall, your storehouse of enjoyment, your blameless paradise,	Dormition II

	τὸ ἀσφαλὲς ὀχύρωμα, τὸ κραταιὸν περιχαράκωμα, τὸν ἰσχυρὸν τῆς ἀντιλήψεως πύργον, τὸν λιμένα τῶν χειμαζομένων, τὴν γαλήνην τῶν τεταραγμένων, τὴν τῶν ἁμαρτωλῶν ἐγγυητὴν, τὴν τῶν ἀπεγνωσμένων προσαγωγὴν, τὴν τῶν ἐξορισθέντων ἀνάληψιν, τὴν τῶν ἐκδιωχθέντων ὑποστροφήν, τὴν τῶν ἀλλοτριωθέντων οἰκείωσιν, τὴν τῶν κατακεκριμένων παράθεσιν, τὴν τῶν καθῃρημένων εὐλογίαν, τὴν δρόσον τῆς ψυχικῆς αὐχμηρίας, τὴν σταγόνα τῆς ἐκτακείσης βοτάνης. «Τὰ γὰρ ὀστᾶ ἡμῶν,	your safe stronghold, your mighty entrenchment, your strong tower of protection, your harbor for the storm-tossed, your calm for those in turmoil, your surety for sinners, access for the hopeless, restoration of the banished, return of the exiles, reconciliation of those alienated, reunion of those condemned, blessing of those convicted, dew for the soul's drought, drop of water for the withering plant ("for our bones," as it is written, "through you rise up like a plant" (Isaiah 66.14 LXX)), the mother	
	ὡς γέγραπται, διὰ σοῦ καθάπερ βοτάνην ἀνατελεῖ·» τὴν τοῦ ἀμνοῦ καὶ ποιμένος μητέρα, καὶ πάντων τῶν ἀγαθῶν γνωριζομένην πρόξενον.	of the lamb and the shepherd, and the one recognized as bringer of all good things.	
360D	Τὴν φθορὰν αὐτοῦ παρεᾷς· ἐπεὶ τοὺς ἐν τῷ κόσμῳ τῆς ἀντιλήψεως ὀρφανοὺς οὐκ ἀφήσεις·	Let its corruption go, since you will not leave those in the world orphaned of your protection;	Dormition III
373B	τί ἄν τις εἴποι περὶ τῆς θεοδοξάστου καὶ πανυμνήτου κόρης τῆς παναχράντου καὶ παναμώμου; Εἰ γὰρ αὕτη πόλις ἔμψυχος τοῦ βασιλέως ἐχρημάτισε Χριστοῦ, δικαίως ἄρα καὶ ὁ ταύτης πανάγιος ναός, οὗ καὶ τὰ Ἐγκαίνια σήμερον ἑορτάζομεν, πόλις δεδοξασμένη ἔστι τε καὶ ὀνομάζεται.	then what should one say about the God-glorified, ever-praised, all-pure and blameless maiden? If she bears the title of living city of the king, Christ, then justly also here most-holy temple, of which we celebrate today the festival, is and is called the glorified city.	Sash

373C	Πόλις οὐκ ἐπιγείῳ καὶ θνητῷ βασιλεῖ πολιτογραφοῦσα τοὺς ὑπὸ χεῖρα· ἀλλὰ τῷ ἐπουρανίῳ, τῷ εἰς ζωὴν αἰώνιον παραπέμποντι, καὶ βασιλείαν τὴν ἑαυτοῦ τοῖς αὐτῷ ἑπομένοις παρέχοντι.	A city not enrolling those under her hand in a mortal and earthly kingdom, but in one which is redolent with heavenly and eternal life, and she represents a kingdom in herself to those who are sworn to her.	Sash
381A 381B	Διὰ τοῦτο καὶ ἡ προστασία σου, ὑπὲρ ἔννοιαν. Τοὺς γὰρ ἀπωσμένους, τοὺς ἐκδεδιωγμένους, τοὺς ἐκπεπολεμωμένους, τῷ σῷ τόκῳ	Therefore also your protection is beyond understanding. For you have reconciled and established the estranged, the one who have given	Sash
	κατήλλαξας καὶ ᾠκείωσας· καὶ υἱοὺς καὶ κληρονόμους πεποίηκας. Σὺ τοὺς καθ' ἑκάστην ταῖς ἁμαρτίαις καταποντιζομένους, χεῖρας βοηθείας ἐκτείνουσα, ἐξέλκεις τοῦ κλύδωνος. Σὺ τὰς τοῦ πονηροῦ κατὰ τῶν σῶν δούλων ἐπαναστάσεις, τῇ κλήσει σου μόνῃ τῇ παναγίᾳ ἀποδιώκουσα διασώζεις. Σὺ τοὺς ἐπικαλουμένους σε ἐκ πάσης ἀνάγκης, ἐκ παντοίων πειρασμῶν προφθάνουσα ἐκλυτροῦσαι, πανάμωμε. Ὅθεν καὶ τῷ σῷ ναῷ σπουδαίως προστρέχομεν· καὶ ἐν αὐτῷ ἑστῶτες, ἐν οὐρανῷ ἑστάναι νομίζομεν.	up, those who had become enemies by your birth-giving you have made children and an inheritance. (*cf.* Rm. 8.17) You have extended your hand of aid to those who have been plunged into the sea of every kind of sin, rescuing them from the waves. You continue to protect your servants from the host of evil, you continue to preserve those who flee only to your holy name. You continue to anticipate ransoming those who call upon you in all needs, and all sorts of temptation, Oh all blameless one. For which reason we speedily flee to your temple; and standing in it we know ourselves to be in heaven.	

There is a homily reported to be by Germanos preached on the deliverance of Constantinople. This homily appears to be unknown to the authors mentioned in this dissertation. It's existence was made know to me by Fr. Gambero after the defense of this dissertation. V. Grumel provides manuscript information as well as a French translation. [39] At present there appears to be no English translation.

[39] V. Grumel, Homélie de sainte Germain sur la délivrance de Constantinople. Mélanges Sévérien Salaville. Vol. xvi. Paris: Institut francais d'études byzantines, 1958.

References to Mary's Role in Redemption in Germanos I Patriarch of Constantinople (715-730)

PG 98 Location	Greek	English	Homily
293C	Σήμερον τῷ ἱλαστηρίῳ ἀνατίθεται ἡ μόνη τοῖς τῶν βρότων ἐσφαλλομένοις διεξαχθεῖσιν ἀμπλακημάτων ἐπιρῥοαῖς, ἱλαστήριον καινόν τε καὶ θεοειδέστατον καθαρτικόν τε καὶ ἀχειρότευκτον χρηματίσασα.	Today she who alone is called the new, god-like, purifying and mercy seat, not made by hands, (cf. Hebrews 9.11) for mortals who have drowned in floods of sin is presented to the mercy seat of the temple.	Presentation I (P Corredentrice 142 ftn. 21)
297D/ 300A	Οἱ προπάτορες τῆς ἀρᾶς ἀπολυθησόμενοι καὶ τῆς ἧς ἐξεβλήθητε τρυφῆς, τὴν οἴκησιν πάλιν ἀποκληρούμενοι· ἆρ' οὐχ τὴν αἰτίαν ὑμνήσετε τῆς σωτηρίας, ἀραρότοις ἐγκωμίοις καὶ μεγίσταις αἰνέσεσιν; ἢ καὶ μάλιστα ὑμῖν ἐστι κεκραγέναι καὶ με σὺν ὑμῖν καὶ πᾶσαν μετ' ἀμφοτέροις τὴν κτίσιν ἀγαλλιᾶσθαι.	Our ancestors who are about to be released from the curse and again inheriting the residence in paradise from which you were cast out: should you not hymn the cause of your salvation, with a fitting encomium and great praises? Indeed you especially ought to shout out, and I with you and with us both all creation [ought] to sing out in joy.	Presentation I (P Corredentrice 141 ftn. 11)
301D	ἡ τὰ τοῦ θανάτου πρόθυρα συνθλῶσα.	you who destroy the doors of death.	Presentation I (P Corredentrice 141 ftn. 12)

304D	Χαίροις τοιγαροῦν τῇ τῆς Ἐδὲμ ἡμῖν θανατηφόρῳ καὶ ψυχοπύρῳ βρώσει γυμνωθεῖσιν, εὐκλεεῖ καὶ ἀχειροτεύκτῳ ἐνδύματι ἐν τῇ σῇ πρὸς τὰ τῶν ἁγίων Ἅγια εἰσδύσει σήμερον ἁλουργοειδῆ στολὴν ἤτοι θεοπερίβλητον ἄφεσιν ἐπαμφιάσασα, ἡ ἄφεσις τῶν παραπτωμάτων τοῖς βορβορώδεσιν ἡμῖν ἐκ Θεοῦ δοθεῖσα, Θεόνυμφε.	Therefore hail, forgiveness of transgressions given by God for us filthy ones, who are denuded by the death-dealing and soul-destroying food of Eden, as you put on the sea-purple robe which represents God-given forgiveness today for your entrance to the holy of holies in your glorious garment not made by hands (*cf.* Genesis 3.17), O bride of God.	Presentation I (P 141 ftn. 17)
305A	Χαίροις, ἡ τῇ τῶν βημάτων σου ρυθμίσει καταπατήσασα τὸν δεινόν μοι ποδηγὸν, κεχρηματικότα πρὸς τὴν παράβασιν σκολιογνώμονα καὶ μισόκαλον ὄφιν διάβολον·	Hail to you who by the rhythm of your footsteps trample down my terrible leader—that serpent with his crooked-minded, good-hating diabolical nature—who has counseled me toward transgression (*cf.* Genesis 3.1-13).	Presentation I (P Corredentrice 142 ftn. 18)
305B	Χαίροις, ἡ νοητικὴν θείαν δρόσον ἡμῖν ἐπιστάζουσα φωτεινὴ νεφέλη, ἡ τῇ τῶν Ἁγίων ἁγίᾳ σήμερον ὑπεισδύσει τοῖς ἐν σκιᾷ θανάτου κατεχομένοις παμφαίνοντα ἥλιον ἐξανατείλασα·	Hail, bright cloud (*cf.* Exodus 19.16) who continues to drop divine spiritual dew upon us (*cf.* Exodus 16.13), you who today by your holy entrance into the Holy of Holies have made to shine the all-brilliant Sun upon those who remain in the shadow of death.	Presentation I (P Corredentrice 142 ftn. 19)
321A	Not found		Annunciation (P Corredentrice 141 ftn. 15)
321B	Χαῖρε, κεχαριτωμένη, ψυχῆς ἀγαλλίαμα, καὶ ὅλου τοῦ κόσμου παγκόσμιον σέβασμα, καὶ ἁμαρτωλῶν ἁπάντων ἡ ὄντως ἀγαθὴ μεσιτεία	Hail full of grace, exceeding great joy of the soul, and object of worship for the whole cosmos, and truly good mediator for all sinners.	Annunciation (P Corredentrice 141 ftn. 13)

324B	Δέδοικα καὶ τρέμω σου τοὺς τοιούτους λόγους· καὶ ὑπολαμβάνω, ὡς ἄλλην Εὔαν πλανῆσαί με παραγέγονας	I am afraid and I tremble at your words. I suspect that you have come to deceive me like another Eve.	Annunciation (P Corredentrice 139 ftn. 6, 140 ftn. 9)
325A	Ἵνα τί, καὶ διὰ τί, καὶ τίνος ἕνεκεν τὸν ἐμὸν εὐαγγελισμὸν ἐπὶ τοσοῦτον ἠπίστησας, δεδοξασμένη; καὶ μέχρι τίνος οὐ πειθαρχεῖς εἰς τὸν ἐξ οὐρανοῦ σοι πεμφθέντα ἄγγελον; Οὐκ εἰμὶ γὰρ ἐγὼ ὁ τὴν Εὔαν πλανήσας.	Why? For what purpose, for what reason, have you distrusted my good news, Glorified one? How long will you disobey the angel that was sent to you from heaven? I am not Eve's deceiver—far from it.	Annunciation (P Corredentrice 139 ftn. 7)
328C	Σωτῆρα τέξεις τὸν Κύριον, τὸν ἕνα τῆς ζωαρχικῆς Τριάδος, καὶ χαρὰν τῷ κόσμῳ προξενήσεις ἀνεκλάλητον, ἣν οὐδεὶς οὐδέποτε ἀγγέλων ἢ ἀνθρώπων προεξένησεν· καὶ ἔσται τὸ ὄνομά σου εὐλογημένον.	You shall bear the Lord, the Savior, who is one of the life-beginning Trinity. You shall bring unexpected joy to the world, which neither angels nor men have ever brought; and your name shall be called blessed.	Annunciation (P Corredentrice 141 ftn. 14)
329C/D	Χριστιανῶν ἁπάντων γενήσῃ κοινὸν ἱλαστήριον· καὶ διὰ τοῦτο πάλιν,	You shall become the common propitiation of all Christians.	Annunciation (P Corredentrice 141 ftn. 16)
336B	Νῦν λέξω Μαρία, ὅτι τοῖς ἴχνεσιν Εὔας σῆς μητρὸς ἐξηκολούθησας. Ἀλλ' ἐκείνη μὲν τοῦ παραδείσου ἀπῳκίσθη, καθότι τὴν ἀκοὴν ἐφήπλωσε τῷ ταύτῃ ψυθιρίσαντι· σὺ δὲ τοῦ οἴκου μου ἐκβληθήσῃ ὡς ὑπεύθυνος.	Now I will say,[40] Mary, that you have followed the path of your mother Eve. She was cast out of paradise because she listened to the whisperer, and you shall be cast out of my house as a guilty woman.	Annunciation (P Corredentrice 140 ftn. 8)

---

[40] Perhaps, I see

348B (349C)	οὐδεὶς ὁ ἐλεούμενος δῶρον, εἰ μὴ διὰ σοῦ, Θεοχώρητε. Τίς γὰρ τῶν ἁμαρτωλῶν ἐπὶ τοσοῦτον ὑπερμαχεῖ; Τίς τῶν ἀδιορθώτων κατὰ τοσοῦτον [ἀντιφωνητικῶς] ὑπεραπολογεῖται;	No one receives the gift of mercy, if not through you, Theochoretos. For who among sinners can prevail to such an extent? Who among those not made upright can speak so strongly in his defense?	Dormition I/II (P Corredentrice 142 ftn. 22)
349A	See the references to development of theme of Mary and Eve		Dormition II (P Corredentrice 140 ftn. 10)
353B	Ἔχεις ἐκ Θεοῦ τὸ μέγα πρὸς θρίαμβον ὕψος· διότι λαὸν αὐτῷ Χριστιανικὸν ἀπὸ σαρκὸς τῆς σῆς συνεστήσω, καὶ τὸ ὁμοιογενές σου, σύμμορφον τῆς θείας αὐτοῦ καὶ ὁμοιωτικῆς εἰκόνος ἀπειργάσω.	For you have from God the great sublime triumph; for which reason you have established a Christian people for him from your flesh, and related by birth to you, you have made conformable to his divinity and to his image which makes us like [him].	Dormition II (P Corredentrice 142 ftn. 20)
There appear to be no other direct references to Mary's role in our redemption in Dormition III nor the Sash. However, one can profitably compare the references to the parallel events, the intercessions and the protection.			

References to the Resurrection & Harrowing of Hell in Germanos I Patriarch of Constantinople (715-730)

PG 98 Location	Greek	English	Homily
301D	Ἰδού σε στήριγμα βλέπω γενησομένην τῶν καταβεβηκότων πρὸς θάνατον.	Behold, I see you as one who will become a support for those who have descended to death.	Presentation I
364C/D	Δημοσιεύει τὴν μετάστασιν, δηλοποιεῖ τὰ παρ' ἀγγέλου πρὸς αὐτὴν δηλωθέντα· δεικνύει καὶ τὸ δοθὲν αὐτῇ βραβεῖον. Ἦν δὲ τὸ βραβεῖον, φοίνικος κλάδος, σύμβολον νίκης κατὰ θανάτου, καὶ ζωῆς ἀμαράντου προεκτύπωμα· τοῦ πιστωθῆναι μετερχομένην, ὅτι καταδυναστεύσειεν τῆς φθορᾶς, ὡς καὶ ὁ ὑπ' αὐτῆς γεννηθεὶς ἐνίκησεν τὸν ᾅδην, Χριστός. Τοιοῦτον τὸ βραβεῖον τοῦ φοίνικος, ἐν ᾧ καὶ οἱ θεοφιλεῖς τῶν Ἑβραίων παῖδες ἐπὶ τὸ πάθος ἐγ) γίζοντι τῷ Χριστῷ, ὡς νικητῇ τούτῳ μέλλοντι γίνεσθαι τοῦ θανάτου, δοξολογητικῶς	She makes public announcement of her translation, she reveals what has been revealed to her by the angel; she shows the prize which was given to her. The prize was a branch, a symbol of victory over death, and a pre-figuration of unwithering life, to confirm that she is going over, that she may prevail over corruption, as also the Christ who received birth from her conquered Hades. Such a prize/branch of a palm-tree, in/ with which also the god-loving children of the Hebrews,	Dormition III

Gregory E. Roth

ἐπέσεισαν, κράζοντες· «Ὡσαννὰ ἐν τοῖς ὑψίστοις·» τουτέστι, Σῶσον δὴ, ὁ ἐν ὑψίστοις. Τὸ γὰρ Ὡσαννὰ παρ' Ἑβραίοις σῶσον δὴ μεθερμηνεύεται. Ὥσπερ οὖν ἐκεῖ τὰ βαΐα τῶν φοινίκων νικητικὸν τὸν τοῦ Χριστοῦ προεμήνυον συμβολικῇ τῇ ὑποδείξει θάνατον, οὕτως καὶ τὸ ἐκ φοίνικος δοθὲν τῇ Θεοτόκῳ βραβεῖον, πληροφόρημα νίκης ὑπῆρχεν θανατοποιοῦ καταφθορᾶς.	when Christ was approaching his passion, as to this one about to become a victor over death, shook with songs of praise, crying out, "Hosanna in the highest;" that is, "Save indeed, [you who are] in the highest." For "Hosanna" among the Hebrews is interpreted as "Save indeed." So as there the branches of the palm-trees foretold the victorious death of Christ with a symbolic demonstration, so also the prize from a palm-tree given to the Theotokos was a fulfillment of victory over death-dealing corruption.	

568

References to Spiritual Life of Germanos I
Patriarch of Constantinople
(715-730)

PG 98 Location	Greek	English	Homily
293A	Τοιγαροῦν σπουδαίως συναπέλθωμεν ἀλλήλους τῇ κοινωφελεῖ σωτηριώδει πανηγύρει τῆς Θεομήτορος προτρεπόμενοι,	So let us eagerly approach together this mutually beneficial, salvific feast of the Mother of God.	Presentation I
296B/C	τρισὶ δὲ περικυκλουμένη ἐνιαυτῶν περιόδῳ τῷ δεκατοῦσθαι Ἰησοῦς ὁ ἐμὸς Κύριος, τοῦ τῆς παραβάσεώς με μολυσμοῦ ἀποκαθαίρει· ἴσως τε ἄλλοις περιοδεύων χρόνοις πᾶσαν νόσον καὶ πᾶσαν μαλακίαν θεραπεύει·	And my Lord Jesus' ministry was for a period of three encircling years, cleansing me from the stain of my transgression and at another time healing every disease and weakness.	Presentation I
301D	Εἴσβλεψον ἐπὶ τὸ καταπέτασμα, ἡ τοὺς τῇ ἀμβλυοποιῷ γεύσει τετυφλωμένους τῇ σῇ ἀστραπῇ φωτίζουσα. Δίδου μοι χεῖράς σε ποδηγοῦντι ὡς βρέφος, καὶ κράτει μου χεῖρα τῷ γήρᾳ κεκμηκότι καὶ τῇ τῆς ἐντολῆς παρεκδύσει γεήφρονι ζήλῳ νενευκότι, καὶ ἄγοις με πρὸς ζωήν. Ἰδοὺ γάρ σε κατέχω βακτηρίαν τοῦ γήρους καὶ τῆς ἀσθενησάσης τῷ ὀλισθήματι φύσεως ἀνόρθωσιν.	Gaze upon the veil (cf. Exodus 26.31ff.), you who enlighten through your lightning flash those who are blinded by their dull-sighted tastes. Give to me your hands as I lead you like a babe and hold my hand exhausted by old age and weakened by earthly-minded zeal in transgressing the commandment, and lead me to life. For behold I keep you as a staff in old age and a prop for the weariness that comes naturally with old age.	Presentation I

Although the words of 301D are placed in the mouth of Zacharias it might well serve to be a parallel to Germnos and a prayer of his to the Theotokos.			
305A	Χαίροις, ἡ τῇ τῶν βημάτων σου ῥυθμίσει καταπατήσασα τὸν δεινόν μοι ποδηγὸν, κεχρηματικότα πρὸς τὴν παράβασιν σκολιογνώμονα καὶ μισόκαλον ὄφιν διάβολον·	Hail to you who by the rhythm of your footsteps trample down my terrible leader—that serpent with his crooked-minded, good-hating diabolical nature—who has counseled me toward transgression (*cf.* Genesis 3.1-13).	Presentation I
317C— 320B	Ἀλλ', ὦ μοι, Δέσποινα, μόνη τὸ ἐμὸν ἐκ Θεοῦ ψυχαγώγημα, τοῦ ἐν ἐμοὶ καύσωνος ἡ θεία δρόσος, τῆς ξηρανθείσης μου καρδίας ἡ θεόρρυτος ῥανίς, τῆς ζοφερᾶς μου ψυχῆς ἡ τηλαυγεστάτη λαμπὰς, τῆς ἐμῆς πορείας ἡ ποδηγία, (317D) τῆς ἀσθενείας μου ἡ δύναμις, τῆς γυμνώσεως ἡ ἀμφίασις, τῆς πτωχείας ὁ πλοῦτος, τὸ τῶν ἀνιάτων τραυμάτων τὸ ἴαμα, ἡ τῶν δακρύων ἀναίρεσις, τῶν στεναγμῶν ἡ κατάπαυσις, τῶν συμφορῶν ἡ μεταποίησις, τῶν ὀδυνῶν ὁ κουφισμὸς, τῶν δεσμῶν ἡ λύσις, τῆς σωτηρίας μου ἡ ἐλπὶς, εἰσάκουσόν μου τῶν προσευχῶν· οἴκτειρόν μου τοὺς στεναγμοὺς, καὶ πρόσδεξαί μου τοὺς ὀδυρμούς. Ἐλέησόν με ἐπικαμφθεῖσα τοῖς δάκρυσι τοῖς ἐμοῖς, (320A) σπλαγχνίσθητι ἐπ᾽	But Oh me, Mistress, my only soul-leader from God, the divine dew of the burning in me, the moisture flowing from God for my parched heart, the bright-shining lamp of my darkened soul, the guide for my journey, (317D) the power for my weakness, the clothing of my nakedness, the wealth of my poverty, the healing of my incurable wounds, the removal of tears, the cessation of groaning, the reversal of misfortunes, the lightening of pains, the release of fetters, the hope of my salvation, hear my prayers: have pity on my groaning, and accept my lamentations. Have mercy on me, bending down to my tears. (320A) Have compassion on me, as mother of the God who loves mankind. Look down and assent to my supplication, fill up my	Presentation I

ἐμοὶ ὡς μήτηρ τοῦ φιλανθρώπου Θεοῦ. Ἐπίβλεψον καὶ κατάνευσον πρὸς τὴν ἐμὴν ἱκεσίαν, ἐκπλήρωσόν μου τὸ ἐκδιψώμενον καταθύμιον, καὶ σύναψόν με τῇ ἐμῇ συγγόνῳ καὶ συνδούλῃ ἐν τῇ γῇ τῶν πραέων, ἐν σκηναῖς τῶν δικαίων, καὶ χορῷ τῶν ἁγίων· καὶ ἀξίωσόν με, ἡ πάντων προστασία καὶ χαρά, καὶ φαιδρὰ θυμηδία, συνευ¬φραν-θῆναι ταύτῃ, δέομαί σου, ἐν τῇ χαρᾷ ἐκείνῃ τῇ ὄντως ἀνεκφράστῳ τοῦ ἐκ σοῦ γεννηθέντος Θεοῦ καὶ Βασιλέως, καὶ τῷ νυμφῶνι αὐτοῦ τῷ ἀφθάρτῳ, καὶ τρυφῇ τῇ ἀλήκτῳ καὶ ἀκορέστῳ, καὶ ἐν τῇ ἀνεσπέρῳ καὶ ἀπεράντῳ βασιλείᾳ. Ναί, Δέσποινα· ναί, τὸ ἐμὸν καταφύγιον, ἡ ζωὴ καὶ ἡ ἀντίληψις, τὸ ὅπλον καὶ τὸ καύχημα, ἡ ἐλπίς μου καὶ τὸ σθένος μου. Δός μοι σὺν αὐτῇ ἀπολαῦσαι τῶν τοῦ Υἱοῦ σου ἀνεκδιηγήτων καὶ (320B) ἀκαταλήπτων δωρεῶν ἐν τῇ ἐπουρανίῳ διαμονῇ. Ἔχεις γὰρ, οἶδα, σύνδρομον τῇ θελήσει τὸ δύνασθαι,	thirsty desire, and join me to my relative and fellow servant[41] in the land of the meek, in the tents of the just (cf. Psalm 118.15), in the choir of the saints (cf. Psalm 116.9); and make me worthy, I beg you, O protection and joy of all and brilliant gladness of heart, to rejoice along with her, in your truly ineffable joy, [because] of the God and King who was born from you, and in his imperishable bridal-chamber, and in the unceasing and insatiable delight, and in the kingdom which has no evening and no limit. Yes, Mistress; yes, my refuge, my life and my support, my armor and my boast, my hope and my strength. Grant me with her to enjoy the inexpressible and unceasing gifts in the heavenly mansion. (320A) For as the mother of the Most High you have, I know, the power which runs along with the will; and because of this I am bold. Therefore may I not be deprived, all-undefiled Lady, of my expectation (cf.	

41 We do not know who this relative of Germanos was, but it must have been a woman who followed a life of service to God. Georges Gharib and Luigi Gambero. Testi Mariani Del Primo Millennio. Roma: Città Nuova Editrice, 1989. 336 nt. 8. While we do not know the name of Germanos' relative this passage is redolent of the final prayers in the Orthodox funeral and memorial service and should be read as one who is familiar with them as Germanos' auditors would have been.

ὡς τοῦ Ὑψίστου μήτηρ· καὶ διὰ τοῦτο τολμῶ. Μὴ οὖν ἀποστερηθείην, πανάχραντε Κυρία, τῆς ἐμῆς προσδοκίας· ἀλλὰ τύχοιμι ταύτης, Θεόνυμφε, ἡ τὴν τῶν ὅλων προσδοκίαν ὑπὲρ λόγον τεκοῦσα, τὸν Κύριον ἡμῶν Ἰησοῦν Χριστὸν, τὸν ἀληθινὸν Θεὸν καὶ Δεσπότην· ᾧ πρέπει πᾶσα δόξα, τιμὴ, καὶ προσκύ-νησις, σὺν τῷ ἀνάρχῳ Πατρὶ, καὶ τῷ ζωοποιῷ Πνεύματι, νῦν καὶ ἀεὶ, καὶ εἰς τοὺς αἰῶνας τῶν αἰώνων. Ἀμήν	Galatians 6.4); but may I obtain this, Bride of God, you who gave birth beyond words to the expectation of all, our Lord Jesus Christ, the true God and Master: to whom is due all glory, honor, and veneration, with the Father who has no beginning, and the life-giving Spirit, now and ever, and to the ages of ages. Amen. (320B)

References to the Sterility in Germanos I, Patriarch of Constantinople (715-730)

PG 98 Location	Greek	English	Homily
293A	καὶ τοῖς ἀδύτοις προκύψαντες εἰσβλέψωμεν παῖδα τὴν πρὸς τὸ δεύτερον καταπέτασμα χωροῦσαν, Μαρίαν τὴν πάναγνον καὶ Θεομήτορα, τὴν ἀκαρπίας στείρωσιν διαλύσασαν, καὶ νομικοῦ γράμματος σκιὰν τῇ τοῦ τόκου χάριτι διελάσασαν.	let us watch the child going toward the second veil, Mary the all-holy Mother of God who put an end to unfruitful sterility, and exchanged the mere shadow of the letter of the law (*cf.* Hebrews 10.1*ff*) through the grace of her birth-giving	Presentation I
293B	Σήμερον Ἰωακεὶμ τὸ τῆς ἀπαιδίας ὄνειδος ἀποσμηξάμενος, ἀναφανδὸν ταῖς λεωφόροις μεγαλαυχικώτατα δείξων πρόεισιν οἰκείαν γονήν, καὶ πάλιν μυσταγωγὸς τῆς κατὰ νόμον ἁγιαστείας δείκνυται.	Today Joachim, who has wiped away the reproach of childlessness, goes openly down the main road boastfully showing off his offspring, and again is shown as a functionary of hallowing according to the Law.	Presentation I
293B	Σήμερον καὶ Ἄννα τὸν τῆς ἀτεκνίας ἐνδελεχισμόν, εὐτεκνίᾳ ἀμείψασα, ἀπλέτῳ χαρμονῇ ἔνθους γινομένη τοῖς πέρασι καρπὸν διακηρυκεύεται κεκτῆσθαι, στέρνοις ἐναγκαλισαμένη τὴν τῶν οὐρανῶν πλατυτέραν.	Today also Anna has exchanged the persistence of barrenness for fruitfulness, and becoming inspired by joy, proclaims to the ends of the earth that she has borne a child, embracing to her bosom the one who is wider than the heavens.	Presentation I

297A	Καὶ προέφθασεν ἡ στεῖρα τε καὶ ἄκαρπος Ἄννα χεῖρα αὐτῆς τῷ Θεῷ διδοῦσα καὶ μεγαλοφωνότατα διαρρήδην βοῶσα· Δεῦτέ μοι, φησὶν, συγχαίρετε, αἵτινές τε καὶ ὅσοι τῇ γεννήσει συνειλεγμένοι, μειζόνως, ἄρτι τὴν ἐξ ἐμῶν σπλάγχνων ἀνατιθεμένῃ Κυρίῳ δῶρον θεοκαλλώπιστον ἡγιασμένον.	And the barren and unfruitful Anna with foresight lifts her hands to God and says in a loud distinct voice, "Come with me, let us rejoice together, all women and men who rejoiced at her birth, even more now, as I dedicate to the Lord this divinely beautiful and holy gift recently received from my own womb.	Presentation I
300C	λάβε τὴν τὸ ὄνειδος ἡμῶν τῆς ἀτοκίας καὶ τὴν στείρωσιν ἐκμειώσασαν·	Accept her who has destroyed the reproach of our barrenness and sterility.	Presentation I
300D	δέχου· δι' αὐτῆς καὶ νόμου ἀπαιδίαν κατακρίνων, ἐλυτρώσω ἡμᾶς ἐνδελεχισμοῦ δεινοτάτου δι' αὐτῆς·	Accept her whom you assigned to destroy our barenness, overcoming through her the barrenness of the Law	Presentation I
308B	Χαίροις, ἡ τῇ σῇ γεννήσει στειρώσεως δεσμὰ λύσασα, καὶ ὀνειδισμὸν ἀτεκνίας λικμήσασα, καὶ νομικὴν κατάραν βυθίσασα,	Hail, you who through your birth released the fetters of sterility, who scattered the reproach of childlessness, and sank the curse of the Law (*cf.* Galatians 3.13)	Presentation I
313A	Εἶτα συνήφθην μὲν ἀνδρὶ, νόμῳ τῷ τοῦ Δεσπότου· εὑρέθην δὲ στεῖρα καὶ ἄγονος ἐφ' ἱκανὸν χρόνον.	Then I was joined to a husband, according to the law of the Lord; but I was found barren and childless for a considerable time.	Presentation II
313B	ἵνα τί ἔθου με παραβολὴν ἐν τῷ γένει μου, καὶ κίνησιν κεφαλῆς ἐν τῇ φυλῇ μου; Ἵνα τί τῆς κατάρας τῶν σῶν προφητῶν μέτοχόν με ἀνέδειξας, δούς μοι μήτραν ἀτεκνοῦσαν, καὶ μασθοὺς ξηρούς; Ἵνα τί μου τὰ δῶρα	Why have you made me an example in my family, and a shaking of the head in my tribe? Why have you declared me a participant in the curse of your prophets, giving me a childless womb and dry breasts (*cf.* Hosea 9.14)? Why	Presentation II

	ἀπρόσδεκτα ὡς ἀτέκνου ἐποίησας; Ἵνα τί μυκτηρισμόν με τοῖς γνωστοῖς, καὶ χλευασμὸν τοῖς ὑπὸ χεῖρα, καὶ τοῖς γείτοσιν ὄνειδος γενέσθαι κατέλιπες; Ἐπίβλεψον, Κύριε· εἰσάκουσον, Δέσποτα· σπλαγχνίσθητι, Ἅγιε. Ὁμοίωσόν με τοῖς πετεινοῖς τοῦ οὐρανοῦ, τοῖς θηρίοις τῆς γῆς, τοῖς τῆς θαλάσσης ἰχθύσιν· ὅτι καὶ αὐτὰ γόνιμά εἰσιν ἐνώπιόν σου, Κύριε. Μὴ χείρων φανείη τῶν ἀλόγων, Ὕψιστε, ἡ κατὰ σὴν ὁμοίωσιν καὶ εἰκόνα ὑπὸ σοῦ γεγονυῖα.	have you made my gifts unacceptable as of a childless [woman]? Why have you left me to become a cause of muttering for my acquaintances, and a mockery for those at hand, and a reproach for my neighbors? Look at [me], Lord; hear [me], Master; have compassion [on me], Holy One. Make me like the birds of heaven, the beasts of the earth, the fish of the sea: because they also are productive before you, Lord. May I not appear worse than the irrational animals, O Most High, I who have been made by you in your likeness and image (*cf.* Genesis 1.26).'	

The following references to Elizabeth in the Annunciation Homily only refer to the sterility that comes of being beyond the age of childbearing. I have included them because they represent a convincing argument on the part of the angel and the of Mary for her virginity even while giving birth to a child.

324C	Ζαχαρίας ὁ προφήτης, καὶ προσφιλὴς τῆς συγγενίδος σου Ἐλισάβετ, ἐξ ἀπιστίας πληροφορήσει σε. Πρὸς ἐκείνην οὖν πορεύθητι, ἵνα μάθης ἐξ ἐκείνου <ἐκείνης> τὰ ἐκείνῳ συμβησόμενα.	Zacharias the prophet and the beloved of your cousin Elizabeth, will convince your unbelief. Go to her so that you may learn from him[42] the things that will happen to him.	Annunciation

---

[42] Perhaps, her

325C	Λέξω σοι τρανῶς, ὅτι καὶ Ἐλισάβετ ἡ συγγενής σου, κατὰ τὸν καιρὸν τοῦτον, υἱὸν ἐν γήρει τέξεται· καὶ πολλοὶ ἐπὶ τῇ γεννήσει αὐτοῦ χαρήσονται καὶ θαυμάσονται· κληθήσεται γὰρ <καὶ κλθήσεται> τὸ ὄνομα αὐτοῦ Ἰωάννης.	I shall tell you clearly, that Elizabeth your cousin at this very moment is about to give birth in her old age to a son, and at his birth many shall rejoice and be amazed, for his name will be called John (cf. Luke 1.19).	Annunciation
333B	Ἠκούσθη σοι ὅτι καὶ Ἐλισάβετ, ἡ τοῦ Ζαχαρίου, καὶ συγγενίς μου, κατὰ τὸν καιρὸν τοῦτον, προφήτην καὶ Πρόδρομον παρ᾽ ἐλπίδα συνέλαβεν. Εἰ μὴ γὰρ <γὰρ μὴ> προφήτης ἐτύγχανεν, οὐκ ἂν διὰ τῶν σκιρτημάτων προσεκύνει τὸν ἐν ἐμοὶ κρυπτόμενον Κύριον.	You have heard that my kinswoman, Elizabeth the wife of Zacharias, has even now conceived beyond hope a Prophet and Forerunner. For if he were not a prophet he would not have leapt to worship the Lord hidden inside of me (cf. Luke 1.40).	Annunciation
No references to sterility or childlessness are to be found in Dorm I, Dorm II, Dorm III or the Sash			

References to Mary as Temple/Throne/ Altar in Germanos I Patriarch of Constantinople (715-730)

PG 98 Location	Greek	English	Homily
293A	ἡ ναὸς ἀκηλίδωτος καὶ ὑπέρτατος μόνη χρηματίσασα τοῦ ἀρχιερέως καὶ τῶν ἁπάντων τελετάρχου Κυρίου	she who alone is called the stainless and greatest temple of the high priest and the Lord of all	Presentation I
293C	Σήμερον ἡ τοῦ θείου ναοῦ πύλη διαπετασθεῖσα, τὴν ἀνατολόβλεπτον καὶ ἐσφραγισμένην τοῦ Ἐμμανουὴλ πύλην εἰσιοῦσαν δέχεται. Σήμερον ἡ ἱερὰ τοῦ ναοῦ τράπεζα λαμπρύνεσθαι ἄρχεται, πρὸς ἀναιμάκτους θυσίας τὴν μεταβίβασιν μετηλλαχυῖα τῇ τῆς οὐρανίου καὶ ψυχοτρόφου ἄρτου τραπέζης θείας προσκυνήσεως μεθέξει καὶ γλυκυτάτῳ ἀσπασμῷ. Σήμερον τῷ ἱλαστηρίῳ ἀνατίθεται ἡ μόνη τοῖς τῶν βρότων ἐσφαλλομένοις διεξαχθεῖσιν ἀμπλακημάτων ἐπιρροαῖς, ἱλαστήριον καινόν τε καὶ θεοειδέστατον καθαρτικόν τε καὶ ἀχειρότευκτον χρηματίσασα.	Today the gate of God's temple is opened to receive the entry of the eastward looking, sealed gate of Emmanuel (cf. Ezekiel 44.1-3). Today the sacred Table of the temple joyfully meets and participates in the true divine table of the heavenly soul-feeding bread and by changing to the worship of the bloodless sacrifice begins to shine. Today she who alone is called the new, god-like, purifying and mercy seat, not made by hands, (cf. Hebrews 9.11) for mortals who have drowned in floods of sin is presented to the mercy seat of the temple.	Presentation I

300A	σὺν τῷ γλυκυτάτῳ ὁμοζύγῳ τὴν ἐξ αὐτῶν ὠδινηθεῖσαν προπέμποντες λαμπαδηφορουσῶν τῶν παρθένων, τὸν ναὸν καταλαμβάνουσι, καὶ διαπετάννυνται πύλαι δεχόμεναι τὴν νοητὴν πύλην τοῦ Ἐμμανουὴλ Θεοῦ,	With the lamp-bearing virgins they reach the temple, whose gates open to receive the mystical gate of God Emmanuel, and the threshold of the temple is blessed by Mary's footsteps.	Presentation I
301B	Ὑμεῖς τὰ τῆς νέας διαθήκης νοητοῦ ναοῦ ἐκλαμπρότατα κέρατα ἐγνωρίσθητε, ἐν τοῖς σφῶν στέρνοις κατίσχοντες τὸ τοῦ ἱεροῦ σφαγίου ἡγιασμένον καὶ θεεγκαίνιστον λογικώτατον θυσιαστήριον. Ὑμεῖς, εἰ μὴ μικρόν τι προφθάντα εἰπεῖν, καὶ Χερουβὶμ ἐγνωρίσθητε τὸ ἱλαστήριον περιθέοντες τῇ τιθηνήσει τοῦ κοσμαγωγοῦ Ἱερέως μυστικώτατα. Ὑμεῖς ὡράθητε ὑπὲρ τὸν πάλαι χαλκευθέντα χρυσὸν πρὸς τὸ τῆς κιβωτοῦ κάλυμμα τὴν τῆς νέας διαθήκης, τοῦ ἐν σταυρῷ ἡμῖν ἄφεσιν ὑπογράψαντος νοητήν τε καὶ θείαν κιβωτὸν	You (Joachim and Anna) have been made known as the shining horns of the new righteous, spiritual temple, holding in your breasts the holy, God-acknowledged, rational altar of the sacred victim. You, if it is not too early to say, have been made known as Cherubim flying around the mercy-seat (cf. Exodus 25.18ff.) with the nourishment of the Priest who supports the universe. You appeared to cover the mystical and holy Ark of the new covenant of Him who on the Cross wrote the forgiveness of our sin, [forming] a covering which far surpasses the one which long ago was wrought of gold to cover the Ark (cf. Exodus 25.10).	Presentation I
301C	Δεῦρο, προπύλαια τοῦ ἁγιαστηρίου ἁγίασον μᾶλλον· οὐ γὰρ σύ, ὡς ἔπος ἔτι φάναι, ταὐτῷ καθαιρομένη ἁγιάζῃ, ἀλλ' ἢ καὶ λίαν ἁγιάζεις.	Come hallow rather the gateway of the holy place, for you, so to speak, are not purified and hallowed by this [gate]: but instead you hallow it more	Presentation I

301D	Δεῦρο, πρόκυψον εἰς ἄδυτον καὶ φρικῶδες ταμιεῖον, ἡ κειμήλιον ἄπλετον καὶ ἀνεξερεύνητον γενησομένη. Εἴσελθε τοῖς τοῦ βήματος προθύροις, ἡ τὰ τοῦ θανάτου πρόθυρα συνθλῶσα. Εἴσβλεψον ἐπὶ τὸ καταπέτασμα, ἡ τοὺς τῇ ἀμβλυοποιῷ γεύσει τετυφλωμένους τῇ σῇ ἀστραπῇ φωτίζουσα.	Come gaze upon the Holy of Holies and the awesome treasury, You who will become the inexhaustible, unsearchable treasure. Come into the entry doors of the Bema, you who destroy the doors of death. Gaze upon the veil (*cf.* Exodus 26.31*ff.*), you who enlighten through your lightning flash those who are blinded by their dull-sighted tastes.	Presentation I
304B	Εὐπρεπές σοι τῷ Χερουβικωτάτῳ θρόνῳ ὁ ἡγιασμένος τόπος εἰς κατοικητήριον.	This holy place is a fitting dwelling for you who are the throne of the Cherubim.	Presentation I
305C	Χαίροις, τὸ τοῦ παμβασιλέως Θεοῦ ἱερότευκτον ἄχραντόν τε καὶ καθαρώτατον παλάτιον,	Hail, sacred, undefiled, most pure palace of the omnipotent God.	Presentation I
305D	ἡ ὄντως χρυσοειδὴς καὶ φωτεινὴ . . . ἑπτάφωτος λυχνία τῷ ἀδύτῳ φωτὶ ὑφαπτομένη καὶ τῷ τῆς ἁγνείας ἐλαίῳ πιαινομένη, καὶ τοῖς ἐν ζόφῳ πταισμάτων ἀχλύϊ τυφλώττουσι αἴγλης ἀνατολὴν πιστουμένη.	Truly golden and brilliant . . . You the seven-lighted lamp stand (*cf.* Exodus 25.31) enkindled by the unapproachable Light and filled by the oil of purity, and giving the rising of its gleam to the blind in the darkness of sin.	Presentation I
308A	Χαίροις, ὁ τοῦ Θεοῦ ἅγιος θρόνος, ἡ θεῖον ἀνάθημα, ἡ δόξης οἶκος, ἡ περικαλλὲς ἀγλάϊσμα, καὶ ἐκλεκτὸν κειμήλιον, καὶ παγκόσμιον ἱλαστήριον, «καὶ Θεοῦ δόξαν διηγούμενος οὐρανός.»	Hail, holy throne of God, the divine gift, house of glory, the most beautiful splendor and elect treasure and universal propitiation, and "heaven declaring the glory of God,"	Presentation I
309A	συνθρόνῳ	sharing the throne	Presentation I

312A	Κόρην ἐξ ἐπαγγελίας αὐτὴν τριετίζουσαν αὐτὴν τριετίζουσαν	A maiden from the promise at the age of three years	Presentation II
321A	σκηνὴ ὡς ἀληθῶς πορφυροποίητος	the true royal tabernacle	Annunciation
321A	ὁ θρόνος ὁ ὑψηλὸς καὶ ἐπηρμένος τοῦ τῶν ὅλων ποιητοῦ	the lofty high throne of the Maker of all	Annunciation
321B	ὁ ναὸς ὁ ἔμψυχος τῆς μεγαλοπρεποῦς δόξης	the living temple of the majestic glory	Annunciation
325A	Θρόνος θεοβάστακτος	the throne which bears God	Annunciation
325A	βασιλικὴ καθέδρα τοῦ ἐπουρανίου Βασιλέως κληθήσῃ	You shall be called . . . the royal seat of the heavenly King	Annunciation
329B	οὐρανὸς γὰρ μέλλεις γενέσθαι καὶ σκηνὴ Θεοῦ ἔμψυχος ναὸς θεοχώρητος,	You are about to become heaven and a God-containing tabernacle, a living temple of God	Annunciation
344C	ἐπειδὴ καὶ οὐρανὸς θεοχώρητος ἀνεδείχθης τοῦ ὑψίστου Θεοῦ	For when you were proved to be a God-containing heaven of the most high God	Dormition I
345B	τὸ σῶμά σου τὸ παρθενικόν, ὅλον ἅγιον, ὅλον ἁγνόν, ὅλον Θεοῦ κατοικητήριον	your virginal body, altogether holy, altogether pure, altogether the residence of God	Dormition I
345B	καὶ ἔμψυχος ναὸς τῆς τοῦ Μονογενοῦς παναγίας θεότητος	a living temple of the all-holy divinity of the Only-begotten One	Dormition I
348A	θεοχώρητον . . . ἀγγεῖον	God-containing vessel	Dormition I
348B	Οἶκος γὰρ αὐτῷ καταπαύσεως σὺ γέγονας σωματικὸς	For you have become a corporeal house of rest for him	Dormition I
356B	Εἰ γὰρ ὁ Σολομώντειος ναός, πάλαι τὸν οὐρανὸν ἐπὶ τῆς γῆς ἐσκιογράφει πόσῳ μᾶλλον ἐμψύχου σοῦ ναοῦ γεγονυίας τοῦ Χριστοῦ, μὴ καὶ τὰς Ἐκκλησίας τὰς σὰς, ὡς ἐπιγείους οὐρανοὺς δικαίως ἔστιν ἀνακομπάζειν;	For if the temple of Solomon formerly made a shadow of heaven on earth how much more when you have become a living temple of Christ, is it not right to adorn your churches as earthly heavens?	Dormition II

361C	Σκεῦος ἐμὸν ἐγένου· οὐ ῥαγώσει τοῦτο σύντριμμα θανατοφθόρου καταπτώσεως	You became my vessel; the fracture of death-corrupting fall will not break this	Dormition III
361D	κιβωτὸν διασωζομένων	an ark for those who are being saved	Dormition III
369A	καταρρίψαι τε τὸν ἔνσαρκον θρόνον μὴ ἐνδοιάσας τοῦ Ὑψίστου	without hesitation to throw down the corporeal throne of the Most High	Dormition III
369A	σκεῦος ὅτι τὸ σῶμα διεγίγνωσκον ὑπάρχειν τῆς ἁγνῆς	because they recognized that the body was the vessel of the pure one	Dormition III
376B	τοῦ Θεοῦ κιβωτὸν	the container of God	Sash
376C	τὸ ἔμψυχον τοῦ Θεοῦ Λόγου προσεγγισάσης κατοικητήριον	near to the dwelling place of the living God	Sash
381C	στάμνε	urn	Sash
381C	τράπεζα	table	Sash
381C	λυχνία	lamp	Sash
381D	τὸ σὲ Κυρίαν καὶ προστάτιν καὶ Δέσποιναν	Lady, patroness and Mistress	Sash

References to Theological Conflicts in Germanos I Patriarch of Constantinople (715-730)

PG 98 Location	Greek	English	Homily
305B	ἴλην τὴν τῶν αἱρέσεων ἐκμειοῦσιν	drown out the company of the heretics.	Presentation I
308C	καὶ Θεὸν πάντων δημιουργὸν εὐπροσδέκτοις καὶ μητροπειθέσι λιταῖς, τοὺς τῆς ἐκκλησιαστικῆς εὐταξίας οἴακας διέπουσα, εἰς ἀκύμαντον λιμένα ἤτοι ἀπόντιστον[43] ἐξ ἐπιρροίας αἱρέσεών τε καὶ σκανδάλων πηδαλιούχησον	the God Creator of all, following the furrows of good ecclesiastical order, steer us from the floods of heresies and scandals to the calm and harbor where ships do not sink.[44]*	Presentation I
317B	«Καὶ γενηθήτω ἄλαλα τὰ χείλη τὰ δόλια, τὰ λαλοῦντα κατὰ σοῦ τῆς δικαίας, ἀνομίαν ἐν ὑπερηφανείᾳ καὶ ἐξουδενώσει·» καὶ ἐξουδενωθήτω ἐν τῇ πόλει σου ἡ τούτων εἰκών· αἰσχυνθήτωσαν, καὶ ἐκλιπέτωσαν, καὶ ἀπολέσθωσαν, καὶ γνώτωσαν ὅτι ὄνομά σοι Δέσποινα.	"And may the deceitful lips be mute, those which speak lawlessness in arrogance and contempt against you the righteous woman" (cf. Psalm 31.19). And let the image of these [people] be brought to naught in your city. Let them be put to shame, and let them die out, and let them perish, and let them know that your name is Mistress (cf. Psalm 83.17-18).	Presentation II

---

43 ἀπόντιστος here only—ἀκαταπόντιστος in Theodore the Studite and Nicholas Mysticus
44 ἀπόντιστος here only—ἀκαταπόντιστος in Theodore the Studite and Nicholas Mysticus

348D	Παυσάτωσαν τῶν αἱρετικῶν οἱ ἀμαθεῖς καὶ ἐμβρόντητοι λόγοι	Let the ignorant and thunderstruck speeches of the heretics cease!	Dormition II
348D	Ἐμφραπέσθωσαν τὰ τούτων ἄδικα χείλη	Let their unrighteous lips be sealed!	Dormition II

356B/C provides a brief view into the issues surrounding the decoration of Church buildings. While some have not read this as an allusion to the iconoclasm of Leo I, I find the implication hard to avoid.
There appear to be no other direct references to specific theological conflicts in Dormition III and the Homily on the Sash. No references to Christian theological conflicts appear in the Annunciation Homily as it is a dialogue.

References to the Virginity of Mary in
Germanos I, Patriarch of Constantinople
(715-730)

PG 98 Location	Greek	English	Homily
293B	Σήμερον ὁ καινότατος καὶ καθαρώτατος ἀμόλυντος τόμος, οὗ χειρὶ γραφησόμενος, ἀλλὰ πνεύματι χρυσωθησόμενος, ταῖς κατὰ νόμον εὐλογίαις ἁγιαζομένη, χαριστήριον δῶρον προσάγεται.	Today a new, pure, unspoiled book which will not be written by hands, but written in gold by the spirit, hallowed with blessings according to the Law, she is brought forward as an acceptable gift.	Presentation I (P—Immac 127 ftn 11)
293C	Σήμερον ἡ τοῦ θείου ναοῦ πύλη διαπετασθεῖσα, τὴν ἀνατολόβλεπτον καὶ ἐσφραγισμένην τοῦ Ἐμμανουὴλ πύλην εἰσιοῦσαν δέχεται.	Today the gate of God's temple is opened to receive the entry of the eastward looking, sealed gate of Emmanuel (cf. Ezekiel 44.1-3).	Presentation I (P—Immac 128 ftn 16)
297D	Πάρεσο, μεγαλόφωνος Ἰεζεκιήλ, τὴν κεφαλίδα θεόθεν κατίσχων τοῦ ζωοποιοῦ Πνεύματος καὶ κεκράζων τὴν εὐφημίαν τῇ ἀνατολοβλέπτῳ καὶ θεοπαρόδῳ ἐσφραγισμένῃ πύλῃ	Come, loud-voiced Ezekiel, holding the divine scroll of the life-creating Spirit and crying your holy words to the eastward oriented and sealed gate (Ezekiel 44:1) which only God goes through;	Presentation I
300B	Πορφυρίζονται στολαὶ τῶν κεράτων τοῦ θυσιαστηρίου τῇ ἁλουργοειδεῖ αὐτῆς καὶ παρθενικῇ ἀμφιάσει.	The vestments of the horn of the altar of sacrifice are made more royal by the purple-hued garment of her virginity.	Presentation I
301A	τὴν τῷ κάλλει τῆς ἑαυτῆς ἀμώμου παρθενίας καὶ ταῖς δροσιστικαῖς μαρμαρυγαῖς τὴν ἅπασαν γῆν καταυγάζουσαν	who in the beauty of her blameless virginity and her dewy sparkling illuminates the whole earth	Presentation I

308C	Ἀλλ᾽, ὦ πανάμωμε, καὶ πανύμνητε, καὶ πανσέβαστε, καὶ πάντων δημιουργημάτων ὑπερφερὲς Θεοῦ ἀνάθημα· ἀγεώργητε γῆ, ἀνήροτε ἄρουρα, εὐκληματοῦσα ἄμπελος, κρατὴρ εὐφραντικώτατε, κρήνη πηγάζουσα, Παρθένε γεννῶσα καὶ Μήτηρ ἀπείρανδρε, ἁγνείας κειμήλιον καὶ σεμνότητος ἐγκαλλώπισμα, ταῖς πρὸς τὸν σόν, τὸν ἐκ σοῦ ἀπάτορα, Υἱόν τε καὶ Θεὸν πάντων δημιουργὸν εὐπροσδέκτοις καὶ μητροπειθέσι λιταῖς, τοὺς τῆς ἐκκλησιαστικῆς εὐταξίας οἴακας διέπουσα, εἰς ἀκύμαντον λιμένα ἤτοι ἀπόντιστον[44] ἐξ ἐπιρροίας αἱρέσεών τε καὶ σκανδάλων πηδαλιούχησον.	But O most blameless and all-laudable, most holy one, offering to God greater than all created things, untilled earth, unplowed field (cf. Ezekiel 19.10), well-pruned vineyard, most joyous wine bowl, gushing spring (cf. Ezekiel 17.6), virgin birth-giver and husbandless mother, treasure of purity and ornament of holiness, by your acceptable and motherly-persuasive petitions to your son, born from you without a father, and the God Creator of all, following the furrows of good ecclesiastical order, steer us from the floods of heresies and scandals to the calm and harbor where ships do not sink.45*	Presentation I
312A	Κόρην ἐξ ἐπαγγελίας, καὶ αὐτὴν τριετίζουσαν, εἰς τὸ τρίτον καταπέτασμα ὡς δῶρον ἄμωμον προσφερομένην, πρὸς τὸ ἐκεῖσε οἰκεῖν ἀπαραλείπτως, καὶ ὑπὸ τῶν πλουσίων τοῦ λαοῦ λιτανευομένην	A maiden from the promise, at the age of three years, is brought as a blameless gift within the third curtain, to live there continuously, and receives petitions from the wealthy men of the people (cf. Psalm 45.13).	Presentation II (P—Immac 127 ftn 14)
312D/ 313A	κόρην προσάγειν σκηνοβατεῖν εἰς τὰ ἄδυτα;	To bring a maiden to make her tent in the sanctuary?	Presentation II

---

44 ἀπόντιστος here only—ἀκαταπόντιστος in Theodore the Studite and Nicholas Mysticus

316C/D	καὶ τότε νεύματι Θεοῦ, καὶ βουλῇ ἱερέων δίδοται περὶ αὐτῆς κλῆρος, καὶ κατακληροῦται Ἰωσὴφ ὁ δίκαιος, καὶ τὴν ἁγίαν ταύτην Παρθένον οἰκονομικῶς ἐκ τοῦ ναοῦ τοῦ Θεοῦ καὶ τῶν αὐτοῦ ἱερέων παραλαμβάνει, πρὸς δελεασμὸν τοῦ ἀρχεκάκου ὄφεως· ἵνα μὴ ὡς παρθένῳ προσβάλῃ τῇ ἀκηράτῳ κόρῃ, ἀλλ' ὡς ἅτε μεμνηστευμένην ταύτην παραδράμῃ.	And then by the assent of God and the counsel of the priests a lot is drawn concerning her, and Joseph the just is allotted, and receives this holy Virgin according to the dispensation from the Temple of God and his priests, to ensnare the serpent who originated evil, so that he should not attack the undefiled maiden as a virgin, but as a betrothed woman he should pass her by.	Presentation II
320B	πανάχραντε Κυρία	all-undefiled Lady	Presentation II
321B	Χαῖρε, κεχαριτωμένη, ὄρος Θεοῦ, ὄρος πῖον, ὄρος κατάσκιον, ὄρος ἀλατόμητον, ὄρος Θεοῦ τὸ ἐμφανές.	Hail full of grace, mountain of God, fertile mountain (*cf.* Psalm 68.15), imposing mountain, uncut mountain, mountain of God's appearing.	Annunciation
324B	Δέδοικα καὶ τρέμω σου τοὺς τοιούτους λόγους· καὶ ὑπολαμβάνω, ὡς ἄλλην Εὔαν πλανῆσαί με παραγέγονας. Ἐγὼ δὲ οὐκ εἰμὶ κατ' ἐκείνην. Πῶς δὲ καὶ ἀσπάζεσαι κόρην, ἣν οὐδέποτε ἐθεάσω;	I am afraid and I tremble at your words. I suspect that you have come to deceive me like another Eve. I am nothing like her. What a greeting you bring to a maiden whom you have never seen before!	Annunciation
324C	Ἐπειδὴ ταῦτα μηνύεις μοι, καὶ μηνύων οὐ παύῃ, λέξω σοι λοιπόν, ὅτι οὐ πιστεύω σου τὸν τοιοῦτον εὐαγγελισμόν· καθότι ἐξουθενῆσαι ἦλθες τὸ παρθενικόν μου ἀξίωμα, καὶ λυπῆσαι τὸν ἐμὸν μνηστῆρα.	Since you are telling this to me, and since you won't stop saying it, for the rest I will say to you that I don't trust this announcement of yours. You come to debase my virginity, and to grieve my betrothed.	Annunciation

325A	Θρόνος θεοβάστακτος, καὶ βασιλικὴ καθέδρα τοῦ ἐπουρανίου Βασιλέως κληθήσῃ, καθότι Βασίλισσα καὶ Δέσποινα, καὶ βασιλέως ἐπιγείου θυγάτηρ τυγχάνεις, καὶ χαρακτῆρα ἔχεις βασιλικόν.	You shall be called the throne which bears God, the royal seat of the heavenly King. As you are Queen and Virgin, and a daughter of [David] the earthly king, so you have a royal character.	Annunciation
325B	Κατὰ τί γνώσομαι τοῦτο, ὅτι ἔσται τελείωσις τοῖς ὑπ' αὐτοῦ γενομένοις, καθότι παρθένος ἀθαλάμευτος ἐγὼ τυγχάνω, καὶ μῶμος ἡδυπαθείας οὐκ ἔστιν ἐν ἐμοί; Δούλη γάρ εἰμι τοῦ Κυρίου τοῦ ποιήσαντός με.	How shall I know this, that what he says[45] will be accomplished? I am an unwedded virgin, and have not experienced shameful, sweet pleasure. For I am the handmaiden of the Lord who created me.	Annunciation
328B	παρθένον ἀπείρανδρον ἀσπαζόμενος, καὶ κόρην ἀπειρόγαμον τοιαῦτα φθεγγόμενος, τὸ ἀληθὲς οἶδας· τὸ πότε, καὶ πόθεν καὶ «Πῶς λοιπὸν ἔσται μοι τοῦτο, ἐπεὶ ἄνδρα οὐ γινώσκω;»	You are greeting an untried virgin, and an unmarried girl you extol. You know the truth: when and where and "How will this happen to me, since I know no man?" (Luke 1.34)	Annunciation
328D	Τέρψις καὶ διόλου γλυκασμός ἐστι τὰ ῥήματά σου, δεδοξασμένη· καὶ διὰ τοῦτό σοι λέξω· ὅτι οὐκ ἐκ θελήματος σαρκός, ἀλλ' ἐκ θελήματος Θεοῦ, καὶ ἐξ ἐπιφοιτήσεως τοῦ ἁγίου Πνεύματος, ἡ σὴ κυοφορία γενήσεται.	At all times your words are sweet and joyous, O blessed one. It is because of this that I will say to you, your pregnancy is due not to the will of the flesh but to the will of God and the descent of the Holy Spirit (cf. John 1.13).	Annunciation
329A	Τίς πληροφορήσει τὸν Ἰωσὴφ, ὅτι οὐκ ἐκ θελήματος ἀνδρός, ἀλλ' ἐξ ἐπιφοιτήσεως τοῦ ἁγίου Πνεύματος ἐγὼ συλλήψομαι; καθότι ἐκ τοῦ αἰῶνος οὐκ ἠκούσθη ὅτι παρθένος ἀπείρανδρος βρέφος τέτοκεν.	Who will persuade Joseph that I shall conceive not by the will of man, but by the descent of the Holy Spirit? For it has never at any time been heard that a virgin has given birth to a child without a man.	Annunciation

---

[45]   From Piana's manuscript

329C	Χαρακτῆρα φέρουσα βασιλικὸν, καὶ εἰς τὰ βασίλεια τῆς ἐμῆς Βηθλεὲμ τιθηνήσασα, καὶ εἰς τὰ ἅγια ἐκ παιδόθεν ἀμέμπτως διαπρέψασα· καὶ παρθένος λοιπὸν τυγχάνουσα, πῶς ἐγὼ μήτηρ ἀκούσω τοῦ παιδός μου;	I am of royal blood, and spent my earliest childhood in the royal house of Bethlehem, and my childhood I spent blamelessly in the temple; and being a virgin up to now, how can I be called the mother of my child?	Annunciation
329D	Ὦ παρθένε, χαρᾶς ἐπουρανίου πρόξενε· τερπνὸν καὶ θαυμαστὸν οἰκητήριον, καὶ τοῦ κόσμου παντὸς ἱλαστήριον, ἡ μόνη κατὰ ἀλήθειαν ἐν γυναιξὶν εὐλογημένη, ἑτοιμάζου λοιπὸν εἰς μυστικὴν Χριστοῦ παρουσίαν.	O Virgin, bringer of heavenly joy, joyful and marvelous dwelling place, and propitiation of the whole cosmos, the only truly blessed one among women (Luke 1.42), prepare yourself for the mystical coming of Christ.	Annunciation
332A	Ἄσπιλόν σε παρέλαβον ἐξ οἴκου Κυρίου, καὶ παρθένον ἀμόλυντον κατέλιπόν σε ἐν τῷ οἴκῳ μου· καὶ τί τοῦτο ὃ νῦν ὁρῶ, μητέρα παρ' ἐλπίδα καὶ οὐ παρθένον τυγχάνουσαν; εἰπέ μοι, Μαρία· τὸ ἀληθὲς ἐν τάχει λέγε μοι.	Undefiled, I received you from the house of the Lord, and an undefiled virgin I kept you in my house. And what is this which I now see, a mother contrary to expectation and not a virgin? Speak to me, Mary. Quickly, tell me the truth.	Annunciation
332C	Γέγραπται ἐν τῇ βίβλῳ Μωϋσέως οὕτως· «Ἐάν τις εὕρῃ τὴν παρθένον, καὶ βιασάμενος κοιμηθῇ μετ' αὐτῆς, δώσει ὁ ἄνθρωπος ἐκεῖνος τῷ πατρὶ τῆς νεάνιδος πεντήκοντα δίδραχμα.» Τί οὖν πρὸς ταῦτα ποιήσεις;	It is written in the Law of Moses. "If one finds a virgin, and lies with her by force, the man shall give to the father of the young woman fifty silver shekels" (Deuteronomy 22.24-25) What will you do with that?	Annunciation
332C	Γέγραπται ἐν τοῖς προφήταις, ὅτι «Δοθήσεται τὸ ἐσφραγισμένον βιβλίον ἀνδρὶ εἰδότι γράμματα, καὶ ἐρεῖ· Οὐ δύναμαι ἀναγνῶναι αὐτό.» Τάχα οὖν, ὡς ἐμοὶ δοκεῖ, ἡ προφητεία αὕτη, περὶ σοῦ ἐλέχθη.	It is written in the prophets, that "they shall give the sealed book to a man who knows letters and he shall say: 'I am not able to read it' (Isaiah 29.11)." Perhaps then as it seems to me, the prophecy was said about you.	Annunciation

333A	Ζῇ Κύριος <ὁ Θεός μου>, ὅτι καθαρά εἰμι, καὶ ἄνδρα οὐ γινώσκω· ὁ γὰρ φανείς μοι, ὡς ἐμοὶ δοκεῖ, ἄγγελος Κυρίου ὑπάρχει, ἀνθρωποσχηματισθείς· καὶ μετ᾽ εὐλαβείας ὡς ἀπὸ διαστήματος ἐξίστατο. Καὶ ἵστατο, καὶ οὕτως ἠρέμα τῇ ἐμῇ ταπεινώσει διελέγετο.	As the Lord lives, I am pure, and have known no man. He who appeared to me, seemed to me to be an angel, being in human form. He stood at a respectful distance. And while standing, he spoke gently to my unworthy self.	Annunciation
333B	Θαυμάζω ἐπὶ σοί, καὶ σφόδρα καταπλήττομαι· καὶ οἶδα ὅτι διαλάλημα γέγονας τοῖς υἱοῖς Ἰσραήλ, καὶ ἐξουδενήσει με Ἀδωναῖ Κύριος, ἀνθ᾽ ὧν παρέλαβόν σε ἐξ ἁγίου Πνεύματος, καὶ ἐξ ἁγίου κατοικητηρίου εἰς τήρησιν, καὶ παρθένον σε οὐκ ἐτήρησα.	I wonder at you, and am greatly amazed, and I know that you have been spoken of among the Sons of Israel, and the Lord Adonai shall hold me in dishonor, for I by the Holy Spirit received you from the Holy Temple to guard, but I have not guarded your virginity.	Annunciation
333D	Κἂν ἐγὼ σιωπήσω τὸ ἁμάρτημά σου, οἱ λίθοι κεκράξονται <ἡ κοιλία σου κεκράξεται> · Καὶ τὰ Ἅγια τῶν ἁγίων μεγάλα βοήσονται· καθότι παρέλαβόν σε εἰς τήρησιν ἐκ τοῦ ἐκείνου καταλεγομένου ἱερέως, καὶ παρθένον σε οὐκ ἐφύλαξα.	Even if I keep quiet about your sin, the stones will cry out.[46] And the Holy of Holies will shout aloud, because I received you for safe keeping from the priest who is enrolled there, and I have not guarded your virginity.	Annunciation
336A	Μὴ γὰρ ἐκ τῆς φωνῆς συνέλαβες; ἐκ τοῦ αἰῶνος οὐκ ἠκούσθη, ὅτι ἀπὸ φωνῆς ῥημάτων ἐκυοφόρησε παρθένος ἀπείρανδρός ποτε· οὔτε οἱ πατέρες ἡμῶν ἀνήγγειλαν ἡμῖν ὅτι τοιοῦτον γέγονεν ἐν ταῖς ἀρχαίαις ἡμέραις.	You did not conceive by a voice, did you? Never has it been heard, that a virgin conceived by the sound of words without a man, nor did our fathers tell us that such an event occurred in the ancient days.	Annunciation

---

[46]   your belly will cry out

336A	Μὴ γὰρ οὐ γέγραπται ἐν τοῖς προφήταις, «Ὅτι Παρθένος ἐν γαστρὶ λήψεται, καὶ παιδίον ἡμῖν τεχθήσεται;» Μὴ <γὰρ> ἔχεις εἰπεῖν ὅτι οἱ προφῆται ψεύδονται; σφάλλῃ λοιπόν, ὦ Ἰωσήφ, ἐπὶ πολὺ μαινόμενος	Is it not written in the Scriptures, "That a virgin shall conceive, and shall bear a child to us" (*cf.* Isaiah 7.14)? You cannot say that the prophets lie, can you? You are mistaken, O Joseph, you are out of your mind about many things.	Annunciation
336D	Πῶς μὴ πτήξω, καὶ τύψω τὴν ὄψιν, ὅτι παρθένον παρέλαβόν σε ἐξ οἴκου Κυρίου μου, καὶ οὐ διετήρησά σε; Πῶς δὲ ἀπὸ τοῦ νῦν προσάξω Κυρίῳ τῷ Θεῷ μου, καὶ ἐκπληρώσω νομικὴν διάταξιν κατὰ τὸ ἐμοὶ εἰθισμένον;	How can I not be frightened, and confounded in my sight? For I received you from the temple of my God as a virgin, and I did not guard you. And how shall I bring gifts to my Lord God and fulfill the customs of the law as I have been accustomed to do?	Annunciation
341B	Εἰ πρὸ γεννηθῆναι παρὰ σοῦ τῆς Παρθένου Μητρός, Υἱὸς οὗτος μονογενὴς τοῦ Θεοῦ, πῶς ὁ Πατήρ φησι πρὸς αὐτόν, «Ἐγὼ σήμερον γεγέννηκά σε;» Δῆλον ὅτι τὸ σήμερον, οὐχὶ τὴν τῆς θεότητος τοῦ Μονογενοῦς πρόσφατον παρίστησι ὕπαρξιν, ἀλλὰ τὴν πρὸς ἀνθρώπους σωματικὴν αὐτοῦ βεβαιοῖ παρουσίαν.	If before being born from you, the Virgin Mother, this one was only-begotten Son of God, how does the Father say to him, "Today I have begotten you"? It is clear that "today" does not represent a new beginning of the divinity of the Only-begotten, but declares his corporeal presence among men.	Dormition I
341C	Ἐπειδὴ γὰρ οὐκ ἀλλότριον τὸ Πνεῦμα τοῦ Πατρός· εὐδοκίᾳ δὲ καὶ ἀποστολῇ τοῦ Πατρὸς ᾤκησεν ἐν σοὶ τῇ Παρθένῳ καὶ Μητρὶ	For since the Spirit is not alien to the Father, for by good will and sending of the Father he has come to dwell in you the Virgin and Mother,	Dormition I
345B	Σύ, κατὰ τὸ γεγραμμένον, «ἐν καλλονῇ·» καὶ τὸ σῶμά σου τὸ παρθενικόν, ὅλον ἅγιον, ὅλον ἁγνόν, ὅλον Θεοῦ κατοικητήριον· ὡς ἐκ τούτου λοιπὸν καὶ ἀλλότριον χοϊκῆς ἀναλύσεως.	You, as it is written, [are] "in beauty" (Cant 2.3 LXX) and your virginal body, altogether holy, altogether pure, altogether the residence of God; so because of this [it is] separated and alien from earthly dissolution.	Dormition I (P—Immac 131 ftn 27)

348D	παρθενίαν σου	your virginity	Dormition II
349A	«Εἰ μὴ ὅτι Κύριος ἐβοήθησεν ἡμῖν,» ἐκ παρθένου σαρκωθείς, «παρὰ βραχὺ παρῴκησεν ἂν,» ἐν τῷ παμφάγῳ τῆς ἀπονεκρώσεως ᾅδη, «τῶν ψυχῶν ἡμῶν»	"If the Lord had not helped us"—he who was incarnate of a virgin—"in a little he would have settled" in the all-devouring Hades of death, the sinking "of our souls"	Dormition II
360A	Καὶ ἡ περὶ τῆς σωματικῆς κοιμήσεως τῆς Ζωοτόκου καὶ ἀειπαρθένου Μαρίας διήγησις	And the exposition concerning the corporeal falling-asleep of the life-bearing and ever-virgin Mary	Dormition III
361C	Μονογενῆ με κεκτημένη, μῆτερ, Υἱὸν, συνοικῆσαί μοι μᾶλλον προτίμησον· οὐκ ἀντιπερισπάσαι γὰρ οἶδα πρὸς ἑτέρου τέκνου διάθεσιν. Ἐγώ σε παρθένον ἀνέδειξα μητέρα· ἐγώ σε καὶ εὐφραινομένην ἐπὶ Τέκνῳ καταστήσω μητέρα	Since you obtained me as your only-begotten Son, O mother, prefer rather to live with me; for I know you have no other child. I showed you to be a virgin mother; I also will make you a mother rejoicing in her Child.	Dormition III
365A	Εἰ οὖν ὑμεῖς γονεῖς ὄντες ἐκ φθαρτῶν καὶ ἐκ ῥύπου συναφείας παίδων, οὐ καρτερεῖτε τούτων πρὸς ῥοπὴν χωρισθῆναι, πῶς ἐγὼ Θεὸν Υἱὸν κεκτημένη, καὶ σπλάγχνα μονομερῆ πρὸς αὐτὸν ἐπέχουσα, διότι χωρὶς ἀνδρὸς αὐτὸν ἀφθάρτως καὶ παρθενικῶς ἐκύησα, μὴ μεῖζον ὑμῶν νενίκημαι παρὰ τῶν σπλάγχνων;	So if you being parents from perishable children and the union of pollution, will not refuse to be separated from these for an instant, how shall I who have obtained God as a Son and maintain my affection singly for him, because without a husband I bore him incorruptibly and virginally, how shall I not be overcome more than you by my affection?	Dormition III
365D/ 368A	ἀνοίγει τούτῳ χαριέντως ὁ τοῦ οἴκου προεστὼς Ἰωάννης ὁ ἀπόστολος, καὶ τὴν Παρθένον ὡς μητέρα ὁ παρθένος εἰς τὰ ἴδια διαπαραλαβὼν ἐξ αὐτοῦ τοῦ Χριστοῦ.	John the apostle, who presides over the house, joyfully opens to him, he the virgin who received the Virgin as mother into his own house from Christ himself (John 19.27).	Dormition III

Mary's virginity is not specifically mentioned in the sash homily. However, many words which are elsewhere in Germanos' homilies and connected with Mary's (perpetual) virginity are present.

Works Cited

Aghiorgoussis, Maximos. "Sin in Orthodox Dogmatic." St. Vladimir's Theological
Quarterly 21.4 (1977).

Ameringer, T.E. The Influence of the Second Sophistic in the Panegyrical Sermons of St. John Chrysostom. A Study in Greek Rhetoric, Patristic Studies. Vol. V. Washington D.C., 1921.

Andrew, and Vittorio Fazzo. Omelie Mariane. Roma: Citta Nuova Editrice, 1987.

Antonopoulou, Theodora. The Homilies of the Emperor Leo VI. Leiden ; New York: Brill, 1997.

Antonopoulou-Kollaros, Christina. Greece; a Study of the Educational System of Greece and a Guide to the Academic Placement of Students from Greece in United States Educational Institutions. [Washington, D.C.,: International Education Activities Group of the American Association of Collegiate Registrars and Admissions Officers], 1974.

Aphthonius. Aphthonii Progymnasmata, ed. Hugo Rabe. Leipzig: B. G. Teubner, 1926.

Arbel, Benjamin, and David Jacoby. Intercultural Contacts in the Medieval Mediterranean. Portland, OR: F. Cass, 1996.

Barber, Charles. "Theotokos and *Logos*: The Interpretation and Reinterpretation of the Sanctuary Programme of the Koimesis Church, Nicaea." Images of the Mother of God: Perceptions of the Theotokos in Byzantium. Ed. Maria Vassilaki. Aldershot, Hants., England; Burlington, VT: Ashgate, 2005.

Barnard, Leslie W. The Graeco-Roman and Oriental Background of the Iconoclastic Controversy. Byzantina Neerlandica; Fasc. 5, 1974.

Bauducco, F.M., S.J. "La mariologia di San Germano." Civiltà Cattolica II (1955): 409-14.

Beck, H.-G. "Die Griechische Kirche im Zeitalter des Ikonoklasmus." Handbuch der Kirchengeschichte. Ed. H.-G. Beck. Vol. III. Freiburg: I. Halbband, 1966.

Blancy, Alain, Maurice Jourjon and the Dombes Group. Mary in the Plan of God and in the Communion of Saints. New York/Mahwa, NJ: Paulist Press, 2002.

Blum, Wilhelm. "Die Theodizee des Patriarchen Germanos I Von Konstantinopel." Vigiliae Christianae 28.4 (1974): 295-303.

Bonner, G., ed. The Homily on the Passion by Melito Bishop of Sardis and Some Fragments of the Apocryphal Ezekiel. London and Philadelphia, 1940.

Bouvy, Edmond. "La fête de l'εἴσοδος où de la présentation de la vierge au temple dans l'église grecque." Bessarione I (1897): 555-62.

—. "Les origines de la fête de la présentation." Revue Augustinienne I (1902): 581-94.

Browning, Robert. The Greek World : Classical, Byzantine and Modern. 1st paperback ed. London: Thames & Hudson, 2000.

Brubaker, Leslie, et al. Byzantium in the Iconoclast Era (Ca. 680-850): The Sources: An Annotated Survey. Birmingham Byzantine and Ottoman Monographs. Vol. 7. Aldershot UK: Ashgate, 2001.

Burgess, T.C. "Epideictic Literature." University of Chicago Studies in Classical Philology 9 (1902): 89-261.

Cameron, Averil. Christianity and the Rhetoric of Empire: The Development of Christian Discourse. Sather Classical Lectures. Berkeley: University of California Press, 1991.

Caputo, John D. Philosophy and Theology. Horizons in Theology. Nashville, TN: Abingdon Press, 2006.

Carli, Luigi. La morte e l'assunzione di Maria Santissima nelle omelie greche dei secoli VII, VIII. Rome: Officium libri catholici, 1941.

Carroll, Michael P. The Cult of the Virgin Mary: Psychological Origins. Princeton, N.J.: Princeton University Press, 1992.

Casagrande, Dominicus. Enchiridion Marianum Biblicum Patristicum. Rome: Cor Unum, 1974.

Chaîne, Marius. Apocrypha De B. Maria Virgine. Rome: K. de Luigi, 1909.

—. Apocrypha De Beata Maria Virgine. Louvain: L. Durbecq, 1955.

—. Apocrypha De Beata Maria Virgine. Louvain: Secretariat du Corpus SCO, 1961.

Chevalier, C. "Les trilogies homilétiques dans l'élaboration des fêtes mariales, 650-850." Gregorianum 18 (1937): 361-78.

Chrystal, James. Authoritative Christianity. The Decisions of the First Six Sole Ecumenical Councils: That Is, the Only Decisions of the Whole Church, East and West, before Its Division in the Ninth Century. Jersey City, N.J.: J. Chrystal, 1891.

Cichecki, Vincent. A Short Outline of the History of the Universal Church: Result of Courses Given in Lusaka in 1990-1992: With Maps and Complete Lists of Popes, Ecumenical Councils, Emperors and Kings of the Roman Empire and of Modern States, Enabling Easy References and Cross References: With References to Zambia, Where Applicable. [Lusaka]: Lusaka Catholic Bookshop, 1994.

Clark, Donald Lemen. Rhetoric in Greco-Roman Education. New York: Columbia University Press, 1957.

Coit, Thomas Winthrop. A Lecture on Ecumenical Councils, Delivered in St. Paul's Church, Troy, N.Y. on Christmas Eve. Hartford: Church Press Co., 1870.

Constantinople (Ecumenical patriarchate), and V. Grumel. Les regestes des actes du patriarcat de Constantinople. [2. éd.]. Paris: Institut francais d'études byzantines, 1972.

Cunningham, Mary B. "Preaching and the Community." Church and People in Byzantium. Eds. Rosemary Morris, et al. Birmingham, England: Centre for Byzantine, Ottoman and Modern Greek studies, University of Birmingham, 1990. 39-40.

—. The Life of Michael the Synkellos. Belfast: Belfast Byzantine Enterprises, 1991.

—. "Innovation or Mimesis in Byzantine Sermons?" Originality in Byzantine Literature, Art and Music: A Collection of Essays. Ed. Anthony Robert Littlewood. vols. Oxford [England]: Oxbow Books, 1995. 67-80.

—. The Meeting of the Old and the New: The Typology of Mary the Theotokos in Byzantine Homilies and Hymns. Studies in Church History, the Church and Mary. Ed. R. N. Swanson. Rochester, NY: Ecclesiastical History Society/Boydell Press, 2004.

Cunningham, Mary B., and Pauline Allen. Preacher and Audience: Studies in Early Christian and Byzantine Homiletics. Leiden & Boston: Brill, 1998.

Daley, Brian J. On the Dormition of Mary: Early Patristic Homilies. Crestwood, NY: St. Vladimir's Seminary Press, 1998.

Daniélou, Jean. The Theology of Jewish Christianity. Translated and edited by John A. Baker. Development of Christian Doctrine before the Council of Nicea ; V. 1. Chicago: H. Regnery Co., 1964.

Davis, Leo Donald. The First Seven Ecumenical Councils (325-787): Their History and Theology. Theology and Life Series; V. 21. Collegeville, Minn.: Liturgical Press, 1990.

Detorakis, Theodorakis. "Αθησαυριστες Λεξεις απο τα Εργα του Πατριαρχη Γερμανου Α'." Lexicographica Byzantina: Beiträge zum Symposion zur Byzantinischen Lexikographie (Wien, 1.-4. 3. 1989). Eds. Wolfram Hörandner and Erich Trapp. Wien: Verlag der Österreichischen Akademie der Wissenschaften, 1991.

Doom, Erin Michael. "Patriarch, Monk and Empress: A Byzantine Debate over Icons." Wichita, Kansas: Wichita State University, 2005.

Dubose, William Porcher. The Ecumenical Councils. 2d ed. New York: The Christian Literature Co., 1897.

Dvornik, Francis. "The Byzantine Church and the Immaculate Conception." The Dogma of the Immaculate Conception: History and Significance. Ed. Edward D. O'Connor. Notre Dame, Ind.: University of Notre Dame Press, 1958.

—. The Ecumenical Councils. Ed.1. New York: Hawthorn Books, 1961.

Ehrhard, Albert. Überlieferung und Bestand der Hagiographischen und Homiletischen Literatur der Griechischen Kirche von den Anfängen bis zum Ende des 16. Jahrhunderts. Texte und Untersuchungen zur Geschichte der Altchristlichen Literatur. Leipzig: J. C. Hinrichs, 1937.

Engelhardt, H. Tristram. The Foundations of Christian Bioethics. Lisse [The Netherlands]; Exton, PA: Swets & Zeitlinger Publishers, 2000.

Esbroeck, Michel van. Collected Studies, Cs472. 1995.?

Evdokimov, Paul. The Sacrament of Love: The Nuptial Mystery in the Light of the Orthodox Tradition. Crestwood, NY: St. Vladimir's Seminary Press, 1985.

—. The Art of the Icon: A Theology of Beauty. Redondo Beach, Calif.: Oakwood Publications, 1990.

—. Woman and the Salvation of the World: A Christian Anthropology on the Charisms of Women. Crestwood, NY: St. Vladimir's Seminary Press, 1994.

—. Ages of the Spiritual Life. Crestwood, NY: St. Vladimir's Seminary Press, 1998.

Evdokimov, Paul, Michael Plekon, and Alexis Vinogradov. In the World, of the Church: A Paul Evdokimov Reader. Crestwood, N.Y.: St. Vladimir's Seminary Press, 2001.

EWTN, "Library Index". 2007. (11/16/2006): Contains selected texts from the Iconoclast Synod of Constantinople (Hiera), as well as the text from the Second Ecumenical Council of Nicaea condemning . . . EWTN (Eternal Word Television Network-Global Catholic Network). February 16, 2007. <www.ewtn.com/library/indexes/COUNCILS. htm>.

Farenga, Vincent. "Periphrasis on the Origin of Rhetoric." Modern Language Notes (94/95): 1033-55.

Flores, Deyanira. "Mary, the Virgin 'Completely and Permanently Transformed by God's Grace': The Meaning and Implications of Luke 1:28 and of the Dogma of the Immaculate Conception for Mary's Spiritual Life." Marian Studies LV.The Immaculate Conception Calling and Destiny (2004): 47-113.

Florovsky, Georges. Christianity and Culture. Belmont, Mass.: Nordland Pub. Co., 1974.

Follieri, Enrica. Initia Hymnorum Ecclesiae Graecae. Città del Vaticano: Biblioteca apostolica vaticana, 1960.

Fortescue, Adrian. "Iconoclasm." The Catholic Encyclopedia. 1910 ed, 1910. Vol. VII.

Freeman, Ann. Theodulf of Orléans: Charlemagne's Spokesman against the Second Council of Nicaea. Aldershot; Burlington, VT: Ashgate/ Variorum, 2003.

Gambero, Luigi. "Germanus of Constantinople, Andrew of Crete, John Damascene:

Their Marian Doctrine and Their Involvement in the Iconoclastic Controversy."

Dayton, OH: International Marian Research Institute, 1990.

—. Mary and the Fathers of the Church: The Blessed Virgin Mary in Patristic Thought. Trans. Thomas Buffer. San Franscisco: Ignatius Press, 1999.

Garland, Landon C., and Vanderbilt University. Discussions in Theology, Doctrinal and Practical. microform. Pub. House of the M.E. Church, South, Nashville, Tenn., 1890.

Geerard, Maurice, ed. Clavis Patrum Graecorum. Vol. III. V. Turnhout: Brepols, 1974-1987.

Germanus. On Predestined Terms of Life. Trans. Charles Garton and Leendert Gerrit Westerink. Arethusa Monographs. Vol. VII. Buffalo: Dept. of Classics, State University of N.Y. at Buffalo, 1979.

Germanus I. Omelie Mariologiche : Le omelie mariane e le lettere sulle sacre immagini. Ed. Vittorio Fazzo. Rome: Città nuova, 1985.

Germanus I. On the Divine Liturgy. Trans. and Intro. by Paul Meyendorff. Crestwood, N.Y.: St. Vladimir's Seminary Press, 1984.

Gero, Stephen. Byzantine Iconoclasm During the Reign of Constantine V, with Particular Attention to the Oriental Sources. Louvain: Corpus SCO, 1977.

Gharib, Georges, and Luigi Gambero. Testi mariani del primo millennio, Roma: Città Nuova Editrice, 1989. 318-90. Vol. II. IV

Gharib, Georges, et al. Germano de Constantinopoli. Testi mariani del primo millennio. Ed. Georges Gharib. Vol. II. Padri e altri autori bizantini (VI-XI sec.). Rome: Città Nuova Editrice, 1988.

Gillet, Lev. "The Immaculate Conception and the Orthodox Church". 1983.

Chrysostom. (August 1 2008). <http://eirenikon.wordpress.com/2008/08/01/the-immaculate-conception-and-the-orthodox-church-4/>.

Gilvin, Brandon. Solving the Da Vinci Code Mystery. St. Louis: Chalice Press, 2004.

Gordillo, M. Mariologia Orientalis. Orientalia Christiana Analecta, 141 (1954)

Grabar, André. L'iconoclasme byzantin: le dossier archéologique. [2e éd.] Paris: Flammarion, 1998.

Grabar, André, and Fondation Schlumberger pour les études byzantines. L'iconoclasme Byzantin; Dossier Archeologique. Paris: College de France, 1957.

Graef, Hilda C. Mary: A History of Doctrine and Devotion. Westminster, Md.; London: Christian Classics. Sheed and Ward, 1985.

Gross, Jules. The Divinization of the Christian According to the Greek Fathers. 1st
ed. Anaheim, Calif.: A & C Press, 2002.

Gross, Jules, at Université de Strasbourg. La divinisation du chrétien d'après les pères grecs: Contribution historique à la doctrine de la grâce. Microform: 1938.

Grumel, V. Les regestes des actes du patriarcat de Constantinople. Paris: Socii Assumptionistae Chalcedonenses, 1932.

Grumel, V. Homélie de sainte Germain sur la délivrance de Constantinople. Mélanges Sévérien Salaville. Vol. xvi. Paris: Institut francais d'études byzantines, 1958.

Hahn, Scott. "Biblical Theology and Marian Studies." Marian Studies LV (2004): 9-32.

Hall, S. G. Melito of Sardis, On Pascha and Fragments. Oxford, 1979.

Hannick, Christian. "The Theotokos in Byzantine Hymnography: Typology and Allegory." Images of the Mother of God: Perceptions of the Theotokos in Byzantium. Ed. Maria Vassilaki. Aldershot, Hants, England; Burlington, VT: Ashgate, 2005.

Hansen, Günther Christian. Theodoros Anagnostes Kirchengeschichte. Berlin: Akademie-Verlag, 1971.

—. Theodoros Anagnostes Kirchengeschichte. Zweite, durchgesehene auflage. ed. Berlin: Akademie-Verlag, 1995.

Hefele, Karl Joseph von. A History of the Councils of the Church: From the Original Documents. 5 vols. Edinburgh: T. & T. Clark, 1883.

—. A History of the Councils of the Church : From the Original Documents. 5 vols. Edinburgh: T. & T. Clark, 1872.

Henn, William. The Honor of My Brothers: A Short History of the Relation between the Pope and the Bishops. Ut Unum Sint. New York: Crossroad Pub., 2000.

Henze, Anton. The Pope and the World: an Illustrated History of the Ecumenical Councils. New York: Viking Press, 1965.

Herrin, Judith. The Formation of Christendom. 1st Princeton paperback printing, with revisions and ill. Princeton, N.J.: Princeton University Press, 1989.

Hopko, Thomas, V. Rev. "Annunciation." Orthodox Church in America. May 23, 2008. <http://oca.org/OCchapter.asp?SID=2&ID=84>.

Hörandner, Wolfram, and Erich Trapp. Lexicographica Byzantina: Beiträge zum Symposion zur Byzantinischen Lexikographie (Wien, 1.-4. 3. 1989). Wien: Verlag der Österreichischen Akademie der Wissenschaften, 1991.

Horvath, Tibor, S.J. Germanos of Constantinople and the Cult of the Virgin Mary, Mother of God, Mediatrix of All Men. De cultu mariano saeculis VI-XI; acta congressus mariologici mariani internationalis in Croatia anno 1971 celebrati. 1972. Pontificia Academia Mariana Internationalis.

Ilarion. Orthodox Witness Today. Geneva: WCC Publications, 2006.

Janin, R., and Institut français d'études byzantines. Les églises et les monastères. Paris: Institut français d'études byzantines, 1953.

Jedin, Hubert. Ecumenical Councils of the Catholic Church. 1st ed. Freiburg: Herder, 1960.

Jeffreys, Elizabeth. Rhetoric in Byzantium: Papers from the Thirty-Fifth Spring Symposium of Byzantine Studies, Exeter College, University of Oxford, March 2001. Aldershot, Hants, England; Burlington, VT: Ashgate, 2003.

John Paul II, Pope. Apostolic Letter "Duodecimum Saeculum" of the Supreme Pontiff John Paul II to the Episcopate of the Catholic Church on the Occasion of the 1200th Anniversary of the Second Council of Nicaea. Washington, D.C.: United States Catholic Conference, 1987.

Jugie, Martin. "Les homélies de Saint Germain de Constantinople sur la dormition de la sainte vierge." Échos d' Orient 16 (1913).

—. Homélies mariales byzantines: textes grecs édités et traduits en latin. Paris: Firmin-Didot, 1922.

—. Theologia dogmatica christianorum orientalium ab ecclesia catholica dissidentium. Paris: Letouzey et Ané, 1926.

—. Le schisme byzantin, aperçu historique et doctrinal. Paris,: P. Lethielleux, 1941.

—. La mort et l'assomption de la sainte vierge, étude historico-doctrinale. Città del Vaticano, 1944.

—. L'immaculée conception dans l'écriture sainte et dans la tradition orientale. Romae: Officium Libri Catholici, 1952.

Kazhdan, A. P. Authors and Texts in Byzantium. Aldershot, Hants., Great Britain; Brookfield, Vt., USA: Variorum, 1993.

Kazhdan, A. P., and Giles Constable. People and Power in Byzantium: An Introduction to Modern Byzantine Studies. Washington, D.C.: Dumbarton Oaks, Center for Byzantine Studies, Trustees for Harvard University, 1982.

Kazhdan, A. P., Anthony Cutler, and Simon Franklin. Homo Byzantinus: Papers in Honor of Alexander Kazhdan. Dumbarton Oaks Papers. Washington, D.C.: Dumbarton Oaks Research Library and Collection, 1992.

Kazhdan, A. P., Lee Francis Sherry, and Christina Angelides. A History of Byzantine Literature, 650-850. Athens: National Hellenic Research Foundation Institute for Byzantine Research, 1999.

Kellner, K. A. Heinrich. Heortologie, oder, Die Geschichtliche Entwicklung des Kirchenjahres und der Heiligenfeste: Von den Ältesten Zeiten bis zur Gegenwart. Vollständig neu bearb. und verm. Aufl. Freiburg im Breisgau: Herder, 1906.

Kellner, Karl Adam Heinrich. Heortology: a History of the Christian Festivals from Their Origin to the Present Day. London, Trench, St. Louis: K. Paul Trubner; Herder, 1908.

Kennedy, George Alexander. The Art of Persuasion in Greece. A History of Rhetoric. Vol. I. Princeton, N.J.: Princeton University Press, 1963.

—. Greek Rhetoric under Christian Emperors. Princeton, N.J.: Princeton University Press, 1983.

—. A New History of Classical Rhetoric. Princeton, N.J.: Princeton University Press, 1994.

—. Progymnasmata: Greek Textbooks of Prose Composition and Rhetoric. Leiden; Boston: Brill, 2003.

Kennedy, George Alexander, and Duane Frederick Watson. Persuasive Artistry: Studies in New Testament Rhetoric in Honor of George A. Kennedy. Journal for the Study of the New Testament. Supplement Series 50. Sheffield: JSOT Press, 1991.

Kennedy, George Alexander, and Hugo Rabe. Invention and Method: Two Rhetorical Treatises from the Hermogenic Corpus. Leiden; Boston: Brill, 2005.

Kimball, Virginia M. "The Immaculate Conception in the Ecumenical Dialogue with Orthodoxy: How the Term *Theosis* Can Inform Convergence." Marian Studies LV (2004): 212-44.

—. "The Immaculate Conception in the Ecumenical Dialogue with Orthodoxy: How the Term Theosis Can Inform Convergence." Mary for Time and Eternity: Papers on Mary and Ecumenism Given at International Congresses of the Ecumenical Society of the Blessed Virgin Mary at Chester (2002) and Bath (2004), a Conference at Woldingham (2003) and Other Meetings in 2005. Eds. William McLoughlin and Jill Pinnock. Leominster: Gracewing, 2007. 219-52.

Kishpaugh, Mary Jerome. The Feast of the Presentation of the Virgin Mary in the Temple: An Historical and Literary Study. Washington, D.C.: The Catholic University of America, 1941.

Krumbacher, Karl. Geschichte der Byzantinischen Litteratur. München: Beck, 1891.

—. Geschichte der Byzantinischen Litteratur. 2. Aufl.: B. Franklin, 1958.

Krumbacher, Karl, Albert Ehrhard, and Heinrich Gelzer. Geschichte der Byzantinischen Litteratur von Justinian bis zum Ende des

Gregory E. Roth

Oströmischen Reiches (527-1453). 2. aufl. ed. München: C.H. Beck (O. Beck), 1897.

Kustas, George L. "The Evolution and Function of Byzantine Rhetoric." Viator (1970).

—. Studies in Byzantine Rhetoric. Thessalonike: Patriarchikon Hidryma Paterikon, 1973.

—. "Rhetoric and the Holy Spirit." Originality in Byzantine Literature, Art and Music: A Collection of Essays. Ed. Anthony Robert Littlewood. vols. Oxford [England]: Oxbow Books, 1995. 29-37.

L'Huillier, Peter. The Church of the Ancient Councils: The Disciplinary Work of the First Four Ecumenical Councils. Crestwood, N.Y.: St. Vladimir's Seminary Press, 1995.

La Piana, George. Le rappresentazioni sacre nella letteratura bizantina dalle origini al sec. IX, con rapporti al teatro sacro d'occidente. Grottaferrata: Tip. italo-orientale "S. Nilo", 1912.

Lafontaine-Dosogne, Jacqueline. Iconographie de l'enfance de la vierge dans l'empire byzantin et en occident. Brussels, 1964.

—. "Iconographie de l'enfance de la vierge dans l'empire byzantin et en occident." Mémoires de la classe des beaux-arts. Collection in-4o, 2. sér., t. 11, fasc. 3. (1992).

Lamza, Lucian. Patriarch Germanos I von Konstantinopel (715-730): Versuch einer Endgültigen Chronologischen Fixierung des Lebens und Wirkens des Patriarchen: Mit dem Griechisch-Deutschen Text der Vita Germani am Schluss der Arbeit. Würzburg: Augustinus-Verlag, 1975.

Lane, A. N. S., A Concise History of Christian Thought. Completely rev. and expanded ed. Grand Rapids, Mich.: Baker Academic, 2006.

Laurentin, René. Table rectificative des pièces mariales inauthentiques ou discutées contenues dans les deux patrologies de Migne. Court traité de théologie mariale. Paris, 1954.

—. The Question of Mary. [1st. ed.] New York: Holt, 1965.

—. The Question of Mary. Techny, Ill.: Divine Word Publications, 1967.

Lebreton, Jules. History of the Dogma of the Trinity from Its Origins to the Council of Nicea. New York: Benzinger, 1939.

Lemaître, Jean Loup, and Musée du pays d'Ussel. Saint Germain de Constantinople à Bort. Ussel Paris: Musée du pays d'Ussel; Diffusion de Boccard, 1999.

Lindberg, Carter. A Brief History of Christianity. Blackwell Brief Histories of Religion. Oxford, UK; Malden, MA: Blackwell Pub., 2006.

List, J. "Studien zur Homiletik Germanos I von Konstantiople und Seiner Zeit." Texte und Untersuchungen zur byzantinisch-neugriechischen Literatur 29 (1939).

Mack, Burton L. Rhetoric and the New Testament. Guides to Biblical Scholarship. New Testament Series. Minneapolis: Fortress Press, 1990.

Malaty, Tadrous Y. Ecumenical Councils and the Trinitarian Faith. Prepratory [sic] ed. [Cairo?]: T.Y. Malaty, 1992.

Mango, Cyril A. The Brazen House: a Study of the Imperial Palace of Constantinople. København: I kommission hos Munksgaard, 1959.

—. "Notes on Byzantine Monuments." Dumbarton Oaks Papers 23 (1969-70): 369-75.

Maria, A.S.Fr., O.C.D. "Doctrina S. Germani Constantinopolitani de morte et assumptione B.V.M." Marianum Annus XV (1953).

Martin, Edward James. A History of the Iconoclastic Controversy. London,

New York: Society for Promoting Christian Knowledge; Macmillan, 1930.

—. A History of the Iconoclastic Controversy. 1st AMS ed. New York: AMS Press, 1978.

Meyendorff, John. Byzantine Theology: Historical Trends and Doctrinal Themes. New York: Fordham University Press, 1979.

Migne, J. P. Patrologiae Cursus Completus, Seu Bibliotheca Universalis, Integra, Uniformis, Commoda, Oeconomica, Omnium Ss. Patrum, Doctorum Scriptorumque Ecclesiasticorum . . . : Series Graeca. Patrologia Graeca. Vol. 98. [Parisiis]: Migne, 1857.

Mimouni, Simon Claude. Dormition et assomption de Marie: histoire des traditions anciennes. Théologie historique. Paris: Beauchesne, 1995.

Mimouni, Simon Claude, and Pierre Maraval. Le christianisme des origines à Constantin. Nouvelle Clio. Paris: Presses universitaires de France, 2006.

Mimouni, Simon Claude, and S. J. Voicu. La tradition grecque de la dormition et de l'assomption de Marie. Sagesses Chrétiennes. Paris: Cerf, 2003.

Molloy, Michael E. Champion of Truth: The Life of Saint Athanasius. New York: St. Pauls, 2003.

Moreschini, Claudio, and Enrico Norelli. Early Christian Greek and Latin Literature: A Literary History. 2 vols. Peabody, Mass.: Hendrickson Publishers, 2005.

Morris, Rosemary, et al. Church and People in Byzantium. Birmingham, England: Centre for Byzantine, Ottoman and Modern Greek studies, University of Birmingham, 1990.

Nicephorus, Ignatius, and Carl de Boor. Nicephori Archiepiscopi Constantinopolitani Opuscula Historica. Leipzig: B. G. Teubner, 1880.

Nicephorus, Lajos Orosz, and British Museum. The London Manuscript of Nikephoros "Breviarium" = Nikephoros "Breviarium"—Ának Londoni Kézirata. Budapest: Pázmány Péter Tudományegyetemi Görög Filológiai Intézet, 1948.

Nicephorus, Norman Tobias, and Anthony R. Santoro. An Eyewitness to History: The Short History of Nikephoros Our Holy Father the Patriarch of Constantinople. Brookline, Mass.: Hellenic College Press, 1994.

Ostrogorsky, G. "Les débuts de la querelle des images." Mélanges Charles Diehl. Vol. I. vols. Paris, 1930. 235-55.

Papaeliopoulou-Photopoulou, Helen e. Tameion anekdoton vyzantinon asmatikon kanonon, or, Analecta hymnica graeca e codicibus eruta orientis christiani. Athenai: Syllogos pros Diadosin Ophelimon Vivlion, 1996.

Parry, Kenneth. Depicting the Word: Byzantine Iconophile Thought of the Eighth and Ninth Centuries. The Medieval Mediterranean: Peoples, Economies and Culture, 400—1453. Ed. Michael Magdalin Whitby, Paul Kennedy, Hugh Abulafia, David Arbel, Benjamin Meyerson, Mark. Vol. 12. Leiden; New York: E.J. Brill, 1996.

"The Passing of Mary." International Standard Bible Encyclopedia, ed. James Orr. Wm. B. Eerdmans Publishing Co. 1939. Accessed May 21, 2008. <http://www.internationalstandardbible.com/A/apocryphal-gospels.html>.

Patrology: V. 4 the Golden Age of Latin Patristic Literature from the Council of Nicea to the Council of Chalcedon. Westminster, Md.: Christian Classics, 1986.

Pentcheva, Bissera V. "The 'Activated' Icon: The Hodegetria Procession and Mary's Eisodos." The Mother of God : Representations of the

Virgin in Byzantine Art. Ed. Maria Vassilaki. Milan London New York: Skira Editore; Thames & Hudson; Abbeville, 2004. 195-202.

—. Icons and Power: The Mother of God in Byzantium. University Park, PA: The Pennsylvania State University Press, 2006.

Perkins, Justin, and Constantin von Tischendorf. Apocalypses Apocryphae Mosis, Esdrae, Pauli, Iohannis. Hildesheim: G. Olms, 1966.

Perniola, Erasmo. La mariologia di San Germano, Patriarca di Constantinopoli. Roma: Edizioni Padre Monti, 1954.

Person, Ralph E. "The Mode of Theological Decision Making at the Early Ecumenical Councils: An Inquiry into the Function of Scripture and Tradition at the Councils of Nicaea and Ephesus." Thesis. F. Reinhardt, Basel., 1978.

Pharmakides, Theokletos. Ho Pseudonymos Germanos. Athenai, 1838.

Phougias, Methodios G. The Person of Jesus Christ in the Decision of the Ecumenical Councils: A Historical and Doctrinal Study with the Relevant Documents Referring to the Christological Relations of the Western, Eastern, and Oriental Churches. Addis Ababa: Central Print. Press, 1976.

Pitra, J. B. Analecta Novissima Spicilegii Solesmensis: Altera Continuatio. 2 vols.

Farnborough, Hants., England: Gregg, 1967.

—. Analecta Sacra Spicilegio Solesmensi Parata. [Farnborough, Eng.,]: Gregg Press, 1966.

"Protoevangelium of James." May 21 2008. <http://www.newadvent.org/fathers/0847.htm>.

Quasten, Johannes. Patrology. Westminster, Md.: Newman Press, 1950.

—. Patrology. 4 vols. Westminster, Md.: Christian Classics, Inc., 1983.

—. Patrology. 4 vols. Allen, TX: Christian Classics, 1986.

Raab, Clement. The Twenty Ecumenical Councils of the Catholic Church. London, New York [etc.]: Longmans, Green, and co., 1937.

—. The Twenty Ecumenical Councils of the Catholic Church. Westminster, Md.: Newman Press, 1959.

Rabe, Hugo, et al. Prolegomenon Sylloge; Accedit Maximi libellus de obiectionibus insolubilibus. Rhetores Graeci. Leipzig: B. G. Teubner, 1931.

Rendina, Claudio. The Popes: Histories and Secrets. Santa Ana, Calif.: Seven Locks Press, 2002.

Ross, Kelley L. "The Bishops of Rome, the Popes; the Patriarchs of Constantinople, Alexandria, Antioch, Jerusalem, Armenia, and the East; Archbishops of Canterbury and Prince Archbishops of Mainz, Trier, Cologne, and Salzburg." December 4, 2007. <http://www.friesian.com/popes.htm#constantinople>.

Rossier, François, S.M. "*Kecharitomene* (Luke 1:28) in the Light of Gen. 18:16-33." Marian Studies LV (2004): 159-83.

Russell, D. A. "Epideictic Literature." Menander Rhetor. Eds. D. A. Russell and Nigel Guy Wilson. vols. Oxford New York: Clarendon Press; Oxford University Press, 1981.

S, B. A Letter Wherein Is Shewed, First What Worship Is Due to Images According to the Second Council of Nice, Secondly, That the Papists Are Very Unjust in Charging Schism on the Church of England, as Also That the Church of Rome Is Most Notoriously Guilty of That Sin. microform. Printed for William Churchill, London, 1680.

Samaha, Brother John M., S.M. "Is There a Byzantine Mariology?" http://www.ignatiusinsight.com/. May 21, 2008.

Schaff, Philip, and Henry Wace. A Select Library of Nicene and Post-Nicene Fathers of the Christian Church. Second Series. New York: The Christian literature company; [etc.], 1890.

Schirò, Giuseppe. Analecta hymnica graeca e codicibus eruta italiae inferioris. Rome, 1966.

Schmemann, Alexander. "Mary in Eastern Liturgy." Marian Studies 19 (1968).

—. "On Mariology in Orthodoxy." Marian Library Studies 2 (1970).

—. The Historical Road of Eastern Orthodoxy. Crestwood, N.Y.: St. Vladimir's Seminary Press, 1977.

—. The Presence of Mary. Mount Hermon, Calif.: Conciliar Press, 1988.

—. "The Virgin Mary." The Virgin Mary: St. Vladimir's Seminary Press, 1995.

Shoemaker, Stephen J. Ancient Traditions of the Virgin Mary's Dormition and Assumption. Oxford Early Christian Studies. Oxford: Oxford University Press, 2002.

Schönborn, Christoph von. God's Human Face: The Christ-Icon. San Francisco: Ignatius Press, 1994.

Ševčenko, Ihor. "A Shadow of Virtue: The Classical Heritage of Greek Christian Literature (Second to Seventh Century)." Age of Spirituality:

A Symposium. Ed. K Weitzmann. vols. New York: Metropolitan Museum of Art; distributed by Princeton University Press, 1980.

Sewell, Elizabeth Missing. History of the Early Church, from the First Preaching of the Gospel to the Council of Nicea. Appletons' Students' Library. New York: Appleton and Co., 1882.

Slaatte, Howard Alexander. The Seven Ecumenical Councils. Lanham, MD: University Press of America, 1980.

Tanner, Norman P. Decrees of the Ecumenical Councils. London & Washington, DC: Sheed & Ward; Georgetown University Press, 1990.

Theophanes, Anastasius, Chronographia, ed. Carl de Boor. 2 vols. Leipzig: Teubner, 1883.

Theophanes, Chronographia: A Chronicle of Eighth Century Byzantium, ed. Anthony R. Santoro. Gorham, Me.: Greek, Roman and Byzantine Studies Conference, 1982.

Theophanes, The Chronicle of Theophanes: An English Translation of Anni Mundi 6095-6305 (A.D. 602-813). Trans. Harry Turtledove. Philadelphia: University of Pennsylvania Press, 1982.

Timiadis, Emilianos. The Ecumenical Councils in the Life of the Church. Joensuun Yliopiston Teologisia Julkaisuja, 9. Joensuu, Finland: Joensuun yliopisto, 2003.

Toon, Peter. Yesterday, Today, and Forever: Jesus Christ and the Holy Trinity in the Teaching of the Seven Ecumenical Councils. Swedesboro, NJ: Preservation Press, 1996.

Tsironis, Niki. "Historicity and Poetry in Ninth-Century Homiletics: The Homilies of Patriarch Photios and George of Nicomedia." Preacher and Audience, Studies in Early Christian and Byzantine Homiletics. Edd. Mary B. Cunningham and Pauline Allen. Boston and Leiden: Brill, 1998.

—. "The Mother of God in the Iconoclastic Controversy." Mother of God: Representations of the Virgin in Byzantine Art. Ed. Maria Vassilaki. vols. Milan: Skira, 2000. 26-39.

—. "From Poetry to Liturgy: The Cult of the Virgin in the Middle Byzantine Era." The Mother of God: Representations of the Virgin in Byzantine Art. Ed. Maria Vassilaki. Milan London New York: Skira Editore; Thames & Hudson; Abbeville, 2004. 195-202.

Vassilaki, Maria. Images of the Mother of God: Perceptions of the Theotokos in Byzantium. Aldershot, Hants, England; Burlington, VT: Ashgate, 2005.

Vermès, Géza. Scripture and Tradition in Judaism; Haggadic Studies. Leiden: E. J. Brill, 1961.

Walz, Christian. Rhetores Graeci, ex Codicibus Florentinis, Mediolanensibus, Monacensibus, Neapolitanis, Parisiensibus, Romanis, Venetis, Taurinensibus et Vindobonensibus. 9 vols. Stuttgart and Tübingen: J. G. Cottae; [etc.,etc.], 1832.

—. Rhetores Graeci, ex Codicibus Florentinis, Mediolanensibus, Monacensibus, Neapolitanis, Parisiensibus, Romanis, Venetis, Taurinensibus et Vindobonensibus. Emendatiores et auctiores edidit. Osnabrück: Zeller, 1968.

Ware, Kallistos. "'The Final Mystery': The Dormition of the Holy Virgin in Orthodox Worship." Mary for Time and Eternity: Papers on Mary and Ecumenism Given at International Congresses of the Ecumenical Society of the Blessed Virgin Mary at Chester (2002) and Bath (2004), a Conference at Woldingham (2003) and Other Meetings in 2005. Eds. William McLoughlin and Jill Pinnock. Leominster: Gracewing, 2004. 219-52.

Weitzmann, Kurt, and Hans Georg Beck. Age of Spirituality: A Symposium. New York [Princeton, N.J.]: Metropolitan Museum of Art; distributed by Princeton University Press, 1980.

Wenger, Antoine. L'assomption de la t. s. vierge dans la tradition byzantine du vie au xe siècle; études et documents. Paris: Institut français d'études byzantines, 1955.

Wenger, A. "Un nouveau témoin de l'assomption: une homélie attribuée à Saint Germain de Constantinople." Revue des Études Byzantines XVI Mélanges Sévérien Salaville (1958).

Wortley, John. "The Byzantine Component of the Relic-Hoard of Constantinople." GRBS 40 (1999): 307-32.

—. "Icons and Relics: A Comparison." GRBS 43 (2002): 161-74.

—. "The Marian Relics at Constantinople." GRBS 45 (2005): 171-87.

Xanthopoulos, Nikephoros Kallistos. "Historia Ecclesiastica." Patrologiae Cursus Completus: Series Graeca. Ed. J-P Migne. Paris: Migne, 1857-66. Vol. 145-147.